TOWARD UNDERSTANDING MACRO-ECONOMICS

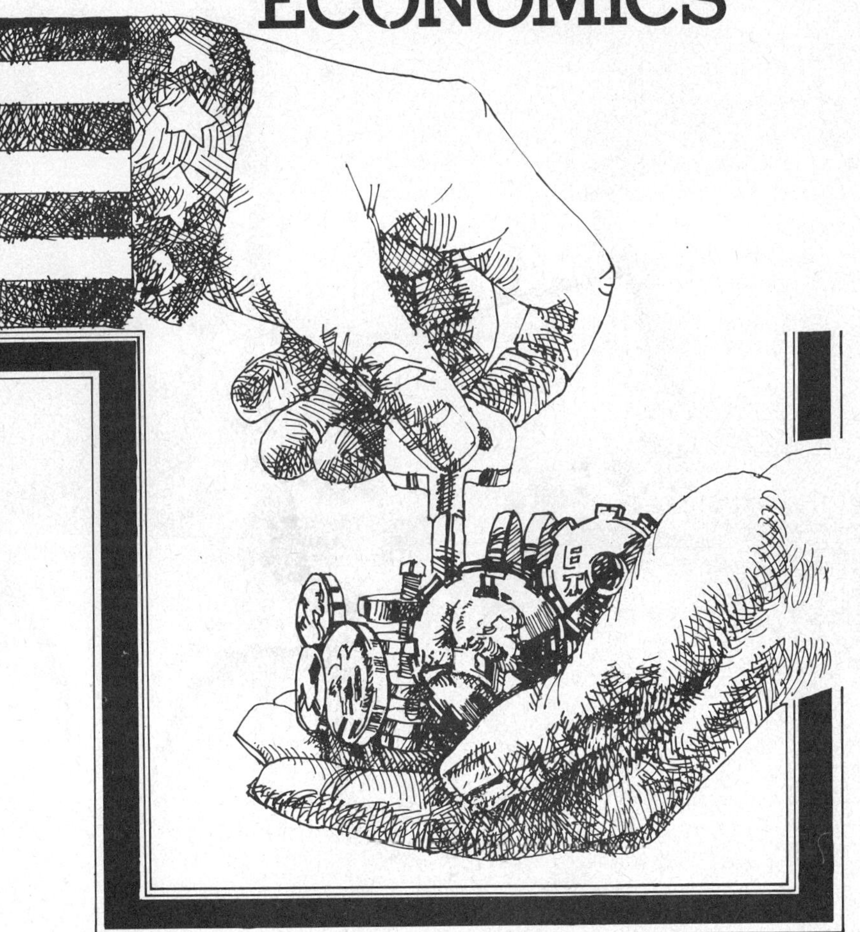

PAUL HEYNE · THOMAS JOHNSON

SCIENCE RESEARCH ASSOCIATES, INC.
Chicago, Palo Alto, Toronto, Henley-on-Thames, Sydney, Paris, Stuttgart
A Subsidiary of IBM

Library of Congress Cataloging in Publication Data

Heyne, Paul T
   Toward understanding macroeconomics.

   Includes index.
   1. Macroeconomics. I. Johnson, Thomas, 1936–
joint author. II. Title.
HB171.5.H466   339   76–22501
ISBN 0–574–19275–1

Material contained herein also appears in books
entitled *Toward Economic Understanding*
and *The Economic Way of Thinking.*

PREFACE

Microeconomics and macroeconomics are not two distinct and unrelated bodies of thought. Surely all economists will agree on that. But what is the precise relationship between them? Which is the foundation and which is the superstructure? The way authors conceive of that relationship determines the way they organize any introductory economics textbook they write.

The authors of this book and its companion volume, *Toward Understanding Microeconomics,* believe that microeconomic principles form the core of economic thought, and that macroeconomics is essentially an application of microeconomic analysis to particularly difficult and pressing problems associated with fluctuations in the aggregate level of economic activity or, in shorthand, the problems of inflation and recession. We gave expression to that conviction in *Toward Economic Understanding,* the larger book from which the present volume has been derived: We presented microeconomics before macroeconomics.

Many introductory courses, however, offer macroeconomics first. We wanted our book to be suitable (a subtle way of saying we wanted it to be adopted) in departments employing the macro-to-micro sequence. We could not make it usable, however, merely by splitting the book with a razor blade and attaching paper covers. We had to present at the beginning of the macro volume the micro foundations we were going to build upon. And that meant those who used both paperbacks would encounter some repetition whichever sequence they chose.

If you are using the two books sequentially, you will want to know where to expect duplication. The first six chapters of this book present in condensed form the introductory chapter plus the most basic concepts from chapters 2–5, 7, 8, 12, and 13 of our *Microeconomics*. We think that students who go through this material a second time will be more likely to say "Now I see" than "We've already done this." We *want* to believe that, of course, and the wish may be father and mother to the opinion.

We think it's also important in this preface to say something about the pedagogical principles informing the book. Our convictions about the best way to introduce students to economics can be briefly summarized:

1. It is economic *theory* that makes economics an illuminating, useful, and fascinating subject.
2. A small amount of economic theory goes a long way and a lot of economic theory often goes nowhere.
3. Theory must be taught in the context of applications if it is to be learned and retained.

We want beginning students to master a set of concepts that will help them think more coherently and consistently about the wide range of social problems that economic theory illuminates. The principles of economics make sense out of buzzing confusion. They clarify, systematize, and correct the daily assertions of journalists, political figures, axe grinders, and barroom pontiffs. And the applicability of the economist's thought-tools is practically unlimited. But students won't come to appreciate any of this unless we persuade them by showing them. And that means we must teach the concepts of economic analysis as ways of answering actual questions which students are asking.

No good teacher of economics has ever found this task an easy one. It requires imagination, insight, a knowledge of current events, the ability to listen attentively, and a sense of perspective, as well as familiarity with the formal techniques of economic analysis. Those are all scarce goods. And it presupposes a conviction on the part of the teacher that economic theory really is useful for something more than answering artificial questions and passing equally artificial examinations.

Perhaps no one would disagree in principle with any of the above. If so, our practice has been far out of step with our precept. One reason is undoubtedly the obsession with formal technique that characterizes so much teaching of economic theory at all levels. The disciple will very rarely rise above the master. And if the masters in our profession are more concerned with form than with content, the effects will be felt at the principles level. We need not debate here the question of how much of what makes it into intermediate and advanced theory texts really belongs there, or how the balance should be struck in graduate theory courses between the logic-mathematics and the economics of theory. For the question of what should go into a beginning course can be answered without resolving the other questions. And that answer is: *very little.*

Most of what might go into a Compleat and Current Compendium of Economic Theory is actually refinement and elaboration of the few fundamental concepts that are useful in enabling us to understand the real world and to evaluate policy proposals. Almost all the genuinely important things that economics has to teach are elementary concepts of relationship that people could almost figure out for themselves if they thought carefully. The vast body of more advanced economics is largely composed of applications of these concepts to specific problems.

Some problems are difficult indeed and test the mathematical, statistical, and policy skills of many good minds. Our challenge, however, is getting people to *appreciate* these few, simple concepts. To do that, we must practice the virtue of restraint. We must attempt less and thereby accomplish more. An introductory course should distinguish itself as much by what it excludes as by what it incorporates. Unless it is our aim to impress students with the esoteric quality of economists' knowledge, we should teach no theory *in the introductory course* that cannot immediately be put to work in some meaningful and hopefully vivid way. Otherwise we drown the beginning student; he is made to thrash about so desperately in such deep water that he doesn't learn to swim a single stroke. Our aim should be to get him swimming and instill in him the confidence that through practice he can learn to swim better.

And so we have omitted a good deal that can be found in most of the fat textbooks through which college students are usually introduced to economics, in order to provide more applications of basic concepts and more dialogue about the social problems to which economic theory is applied. We don't present the fundamentals of accounting or the history of the labor movement, and we don't explain social security benefits, rates of population growth, or the differences between common and preferred stock. We think those are all useful things to know, but we don't want them in an introductory economics text where too many dates, definitions, and data can easily get in the way of understanding. And it's *understanding* that we're after, as the title of the book suggests.

We have, however, given more attention to political and ethical questions than most textbooks do. *Homo oeconomicus* is a fiction in which no good economist has ever believed. Economic decisions are made by real people who do not live by bread alone and whose economic activities occur in social and political contexts. Economics becomes a more difficult subject when we admit that, but it also becomes more challenging and meaningful.

Reviewers of these pages who agreed wholeheartedly with our philosophy did not always agree with us about particular omissions and inclusions. Sometimes we took their advice and sometimes we did not;

judgments on relevance and relative importance inevitably vary. Many of our most difficult decisions were made easier by the knowledge that this book will usually be found in the company of teachers who can amend our mistaken judgments, correct our limited vision, and assure students that nothing is certain merely because it's in print.

One of our most heartening experiences in the preparation of this book was discovering how many teachers of economics around the country were willing to help and how much we could learn from them. They have proved to us that a *community* of scholars still lives in this era of disciplinary professionalism, and we are deeply grateful for their unselfish assistance. We are particularly indebted to Donald A. Wells of the University of Arizona who counseled and cautioned us extensively in the organization of chapters 2 through 7. This is a much better book because of his advice, and it would probably be better still had we been willing to incorporate more of his suggestions. But new insights must be grafted onto older ones. We know that we often err; we hope it's because we're still learning.

PAUL HEYNE

THOMAS JOHNSON

CONTENTS

1

THE ECONOMIC WAY OF THINKING

"Non-economists tend to be too academic. They abstract too much from the real world."

That isn't the way you usually hear it. Businessmen and college students who have sampled the writings or the courses of professional economists have all too often gone away with the suspicion that what they learned was "purely theoretical." Interesting intellectual exercise, perhaps, but not very helpful to anyone who wants to understand how an economy actually works. If you have heard comments to that effect, and are more than half-convinced of their truth, there is little chance we will persuade you otherwise in a short introductory chapter. The authors have found economics exciting and important for anyone who wants to understand the problems and possibilities of our society, but your own experience with this course will have to provide the test of that judgment.

It might be helpful, though, if you reflected for a moment on the quotation with which we began. People who sneer at "fancy theories" and prefer to rely on common sense and everyday experience are often in fact the victims of extremely vague and sweeping hypotheses. This morning's newspaper contains a letter from a young person in Pennsylvania who was once "one of a group of teenage pot smokers. Then a girl in the crowd got pregnant. Her baby was premature and deformed and needed two operations." The newspaper's adviser to the teenage lovelorn printed that letter approvingly, as evidence that the price of smoking marijuana is high.

Perhaps it is. But suppose the writer of that letter had written: "Then the Pittsburgh Steelers won the Super Bowl and the Philadelphia Flyers took the Stanley Cup." Everyone would object that those events had nothing to do with the group's pot smoking. But how do we know that? If the mere fact that the young girl's misfortunes followed her pot smoking is evidence of a causal relationship, why can't we also infer a causal relationship in the case of the Steelers and the Flyers?

The point is a simple but important one. We cannot discover, prove, or even suspect any kind of causal relationship without having a theory in mind. Our observations of the world are in fact drenched with theory, which is why we usually make sense out of the buzzing confusion that our eyes and ears pick up. We actually observe only a small fraction of what we "know," a hint here and a suggestion there; the rest we fill in from the theories we hold, small ones and broad ones, vague and precise ones, well tested and poorly tested, widely held and sometimes peculiar, carefully reasoned and dimly recognized.

I. M. D. Little is a distinguished British economist who wrote the sentences with which this chapter began, in an article describing his experiences as an adviser to the British Treasury. Here is the paragraph from which they were taken:

> Economic theory teaches one how economic magnitudes are related, and how very complex and involved these relationships are. Non-economists tend to be too academic. They abstract too much from the real world. No one can think about economic issues without some theory, for the facts and relationships are too involved to organize themselves: they do not simply fall into place. But if the theorist is untutored, he is apt to construct a very partial theory which blinds him to some of the possibilities. Or he falls back on some old and over-simple theory, picked up from somewhere or other. He is also, I believe, apt to interpret the past naively. *Post hoc ergo propter hoc*[1] is seldom an adequate economic explanation. I was sometimes shocked by the naive sureness with which very questionable bits of economic analysis were advanced in Whitehall. Of course, economists may be too academic in another sense: they may not appreciate administrative difficulties, or may lack a sense of political possibility. But then, there is no danger of these things being overlooked.[2]

Thinking Like an Economist

Economics is basically a way of thinking. The theories of economists, with surprisingly few exceptions, are simply extensions of the assumption that individuals choose those options which seem to them most likely to secure their largest net advantage. *Everyone*, it is assumed, acts in accordance with that rule: miser or spendthrift, saint or sinner, consumer or seller, politician or business executive, cautious calculator or spontaneous improviser.

---

1. Literally, "After this, therefore because of this"; the logical fallacy of assuming that A must have caused B if A preceded B in time. The argument of the penitent Pennsylvania pot smoker is an example.

2. I. M. D. Little, "The Economist in Whitehall," *Lloyds Bank Review*, April 1957.

Economic theory, we said, is *simply* an extension of that assumption. But "simply" is a treacherous word. Did you ever have a math instructor who began: "To solve this kind of problem, we simply . . ."—when it wasn't simple to you at all? The economic way of thinking is somewhat like that. The basic assumption resembles a magician's top hat: It seems to be empty; but in practiced hands it produces a fascinating array of surprises. And once you've seen for yourself how it's done, you can go back home and astonish all your friends.

The simile of the magician's top hat is apt in another way. Economics has a reputation for being mysterious and incomprehensible. And because the subject utterly baffles so many who study it, economics has also acquired a reputation for being difficult, dull, and irrelevant. This book developed out of a growing suspicion that students have found economic theory to be mystifying and tedious largely because we economists have tried to teach them too much. We have dazzled them with complex theorems and exercises in pure logic instead of helping them to see how much their world is illuminated by economic theory.

Controversy and Consensus

A number of jokes have been floating around for a long time about the inability of economists to agree. The one most often quoted says that if all the economists in the world were laid end to end, they would reach . . . no conclusion. The jokes have been revived in recent years as policy-makers struggled with the simultaneous problems of rising unemployment and rising prices, and economists could not agree on a solution. But a more careful look at the opinions of economists reveals a range of disagreements that is actually quite small when compared with the vast area of consensus. There are two principal explanations for the erroneous belief that economists rarely agree.

One, of course, is the fact that disagreement by its very nature receives more publicity. People don't spend much time discussing points on which they agree: it's both more challenging and more fruitful to move on into disputed questions and into areas where advancing knowledge has not yet produced consensus. Because the economics profession in the United States makes little effort to carry on controversy in secret (would we want it any other way in a democratic society?), disagreement looks much more substantial than it actually is. In addition, newspapers, magazines, and television commentators are generally more eager to publicize dissent than consensus. There's a much better market for criticism than there is for words of approval. And so an economist who wants to argue that his colleagues are off on the wrong track is more likely to obtain a forum for his views than is an economist eager to praise the accomplishments of his discipline.

A second explanation for the tide of popular suspicion is the public's obsession in recent years with one particular economic problem: achieving aggregate stability, or checking inflation while avoiding a rise in unemployment. That is, of course, a highly visible and well publicized problem (or pair of problems). It is also an extraordinarily complex problem. How can anyone understand and prescribe for a problem created by the interaction of so many powerful and unpredictable forces? Congress, the president, the Federal Reserve Board, world food production, population growth, the weather, cartels of oil producers, international politics, labor unions, large corporations, environmental groups, the millions of producers, consumers, savers, and investors all have an impact on the price level and employment.

Some of the public's current disillusionment with economics is attributable to the thoroughly unrealistic expectation that economists ought to be able to predict and control the variables listed in the preceding paragraph. When put in that way, the expectation is absurd. By failing to recognize how much knowledge may in fact be required for the achievement of price and employment stability, we have allowed ourselves to harbor extravagant expectations. At the same time it should be admitted that those economists who eagerly claimed credit for the relatively stable price levels and low unemployment in the 1960s helped create the extravagant expectations and consequent disillusionment of the 1970s.

The economics profession is now hard at work on a variety of fronts trying to locate and describe the factors responsible for rapid price inflation and surges of unemployment. Some of the consensus that developed in the 1960s has been disrupted; certain large scale generalizations from which many hoped to construct effective stabilization policies have been called into question; more detailed knowledge is now being sought in many directions. And the resulting scene, understandably enough, seems to the lay observer more chaotic than it actually is.

But it just isn't true that economists always disagree. Consensus among economists is the invisible part of the iceberg and disagreement is the visible but far less weighty tip. When it comes to the understanding of economic systems and the recommendation of economic policies, the important divisions of opinion in our society are less likely to be among economists than between those who have learned to use the economic way of thinking and those who have not.

2

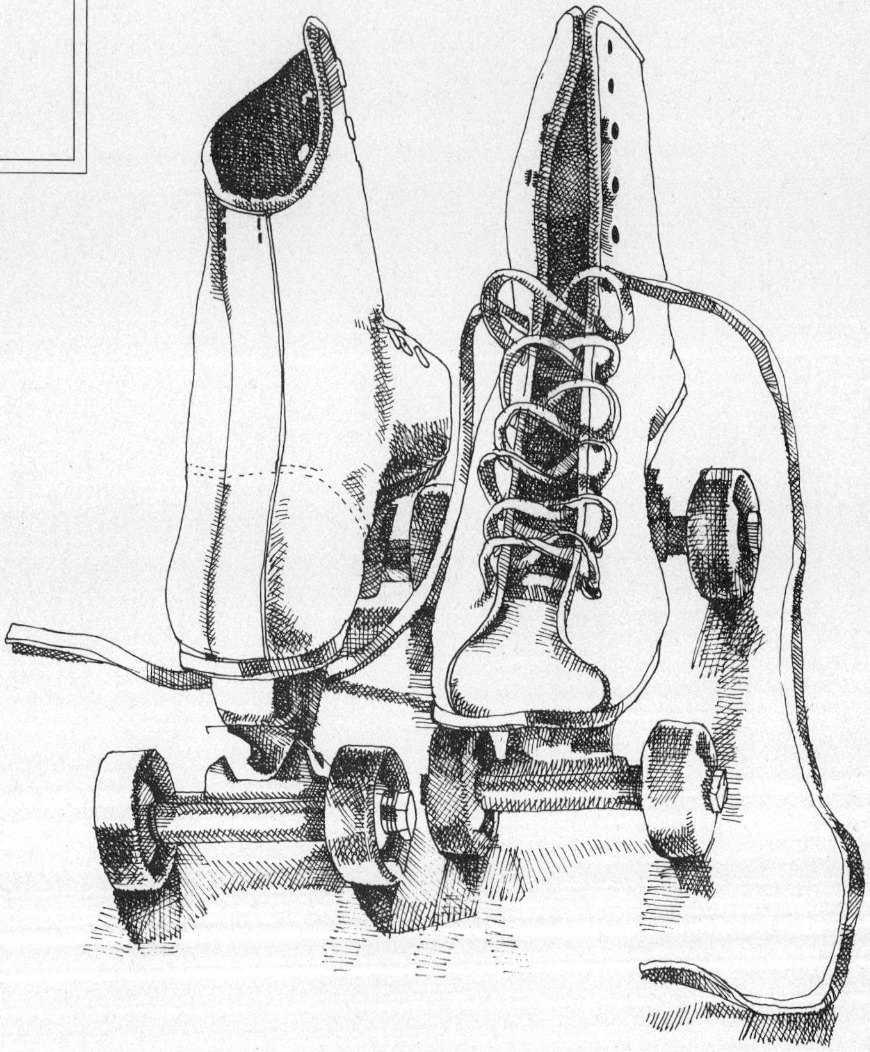

SUBSTITUTES EVERYWHERE

The concept of demand

You must have read or heard statements like these many times in your life:

1. Fire safety requires that there be two exits from each apartment unit.

2. Our state will need large amounts of additional water in the coming decade.

3. All citizens should be able to obtain the medical care they need regardless of ability to pay.

Fire safety, water, and medical care are certainly desirable things—what the economist calls "goods." But each of those statements is highly misleading. What's wrong with them?

The misleading element common to all three is the notion of *necessity*.

Take the first one. Will apartment dwellers who live in units with only one exit all be injured or killed by fires? Of course not. It's just that the risk is greater with one exit than with two. But then why not three exits? Or four? Why not go the whole route and make the outside walls nothing but doors? The answer is that, while fire safety is a good, it isn't the only good apartment dwellers are interested in. Low rental costs and low heating and cooling costs are also goods, to say nothing of protection from burglars

who notice that multiple exits are also multiple entrances. Moreover, there are other and perhaps better ways to increase fire safety. Extinguishers, alarm sprinklers, and large ashtrays also reduce the risk to apartment dwellers of injury or death from fire. If more than one exit is required, why not also require a fire extinguisher on every wall?

That sensible-sounding statement about apartment exits overlooks three interrelated facts: (1) Most goods are not free but can only be obtained by sacrificing something else that is also a good. (2) There are substitutes for anything. (3) Intelligent choice among substitutes requires a balancing of additional costs against additional benefits.

FROM "NEEDS" TO DEMAND

Now go back and look at the other two statements. "Our state will need large amounts of additional water in the coming decade." Does any state really need large amounts of additional water? Dams and reservoirs, pipelines, and desalinization plants are ways of obtaining more water. But they have costs. Do the benefits justify the costs? If you think there are no substitutes for water, then you are thinking too academically. You have abstracted unrealistically from the real world. Probably you are assuming that water is used primarily for drinking, whereas in fact the overwhelming bulk of the water consumed in the United States goes for other uses. What are some of the substitutes for water in such places of chronic scarcity as Arizona and Southern California? How about browner lawns, dirtier automobiles, more tennis courts to replace golf courses, and more land in cactus and less in cotton?

You will be able to make much more sense out of the water problem if you keep in mind that entities like *states* or *cities* never really want anything. Wants and goals are always attached ultimately to individuals. When someone says "The people want . . ." what does he mean? That all the people want it? A majority? Those who count? It is usually a good rule in analyzing statements like those above to ask: *Who* wants the good? And would they still want it if they had to pay the cost of getting it?

The third statement sounds humanitarian and liberal. All citizens should be able to obtain the medical care they need regardless of ability to pay." But how much medical care does any person need? We might all agree that a man with an inflamed appendix and no money should have his appendectomy completely at the taxpayers' expense if he is unable to meet any of the cost himself. But what of the man with a splinter in his finger? The services of physicians are not free goods, and they would not become free goods even if every physician treated his patients without charging a fee. There just would not be enough physicians to go around if everyone consulted a doctor for every minor ill. The lower the price of visiting a physician, the more frequently people will substitute a trip to the doctor for such other remedies as going to bed, taking it easy, or waiting and hoping. One could rather confidently predict that lower monetary fees would result in higher fees of other sorts, like waiting in line for many hours.

The Concept of Demand

"Needs" turn out to be mere *wants* when we inspect them closely. That's an important difference, for in the case of wants we may ask: "How *urgently* are they wanted?" Economists get at this question through the concept of *demand*. Demand is a concept that *relates amounts that are purchased to the sacrifices that must be made to obtain these amounts.*

Ask yourself the following questions: How many phonograph records do you want to own? How many times do you want to go out to dinner in a year? What grade do you want from this course?

If you can answer any of those questions, it is because you have assumed some cost in each case. Suppose you said you want an A from this course and plan to get one. What difference would it make if the price of an A went up? The teacher isn't taking bribes; the price of an A *to you* (that's what counts) is the sacrifice you must make to obtain it. Would you still want an A if it required twenty hours of study a week, while a B could be had for just one hour a week? You might still want it, but you would probably not be willing to buy it at such a high price when a fairly good substitute, a B, is so much cheaper. And that is what counts. Human wants

seem to be insatiable. But when a want can only be satisfied at some cost—that is to say, by giving up the satisfaction of some other wants to obtain it—we all moderate our desires and accept less than we would like to have.

The phenomenon of which we're speaking is so pervasive and so fundamental that some economists have been willing to assign it the status of a law: the law of demand. This law asserts that there is a negative relation between the amount of anything that people will purchase and the price (sacrifice) they must pay to obtain it. At higher prices, less will be purchased; at lower prices, more will be purchased.

Would you agree that this generalization can be called a *law*? Or can you think of exceptions? Genuine exceptions are rare at best. Why would anyone be indifferent to the sacrifices he must make? Or prefer more sacrifice to less? That's what a person would be doing if he took more of something as the cost of obtaining it increased.

Alleged exceptions to the law of demand are usually based on a misinterpretation of the evidence. A masochist, for example, would not provide an exception, because pain is for him a good and not a sacrifice. But what of the familiar case where the price of something rises and people increase their purchases in anticipation of further price rises? If you think about it carefully you will see that this is not an exception to the law of demand. The expectation of higher prices in the future, created by the initial price rise, has increased people's current demand for the item. It is not the higher price but the changed *expectations* that have caused people to buy more. We would observe something quite different if the initial price increase did *not* create those changed expectations. Another possibility is that changes in the price of substitutes or in available income have not been considered. When the price of beans goes up but the price of hamburger goes up even farther, people may buy more beans because they are now *relatively* cheaper.

It has sometimes been argued that certain prestige goods are exceptions to the law of demand. For example, people supposedly buy mink coats because their price is high, not low. No doubt there are people who buy some items largely to impress others with how much they can afford to pay. And people sometimes, in the absence of better information, judge quality by price, so that over a limited range, at least, their willingness to purchase may be positively rather than negatively related to price.

Even these seeming exceptions can be explained in a way consistent with the law of demand. People may be purchasing prestige rather than mere mink or judging quality by price because they have no better information. But we are not interested in rare curiosities. Whether or not you are willing to call it a law, the fact is undeniable and extremely important: increases in the price of goods will characteristically be accompanied by decreases in the total amount purchased, and decreases in price will char-

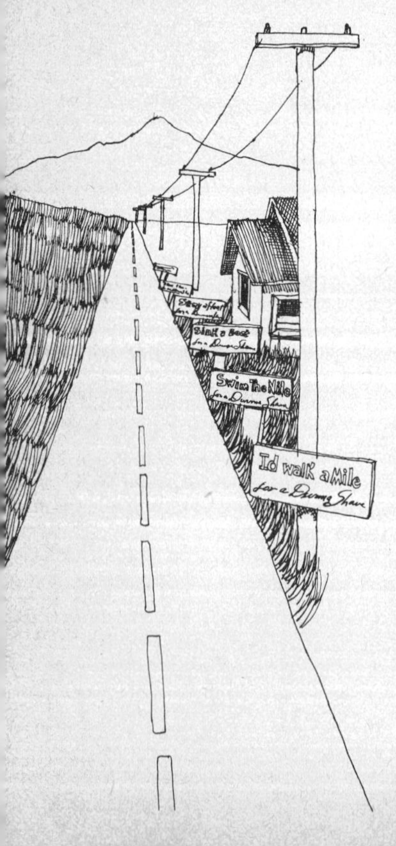

acteristically be accompanied by increases in the amount purchased. It is a serious mistake to overlook this pervasive fact.

Money Costs and Other Costs

The price in money that must be paid for something is not a complete measure of its cost to the purchaser. Sometimes, indeed, it is a very inadequate measure, as in the case of the student who wanted an A. Economists know this at least as well as anyone else. The concept of demand definitely does not suggest that money is the only thing that matters to people. Confusion about this point has done so much to create misunderstanding that we might profitably take a moment to clarify the matter.

Consider the case of a man buying soft drinks. Assume that he can purchase them in either returnable bottles or throwaway bottles, and that a six-pack of throwaway bottles is priced at 90¢, while a six-pack of returnable bottles is priced at 80¢ plus an 18¢ deposit. Which will he buy? Which is cheaper?

It depends on the cost to him, of which the retailer's price is only one element. If he doesn't mind saving and returning bottles—that is, if the cost to him of doing so is low—he will probably find the returnable bottles cheaper and will buy them. On the other hand, if he lives in an apartment with very limited storage space, gets to the store rarely, consumes large quantities of soft drinks, and has a waste-disposal chute a few steps from his door, he may well find the throwaway bottles cheaper and will purchase them in preference to returnable bottles.

Now suppose that our hypothetical apartment dweller with a passion for pop attends an ecology conference and comes away convinced that we must recycle to survive. The cost to him of using throwaway bottles suddenly jumps, for now he suffers pangs of guilt every time he tosses a bottle in the waste-disposal chute. The added cost in moral regret may be sufficient to induce him to switch to returnable bottles.

Or it may not. Suppose that he is going on a camping trip and wants to take along a dozen bottles of pop. He must backpack them into his camp site, and backpack the empties out again if he returns the bottles. The added cost of carrying a dozen empties may be enough to overcome the added cost of an uneasy conscience so that, in this case at least, he reverts to throwaway bottles. (Hopefully he throws them in a trash can.)

But let's change the last situation. Suppose the price of throwaway bottles is not 90¢ but $1.00, $1.20, or $1.80. At some price we may confidently expect that the cost of transporting empties will become less than the combined cost of buying throwaway bottles and living with guilt. (Of course, the deposit on returnables will have to rise, too, or he will just use and discard returnable bottles.)

There are several lessons to be drawn from this tale of the pop bottles. To assert that people purchase less of anything as the cost to them increases does not imply that people pay attention only to money, or that people are selfish, or that concern for social welfare does not influence economic behavior. It does imply that people respond to changes in cost and—a crucial implication—that a sufficiently large change in price can be counted on to tip almost any balance. When someone says that Americans won't give up the convenience of throwaway bottles and cans unless the government outlaws them, he overlooks several possibilities. A widespread change in attitude toward the environment could overcome the cost of being inconvenienced. And a sufficiently large tax on throwaway containers (call it a deposit if you wish) would make convenience a luxury too expensive to enjoy very frequently.

The essential point in all this is that the money price of obtaining something is only one part, and occasionally even a very small part, of its cost. What the law of demand asserts is that people will do less of what they want to do as the cost to them of doing it increases, and do more as the cost decreases.

A Useful Device

Many of the most useful concepts in economics can be conveniently expressed by means of graphs.

Suppose that we somehow obtained the following data on the relation between the price per gallon of water and the number of gallons that would be consumed (not swallowed!) per day in New York City at each of these different prices:

Price Charged the Consumer per Gallon	Millions of Gallons Consumed per Day
$.0035	60
.0028	80
.0021	120
.0016	160
.0012	200
.0009	240
.0003	360
.0001	450
.0000	510

We have graphed these values in figure 2A. The dots express graphically the data from the demand schedule above. If you are not accustomed to working with graphs, study figure 2A until you understand exactly how it was constructed from the demand schedule.

The graph of figure 2A also *adds* something to the information contained in the schedule. We have connected the dots by means of straight lines. The assumption underlying this procedure is that the price can be changed by very small amounts and that there will result small continuous changes in the daily consumption of water. When dealing with the total demand of a large number of consumers, it will be easy to find an individual who makes no response to a small price increase. But you can also find important changes, such as the man who gets his leaky toilet fixed.

Now use the demand curve in thinking through the following questions. (By the way, it is called a demand *curve* even though it is composed exclusively of straight lines. A straight line is simply a curve that doesn't. Like a baseball pitcher's curve that failed to "break.")

1. How much water do New Yorkers "need"? How much will they consume per day if the price of water is zero? Is there an important difference between the two questions?

2. If the price of water has been set for many years at $.0008 per gallon, how much water will the city authorities say that New Yorkers need per day? What are they assuming when they say this?

3. Suppose that New York's reservoirs are being rapidly depleted, and experts predict that the supply will become critically low before fall unless daily consumption is reduced to 180 million gallons. How could the city's water managers obtain this desired reduction in consumption?

4. Notice by how much water consumption would increase if the price were originally $.0035 and were then decreased to $.0003. Do you think that residents of the city would increase their *drinking* by this amount? How might the additional 300 million gallons per day be used?

Time Is on Our Side

If you are at all the suspicious sort of person, you will have wondered whether water consumption really would or could change in response to price changes by as much as the demand curve indicates. Changes take time. And that is an important observation. Changes in the amount purchased will be greater for any given price change the longer the time period allowed for adjustment.

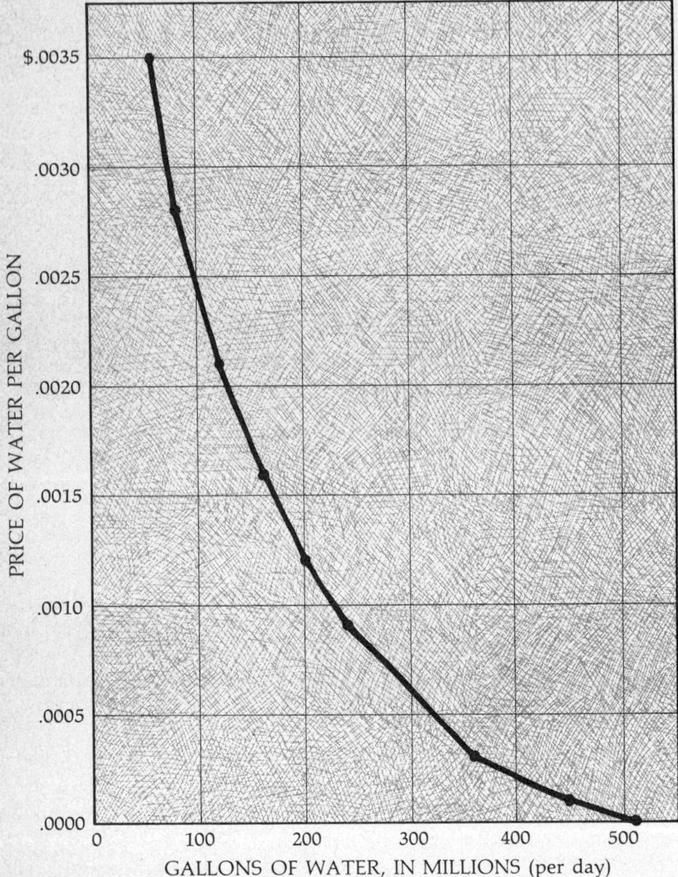

Figure 2A Demand for water

Check this out for yourself with a mental experiment. Suppose the price of water has been $.0003 a gallon for twenty years and it is raised overnight to $.0028. What substitutions for water will be made *right away*? What substitutions would you expect to observe after a month or two had passed? What substitutions would you expect to observe over the next ten years—assuming that everyone expects the price to remain at the higher level?

Try a similar mental experiment with the price of gasoline. Suppose that the federal government levied an additional tax on gasoline of 50¢ per gallon. How do you think this would affect the amount purchased in the subsequent week? In the subsequent six months? After four years had elapsed?

By taking our examples almost entirely from the area of household decisions, we may have obscured the important fact that customers include producers as well as consumers. Business firms use water and gasoline, too, and they sometimes use so much that they are exceptionally sensitive to price changes. You'll be neglecting some of the major factors that cause demand curves to slope downward to the right if you overlook the contribution producers make to the demand for many goods. In the case of water, location decisions are often made on the basis of the expected price of water, and those decisions then affect the quantities demanded in different geographic areas.

But it takes time for customers to find and begin to use substitutes. It also takes time for producers to devise, produce, and publicize substitutes. As a result, the amount by which people increase or decrease their purchases when prices change depends very much on the time period over which we are observing the adjustment. Occasionally even a rather large price increase (or decrease) will lead to no significant decrease (or increase) in consumption—*at first.* And this sometimes causes people to conclude that price has no effect on consumption. A very mistaken conclusion! Nothing in this world happens instantaneously. Man, creature of habit that he is, must be allowed a little time to prove that there are substitutes for anything.

Economizing Behavior

The concept of demand is central to the economic way of thinking because it interprets the behavior of producers as well as consumers. Producers must also choose constantly among substitutes in the process of organizing production; for producers as well as for consumers there are substitutes for everything; the demand curves for riveters, turret lathes, industrial sites, marketing agents, and all the infinite paraphernalia of production slope downward to the right just as do the demand curves for passenger automobiles, medical care, and soda pop in returnable bottles. The theory of demand is not so much the theory of consumer behavior as it is the theory of *economizing* behavior. And *everyone* economizes: the trade association lobbyist in Washington urging Congress to exclude foreign competitors as well as the supermarket shopper hesitating between pickled herring and smoked oysters. Economics explains how the economizing behavior of individuals is coordinated in a system of social cooperation.

PRICES, INCOME, AND DEMAND

It is extremely cumbersome to talk about "the amount by which people increase or decrease their purchases when the price changes." But this is an important relationship with many useful applications. So economists have invented a special phrase that summarizes the relationship. The formal title of the concept is *price elasticity of demand.*

That's an appropriate name. Elasticity means responsiveness. If the amount of any good that people purchase changes substantially in response to a small change in price, demand is said to be elastic. If even a very large price change results in little change in the amount purchased, demand is said to be inelastic.

Price elasticity of demand is defined precisely as *the percentage change in quantity demanded divided by the percentage change in price.* Thus, if a 10% increase in the price of eggs leads to a 5% reduction in the number of eggs sold, the elasticity of demand is 5% divided by 10%, or .5. To be completely accurate, it is *minus* .5, since price and amount purchased vary inversely. But for simplicity we shall ignore the minus sign and treat the coefficients of elasticity as if they were positive.

Whenever the coefficient of elasticity is greater than one (ignoring the sign)—that is to say, whenever the percentage change in quantity is *greater* than the percentage change in price—demand is said to be elastic. Whenever the coefficient of elasticity is less than one, which means whenever the percentage change in quantity is *less* than the percentage change in price, demand is said to be inelastic. Compulsive learners will want to know what is said when the percentage change in quantity is exactly equal to the percentage change in price, so that the coefficient of demand elasticity is exactly one. You may file away the information that demand is then *unit elastic.* (Economics is a very systematic discipline.)

You can begin to familiarize yourself with the uses of this concept by asking whether demand is elastic or inelastic in each case below. The cases are discussed in the subsequent paragraphs.

1. "People aren't going to buy much more no matter how far we cut the price."

2. "This is a competitive business. We would lose half our customers if we raised our prices by as little as 2%."

3. The demand for salt.

4. The demand for Morton's salt.

5. The demand for Morton's salt at the Kroger Store at Fifth and Main.

6. "The university's total receipts from tuition would actually increase if they cut the tuition rates by 20%."

7. "It's odd but true. Wheat farmers would gross more money if they all got together and burned one-quarter of this year's crop."

8. If the statement in 7 is true, does it follow that they could gross even more money by burning one-half of the crop?

Price Elasticity in Practice

1. "People aren't going to buy much more no matter how far we cut the price." If a businessman doubts that even a very large price decrease will do much to increase his sales, he believes that his demand is highly inelastic. He will not want to lower his price under such circumstances for he will lose more through the lower price than he will gain through the larger volume. But if people don't respond very much to a price cut, will they also be relatively insensitive to a price hike? If they are, a businessman out to increase his income will want to raise his price. Businessmen typically complain that prices are too low. Then why don't they raise their prices? It's a free country, isn't it? The answer, of course, is that they would usually lose too many customers if they did so. It is the elasticity of demand that determines whether or not a businessman can add to his money receipts by raising his prices.

2. "This is a competitive business. We would lose half our customers if we raised our prices by as little as 2%." The businessman making this statement is saying in effect that he faces a highly elastic demand: A 50% decline in quantity demanded would follow a mere 2% increase in price. The coefficient of elasticity is 25. The demand is very elastic indeed. Another way of putting it would be to say that his customers are extremely sensitive to any price change. And that makes it difficult for him to raise his prices, however eager he might be to do so.

3. The demand for salt. What makes demand curves elastic or inelastic? The availability of good substitutes is clearly an important factor. Another is the importance of the item in the budget of purchasers. If the expenditure on some good is large relative to the income or wealth of the purchaser, he will be more sensitive to any change in its price. Isn't that true from your own experience? Suppose you smoke and also attend movies twice a week. A book of matches costs a penny and movies $2.50. It is not likely that a 200 percent increase in match prices will have much effect on

your smoking. But a 50 percent increase in the price of movies would substantially affect your movie going if you have a typical student's income.

Apply this to table salt. One pound of salt lasts a long time and costs less than 10¢. So who cares? Housewives will be relatively insensitive to any change in the price of salt. Moreover, salt has few good substitutes. You would not be inclined to put sugar on your eggs if the price of salt rose dramatically, just as you would not cut the pepper and double the salt if the price of salt fell substantially.

Adam Smith, often called the founder of modern economics, observed in *The Wealth of Nations* (1776) that "salt is a very ancient and very universal subject of taxation. . . . The quantity annually consumed by any individual is so small, and may be purchased so gradually, that nobody, it seems to have been thought, could feel very sensibly even a pretty heavy tax upon it." Moreover, salt was one of "the necessaries of life" in Smith's terminology. We can object to the term *necessary* and express Smith's meaning more accurately: salt has few good substitutes. The result is a highly inelastic demand and an apparently irresistible temptation to governments in ancient times to levy taxes on salt.

But it's possible to exaggerate the inelasticity of even the demand for salt. Householders in wintry regions sometimes sprinkle table salt on their sidewalks or porch steps to melt the ice. If salt were ten times as expensive, many would substitute chopping and scraping for salt.

4. The demand for Morton's salt. Why would the demand for Morton's salt be less inelastic than the demand for salt? Because there are substitutes—namely, other brands of salt. The Morton Salt Company is not in the privileged position of ancient governments, which could raise the price of *all* salt. If someone in the marketing department at Morton chanced to read Adam Smith and was inspired by him to double the price, the grocery stores that are Morton's customers would tend to shift their purchases to other salt manufacturers.

5. The demand for Morton's salt at the Kroger Store at Fifth and Main. If there are more good substitutes for Morton's salt than for salt, there are even more good substitutes for the Morton's salt sold at the local Kroger store. We have moved from a very inelastic to what is probably a highly elastic demand for the same quantity. And that is why you aren't victimized when you purchase salt. You might be willing to pay $2 a pound if salt was not available at a lower price. But fortunately for you, there are many options. A seller who tried to take advantage of the fact that the total demand for salt is highly inelastic would lose his customers. The demand for *the salt he sells* will be quite elastic.

People often make the mistake of assuming that those who sell "vital necessities" could get away with charging almost any price they chose.

We have learned to be suspicious of the phrase *vital necessities.* Now we see again the grounds for this suspicion. Food has as good a claim as anything to the title "vital necessity." But the relevant fact is that *no one buys food.* Housewives do not purchase a pound of "food"; they buy a pound of hamburger, or bacon, or calf's liver. And there are many sellers selling many kinds of food. All of which means that there are excellent substitutes for specific food commodities, and hence demand curves are highly elastic. So sellers are for the most part closely constrained in the prices they can charge.

Remember also what was said in the last chapter about the importance of *time:* greater substitution will occur in response to a price change the more time elapses. We can now express the same thought another way: Demand curves are more elastic over longer than over shorter periods. Gasoline provides an excellent example. If the federal government pushed up the price of gasoline across the board by imposing a large additional tax, motorists would at first grumble but pay. Then they would begin to form car pools and investigate public transportation. Still later some would move in order to be closer to work. When they replaced their present cars, many would switch from eight cylinders to four. Automobile manufacturers would meanwhile be shifting toward greater production of economy cars and less production of gas-guzzlers. Some technological changes to reduce gasoline consumption that were not economical on balance at the former price of gasoline would become economical at the higher price. These are the kinds of factors that make demand curves more elastic in the long run.

6. "The university's total receipts from tuition would actually increase if they cut the tuition rates by 20%." The university's total receipts from tuition are the product of the tuition rate and the number of students who enroll. If a 20% decrease in the tuition rate results in an increase in tuition receipts, then there must have been a *more than* 20% increase in enrollment. The percentage change in quantity demanded is greater than the percentage change in price, so demand is elastic.

This suggests a simple way of thinking about elasticity. Keep in mind that the quantity demanded will always move in the opposite direction from the price. So if a price change causes *total receipts* to move in the *opposite* direction from the price change, demand must be elastic. The change in the quantity purchased has to be larger in percentage terms than the price change, because total receipts are nothing but the product of price and quantity. And that is the definition of an elastic demand. If a price change causes *total receipts* to move in the *same* direction as the price change, demand must be inelastic. The change in amount purchased was not large enough to outweigh the change in price. And that is the meaning of an inelastic demand. You can satisfy yourself that this relationship holds by running through a numerical example.

Assume that 1000 students will enroll if the tuition is $500 per year, but only 900 will enroll if the tuition is $600 per year. Is the demand elastic or inelastic within this range of tuition charges? We notice that the university's total receipts change *in the same direction* as the price change: 1000 × 500 is less than 900 × 600. So the demand is inelastic by the rule given above. We can confirm this with a little arithmetic. The percentage change in quantity demanded is 100 enrollments divided by 950. (A percentage change is the change divided by the base: we chose the average of 1000 and 900 as the base, because we want to get the same answer whether we raise the price from $500 to $600 or lower it from $600 to $500.) The percentage change in price is $100 divided by $550—where we again use the average of the two values between which we're moving as the base. The coefficient of elasticity is $^{11}/_{19}$, or .58.

Now assume instead that enrollment falls from 1000 to 800 as a result of the tuition increase from $500 to $600. In this case total receipts and price are moving *in opposite directions*: 1000 × 500 is greater than 800 × 600. So the demand must be elastic. A few calculations will verify this conclusion. The percentage change in quantity is now 200 divided by 900; the percentage change in price is again 100 divided by 550. (The units don't matter; they cancel out.) The coefficient of elasticity is $^{11}/_9$, or 1.22.

Do not jump to the conclusion that the university will always be in a better financial position, given an elastic demand, if it lowers its tuition. True, lower tuition charges will mean larger receipts whenever demand is elastic; but a larger enrollment probably also means larger costs. The university must decide in such a case whether the addition to total receipts will be larger than the addition to total costs.

7. "It's odd but true. Wheat farmers would gross more money if they all got together and burned one-quarter of this year's crop." The logic of number 6 applies also here. Farmers can only gross more money while

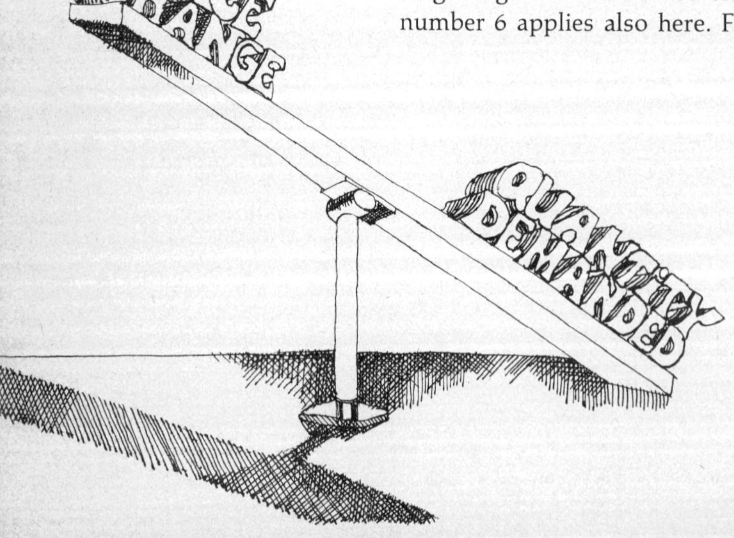

selling less wheat if the percentage change in price is greater than the percentage change in the amount sold. Demand would have to be inelastic.

Farmers may never have heard about elastic or inelastic demands. But when they lobby for government controls on production, they are usually very much aware of the relation between price and the amount that is sold. You can, like Molière's famous M. Jourdain who spoke prose for forty years without knowing it, make good use of demand elasticities without ever having heard the term.

8. Could wheat farmers do even better by burning one-half of the crop? The elasticity of demand will almost certainly not be the same at all the different positions along a demand schedule or curve. As a general rule, demand will be more elastic at higher prices (and smaller quantities) than at lower prices (and larger quantities). Why? Basically because people tend to be more sensitive to price changes when the price in question is large (relative to their incomes) than when it is small. Consequently, if farmers somehow agreed upon a scheme for destroying wheat in order to raise its price, at some point they would run into an elastic demand. And as soon as the demand turned from inelastic to elastic, total receipts would go down as a consequence of further price increases.

This relationship may become clearer to you if you examine a straight-line demand curve. Along the upper left portion of the demand curve, any price change of a given amount will be a *smaller percentage change* than it will be along the lower right portion of the curve. At the same time, the *percentage change* in quantity demanded will be getting *larger* as we move from the lower right portion of the curve to the upper left. Since elasticity of demand is the ratio of these percentage changes, the coefficient of elasticity must be increasing continuously as we move up and back along a straight-line demand curve.

The Myth of Vertical Demand

But enough of such technicalities. In the three statements with which we began this chapter, what was being implicitly assumed about the elasticity of demand? Our objection to each statement, you recall, was that it ignored the fact that all goods have substitutes and that substitution does occur when prices change. In other words, demand curves are *not* completely inelastic. A completely inelastic demand curve would graph as a vertical line. You would be wise not to look for such demand curves in the real world.

You would also be wise to look out for people who argue as if completely inelastic demand curves are the rule. There is no such thing as a completely inelastic demand over the entire range of possible prices. Most purchasers will respond at least a little to changes in the cost to them, and *all* purchasers would respond to a sufficiently large change. If this seems too obvious to bother mentioning, consult your daily newspaper for evidence that it is by no means obvious to everyone. Well-intentioned people and some not so well intentioned talk constantly of basic needs, minimum requirements, and absolute necessities.

Demand curves are rarely as inelastic as orators suppose. That does not imply, of course, that they are always elastic. That is a more difficult question to be answered by looking at each case. But it is a very important question for anyone who wants to decide how well our economic system functions.

Estimating Elasticity

When the oil exporting countries of the Middle East imposed their embargo on sales to the United States in 1973, the price elasticity of demand for gasoline became an issue in the newspapers. Some gloomily predicted a short run elasticity as low as .2, which means that a 20% reduction in sales would require a 100% increase in the price of gasoline. Optimistic estimates predicted an elasticity of .4, in which case a 50% increase in price would still be necessary to reduce consumption by 20%. Other estimates tended to range between .2 and .4. Let's take a look at the difference that elasticity makes.

The average retail price of gasoline in 1972 was very close to 36¢. Under the most optimistic estimate cited above, the price would have to rise to 54¢ to cut purchases back to available supply if the supply were reduced by 20%: a 20% reduction in quantity demanded divided by a 50% increase in the price yields an elasticity coefficient of .4. With a demand elasticity of only .3, the price would have to rise to 60¢. And it would have to go all the way to 72¢ under the conditions of the most unfavorable estimate, an elasticity of .2.

None of these estimates was put forward in 1973 with a great deal of confidence; we simply had no experience in the United States with changes of this magnitude in the price of gasoline. And extrapolation is risky in cases of this sort. The fact that a 10% price increase has in the past led to a 3% reduction in consumption does not mean that a 100% increase will yield a 30% reduction. We can be certain, in fact, that if the relative price of a good rises far enough, the demand for it will eventually become elastic. That is because at higher prices any good makes a larger dent in people's budgets and they consequently become more sensitive to changes in its price. Someone with a weekly take home pay of $150 may ignore the fact that he is now spending $9 a week rather than $6 on gasoline

AN IMPORTANT NOTE ON *RELATIVE* PRICES

From the beginning of the book, whenever we've talked about a change in the price of some good we've meant a change in its *relative price: its price in relation to other goods.* For the last decade or so the United States has experienced a general rise in prices. The average of *all* prices has been going up. Now if all prices rise by the same percentage, then relative prices do not change at all. Since we're trying to understand the way in which relative prices guide consumer and producer decisions, we have to distinguish the change in a good's price that was caused by general inflation from the change caused by an alteration in the scarcity of that particular good.

Take the case of gasoline prices. An increase from 36¢ per gallon for regular at the beginning of 1972 to 58¢ at the end of 1974 was a 61% increase (using the original price as the base). But the average of *all* prices paid by consumers rose 26% over this period. The increase in the relative price of gasoline was therefore only about 35%. That is equivalent in its effects to an increase of only $12\frac{1}{2}$¢, from 36¢ to about 48¢.

Or take the price changes from 1955 to 1974. The average price of gasoline in 1955 was 29¢. From 29¢ to 58¢ is a 100% increase. When we deduct the rate of increase in the general price level between 1955 and 1974, however, the change in the relative price of gasoline was only about 6%. In short, gasoline was not actually much more expensive in 1975 at 58¢ than it had been in 1955 at 29¢ a gallon. And it's the relative price that matters.

because its price has gone up; he is less likely to ignore an increase from $20 to $30 in his expenditures for gasoline. His budget is more likely to compel a cut in gasoline consumption in the second case. And every gallon not consumed will now free a larger portion of his income for other purposes.

Income and Demand

One of the reasons for the low elasticity of demand for gasoline is that its price *relative to income* in the United States had been falling for many years. The average price of gasoline was about 29¢ a gallon in 1955 when per capita disposable income was $1666. This means that it took $145, or

---

A TECHNICAL NOTE ON
THE CALCULATION OF PERCENTAGE CHANGES

Is a price increase from 36¢ to 72¢ a 100% increase? That depends on how you interpret percentage changes, a matter on which there is unfortunately no uniform practice. Note that a decrease from 72¢ to 36¢ is only a 50% change—when we use the original value as the base in calculating the percentage change. For some purposes that is a misleading way of handling percentage changes because it arbitrarily makes every increase seem larger than an identical decrease. The bias arises from the fact that when the original value is chosen as the base, a smaller base is always used for increases than for decreases. We have already suggested a way to avoid this bias: by selecting as the base neither the original nor the subsequent value but the average of the two. Then the percentage change will be the same going up as coming down. By *this* method of calculation a 100% increase from a price of 36¢ is an increase to $1.08 and a 100% decrease from $1.08 returns the price to 36¢. The change in price of 72¢ is exactly 100% of the average of $1.08 and 36¢. The point is worth your attention because percentage changes are a common way of making comparisons; but the comparisons can be quite misleading when the percentage changes are large and the precise method by which they were calculated is not stated. For small percentage changes the bias introduced through choice of a base is less significant.

8.7% of per capita disposable income, to buy 500 gallons of gasoline in 1955. For 500 gallons of gasoline to use up 8.7% of income in 1973, its price would have had to be 73¢ a gallon. So it's not surprising that the driving habits of Americans did not change drastically in 1974 even when the price of gasoline rose to about 60¢ a gallon.

The elasticity of demand for a good will depend, then, upon its price *relative to income* as well as upon the range of available substitutes. The low elasticity of demand for gasoline results from the fact that its price has been declining substantially relative to income for many years and that the substitutes for gasoline don't appeal strongly to a lot of people. Let's apply this reasoning to a hypothetical case. Suppose we want to make ourselves less vulnerable to political blackmail by oil exporting nations. A more elastic demand reduces vulnerability. We could increase the elasticity of demand by raising the price of gasoline substantially (through an additional federal tax) or by improving the quality of such substitutes as public transportation systems, which use far less fuel per passenger ride. The higher cost of driving would presumably increase the demand for public transportation, and the tax could be used to finance improvements that would in turn make public transportation a more attractive substitute.

The other principal factor upon which demand elasticity depends is time, as we've mentioned previously. Time permits consumers to search out acceptable substitutes and gives producers a chance to contrive new ones. Elasticity is a measure of responsiveness or flexibility, and everything is more flexible over a longer than a shorter time. Some of the 1973 estimates on the elasticity of demand for gasoline *given one year* for adjustments to occur were in the vicinity of .8. A 20% reduction in the quantity demanded would require only a 25% increase in the price if elasticity were .8.

Demand versus Quantity Demanded

In using the concepts of demand and elasticity it's important to keep an eye on other factors that may be changing along with the price. Elasticity measures the responsiveness of the quantity demanded to changes in the price on the assumption that nothing has occurred to change the demand curve itself. The demand curve for any good depends upon people's tastes and preferences, their incomes, and the properties of substitutes. *With the demand curve given and constant,* the specific quantity that will be demanded depends upon the price.

You can avoid a very common confusion by carefully observing the distinction between *demand* and the *quantity demanded.* Demand is a relation between quantity demanded and price. The demand for gasoline is expressed by a series of prices and a series of corresponding quantities that would be demanded (or amounts that would be purchased) at those prices during some period of time, expressed either in a schedule or a curve. A movement from one row (or line) of the schedule to another, or from one point on the curve to another, should always be called a change in the *quantity demanded,* not a change in the *demand.* The latter would be a change in the schedule itself, a shift in the curve caused by a change in tastes and preferences, or income, or the perceived properties of substitutes. The relative prices of substitutes are among their most important properties.

If this seems a terribly abstract or pedantic distinction, try your hand at locating the error in the following argument. It arises from a failure to observe the distinction.

If the government puts a large new tax on gasoline so that its price goes up, the demand will fall. But when the demand for anything falls, its price tends to fall. So we can't be sure that the tax will actually raise the price of gasoline.

Can you spot the error? It's in the main clause of the first sentence. The demand will *not* fall. Only the *quantity demanded* will fall. So the next two sentences are mistaken conclusions. When the quantity demanded falls in response to the price increase, that's the end of the matter. Of course, the higher price may over time call forth new substitutes, and the appearance of new substitutes is capable of causing the demand curve to shift—a true change in demand.

If a combination of rising incomes, environmental concern, and new interest in outdoor exercise induces more people to want bicycles, the demand for bicycles will increase. And both the price and quantity demanded may well increase as a consequence. This actually occurred in 1971. You have grasped the distinction between demand and quantity demanded if you see clearly why this in no way contradicts the law of demand. An increase in demand, or a shift upward and to the right in the demand curve, will pull up both price and quantity demanded. But it was still true with the high demand of 1971, as it had been with the low demand of 1969, that a smaller quantity of bicycles was demanded at higher than at lower prices. And this is what the law of demand asserts.

Income Elasticity of Demand

Price elasticity of demand is the oldest child in a rather large family of elasticity concepts. The size of the family should not surprise you. Economics is useful because change occurs; it attempts to predict or understand the consequences of changes. Elasticity concepts provide a way of focusing on particular change relationships and of discussing them in quantitative terms. So new children are born regularly into the elasticity family as economists pursue their varied investigations. We won't try to introduce you to the whole family (an impossible task anyway given the birth rate), but one more member is worth meeting.

Income elasticity of demand is a close companion to price elasticity of demand. Its definition is analogous: *the percentage change in quantity demanded divided by the percentage change in income.* If a 20% increase in your income leads to a 15% increase in your expenditures on housing, the income elasticity of your demand for housing is $\frac{3}{4}$ or .75. Notice that the coefficient of elasticity in this case could be greater than unity, between zero and unity, or less than zero (negative). If a 20% increase in your income leads to an 80% reduction in your oleomargarine consumption (because you're now buying butter), the elasticity coefficient will be minus 4. We cannot ignore the algebraic sign in the case of income elasticity of demand; for while more income *permits* more consumption, it need not *result* in more consumption of any particular commodity. Suppose that we put income on the vertical axis as we did with price. Curves expressing the relationship between *price* and quantity demanded slope downward to the right, expressing the inverse relationship between these two variables and yielding negative coefficients of elasticity. But a curve that shows the relationship between *income* and the quantity demanded of some good can slope upward to the right or be vertical or slope upward to the left. A single such curve, expressing, say, the responsiveness of Homer Iliad's weekly hamburger purchases to changes in his income, might well resemble a backward "C". The income elasticity of Homer's demand for hamburger could thus be shown as positive, zero, or negative, depending on the income range under consideration. Let's reflect on Homer's habits to convince ourselves that this is quite plausible.

When Homer's income was very low, he yearned for meat but could rarely afford it. When he got a 5% raise, he doubled his consumption of hamburger, displaying an income elasticity of demand of 20 (100% divided by 5%). Homer's coefficient declined as his income rose further, both because any absolute change in income is a smaller percentage change when income is higher and because at higher income levels Homer could afford more expensive cuts of meat. As Homer's income rose still further he eventually reached a point where more income didn't lead to any more hamburger consumption at all. As his wealth increased, Homer began substituting steaks and roasts for hamburger, something he would have liked to do even when he was poor but couldn't do because he wasn't wealthy enough.

When the quantity of a good demanded decreases as income increases, the good is called an *inferior good.* This is a technical term and not a judgment about intrinsic value. Almost any good could be an inferior good for someone at some income level. For a rich man who buys a Cadillac annually but then becomes *filthy* rich and shifts to a Rolls Royce annually, a Cadillac is an inferior good. You could easily find similar if less spectacular cases from your own experience.

Once Over Lightly

Every good has substitutes: other goods which will be used in its stead when the cost of using the original good rises, other goods for which the original good will substitute when *their* relative cost goes up.

By talking about "needs," we can sometimes win arguments we might otherwise lose. "Needs" are actually wants of many different urgencies.

People want more or less of a good as the *cost to them* decreases or increases.

The concept of *demand* is preferable to the concept of *need* because demand relates the amounts that are purchased to the sacrifices that must be made to obtain these amounts.

The "law of demand" asserts that more will be purchased at lower prices, less at higher prices—assuming that something in addition to the price has not changed to offset this consequence.

The money cost of a good is only one part of the cost that affects people's decisions.

A sufficiently large change in money cost (price) can usually overcome the effects that nonmoney costs exert on people's decisions.

A change in price will usually induce a larger change in amounts purchased when more time is allowed for consumers and producers to learn about and invent new substitutes.

Price elasticity of demand is a measure of the percentage change in the quantity of a good demanded relative to the percentage change in its price.

Demand is (price) elastic when the percentage increase in quantity demanded is greater than the percentage decrease in price. Demand is inelastic when the percentage change in quantity demanded is smaller than the percentage change in price.

Price elasticity of demand depends upon the importance of the price relative to one's income, but even more upon the quality and price of available substitutes.

More separate sources of supply for a good imply better substitutes for any particular unit of the good and hence a more elastic demand.

Total receipts or expenditures move in the opposite direction from price when demand is elastic and in the same direction as price when demand is inelastic.

The concept of "needs" implies a perfectly inelastic demand curve—an extremely rare phenomenon.

Changes in income cause demand curves to shift. The income elasticity of demand for a good is the percentage change in the quantity demanded divided by the percentage change in income. It can vary over a wide range of negative or positive values.

The demand for a good refers to the *schedule of relationships* between price and quantity demanded and must be distinguished from the quantity or amount that is demanded. The quantity of a good demanded changes with its price. But a true change in demand will alter *both* price *and* quantity demanded.

It is the *relative* price of a good, its price in relationship to the prices of other goods, which determines the quantity demanded at various prices and income levels.

The technical term *inferior good* refers to any good for which the quantity demanded varies inversely with income. This term does not evaluate the quality of a product.

The concept of demand forms the basis for the theory of *economizing behavior*, behavior aimed at obtaining as much as possible from what is available.

QUESTIONS FOR DISCUSSION

1. Assume that Congress has decided to reduce consumption of nonreusable containers in order to preserve Spaceship Earth. Evaluate the following arguments that might be used in the discussion of how to go about achieving this goal.

   (*a*) "We know we cannot survive unless we stop using things and then discarding them. The only sensible approach, therefore, is a legal ban on all nonreusable containers of any kind."

   (*b*) "People will do the right thing once they understand the problem. I don't think we should start passing laws. We should assume that the American people are public-spirited and we should educate them to the facts."

   (*c*) "It has been proposed by some that we place a tax on the manufacture of containers to encourage deposit-and-return. This would not work because people just would not care about the tax. Moreover, a tax says in effect that it's all right to pollute if you're rich, but not if you're poor."

2. Most systems of hospitalization insurance substantially reduce the cost to the patient of hospitalization, sometimes to zero. How does this affect hospital use? Why? Evaluate the argument that it does not affect hospital use since "no one gets sick just because hospitals are cheap, or avoids getting sick because they're expensive."

3. In 1967 the president of the American Medical Association was quoted as saying that medical care was a privilege and not a right. Today the AMA officially proclaims that "health care is the right of everyone." What quantity and quality of health care do you suppose they're talking about?

4. If the government forbids motorists to drive more than 55 miles per hour, does everyone stay within the 55 mile limit? What are the costs of going faster? What are some of the costs of going faster that do not fall on the speeding motorist? Do these latter costs affect motorists' decisions? Why might the fact that faster driving uses up more of the nation's scarce petroleum reduce the speed of some drivers but not others?

5. Why do people live in New York City if the costs of doing so—high rents, noise, dirt, congestion, the risks of being robbed or assaulted—are

so high? Is it true that most of them "have no choice"? What do you think would happen if the costs listed above were significantly reduced?

6. One of the recurring themes of this book will be the *informational role* performed by prices. People learn about increased scarcities by paying attention to prices. How did most Americans discover in 1974 that the Arab nations were buying more sugar, the sugar beet crop in the Soviet Union had fallen short of expectations, and hurricanes had reduced the sugar cane harvest in the Gulf of Mexico region? What did people do when they found out? Why? (One of the articles reprinted in the appendix, "The Use of Knowledge in Society" by the 1974 Nobel prizewinner F. A. Hayek, is a thoughtful exploration of the price system as a social device for economizing effectively with very little information.)

7. John loves butter and thinks that margarine tastes like soap. George can't tell the difference. Whose demand for butter is likely to be more elastic?

8. Would the elasticity of a crowd's demand for cold lemonade be affected by the proximity of a drinking fountain?

9. How do you think the development of other copying machines affected the elasticity of demand for Xerox machines?

10. Is the demand for prescription drugs elastic or inelastic? Why? Do you agree with the statement sometimes made that the prices charged for prescription drugs can be freely set by the manufacturers, since people must buy whatever the doctor prescribes?

11. How does ignorance affect elasticities of demand?

12. How might the development of science and technology affect demand elasticities?

13. Does a society's transportation system in any way affect elasticities of demand? How?

14. The demand for aspirin at currently prevailing prices seems to be highly inelastic. What do you think would happen to the elasticity of demand if the price of aspirin relative to everything else were five times as high? Fifty times as high? Why?

15. Higher prices for beef, automobiles, or television sets will lead to a reduction in the *amount of each demanded.* Think of some specific changes (such as in tastes, prices of substitutes, quality of complements) that would cause the *demand* for each to increase so that more might actually be demanded at higher prices. Why is this completely consistent with the law of demand?

16. A change in expectations can cause a change in demand. Explain how this could lead to a situation where a price decline was followed by a *decrease* in the amount purchased.

17. Lucy Borgia earned money for school last summer by working during June,
July, and the first two weeks of August for $3.00 an hour. She quit her job
on August 15 in order to take a vacation at Ocean Beach. This coming
summer, the firm for which she worked has offered her a much better position paying $4.50 an hour. Explain why the higher wage rate might induce
Lucy to eliminate her vacation this summer *or* might induce her to spend
the entire month of August at Ocean Beach.

How is the price of a vacation related to the available wage? Use the concept
of income elasticity of demand to interpret Lucy's decision if she elects
to take twice as much vacation this year despite the fact that a unit of vacation is half again more expensive that it was last year.

3

SCARCITY AND THE PRICE SYSTEM

No one blames the thermometer for low temperatures or seriously proposes to warm up the house on a cold day by holding a candle under the furnace thermostat. People do, however, often blame high prices for the fact of scarcity and act as if scarcity could be eliminated by pushing down prices through legislation or by moralizing.

To the lover of lobster, its high price does indeed look like the cause of its scarcity. Lobster rarely appears in our house because its price is high. But what would happen if the lobster lovers' lobby pushed a bill through Congress which placed a ceiling price on lobster well below the currently prevailing price? Would lobster be any less scarce? Lobster fans would now *want* to buy more lobster. But would they succeed? The low ceiling price might in fact cause lobster to disappear from most of the stores in the country.

Contrary to the doctrine now being propounded by some who are impressed with the enormous wealth of the United States, even we, the wealthiest people in the world, have not ended scarcity. Nor is it likely that we ever shall. We may learn to be more content with fewer material goods, or we may manage to produce and distribute material goods in such abundance that no one any longer gives much thought to acquiring more. But even then we would not have abolished scarcity. For the present and the foreseeable future, we shall have to live with the fact that the means of satisfying our wants fall far short of the wants themselves.

So we must *economize.* We must allocate our resources intelligently to obtain from what we have as much as possible of what we want. We must learn to *manage* scarcity since we cannot hope to abolish it. The management of scarcity does include scaling down or otherwise altering wants as well as expanding production. It's often possible to loosen the pinch of scarcity merely by reevaluating one's objectives and discovering that a particular goal really isn't worth the cost of attaining it, or that the want behind the desire for some good can actually be satisfied in another and less difficult way. But the management of scarcity, especially in an economy as large and diversified as ours and with as many different resources and infinitely varied preferences, will remain an enormously complex social task. In this chapter we want to gain an understanding of those complexities by exploring some of the implications of scarcity. We shall notice that scarcity is quite different from shortage, and that something can be scarce even when a surplus of it exists.

THE MEANING OF SCARCITY

The climate of Gazebo, a fictitious South Sea Island, is perfect for growing both oranges and pineapples. But since there are far more pineapple plants than orange trees on the island, 50,000 pineapples are harvested each month and only 5000 oranges. Which is more scarce?

We cannot tell from the information given. Scarcity is a *relationship.* If the people of Gazebo love pineapples and hate oranges, pineapples could be more scarce despite their greater abundance. Scarcity is a relationship between availability and desirability, or between supply and demand. If pineapples in Gazebo were considered unfit for human consumption, and there was no way to sell them to others, they would not be scarce at all. No one speaks of the scarcity of garbage—except hog farmers, perhaps, for whom garbage is not garbage.

If everyone can have all that he wants of some good without being required to sacrifice anything else that is also wanted, that good is not *scarce. It is a* free good. There are obviously not many free goods available in our society, despite the song that says the best things in life are free. Perhaps the best things in life cannot be purchased with money; but that does not make them free goods.

If anything is scarce, it must be rationed. That means that a criterion of some kind must be established for discriminating among claimants to determine who will get how much. The criterion could be age, eloquence, swiftness, public esteem, willingness to pay money, or almost anything else. We characteristically ration scarce goods in our society on the basis of willingness to pay money. But sometimes we use other criteria in order to discriminate.

Harvard College each year has many more applicants than it has places in the freshman class, so Harvard must ration the scarce places. It discriminates on the basis of high school grades, test scores, recommendations, and other criteria.

Only one person at a time can be president of the United States. Since many more people than that want the position, we have evolved an elaborate system of discrimination in the form of conventions and elections. Although there is considerable doubt about just what the criteria for discrimination are, the system does discriminate. We end up every fourth year with only one satisfied candidate.

Joe College is the most popular man on campus and has coeds clamoring for his favor. He must therefore ration his attentions. Whether he employs the criterion of beauty, intelligence, geniality, or something else, he must and will discriminate in some fashion.

But the other side of discrimination is competition. Once Harvard announces its criteria for discrimination, freshman applicants will compete to meet them. The criteria for selecting a president are studied carefully by the hopefuls who begin competing to satisfy those criteria long before the election year. If the coeds eager to go with Joe College believe that beauty is his main criterion, they will compete with one another to seem more beautiful.

Competition is obviously not peculiar to capitalist societies or to societies that use money. The point is of fundamental importance: *competition results from scarcity* and can only be eliminated with the elimination of scarcity. Whenever there is scarcity, there must be rationing. Rationing is allocation in accord with some criteria for discrimination. Competition is merely what occurs when people strive to meet the criteria that are being employed.

Of course, the criteria employed do make a difference. If a society rations on the basis of willingness to pay money, members of that society will strive to make money. If it uses physical strength as a primary criterion, members of the society will do body-building exercises. And if the better colleges and universities use high school grades as an important criterion for selection, high school students will compete for grades. They might be competing for grades to acquire other goods as well (status among classmates, compliments from teachers, use of the family car); but it is odd for colleges to complain of grade grubbers when their own rationing criteria promote grade grubbing.

Scarcity and Prices

Monetary prices are the most common rationing device in our society. The high price of lobster both reflects the fact that lobster is scarce *and* rations out to eager gourmets the limited quantity available. What happens when the price of lobster is not allowed to rise to the level that reflects its actual scarcity? Suppose that our lobster lovers' lobby managed to get a law through Congress setting $1 a pound as the maximum price that could be charged for lobster.

The quantity demanded would immediately increase. Lobster lovers would race to the grocery stores in anticipation of inexpensive epicurean delights. But many would find only frustration. Someone else would have gotten there first. The lower price does nothing to increase the number of lobsters available and, in the long run, it will reduce the amount of lobster that reaches the grocery stores and fish markets as lobstermen find it more profitable to do something other than trap lobsters. The lobster lovers' lobby did nothing to make lobster less scarce. They only suppressed the rationing device. They put ice cubes on the thermometer, so to speak; they did not turn on the air conditioning. They mistook a symptom (the high price) for the cause of their discontent (the scarcity of lobster).

But since lobster is still scarce, it must still be rationed. When price was prevented from serving as the discriminatory criterion, swiftness took its place. Those who were first to the stores took home the lobster, and the rest had none. Later on we might expect friendship with the butcher or fishmonger to become an important discriminatory criterion. And if this

happens we would expect the social popularity of these tradesmen to increase as lobster lovers start competing to satisfy the new rationing system. Fishmongers will be seen at all the more glittering social events, and party givers will call months in advance to be sure of their butcher's presence. Proximity to Maine will be another rationing device. Why pay the cost of shipping lobster any farther if New Englanders are willing to buy all that is available? When the lobsters no longer come to the people, the people will have to go to the lobsters.

Copper in Klutz

Scarcity is an inescapable fact of life, but shortages are avoidable. *A shortage is defined by economists as a situation in which the quantity demanded is greater than the quantity supplied.* Since the quantity demanded depends on the price (later we shall see that the quantity supplied also depends on price), it is possible to eliminate any shortage merely by allowing the price to rise.

We can see what this means and gain further practice in working with graphs by using figure 3A. The following discussion will be understood easily by anyone who follows it with a finger on figure 3A. The line labeled OD is the original demand for copper in the hypothetical country of Klutz. It shows the number of pounds of copper that will be purchased each month in Klutz at prices between roughly $1.35 and $.25 per pound. The line labeled LD is the demand for copper in Klutz at some later date. It is the demand after a major change (an expansion, let us say, in the country's electrical supply network) causes copper users to be willing to pay more to obtain any given quantity of copper. Another way of describing the difference between OD and LD is to say that, with LD, copper users want to buy more copper than before at each and every price.

We might begin by asking how much copper was needed in Klutz at OD. The question is meaningless, of course. Klutz has a highly developed economy and every industrialized economy uses large amounts of copper. But it is still misleading to say that Klutz needs any particular amount of copper per month. As the graph indicates, more or less will be demanded as the price is lower or higher.

Suppose now that exactly 10,000 pounds of copper become available to Klutz users each month. Will this be enough? Will there be a shortage of copper? Not if the price is 85¢ per pound. At this price copper users will want to buy 10,000 pounds per month, exactly the amount available.

What would happen if the monthly supply fell for some reason to 8000 pounds? If the price did not rise, some prospective purchasers of copper would be unable to obtain as much as they want. In order to get more, some would offer to pay a slight premium, and the price would rise. It

---

CAN PRICE CONTROLS *RAISE* PRICES?

What happens when the government "freezes" prices? One consequence is that certain items disappear from the market. Any item whose price is frozen below the market clearing level will be in short supply and hence not always available to purchasers looking for it. Beyond that, however, price controls tend to cause the gradual disappearance of just barely profitable goods. Often these are "bottom of the line" commodities: cheaper grades of paper, lumber, or fabric and many other low-quality items that are demanded for uses where higher quality serves little purpose. If a firm isn't able to produce as much as it can sell, it will concentrate its resources on producing the items that generate the largest profit. This often compels other producers to adopt inefficient production techniques that raise costs and prices. An example is the steel products company forced to use beautifully grained hardwood lumber in its shipping pallets because the grade it formerly used is no longer available.

A question: Has a price freeze really frozen prices when buyers can't obtain the items they want and have to accept (and pay for) goods with more quality than they can use?

---

would tend to continue rising as long as anyone who was willing to pay a higher price (if necessary) could not obtain all the copper he wanted at the existing price. But as the price rises, some prospective purchasers alter their plans. They decide they now want less copper than they originally planned to purchase. The price is bid up by the competition of those who want more than is available to them. And as it rises, the amount demanded declines. At a price of $1.05 per pound, the quantity demanded equals the quantity supplied. $1.05 per pound is the *equilibrium price* for the new situation of reduced supply. It is the price that "clears the market." This means that all purchases that people want to make *at the prevailing price* can be made, while purchases that people are willing to make only at some lower price cannot be made.

What would have occurred if the government of Klutz had decided that copper was an essential commodity and therefore its price could not be allowed to rise? When the supply fell from 10,000 pounds per month to 8000 pounds, a shortage would have appeared: the quantity demanded at the legally fixed ceiling price would exceed by 2000 pounds per month the quantity supplied. The shortage is a clear consequence of the ceiling price and can be eliminated by removing the ceiling.

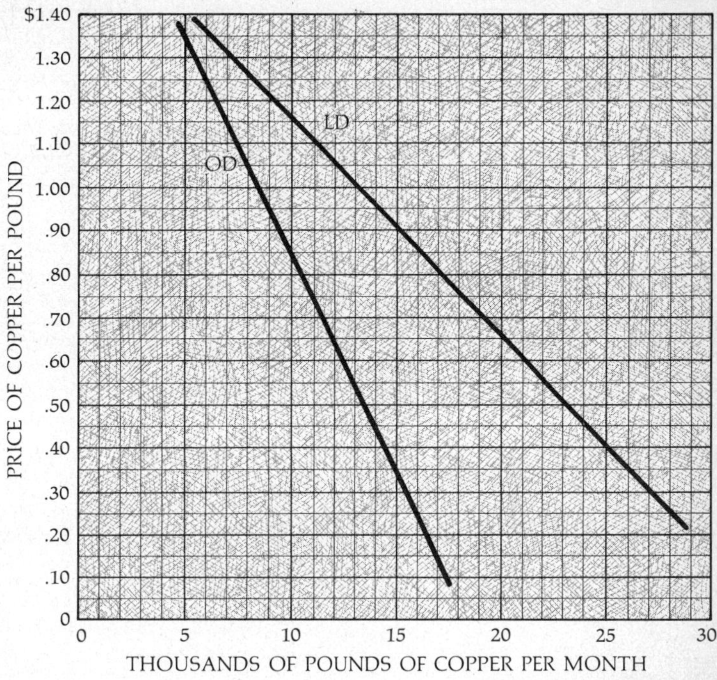

Figure 3A Copper in Klutz

Suppose that with the supply at the lower level of 8000 pounds and the price effectively fixed at 85¢ per pound, the demand shifts from OD to LD. How large will the shortage now be? Purchasers will want to buy 16,000 pounds. The shortage will therefore be 8000 pounds per month.

Would you like to see a shortage turn into a surplus before your very eyes? Let the demand continue at LD and the monthly supply at 8000 pounds. And let the government of Klutz now decide that since copper is an essential commodity its price must be supported at $1.30 a pound. If you wonder how a government can argue first for a low maximum price and then for a high minimum price both on the grounds that copper is an essential commodity, remind yourself once again that those who talk about "essential" commodities are often not much interested in logical conclusions.

If the government supports the price of copper at $1.30 a pound by offering to buy for stockpiling all of the supply which cannot be sold at that price, then 1000 pounds will have to be added each month to the government's stockpile. *Voilà!* A surplus. It's easy once you learn the trick, as many governments other than that of Klutz have often demonstrated. *A surplus, in case you are still looking for the formal definition, is a situation in which the quantity supplied exceeds the quantity demanded.*

THE CONCEPT OF "EQUILIBRIUM"

A price at which the quantity of a good demanded equals the quantity offered for sale is called an *equilibrium price*. The price is said to be "at equilibrium" or "in equilibrium" because the various factors pushing it in each direction just balance each other at that price. When the quantity demanded equals the quantity supplied, those who would like to see the price at a higher or lower level don't have the ability to make it go higher or lower; and those who have the ability lack the desire.

In Figure 3A, when suppliers have 10,000 pounds they want to sell and demand is OD, the equilibrium price is 85¢. Sellers would like to get more; but any seller who holds out for more than 85¢ won't find a buyer. Demanders would prefer a lower price; but no copper will be available to those bidding less than 85¢.

Economists make frequent use of the equilibrium concept. But equilibrium is a theoretical construct to assist us in thinking clearly; it is not something we can observe. Economists would say that a price of 60¢ with the supply fixed at 10,000 pounds and the demand at OD is a *disequilibrium* price because some suppliers *and* some demanders would prefer a higher price. If purchasers are willing to pay more, the price will presumably rise from the 60¢ level.

But if the government threatens to fine or imprison any purchaser who pays more than the legal ceiling price, can we be sure that purchasers will in fact be willing to pay more than 60¢ a pound? With legal penalties taken into account, perhaps the 60¢ price is an equilibrium price by the definition above.

The point is that equilibrium or disequilibrium depends upon which factors we choose to include in our analysis. Almost any price might qualify as an equilibrium price under the appropriate assumptions. We shall see both in chapter 20 and chapter 23 that the equilibrium concept can confuse discussion at times by concealing critical assumptions.

Notice that copper is still scarce despite the surplus. Surpluses do not necessarily mean that scarcity has been overcome. They may only mean that prices are not being allowed to decline. It's tempting to assert that just as any shortage can be eliminated by a large enough increase in price, so any surplus can be eliminated by a large enough decrease in price. But that could be misleading unless you realize that the price decrease might have to be so large as to make the equilibrium price negative. Suppliers might have to pay demanders to take the commodity away. If that sounds silly, how do you think we eliminate surpluses of trash?

Supply Curves: A Brief Introduction

We've been assuming in the copper case that the problem is to allocate a *monthly output* of copper among competing demanders. That assumption simplifies the exposition. But you know very well that the output of goods like lobster or copper is not fixed and unalterable. We mentioned a few paragraphs back, in parentheses, that the quantity supplied also depends upon the price. In other words, there are supply curves as well as demand curves. Chapter 4 will launch us into reflection on the nature of costs and the relationship between costs and supply curves. But a little anticipation at this point will be helpful.

Figure 3B adds a supply curve (S) to figure 3A. It's a relatively inelastic supply curve: throughout the range of quantities and prices shown, a change in price will be accompanied by a smaller percentage change in the quantity supplied.

Price ceilings and price supports will lead to even larger shortages and surpluses when the quantities supplied as well as those demanded are reponsive to price changes. Look at figure 3B. With demand at LD, the market clearing price will be 95¢ a pound. An effective price ceiling of 80¢ would create a monthly shortage of 4000 pounds, by inducing demanders to want an extra 3000 pounds each month while prompting suppliers to reduce their offerings by 1000 pounds per month.

PRICE RATIONING AND NON-PRICE RATIONING

Shortages and surpluses that persist for any extended period of time will almost always be found to be a consequence of failure to allow prices to perform their rationing function. Since rationing is a necessary consequence of scarcity, some other method of rationing will come into play when a price is set at a level that does not reflect actual scarcity. A few years ago the United States government tried to hold down the price of copper in the face of rising demand and a diminished supply. New discriminatory criteria came into operation, such as willingness to stand in line, ability to influence sellers, and dishonesty (thefts of copper increased significantly). Are these rationing devices any better than price?

It is hard to see in what way they might be better. One important consequence of rationing by means of price is that it allocates the scarce commodity to those who are willing to pay more. If you assume that some

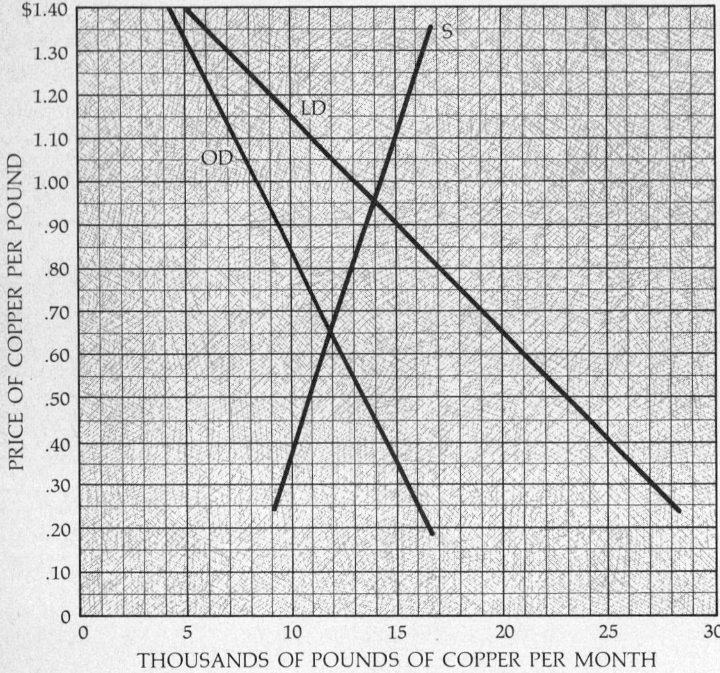

Figure 3B Supply and demand
for copper

prospective buyers are willing to pay more than others because they plan
to use the copper in products for which consumers are willing to pay
more, rationing by means of price has a tendency to allocate scarce commodities toward those uses for which consumer demand is greatest. And
that makes sense.

Remember the law of demand and the phenomenon of substitutability
on which it ultimately rests. At a low, fixed price, copper users have little
incentive to economize in its use by finding copper substitutes. When the
price of copper is allowed to rise, a long chain of substitutions is set in
motion. Home builders may cut down on the number of bathrooms, for
example, in order to hold down the cost of the houses they are constructing. New home buyers may look at the cost of an additional bathroom
and decide, all things considered, that three aren't really much better than
two. Scarcity calls for economizing. Higher prices for copper encourage
everyone who uses it to do exactly that.

Economics and Politics

Price rationing is for the most part an impersonal process. When the
price of gasoline rises as a result of a larger demand or a smaller supply,

those who are willing to pay the higher price get as much gasoline as they want and those who are unwilling do without. Race, sex, religion, political beliefs, length of hair, character, and temperament are irrelevant.

A price ceiling set below the market clearing level alters the situation. Since station operators will now have more customers than they are able to satisfy, they can, if they wish, discriminate in favor of regular customers. Or they can discriminate against afternoon and weekend customers by opening their pumps only on weekday mornings. This also has the effect of discriminating against people who work from eight to five: they must purchase gasoline on the way to work, and that forces them to leave home earlier and burn up both gasoline and patience in long queues. Rationing systems of this kind are highly arbitrary and offend most people's sense of justice. Rationing by queuing is also inefficient, since the real costs that are borne by those who must wait in line are dead weight costs; the cost of waiting in line does not become income for someone else as does a higher money price.

And so private rationing systems devised by sellers usually lead to a demand for rationing through the political process. What are the principal advantages and disadvantages of political rationing?

Its main advantage lies in the fact that people tend to regard political rationing as basically equitable, at least in its early stages. When the government takes over and allocates scarce supplies, everyone gets his "fair share"; at least everyone is *more likely* to get his fair share than under other systems. Or so many people apparently believe. The belief is important whether it is true or not. But political rationing systems seem to have rather short useful lives. It is extraordinarily difficult to devise a system for allocating gasoline and diesel fuel that will guarantee adequate supplies to "essential" users, distribute what remains in an equitable fashion, and protect the interests of firms in the supply system. Truck drivers will not agree, for example, that agriculture is a more "essential" industry than transportation. And if they aren't given what they want and sincerely believe they deserve, truck drivers will feel justified in demonstrating how essential their services are by going on strike. They also know that a 55 mile per hour speed limit on large trucks that have been designed for higher cruising speeds forces them to burn more fuel, not less, and they resent being compelled to pay these higher costs just so motorists won't have to bear the indignity of being passed by a truck. Of course, the 55 mile limit will not stick if too many motorists conclude that it is unfair, which they are more likely to do if they are frequently passed on the high-way by large trucks. So how do the government rule makers arrive at efficient and equitable decisions that are also *perceived* as efficient and equitable?

They will inevitably rely on past allocations as a basic guide. For example, they may allocate to each geographic area for the current year

some percentage of the quantity it consumed last year. That seems fair at first glance, a reasonable way of spreading the shortage. But it is not fair at all when the shortage has itself altered the geographic pattern of consumption. As a direct consequence of a gasoline shortage, for example, fewer motorists take long trips. With fewer people on the highways, the demand may actually decline in rural areas along major highways while rising in urban areas, leading to patterns of surplus *and* shortage. That is neither efficient nor equitable.

According to a February 1974 wire service story, the mayor of a West Virginia coal town decreed that any gasoline truck passing through the city would be stopped and unloaded. In itself the incident means little; as a symptom of the basic disadvantage of political rationing it may be significant. When government allocates scarce resources, an impersonal rationing system is replaced by one managed by human beings in a very visible way. What people might previously have accepted as unfortunate but inevitable, like "acts of God," now come to be seen as under human control and therefore avoidable. Criticism focuses on the government allocators; the inequities of their decisions, real or imagined, are widely advertised; the system is increasingly regarded as "fixed" and therefore unjust; and laws perceived as unjust do not command allegiance. The West Virginia mayor no doubt felt himself fully justified in confiscating some other area's gasoline for the sake of his community. But rationing on the basis of a lot of individual and highly biased perceptions of efficiency and equity is clearly not a viable system in the long run.

Perhaps the most significant feature of the government price and wage controls introduced in August 1971 and retained in a wavering fashion into 1974 was precisely that they wavered. They were imposed with fanfare. That apparently quieted the rumblings of those who believed the government had an obligation to control "price gouging" and check inflation. They were then quietly relaxed. That enabled prices to continue performing their allocative function. This is hardly an ideal procedure. But the intelligence and understanding, or ignorance and misunderstanding, of citizens finally determine the shape of public policy in a democratic society.

Once Over Lightly

Scarcity is a relationship between availability and desirability. A good is scarce when there is not enough available for everyone to have all that he wants at no cost.

Scarce goods must be rationed in some way.

Every rationing system must employ criteria of some kind to discriminate among those who want scarce goods.

Competition is the attempt to satisfy whatever discriminatory criteria are being used to ration the scarce goods.

Rationing by the criterion of monetary price encourages people to acquire money. The social consequences of this will largely depend on the discriminatory criteria that must be satisfied in a society in order to obtain monetary income.

A shortage of a good exists when the quantity demanded is greater than the quantity supplied (at a given price). A shortage can always be eliminated by a sufficiently large price increase.

A surplus of a good exists when the quantity supplied is greater than the quantity demanded. If a surplus still existed when the price of a good was zero, that good would not be scarce.

Rationing a good by means of monetary price discriminates in favor of those who receive high monetary incomes, whether through diligence, luck, genius, or knavery. But it also discriminates in favor of those who want the good more strongly and are therefore willing to give up a larger portion of their monetary income to obtain it.

An equilibrium price is a price that adjusts the *intentions* of buyers and sellers until the quantity people want to purchase is equal to the quantity people want to sell. Economists make extensive use of the equilibrium concept as a way of predicting the consequences of particular sets of circumstances. An equilibrium is never observed; it is deduced from the assumptions the analyst is using and may therefore change if the assumptions are expanded or otherwise altered.

QUESTIONS FOR DISCUSSION

1. Many ceiling prices were fixed by law in World War II. How were scarce goods rationed?

2. Why was the sale or barter of ration stamps in World War II prohibited? Who would gain and who would lose if citizens were allowed to exchange ration allotments?

3. State colleges and universities usually set a very low tuition. How do they ration scarce facilities? Who do you think gains from this system? Why might professors and administrators of state schools prefer *not* to have scarce facilities rationed by means of higher price (tuition)?

4. There are no toll charges for driving on many urban expressways during the rush hour. How is the scarce space rationed?

5. Parking space is often sold on college campuses at a zero price. How is the scarce space rationed? If all students who bring cars onto the campus are

charged $10 a year by the college as an automobile registration fee, is the fee a rationing device?

6. If the supply of turkeys in a particular November turned out to be unusually small, do you think a turkey shortage would result? Why or why not?

7.   (*a*) There is currently much concern about a growing surplus of college teachers. How could the surplus be reduced or eliminated? Do you think this is likely to occur? Why or why not?

   (*b*) Notice that a surplus of college teachers can also be viewed as a shortage of college teaching positions. How will the scarce supply of positions be rationed if the price (salary of teachers) is not allowed to perform this function?

8. How do you account for the fact that people were deeply concerned about world food shortages in 1974 when only five years earlier the governments of Australia, Canada, and the United States had been worrying about surpluses?

9. If you travel through the Western states in the summer, you are much more likely to encounter a shortage of camping spaces than of motel rooms. Why?

10. The government did not impose controls on sugar prices in 1974, and the price per pound rose about 600%. Did the high price cause any more sugar to be available in 1974 than would have been available at a lower, controlled price? Do you think there would have been any refined sugar available on grocers' shelves if the government had frozen the price near its original level? Where would it have gone?

4

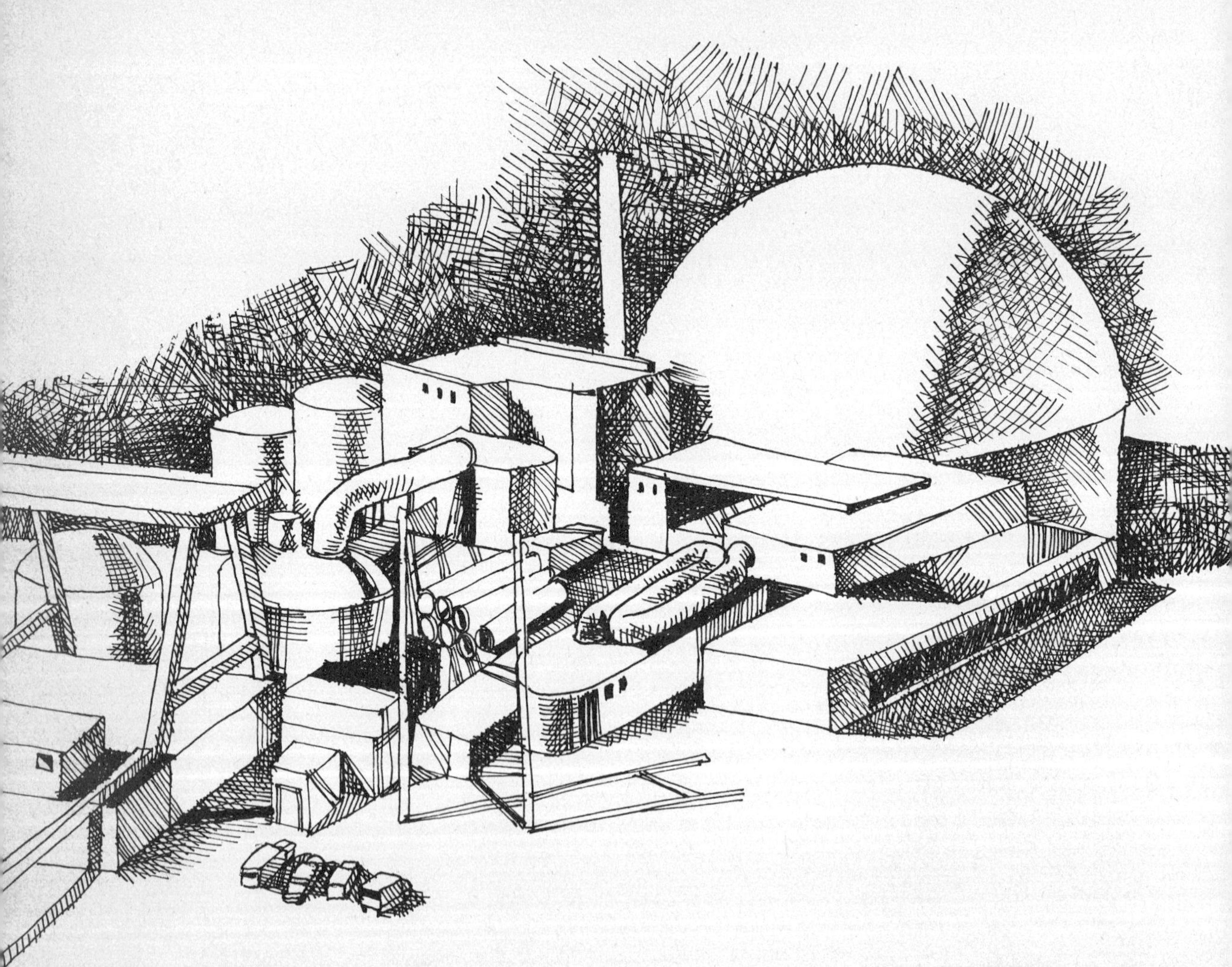

OPPORTUNITY COST
AND THE SUPPLY OF GOODS

Most of our attention has been focused until now on demand. We've been looking at the way in which prices ration available supplies by persuading people to substitute alternative goods. But what determines the available supplies, or the amount of each good offered for sale?

The answer is *cost*. But this reply raises as many questions as it answers once you begin to think about it. What do we mean by *cost*? We shall try to convince you in this chapter that it makes sense to think of *cost as the value of sacrificed opportunities*. Economists call this concept *opportunity cost*, and it ties together, as we shall see, the law of demand and the principles governing supply.

CHOICE AND OPPORTUNITY COST

The following exchange occurs in a college dormitory on a Monday night in the fall:

"Hey, Jack, do you want to go see the new Bergman movie? It closes after tonight."

"Golly, I'd love to but I can't. We've got a Russian test tomorrow and I'll flunk if I don't cram some vocabulary."

"Forget it. You can borrow my vocabulary cards in your free period tomorrow. An hour with the cards right before class is a B for sure."

"Well—trouble is the Redskins and Miami are on TV tonight and I'd rather watch the game if I don't have to study."

"We'll go at six and be back for the kickoff."

"All right. Just let me see how much money I've got. . . . Five, six, seven, eight dollars—to last until I get paid on Thursday. And I'm out of meal tickets!"

"Eat peanut butter sandwiches! I thought you wanted to see the movie."

"I do. O.K. I'll let my stomach shrink a little until Thursday. Should we leave at quarter to six?"

The real cost of any action (going to a movie, buying a pair of jeans, manufacturing a lawnmower, moving to Halifax, raising beef cattle, building a hardware store, taking out an insurance policy) is the value of the alternative opportunity that must be sacrificed in order to take the action. The cost for Jack of going to the movie was at first calculated as a passing grade (given up!) in Russian. When his friend showed him how to reduce that cost, Jack looked at the next most valuable opportunity he would have to sacrifice if he went to the movie: watching the Monday night football game, a game he particularly wanted to see. His friend eliminated that cost for him and Jack turned to the money cost. But money wasn't the real cost. The real costs that dollars and cents represent are the opportunities given up when the money is spent in one way rather than another. The two dollars Jack will spend for the movie represent some meals he would have liked to eat but is willing to sacrifice in order to see the film.

The theory of supply in economics is not essentially different from the theory of demand. Both assume that decision makers face alternatives and choose among them, and that their choices reflect a comparison of the benefits anticipated from the alternatives. The logic of the economizing process is the same for producers as it is for consumers.

Producers' Costs as Opportunity Costs

When we think about producers' costs, asking ourselves for example why it costs more to manufacture a ten-speed bicycle than a redwood picnic table, we tend to think first of *what goes into* the production of each. We think of the raw materials, of the labor time required, perhaps also of the machinery or tools that must be used. We express the value of the inputs in monetary terms and assume that the cost of the bicycle or the table is the sum of these values. That isn't wrong. But it leaves unanswered the question of why the inputs had those particular monetary values. The concept of opportunity cost asserts that those values reflect the value of the inputs in their next best uses, or the value of the opportunities foregone by using the inputs in the production of bicycles and picnic tables.

The manufacturer's cost of producing a bicycle will be determined by what he must pay to obtain the appropriate resources. He must bid these resources away from alternative uses. Insofar as these resources have other opportunities for employment, he must pay the value of the best such opportunity. The value of these foregone opportunities thus becomes the cost of manufacturing a bicycle. This makes excellent sense. For the meaningful cost of obtaining one more bicycle is the value of what must be given up or sacrificed or foregone in order to obtain that bicycle.

Consider the case of the picnic table. Part of its cost of production is the price of the redwood. Assume that the demand for new housing has increased recently, and that building contractors have consequently been purchasing a lot more redwood lumber. If this causes the price of lumber to rise, the cost of manufacturing a picnic table will go up. Nothing has happened to affect the physical inputs that go into the table, but its cost of production has risen nonetheless. For houses containing redwood lumber are now more valuable than formerly, and the table manufacturer must pay the opportunity cost of the lumber he wants to put into his picnic tables.

The concept of opportunity cost explains also how labor enters into production costs. A worker must receive from his employer a wage that persuades him to turn down all other opportunities. A skilled worker will be paid more than an unskilled worker because and only insofar as those skills make him more valuable somewhere else. A worker who can install wheel spokes while standing on his head and whistling "Dixie" is marvelously skilled. But our bicycle manufacturer will not have to pay him additional compensation for that skill *unless* his unusual talent makes him more valuable somewhere else. That could happen. A circus might bid for his talents. If the circus offers him more than he can obtain as a bicycle producer, his opportunity cost to the manufacturer rises. In that case the manufacturer will probably wish him goodbye and good luck and replace him with another worker whose opportunity cost is lower.

If the National Basketball Association and the American Basketball Association merge into one league, what happens to the opportunity cost of physically coordinated seven-footers? With two leagues, each player has two teams bidding for his services. What either team must pay to get him is determined by what the other team is willing to pay and is based on its estimate of his value to the franchise. If the leagues merge, however, the right to hire a particular player is assigned to a single team, and the opportunity cost of a well coordinated seven-footer will fall to the presumably much lower level of his value in other lines of work. It's not surprising that owners of professional basketball teams prefer one league to two.

Let's take a less unusual case. If a large firm employing many people moves into a small town, the cost of hiring grocery clerks, bank tellers, secretaries, and gasoline station attendants in the town will tend to go up.

Why? Because grocery stores, banks, offices, and gasoline stations must all pay the opportunity cost of the resources they employ, and more valuable opportunities will have been created for these people by the entrance of the new firm. Suppose the new firm is interested in hiring women exclusively; only the opportunity cost of hiring women will increase at first. But that will pull women out of some jobs and thereby create additional opportunities for men, so that the opportunity cost of male workers will also tend to rise.

The resource that most clearly illustrates the opportunity cost concept is probably land. Suppose you want to purchase an acre of land to build a house. What will you have to pay for the land? It will depend on the value of that land in alternative uses. Do other people view the acre as a choice residential site? Does it have commercial or industrial potentialities? Would it be used for pasture if you did not purchase it? The cost you pay for the land will be determined by the alternative opportunities that people perceive for its use.

Do Costs Determine Prices?

When sellers announce a price increase to the public, they like to point out that the increase was compelled by rising costs. *The Wall Street Journal* publishes frequent announcements of this kind, and it's rare indeed when the announcement fails to include an expression of regret that higher costs made this unfortunate step necessary. But is it true that costs determine prices?

Does it make sense to claim, for example, that the price of haircuts has gone up because barbers' wages have risen? If people weren't willing to pay a high price for a haircut, how could barbers' wages rise? The price people are willing to pay to have their hair cut professionally is one important factor that causes costs—that is, wages—to be what they are.

Plastic surgeons receive high incomes because they command a high price for their services. Is this why it costs so much to have a face lift? Not exactly. The causal relationship also runs in the opposite direction. It's the fact that people are willing to pay a high price for cosmetic surgery that makes the cost of hiring a plastic surgeon so high. Few people have the requisite skills, of course, and their acquisition is difficult and time-consuming. That's why the demand for cosmetic surgery raises the income of the surgeons rather than merely increasing the number of people willing and able to provide the service. But the cost of a plastic surgeon is obviously not something independent of the demand for plastic surgery.

When the owners of professional football teams announce in the summer that ticket prices will be raised in the fall, they like to blame this tear-

fully on rising costs, especially the high wages that must be paid to the players. But why do the players receive such high wages? It can't be that their work is so dangerous and grueling because it was just as dangerous and grueling in the days when players received only a few hundred dollars for the season. It's the demand, the willingness of many people to pay high prices to watch, that has pulled up the costs by making football players such valuable productive resources to the owners of professional teams. Soccer players in the United States receive far less, not because they work less hard, but because soccer isn't that popular in this country.

All three examples illustrate the same point. It is misleading to say that costs determine prices because the prices people will pay for goods also determine the cost of the resources used in their production. In short, the costs of productive resources like labor and land are prices determined by demand. This is what's meant by calling them opportunity costs.

We can just as easily argue that the prices of consumer goods are in reality costs, opportunity costs that measure the value of the goods in alternative uses. Take the case of lobster tails. Lobsters are, unfortunately, scarce. More lobsters will be brought to market as higher prices offer larger incentives to lobster fishermen; but the demand in recent years has increased considerably faster than the output and the price has consequently risen sharply. Figure 4A illustrates what has occurred.

The higher price can be viewed as the opportunity cost of the resources engaged in bringing lobsters to market. But when the lobsters have all been brought to market on a given day, so that the supply is, for that day at least, completely inelastic, then the price can be viewed as the opportunity cost of the last potential purchaser who was persuaded by the high price to do without lobster. Think of it as follows: Lobster tails have many alternative uses, at least as many as there are potential lobster eaters. Lobsters by and large have only one function, it is true, from the aggregate point of view. (We're notorious for ignoring the values and preferences of the lobster.) But the consumption of a lobster by one gourmet prevents its consumption by another. Lobster lovers in effect bid against one another for the limited supply. As the price rises, more and more potential consumers are reluctantly persuaded to do without. The price that clears the market, that makes the quantity demanded equal to the quantity supplied, will be the price that just barely persuades the most reluctant of the disappointed lobster lovers to go home from the seafood market with ocean perch or flounder fillets. It is *his* opportunity cost that is expressed by the market clearing price.

The point of all this is that people don't pay what lobster is worth to them but rather what lobster is worth in its most valued alternative use: as food for the consumer who was just barely deterred by the price from making a purchase. It's the opportunity cost of this disappointed lobster

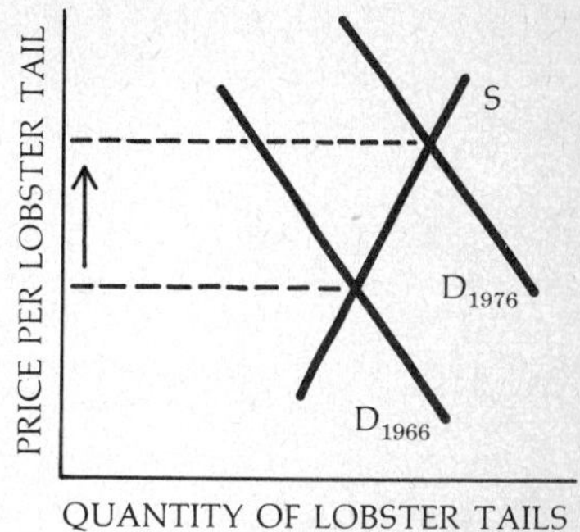

Figure 4A Supply and demand of lobster tails

lover that the price reflects, as well as the opportunity costs of the resources used to bring additional lobsters to market.

How many people realized in late 1974 when they were paying 75¢ a pound for sugar that the price was equal to the cost? Not the growers' cost, of course, but the opportunity cost of those sugar and candy bar lovers who were finally persuaded by the rising price to sacrifice the sweets they craved.

The Concept of Marginal Cost

One of the economist's favorite words is *marginal*. It means in economics exactly what it means in everyday speech: situated on the border or edge. The concept is of fundamental importance in economic thinking, because economic decisions, like all effective decisions, always involve *marginal*

comparisons. That is to say, they always have to do with movements at the border, with positive or negative *additions.* A synonym for marginal, in fact, is *additional.* What will be the *additional,* or *marginal,* cost that results from this decision? And how does it compare with the marginal cost of alternative decisions?

If you think about it for a moment, you will discover that opportunity costs are always marginal costs. The term *marginal cost* does no more than bring into strong relief an aspect of opportunity cost thinking. That aspect is so important, however, that we shall want to make frequent use of the term. Later on we shall talk about marginal other things.

Marginal Does Not Mean Average

A student will have no difficulty with the marginal concept if only he does not get it mixed up with the notion of an *average.* You may have no intention of confusing marginal with average; if so, what follows may only plant in your head the seeds of a bad idea. Let's hope it doesn't. A simple production schedule of a hypothetical zerc manufacturer will illustrate the distinction:

Number of Zercs Produced	Total Cost of Producing Zercs
42	$4200
43	4257
44	4312
45	4365

A little long division reveals that the average cost (total cost per unit) if 42 zercs are produced is $100; it is $99 for 43 zercs, $98 for 44, and $97 for 45. A little subtraction reveals, however, that the cost of producing the 43rd zerc is not $99 but $57. The incremental expenditure, or the extra cost, incurred by producing the 43rd zerc, is its marginal cost. The marginal costs of the 44th and 45th zercs are $55 and $53 respectively. It is clear that marginal cost can be more or less than average cost and can even differ substantially from average cost. It should also be clear that for a zerc manufacturer trying to make production decisions, it is the marginal costs that should guide him. Shall we produce more? Or less? Marginal cost is the consequence of action; it should therefore be the guide to action.

Is a businessman then not interested in average costs? Unless a businessman can cover all his costs from revenue, he will sustain a loss. He won't willingly commit himself to any course of action unless he anticipates being able to cover his total costs. He might therefore set up the problem in terms of anticipated production cost per unit against anticipated selling price per unit. But notice that the *anticipated* costs of any decision are really *marginal* costs. Marginal cost need not refer to the additional cost of a single unit of output. It could also refer to the additional cost of a batch of output, or the addition to cost expected from a decision regarding an entire process. Decisions are often made in this "lumpy" way.

For example, no one plans to build a soda-bottling factory expecting to bottle only one case of soda. There are important economies of size in most business operations, so that unless a businessman sees his way clear to producing a large number of units, he will not produce any. He won't enter the business. He won't build the bottling factory at all. The entire decision—build or don't build, build this size plant or that, build in this way or some other way—is a marginal decision at the time it is made. Remember that additions can be very large as well as very small.

Whether or not the businessman casts his thinking in terms of averages, it is marginal costs that guide his decisions. Averages can be looked at after the fact to see how well or poorly things went, and maybe even to learn something about the future if the future can be expected to resemble the past. But this is history—admittedly an instructive study—while economic decisions are always made in the present with an eye to the future.

EFFICIENCY AND COMPARATIVE ADVANTAGE

Is a diesel locomotive more efficient than a steam locomotive? Most people would say yes. But what reasons would they give for their answer?

If efficiency is to have any precise meaning, it must be understood as a ratio of one thing to another. Engineers use a definition of efficiency that seems to satisfy this test. They define efficiency as the ratio of the work done by a machine to the energy supplied to it, and that ratio is usually expressed as a percentage. From the engineering standpoint, the diesel locomotive is therefore more efficient than the steam locomotive because, per unit of potential energy contained in its fuel, the diesel does more work.

This definition is somewhat unsatisfactory, however, when we think about it more critically. Efficiency cannot be simply the measure of energy output to energy input because, by the laws of thermodynamics, that ratio is always unity for any process. It is rather a measure of *work done* in relation to energy input. But what constitutes "work done"? Doesn't that depend on what is *wanted*? What qualifies as "work"? Engineers actually call a steam engine less efficient than a diesel because with a steam engine a higher percentage of the energy input is *wasted*. Strictly speaking, however, even wasted energy does work. It just doesn't do any *useful* work. That means it doesn't do work that anybody *wants* done. All of which implies that efficiency is not a purely objective or technological matter, but depends inevitably upon valuations.

It is sometimes said that our society places too high a value on efficiency. That's almost like saying that we place too high a value on what we value, which doesn't make much sense. We may be excessively infatuated with technology, but that is quite another matter. A mindless obsession with technology is very different indeed from a concern for efficiency.

The Meaning of Efficiency

Efficiency is inescapably an evaluative term. It always has to do with the ratio of the *value* of output to the *value* of input. Efficiency will always have an objective component, of course; our likes and dislikes don't determine the potential heat in a pound of fuel. But physical facts *by themselves* can never determine efficiency. It follows that the efficiency of any process can change with changes in valuations, and because everything depends upon everything else, any change at all in any subjective preference is in principle capable of altering the efficiency of any process.

Let's go back to the question of the relative efficiency of diesel and steam locomotives. Each can be put into operation only with the use of a large number of inputs: not only coal or oil and locomotive operators, but also all the inputs used in manufacturing the locomotives, the inputs that went into the fabrication of these inputs, the inputs that went into the fabrication of the products that were inputs in the process of producing the products that were inputs in the manufacture of the locomotives, and so on without any discernible limit. Anything that changes the value of anything that contributes to a locomotive's operation can in principle alter its efficiency.

We don't need any far-fetched illustrations to make the essential point. An increase in the price of oil relative to coal, if it is large enough, can by itself transform their relative efficiencies so that a coal-fired steam locomotive becomes more efficient than a diesel. It follows that these relative efficiencies depend on the demand for and supply of oil and coal, and hence on such factors as the motoring habits of the general public, the political situation in oil-producing countries, United States policy on import quotas, and the value placed on the environmental effects of strip mining coal. Perhaps it never occurred to you that the relative efficiency of the old steam locomotive was affected by the efforts of the United Mine Workers!

To test your grasp of the principle at work here, examine each of the statements below. Ask yourself what kind of change would be capable of creating or reversing the situation. The possibilities are limited only by your imagination.

1. Math can be taught more efficiently with programed textbooks than with teachers.

2. It is more efficient to cultivate corn with a tractor than by hand.
3. It is inefficient to use trained lawyers as court stenographers.
4. It is more efficient to cut down trees with a chain saw than with an ax.

If you thought through these statements, you should have noticed the possibility that changes in printing costs or teachers' salaries, tractor prices or farm labor wages, alternative opportunities available to people trained in law and in shorthand, and even, in the fourth case, changes in attitudes toward noise in the forests are capable of altering relative efficiencies. If you failed to notice these things and more, try again at the conclusion of this chapter.

Some Myths Concerning Wealth

Trading has long had an unsavory reputation in the Western world. This may reflect the enormous influence of Aristotle and his medieval followers, who thought there was something unnatural about exchange for monetary gain; but it is more likely the result of a deep-seated human conviction that nothing can *really* be gained through mere exchange. Agriculture and manufacturing are believed to be genuinely productive: they seem to create something genuinely new, something additional. But trade only exchanges one thing for another. It follows that the merchant, who profits from trading, must be imposing some kind of tax on the community. The wages or other profit of the farmer and artisan can be obtained from the alleged real product of their efforts, so that they are entitled in some sense to their income; they reap what they have sown. But the merchant seems to reap without sowing; his activity does not appear to create anything and yet he is rewarded for his efforts. Trading, some have thought, is social waste, the epitome of inefficiency.

This line of argument strikes a deeply responsive chord in many people who still retain the old hostility toward the merchant in the form of a distrust of the "middleman." Everybody wants to bypass the middleman, who is pictured as a kind of legal bandit on the highways of trade, authorized to exact his percentage from everyone foolish or unlucky enough to come his way.

However ancient or deep-seated this conviction of the unproductiveness of trade, it is completely erroneous. There is no defensible sense of the word *productive* that can be applied to agriculture or manufacturing but not to trading. Exchange is productive! It is productive because it promotes greater efficiency in resource use.

Many have taken a fatal wrong turn at the very beginning in considering this question by assuming that exchange, unless it is fraudulent or coerced, is always the exchange of *equal values.* It just isn't so. The exact reverse is true: Exchange is never an exchange of equal values. *If it were, it would not occur.* In an informed and uncoerced exchange (and that is the kind we want to consider), both parties gain by giving up something of lesser for something of greater value. If Jack swaps his basketball for Jim's baseball glove, Jack values the glove more than the ball and Jim values the ball more than the glove. Viewed from either side, the exchange was unequal. And that is precisely the source of its productivity. Jack now has greater wealth than he had before, and so does Jim. The exchange was productive because it increased the wealth of both parties involved.

"Not really," comes a voice from the rear. "There was no real increase in wealth. Jack and Jim feel better off, it's true; they may be happier and all that. But the exchange didn't really produce anything. There is still just one baseball glove and one basketball."

We must be respectful but wary toward that small voice. What does wealth consist of? What constitutes production? Many people have drifted into the habit of supposing that an economic system produces "material wealth," like cars, houses, basketballs, breakfast cereals, and ball-point

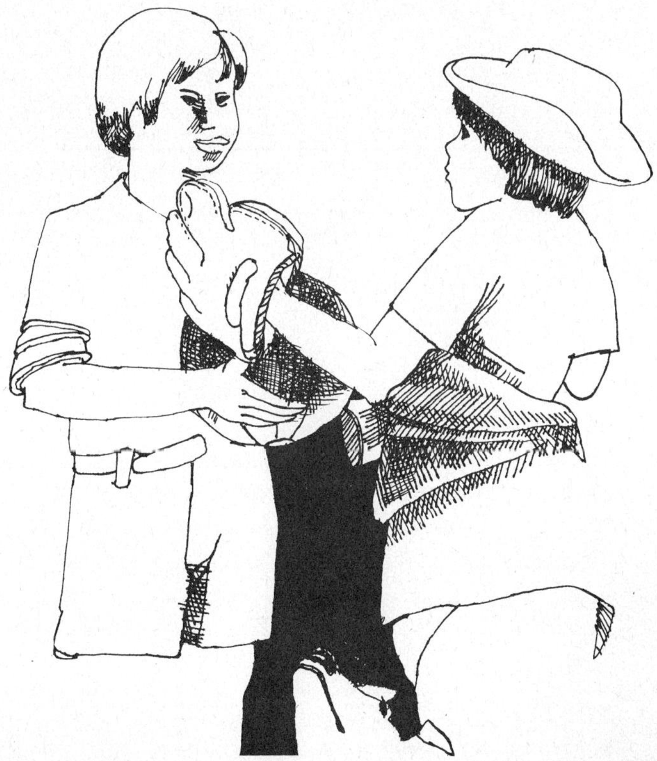

pens. But none of these things is wealth unless it is available to someone who values it. Additional water is additional wealth to a farmer who wants to irrigate; it is not wealth to a farmer caught in a Mississippi River flood. A food freezer may be wealth to an American housewife but not to an Eskimo. The crate in which the freezer was delivered is trash to the house-wife but a treasure to her small son who sees it as a playhouse.

Economic growth consists not in increasing the production of *things,* but in the production of *wealth.* Material things can contribute to wealth, obvi-ously, and are in some sense essential to the production of wealth. (Even such "nonmaterial" goods as love and peace of mind do, after all, have some material embodiment.) But there is no necessary relation between the growth of wealth and an increase in the volume or weight or quantity of material objects. The indefensible identification of wealth with only material objects must be rejected at root. It makes no sense. And it blocks understanding of many aspects of economic life.

So the small voice from the rear was confused. Both Jack and Jim do have greater wealth after their exchange, and in a sense no different from the sense in which each would have greater wealth if a ball and a glove rained down on them like manna. For people who hate sports, of course, such a rainfall would not be wealth but an unnatural disaster.

Recall what we concluded earlier about efficiency: it is measured by the ratio of one *value* to another, not by physical ratios of any sort. You can think of Jack and Jim's exchange as an act of production. Jack used the basketball as an input to obtain the output of a baseball glove. For Jim the glove was the input and the ball the output. The result of the productive process (the exchange) was an output value greater than input value for both parties. Nothing further is required to make an activity productive. The exchange expanded real output.

Efficiency and the Gains from Trade

The preliminary work has been done. We're ready now to introduce you to the principle of *comparative advantage,* a concept that sums up almost everything we've been talking about thus far. We'll allow Smith and Brown to make the introduction. They are suburban neighbors, each with a large lawn and a sizable flower garden. Every Saturday afternoon during the summer, Smith and Brown reluctantly go out to mow their lawns and weed their gardens.

But Smith always finishes earlier despite the fact that the lawns and gardens are identical in size. He is a strong and agile man who can mow his lawn in 40 minutes and weed his garden in 80 minutes. Brown takes two hours to mow his lawn and another two hours to weed his garden, so he is still toiling while Smith is sipping lemonade. You should have these data clearly before you as you proceed, so we'll summarize them in a little table:

Smith

Lawn:	40 minutes
Garden:	80 minutes

Brown

Lawn:	120 minutes
Garden:	120 minutes

We're ready for the question: Is it possible for either or both to get to the lemonade sooner on Saturday by engaging in a little trade?[1] We're all familiar with the advantages of specialization. If the mason builds the carpenter's chimney and the carpenter builds the mason's garage, they each gain by taking advantage of their own and the other party's special skills. That's familiar enough.

But it doesn't seem to fit the case of Smith and Brown. For Brown appears to have no special skills, to be less efficient than Smith in both mowing and weeding. So it would appear, but appearances are misleading.

Suppose that Smith gave up all weeding and instead confined his yard-work to mowing first his own lawn, then Brown's. He could then finish his yard work in just 80 minutes, a gain of 40 minutes for Smith. If Brown meanwhile weeded both gardens, he would still be working 240 minutes, for no gain or loss. Smith has gained from trade with Brown and without inflicting any loss on Brown.

The Principle of Comparative Advantage

What happened? Nothing very unusual. Smith just happens to be a more efficient mower than Brown and Brown a more efficient weeder than Smith. Like the mason and the carpenter. So each specialized in that activity in which he was more efficient and they exchanged services. Each pursued his comparative advantage, which means that he specialized in the activity in which he was more efficient. It is a *comparative* advantage, because each is more efficient in one activity than the other activity only *in comparison* with his neighbor. But that is what matters.

Whoa! The small voice from the rear is stirring again. "But Brown is *not* a more efficient weeder than Smith. The clumsy slob is less efficient than Smith in *both* activities." That small but helpful voice has erred again.

---

1. We shall assume that neither Smith nor Brown has a preference for one kind of chore over the other and that the use of different tools is not a factor in the problem. Dropping these assumptions would add complexity without affecting the underlying principles.

It just is not true that Brown is less efficient than Smith in both activities. He really is more efficient than Smith in weeding.

Proof is provided by the arithmetic calculation which shows that Smith added to his wealth (his lemonade sipping time) by specializing in mowing and then trading with Brown. And he did not do it at Brown's expense, for Brown's wealth was not reduced. No such gain would be possible if Brown were not more efficient than Smith in weeding—which implies, of course, that Smith is *less* efficient than Brown in weeding.

Nonsense? No—just a momentary paradox. The paradox disappears when we remember to wear the spectacles of opportunity cost. What is the cost to Smith of weeding a garden? It is two lawns left unmowed. And the cost to Smith of mowing a lawn is one-half a garden unweeded. The cost of anything is the opportunity thereby foregone; the cost of weeding is therefore to be expressed in this case in terms of mowing, and the cost of mowing in terms of weeding.

What about Brown? The cost to him of mowing a lawn is one garden left unweeded and the cost of weeding a garden is consequently one lawn left unmowed. We can now determine who is the more efficient or lower-cost producer of weeded gardens by comparing relative costs.

The cost of a garden weeded by Smith is two lawns unmowed. For Brown it is one lawn unmowed. One is less than two. Brown is therefore the lower-cost or more efficient producer of weeded gardens.

We aren't just playing with words, as demonstrated by the crucial fact that either or both can increase their wealth if Brown specializes in weeding and the two engage in trade. Common sense resists this conclusion only because Brown takes *more time* to weed a garden than does Smith. Suppose, someone objects, that we express the costs in man-hours. Then Brown's cost will be one and one-half times as high as Smith's, and common sense will be salvaged. But only at the expense of everything we have argued for! Such an approach assumes that the real measure and determinant of value is the labor embodied in a commodity. But the assumption fails completely to explain relative prices. The cost of any commodity, in the economist's way of thinking, is not what is embodied in it, but what is given up in order to obtain it. It is the value of what is sacrificed, or of the opportunities foregone.

But could we not take leisure, the third good in our problem, as the measure of cost? Let's examine this possibility. Smith gives up 80 minutes of leisure to weed a garden, Brown gives up 120. By this measure Smith is the more efficient producer of weeded gardens and common sense is again salvaged.

You may take this route if nothing else will satisfy you. But if you take it too far you will end up in confusion. Since leisure or lemonade-sipping time is a valued opportunity, the cost of mowing a lawn or weeding a garden can legitimately be expressed in terms of the leisure time given up. But the fact that Smith sacrifices less leisure than Brown to do a job does not prove that Smith is more efficient in some absolute sense. For Smith's leisure may be more valuable than Brown's! It makes sense to measure costs ultimately in terms of leisure only if we believe that leisure is "the ultimate good" *and* if we can assume that an hour of leisure is of equal value to everyone. This sort of absolutism does have a psychological appeal. There is a streak of egalitarianism in almost everyone which wants to assert that one person's leisure counts for exactly as much as any other's. And that conviction is remarkably resistant to all sorts of evidence suggesting that it just isn't so. Question 24 at the end of this chapter has been included for everyone who has trouble freeing himself from the presupposition that labor time or its opposite, leisure, is the proper ultimate measure of cost. And it's important to shake loose from the presupposition because opportunity cost thinking recognizes *no* absolute measures of value: the value of *every* good must finally be expressed in terms of other goods.

The Terms of Trade

We stated a few paragraphs back that Smith or Brown or both can gain from specialization and exchange. In the one case we worked through, Smith appropriated the entire gain. That was a result of the specific terms of trade: the relative prices at which mowing and weeding were exchanged. The terms of trade were one garden for one lawn. At that price, Smith appropriated the entire gain from trade.

Satisfy yourself that you understand what we're doing by calculating the terms of trade that would assign the entire gain to Brown. If Brown weeded his own garden plus only half of Smith's, Brown would be working 180 minutes altogether. Smith would be left with two lawns to mow (80 minutes) plus half of his garden to weed (40 minutes), so he would be no better or worse off. The terms of trade that assign the whole gain to Brown are thus

$$1 \text{ L} = \tfrac{1}{2} \text{ G, or } 1 \text{ G} = 2 \text{ L}$$

The argument is consistent with what you know about relative prices. The people who gain from an increase in the price of a good relative to other goods are those who specialize in its production. Brown likes to see the price of a weeded garden rise from one mowed lawn to two for the same reason that any producer likes to see the price of his specialty increase.

Of course, at some intermediate price ratio they could share the gain from trade. If

$$1 \text{ L} = \tfrac{3}{4} \text{ G, or } 1 \text{ G} = 1\tfrac{1}{3} \text{ L}$$

Smith could gain 20 minutes and Brown 40 minutes from specialization and trade. (Don't conclude that Brown gains more! That requires the doubtful assumption that leisure is equally valuable to both. Turn to question 24 for the antidote.)

A Summary of Principles

The principles illustrated here have far-reaching implications. Let's list some of them:

Wealth can be increased by means of trade.

People specialize because they can increase their wealth by doing so. They specialize in activities in which they have a comparative advantage.

Relative prices help people to determine where their comparative advantages lie.

Relative prices determine the distribution of income or the gains from specialization and trade.

Anything that prevents voluntary exchange promotes inefficiency by preventing the specialization that increases total wealth.

Comparative Advantage, the Economist's Umbrella

The term with which economists summarize everything we have been discussing in this chapter is *comparative advantage.* It might even be thought of as a term to summarize the entire collection of concepts presented thus far. To pursue comparative advantage means simply to sacrifice that which is less valuable for the sake of something more valuable.

Why do demand curves slope downward to the right? Because people pursue their comparative advantage. A rise in the price of any good means that its users will now be able to obtain the satisfaction it provides at a *relatively lower cost* by using some substitute.

How is the opportunity cost of any resource established? Through the pursuit of comparative advantage. People bid for a resource after estimating the potentiality of that resource *relative to other resources* for providing whatever it is they're after.

Why are only marginal costs relevant to decision making? Because marginal costs reflect the *comparative advantages of alternative decisions.*

It is comparative advantage—the advantage resources have over other resources in particular uses relative to other uses—that determines the most efficient way to employ a society's resources. And the pursuit of comparative advantage will lead decision makers actually to employ resources in the most efficient way *if* the relative costs decision makers must pay reflect opportunity costs.

The economic way of thinking may at root be nothing more than the ability to think consistently in terms of comparative advantage.

Once Over Lightly

The real cost of any good is the value of what must be sacrificed in order to obtain it. Economists call this its opportunity cost.

Insofar as resources can only be obtained through competitive bidding, costs of production will reflect the value in alternative uses of the resources employed in producing the goods.

The value of a human being may be infinite; but the wages of human beings in any task will be much closer to the value of their services in alternative employments than to infinity.

Budget costs are not always real costs because they sometimes overlook or conceal opportunity costs. People in business for themselves often overlook the opportunity costs of the resources they themselves own.

The law of demand and opportunity cost are opposite sides of the same coin. The monetary price of a good expresses the value of other goods the purchaser could have obtained with that sum if he had not purchased this particular good. The price that must be bid to obtain it also expresses the value of that good to the last unsuccessful bidder who gave up his opportunity to have the good when the price rose too high. Because prices express forsaken opportunities, less will be purchased at higher prices and more at lower prices.

Demand determines costs. Costs determine prices. Prices for alternative goods determine the demand for particular goods. Everything depends upon everything else in the opportunity cost way of thinking.

The cost of a decision is the value of the opportunities foregone if that decision is made.

Opportunity costs are marginal costs, not average costs; they are the additional costs the decision entails.

Cost calculations, like all economizing decisions, must be made by looking to the future, not to the past.

Efficiency depends upon valuations. While physical or technological facts are certainly relevant to the determination of efficiency, they can never by themselves determine the relative efficiency of alternative processes. Efficiency depends upon the ratio of output *value* to input *value.*

Exchange creates wealth, because voluntary exchange always involves the sacrifice of what is less valued (input) for what is more valued (output). Exchange is as much a wealth-creating transformation as is manufacturing or agriculture.

People specialize in order to exchange and thereby increase their wealth. They specialize in activities in which they believe themselves to have a comparative advantage.

Comparative advantage is determined by opportunity costs. No person, no group, no nation can be more efficient than another in *every* activity, for even the most highly productive agents must have some activities in which they are *less* highly productive. If you're four times as intelligent as someone else, three times as strong, and twice as beautiful, then the other person has a comparative advantage in beauty—and you, handsome as you are, have a comparative *dis*advantage in beauty.

Relative prices help people decide where their comparative advantages lie insofar as relative prices reflect opportunity costs.

Relative prices also determine the distribution of income or the gains from specialization and trade.

QUESTIONS FOR DISCUSSION

1. What effect would the expectation of a continuing high price for soybeans have on the price of field corn? How does the concept of opportunity cost aid us in seeing the relationship?

2. What is the cost per ticket to a professional baseball club that offers 50 "free" tickets to an orphanage? Does it matter *for what game* the tickets are offered?

3. Why did the cost of hiring domestic servants increase dramatically during World War II? What would you have replied to people who said that servants "just weren't available"?

4. Some people contend that the ending of the military draft reduced college enrollments. Use the concept of opportunity cost to defend this argument.

5. If the federal government and private foundations allocate large sums for research, will this tend to benefit or harm a small college whose faculty either does no research or cannot land any research grants? Why?

6. By taking an airplane one can go from D to H in one hour. The same trip takes five hours by bus. If the air fare is $30 and the bus fare is $10, which would be the cheaper mode of transportation for someone who could earn $2 an hour during this time? For someone who could earn $10 an hour? $5 an hour?

7. Why might a multinational corporation with identical plants in two different countries pay different wage rates to workers in the two countries even though their skill levels were the same? Does this strike you as unjust? Why might the *higher paid* workers object?

8. Think about the cost of television commercials. What enters into the cost of a 30-second commercial plugging Friendly Fred's Ford Dealership? How do you explain the fact that the same commercial will cost $90 on Wednesday morning but $1600 on Saturday night right before "All in the Family"? Local television stations are often asked to donate time for public service spots. Does this cost the station anything? Do you think stations are more willing to donate time on Sunday morning than on weekday mornings because the owners are religious?

9. A recent news report from London stated that British doctors, while dissatisfied with some aspects of their country's National Health Service, generally appreciated the fact that they could treat patients under this system "without regard to cost." Comment.

10. Physicians in the United States must typically go through four or more years of training after college before they can practice. Does this cost affect the prices doctors receive for their services? Explain.

11. An airline is thinking about adding a daily flight from Denver to Billings. It has estimates of the number of passengers who would use the flight. What costs should and should not be considered in deciding whether the anticipated revenue is sufficient to make the flight profitable?

12. The Board Chairman of the Tennessee Valley Authority complained in November 1974 that "prices charged for coal in today's market bear no reasonable relationship to the cost of producing it." What do you think he meant by cost of production? He also complained that TVA got no response

when it asked for competitive bids from coal producers: "They don't need to compete because they can sell all the coal they want at their prices." If that's true, is it possible for the price of coal to be higher than its opportunity cost? What opportunities were determining the price TVA had to pay for coal? He also commented: "This country cannot afford to let something as vital to our well-being as coal be used to maximize profits." Do you think the prices charged for coal were harmful to the national well-being? What price structure for coal is most in the national interest?

13. In its 1973 annual report Phelps Dodge Corporation said it would exhaust the copper in Lavender Pit (Arizona) by mid-1974 and close the mine at that time. But the June 1974 price of copper was 25% higher than the January price, and the mine kept on operating. Did the higher price put additional copper in the pit? What would a geologist mean by the statement, "I can't tell you how much ore is in that mountain until I know the price of copper"?

14. The American Petroleum Institute estimated that proved U.S. oil reserves at the beginning of 1975 were 34.25 billion barrels. Petroleum geologists have estimated that 300 billion barrels of oil lie beneath the ground in fairly well known locations within the United States. How would you reconcile these two vastly different estimates? The API defines "proved reserves" as the amount of oil likely to be recoverable from known reservoirs *under current economic conditions.* Can you suggest an easy way to increase the nation's proved reserves?

15. A Department of Agriculture official said early in 1975 that farmers were no longer pouring on all the fertilizer the ground will take because of the sharp rise in fertilizer prices. Why might higher prices cause a particular farmer to use *less* fertilizer rather than cut out its use altogether? How will higher fertilizer prices affect U.S. agricultural output? Do you think price controls on fertilizer would help maintain U.S. farm output and thus hold down food prices? (Hint: The U.S. government had put a ceiling price of $75 a ton on domestic sales of a certain phosphate fertilizer at a time when foreign buyers were offering to pay $110 a ton.)

16. Is it more efficient to build dams with lots of direct labor and little machinery or with lots of machinery and little labor? Why might the answer vary from one country to another?

17. Which is more efficient: Japanese agriculture with its carefully terraced hillsides, or American agriculture with its far more "wasteful" use of land? How have relative prices in the two countries brought about these different methods of farming? How have opportunity costs entered into the formation of these relative prices?

18. Attorney Fudd is the most highly sought-after lawyer in the state. He is also a phenomenal typist who can do 120 words per minute. Should Fudd do his own typing if the fastest secretary he can obtain does only 60 words per minute? Prove that Fudd is *not* twice as efficient as his secretary at typing, that he is in fact *less* efficient at typing, and that he should therefore retain a secretary.

19.   The dean knows that Professor Svelte is the most capable administrator in his department, far more capable than Professor Klunk. Can you think of any reasons (related to efficiency rather than nepotism) for nonetheless appointing Klunk over Svelte as department chairman?

20.   Have you ever noticed how few gasoline stations are found in the center of large cities? With such heavy traffic one ought to be able to do an excellent business. Why then are there so few?

21.   The key to question 20 is the high price of land in the center of large cities. Would it make sense for the city government, which has the right of eminent domain, to take over some of this land in order to provide "vitally needed service stations"?

22.   It has often been claimed that under a capitalist system business firms will sometimes continue to use obsolete equipment rather than the new, "most efficient" equipment because they have a lot of money tied up in the old equipment. Does this make sense? What is the relevance to such decisions of "money tied up"? Would an efficient enterprise manager want to behave differently under a socialist system?

23.   You own and occupy a large brick house in an old residential neighborhood. The area is being rezoned to allow multiple-family occupancy and apartment buildings. How would you go about deciding whether to (*a*) continue to occupy the house as a single-family dwelling, (*b*) divide the house into several apartments, or (*c*) tear down the house and erect a new apartment complex? If you were to choose *b*, could you be accused of retarding the economy by failing to adopt the most up-to-date equipment because of your vested interest in obsolete equipment? Does this differ from problem 22?

24.   Here is a problem for those still infatuated with a labor-or-leisure theory of value. Suppose we want to verify the hypothesis that, since "a man's a man for a' that," one hour of Brown's leisure is equal in value to one hour of Smith's leisure. We gather the following evidence:

(*a*) We ask them. Brown says his leisure is worth more because he is fat and lazy. Smith agrees that Brown's leisure is worth more.

(*b*) While Smith and Brown are sipping lemonade together, Jones across the street offers them $10 apiece to work for an hour cleaning his garage. Smith accepts with alacrity, but Brown says he won't do it for less than $20.

(*c*) Smith often walks home from work because he has, as he says, "nothing better to do." Brown would take a cab if his car were in the shop because he is always eager to get home.

(*d*) Smith daydreams while sipping lemonade. For Brown, this is a time for imaginative creativity; he thinks up all kinds of useful ideas for the employee suggestion box at the office.

If all this evidence is not sufficient to refute the hypothesis that Smith's leisure and Brown's leisure are of equal value, what possible evidence *could* refute it? If there is no way at all of refuting or confirming a hypothesis, does the hypothesis assert anything? If it asserts nothing, why retain it? You might still want to retain a hypothesis that can be neither proved nor disproved on the basis of existing data if it is useful in some way; we do speak of "useful hypotheses." But of what use is the hypothesis that every person's leisure is equal in value to everyone else's leisure? It is seriously misleading for many purposes, and it contains implications that are contrary to a great deal of evidence.

5

UNCERTAINTY AND
THE ALLOCATION OF RESOURCES

When Richard Nixon addressed the nation on television in August 1971 to announce several abrupt changes in the direction of government economic policy, he made six disparaging references to speculation or speculators. It's politically risky to blame business, labor, consumers, other nations, or the government's own policies for creating economic problems. But it's always safe to blame speculators. Ordinary citizens are producers who earn their income by contributing to the welfare of society. Speculators, on the other hand, are unprincipled parasites who get rich at other people's expense.

Right? Almost totally wrong. We are all speculators, for speculation is an unavoidable aspect of every economizing decision. And the profit that successful speculators receive is unearned income only if we believe that people who assume the risk that others don't want to bear are not performing a socially useful function. The truth of the matter, however, is that we live in a world of uncertainty and are therefore compelled to make choices that will affect our future without knowing for sure just how they will do so. Every economizing decision entails a comparison of *expected* benefits and *expected* costs in situations characterized by incomplete information. Information is a scarce good which cannot be acquired costlessly and for which there are substitutes.

INFORMATION AS A SCARCE GOOD

Let's take a simple example. Suppose you want to sell your house for as much as you can get. The appropriate buyer will be the one person in

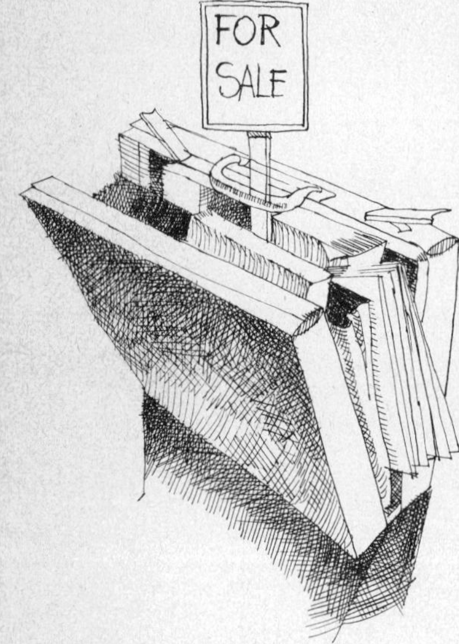

the world willing to pay the highest price. That seems obvious. What isn't obvious is how you find him. You are presumably not omniscient, so you will never even discover the existence of many potential purchasers. It is almost a certainty, therefore, that when you finally do sell, you will not have found that one buyer willing to pay the very top price. Does this imply that you should keep searching indefinitely?

Information is a scarce good with its own costs of production. It simply does not pay to go on acquiring information forever before acting. A rational seller will continue acquiring information, therefore, only so long as the anticipated marginal gain from doing so is greater than the anticipated marginal cost of acquiring information. A rational buyer will behave in the same way. And this is the principal reason that people employ real estate agents in selling or buying houses. Both sellers and buyers can gain from using the services of a realtor because the realtor enables them to obtain additional information at low cost. When you think about it, this seems in fact to be the primary function of middlemen: they promote efficiency and hence increase wealth by acting as low-cost producers of valuable information. Realtors provide sellers and buyers with better opportunities than they would otherwise have, by putting them in possession of additional information. That is a valuable service. (It's true that only the seller actually "hires" the realtor. But the fact that buyers go to them and make use of their multiple-listing services shows that realtors provide a service to buyers, too.)

Suppose you own ten shares of General Electric stock and want to sell it. You could go around to your friends and try to peddle it or you could put an ad in the newspaper. But it is very likely that you would obtain a higher price by using the services of a middleman, in this case a stockbroker. No doubt if you advertised long enough you could find a buyer willing to pay the price the stockbroker obtained for you. But it is most improbable that the cost of your search would be less than the broker's fee.

"Getting it wholesale" is a popular pastime for many people who think that they're economizing. Perhaps they are. If they enjoy searching for bargains (and many people do), then they may well gain from their activities. But for most people, retailers are an important low-cost source of valuable information. The retailer's inventory reveals something of the range of opportunities available, information that is often difficult to obtain in any other fashion.

The same is true for job-placement agencies. Many people resent the fee charged by private agencies for finding them a job. But unless they felt that the information obtained through the agency was worth more than the fee, they would presumably not have used the agency's service. Employers are also willing to pay for such services, and for exactly the same reason.

A large part of the middleman's bad press stems from our habit of comparing actual situations with better but nonexistent ones. The exchanges we make are rarely as advantageous as the exchanges we could make if we were omniscient. So we conclude that the middleman takes advantage of our ignorance. But why look at it in that way? Using the same argument, one could say that the doctor takes advantage of your illnesses, and that he should receive no return for his services because he would be unable to obtain a return if you were always healthy. That is both true and irrelevant. We are neither always healthy nor omniscient. Physicians and middlemen are consequently producers of real wealth. Other prestigious persons performing similar services are lawyers, teachers, preachers, and corporation executives.

Markets Create Information

Supply and demand, or the market process of competing bids and offers, creates indices of value for decision makers by placing price tags on available resources. The capacity of the market to generate high-quality information at low cost is one of its most important but least appreciated virtues. Middlemen are important participants in this process.

"But what is 'the market'?" you may ask. That's a good question and not an easy one to answer in a few words. The market is clearly not a place, though it may sometimes be closely identified with a particular place. Nor is it anything one can observe in the usual sense of observation. It is finally just a set of interrelationships, or what we called a "process of competing bids and offers." Some markets, like stock markets and commodity-markets, are "well organized," which means that the bids and offers of prospective buyers and sellers are rather comprehensively assembled so that a single price tends to be established for all transactions over a wide geographic area. The market for used furniture, on the other hand, is relatively unorganized. Transactions take place at prices that vary greatly, because buyers and sellers are not in extensive contact. The market for retail groceries falls somewhere between these extremes. Hamburger prices will consequently vary more over a given area at one time than livestock prices, but less than used furniture prices.

It is sometimes said that stock markets and commodity markets are more nearly "perfect" than retail grocery markets and used furniture markets. This is a misleading way to describe the difference, however, because it implies that the latter markets *ought to be changed* (perfection is better than imperfection). Remember, however, that such a recommendation makes sense only if the costs of improving the markets are less than the gains from more efficient exchange made possible by the improvement.

In every case, however, the relationships between buyers and sellers, whether constant and extensive or sporadic and scattered, generate prices. Each such price is a piece of potentially valuable information to other people concerning available opportunities. The more such prices there are and the more widely they are known, the wider the range of opportunities available to others.

Opportunity costs consequently decline because markets exist, which is really a way of saying that the range of opportunities available to decision makers expands. And that is a way of saying that wealth increases or that economic growth occurs. And is that not what we finally mean by an increase in wealth? A wider range of available opportunities? The freedom and the power to do more of what one wants to do?

Those who make markets—middlemen, brokers, arbitrageurs—facilitate exchange by specializing in the production of information. They do so presumably because they believe themselves to have a comparative advantage in information production. Anyone who thinks that he "knows better" is free to take advantage of his knowledge—unless, as so often occurs, legal restrictions are imposed on trading. A society that prohibits exchange or suppresses markets, whether from hostility to the trader or for some other reason, denies useful information to its members.

Speculators Everywhere

All of this casts a new light on the phenomenon of speculation. The dictionary defines speculation as "trading in the hope of profit from changes in the market price." That's good enough for our purposes. The most celebrated (or, more accurately, the most execrated) speculator is probably the Wall Street "bear." He "sells short," that is, sells shares of stock he does not currently own for future delivery. He believes that the stock will go down in price, so that when the time comes for him to deliver, he can purchase the share at a low price and sell them at the previously agreed-upon higher price.

A more important speculator is probably the commodity speculator, who may trade in such items as wheat, soybeans, hogs, lumber, sugar, cocoa, or copper. He buys and sells "futures." These are agreements to deliver, at some specified date in the future, amounts of a commodity at a price determined now.

These are the spectacular speculators whose feats make the financial pages. A less publicized speculator is you yourself. You are buying education now, partly in the hope that it will increase the value of the labor services you'll be selling in the future. But the future price of your services could turn out to be too low to justify your present investment.

Another familiar speculator is the housewife who reads that the price of sugar is expected to rise and responds by loading her pantry with a two-year supply. If the price of sugar rises far enough, she gains. If it does not, she loses. She has tied up her wealth in sugar, thereby cluttering her shelves and depriving herself of the opportunity to purchase more valuable assets—an interest-bearing savings account, for example.

The motorist who fills his tank when he sees a sign advertising gasoline at two cents a gallon less than he's accustomed to pay is speculating; the price may be four cents lower two blocks ahead. And the motorist who drives on an almost empty tank in hope of lower prices up ahead is a notorious speculator.

When you begin to think about it carefully you discover that every consumer purchase is a speculative venture. The consumer pays a sum of money in anticipation of a future stream of services, and those services will often not be as satisfactory as he expected when he made the purchase. The loaf of bread may prove moldy when he opens it or just less tasty than he had hoped; the new roof may leak in a driving rain; the articles in the magazine to which he took out a twelve-month subscription may turn out to be dull and uninformative; the movie rated G may give his children nightmares for a week.

What are we going to do about it? Sometimes, if we prefer, we can reduce our risk by persuading the sellers from whom we purchase to accept more of the risk. We may, for example, refuse to purchase an automobile unless the seller guarantees it against a wide range of potential defects. We may purchase clothing exclusively from merchants who are willing to refund our money if we're dissatisfied. We may purchase a service contract along with our new washing machine, which means that we accept the payment of a small, fixed sum as insurance against the risk of a large repair bill. This last example makes it quite clear that we aren't obtaining something for nothing. If they believe it is in their interest to do so, people will accept the risks that others don't want to bear. They must therefore be able to anticipate a larger net return from assuming risk than from not doing so.

Consequences of Speculation

But what about those "professional" speculators whom most people seem to have in mind when they condemn the greed and unearned profits of speculators? "Commodity speculators exploit natural disasters," it is often said, "by driving up prices before the disaster occurs. And sometimes the expected disaster never even materializes." That is true. But it is only one small and misleading part of the truth. Suppose evidence begins to accumulate in early summer that the fungus called corn leaf blight is spreading to major corn-producing areas of the Midwest. A significant percentage of the year's corn crop could be wiped out as a result.

People who think this is likely to occur will consequently expect a higher price for corn next year. This expectation will induce some people to hold some corn out of current consumption in order to carry it over into the next crop period when, they believe, the price will be higher. That is speculation.

Notice how many different parties engage in such speculation: farmers who substitute other livestock feed for corn in order to maintain their corn stocks at a higher level, either to avoid having to buy corn next year at a higher price or in order to sell then at the higher price; industrial users who increase their inventories now while the price is relatively low; plus people who might not know a bushel of corn from a peck of soybeans but who hope to make a profit from buying cheap now and selling dear later. There are well-organized commodity markets to facilitate this kind of transaction. The effect of all these activities is to reduce the currently marketed supply of corn; the price consequently rises. And just as the critic protested, it rises before the disaster occurs.

But that is only a part of the picture. These speculative activities cause corn to be transported *over time* from a period of relative abundance to one of greater scarcity. The price next year, when the blight is expected to have its effects, will therefore be lower than it otherwise would be. Speculators thus even out the flow of commodities into consumption and diminish price fluctuations over time. Since price fluctuations create risks for those who grow or use corn, speculators are actually reducing risk to others. More accurately, they are purchasing risk (in hope of a profit) from others less willing to take risk (and willing to pay something in the form of reduced expected returns to avoid it).

Prophets and Losses

All this assumes, however, that the speculators are correct in their anticipations. What if the expected poor harvest fails to materialize? What if an unusually large crop appears instead? Then the speculators are transporting corn from a period of lesser to a period of greater abundance and thereby magnifying price fluctuations. This is clearly a misallocation of resources, involving as it does the giving up now of some high-priced corn for the sake of obtaining later an equal amount of low-priced corn. That is not socially profitable.

But neither is it profitable for the speculators. They will sustain losses where they had hoped for gains. We should not expect them, consequently, to behave in this fashion *except as a result of ignorance.* Are speculators likely to be ignorant?

No one is omniscient. And speculators make mistakes. (Why would they otherwise be called speculators?) But living as we do in an uncertain world, we have no option but to act in the presence of uncertainty. No one escapes uncertainty and the consequences of ignorance by refusing to act or to think about the future. And if anyone thinks he knows more than the speculators, he can counter them at a profit to himself by betting against them. It is interesting and somewhat revealing to note that those who criticize speculators for misreading the future rarely give effective expression to their own supposedly greater insight by entering the market against them. Hindsight, of course, is always in copious supply—and the price is appropriately low.

As we have repeatedly tried to show, information is a scarce good. Better information means greater efficiency because it provides a wider range of opportunities and hence expanded scope for the exploitation of comparative advantage. Speculators provide information. Their offers to buy and sell express their judgments concerning the future in relation to the present. The prices generated by their activities are, like all prices, indices of value: information for decision makers on present and future opportunity costs. This information is at least as important to conservatives as it is to gamblers. It is true that the information they provide is "bad" information when the speculators are wrong. But harping on this is again a case of comparing one situation with a better but unattainable situation. Anyone who thinks he can read the future better than the speculators is free to express his convictions with money, profit from his insight, and benefit society in the process.

Meanwhile those whose ordinary business activities involve them in the use of commodities that are speculatively traded do make effective use of the information generated by the speculators. Farmers employ the prices predicted in the commodity exchanges to make planting decisions, for example. And those who use goods not ordinarily thought of as speculative commodities also take advantage of the information generated by speculators. For we all use prices as information; and prices reflect competing bids and offers inevitably based to a large extent on a (speculative!) reading of the future.

Price Takers and Price Searchers

In talking about the functions that relative prices perform, we have generally been assuming until now that sellers must accept the prices established in the market by the competing bids and offers of buyers and all other sellers. This is not in fact the way most prices are established. More often than not sellers must choose the prices at which they will offer their products. And this, too, is a speculative activity. Let's examine the

situations of the United States Steel Corporation and a wheat farmer from central Kansas when they decide what prices to ask for their products.

Take the case of the wheat farmer first. Suppose he consults the financial pages of his newspaper or tunes in for the noonday market reports and finds that number 2 ordinary hard Kansas City wheat opened at $3.25 per bushel. That news may disappoint or delight him, but there is almost nothing he can do to change it. If he decides that the price is an excellent one, and sells his entire crop for immediate delivery, the market will feel scarcely a ripple. Even if he is one of the biggest wheat farmers in the state, he is still such a small part of the total number of those offering to buy or sell wheat that he cannot affect the price. The difference between what the closing price will be if he sells all of his crop, and what it will be if he sells only half of it, will not be as much as $\frac{1}{4}$¢.

Economists therefore call the wheat farmer a *price taker.* He cannot affect the price by his own actions. The price at the local grain elevator is determined by the actions of many buyers and sellers all over the country. If the farmer exercises his legal right to put a price tag on his wheat 2¢ higher than the market decrees, he will sell no wheat. And since he can sell all the wheat he has at the going price, he has no incentive to offer to sell any wheat at less than the going price. Price takers face perfectly elastic demand curves, or what for all practical purposes amount to perfectly elastic demand curves. The demand curves are horizontal at the going price.

Most businessmen are not in this position. They can raise their prices if they choose, without losing all their sales. And they cannot, as can the farmer, always sell everything they're capable of producing without lowering their prices. At higher prices they will sell less, at lower prices they will be able to sell more. They must choose a price or set of prices. Economists therefore call them *price searchers.*

The United States Steel Corporation is a price searcher. But now we must be careful. United States Steel does not, as many commentators have suggested, set its prices in disregard of supply and demand. Supply depends on cost, and cost is taken into account by every price searcher. The supply capabilities and intentions of other steel producers will also be considered. Demand curves are never completely inelastic, so demand must be taken into account if the price searcher hopes to find what he is looking for, which is presumably the most profitable price to set. The current and prospective demands for such other products as aluminum, plywood, plastic, and cement are also relevant information to the searcher for a proper steel price, since any or all of these products may turn out to be substitutes for steel.

And sometimes United States Steel errs significantly when it sets its prices. Pricing decisions, like production decisions, are based on expected marginal costs and expected demand in the absence of complete information. Demand may turn out to be weaker than anticipated so that the corporation finds its output inventories growing in an unplanned and undesired way. Or demand may prove stronger than anticipated so that the steel produced and marketed could have been sold at a higher and more profitable price. Costs, too, may in fact be different from what they were expected to be. Higher than anticipated marginal costs *may* call for higher selling prices; lower costs than were anticipated *may* allow for price reductions that will increase the firm's net revenue if demand is sufficiently elastic.

Price searchers make mistakes and mistakes by definition reduce the seller's net revenue. But even after a mistake has been recognized the seller will not be sure of what to do. It's often costly to change a printed price list; in addition to the printing and mailing costs, the firm risks the responses of angered customers when prices are hiked and of threatened competitors when they are reduced. These expected costs must be set against the costs expected to be associated with maintaining the original but poorly chosen set of prices—costs of carrying large inventories, of closing the plant for two weeks, or of losing additional sales revenue. Pricing is indeed for most business firms a speculative activity.

SPECULATION, PROFIT, AND INTEREST

Why are we placing so much emphasis on the essentially speculative nature of economic decisions? The answer is that no economic system can be adequately understood by someone who fails to see that risk is unavoidable in an uncertain world, that a large number of major economic problems are at least in part the consequence of uncertainty, and that the way in which society assigns risks or allows people to buy and sell risk will to a large extent determine the manner in which its economy functions. The future-oriented character of all economizing decisions requires us to look very closely at the concept of profit. But before we can do that we must examine something else with which profit is sometimes confused, the phenomenon of interest.

Why Is Interest Paid?

Interest is the difference in value between present and future goods. Once you understand why present goods are more valuable than goods in the future, you realize that interest is not something peculiar to capitalist economies, or a consequence of the avarice and monopoly power of bankers and other money lenders, or something that could be eliminated just by making more money available. Interest rates are generally talked about as if they were the cost of borrowing money, because money is the usual means by which people acquire possession of present goods. But interest would exist in an economy that used no money at all, since it is fundamentally the difference in value between present and future goods.

Why are present goods more highly valued than goods in the future? This is a question that has intrigued a number of the most distinguished minds in the history of economics, and the higher subtleties of the problem still arouse controversy in some quarters. Two facts stand out, however, whose significance can be readily grasped.

Time Preference

In the first place, individuals have on the average *a positive rate of time preference.* That is to say, people tend to place a higher subjective value on consumption in the near future than on consumption in the more distant future. Some have interpreted this as evidence of shortsightedness, or of inability to imagine the distant future with as much vividness and force as one contemplates the immediate future, or of an innate human tendency to view the future through rose-tinted glasses. Each of these interpretations casts suspicion on the ultimate "rationality" of time preference. On the other hand, given the facts of human mortality and all the contingencies of life, it is not necessarily irrational or shortsighted to prefer a bird in the hand to two in the bush. Moreover, if people have reason to believe that their income will increase over time, they could very logically

conclude that giving up something now entails a larger subjective sacrifice than giving up quite a bit more of the same thing at a future date when one's income is expected to be larger. Whatever the explanation or explanations, however, there can be no doubt that people do display positive rates of time preference. To obtain 100 strawberries today, a person may be willing to give in exchange 115 strawberries one year from now. Conversely, such an individual could be persuaded to give up 100 strawberries now only by the promise of 115 strawberries or more one year hence. He displays a 15% rate of time preference. While these subjective rates of time preference vary widely from individual to individual and from one culture to another, on average they are positive in every known society. This by itself would be sufficient to create a premium on present goods over future goods and thus a positive rate of interest.

The Productivity of Capital

The second main factor making for positive interest rates in a society—though perhaps it is only another aspect of the factor already discussed—is *the potential productivity of goods.* Suppose that Robinson Crusoe, a familiar figure in economists' arguments, can only keep himself alive from day to day by digging for clams. Five clams a day will barely enable him to keep body and soul together. And five clams a day is the most he can obtain by digging with his hands during every working hour. If he had a shovel, however, he could increase his daily output to ten clams. But a week's work is required to manufacture a suitable shovel. Since Robinson would starve if he took a week off from digging in order to make the shovel, he cannot attain this higher income level.

It is clear in such a case that Robinson would be eager to obtain 35 extra clams, and willing to give in return more than 35 clams in the future, for the opportunity to increase his productivity by first making a shovel. The shovel is *capital* for Robinson, by which we mean *produced goods intended to be used for the production of future goods.* And it is the shovel's value as capital—that is, its present productivity in the creation of future goods—that causes Robinson to want it and makes him willing to pay a premium to obtain it.

Consequences of Uncertainty

When we begin to think about all the different rates of interest that lenders charge, we quickly encounter the interesting problems raised by uncertainty. Suppose that Joe Jones puts $100 into a savings account on January 1. The bank promises 5% interest and Joe is confident that the bank will neither fail nor renege on its commitment. On December 31 he withdraws $105. He earned $5 in interest, a payment for the use of his savings. He was able to earn interest because some people wanted to borrow and were willing to pay a premium in the future in order to obtain goods in the present.

Now suppose that he lends the same $100 to a business firm that promises to pay him $5 per year for each year he leaves his funds with the firm and gives him a bond as evidence of its obligation. The firm uses his savings, we may assume, to purchase capital. This doesn't seem to differ in any significant way from the preceding case. Joe has once again received 5% per year for the use of his savings. And everyone will in fact call the $5 interest because it is a contractual obligation of a fixed amount.

Let's vary the situation once again. This time Joe lends the firm $100 and receives in return a share of common stock. Now Joe is not entitled to receive any fixed amount. Ownership of the stock entitles him merely to a share of the firm's earnings. The firm may do poorly and pay him only $2 in dividends over the year, or it may do very well and pay him $15 in dividends. That won't be called interest by most people because it was not a fixed, contractual obligation. But a good case can be made, from a functional standpoint, for applying the interest label to $5 of the dividends. For if 5% is the going rate at which the firm can borrow, and 5% is the rate of return that lenders like Joe can fairly confidently expect from lending their funds at little risk, then 5% is the opportunity cost of lending funds to firms for capital acquisitions. It is what the lender sacrifices by letting any borrower have his savings. It is what he will therefore demand as a condition of making the loan.

Unless he wants to make more than 5% and is willing to accept greater risk in the effort to do so! But if the firm subsequently pays only $2, Joe *sustains a loss.* He loses the extra $3 he could have obtained pretty much as a matter of course by purchasing a bond or putting his money in the bank. If the firm pays $15, Joe *makes a profit.* The profit is $10, not $15: the amount over and above what is available with a very high degree of certainty. To grasp the point we're making here, you must ask yourself why people lend money at 5% when there are opportunities to lend at 15%. The answer is that they can't be certain of the 15%. It might well be less, perhaps a good deal less. The higher rate of return is reserved for people who are willing to take more risk. But that implies, of course, that the higher return *was not generally anticipated.* The generally anticipated return, the rate of return that is rather confidently expected, may be thought of as the interest portion of the return. The remainder is profit.

Profit as the Consequence of Uncertainty

We are defining profit here as *the difference between the outcome that was generally anticipated when a decision was made and what finally happened.* It is not the same as interest, which is the social rate of preference for present over future goods and hence the opportunity cost of obtaining present goods. By this definition, profit as distinct from interest is not a cost at all. It is something that appears because the future is uncertain. If there were no uncertainties in life, there would never be a divergence between anticipation and realization, and there would be, by this definition, no profits at all—and no losses, since a loss is simply a profit with a minus sign, like the $3 Joe lost when the firm paid him only $2 in dividends.

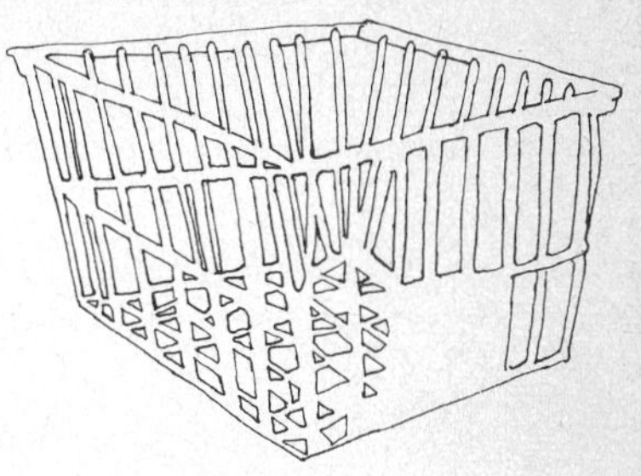

What Function Does Profit Perform?

The core of the argument is that profit in this sense is something quite different functionally from other kinds of income. The payment that induces someone to supply labor services is a wage. The payment that induces someone to supply the services of his money, or better, the services of what this money can obtain, is interest. These payments must be made because they are true costs of doing business. A manufacturer cannot obtain the services of people or physical property unless he is able to bid them away from alternative employments by paying their opportunity cost. But there is a kind of income that seems *both unnecessary and inevitable:* the income that accrues to people because decisions are always made in the present but only justified in the future, and the future is uncertain. "Unnecessary and inevitable" is a strange combination. But think about it.

When businessmen and others talk about the "necessity for profits," as they often do, they are almost certainly not using the word *profit* in the way that we are now defining it. A business firm will not be able to operate unless it can obtain funds with which to hire services. In that sense, such funds are necessary. It can obtain funds only by generating revenue from sales or by borrowing. It will be unable to borrow unless potential lenders believe that future sales will generate sufficient revenue to allow payment of interest on the loans. It will be easy for the firm to obtain funds if people are anticipating very large future net revenues from its operation, but difficult for it to do so if people generally are pessimistic about the firm's prospects. This is all that businessmen mean, or ought to mean, when they speak of the necessity for profits: the need for enough revenue and prospective revenue to enable the firm to pay the opportunity cost of the services required for continued operation. This much is "needed" because the business firm will not be able to operate indefinitely without it.

We must keep in mind at the same time that the *potential* of profit is an important stimulus to action. If profits could somehow always be confiscated, we would certainly observe less innovation in society and fewer resources devoted to exploration and experiment. But there is a very big difference between a *potential* profit and a profit in the pocket. The potential of a profit prompts people to search for more efficient ways of combining resources, new products for which there might be a social demand, and organizational innovations that promise to increase efficiency. If they succeed, they benefit society and receive a profit. But they may fail, and in that case they will sustain a loss.

So no business *must* make a profit. At the same time, profits and losses are inevitable. As long as there is uncertainty about the future, there will be divergencies between anticipated outcomes and what actually does occur, divergencies that will create profits and losses. Nor is this true only for business firms. Profits and losses can and do appear almost anywhere, for anyone at all, and not just for business firms, commodity speculators, or those who lend money. Aerospace engineers suffer losses when the federal government cuts back on the space program and cancels the SST (supersonic transport). College professors receive profits when the federal government decides to spend huge sums on higher education. Authors make a profit when they hit on a product that captivates the public. And highly trained astrologers took a loss when people abandoned the belief that the stars shape individual destiny—just as some of their intellectual descendants have recently made profits from an unexpected return to older persuasions.

What Tomorrow Is Worth Today

Income in the future, besides being uncertain, is not worth as much as income now. That's what the interest rate asserts. If the pure interest rate, which means the nominal rate minus any premium for risk, is 3%, then any person with $100 now can have $103 one year from now. All he must do is surrender for a year $100 of his power to purchase goods. Whether he thinks that's a fine bargain will depend upon his personal rate of time preference.[1] Those who discount the future at less than 3% per year will want to surrender present for future purchasing power at that rate of

---

1. Any discussion of interest rates and the relative values of present and future goods will be misleading unless all parties to the discussion are making similar assumptions about the future behavior of the general price level. In a period of long continued inflation, discussion gets confused by the implicit adoption of different expectations about future prices. If you chuckled derisively at the suggestion in the text above that 3% per year was a fine bargain, that may be because you have never experienced a stable price level and you're assuming that inflation is going to continue at 5% per year or so. But a 5% annual increase in the price level is the same thing as a 5% annual decrease in the value of money. That means that $103 one year from now in return for $100 now would be a *real* interest rate of minus 2%. And that would *not* be a fine bargain. We are assuming no change in the value of money, or general price stability, in this chapter, and it's important for you to know that and keep it in mind. This is another instance of the problems created for economic analysis by the experience of inflation. We discussed the problem earlier in chapter 2, page 23, under "An Important Note on *Relative* Prices." You may want to review those paragraphs.

interest. Those who discount the future at more than 3% will want to acquire present command over goods at that rate in exchange for the surrender of future command over goods.

But if the prevailing rate of interest is 3%, then future income should always be discounted at a rate no less than that. Even if you have a zero rate of time preference, so that you value future goods equally with present goods, present goods will have a higher value for you because they grow over time into more goods. At 3%, $100 now becomes $103 after one year.

It follows, then, that $103 to be received one year from now is only worth $100 in present value. The calculation in this case is so simple that it seems silly to write it out; but discounting calculations are not always so obvious, and the simple case provides the basis for understanding more complex cases.

$100 times 1.03, which is one plus the rate of discount, equals $103, the value one year from now of $100 in present value. The value of a present $100 after two years will be $100 times 1.03 multiplied again by 1.03, or $100 times 1.03. This is simply the familiar rule for calculating compound interest.

It follows, then, that $100 eight years from now will be $100 times 1.03^8 or $126.68. Conversely, $126.68 to be received at the end of eight years has a present value of $100: $126.68 divided by 1.03^8 equals $100.

The arithmetic is tedious, even with the aid of a calculator, so that people who must do this kind of discounting often employ tables that enormously simplify the calculations by showing present values of future amounts at various interest rates. But our emphasis here is on the concept rather than the process of calculation. Economizing decisions compare *present* values of *expected* outcomes. A meaningful comparison of future outcomes requires that they be translated into present value terms through discounting at an appropriate rate of interest.

Once Over Lightly

An opportunity of which you're unaware is not a real opportunity. Information is therefore a valuable resource whose possession enables people to increase their wealth.

Information is a scarce good whose production usually entails costs. The efficient decision maker accumulates additional information only as long as the anticipated marginal benefit is greater than the marginal cost.

A great deal of economic activity is best understood as a response to the fact that information is a scarce good. The much abused "middleman" is in large part a specialist in information production. Just as the real estate broker enables prospective buyers and sellers to locate one another, so the typical retailer provides customers with knowledge of the goods sellers are offering and brings sellers into contact with those who want the sellers' offerings.

The common habit of viewing the middleman as an unproductive bandit on the highway of trade stems from the erroneous assumption that information is a free good.

Everyone who makes a decision in the absence of complete information about the future consequences of all available opportunities is a speculator. So everyone is a speculator.

People who think they know more than others about the relationship between present and future scarcities will want to buy in one time period for sale in the other. If they are correct, they gain from their superior insight and also transport goods through time from periods of lesser to periods of greater scarcity. If they're wrong in their predictions, they perversely move goods from periods of greater to periods of lesser scarcity and suffer the penalty of a personal loss on their transactions.

Because prices are summary indicators of scarcity, they are valuable information. Those whose buying and selling activities create prices are generating information that is useful to others.

A useful distinction to make in trying to understand how prices are established is the distinction between *price takers* and *price searchers*. The price taker must accept the price decreed by the market. His buyers have such excellent substitutes for his product that any attempt to raise the price or otherwise shift the terms of sale in his own favor will leave the seller with no customers at all. The price searcher, on the other hand, can sell different quantities at different prices and must therefore search for the most advantageous price. Price searching is a speculative activity.

Insofar as interest represents an opportunity cost, it must be distinguished from profit. Interest is the difference in value between present and future goods. It is usually attached to money simply because money represents general command over present or future goods.

The rate of interest in a society is typically positive because present goods are more valuable than future goods. This reflects positive rates of time preference and the fact that goods *now* can often be employed to create more goods *later*—capital is productive.

Because economic decisions are always made *in anticipation of future costs and benefits,* they are often mistaken. The difference between generally expected and actual outcomes, due to uncertainty, creates profits and losses.

The potentiality of a profit encourages risk taking and innovation on the part of those who hope to appropriate the difference between generally anticipated and actual outcomes. The way in which a society assigns profits and losses will affect people's behavior.

Meaningful comparisons over time among different values require that future values be discounted at whatever rate of interest most adequately reflects the opportunities available to the decision maker.

A judgment as to whether or not particular income has been earned by its recipient depends both upon conceptions of social justice and an analysis of the functions which the possibility of profit performs. "Windfall" profits may be "justified" if the possibility of obtaining them encourages socially desirable behavior such as risk taking and the search for information.

QUESTIONS FOR DISCUSSION

1. If you found that you could reduce your bills for new clothing 10% by buying exclusively from catalogs, would you do it? Are there some articles of clothing you would be more willing to buy from a catalog than others? Why? What kinds of information does a clothing retailer supply?

2. Evaluate the following paragraph from a newspaper article:

   > One sure way to save money on groceries is to eliminate the middleman by buying directly from farmers and other suppliers. That is what a group of socially motivated and normally hungry people have decided to do by forming a grocery cooperative.

3. Would you expect prices for goods of similar quality offered in garage sales to vary more than prices for goods offered in regular retail outlets? Why?

4. A man approaches you in a busy airport terminal, shows you a handsome wristwatch which he says is worth $135, and offers to let you have it for $25. Would you buy it? Would you be more willing to buy it if you had better information? What do you "know" when you buy a watch from an established local jeweler that you do not know in this situation?

5. Are you speculating when you buy fire insurance on your home? Could you save money by getting together with your friends to form an insurance cooperative, thereby eliminating the necessity of paying something to a middleman (the insurance company)? What kinds of useful information do insurance companies provide?

6. You find out in late December that you can probably make $1000 on a business deal if you can gain the good will of a client by getting him two tickets to the Super Bowl game. You manage to buy two well-located seats from a scalper for $250. Were you cheated by the scalper? Would you be glad that scalpers exist? Why do so many people dislike scalpers intensely?

7. Is the college you're attending a price searcher? How much freedom does it

have in setting the tuition rate you will pay? Does it ever make mistakes in setting its prices?

8. Those who use the term "administered prices" do not include in this classification the prices charged by grocery stores. Nonetheless a grocer stamping prices on his products seems clearly to be "administering" his prices. Can you suggest criteria that would enable us to distinguish "administered" from "nonadministered" prices?

9. You purchase for $950 a $1000 government bond maturing one year from the date of purchase. Will you make a profit if you hold the bond to maturity? Will you make a profit if there is a sharp, general increase in prevailing interest rates a week after your purchase? What effect will this have on the price you can obtain from selling your bond in the market?

10. Humbert and Ambler are very different personalities. Humbert likes to eat, drink, and be merry and let the future care for itself. He suspects the world is liable to disintegrate in a few years anyway. Ambler is only twenty-one years old but is already planning conscientiously for his retirement years. What would you predict about their respective rates of time preference? How do people of Humbert's type benefit from the existence of people like Ambler, and vice versa?

11. What effect would you expect the rate of technological innovation in a society to have on the level of interest rates? Why?

12. The Corps of Engineers estimates that a canal between Tussle and Big Stone would save shippers $500,000 per year. The canal would cost $20 million to construct and $200,000 per year to maintain.

   (*a*) Is it correct to say that the canal is a good investment in the long run because it will save society a net $300,000 per year and eventually that will come to more than the $20 million construction cost?

   (*b*) About how low would the interest rate have to be to make the canal a profitable investment? (The canal would not be profitable if the interest payments ate up the saving to shippers minus maintenance costs.)

   (*c*) "The advantage of having the government build the canal is that government can do things that are in the public interest while private enterprise is constrained by narrow considerations of profitability." Evaluate that argument.

13. "A wealthy society has little difficulty paying interest. But in a poor country with almost no capital, economic planners cannot afford to take interest charges into account in their calculations." What's wrong with that argument?

14. "When lenders extend credit to high risk borrowers, they must raise the interest rates they charge low risk borrowers in order to cover their losses from defaults." Do you agree?

15. What arguments can you offer to support the establishment of legal ceilings on interest rates?

16. Why would an agricultural economist conclude that the benefits of a government price-subsidy plus acreage-restriction program accrue largely to the owners of the land *at the time the program was started?*

17. In the spring of 1963 Fidel Castro announced a sugar production goal for 1970 of 10 million tons. As the target date approached, and it began to appear that this much publicized target might not be attained, the Cuban government transferred labor and other resources in large amounts from the production of alternative goods into the production of sugar. The goal was still missed by a large margin. How do you suppose the consequent loss was distributed? How would the profit have been distributed had this decision turned out *better* than anticipated?

6

SUPPLY AND DEMAND IN LABOR MARKETS

When incomes are rising, that's good; we're getting wealthier. When prices are rising, that's bad; the purchasing power of our income is falling and so we're getting poorer. It seems as if we should all cheer for higher incomes and lower prices.

THE DEMAND FOR AND SUPPLY OF LABOR

The catch is that incomes and prices are opposite sides of the same coin. The incomes of physicians are obviously a function of the prices people pay for medical care; the incomes of barbers depend on the price of haircuts. In these cases the connection is obvious because it is relatively direct. But where the connection is less obvious and direct, it is still important. The incomes of construction workers come from the prices people pay for new homes, offices, and factories, as do the incomes of construction contractors and those who supply materials to the building trades. The prices people pay for new automobiles become income for General Motors' assembly-line employees, shareholders, and managers, plus all the employees and shareholders of General Motors' many suppliers.

But don't jump to the conclusion that higher prices for a good necessarily mean larger incomes for its producers. The law of demand asserts that less will be purchased at higher prices. Higher haircut prices, to take the sim-

plest example, might mean less rather than more income for barbers, depending on the elasticity of demand for professional haircuts. That elasticity will in turn depend on how many substitutes there are for barber shops (home clippers, longer hair, a seedy look, and so on).

Most people obtain income by selling the services of the productive resources they own. The demand for productive resources is derived from the demand for the goods these resources are capable of producing. It's quite simple and fairly obvious. But it's also, to judge from the kinds of public policy recommendations one reads and hears, not very widely understood.

How would you evaluate the following arguments?

1. "A sizable increase in the legal minimum wage would go a long way toward reducing poverty."

2. "The ominous threat of automation is hanging over our society. We are not far from the time when a majority of the labor force will be unable to find work at all, because machines are so much more productive than people."

Marginal Productivity and the Demand for Labor

Let's look at the first argument. We are often told that opposition to legal minimum wages is evidence of insensitivity toward poverty. But it's not that simple. A wage is a price, the price of a productive resource. It's also the basis of a human being's income, of course; we're not denying that at all. But from the standpoint of those who hire workers and pay their wages, the wage is a price or cost. The law of demand reminds us that price and quantity purchased tend to move in opposite directions. Won't they do so also in the case of a legally imposed wage increase?

Here is the widely unrecognized consequence of raising wages by law. If the legal minimum is no higher than what employers are already paying, it has no effect. It will have an impact only if some covered employers are paying less than the legal minimum. But when these employers must raise the wage they pay, will they continue to hire as many employees?

Employers hire resources on the basis of some estimate of the probable contribution that resource will make. What will the employment of this resource add to the value of the firm's operation? The phrase economists use is *marginal productivity*, which means the additional value created by the use of the additional productive resources. If the employer wants to increase his wealth, he will only hire resources whose value to his operation is expected to exceed the additional cost he will incur by hiring that resource. This is the general rule for maximizing net revenue: Take those actions and only those actions whose expected marginal revenue is greater than their expected marginal cost. An increase in the legal minimum wage raises the marginal cost of some employees to some employers. We can predict that some employers will consequently choose to hire fewer workers. They will lay off or not replace workers whose estimated marginal productivity is below their now higher employment cost.

Unskilled workers can consequently be hurt by a high legal minimum wage. Teenagers are also hurt by such laws, because employers often place a low estimate on the value of their contribution. Some workers will be paid the higher wage and retained; they're better off. But those who are deprived of work opportunities by the legal minimum are clearly made worse off. So it is not at all obvious that increasing the legal minimum wage reduces poverty.

The Fear of Automation

What are we to make of the second argument above, that machines are destroying jobs? The first question to ask is, What does it mean to say that "machines are more productive than people"? Employers aren't interested in mere physical or technical capabilities; they're interested in the relation between marginal revenues and marginal costs. A machine is more efficient than a person, and hence will be substituted for a person, only if the *value of the machine's marginal product relative to its marginal cost* is greater than the same ratio for a person. That implies, among other things, that wage rates play an important part in shaping the speed and direction of technological change in the economy.

It would be a serious mistake to suppose, for example, that automatic elevators largely replaced elevator operators in the United States over the last two decades merely because of improvements in technology. Time, energy, and money were spent to develop automatic elevators and owners of buildings installed them because of benefit-cost estimates they made, not because automatic elevators are new and shiny. In some other society where the wage rates (opportunity costs) of elevator operators are quite low, elevators run by trained operators may still be more efficient than automatic elevators.

The fear that our society or any society may run out of jobs is an odd kind of fear. A job, after all, represents an obstacle to be overcome. A society that had run out of jobs for people to do would have come very close to overcoming scarcity; and that would be something to cheer, not to fear. We are not in any such fortunate situation. As technological innovations increase the productive potential of our economy, labor resources are released from some employments and made available for others. The automatic or self-service elevator made it possible for people who were formerly employed in transporting passengers up and down to do something else, to make some other and additional contribution to our total output of goods and services.

MARGINAL PRODUCTIVITY AND
THE DEMAND FOR A RESOURCE

A simple numerical example may help you visualize the relationship between the marginal productivity of a resource and the derived demand for it.

A farmer obtains the following yields of corn from the use of hired labor. We'll assume that all other inputs and costs remain the same. Note that the marginal values are *in between* the totals to indicate that they are the effect of *changing* from one level of hiring to another. The farmer can obtain 1000 bushels without hiring any labor because he is working on the farm as well as managing it. To calculate the final column we have assumed a price of $3 per bushel for corn.

Man-Months of Hired Labor	Bushels of Corn	Marginal Corn Product	Marginal Dollar Product
0	1000		
		160	480
1	1160		
		80	240
2	1240		
		40	120
3	1280		
		20	60
4	1300		

The marginal revenue to this farmer is $480 from employing one worker, $240 when he employs a second, and so on. The marginal revenue product states the value to the farmer of using various quantities of hired labor. It is therefore his derived demand for hired labor: derived both from the physical productivity of labor and the demand for his corn (a perfectly elastic demand at $3 per bushel).

If we assume that he can use fractional inputs, the curve below expresses his demand for hired labor. You can read off the quantities he would demand at any monthly wage rate (marginal cost).

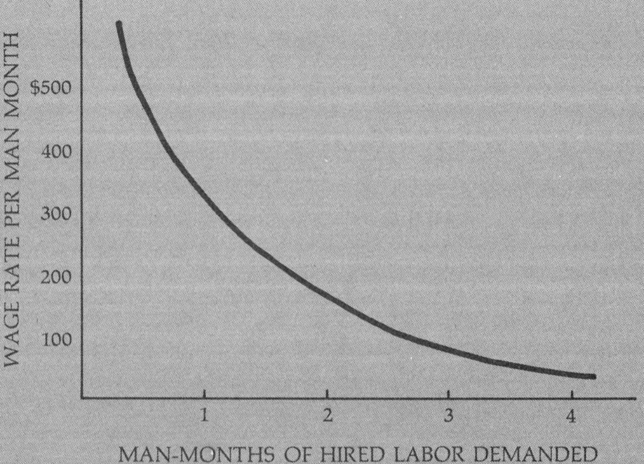

The reallocation of labor in response to changed circumstances, even though it increases the total value of society's output, does lead to a loss of wealth for some people. A rising demand for labor attracted some elevator operators into more remunerative employments and pulled up the wages of the rest. Automatic elevators were in part a response to this situation. But as they were introduced, some elevator operators found themselves pushed rather than pulled: deprived of their present jobs and compelled to accept less desirable alternatives, rather than attracted away from their present positions by better opportunities. Such people suffered, at least temporarily, a loss in wealth. They were forced to incur the cost of searching for new employment, and they were not guaranteed that the new job would be better than the old. Resistance to technological change and the fear of automation or cybernation is therefore quite understandable. Even college professors have been known to speak harshly about the introduction of such technological innovations as videotaped lectures and teaching machines.

Keep in mind, however, that prices and wages are important variables in such processes of adjustment and reallocation. If prices and wages are inflexible or change only very slowly, a larger part of the adjustment burden will be shifted onto something else.

To illustrate: Suppose that a technological breakthrough occurs in automobile production. A manufacturer named Henry Ford finds that he can produce as many automobiles as before, using half as many workers, by employing a moving assembly line. Suppose further that, at existing resource prices, the assembly-line technique cuts the cost of producing these automobiles by 25%. There will be fewer employment opportunities in automobile assembly as a result—at least at first. But if the price of the final product is then reduced, as a consequence of the reduction in cost, and if the demand for automobiles proves sufficiently elastic, there may eventually be more rather than fewer jobs available for automobile assembly workers. That is exactly what did happen. In addition, a reduction in the wages that must be paid to such workers would diminish the manufacturer's incentive to substitute machinery for direct labor; this, too, could alleviate the disemployment effect of the new technology. That has happened much more rarely.

A decline in the demand for anything results in a lesser decline in the quantity demanded if its price falls. This should be kept in mind whenever you are trying to assess the consequences of any change in technology, organization, or the composition of demand. As a matter of demonstrable fact, many prices and especially wages are "sticky," most notoriously when they are subjected to downward pressure. Such stickiness or inflexibility may have advantages, but it also has obvious disadvantages. In the early 1970s, the demand for many kinds of engineering skills fell to unexpectedly low levels. The more that the wages of engineers decline in response to such a change, the larger will be the number of job opportunities still available for engineers. Wage structures that are relatively rigid in a downward direction will leave employed engineers largely unaffected by the changed circumstances; but more engineers than otherwise will be unemployed.

The Supply of Labor

Let's take a look at the supply side of the picture. The amount of time people supply to the labor market can be viewed as the time left over after each person reserves the amount of nonmarket time demanded. Since this nonmarket time is conventionally called leisure by labor economists, we shall use that term. Remember when it is used, however, that it includes all nonmarketed uses of time, from bird watching to sleeping, from studying advanced mathematics to following television serials, from shooting pool to soliciting funds for the March of Dimes.

The demand for leisure can be analyzed by means of the concepts introduced earlier. The price of an hour's leisure, or its opportunity cost, is approximately equal to the available hourly wage rate.[1] People will choose not to be currently employed (that is, to maximize their "purchases" of leisure) when they find the price of leisure sufficiently low. Putting the matter more conventionally: people will offer to supply less of their time to the labor market (purchase more leisure) the lower the wage they expect to obtain. That's just the familiar law of demand. The higher the price of any good (in this case, leisure), the more likely it is that people will choose a substitute (money income and what it will buy).

But that is only part of the picture, because the wage rate is an important component of the income on the basis of which people choose among alternative goods. The concept of income elasticity of demand reminds us that, as people's incomes change, their *demand curve* for particular goods may also change. In the case of leisure, an increase in its price which would cause people to want less entails also an increase in their incomes which may cause them to want more. Since leisure is surely not an inferior good in the technical sense (a good for which the demand decreases as income increases), the higher price of leisure may result in increased purchases of leisure. Higher wage rates, in short, may mean less time supplied to the

---

1. The equality is only approximate for several reasons. Because workers can rarely choose precisely the number of hours they want to work, they cannot equate exactly the marginal cost and the marginal benefit of leisure. Moreover, someone who supplies no labor at all to the market must be placing a marginal value on leisure that is *greater* than the available wage rate.

labor market. Which effect—the substitution effect due to the change in price or the income effect, which is also due to the change in price—will control the direction of people's response to higher wage rates?

There is no consistent evidence showing that, for a given time and locale, higher wage workers do choose to work fewer hours. However, as wage rates in the United States increased during the first half of this century, there was a notable reduction in the average number of hours worked per day and days worked per week. Apparently the demand for leisure did increase as wage income increased, and by more than enough to counter the increased opportunity cost of leisure implicit in the higher wage rates.

We must keep in mind, however, that the hours of work an individual supplies to the market will depend not only on the relative valuations placed upon rest and recreation versus money income and the goods it can purchase, but also on the value assigned to nonmarket opportunities to produce goods. Such goods might include homemade bread, a freshly painted house, or additional education. It follows that as ways are found to produce these goods more quickly in the home or more efficiently outside the home, or as the value that the culture places on household work declines, more time will be offered for sale in the labor market. One very important good produced during leisure time is information about alternative job opportunities. Searching for a better job is often a highly productive way in which to use one's leisure.

Two Supply Curves

Amelia and Bruce are both 20 years old, both have experience as taxicab operators, and both are licensed to drive a cab in the city where they live. But their situations are otherwise quite different. Amelia lives alone in a furnished room one block from the downtown garage of a taxi company. Since it doesn't cost her anything to commute and she has no other attractive job opportunities, Amelia would be willing to drive a taxi for about 30 hours a week if she was offered $2.50 per hour. She would prefer a higher wage, of course, but she would be willing to drive 30 hours for $2.50. Amelia is tired after 5 or 6 hours of hacking, but if she was offered $3.00 per hour, she would be willing to work up to 40 hours a week. She would put up with the fatigue and monotony because she could then afford to rent a larger room, take in more shows, and eat out more frequently. If she could earn $5.00 per hour she would be willing to work as many as 50 hours a week; she could then fulfill her dream of a customized van with quadraphonic tape deck, llama hair rug, and complete cooking facilities. However, if Amelia was able to earn $6.00 per hour, she would

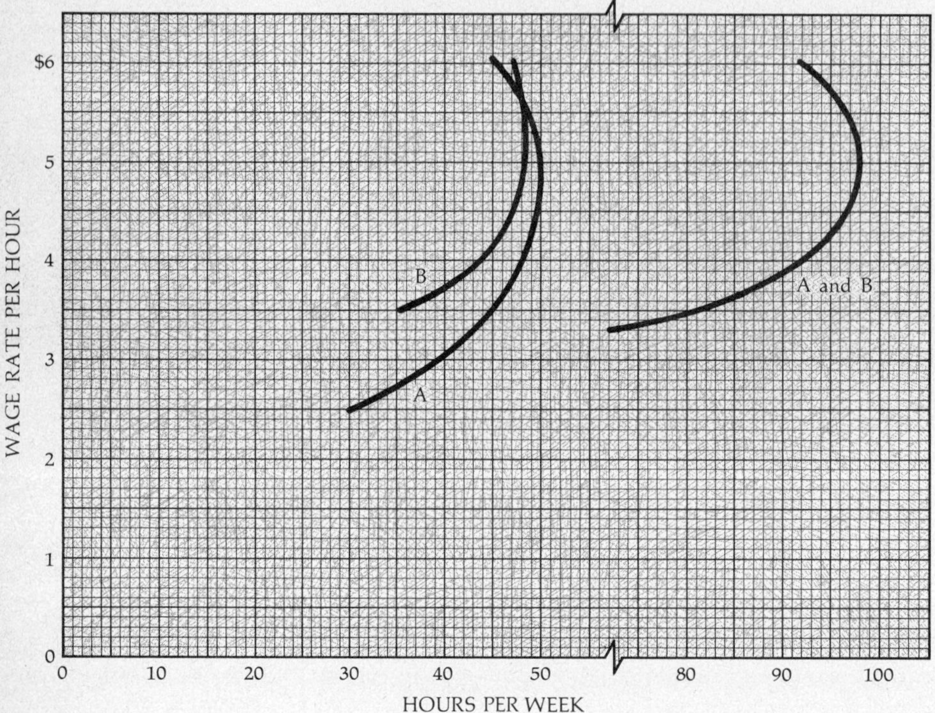

Figure 6A. The labor supply of two workers

not want to work more than 50 hours per week. She would become willing at that wage rate to clock out early at times and to be satisfied with a 45 hour week and more time in the van. Amelia's labor supply schedule is shown as curve A in figure 6A.

Bruce is in a different situation. He lives at home with his parents near the outskirts of the city and would have to commute downtown for the taxi driving job. He knows he can earn about $20 a week from baby-sitting jobs. With room and board furnished he has in effect a comfortable income without working in the market. And so it would take at least $3.50 per hour to get him to drive a taxi. At $3.50 per hour he would be willing to drive 35 hours per week. Rather than prolong the story, we'll just say that the goods Bruce wants require combinations of money income and time that are different from the mixtures required for the goods Amelia wants, and so his response to an increase in wage will be different from Amelia's. Bruce's labor supply schedule is shown as curve B in figure 6A.

Those curves are plausible. An increase in the wage rate will usually get workers to supply more hours when wage rates are relatively low because it makes leisure a more expensive good. But the positive response to wage rate increases tends to diminish as the wage becomes higher

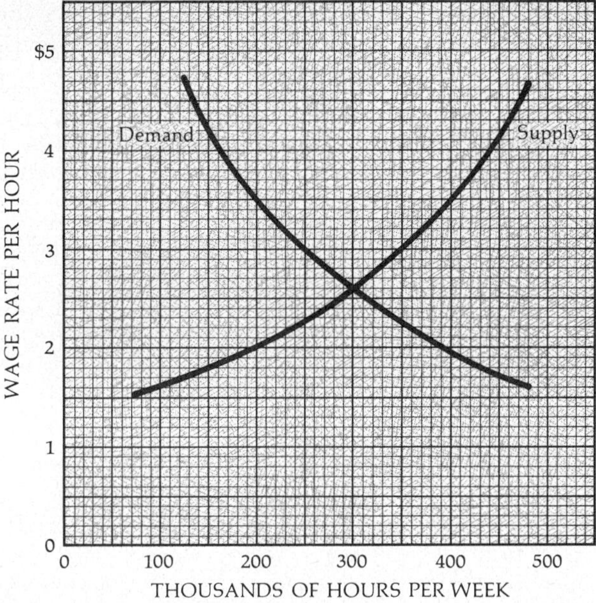

Figure 6B. A labor market

because the larger income associated with high wage rates increases the demand for leisure. Above some wage rate further increases may actually cause the worker to supply fewer hours per year.

The Larger Picture

Since individuals are all different, the supply of labor in a market will not necessarily have the same shape as the curve for an individual. One of the most important effects of an increase in the wage rate is to bring more workers into the market. In figure 6A, Amelia starts supplying labor to the market at a wage of $2.50 per hour and Bruce comes in at $3.50 per hour. When we add the two supply curves by summing them horizontally we get the curve labeled A and B. The individual supply curves of all workers *and potential workers* may well be such that when they are added together the *market* supply curve does not bend backward. This reasonable assumption seems to correspond with what we can observe in most labor markets. A market supply curve for workers and potential workers is shown in figure 6B.

The wage in this market will be determined by the market demand and supply. As we have drawn the curves, a wage rate of $2.60 per hour would equate the hours of work demanded with the hours supplied.

Suppose now that a minimum wage law is enacted which sets the minimum at $3.00 per hour. What will happen in the labor market in figure 6B? Employers will demand only 250 thousand hours of work per week instead of 300. Whether the fewer hours of work will yield more total income to all of the workers in the market depends upon the elasticity of demand. If the demand is elastic between $2.60 and $3.00 per hour, the total income to workers will decrease. The demand will have to be inelastic for the increase in the minimum wage to increase the total income of workers.

But that isn't yet the whole story. When people learn about the higher wage rate, new workers will want to enter the market. And some already working will want to work longer hours. The hours supplied per week will increase to 350 thousand. The net result will be 100 thousand more hours supplied than employers are willing to pay for at the minimum wage of $3.00 per hour. Would you want to call that a shortage of jobs or a surplus of workers? By whichever name, part of that 100-thousand-hour discrepancy will probably show up in the official unemployment figures as a "statistical fact."

Facts as Interpretations

"You can't argue with the facts," we often say. But facts aren't always as "hard" or clear as we suppose. Our experiences have to be interpreted before they become meaningful, and what we take to be "hard facts" are often in reality complex and sometimes highly questionable interpretations of events. There are many mirages in the study of social phenomena.[1]

How did you know in 1974 that the United States economy was going through a period of inflation? Inflation means a rising level of money prices. But some prices may be going up while others are not. How many prices have to rise and by how far must they rise before we have inflation? While we may rely in part on our own experience as customers, most people consult the Consumer Price Index to find out what's happening to the level of money prices. But the Consumer Price Index, as we shall see in the next chapter, is a construct of theorists and statisticians in the Department of Labor. It has been constructed on the basis of careful empirical studies and well-reasoned theories by a lot of competent and

---

1. There is no consensus among users of English on the distinction between "facts" and "data." But the Latin origins of the words point to a distinction that we ought to notice, whatever vocabulary we use to describe it. *Fact* comes from a word meaning "to make" (as does *factory*, a place of making). *Datum,* the singular of *data,* comes from a word which means "to give." *Data* might thus be thought of as the things given, the actual events, and *facts* as what we make of the data, our interpretation and understanding of what is given to experience. One's point of view, angle of vision, theoretical framework, and other presuppositions will help determine which "facts" emerge from the "data."

conscientious people. But it is *not* something that is simply *given* and with which one cannot argue.

How did you discover in 1974 that the economy was simultaneously entering a recession? The recognition of recession is even more difficult than the recognition of inflation. A recession generally means a declining level of production in the economy as a whole. Sometimes, however, it means only a slowdown in the rate of increase in the level of production. Moreover, industries and firms expand and contract production for many reasons, and they do not do so in perfect unison. Even during a deep and prolonged recession, production may be expanding in some industries or areas of the economy while it is declining in most. In chapter 8 we'll introduce you to the National Income and Product Accounts, the information that most people use is deciding what is currently happening to aggregate production. We shall discover that gross national product is also a theoretical construct and not simply a "hard fact."

The most widely used measure of recession, however, and the one that arouses the greatest public concern, is the level of unemployment. This is attested to by the title of the most prominent piece of federal legislation directed toward the control of aggregate fluctuations, the Employment Act of 1946. Although this act grew out of the Full Employment Bill of 1945, it does not call for "full employment." The responsibility of the federal government under the 1946 act is to maintain "maximum employment, production, and purchasing power."

"Full employment" is an unrealistic target if one takes it literally, and a vague target if one does not. The goal of "maximum employment" escapes the charge of being unrealistic, but fares no better than "full employment," when we try to give it a clear and definite meaning. That does not imply the goal is either illusory or unimportant. It does mean that we ought to inquire carefully into the nature of employment and unemployment and examine critically the concepts we use to measure them.

Measuring the Labor Market

Let's look at some numbers provided by the Bureau of Labor Statistics in the United States Department of Labor to get an initial sense of the problems. In December 1974 the BLS sampling techniques yielded the following figures on the labor force, employment, and unemployment. We have added the Bureau of the Census estimate of 1974 population.

Population (1974 average)	211,909,000
Labor force	94,015,000
Employment	87,414,000
Unemployment	6,601,000

If 87.4 million people were employed out of a total population of 211.9 million, then 124.5 million people were *not* employed in December 1974. But unemployment totaled only 6.6 million. So there is clearly a substantial difference between being *not* employed and being *un*employed.

The Noninstitutional Population and the Labor Force

The number of those unemployed, according to BLS estimates, is the difference between the total labor force and the number employed. The question then becomes, Who is included in the labor force and who is not? Everyone under sixteen years of age or an inmate of a penal or mental institution, sanitarium, or home for the aged, infirm, or needy is automatically excluded. That eliminates from the labor force some people who are actually doing work for pay; but the omission is relatively minor. The BLS calls the group that's left the *noninstitutional population.* In December 1974 the noninstitutional population was 150,827,000, or approximately 70% of the total population.

But only 62% of the noninstitutional population was included in the labor force. By what criteria were some included and others left out? The BLS excludes from the labor force, and hence from the ranks of the officially employed or unemployed, all those who are retired, engaged in their own housework, not working while attending school, unable to work because of long-term illness, discouraged from seeking work because of personal or job-market factors, or voluntarily idle. That's a highly diverse list of criteria. Much worse, some of the criteria have extremely fuzzy edges. What's the difference between someone voluntarily idle and someone neither working nor seeking work because of discouragement growing out of personal or job market factors? What's the difference between someone seeking work (and hence in the labor force) but doing so in a half-hearted way, and someone not seeking work (and hence not in the labor force) who would be willing to take a job if the right one came along? There would seem to be an important difference between someone who retires voluntarily and someone who is retired against his wishes; but neither one is in the labor force and so neither is counted among the unemployed.

The Bureau of Labor Statistics divides the labor force into the employed and the unemployed by putting each member into one of four categories: (1) all those working for pay or working more than 15 hours a week without pay in a family-operated business; (2) those temporarily absent from work because of illness, accident, strikes, or a similar cause; (3) those who are not working but are waiting to be recalled after a layoff, or waiting to start a new job within 30 days; (4) those not working but actively seeking employment. Categories 1 and 2 make up the officially employed; categories 3 and 4 make up the officially unemployed.

One who is minded to quibble can always find nits to pick even in the most carefully constructed definitions. There are excellent reasons, however, for looking critically at official employment and unemployment concepts. Each month the BLS releases and the news media publicize the current unemployment rate: the total of those officially unemployed expressed as a percentage of the civilian labor force. (The civilian labor force is the total labor force minus all those in the armed forces.) The civilian labor force in December 1974 was 91,803,000. With 6,601,000 unemployed, the official unemployment rate for the month was therefore 7.2%. When that figure was published in January 1975, political pressure intensified for some kind of government action to stimulate employment. If the concepts of the labor force, the employed, and the unemployed contain serious ambiguities—as they do—the official unemployment rate can be a misleading guide and spur to action. That is why we want to look at the patterns of behavior these concepts are attempting to summarize.

Think for a moment about the language of the 1946 Employment Act, which calls for policies to secure "maximum employment." Surely Congress did not mean what the words suggest if taken literally, that as many people as possible ought to be employed. The goal of the Employment Act is enough jobs to satisfy the demand of those who *want* jobs. But more people will want jobs the more attractive those jobs are, all things considered, and the more eager they are for additional income. The number of people who want jobs is not any fixed percentage of the noninstitutional population. It is rather a consequence of the options people perceive and the choices they make. The only defensible public policy toward employment is therefore one which aims at improving the range of opportunities available to the population. And that, quite obviously, is not a clear and precise target.

UNIONS AND THE LABOR MARKET

Where do unions fit into all of this? Economic theorists have often been criticized for treating unions as an afterthought in their analysis of labor markets. Part of the reason is that union goals and behavior cannot be fitted easily into the framework of economic analysis. Because the policies of particular unions are shaped by internal political processes as well as by the preferences of individual workers and employers, some economists have chosen to assign the analysis of union behavior to political scientists and sociologists. But unions play an important role in affecting labor market variables, and ignoring them entails a serious omission.

Table 6A EMPLOYMENT STATUS OF THE NONINSTITUTIONAL POPULATION, HOUSEHOLD DATA (Numbers in thousands)

	Employment status	Not seasonally adjusted			Seasonally adjusted					
		Apr. 1974	Mar. 1975	Apr. 1975	Apr. 1974	Dec. 1974	Jan. 1975	Feb. 1975	Mar. 1975	Apr. 1975
	TOTAL									
1	Total noninstitutional population[1]	150,283	152,646	152,840	150,283	152,020	152,230	152,445	152,646	152,840
2	Total labor force	91,736	93,593	93,564	92,567	94,015	94,284	93,709	94,027	94,457
3	Participation rate	61.0	61.3	61.2	61.6	61.8	61.9	61.5	61.6	61.8
4	Civilian noninstitutional population[1]	148,040	150,447	150,645	148,040	149,809	150,037	150,246	150,447	150,645
5	Civilian labor force	89,493	91,395	91,369	90,324	91,803	92,091	91,511	91,829	92,262
6	Participation rate	60.5	60.7	60.7	61.0	61.3	61.4	60.9	61.0	61.2
7	Employed	85,192	83,036	83,549	85,787	85,202	84,562	84,027	83,849	84,086
8	Agriculture	3,437	2,988	3,171	3,515	3,339	3,383	3,326	3,265	3,238
9	Nonagricultural industries	81,756	80,048	80,377	82,272	81,863	81,179	80,701	80,584	80,848
10	Unemployed	4,301	8,359	7,820	4,537	6,601	7,529	7,484	7,980	8,176
11	Unemployment rate	4.8	9.1	8.6	5.0	7.2	8.2	8.2	8.7	8.9
12	Not in labor force	58,547	59,053	59,276	57,716	58,006	57,946	58,735	58,618	58,383
	Males, 20 years and over									
13	Total noninstitutional population[1]	63,712	64,730	64,812	63,712	64,462	64,552	64,644	64,730	64,812
14	Total labor force	51,738	52,311	52,320	51,912	52,414	52,244	52,150	52,136	52,414
15	Participation rate	81.2	80.8	80.7	81.5	81.3	80.9	80.7	80.5	80.9
16	Civilian noninstitutional population[1]	61,897	62,997	63,080	61,897	62,690	62,824	62,911	62,997	63,080
17	Civilian labor force	49,924	50,579	50,588	50,097	50,642	50,515	50,417	50,403	50,683
18	Participation rate	80.7	80.3	80.2	80.9	80.8	80.4	80.1	80.0	80.3
19	Employed	48,104	46,612	46,901	48,341	47,961	47,490	47,288	46,990	47,123
20	Agriculture	2,508	2,310	2,401	2,506	2,451	2,422	2,475	2,421	2,399
21	Nonagricultural industries	45,596	44,302	44,500	45,835	45,510	45,068	44,813	44,569	44,724
22	Unemployed	1,820	3,966	3,688	1,756	2,681	3,025	3,129	3,413	3,560
23	Unemployment rate	3.6	7.8	7.3	3.5	5.3	6.0	6.2	6.8	7.0
24	Not in labor force	11,973	12,419	12,492	11,800	12,048	12,309	12,494	12,594	12,397
	Females, 20 years and over									
25	Civilian noninstitutional population[1]	70,139	71,266	71,358	70,139	70,961	71,061	71,167	71,266	71,358
26	Civilian labor force	31,611	32,789	32,756	31,612	21,305	32,556	32,326	32,637	32,845
27	Participation rate	45.1	46.0	45.9	45.1	45.5	45.8	45.4	45.8	46.0
28	Employed	30,159	30,073	30,145	30,033	29,992	29,932	29,719	29,877	30,007
29	Agriculture	494	374	414	541	454	524	474	443	453
30	Nonagricultural industries	29,666	29,699	29,731	29,492	29,538	29,408	29,245	29,434	29,554
31	Unemployed	1,452	2,716	2,611	1,579	2,313	2,624	2,607	2,760	2,838
32	Unemployment rate	4.6	8.3	8.0	5.0	7.2	8.1	8.1	8.5	8.6
33	Not in labor force	38,528	38,477	38,602	38,527	38,656	38,505	38,841	38,629	38,513

Table 6A—*continued*

Employment status	Not seasonally adjusted			Seasonally adjusted					
	Apr. 1974	Mar. 1975	Apr. 1975	Apr. 1974	Dec. 1974	Jan. 1975	Feb. 1975	Mar. 1975	Apr. 1975
Both sexes,16–19 years									
34 Civilian noninstitutional population[1]	16,004	16,184	16,207	16,004	16,157	16,152	16,168	16,184	16,207
35 Civilian labor force	7,958	8,027	8,025	8,615	8,856	9,020	8,768	8,789	8,734
36 Participation rate	49.7	49.6	49.5	53.8	54.8	55.8	54.2	54.3	53.9
37 Employed	6,929	6,351	6,503	7,413	7,249	7,140	7,020	6,982	6,956
38 Agriculture	435	304	357	468	434	437	377	401	386
39 Nonagricultural industries	6,494	6,047	6,146	6,945	6,815	6,703	6,643	6,581	6,570
40 Unemployed	1,029	1,677	1,522	1,202	1,607	1,880	1,748	1,807	1,778
41 Unemployment rate	12.9	20.9	19.0	14.0	18.1	20.8	19.9	20.6	20.4
42 Not in labor force	8,046	8,157	8,182	7,389	7,301	7,132	7,400	7,395	7,473
WHITE									
43 Civilian noninstitutional population[1]	130,922	132,879	133,039	130,922	132,356	132,553	132,720	132,879	133,039
44 Civilian labor force	79,415	81,108	81,113	80,089	81,338	81,706	81,071	81,546	81,825
45 Participation rate	60.7	61.0	61.0	61.2	61.5	61.6	61.1	61.4	61.5
46 Employed	75,950	74,243	74,711	76,470	76,106	75,555	75,043	75,039	75,193
47 Unemployed	3,465	6,865	6,402	3,619	5,232	6,151	6,028	6,507	6,632
48 Unemployment rate	4.4	8.5	7.9	4.5	6.4	7.5	7.4	8.0	8.1
49 Not in labor force	51,507	51,771	51,926	50,833	51,018	50,847	51,649	51,333	51,214
NEGRO AND OTHER RACES									
50 Civilian noninstitutional population[1]	17,118	17,568	17,606	17,118	17,452	17,484	17,527	17,568	17,606
51 Civilian labor force	10,078	10,286	10,256	10,196	10,389	10,464	10,387	10,364	10,401
52 Participation rate	58.9	58.6	58.3	59.6	59.5	59.8	59.3	59.0	59.1
53 Employed	9,242	8,792	8,837	9,296	9,090	9,057	8,989	8,893	8,886
54 Unemployed	835	1,494	1,418	900	1,299	1,407	1,398	1,471	1,515
55 Unemployment rate	8.3	14.5	13.8	8.8	12.5	13.4	13.5	14.2	14.6
56 Not in labor force	7,041	7,281	7,350	6,922	7,063	7,020	7,140	7,204	7,205

Source: Bureau of Labor Statistics.

Note: Data relate to the noninstitutional population 16 years of age and over. Total noninstitutional population and total labor force include persons in the Armed Forces.

1. Seasonal variations are not present in the population figures; therefore, identical numbers appear in the unadjusted and seasonally adjusted columns. (For an explanation of seasonal adjustments, see page 157.)

Table 6B MAJOR UNEMPLOYMENT INDICATORS, SEASONALLY ADJUSTED, HOUSEHOLD DATA

	Selected categories	Number of unemployed persons (In thousands)		Unemployment rates					
		Apr. 1974	Apr. 1975	Apr. 1974	Dec. 1974	Jan. 1975	Feb. 1975	Mar. 1975	Apr. 1975
1	Total, 16 years and over	4,537	8,176	5.0	7.2	8.2	8.2	8.7	8.9
2	Males, 20 years and over	1,756	3,560	3.5	5.3	6.0	6.2	6.8	7.0
3	Females, 20 years and over	1,579	2,838	5.0	7.2	8.1	8.1	8.5	8.6
4	Both sexes, 16–19 years	1,202	1,778	14.0	18.1	20.8	19.9	20.6	20.4
5	White, total	3,619	6,632	4.5	6.4	7.5	7.4	8.0	8.1
6	Males, 20 years and over	1,431	2,912	3.2	4.7	5.5	5.6	6.2	6.4
7	Females, 20 years and over	1,262	2,333	4.6	6.5	7.7	7.6	8.0	8.2
8	Both sexes, 16–19 years	926	1,387	12.0	15.9	18.4	17.5	18.1	17.8
9	Negro and other races, total	900	1,515	8.8	12.5	13.4	13.5	14.2	14.6
10	Males, 20 years and over	327	650	6.4	9.3	10.5	11.1	11.8	12.6
11	Females, 20 years and over	300	478	7.2	10.9	11.0	10.9	11.2	11.2
12	Both sexes, 16–19 years	273	387	30.5	37.7	41.1	36.7	41.6	40.2
13	Household heads	1,593	3,194	3.0	4.6	5.2	5.4	5.8	6.0
14	Married men, spouse present	966	2,226	2.4	3.8	4.5	4.7	5.2	5.6
15	Full-time workers	3,583	6,824	4.6	6.8	7.7	7.8	8.3	8.7
16	Part-time workers	982	1,395	7.6	9.6	10.5	10.3	10.9	10.4
17	Unemployed, 15 weeks and over[1]	875	2,403	1.0	1.4	1.7	2.0	2.2	2.6
18	State insured[2]	2,118	4,494	3.3	4.8	5.5	5.9	6.4	6.8
19	Labor force time lost[3]	—	—	5.7	7.9	8.9	8.9	9.6	9.7
	OCCUPATION[4]								
20	White-collar workers	1,224	2,094	2.9	4.1	4.6	4.5	4.6	4.7
21	Professional and technical	283	450	2.3	2.5	2.9	3.2	2.9	3.4
22	Managers and administrators, except farm	148	295	1.6	2.6	3.3	2.7	2.7	3.3
23	Sales workers	188	342	3.3	6.0	5.7	5.3	6.0	5.8
24	Clerical workers	605	1,007	3.9	5.4	6.3	6.2	6.6	6.2
25	Blue-collar workers	1,989	4,156	6.3	9.3	11.0	10.9	12.5	13.0
26	Craft and kindred workers	469	1,074	3.9	6.1	7.0	6.5	8.7	9.0
27	Operatives	1,033	2,248	6.9	10.7	13.1	13.3	14.1	14.9
28	Nonfarm laborers	487	834	10.3	13.0	14.3	14.1	16.2	17.2
29	Service workers	689	1,015	5.8	7.1	8.1	7.7	8.5	8.2
30	Farm workers	86	118	2.7	2.4	3.6	3.0	4.5	4.0

Table 6B—*continued*

	Selected categories	Number of unemployed persons (In thousands)		Unemployment rates					
		Apr. 1974	Apr. 1975	Apr. 1974	Dec. 1974	Jan. 1975	Feb. 1975	Mar. 1975	Apr. 1975
	INDUSTRY[2]								
31	Nonagricultural private wage and salary workers[5]	3,422	6,582	5.2	7.7	8.7	8.8	9.3	9.8
32	Construction	449	832	9.9	14.9	15.0	15.9	18.1	19.3
33	Manufacturing	1,075	2,638	5.0	8.9	10.5	11.0	11.4	12.2
34	Durable goods	625	1,651	4.9	8.7	10.5	10.9	11.3	12.8
35	Nondurable goods	450	987	5.1	9.1	10.3	11.1	11.6	11.4
36	Transportation and public utilities	153	320	3.1	3.9	5.9	5.2	5.6	6.6
37	Wholesale and retail trade	957	1,525	6.0	8.1	8.5	8.0	8.7	9.1
38	Finance and service industries	767	1,226	4.3	5.4	6.2	6.5	6.7	6.6
39	Government workers	421	569	2.9	3.2	3.4	3.6	3.9	3.8
40	Agricultural wage and salary workers	112	167	7.9	7.9	10.2	8.8	12.0	12.6
	VETERAN STATUS								
	Males, Vietnam-era veterans[6]:								
41	20 to 34 years	286	593	5.0	7.6	9.0	8.8	9.0	9.9
42	20 to 24 years	114	239	9.2	15.6	19.7	17.3	17.5	22.8
43	25 to 29 years	139	241	4.3	6.7	6.9	7.4	8.1	7.3
44	30 to 34 years	33	113	2.7	3.7	6.1	5.9	5.2	6.8
	Males, nonveterans:								
45	20 to 34 years	752	1,471	5.6	8.1	8.6	9.5	10.5	10.4
46	20 to 24 years	440	920	7.4	10.4	11.6	12.6	14.7	14.5
47	25 to 29 years	178	284	4.7	7.2	7.2	8.6	8.5	6.9
48	30 to 34 years	134	267	3.7	5.1	5.1	5.1	5.5	7.2

Source: Bureau of Labor Statistics

1. Unemployment rate calculated as a percent of civilian labor force.
2. Insured unemployment under State programs; unemployment rate calculated as a percent of average covered employment.
3. Man-hours lost by the unemployed and persons on part time for economic reasons as a percent of potentially available labor force man-hours.
4. Unemployment by occupation includes all experienced unemployed persons, whereas that by industry covers only unemployed wage and salary workers.
5. Includes mining, not shown separately.
6. Vietnam-era veterans are those who served after August 4, 1964.

The Context of Union Policies

We must remember at the beginning that although unions *bargain* with employers, unions are not *competing* with employers. It is more correct to say that unions attempt to become the exclusive seller of a particular input to the production processes of employers or that they attempt to eliminate competition among employees. The position of unions is analogous to that of steel producers who want to sell to automobile makers. The steel companies do not compete against the automobile companies; they compete rather against other steel companies and against companies that produce substitutes for steel.

A major difference between the steel companies and the United Automobile Workers, both of which are selling inputs to automobile makers, is that the UAW must deal with conflicting interests among its current and potential members. Higher wage rates will mean fewer employment opportunities. How shall the union compromise between the desire of some for more jobs and the desire of others for higher wages? Workers who never obtain jobs in the automobile plants because of the high wage rates negotiated by the union can perhaps be ignored by union leaders; but unemployed union members have a vote and so their interests must be considered. Executives of steel companies, by contrast, don't have to weigh the preferences of the iron ore that must wait longer in the ground before finding employment if the price of steel is raised.

The goals and practices of unions often differ systematically between the two major types of labor union that exist in the United States. *Craft unions* are those with formal apprenticeship programs that train new members in specialized and fairly clearly defined skills. Craft unions include, among others, plumbers, carpenters, pipe fitters, and electricians. Members of a craft union belong to the union organizing their craft regardless of the employer for whom they work. Because some jobs are difficult to classify by craft, some crafts are represented by more than one union. The jurisdictional disputes that subsequently arise between craft unions are further evidence that unions are not competing against employers but against those who sell substitutes for their members' productive services.

Industrial unions are organizations of all the workers in a particular industry without regard to the kind of task they perform. Sometimes industrial unions will exempt those who work at crafts for which specific craft unions exist, but at other times industrial unions will attempt to include the craft workers employed in the industries they have organized. This is another prominent source of jurisdictional disputes between unions. The United Automobile Workers, the United Steel Workers, and the United Mine Workers are examples of major industrial unions.

Because of their control over the apprenticeship programs that are the means to certification as a skilled worker, craft unions can control the supply of workers available to employers. If they can also limit employers' options for substituting other workers or capital for the services of their members, craft unions will have substantial market power. And craft union members do in fact tend to be well paid. Industrial unions, on the other hand, must accept as members whomever the industry hires. Unable effectively to limit the supply of potential employees, industrial unions are reduced to bargaining for higher wages while insisting on the seniority rights of members in order to prevent employers from substituting workers who would accept a lower wage.

The Effects of Unions

To most people it seems obvious that unions raise the income of workers. Economists aren't that sure. If fewer workers are demanded at higher wage rates and the demand for labor is elastic, the total wage bill will decline as a result of union success in bargaining for higher wages. The workers still employed in the organized crafts or industries will gain. But those excluded from employment by the higher wage rates will lose. They will be forced to accept employment elsewhere on less advantageous terms.

The question of the effect of unions on wages divides into at least three separate questions: (1) What has been their effect on the average level of money wages? (2) What has been their effect on the average level of real wages? (Insofar as prices increase as a consequence of wage increases, real wages do not increase.) (3) What has been their effect on the relative wages of unionized and nonunionized workers? Professor H. Gregg Lewis investigated the last question in a major study published in 1963, *Unionism and Relative Wages in the United States*. After examining more than twenty different industries and crafts, he concluded that, apart from periods of unusually rapid inflation, unions increased their members' wages relative to nonunion workers by at least 10%, and lowered the relative wages of nonunion workers by about 2%. He also concluded that the relative effect of unions has not been larger than 20% at any time since the late 1930s. The impact of unionism on relative wage inequality among all workers has been small, less than 6%, with the direction of the effect (toward more or less inequality) uncertain. During periods of unusually rapid inflation, the relative wages of unionized workers have lagged behind the wage increases of nonunion workers, because the length of union contracts has tended to lock members into relatively infrequent wage increases.

It also appears that the effect of unionization on the total share of national income going to labor has been small. The portion of the civilian labor force that was unionized grew from 3% to 22% between 1900 and

1945. Since then it has fluctuated between 22% and 26%, with the peak of 26% occurring in 1953. During the same period labor's share of national income has increased very slightly, from about 70% during the decade 1900–1909 to about 77% during the decade 1930–1939, and has remained fairly constant since. A slightly different measure, the ratio of wage and salary income to total nonagricultural personal income, varied between .65 and .75 during the period 1930–1974. Thus there is no evidence to show that increasing unionization has substantially enlarged the share of national income going to employees.

Many Americans believe that labor unions have been an important force in raising the income and improving the job conditions of working people, and that without them the benefits of economic growth in the United States over the last century would have been much less widely dispersed. It is difficult to separate the effects of unions from the effects of other factors, such as rising productivity, that have also been operating to alter wages and working conditions. Unions often receive credit (or blame) for changes that would have taken place without them, though perhaps not at quite the same time or in exactly the same way. Economic theory cautions against exaggerating the impact of unions. They must pursue their objectives within the constraints imposed by the demand for labor. A higher price for any input means a smaller quantity of it will be demanded, so that unions are far from being able to redistribute income as they please.

One very important source of restraint on union power is the competition faced by the employers with whom unions bargain. Firms that are price takers cannot raise their prices to cover union-won wage increases, so that any gains must come from the returns that would otherwise have gone to the owners of other productive resources employed in the business. But over a longer period of time these resources will not be available to cooperate with unionized workers if they are not adequately compensated. The firms with whom unions bargain may go out of business or be replaced by nonunion firms. This constraint is not really avoided if the union organizes *all* the firms in an industry. These firms will still have an incentive to shift toward labor-economizing production processes, and they will still be facing competition from firms in other industries.

The possibilities for substitution in both production and consumption are enormous and extremely difficult for unions to control. Even when firms are price searchers, so that they can to some extent increase their prices to cover higher wages, the higher prices will reduce the quantity of the product demanded and hence the demand for labor to produce that product. If a union organizes an industry of price-taking firms, the union may in effect search for the optimal price for the industry's product with the same result: the higher the price, the less product sold and the fewer workers hired.

Table 6C TOTAL MEMBERSHIP IN NATIONAL UNIONS AND EMPLOYEE ASSOCIATIONS IN THE UNITED STATES, 1970

Membership and unions		Number of members
Membership claimed by all national and international unions with headquarters in the United States....................		20,690,000
Less: number outside the United States.............		1,470,000
Membership of national and international unions in the United States...........................		19,220,000
Add membership of locals directly affiliated with AFL-CIO......................	62,000	
Add membership in single firm and local unaffiliated unions............................	475,000	537,000
Total union membership...........................		19,757,000
Add membership of professional State employees associations	1,868,000	
Less: number outside the United States.............	8,000	
Add membership of municipal employee associations[1]........................	235,000	
Total association membership		2,095,000
Total union and associations membership in United States........................		21,852,000

Source: Bureau of Labor Statistics.

1. See Municipal Public Employees Associations (BLS Bulletin 1702, 1971). Membership adjusted to account for duplication.

Federal Labor Legislation

When Congress passed the National Labor Relations Act (Wagner Act) in 1935, it became the official policy of the federal government to promote unionization of employees and collective bargaining. Many of the tactics previously used by employers to resist the organization of their workers or to avoid bargaining with unions over wages and working conditions were declared to be "unfair labor practices."[1] The legislation was signifi-

1. Unions are exempt from the Sherman Act's prohibitions of combinations in restraint of trade or attempts to monopolize (unless they combine or conspire with employers). The Supreme Court ruled in 1941 that Congress could not simultaneously intend to promote collective bargaining *and* to subject unions to the Sherman Act. The Court's decision invited Congress to clarify its intentions through further legislation if this ruling was incorrect.

cantly amended in 1947 (Taft-Hartley Act) to include a list of "unfair labor practices" in which unions were forbidden to engage; but the basic policy of encouraging collective bargaining was not altered. The consequences of this policy, as we have suggested, are difficult to determine with precision or confidence. The notion that employees acquire property rights in jobs for which they have been hired has undoubtedly increased job security for employed workers and reduced the extent to which workers are treated arbitrarily by employers and supervisors. The development of union-enforced grievance procedures in many industries and crafts is one major consequence of the National Labor Relations Act.

But the gains have not been made without some costs: systems of job classification and assignment that promote waste; restrictions on the power of managers to innovate; reduced opportunities for workers not fortunate enough to obtain craft certification or jobs in firms organized by powerful industrial unions. Have unions also been responsible, as some argue, for higher unemployment rates? Or have they been, as far more people seem to believe, a major cause of inflation in the period since World War II? The last two questions relate to the topics of the following chapters. But we will not be in a good position to answer them until we have inquired more deeply into the nature and causes of fluctuations in the aggregate level of economic activity.

Once Over Lightly

Income is ordinarily obtained by selling the services of productive resources. The price any resource can command will be determined by the demand for the goods it produces and the marginal productivity of the resource. The marginal productivity of a resource is the additional contribution it makes to the production of wealth.

The law of demand applies to productive resources as well as to other goods. The higher the price of a particular resource, the more actively will people look for substitutes.

The demand for labor is determined by employers' estimates of the marginal contribution labor will make to revenue in particular production processes.

Economic analysis of labor markets assumes that people choose whether or not to seek work and to accept or reject particular job offers by weighing the attractiveness of leisure against its opportunity cost. Leisure in this context means all nonmarket uses of time, and the opportunity cost of leisure is the wage rate that is sacrificed.

At higher wage rates, leisure becomes more expensive and so tends to be purchased less, which is to say that people supply more time to the labor market. This may be called the substitution effect of the increase in the price of leisure: people choose to substitute for leisure more of the goods that money income can buy. But an increase in the price of leisure has another important effect that tends to nudge choice in the opposite direction. An increase in the price of leisure, corresponding to an increase in the wage rate, implies an increase in income. The demand curve for leisure may shift upward to the right as income increases, so that ultimately more rather than less leisure is "purchased" when its price rises.

Since people choose, by comparing the expected cost and value to them of alternative opportunities, whether or not to enter the labor force and whether or not to accept a particular job offer, employment and unemployment are the consequence of people's choices in given situations.

The common notion that the owners of productive resources compete against the purchasers of these resources is seriously misleading. Employees, for example, do not compete against employers but against other employees and potential employers. Unionization, while it may have other goals as well, is an attempt to restrain competition *among* workers.

Labor unions attempt to control the supply of labor to employers and to limit competition for jobs among employees. Unions do not single-mindedly pursue higher wage rates, however, because this goal conflicts with the goal of more employment opportunities. Internal political processes will therefore shape the goals and behavior of particular unions.

An important distinction to make in predicting union behavior is the distinction between unions that can control entry to the occupation and those that cannot. Craft unions typically have more market power than industrial unions, because they can more directly limit the number of workers who are certified as eligible for particular jobs.

The fact that collective bargaining affects employment as well as wage rates means that unions affect the distribution of income among workers as well as the distribution between wage earners and employers or owners of other productive resources. The numerous possibilities for substitution in production and consumption when particular wages rise set closer limitations upon union power than the public commonly assumes.

QUESTIONS FOR DISCUSSION

1. For many years federal minimum-wage legislation completely excluded workers in agriculture or domestic service. Yet the average wages paid to these workers ranked at the very bottom of the wages paid in the American economy. How do you explain the seeming inconsistency in this exclusion?

2. Teachers began encountering serious job shortages in the early 1970s after many years of rising demand for their services. An intensified interest in unionization has been observed. What can unionization accomplish for

teachers in a highly unfavorable job market? Whom is it likely to benefit and whom will it harm?

3. "Farmers complaining that they can't get field hands now that the bracero program has been curtailed aren't sincere," said an official of the United Packinghouse Workers Union. "About one-third of the unemployed in Los Angeles are former farm workers, and the farmers could get them back if they'd make wages and working conditions attractive enough." Do you think the farmers are insincere? Could they get enough workers if they tried harder? Explain.

4. In 1940, according to the Bureau of Labor Statistics, there were 9,540,000 persons employed in agriculture. The population of the United States in 1940 was 132,122,000. In 1970 the corresponding figures were 3,462,000 farmers in a population of 205,395,000. Thus in 1940 it took one farmer to provide agricultural produce for every 14 Americans. Thirty years later one farmer could take care of almost 60 people.

    (*a*) What made this dramatic change possible?

    (*b*) What happened to the "excess" farmers? Where did they go?

    (*c*) What factors induced people to move out of agricultural employment?

5. Under a closed-shop arrangement, employers may only hire workers who are already union members. Under a union-shop arrangement, employers may hire whomever they please but the employees must then join the union. What different effects would you expect these alternative arrangements to have on wages? On employment? On discrimination by the union against members of minority races? Why?

6. College professors in the United States have never had an effective union. Then why did their average wage rise spectacularly in the 1960s? How might college professors have used unionization to obtain even larger salary increases over this period? Why might some professors be interested in a law that prohibited anyone without an earned doctorate from teaching in colleges? What consequences would you predict if a few states passed such a law?

7. The questions below ask you to think critically about the relationships between the total population, the noninstitutional population, and the labor force.

    (*a*) Is it desirable or undesirable for the noninstitutional population to decrease relative to the total population? Explain your answer.

    (*b*) Why do you suppose that the BLS in 1947 raised the cutoff age level for inclusion in the noninstitutional population from fourteen to sixteen? Do you think it should be even higher today? Why or why not?

    (*c*) What would happen to the rate of labor force participation (the total labor force as a percent of the noninstitutional population) under each of the following circumstances?

    (i) Sudden, large-scale layoffs occur in major manufacturing industries.

    (ii) The government puts effective pressure on employers to end sex discrimination in hiring.

    (iii) Educational reforms increase the ratio of learning to teaching in the schools and also make schooling a more enjoyable experience.

    (iv) The public becomes convinced that additional years of schooling are not likely to result in better job opportunities.

    (v) Changes in life style occur and people move toward greater participation in family and community projects and less purchasing of commodities and services (for example, more neighborhood softball teams and less attendance at professional baseball games; more church suppers and fewer restaurant meals; neighborhood sharing of lawnmowers, washers and driers, car pools and swimming pools).

    (vi) Inflation raises substantially the cost of food, clothing, and housing.

8. A plumbers local in Fort Lauderdale, Florida, voluntarily lowered the hourly rate for union workers on low-rise construction projects from $10.70 to $6.90 an hour (in June 1972). The $10.70 rate continued to apply to high-rise construction. The business manager of the union said this was being done to curb inflation and help home owners. Do you think it might also have been done because nonunion plumbers were available in the area at $4.50 to $5 an hour? Why do you suppose the union did not lower the rate on high-rise construction work?

9. Economists generally assume that business firms try to maximize profits. What do unions try to maximize? Wage rates? The wage bill (wage rates times the number employed)? Is the maximization assumption useful in the analysis of union behavior?

10. Why is a union of textile workers in New England willing to spend money to organize textile workers in North Carolina? Why do unions fight for increases in the legal minimum wage even though all their members are being paid more than the minimum wage? Why do unions oppose exempting teenagers from coverage under the minimum-wage laws? Do you agree that each of these cases shows "the class solidarity of unionized workers"? Who would be threatened by failure to secure each of the objectives mentioned? What do these cases suggest by way of an answer to the question, With whom do unions compete?

11. Craft unions in the United States have long been notorious for discriminating against blacks. Industrial unions, on the other hand, have a record of actively supporting legislation directed against racially discriminatory practices in society? How would you explain this difference?

7

FLUCTUATIONS IN
EMPLOYMENT AND UNEMPLOYMENT

The fear that our society or any society may run out of jobs was criticized in chapter 6. We argued there that jobs represent obstacles to be overcome, and that a society without jobs for people to perform would have come close to abolishing scarcity. Such a situation would be an occasion for rejoicing. Neither the United States nor any other contemporary society is in such a happy position.

Throughout the discussion in chapter 6, however, we left out of account a phenomenon that has puzzled and disturbed students of economic systems for more than two centuries. It used to be called the *trade cycle,* and later on the *business cycle.* Those terms began to disappear from use as economists came to have increasing doubts about the regularity of such fluctuations. The word *cycle* has connotations of predictable recurrence, connotations that may be misleading and that can be avoided by substituting a more neutral phrase, such as "fluctuations in the aggregate level of economic activity."

Whatever the fluctuations are called, there can be no doubt about their existence and importance. If those who work for wages entertain some irrational anxieties about the disappearance of job opportunities, they may also have substantial grounds for completely rational fears. Our insistence that there is no overall scarcity of jobs seems to be flatly contradicted by the experience of every industrialized nation with recessions and depressions.

In the 1930s, the study of such fluctuations, their causes and their cures, came to be called *macroeconomics,* from the Greek word *makros,* meaning "large." The remainder of economics was then referred to as *microeconomics,* from *mikros,* meaning "small." There are serious ambiguities in this use of terms, and some dangers. The beginning student ought to know that many economists would call chapters 2–6 microeconomics, and chapters 7–18 macroeconomics. You won't go far wrong if you understand macroeconomics to mean the study of fluctuations in the aggregate level of economic activity, or the study of recessions and depressions, inflation, and aggregate growth or decline.

INTERPRETING UNEMPLOYMENT DATA

We argued in Chapter 6 that employers will purchase productive resources as long as their expected marginal contribution to revenue is greater than the expected marginal cost. While the marginal productivity theory does not provide a complete theory of the demand for labor, it does provide important insights into the way labor markets operate. It must be used with caution, however, and with attention to the actual range of options that employers encounter. Hiring and discharging workers when wages change or when their marginal dollar product shifts is not a cost-less action.

An employer usually expects to incur costs in finding appropriate workers and equipping them with the skills they must have to be effective in particular positions. The costs of advertising, interviewing, testing, and filling out forms are investments that employers must make to obtain workers. Moreover, in an organization of any complexity, there are many things to be learned before workers' productivity can reach the level expected when they were hired. They may have to learn, for example, the names of associates, the formal and informal rules of social conduct, the location of specific tools and facilities, the procedures to be followed in requisitioning materials, making a sale, taking sick leave, reporting progress or trouble, replacing a light bulb, and so on. An employee who leaves after acquiring this job-specific training represents a loss to the employer of what may be a significant investment. That's why labor turnover can be quite costly and why employers often try to retain certain workers even though their marginal dollar product is expected to be temporarily below their marginal cost.

But employers have other options, too. In some circumstances they will hire on a day-by-day or even hour-by-hour basis. When the driver of a moving van arrives in town with your furniture, he will go to a labor pickup point and hire some workers for just a few hours to help him unload. Farmers may hire laborers in a similar manner. A few skilled occupations are organized so that an employer can obtain skilled workers

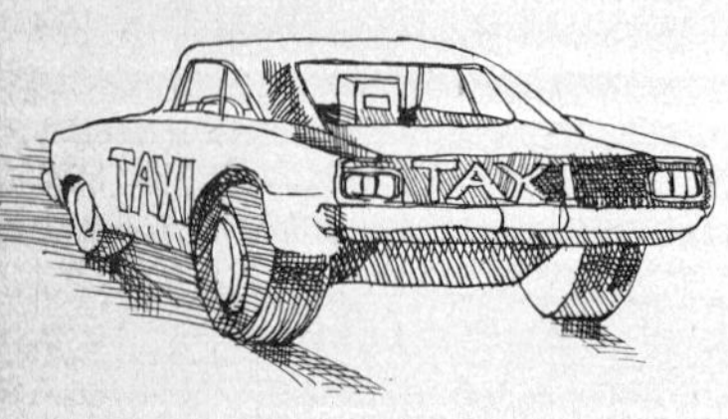

on a short-term basis through the union hiring hall. The appropriate union certifies the qualifications of the carpenter, electrician, or plumber. The common feature in each of these cases is that the employer invests very little in finding and training workers. If employers know they can hire practically identical workers at the going wage with little cost of search or training, they may elect not to keep such workers on the payroll on the days when they cannot be used to produce revenue at least equal to their wages.

Sometimes these kinds of markets become so flexible that workers are hired for only a few minutes at a time. You hire a taxi driver and his vehicle for only a few minutes and, unless you've traveled to a remote destination from which you intend to return very soon, you fire him and hire another for your next trip. Many consumer services are arranged on this basis. We typically think of those who provide such services as being self-employed; but they are actually being employed by the consumers of their services.

"So what does all this have to do with unemployment?" says an impatient voice from the back of the room. Suppose you were going to spend the summer working at a dude ranch in Wyoming and you didn't have room to take along your bicycle and stereo set. As a result they would be unemployed over the summer. Would you lay them off for the summer or retain them on the payroll? In other words, would you sell them before leaving and then purchase replacements in the fall? Or would you expect the expenses of selling and repurchasing to be greater than the opportunity cost of keeping them during the summer? For exactly the same reasons an employer may retain an employee during a period of slack business; he expects the value of the worker's marginal product to exceed the wages again in a short while and he believes it would be costly to find and train a replacement.

This provides at least a partial explanation for some of the observed employment phenomena during a recession. More highly skilled workers and those with more job-specific training have lower layoff and un-employment rates during a recession, and their unemployment rates start to rise sometime after those of other workers. It is well known that product per employee-hour tends to decline during recessions while unit labor costs rise. (See figure 7A.) The notion of employer investment in employees explains this phenomenon.

"Involuntary" Unemployment

The Bureau of Labor Statistics maintains a statistical series on un-employment in our economy going back to 1929. The data are based on household interviews conducted in accordance with accepted sampling procedures. The estimated totals for the economy are shown in Table 7A,

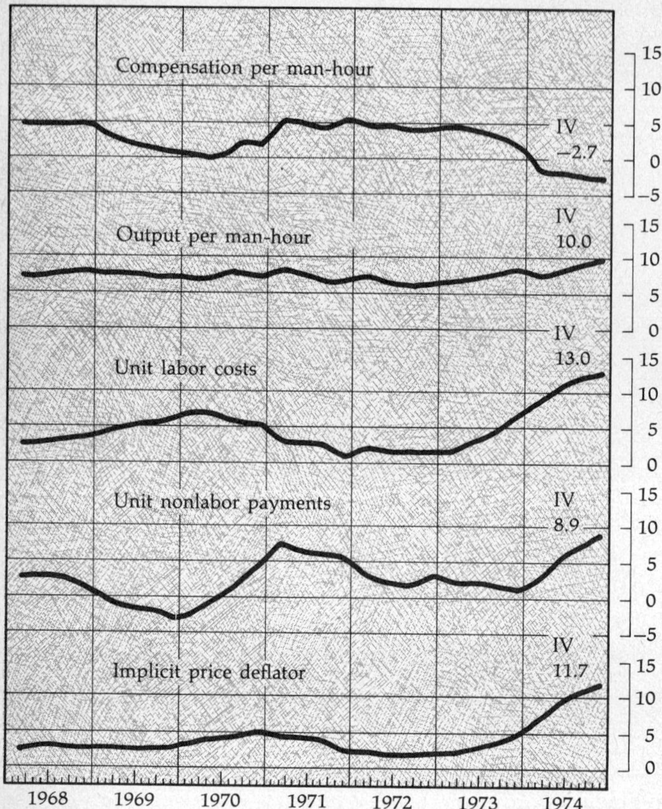

Source: *Productivity in the Private Economy, First Quarter 1975*, U.S. Department of Labor, Bureau of Labor Statistics, April 24, 1975

Figure 7A Productivity, hourly compensation, unit costs and prices—nonfinancial corporations (percent change from same quarter a year ago)

and a wealth of detail on more recent years is presented in Figures 7B through 7Q. The data recount a disturbing history.

The civilian labor force, you will recall, is defined to include everyone over the age of sixteen (over fourteen until 1947) not an inmate of an institution or in the armed forces, and either employed, actively seeking employment, or waiting to be recalled to employment. Table 7A shows in the first two columns the total number of people in the civilian labor force classified as unemployed in each year from 1929 to 1974, and the same figure expressed as a percentage of the civilian labor force. The figures are annual averages based on monthly survey data, and are given to the nearest thousand. What do they tell us?

A good place to begin asking that question is with the data for 1942–1945, the years of World War II. No one claims that the United States had an unemployment problem during those years. Yet even in 1944,

Table 7A EMPLOYMENT AND UNEMPLOYMENT, 1929–1974

Year	Unemployed (in thousands)	Percentage of Civilian Labor Force	Employed (in thousands)	Percentage of Noninstitutional Population
1929	1,550	3.2%		
1930	4,340	8.7		
1931	8,020	15.9		
1932	12,060	23.6		
1933	12,830	24.9		
1934	11,340	21.7		
1935	10,610	20.1		
1936	9,030	16.9		
1937	7,700	14.3		
1938	10,390	19.0		
1939	9,480	17.2		
1940	8,120	14.6		
1941	5,560	9.9		
1942	2,660	4.7		
1943	1,070	1.9		
1944	670	1.2		
1945	1,040	1.9		
1946	2,270	3.9		
1947	2,311	3.9	57,039	55.2%
1948	2,276	3.8	58,344	55.8
1949	3,637	5.9	57,649	54.6
1950	3,288	5.3	58,920	55.2
1951	2,055	3.3	59,962	55.7
1952	1,883	3.0	60,254	55.4
1953	1,834	2.9	61,181	55.3
1954	3,532	5.5	60,110	53.8
1955	2,852	4.4	62,171	55.1
1956	2,750	4.1	63,802	56.1
1957	2,859	4.3	64,071	55.7
1958	4,602	6.8	63,036	54.2
1959	3,740	5.5	64,630	54.8
1960	3,852	5.5	65,778	54.9
1961	4,714	6.7	65,746	54.2
1962	3,911	5.5	66,702	54.2
1963	4,070	5.7	67,762	54
1964	3,786	5.2	69,305	54.5
1965	3,366	4.5	71,088	55.0
1966	2,875	3.8	72,895	55.6
1967	2,975	3.8	74,372	55.8
1968	2,817	3.6	75,920	56.0
1969	2,831	3.5	77,902	56.5
1970	4,088	4.9	78,627	56.1
1971	4,993	5.9	79,120	55.5
1972	4,840	5.6	81,702	56.0
1973	4,304	4.9	84,409	56.9
1974	5,076	5.6	85,936	57.0
1975	7,830	8.5	84,783	55.3

Source: Bureau of Labor Statistics.

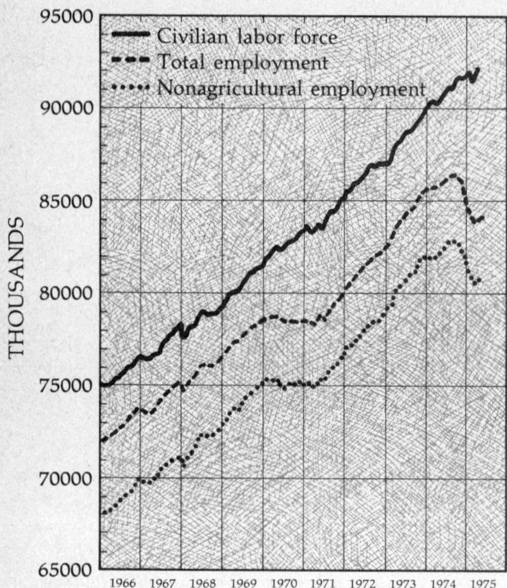

Figure 7B Labor force and employment

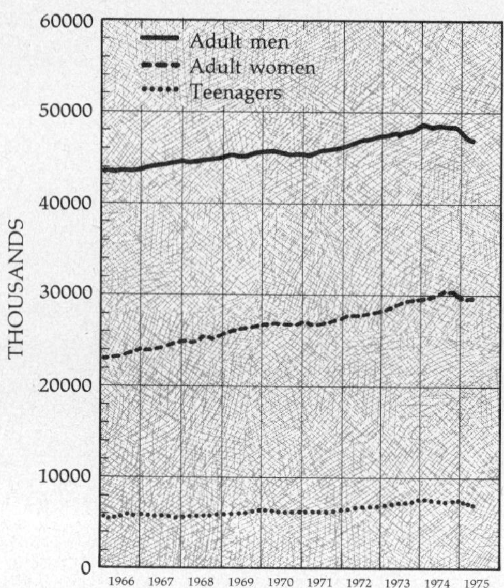

Figure 7C Total employment

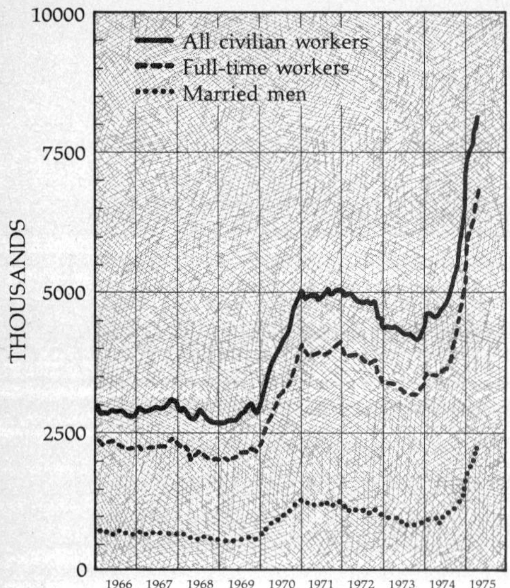

Figure 7D Unemployment

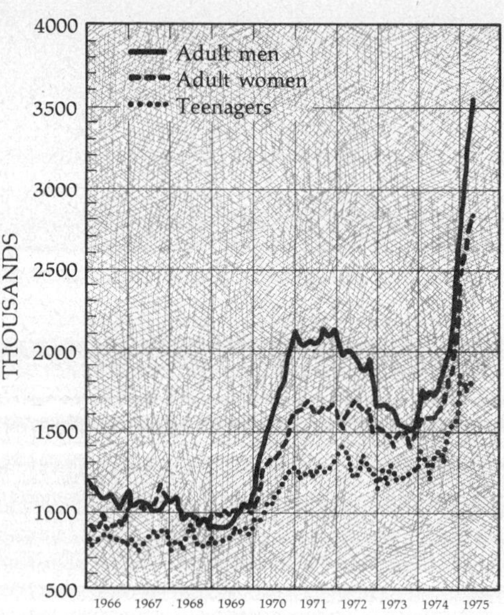

Figure 7E Unemployment

Source of figures 7B–7Q: Bureau of Labor Statistics. (All data seasonally adjusted)

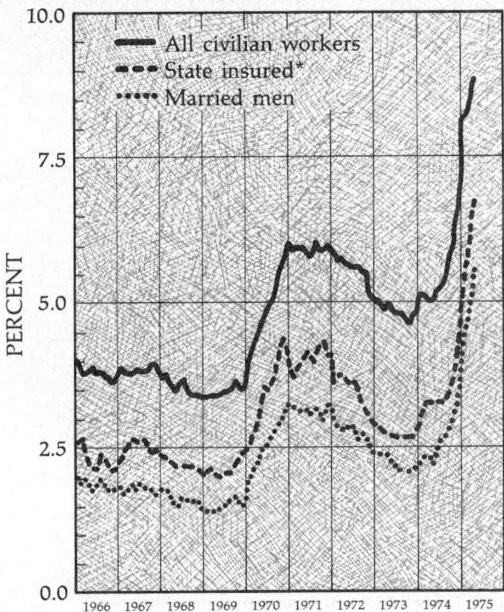

Figure 7F Unemployment rates

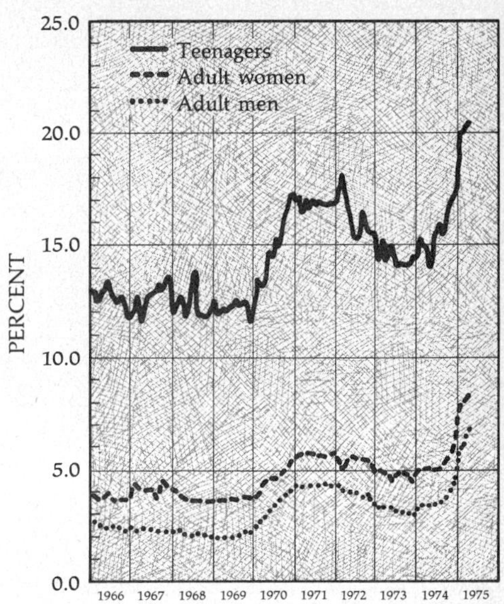

Figure 7G Unemployment rates

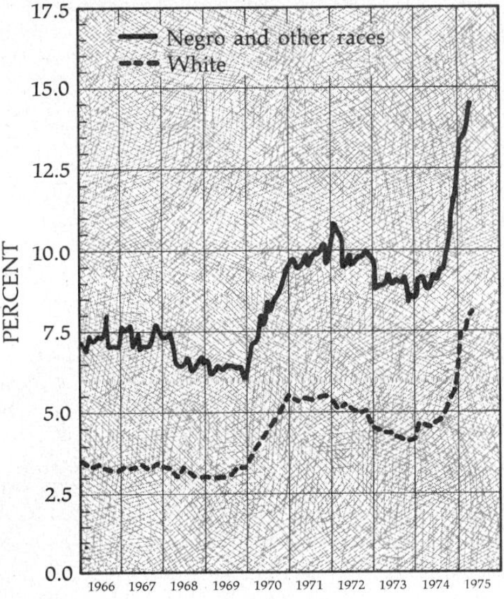

Figure 7H Unemployment rates

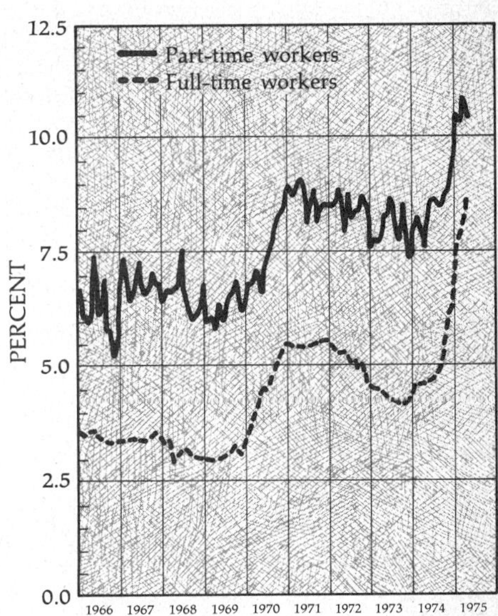

Figure 7I Unemployment rates

*State insured unemployment rate pertains to the week including the 12th of the month and represents the insured unemployed under state programs as a percent of average covered employment. The figures are derived from administration records of unemployment insurance systems.

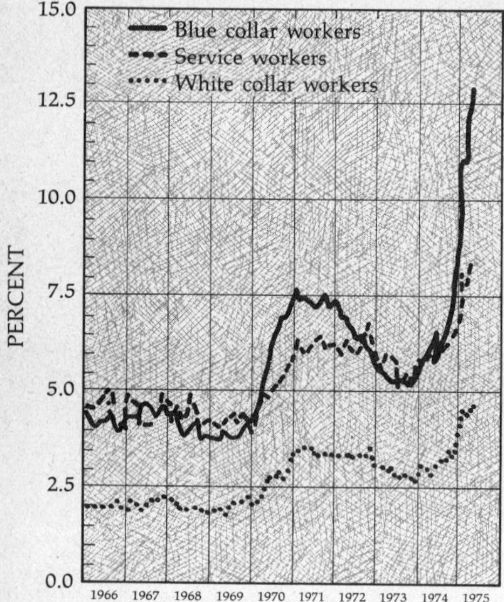

Figure 7J Unemployment rates

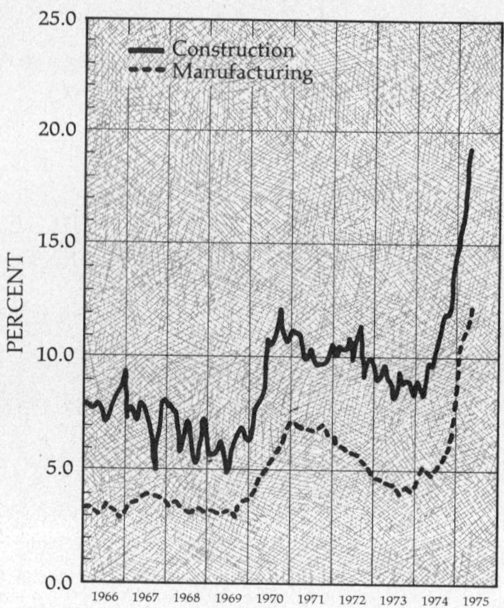

Figure 7K Unemployment rates

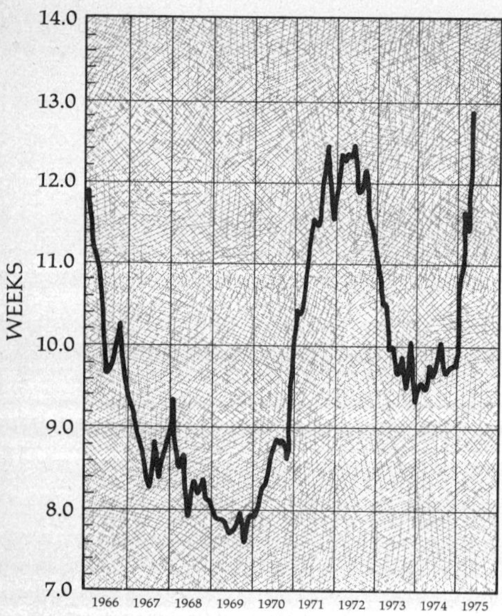

Figure 7L Average duration
of unemployment

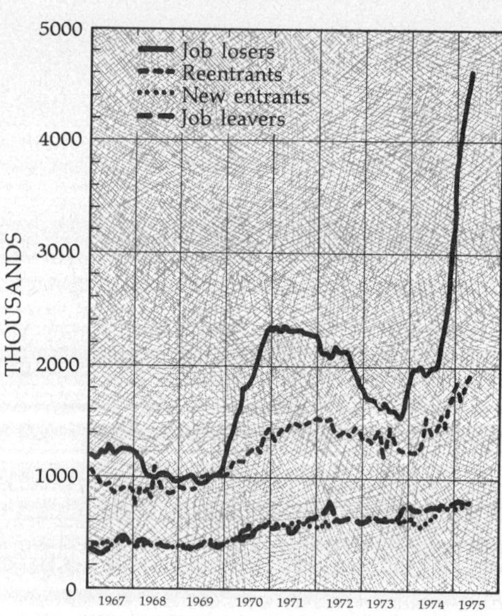

Figure 7M Unemployment by reason

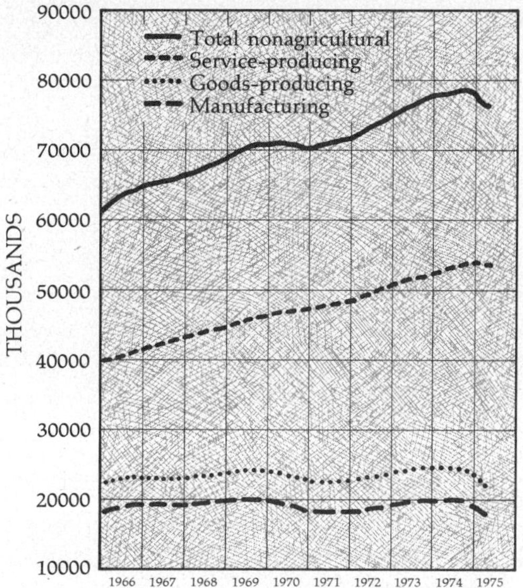

Figure 7N Employment

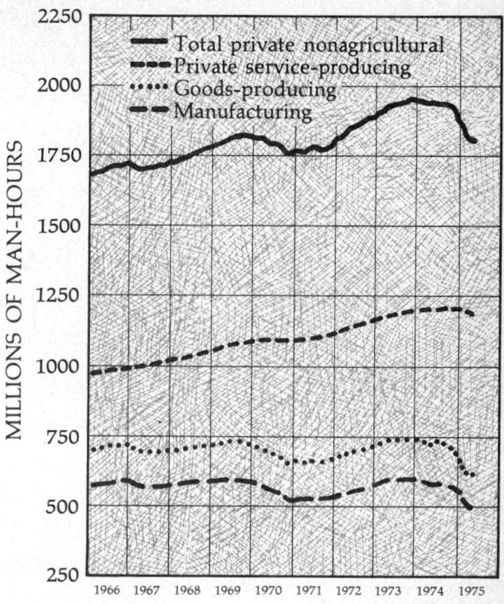

Figure 7O Man-hours worked

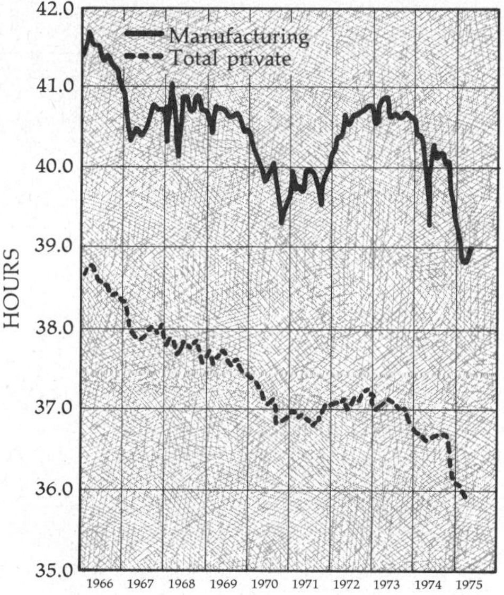

Figure 7P Average weekly hours

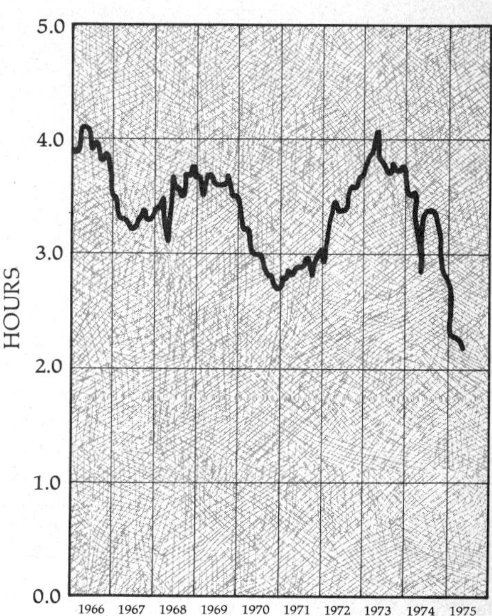

Figure 7Q Average weekly overtime hours in manufacturing

Note: Figure 7N and 7O relate to production of nonsupervisory workers; figure 7P relates to production workers. Data for the two most recent months are preliminary in figure 7M–7P.

when people were being urged to leave school and take a job, to come out of retirement, to work six- and seven-day weeks, 1.2% of the labor force was classified as unemployed. Anyone who lived through those years would have trouble believing that 670,000 people could not find jobs in 1944. What was happening?

People were *looking* for work in 1944 not because they couldn't find employment, but because they wanted *better* jobs than the ones they already knew about. They were unemployed *by choice* and not involuntarily. And that leads to the somewhat controversial proposal that we shall now offer and defend: People are always unemployed by choice. Those whom the BLS statisticians count as unemployed have chosen this status because it presents, in their judgment, the best available option.

Don't jump to unwarranted conclusions. We aren't supporting the notion that unemployment is due to laziness, or that everyone could find a satisfactory job if only he resolved to do so. Nothing like that is implied by the assertion that unemployment is a consequence of choice, something *chosen as the best available opportunity.* This is simply a way of thinking about unemployment that provides a more comprehensive picture than the usual notion that people can be involuntarily unemployed.

When an airplane manufacturer tells an engineer in his employ that he is being laid off at the end of the week, the engineer will make plans. Because there *are* work opportunities available, he *could* begin a new job the next day. But it is not probable that he could the very next day go to work at another job with net advantages equal to the one from which he has been laid off, or even very close. The condition of his finding a new job immediately might be a willingness to work for a small fraction of his previous wage or in some occupation that he intensely dislikes. If an engineer laid off on Friday refused to go to work on Monday as a restaurant dishwasher for $2.00 an hour (which we are now assuming to be the best option available to him for Monday), he would become officially unemployed inasmuch as he *chose* not to take the dishwashing job.

At the same time we should probably all agree that he would be foolish *not* to become officially unemployed. There are almost certainly better opportunities not yet available because they are not yet known to him. If he takes a job that pays $4000 a year in order to avoid being counted as unemployed, he reduces his opportunities to search for a better job. The value to him of time spent searching may well be greater than $2 an hour. He may even value just fishing for a few weeks at more than $2 an hour. If he has some savings accumulated, or his wife has a good job, or he is fairly certain that another engineering position will become available shortly, voluntary unemployment could be a very sensible choice for him.

Why stress the voluntary nature of unemployment? What's the point? The point is the fundamental ambiguity, bordering on meaninglessness, of the concept of involuntary unemployment. As long as useful work remains to be done—and that covers every place and time with which we are familiar—employment opportunities exist, including opportunities for self-employment. (Notice that the official definition misleadingly counts as unemployed those persons who are working around the house while looking for more attractive opportunities elsewhere.) Of course, available opportunities may be far below the individual's expectations; they may not yield an income on which he could begin to support himself adequately; and they may—a crucial point—promise a lower marginal benefit than he anticipates from continued job searching. The possibilities are many. Choice is therefore crucial. But the concept of *involuntary* unemployment covers over the important factor of choice. That is why we have rejected it in favor of the working postulate that every unemployed person *chooses* that status. For some people, the choice will be a dismal one. But the problem for them and for society is that these people must choose among a set of very poor options; the problem is *not* that no work at all is available.

It follows, then, that 670,000 persons were unemployed on an average throughout 1944 because this number of people preferred unemployment. Why? For the most part they were out of work in order to obtain a better job. They were looking or waiting. That obviously does not make them lazy or foolish. It doesn't even make them unpatriotic. Wartime demands called for numerous reallocations of labor among jobs. The individual who was looking for a higher-paying job in 1944 can also be viewed as someone trying to move from a socially less-valued to a socially more-valued task, with the competitively determined wage reflecting social priorities.

But what of 1933? Were 13 million people voluntarily unemployed? One in every four members of the labor force? Yes, strange as that answer may sound at first. They were for the most part unhappy, frustrated, and often desperate. Something had gone radically wrong with the economic system. The value of available job opportunities had diminished spectacularly and rapidly after 1929. This was the crux of the unemployment problem. Opportunities for gainful employment were so unattractive that almost 13 million people eager for job income had no better option than to be unemployed, despite the personal and family distress that this entailed.

Once again, with all the emphasis we can muster: in defining unemployment as a consequence of choice, we are *not* assigning moral fault or minimizing the often tragic consequences of depressions. We are rather incorporating this problem, too, within the general analytical framework of economics, where action is assumed to result from choice of the best available opportunity, even in situations where the best opportunity available is a distressingly poor one.

Employment Rates and Labor Force Participation

During 1974 an average of 5.6% of the civilian labor force was unemployed, as measured by the Bureau of Labor Statistics. In 1966 the corresponding figure had been only 3.8%. May we conclude that the employment picture was more favorable in 1966 than in 1974? Let's take a closer look at the data for those years before answering.

In 1966, 57.8% of the noninstitutional population was officially included in the civilian labor force: those working, waiting to be recalled to work, or actively seeking employment. In 1974, by contrast, 60.3% of the noninstitutional population was in the civilian labor force. In other words, a considerably larger portion of the eligible population wanted jobs in 1974 than in 1966. Moreover, despite the higher unemployment rate in 1974, a larger percentage of the eligible population actually held jobs in 1974 than in 1966. The *employment* rate, defined as the percentage of the non-institutional population holding civilian employment, was 55.6% in 1966 and 57% in 1974. It turns out that while the unemployment rate was much worse in 1974 than in 1966, the employment rate was actually higher in 1974.

Which is the more meaningful measure of the job situation? There is no simple way to answer that question. The employment rate can rise right along with the unemployment rate, which just says that the labor force is increasing faster than unemployment is increasing. That occurred between 1966 and 1974. Was it a desirable or undesirable development? Is it a good sign or a bad sign when a large percentage of the population chooses to enter the labor market? The answer depends on why they made that choice.

In each of the imaginary cases below, people's choices are altering the labor force participation rate. The examples were constructed to convince you that neither entrance into nor exit from the labor force is in itself a good thing, but that the desirability or undesirability of changes in the labor force participation rate depends on the circumstances underlying people's choices.

1. David Ricardo retires from his job as a stockbroker, because he can live comfortably on his accumulated savings and he wants to spend more time in public service.

2. Arthur Mommeter, who retired seven years ago at age 65, starts looking for work again, because inflation has eaten up so much of his savings.

3. Jack Daniels turns to the bottle after losing his job and refuses even to look for work.

4. Gloria Greer, whose husband is a wealthy lawyer, takes a job after thirteen years of marriage, because she wants something more challenging to do than keep house for Mr. Greer.

5. Elizabeth Bennett reluctantly accepts a temporary job as a waitress when her husband's unemployment compensation runs out.

6. John London quits school and signs on with a logging crew, because he finds the forest more healthful, interesting, and profitable than college.

7. Virginia Fox enrolls in college full time, because she hasn't been able to find a good job after looking for six months.

8. Delmar Monte takes a full-time job in the cannery while attending school, because the canning company has boosted wage rates in an effort to get more help.

IS UNEMPLOYMENT VOLUNTARY OR INVOLUNTARY?

Many economists do not agree that it is useful to view all unemployment as voluntary. Some have argued that the attempt to eliminate the concept of involuntary unemployment from discussion is at best an unwarranted stretching of the meaning of words, at worst a disguised attempt to persuade people that unemployment is not a serious social problem and that public policy can therefore adopt a tolerant attitude toward it. Students encountering this mode of analysis for the first time are likely to agree: They will suspect that someone is either trying to get rid of a problem by verbal juggling or else trying subtly to insinuate that people are unemployed through their own fault. Why not conform to conventional usage and agree to call some unemployment involuntary?

But those who retain the concept of involuntary unemployment run into problems, too. First of all, how will they classify those people who are not employed and are not actively looking for work because they don't believe they could find an acceptable job? Are they involuntarily unemployed? As far as the BLS is concerned, they are not unemployed at all because they are not in the labor force. We know, however, that the BLS data understate the problem by missing all those workers who have left the labor force out of discouragement. But how shall we draw the line between those for whom not working entails severe hardship and those who feel no urgency about finding a job but nonetheless would accept employment if the right opportunity arose? We shall certainly want to draw some such line. But is there any way to do so that does not pay fundamental attention to the opportunities among which different people are *able to choose?* And that takes us back to the view that unemployment is chosen and hence voluntary.

A second difficulty is that of deciding what portion of measured unemployment shall be counted as a problem. For policy purposes, a part of the officially measured unemployment is universally regarded as voluntary: that part which reflects "normal" turnover between jobs or people in the process of "changing" jobs. The accepted term for that is *frictional unemployment.* But how is frictional unemployment to be distinguished in practice from involuntary unemployment, the unemployment that calls for corrective social policy? The standard procedure is simply to pick some percentage (2% or 3% or 4%) and to say that we have a problem whenever unemployment rises above this "unavoidable" minimum.

But with this procedure, the amount of problem unemployment is as arbitrary as the percentage figure chosen to "define" frictional unemployment. And the unemployment problem can be eliminated (or aggravated) simply by agreement to raise (or lower) the magic number. As a matter of historical fact, the percentage used to "define" frictional unemployment in the United States has drifted upward from about 2.5% or 3% in the early 1950s to 5% or more in the mid-1970s. In other words, unemployment levels that would have created consternation and calls for urgent action in the 1950s are now widely accepted as appropriate targets for policy. The concept of involuntary unemployment provides no bulwark against complacency in the face of rising unemployment, because it is logically linked to the concept of frictional unemployment, which in turn is little more than a fudge factor. The question remains, What is the appropriate level of frictional unemployment and why is this level to be deemed acceptable?

It seems to us far more useful to consider all unemployment as the product of choice and to ask: Why do people choose as they do? Why do opportunities for choice suddenly expand or decline? Why do some people have such a terribly poor range of choices? What can be done to enlarge and improve available opportunities, especially for those whose choices are severely constrained?

At the very least, this way of looking at the problem does not seem any more open to political abuse than the conventional approach. And it is conceptually clearer, more comprehensive, and more consistent.

Employment Rates or Unemployment Rates?

A former commissioner of Labor Statistics, Geoffrey H. Moore, suggested in a recent article in the *Wall Street Journal* (May 9, 1975) that the employment rate might provide a more objective and reliable measurement of the job situation than the unemployment rate. The two variables necessary to calculate the employment rate are total civilian employment and the noninstitutional population, both of which can be objectively measured without great difficulty. The unemployment rate, by contrast, is the number waiting to be recalled or actively seeking employment divided by the civilian labor force; both of these magnitudes are difficult to measure objectively, because "actively seeking employment" is not a clear-cut status.

The fourth column of table 7A on page 123 shows the employment rate in the United States in each year since 1947. (Data prior to 1947 would not be comparable without major adjustments, because the minimum age for being counted in the noninstitutional population was raised in 1947.) Compare the two columns and ask yourself whether it makes much difference whether we consult the employment or unemployment rate in making public policy.

We'll provide one argument on each side. In March 1975 the *un*employment rate was 8.7%, worse than it had been in any recession since the years prior to World War II. But that was not nearly as great a cause for alarm as many people thought; the *em*ployment rate in the same month was 54.9%, higher than it had been in the recession years of 1949, 1954, 1958, and 1961. If the March 1975 *un*employment rate had been lowered only to 7.6%, everything else remaining unchanged, the *em*ployment rate for the month would have been at a higher level than actually prevailed in the low unemployment year of 1966.

On the other hand, the surprisingly high *em*ployment rate in March 1975 was the result of an exceptionally high rate of participation in the labor force, which may in turn have been due to the persistence of inflation and increasing unemployment. (Consult the cases above of Arthur Mommeter and Elizabeth Bennett to see how inflation and unemployment can each cause the labor force to increase.) By looking at *em*ployment rather than *un*employment rates, we may be allowing people's response to a problem to obscure the gravity of the problem.

Both arguments have merit. The wisest procedure may be to understand the concepts upon which each measurement is based and use good judgment thereafter. Neither an increase in the employment rate nor a decrease in the unemployment rate is necessarily a good thing. Economic improvement consists of an extension of the range of alternatives available to a society. The goal is more and better choices for people.

DISSECTING UNEMPLOYMENT DATA

It was a significant achievement when we were able to obtain reliable data on unemployment to substitute for casual estimates based on fragmentary evidence, estimates that provided little guidance to policymakers because they could so easily be disputed. Tables 6A and 6B and figures 7B through 7Q begin to reveal the detailed nature of the available data on unemployment. The BLS breaks the aggregates down to provide information on employment and unemployment by age, sex, and race; by selected groups such as experienced workers, household heads, married males, full and part-time workers, blue-collar workers; by duration of unemployment, from less than five weeks to more than half a year. And the Office of Manpower Administration, also in the Department of Labor, publishes extensive data on unemployment insurance programs: workers covered, claims paid, benefits exhausted. We have available a remarkably comprehensive and detailed picture of the dimensions of the unemployment problem in the United States.

But the picture, in some respects, is like a surrealist painting: vivid in detail and full of recognizable objects but somewhat disconcerting when one tries to make sense out of it.[1] The analogy must not be pressed, however, for paintings aren't required to make sense in the same way that economic data are. But what *do* the data mean? More specifically, what kind of *problem* is presented by the unemployment levels depicted?

Our concern at the moment is not with the 1930s and 1940s, but with the unemployment figures in subsequent years. What does it mean, for example, that almost 5 million people were unemployed in 1971? It does not mean, first of all, that 5 million households were without income. The average unemployment rate in 1971 for household heads was only 3.6%, and in most of these households there was income from other sources. Among married men the unemployment rate was 3.2%. On the other hand, it was 7.4% among blue-collar workers and a disturbingly high 10% among nonwhite members of the labor force. Among teenagers (16–19 years old) it was 16.9%. The aggregate figure of 5.9% obviously conceals a lot of important variation.

Let's take a look at data on duration of unemployment in 1971. The average (mean) duration was 11.3 weeks. Of the almost 5 million unemployed, about 45% were without jobs for less than five weeks. But a little more than 10% of these people were unemployed for more than half the year. Why did some go back to work quickly while others found no work for long periods of time? The figures on long-term unemployment actually understate the problem. For once a person withdraws from the labor force, he's no longer counted as unemployed. And workers who don't find employment within six months are often discouraged enough to quit looking, so that they drop out of the labor force and hence out of the unemployment figures. We referred above to the well-known phenomenon of extremely high unemployment rates among nonwhites. Does that explain why in the quarter century after 1948 labor force participation rates of nonwhite adult males dropped from 97.2% to 92% among those 35–44 years old and from 94.7% to 86.9% among those 45–54 years old? (The corresponding changes for white males were only 98% to 97% and 95.9% to 94.7%.) People who cannot find what they're looking for may eventually give up.

One more set of data will add significantly to the picture. In 1971 almost 60 million people worked at jobs covered by some kind of government-operated or -assisted system of unemployment compensation. That's slightly more than 70% of the civilian labor force. The average weekly

---

1. If you've never seen a painting by the late Belgian surrealist René Magritte, look him up on your next trip to the library. You may find yourself captivated by an intriguing painter. And you'll discover the force of this analogy.

check received by workers entitled to unemployment compensation was $54. But only 2.3 million unemployed workers, or less than half the total, received any of these benefits. The picture is again one of enormous differences, with some unemployed workers receiving benefits that, partly for tax reasons, left them almost as well off financially as when they were working, and others receiving nothing.

Clearly the unemployment problem in the United States is not a simple one. And this is the point we want to stress in asking what the BLS figures on unemployment *mean.* In using these data for policymaking purposes we must be continually aware that particular people are unemployed for very different reasons and with quite different social and personal consequences, and that no single government policy is capable of solving *the* unemployment problem because it isn't a single problem.

Largely as a result of our experience in the 1930s with prolonged, large-scale unemployment associated with low levels of private spending and huge amounts of unused productive capacity, economists and other students of economic policy have focused on the relation between unemployment and the total market demand for commodities and services. This emphasis, as we shall see in subsequent chapters, produced a great deal

of theoretical and empirical work on the causes and cures of aggregate economic fluctuations. But unemployment has other causes as well, causes on which we want to reflect before launching into our analysis of aggregate demand, Keynesian economics, monetary disturbances, and fiscal and monetary policy.

Job Turnover and Labor Force Attachment

In 1971 only 46% of those listed as unemployed had lost their jobs or been laid off. The other 54% were either entering the labor force for the first time, reentering it after a period of absence, or had quit their last jobs. Moreover, job turnover has long been high in the United States. Total hirings and separations among employees in manufacturing, for example, consistently run above 4% of the labor force per month. We can translate that loosely by saying that one out of every 25 workers in manufacturing can be expected to leave his job for some reason in the next 30 days. Unless these job leavers drop out of the labor force altogether, they will add to the unemployment totals until they go to work at a new job.

These figures suggest that much of our measured unemployment can be attributed to weak job attachment among a substantial number of workers. That thesis is supported by other evidence.

Teenage Unemployment

The unemployment rate among teenagers has long been many times higher than the national average. In part that results from the general absence in this country of programs for matching up available jobs with young people as they leave high school. High school counselors are diligent college placement officers, but they are less effective in serving those who want to go to work when they graduate or leave school. This is not to blame the counselors. They have for the most part received little encouragement or assistance from employers, parents, or the students themselves.

But there is more to the teenage unemployment picture. A large proportion of the jobs available to teenagers are simply not attractive. They don't pay much more than the legal minimum and they offer no hope of advancement. They are seen as dead-end jobs, something to be done to earn a little money but not the beginning of careers. The attractiveness of a particular job depends, of course, on the alternatives. Most teenagers have few financial obligations and many continue to live with their parents, so they can afford to quit a job and take their time about finding another. Since there are usually plenty of equally attractive (or unattractive) jobs around, they are not much deterred from quitting by the fear that they won't be able to get something just as good if they change their minds.

Moreover, many unemployed teenagers look for jobs, full or part time, while attending school, and still others only flirt with the job market because they're simultaneously flirting with the possibility of going back to school or joining the military service or maybe getting into some kind of vocational training program. The common element in all these factors is the low urgency assigned to remaining at the current job or taking another at the first opportunity.[1]

We don't mean to suggest by this analysis that teenage unemployment is not a serious social problem. We are rather trying to find out just what kind of problem it is. It is not, except in rare instances, a problem of no work to be had by those who must have income to meet their obligations. But a society that is unable to provide a substantial number of its young people with jobs they think are worth pursuing, jobs with live prospects for advancement or meaningful work, does have a serious problem. In recent years the problem may even have become more acute and widespread as college students, too, leave school and find that even a bachelor's degree no longer guarantees an attractive job offer. There is evidence that the scenario sketched above for 16–19-year-olds is beginning to be reenacted by 20–24-year-olds.

ON "RETIRING" AT TWENTY OR AT SIXTY

One of the authors has done research on time and income allocation over the course of people's lifetimes. He found that an interesting pattern emerges after formal schooling is complete.

People who are more impatient than society (that is, who discount the future at a rate higher than the market rate of interest) will devote an *increasing fraction* of their time to work as they get older. They will work less when young and may not plan to retire.

People who are less impatient than society (whose internal rate of time discount is below the market rate of interest) will devote a *decreasing fraction* of their time to work as they grow older. They will work hard when young and plan for their retirement.

Is one inherently superior to the other? Yet the less impatient frequently do condemn those who are more impatient.

---

1. Martin Feldstein has suggested: "Perhaps much of the high turnover and voluntary labor force withdrawal among young non-students reflects an attempt to enjoy the same freedom and occupational irresponsibility that we take for granted in our student population of the same age." Why not? This analysis of unemployment data and their meaning owes much to Feldstein's discussion of "The Economics of the New Unemployment," based on a study he submitted to the Joint Economic Committee of the Congress in 1973 and published in *The Public Interest,* Fall 1973.

In 1971 one out of every four labor force participants listed as unemployed was a teenager; in 1973 it rose to two out of every seven. That's certainly a significant fact to keep in mind when asking about the meaning of our unemployment figures. But what about the other three out of four or five out of seven? Why are they unemployed?

Abilities and Opportunities

When we begin to break down the data we discover that there are several reasonably distinct causes of unemployment among older workers, and that this diversity of causes creates different kinds of problems that will probably require for their solution quite different policy approaches.

To begin with, some workers are close to unemployable. They may have low skills, physical disabilities, emotional problems, or simply such poor work habits that few employers would want to take them on at any positive wage.

Then there are workers, again often with low skills and poor work habits, who are unwilling to accept or to remain for long at the jobs employers are willing to give them. Martin Feldstein reports on a program initiated in Boston in 1966 to provide jobs for very low-skill workers. About 15,000 were referred to employers and 70% of these received job offers. But 45% of the job offers were rejected, and half of those who did accept were no longer on the job after one month. A high proportion of these separations was initiated by the workers themselves. Many workers in this category are probably not even listed as unemployed, because they have withdrawn from the labor force. So in this case the BLS data probably understate the problem. But exactly what *is* the problem? Extravagant expectations or inadequate opportunities? Whichever alternative we elect, the situation results in poverty for a substantial number of such individuals and in many cases their dependents as well. The problem is genuine. But how should we set about solving it?

Points of View and Bias

The language of the preceding paragraph may have suggested that workers with low skills or poor work habits are themselves to blame for their situation. There are people eager to argue that a lack of ambition or personal responsibility is the root cause of a substantial amount of national unemployment. It is particularly easy for white, middle-class males to think in this fashion, and thereby to overlook the possible role of the labor market itself in creating the problem. Substantial evidence exists to support the view that hiring practices in the United States have helped to create the problem. Discrimination by employers *and fellow employees* on the basis of such factors as race and social class has tended to confine some workers to the least attractive jobs: the ones with low pay, poor prospects for advancement, little chance to acquire skills, and a low probability of permanent employment. It isn't surprising that such workers develop a weak attachment to the labor force, tend to be relatively unskilled, and display work habits that make them unattractive to employers. But what is cause and what is effect?

Social scientists are usually reluctant to enter into a discussion of "blame" or "fault." But intelligent policy formulation requires attention to causes and almost any discussion of causes, when we're looking at social phenomena, presupposes some notion of responsibility—which in practice is very difficult to distinguish from notions of credit or blame. Because the economic way of thinking is rooted in the concept of individual choice, it tends to postulate individual responsibility for any actions that people take. This is not so much explicitly stated as presupposed. But it begs an important question: Do individuals create society? Or does society create individuals? Shall individuals or society be held responsible for the misfortunes that people encounter? That is the larger question underneath numerous contemporary public policy disputes, not just disputes over policies to deal with unemployment. It is a question, of course, that people have been debating for centuries and one that none of us is likely to resolve. We can at least be alert to the fact that the emphasis we place upon either of these poles—the individual or society—will influence our interpretation of fact and hence the policy conclusions to which we come. In such a situation there may be no better remedy than a determination to remain open to alternative points of view and to give sympathetic attention to opposing analyses.

There is an additional component of our unemployment totals where individual choice is clearly involved but where the choices would not be widely regarded as intolerable. The problem—insofar as it is a problem—may have been created by our unemployment compensation system, our way of taxing wage income, the prevalence of families with more than one wage earner, and the fact that the demand for leisure tends to increase at higher income levels.

Imagine a man laid off who is eligible for unemployment compensation and whose wife is working. He loses the income from work. But he receives as compensation one-half his regular wage. Moreover, this income is not subject to income or social security taxes so that the actual reduction in his income will be considerably less than half. How eager will he be to return to work? A worker loses his eligibility for unemployment compensation if he refuses to accept a job to which he has been referred as long as that job is comparable to the one he lost; so the system doesn't provide automatic paid vacations. But it's possible to behave during a job interview in a way that reduces the probability of a job offer. The point

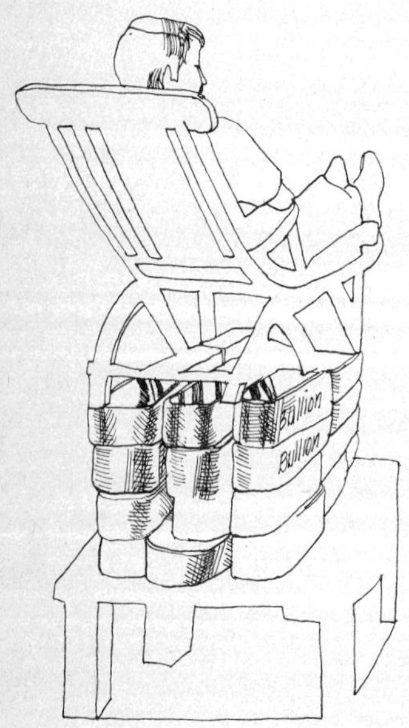

of this analysis, in any event, is not to argue that some of the officially unemployed are goldbricking but to suggest that unemployment of limited duration is not experienced as an economic disaster by *all* those who are laid off.

Toward Clarity of Goals

So the BLS statistics on employment and unemployment require considerable dissection and interpretation before they can serve as a guide to policy. No one has ever suggested that government policy should aim at a zero unemployment rate, a target that wasn't even reached at the height of World War II. *Some* unemployment is universally accepted as necessary if workers are to be allowed freedom of choice and if the labor market is to function as a system for reassigning workers in an economy characterized by continual change both in technology and in the composition of demand for products. How much unemployment ought to be accepted, not as a problem but as a condition of freedom and fluidity? The answer can't simply be stated as a percentage. The tolerable or desirable minimum level of unemployment should and will increase as the opportunity cost to workers of being unemployed goes down.

Moreover, there are many among the unemployed who will not readily find work even if the aggregate demand for labor increases. It may prove much more difficult to devise effective and politically acceptable ways to offer income and work to many of the unemployed than we currently realize. So government actions aimed at creating or maintaining a high and steadily expanding demand for labor, important as they may be, cannot be the whole of our labor policy.

Once Over Lightly

The study of aggregate fluctuations in the level of economic activity, or of recessions and inflations, their causes and cures, is widely known as *macroeconomics.*

Macroeconomics makes extensive use of statistical series on prices, output, income, and employment. Intelligent use of this information requires understanding of the theories and concepts that have been used to construct the series.

The most widely used measure of recession and perhaps the most politically significant index of aggregate economic activity is the unemployment rate calculated each month by the Bureau of Labor Statistics.

The key concepts for understanding the unemployment rate are the noninstitutional population and the labor force. To be officially unemployed one must be in the labor force, and to be counted in the labor force one must first be included in the noninstitutional population. The noninstitutional population includes all those over sixteen years of age who are not inmates of institutions. The labor force includes all members of the noninstitutional population who are either working, absent for such reasons as illness, strikes, or accidents, waiting to resume a job or begin a new one, or actively looking for work. The official unemployment rate is the sum of the latter two categories divided by the civilian labor force (the total labor force minus members of the armed forces).

The total of those unemployed can and sometimes does rise at the same time as the total of those employed. This implies that the labor force is increasing faster than unemployment is increasing. Sometimes an increase in unemployment may even cause a further increase in unemployment by stimulating a higher rate of labor force participation.

The employment rate is the total number of people in civilian employment divided by the noninstitutional population. For some purposes this is a better measure of the job situation than the unemployment rate, because the defining concepts can be more easily and objectively measured.

The notion that unemployment results from people's choice of the best option available to them is consistent with empirical data on rates of labor force participation and the frequency and duration of unemployment for different categories of the population. The only defensible goal for employ-ment policy is improvement of the range of opportunities available to people.

The aggregate level of economic activity is one factor determining job opportunities. But while the demand for labor is determined by employers' estimates of the marginal contribution labor will make to revenue in par-ticular production processes, employers may retain workers whose mar-ginal dollar product is expected to be *temporarily* below their marginal cost when the cost of finding and training new workers is substantial.

QUESTIONS FOR DISCUSSION

1. "Full employment" of the labor force is often said to be an important goal for government economic policy.

    (*a*) What is meant by full employment of the labor force? Would you favor policies to secure *full* employment at all times?

    (*b*) Why do you think it is that economic commentators tend to define employment as 96% to 97% employment of the labor force? (That is, we are deemed to have achieved full employment when the BLS data show that unemployment is down to 4% or at best 3% of the labor force.) How do they know that it should be 96% rather than 95% or even less?

(*c*) Are the people being counted as unemployed in a period of full employment (as defined above) voluntarily unemployed? Can you find evidence to support the claim that jobs are always available?

(*d*) If the BLS unemployment figure rises to 6%, are all the unemployed still to be thought of as voluntarily unemployed? Defend your answer.

2. Can there be "overfull" employment?

(*a*) Suppose that the vacancy rate on apartments in a large city is less than 1%. What undesirable consequences might be associated with such a full level of apartment employment? Would you enjoy moving to a city with such a low vacancy rate?

(*b*) If you are driving on only 80% of the automobile tires you own, is the spare tire unemployed? Would you like to be driving with your tires at "full employment"? Across the Great Salt Lake Desert?

3. Jones is a tool and die maker earning $8 an hour. He is suddenly laid off.

(*a*) He frequents employment agencies, reads want ads, and follows up leads on tool and die making jobs for two weeks. Is he involuntarily unemployed during this time?

(*b*) At the end of the two weeks he is offered a job driving a bread truck that pays $4.50 an hour. He turns it down. Is he involuntarily unemployed?

(*c*) He receives an offer of a job as a tool and die maker in a city 125 miles away. He turns it down because his teenage children don't want to change high schools. Is he involuntarily unemployed?

(*d*) After three months of searching, Jones becomes discouraged and quits looking. Is he involuntarily unemployed? Or is he no longer in the labor force?

4. Which of the following situations does *not* result in voluntary unemployment?

(*a*) Smith quits his job because his employer requires him to start work at 4 A.M.

(*b*) Smith is fired when he refuses to do something that his employer orders him to do but which he considers unethical.

(*c*) Would your answer be different if the act ordered by Smith's employer were also illegal?

(*d*) Smith is told that he can continue in his job only if he accepts a 75% cut in wages; he quits.

5. A person who is laid off from his job goes to work for himself (becomes self-employed) "producing" information about alternative job opportunities. How long he will remain self-employed in this way depends on his "productivity" (is he generating what he considers valuable information?)

and the opportunity cost of this self-employment. (He'll want to continue as long as his anticipated marginal revenue exceeds anticipated marginal cost.) How will the duration of measured unemployment be affected by

(*a*) unemployment compensation?

(*b*) food stamp programs?

(*c*) persistent rumors that many large firms are beginning to hire?

(*d*) a spirit of confidence and optimism?

6. Are the hypothetical individuals who made each of the statements below voluntarily or involuntarily unemployed? How would they be classified by most people? Why would you agree or disagree with the usual classification? It is important to notice that statements such as *h* and *i* may not express different situations at all. "I don't want to work (at any job I can find)" may mean "I can't find a job (at which I want to work)."

(*a*) "I quit my job and I'm going to remain unemployed until I find a job that pays $1000 for ten hours' work a week."

(*b*) "I was laid off last month. I had a great job as marketing consultant to a franchising chain. They paid me $1000 a week for about ten hours of work. I'm going to keep looking until I find another job like that one."

(*c*) "I decided I could no longer be a part of the military-industrial complex; so I quit my job. I'm looking now for an engineer's position that doesn't require me to participate in murder, pollution, and mind-raping."

(*d*) "When Boeing laid me off, I figured I could quickly find another job in engineering. But now I don't care. I'll take any job at all that pays what I used to get."

(*e*) "I've been out of work for six months and I'm pretty desperate. I'll do anything that's legal to get food for my family. But I have an invalid wife and five small children, so I can't take any job that pays less than $100 a week."

(*f*) "I could get any one of a dozen jobs tomorrow. But I don't want to. I'm eligible for three more months of unemployment compensation, so I'm just going to take it easy until the checks run out. Oh, if something really good turned up, I'd take it, of course."

(*g*) "I could get any one of a dozen jobs tomorrow. But I don't want to. I'm eligible for three more months of unemployment compensation, so I'm just going to spend my time really looking. I'm going to use those three months to find the very best job I can possibly get."

(*h*) "I don't want to work."

(*i*) "I can't find a job."

7. Is the cost to an employer of finding and training workers part of his sunk costs or of his marginal costs? What is the significance of this distinction in explaining layoff policies during a recession?

8

MUDGES GENERAL STORE
Special Sa
Coca-Cola
LUMBER SALE
NAILS
PAINT
ICE CREAM
POPSICLE
5¢
Double-dip CONES
Fresh Fruit
HAIRCUT... 50
FLAT-TOP ... 75
SHAVE ... 50
SHAMPOO... 55

TOTAL OUTPUT AND
THE PRICE LEVEL

The experience of the Great Depression lent added impetus to private efforts that had begun in the United States around 1920 to compile reliable information on the overall performance of the economy. The best-known statistical series evolving out of these efforts is the national income and product accounts compiled by the Bureau of Economic Analysis (called the Office of Business Economics until 1972) in the United States Department of Commerce. If you read only the front page of the daily newspaper, you will have heard about gross national product. This is the most comprehensive item in the Department of Commerce accounts and the one most frequently quoted. Some people watch the behavior of GNP, as it is familiarly known, with the intensity of small boys on the morning of a picnic listening to the weather report.

MEASURING TOTAL OUTPUT:
THE INCOME AND PRODUCT ACCOUNTS

What is the *gross national product?* It is *the market value of all the final goods produced in the entire economy in a year.* (The term *goods* includes both commodities and services.) In 1974 the gross national product of the United States was $1406.9 billion. That number and most of the other numbers in this chapter and the preceding one are subject to minor revisions for recent months, quarters, or years as more complete estimates become available. But the revisions very rarely entail significant changes that alter our basic conception of what has been occurring.

What does GNP attempt to measure? And what can we learn by examining its behavior over time? We shall necessarily simplify. If you don't trust simplifications, you may consult the January 1976 issues of the *Survey of Current Business,* a publication of the Bureau of Economic Analysis, where you will find a detailed description of the accounts and enough numbers to keep you thoroughly occupied for days.

Total Output Is Total Income

As the phrase "income and product" suggests, there are two ways to look at the statistics in the system of accounts. Calculated in one way, they measure *the value of what is produced.* On the other side of the coin, they measure the *income earned* by the producers. The value created in one year by all the productive resources of the nation will be equal to the income made available to the owners of those resources, after appropriate adjustments. The reason, of course, is that real income can come only from output and that every output constitutes income for someone. This necessary link between income and output (or product) provides part of the logical foundation for a method of analyzing aggregate fluctuations that we'll be examining in subsequent chapters.

Gross national product in 1974 was calculated at $1406.9 billion. The income made available to individuals and households in 1974, for them to spend or save, was $983.6 billion. This latter figure is labeled *disposable personal income.* (It's often referred to simply as *disposable income.*) The difference between the two arises from deductions that governments and businesses make from the total value of output before it becomes available as disposable income. Business firms retain some of the income (output) produced in order to cover wear and tear on capital equipment associated with the year's production; in addition, corporations characteristically retain a portion of their net earnings rather than pay it all out to owners. Governments levy taxes of various sorts, and this is, as everyone knows, a very large deduction from gross income. But governments and, to a much lesser extent, private firms, also pay out income to persons in what are called transfer payments. In the income and product accounts, these are income payments to persons that are *not* made in return for productive services being currently rendered; pensions, social security benefits, and welfare payments are examples. The sum of these deductions, net of the additions, roughly makes up the difference between gross national product and disposable income.

The magnitude of the difference—$1406.9 versus $983.6 billion in 1974—may prompt you to look skeptically at our previous assertion that output equals income "after appropriate adjustments." An elephant is just like a rabbit, too, "after appropriate adjustments." But the differences are also income. Taxes are income claimed by government, and the deductions made by business firms are their attempt to hang on to some income rather than pay it all out to the owners of the firms. If we think of the economy as divided into three sectors—consumers, business firms, and government—we can calculate the approximate portion of the year's output (gross national product) claimed as income by each sector. Consumers received disposable income of $983.6 billion in 1974, which was about 70% of the gross national income. Tax revenue minus government transfer payments approximated 18% of gross national product, and this we could call the net income of government. Business firms appropriated as their income the remaining 12%. (Be careful. That 12% implies nothing about the relative importance of the business sector. It is roughly the sum of undistributed corporate profits and depreciation allowances. We have called this *business income,* because it is income not at the disposal of consumers or government.)

Where Did the Output Go?

Income is desired because it permits the purchase of commodities and services. Who finally purchased the 1.4 trillion dollars worth of goods produced in 1974? A slightly different classification system may be used to answer this question. The potential purchasers of goods may be divided into consumers, government, and investors. Personal consumption expenditures by Americans in 1974 came to $885.9 billion. Federal, state, and local government purchases of goods totaled $301.1 billion. Domestic investors purchased $212.2 billion. And the remaining $7.7 billion was our net exports to foreign consumers, investors, or governments.

Investment is a key concept in economics and is defined as *the purchase of capital. Capital means goods that will be employed in the production of future commodities or services.* The distinction between an investment expenditure and a consumption expenditure will inevitably be somewhat arbitrary. An amateur tennis player purchases a racket for the sake of the future services he expects it to provide. Is the racket a consumption or an investment good? Family automobiles are also purchased for the sake of future services. A kitchen blender is an investment inasmuch as it is obtained for the sake of the goods it will produce in the future. But the income and product accounts nonetheless classify all these purchases as consumption

expenditures except when they are made by business firms. If you buy a water cooler for your patio, that's a consumption expenditure. If one is purchased for the office where you work, that's an investment expenditure. The only such purchase by households that qualifies as investment in these accounts is the purchase of new housing. Here the stream of services extends so far into the future that it seems unduly misleading to count the purchase of a new residence as consumption. But the difference between automobiles and residences is one of degree. Consumers, of course, usually don't worry about these fine accounting distinctions, and consider the purchase of a durable household good an investment. People say, quite correctly, that they "invested" in a clothes dryer, or a dining-room set, or new carpeting. That is completely consistent with our definition of investment. But accountants must make distinctions even when they are somewhat arbitrary.

The components of investment as measured by the Bureau of Economic Analysis are (*a*) residential construction, (*b*) purchases of new business structures (offices, factories, stores), (*c*) purchases of new durable equipment (machinery), and (*d*) net additions to business inventories. The last item makes sure that everything produced is counted as purchased by someone. If a business firm finds itself unable to sell all the output it has produced, it is considered to have purchased that output itself and added it, perhaps reluctantly, to inventory.

In 1974 these components of investment were calculated as follows:[1]

Residential construction	$54.6 billion
Nonresidential construction	54.4
Producers durable equipment	93.5
Addition to business inventories	9.7
	$212.2

Foreigners imported $144.2 billion of American goods in 1974 while the U.S. was importing $136.5 billion in foreign goods. So net exports (exports minus imports) took $7.7 billion of goods, the last component of gross national product. The significance of this component may vastly exceed its size; but that question will be reserved until chapter 14.

The sum of consumer, government, investor, and net foreign purchases of new goods in 1974 was $1406.9 billion, the exact amount calculated as the gross national income. To be perfectly honest, the totals will never match exactly, because there are bound to be errors and omissions in the measurement of such vast and variegated quantities as total national income and total expenditures on new goods. But since they are equal by definition, the Bureau of Economic Analysis adjusts national income with a fudge factor which it calls Statistical Discrepancy.

The Historical Record

The history of gross national product and some of its components since 1929 is summarized in table 8A. All figures represent billions of dollars, and are rounded to the nearest tenth of a billion.

As we noted earlier, recessions and depressions are marked by an increase in measured unemployment. They are also marked, as we would expect, by a decline in the rate of growth of gross national product. If you pick out from table 7A the years since World War II in which unemployment rose sharply, you will find that they are years in which gross national product either declined from the previous year (1949), remained basically unchanged (1954), or rose by a substantially smaller percentage than in the immediately preceding years (1958, 1961). The years 1970 and 1974 only *appear* to be an exception: the decline in GNP in these years is concealed by a rapid rise in prices (of which we'll say more a bit later). The decade of the 1930s has a whole sad history of its own.

---

1. Components do not always sum to the total in data of this type if the component figures have been rounded off.

Table 8A   GROSS NATIONAL PRODUCT AND COMPONENTS
(in billions of dollars)

Year	Gross National Product	Personal Consumption Expenditures	Gross Private Domestic Investment	Net Exports of Goods and Services	Government Purchases of Goods and Services	DISPOSABLE PERSONAL INCOME
1929	103.1	77.2	16.2	1.1	8.5	83.3
1930	90.4	69.9	10.3	1.0	9.2	74.5
1931	75.8	60.5	5.6	.5	9.2	64.0
1932	58.0	48.6	1.0	.4	8.1	48.7
1933	55.6	45.8	1.4	.4	8.0	45.5
1934	65.1	51.3	3.3	.6	9.8	52.4
1935	72.2	55.7	6.4	.1	10.0	58.5
1936	82.5	61.9	8.5	.1	12.0	66.3
1937	90.4	66.5	11.8	.3	11.9	71.2
1938	84.7	63.9	6.5	1.3	13.0	65.5
1939	90.5	66.8	9.3	1.1	13.3	70.3
1940	99.7	70.8	13.1	1.7	14.0	75.7
1941	124.5	80.6	17.9	1.3	24.8	92.7
1942	157.9	88.5	9.8	.0	59.6	116.9
1943	191.6	99.3	5.7	−2.0	88.6	133.5
1944	210.1	108.3	7.1	−1.8	96.5	146.3
1945	211.9	119.7	10.6	−.6	82.3	150.2
1946	208.5	143.4	30.6	7.5	27.0	160.0
1947	231.3	160.7	34.0	11.5	25.1	169.8
1948	257.6	173.6	46.0	6.4	31.6	189.1
1949	256.5	176.8	35.7	6.1	37.8	188.6
1950	284.8	191.0	54.1	1.8	37.9	206.9
1951	328.4	206.3	59.3	3.7	59.1	226.6
1952	345.5	216.7	51.9	2.2	74.7	238.3
1953	364.6	230.0	52.6	.4	81.6	252.6
1954	364.8	236.5	51.7	1.8	74.8	257.4
1955	398.0	254.4	67.4	2.0	74.2	275.3
1956	419.2	266.7	70.0	4.0	78.6	293.2
1957	441.1	281.4	67.9	5.7	86.1	308.5
1958	447.3	290.1	60.9	2.2	94.2	318.8
1959	483.7	311.2	75.3	.1	97.0	337.3
1960	503.7	325.2	74.8	4.0	99.6	350.0
1961	520.1	335.2	71.7	5.6	107.6	364.4
1962	560.3	355.1	83.0	5.1	117.1	385.3
1963	590.5	375.0	87.1	5.9	122.5	404.6
1964	632.4	401.2	94.0	8.5	128.7	438.1
1965	684.9	432.8	108.1	6.9	137.0	473.2
1966	749.9	466.3	121.4	5.3	156.8	511.9
1967	793.9	492.1	116.6	5.2	180.1	546.3
1968	864.2	536.2	126.0	2.5	199.6	591.0
1969	930.3	579.5	139.0	1.9	210.0	634.4
1970	977.1	617.6	136.3	3.6	219.5	691.7
1971	1054.9	667.1	153.7	−.2	234.2	746.4
1972	1158.0	729.0	179.3	−6.0	255.7	802.5
1973	1294.9	805.2	209.4	3.9	276.4	903.7
1974	1406.9	885.9	212.2	7.7	301.1	983.6

Source: Bureau of Economic Analysis. Benchmark revisions published in 1976 are only reflected above in data for 1974. Publication of revised estimates for 1929–74 was expected to be completed by midyear 1976.

RECESSION OR DEPRESSION?

What's the difference between a recession and a depression? According to the tired old joke, it's a recession when your neighbor loses his job and a depression when you lose yours. There is actually no agreed upon statistical measure that precisely defines a recession or a depression. By common consent, the National Bureau of Economic Research, a private nonprofit research organization that has been measuring aggregate economic fluctuations for more than half a century, makes the "official" determination of recession. The bureau, however, does not even employ the category of depression. What is widely known as the Great Depression of the 1930s is treated by the NBER as two recessions (1929–33 and 1937–38) with associated periods of recovery.

The Structure of the Income and Product Accounts

In addition to gross national product and disposable personal income, the Bureau of Economic Analysis calculates three other measures of the nation's annual income and product flow. Because they are sometimes mentioned in the public press, they will be briefly described here.

Personal income is disposable personal income prior to the subtraction of personal taxes.

National income is a bit confusing in that the term is sometimes used to describe the entire system of accounts while also referring to one particular concept within the system. National income in the latter and narrow sense is the total income earned by owners of productive resources, or the total of wages, profits, rental income, and interest income. The BEA computes it by adding together the compensation of employees; the net income of professionals, farm proprietors, and unincorporated businesses; corporate profits; rental income earned by persons; and net interest.

Net national product is gross national product after allowances for capital consumption have been deducted. These allowances are a rough measure of the value of productive equipment used up in the process of turning out a year's goods. Consequently net national product would be a better measure of annual output than gross national product were it not for one drawback: the measurement of capital consumption allowances (or depreciation) is very rough indeed, inconsistent from year to year, and arbitrary at the outset in deciding what shall count as capital.

Given the ultimate identity in the value of income and output, or the fact that they are merely two views of the same thing, why aren't net national product and national income identical? Net national product is the nation's (net) output calculated in terms of expenditures for final products. National income is the same thing calculated by means of the receipts of those who sell the final products. Aren't these the same? They would be except for sales taxes, certain transfer payments made by business firms, some complications introduced by government business operations and subsidies, and the statistical discrepancy which equates income to output. The difference between net national product and national income, then, is primarily the amount of indirect business taxes (a somewhat more inclusive category than sales taxes as usually understood). In 1974 net national product was $1272.9 billion and national income was $1141.1, with indirect business taxes comprising 96% of the difference.

What about the relation between national income and personal or disposable personal income? That's a little more complicated but simple enough in principle. National income is the total of wages, profits, interest, and rent earned from the sale of new products. Disposable personal income is the income that actually becomes available to persons or households to spend or save. A large chunk of national income goes to taxes, especially corporate profits taxes, social security taxes, and personal income taxes. In addition, corporations retain a portion of their earnings as undistributed corporate profits. Then there are two additions to the income stream that in 1974 more than made up for the subtractions: transfer payments by business or government (but especially by government) and the net interest paid by the government and by consumers. It would take too long to explain why the BEA treats government and consumer interest payments as transfer payments rather than as contributions to national income. Unless you decide to specialize in national income accounting, you had better just accept it as one of those odd facts of classification, such as the ladybugs which entomologists say are actually beetles rather than bugs.

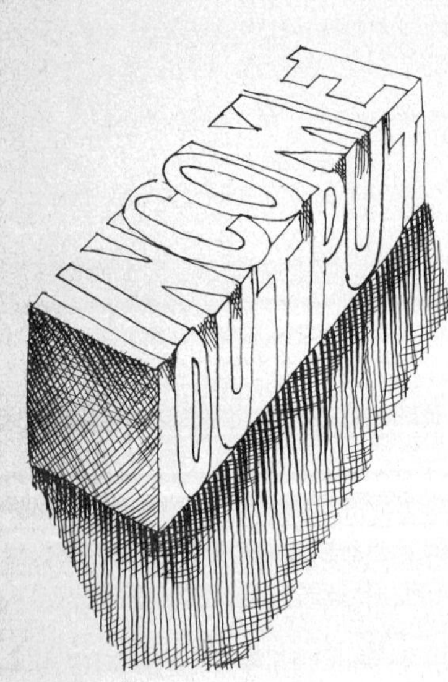

Table 8B presents the skeleton of the income and product accounts for selected years from 1929 through 1974 and quarterly data for 1974. Note that the quarterly data are *seasonally adjusted* totals at *annual rates*. (If the meaning of those terms is not intuitively clear, read the accompanying insert.) Undistributed corporate profits and corporate profits taxes are subtracted from national income by first subtracting the total of corporate profits and then adding dividends, since the sum of dividends, taxes, and retained earnings is the total of corporate profits. Notice that what the Bureau of Economic Analysis calls personal outlays differs from personal consumption expenditures by the total of consumer interest payments and personal transfer payments to foreigners. These last two components of personal expenditures are not regarded as purchases of final goods and hence do not enter into the expenditures that sum to the gross national product.

Table 8B RELATION OF GROSS NATIONAL PRODUCT, NET NATIONAL PRODUCT, NATIONAL INCOME, PERSONAL INCOME, AND DISPOSABLE PERSONAL INCOME

Item	1929	1933	1941	1950	1970	1971	1972	1973	1974	1974 I	1974 II	1974 III	1974 IV
Gross national product	103.1	55.6	124.5	284.8	977.1	1,054.9	1,158.0	1,294.9	1406.9	1370.9	1391.0	1424.4	1441.3
Less: Capital consumption allowances	7.9	7.0	8.2	18.3	87.3	93.7	102.9	110.8	134.0	126.9	131.1	136.1	142.1
Equals: Net national product	95.2	48.6	116.3	266.4	889.8	961.2	1,055.1	1,184.1	1272.9	1244.0	1259.9	1288.3	1299.3
Less: Indirect business tax and nontax liability	7.0	7.1	11.3	23.3	93.5	102.7	110.0	119.2	127.3	123.3	126.6	129.6	129.5
Business transfer payments	.6	.7	.5	.8	4.0	4.3	4.6	4.9	5.8	5.6	5.8	5.9	6.0
Statistical discrepancy	.7	.6	.4	1.5	−6.4	−2.3	−3.8	−5.0	−.6	−6.2	−1.6	2.4	2.9
Plus: Subsidies less current surplus of government enterprises	−.1		.1	.2	1.7	1.1	2.3	.6	.7	1.0	.5	.9	.4
Equals: National income	86.8	40.3	104.2	241.1	800.5	857.7	946.5	1,065.6	1141.1	1122.3	1129.6	1151.3	1161.3
Less: Corporate profits and inventory valuation adjustment	10.5	−1.2	15.2	37.7	69.2	78.7	92.2	105.1	91.3	99.6	94.3	89.2	82.0
Contributions for social insurance	.2	.3	2.8	6.9	57.7	63.8	73.0	91.2	102.9	100.2	101.9	104.4	105.0
Excess of wage accruals over disbursements					.0	.6	.0	−.1	−.5	.0	−.6	−1.5	.0
Plus: Government transfer payments	.9	1.5	2.6	14.3	75.1	89.0	98.6	113.0	134.5	123.5	130.7	138.4	145.5
Net interest paid by government and consumers	2.5	1.6	2.2	7.2	31.0	31.2	33.0	38.3	35.8	34.2	35.3	36.4	37.3
Dividends	5.8	2.0	4.4	8.8	24.7	25.0	27.3	29.6	31.1	30.0	30.9	31.7	31.7
Business transfer payments	.6	.7	.5	.8	4.0	4.3	4.6	4.9	5.9	5.6	5.8	5.9	6.0
Equals: Personal income	85.9	47.0	96.0	227.6	808.3	864.0	944.9	1,055.0	1154.7	1115.9	1136.6	1171.6	1194.8
Less: Personal tax and nontax payments	2.6	1.5	3.3	20.7	116.6	117.6	142.4	151.3	171.2	162.1	168.4	175.3	178.9
Equals: Disposable personal income	83.3	45.5	92.7	206.9	691.7	746.4	802.5	903.7	983.6	953.8	968.2	996.3	1015.9

Source: Bureau of Economic Analysis. Benchmark revisions published in 1976 are only reflected above and in Table 8C in data for 1974. Data on capital consumption allowances and corporate profits for 1974 reflect a significant change in the method of estimating capital consumption.

Table 8C NATIONAL INCOME
(in billions of dollars)

Item	1929	1933	1941	1950	1970	1971	1972	1973	1974
National Income	**86.8**	**40.3**	**104.2**	**241.1**	**800.5**	**857.7**	**946.5**	**1,065.6**	**1141.1**
Compensation of employees	**51.1**	**29.5**	**64.8**	**154.6**	**603.9**	**643.1**	**707.1**	**786.0**	**873.0**
Wages and salaries	*50.4*	*29.0*	*62.1*	*146.8*	*542.0*	*573.6*	*626.8*	*691.6*	*763.1*
Private	45.5	23.9	51.9	124.4	426.9	449.5	491.4	545.1	603.0
Military	.3	.3	1.9	5.0	19.6	19.4	20.5	20.6	22.3
Government civilian	4.6	4.9	8.3	17.4	95.5	104.7	114.8	126.0	137.7
Supplements to wages and salaries	*.7*	*.5*	*2.7*	*7.8*	*61.9*	*69.5*	*80.3*	*94.4*	*110.0*
Employer contributions for social insurance	.1	.1	2.0	4.0	29.7	33.1	38.6	48.4	55.5
Other labor income	.6	.4	.7	3.8	32.2	36.4	41.7	46.0	54.5
Proprietors' income	**15.1**	**5.9**	**17.5**	**37.5**	**66.9**	**69.2**	**75.9**	**96.1**	**85.1**
Business and professional	9.0	3.3	11.1	24.0	50.0	52.0	54.9	57.6	59.5
Farm	6.2	2.6	6.4	13.5	16.9	17.2	21.0	38.5	25.6
Rental income of persons	**5.4**	**2.0**	**3.5**	**9.4**	**23.9**	**25.2**	**25.9**	**26.1**	**21.0**
Corporate profits and inventory valuation adjustment	**10.5**	**−1.2**	**15.2**	**37.7**	**69.2**	**78.7**	**92.2**	**105.1**	**91.3**
Profits before tax	*10.0*	*1.0*	*17.7*	*42.6*	*74.0*	*83.6*	*99.2*	*122.7*	*132.1*
Profits tax liability	1.4	.5	7.6	17.8	34.8	37.5	41.5	49.8	52.6
Profits after tax	*8.6*	*.4*	*10.1*	*24.9*	*39.3*	*46.1*	*57.7*	*72.9*	*79.5*
Dividends	5.8	2.0	4.4	8.8	24.7	25.0	27.3	29.6	31.1
Undistributed Profits	2.8	−1.6	5.7	16.0	14.6	21.1	30.3	43.3	48.4
Inventory valuation adjustment	.5	−2.1	−2.5	−5.0	−4.8	−4.9	−7.0	−17.6	−38.5
Net Interest	**4.7**	**4.1**	**3.2**	**2.0**	**36.5**	**41.6**	**45.6**	**52.3**	**70.7**

Source: Bureau of Economic Analysis. Data for 1974 reflect benchmark revisions published in 1976 and are therefore not strictly comparable with preceding years.

Table 8C shows the composition of national income (in the narrow sense) for the same years.

What Are We Actually Measuring?

The numbers in the tables of this chapter were all constructed by diligent effort and not just "discovered" in the way a child discovers crickets while aimlessly turning over rocks. They were put together by statisticians who wanted answers to certain kinds of questions and knew what they were looking for. The numerical data in the *Monthly Labor Review* or the *Survey of Current Business* represent many prior decisions about what should

SEASONAL ADJUSTMENTS

In June of each year the labor force increases more rapidly than available jobs as students seek summer employment. In December available jobs increase more rapidly than the labor force as employers look for temporary Christmas help. Measured unemployment will consequently tend to rise each June and to fall in December. The Bureau of Labor Statistics "corrects" its monthly data to compensate for such changes by means of what are called *seasonal adjustments.* The letters "S.A." accompanying monthly or quarterly economic data mean that the figures for each month or quarter have been adjusted to eliminate changes caused by seasonal fluctuations. This permits the data to show underlying trends more clearly.

Another common technique for making data easier to interpret is to state certain kinds of flows or rates of change on an *annual basis.* Quarterly data on gross national product, for example, are always presented at "seasonally adjusted annual rates"; the figures show how large GNP would be if the seasonally adjusted level in a particular quarter persisted for twelve months. Similarly, monthly changes in the Consumer Price Index are sometimes multiplied by twelve to show the rate of change on an annual basis. You're doing much the same thing when you read that you're being charged $1\frac{1}{2}\%$ per month interest on your unpaid Master Charge balance and you multiply by twelve to determine that you're paying 18% interest on an annual basis, which is the way interest rates are generally stated.

be counted, how measurements and estimates should be made, and how conflicting criteria should be employed. We'll be able to use these data more intelligently if we understand something of the way in which they're put together and what they do *not* tell us as well as what they do.

We defined gross national product as the value of all the final goods produced in the United States during a single year. In doing so we glided quickly past a fundamental question: What counts as a final good and what does not? Which commodities and services get included in the computation of GNP?

A lot of the activities carried on within families produce goods in the sense of commodities or services that satisfy wants, but the GNP statisticians ignore most of them. They count only the products sold in markets —with a few carefully chosen exceptions. If you purchase a haircut from

the barber, that haircut counts in GNP; but if you get an even better haircut from your mother or your roommate, it adds nothing to GNP. If you
drive your car everywhere and then join a health spa to get in shape, the
gasoline you consume *and* the sauna you rent both make it into GNP. If
you choose instead to keep in shape by selling your car and walking a lot,
GNP will fall even though you're just as healthy and perhaps a lot happier.
The person who enjoys working with wood may obtain intense satisfaction
as well as a better bookcase by building his own, but only the wood, nails,
and shellac he buys will be counted in GNP. The reason is simple: There
is no satisfactory way to assign value to all the want-satisfying activities
that go on in the family or that people perform for themselves or for one
another without any exchange of money. So they are excluded from the
calculation of GNP.

Gross National Welfare?

But doesn't this reduce gross national product to a woefully inadequate
measure of social welfare? That's a very odd question; but it's often asked
today. It's as odd as asking whether failure to include television watching
as time spent in school doesn't lead to an underestimate of learning. Both
questions are misconceived, because learning is not synonymous with
schooling and gross national product was never intended to be a measure
of gross national welfare. The point must be stressed both to those who
revere GNP far beyond its deserts and to those who want to make it worthy
of such reverence by transforming it into something it simply cannot
become.

The Bureau of Economic Analysis has long insisted that GNP is not a
measure of social welfare and has openly advertised the limitations on
what GNP purports to measure. For example, the BEA measures all commodities exchanged for money at their market prices while freely admit-
ting that relative prices are not always reliable indicators of the contribution made by particular products to social welfare. It does not count in
GNP the sale of such illegal products as heroin, but with no implication
whatsoever that the legalization of heroin would add to national welfare,
though it would indeed add to the gross national product. It includes only
final goods and does not include in its calculations those intermediate goods
that businesses purchase to use as inputs in the production of other goods
—the steel, for example, purchased by a car manufacturer—on the grounds

that this would lead to double counting. The steel will enter GNP by contributing to the final automobile. But the BEA has deliberately refused to extend the same argument to the food consumed by workers, although the food consumed by a worker is, at least in part, also an intermediate product. If someone objects that the contribution of food to welfare is exaggerated by the BEA's assumption that people eat only for pleasure, the BEA has an easy answer: It makes no such assumption and it is not even attempting to measure national welfare. The people who are today protesting that GNP doesn't measure social welfare are only agreeing with what the compilers of the data have long been saying.

In recent years, as an extension of the social welfare protest, some have begun to argue the desirability of adjustments in our methods of calculating GNP that would make it reflect changes in the quality of the environ-

NATIONAL INCOME AND "VALUE ADDED"

The total cost of any business enterprise can be thought of as the sum of its payments for the inputs it uses: goods purchased from other firms; supplies of labor, land, capital, and risk; and the services provided by government. This total for any firm will exceed its contribution to the national income or output by the amount of the first item in that list, the payments made to other firms for goods used in the production process. This portion of the firm's final output was contributed by the firms from which it purchased. If we regard taxes as the obligations of those who receive income, then the *value added* by any firm, or its specific contribution to the national income, is the total of its income payments to suppliers of labor, land, capital, and risk. And that is the definition of national income in the narrow sense. Table 8C shows the items that make up the total of these income payments by all business firms.

When indirect business taxes and capital consumption allowances (plus the few minor items discussed above and shown in table 8B) are added to national income, the total must by definition be equal to the sum of consumer, investor, government, and net foreign purchases of final goods. The statistical discrepancy takes care of any actual difference.

This provides another way of showing the conceptual identity of income and output and the reason for excluding intermediate goods from the calculation of the gross national product.

ment. One proposal would have the BEA *deduct* from gross national product the cost of expenditures undertaken to clean up the environment. The argument in this case is that GNP rises when copper is smelted to reflect the value of the copper; it should not rise still further, as now occurs, when people buy paint to cover the grime that the smelting process scatters on their houses. Another proposal would have the BEA *add* something to GNP when a smelter closes down, to reflect the added satisfaction that people now obtain from living in a less odorous environment. What these proposals have in common is dissatisfaction with the way environment-affecting activities are reflected or not reflected in the national income and product accounts. But what they also have in common is confusion about the nature and functions of these accounts. And that confusion is reflected in the opposite direction in which the two proposals move. The first wants to *subtract* from GNP the *cost* of a better environment, the second wants to *add* to GNP the *benefits* of a better environment. Let's ask a hard question of each.

Doesn't the first proposal imply that the BEA should also deduct from GNP all business expenditures that improve working conditions and all household expenditures on shrubbery and lawn fertilizer? Doesn't the second proposal imply that the BEA should add something to GNP for bright, sunny days in January and cool breezes in August? Is there any logical cut-off point once we start moving in either direction? Remember that in the absence of defensible criteria to guide our measurements, we don't know what the measurements mean. And if that's the case, what good are our new and "improved" numbers? They will manage only to make the old and unimproved numbers less reliable while fooling gullible people into believing that we know what we're doing to the environment because we have a set of numbers before us.

There is a harsh fact well known to those who toil at construction of the income and product accounts but rarely recognized by their critics: the basic data from which the accounts are constructed are largely of the type that require no philosophical judgments on the part of the data suppliers. These people provide data on actual expenditures and on dollar and cents receipts, data which they are well qualified to provide. A concept of GNP that attempted to measure changes in welfare would require the BEA to ask questions that are extraordinarily difficult even to ask and that would in practice be answered so arbitrarily as to make the data base almost meaningless. Try a little mental experiment if you want to appreciate the problem. Imagine the difficulties you would encounter if you tried to determine, through a survey questionnaire, the average *welfare* of your classmates. Think how much easier it would be to determine their average income.

The BEA statisticians and economists are not afraid of a challenge. If they decide that the failure to include some difficult-to-measure activity will significantly reduce the meaningfulness of their computations, they will attempt to measure and include it. So they do include in gross national product the food produced and consumed on farms, even though it isn't sold in the market, because failure to do so would seriously understate agricultural income. They also include the estimated rental value of owner-occupied housing because, if they did not, shifts between owner-ship and rental could cause misleading changes in the measure of national output. The wages and salaries that employers sometimes pay in kind (room and board, for example) are also counted, even though these goods are not sold in the market, because compensation of this kind is taken into account in wage bargaining. You may be interested to know that they do not count television programs as final commodities or services; commercial television programs enter the GNP accounts as intermediate goods—as business purchases of advertising—and are thus reflected only as a component in the total expenditures for the advertisers' products. The BEA people are aware that this means personal consumption expenditures may appear to decline when people shift from attending movies to watching television. But how much difference does it make and what would be the cost of correcting the error? The bureau's statisticians are willing to adjust their methods of computation whenever the benefits of doing so seem large enough to offset the added uncertainties from including yet another component whose value must be estimated because it is not sold in the market.

The Uses of GNP Data

If GNP doesn't measure social welfare and is a very clumsy tool for keeping track of environmental changes, of what use *are* the income and product accounts? That depends on whom you ask. Some business executives claim that they find the data useful in planning and forecasting. Governments make use of the data to anticipate tax revenues; the revenue from an income tax depends, after all, on income levels as well as on the tax rate, and the revenue from sales taxes also depends on the behavior of variables whose course is charted in the income and product accounts. Economists use the data to construct and test theories, to confirm what they already suspect, to compose multiple choice questions for college students, and simply for the comprehensive picture that a bird's-eye view can give (even if the bird happens to be color-blind and lacking in depth perception). Journalists use the data to explain to lay audiences the mysteries of prosperity and recession and no doubt on occasion to disguise essential ignorance behind an impressive array of numbers. But all intelligent users approach the data with caution.

Because of all the conventions that enter into the computation of GNP, it is not a useful device for making international comparisons, except in the hands of someone who knows a great deal about the details of national income accounting in the countries being compared. For much the same reason it ought to be used cautiously when making comparisons over long periods of time even within a single country; its focus on production for market and neglect of home production leads to an exaggerated picture of the rate of growth in output over time. Moreover, the *aggregate* character of the data will always be kept in mind by judicious users. The upward (or downward) movement of a composite does not imply anything about the direction of movement of a particular component; industries can founder and firms go bankrupt while GNP is rising smartly, just as it's possible for some firms or whole industries to prosper during a recession. And the data should *not*—we repeat—be used as an index of welfare.

A System of Welfare Indicators

No sensible person will doubt for a moment that social welfare is more important than the production of commodities and services. In fact, welfare is a concept far too important and complex to be compressed and distorted into a form suitable for packaging in the income and product accounts. The federal government officially acknowledged this in 1969, when the Department of Health, Education, and Welfare published a booklet entitled *Toward a Social Report.* The introduction is worth quoting:

> The Nation has no comprehensive set of statistics reflecting social progress or retrogression. There is no Government procedure for periodic stocktaking of the social health of the Nation. The Government makes no Social Report.
>
> We do have an Economic Report, required by statute, in which the President and his Council of Economic Advisors report to the Nation on its economic health. We also have a comprehensive set of economic indicators widely thought to be sensitive and reliable. . . .
>
> Indeed, economic indicators have become so much a part of our thinking that we have tended to equate a rising National Income with national well-being.

But this is a wholly unwarranted equation, the introduction goes on to argue, because income and disaffection *can and do* increase together. *Toward a Social Report* then suggests seven areas in which better data might be gathered and new questions asked by those who want to complement the economic indicators of the income and product accounts with a system of welfare indicators.

> 1. Health and illness: Are we becoming healthier while we're spending more money on medical care?

2. Social mobility: Have we made progress toward equality of opportunity?

3. Physical environment: What's happening to the settings within which we live as the average level of personal wealth continues to rise?

4. Income and poverty: How well does our society distribute economic goods among its members?

5. Public order and safety: How much do we suffer from crime and the fear of violence?

6. Learning, science, and art: How much do they contribute toward the enrichment of our lives?

7. Participation and alienation: How are we faring with respect to justice, and what is happening to our sense of community?

These questions will be far more difficult to answer than the limited and manageable questions asked by the Bureau of Economic Analysis. We think they're very much worth asking. But we don't believe that the income and product accounts are the right place to look for the answers. And we shudder whenever we hear someone talking as if those accounts do measure welfare; for money and happiness are surely not synonymous, and the production of marketable commodities and services is certainly not a satisfactory indicator of social well-being.

MEASURING CHANGES IN THE PRICE LEVEL

One more system of scorekeeping has to be introduced. All our talk about prices in preceding chapters has been about *relative* prices, or the ratios at which goods exchange for one another. Though we expressed these ratios in terms of money, we were not really interested in how much *money*, but rather in how much of *other goods,* had to be sacrificed to obtain some good in question. Thus we have so far said nothing about inflation. But inflation is an important problem and a major issue in the study of aggregate fluctuations and the struggle for economic stability.

Three Price Indices

The Bureau of Labor Statistics accumulates data on the average behavior of prices and publishes these in the form of price indices. The best known such index is the Consumer Price Index, which hits the front page of the newspapers every month during periods of substantial public concern about inflation. Another index, and one more useful for some purposes, is the Wholesale Price Index compiled by the Bureau of Labor Statistics. This is not, as the name suggests, an index of wholesale prices or the

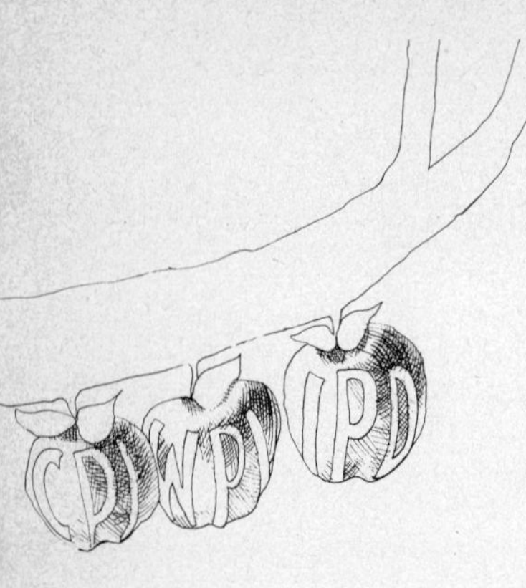

prices paid by retailers. It is simply a measure of changes in the market prices of a long list of such basic agricultural and industrial commodities as processed foods and feeds, textile products, hides, fuels, chemicals, lumber, metals, machinery, and so on.

A third widely used index of prices is the Implicit Price Deflator for gross national product constructed by the Bureau of Economic Analysis. It reflects changes in the average prices of all new production of final goods, or all the items that contribute to the total of GNP. Table 8D summarizes all three indices from 1929 through 1974. (Note that the base years are different for the two Implicit GNP Deflators.)

You can see clearly that prices fell sharply at the onset of the Great Depression. They fell slightly in the 1949 recession. But in 1954, 1958, and 1961 the consumer price index and the GNP deflator defied expectations by moving upward as employment moved downward. Inflation mixed with unemployment, a major concern after 1970, first showed its head in the 1950s.

Wars seem to promote inflation. The year 1951 shows the consequences of the Korean War; and prices began rising in the 1960s concurrently with escalation of the war in Viet Nam. While prices rose during World War II, they rose even more rapidly in the years right after the war.

The wholesale price index seems to respond more vigorously to changing conditions than does the consumer price index. It falls farther and rises faster. But look at the remarkable stability of the WPI from 1958 to 1964, when the CPI was creeping persistently upward. Was "the" price level rising in this period? It has been argued that it was not, but that the CPI was rising because consumers were shifting from commodities to services whose output could not be expanded very rapidly and whose quality improvements are more difficult to measure.

Real and Apparent Change

If prices are rising over time, figures on gross national product and its components will overstate actual increases in the output of goods from year to year. To obtain a truer picture of the expansion in the nation's output and income, GNP data must be adjusted by an index of prices. The implicit price deflators constructed by the Bureau of Economic Analysis are used to transform GNP data into dollars of constant purchasing power. Gross national product in 1958 prices for selected years from 1929 to 1960 and for each year from 1960 to 1974 is given in table 8E.

That isn't nearly as impressive as the somewhat misleading picture in table 8A. Gross national product actually fell in 1970 and 1974. The apparent increase shown in table 8A was due to inflation; the real value

Year	Consumer Price Index (1967 = 100)	Wholesale Price Index (1967 = 100)	Implicit GNP Deflator (1958 = 100)	(1972 = 100)
1929	51.3	49.1	50.6	
1930	50.0	44.6	49.3	
1931	45.6	37.6	44.8	
1932	40.9	33.6	40.2	
1933	38.8	34.0	39.3	
1934	40.1	38.6	42.2	
1935	41.1	41.3	42.6	
1936	41.5	41.7	42.7	
1937	43.0	44.5	44.5	
1938	42.2	40.5	43.9	
1939	41.6	39.8	43.2	
1940	42.0	40.5	43.9	
1941	44.1	45.1	47.2	
1942	48.8	50.9	53.0	
1943	51.8	53.3	56.8	
1944	52.7	53.6	58.2	
1945	53.9	54.6	59.7	
1946	58.5	62.3	66.7	43.9
1947	66.9	76.5	74.6	49.7
1948	72.1	82.8	79.6	53.1
1949	71.4	78.7	79.1	52.6
1950	72.1	81.8	80.2	53.6
1951	77.8	91.1	85.6	57.3
1952	79.5	88.6	87.5	58.0
1953	80.1	87.4	88.3	58.9
1954	80.5	87.6	89.6	59.7
1955	80.2	87.8	90.9	61.0
1956	81.4	90.7	94.0	62.9
1957	84.3	93.3	97.5	65.0
1958	86.6	94.6	100.0	66.1
1959	87.3	94.8	101.7	67.5
1960	88.7	94.9	103.3	68.7
1961	89.6	94.5	104.6	69.3
1962	90.6	94.8	105.8	70.6
1963	91.7	94.5	107.2	71.6
1964	92.9	94.7	108.9	72.7
1965	94.5	96.6	110.9	74.3
1966	97.2	99.8	113.9	76.8
1967	100.0	100.0	117.6	79.0
1968	104.2	102.5	122.3	82.6
1969	109.8	106.5	128.2	86.7
1970	116.3	110.4	135.2	91.4
1971	121.3	113.9	141.4	96.0
1972	125.3	119.1	146.1	100.0
1973	133.1	134.7	154.3	105.9
1974	147.7	160.1	170.2	116.2

Source: Bureau of Labor Statistics and Bureau of Economic Analysis. The Bureau of Economic Analysis changed the base year for the GNP Deflator to 1972 in series revisions published in 1976.

	Table 8E ADJUSTED GROSS NATIONAL PRODUCT	
Year	Gross National Product in 1958 Prices	Percentage Change from Preceding Year *Shown*
1929	$203.6 billion	———
1933	141.5	−30.1%
1939	209.4	48.0
1944	361.3	72.5
1950	355.3	−2.7
1955	438.0	23.7
1960	487.7	11.3
1961	497.2	1.9*
1962	529.8	6.6
1963	551.0	4.0
1964	581.1	5.5
1965	617.8	6.3
1966	658.1	6.5
1967	675.2	2.6
1968	706.6	4.7
1969	725.6	2.7
1970	722.5	−0.4
1971	746.3	3.3
1972	792.5	6.2
1973	839.2	5.9
1974	821.1	−2.2

Source: Bureau of Economic Analysis
*Prior percentage changes are for periods greater than one year.

of goods produced in those years declined from the preceding year. This is consistent with what we know about the rising level of unemployment in both years and the labeling of each as a recession year.

The "Cost of Living Index"

Ordinary citizens experience inflation directly when they find that their income no longer stretches as far as it used to. They experience it indirectly when they pick up their newspapers and read that the Consumer Price Index rose 1.6 points in the past month or that it shows inflation increasing at a 14% annual rate. That's significant news for a lot of people. Household budget makers slump a little lower and think a little longer about new ways to cut corners. More than five million workers get ready for an increase in their hourly wage, because the "cost of living index" has been incorporated into many labor contracts under what are called escalator clauses: when the index of consumer prices goes up, employers increase wages. About thirty million Americans receiving Social Security can anticipate an increase in those payments, because we now use the CPI to adjust Social Security benefits. Politicians in office tremble at the news because the public expects government to prevent such things somehow. Business executives take an anxious look at their inventories and an equally anxious look at the statements being made by politicians, because they know that a rapidly rising consumer price index can lead to significant changes in both the economic and the political environment within which business operates.

An economic indicator as important as the Consumer Price Index ought to be well understood by the public. The aim of the Bureau of Labor Statistics is to provide a measure of changes in the average prices of representative goods regularly purchased by typical wage and salary earners living in cities. Don't nod too quickly. That's not quite the same as measuring *the* price level.

There's obviously no practical way to keep track of *all* prices. The BLS must use sampling procedures that it hopes will adequately portray the price movements of all those goods whose prices it's trying to summarize. But it makes no attempt to measure the prices of every kind of good. The CPI is a *consumer* price index and not an index of prices paid for raw materials or for the other intermediate goods purchased by businesses. Moreover, it's not even a measure of prices paid by *all* consumers; it tries to determine the prices paid for consumer goods by urban wage earners and clerical workers. Even that, though, is an impossible task, since no two families buy exactly the same collection of goods each month.

So the BLS must begin by deciding exactly which goods will be included in its periodic sampling of prices. More than 400 separate items are currently used to construct the CPI. Here are some of them, just to give you the flavor: restaurant meals, cinammon rolls, liverwurst, cucumbers, pretzels, furnace repairing, sofas, baby sitting, socks, slacks, sneakers, new and used automobiles, cough syrup, psychiatric services, aerosol shaving cream, 35-millimeter color film, evening bowling fees, and funeral services. The entire list can be inspected in the statistical tables at the back of any issue of the *Monthly Labor Review*.

The Problem of Weighting

Far more items must necessarily be excluded than can be incorporated into the BLS samples. A lot of thought and investigation goes into the choice of representative goods, goods that typical families will regularly purchase and that will accurately reflect also the prices of all the goods excluded from consideration. But an even tougher decision still has to be

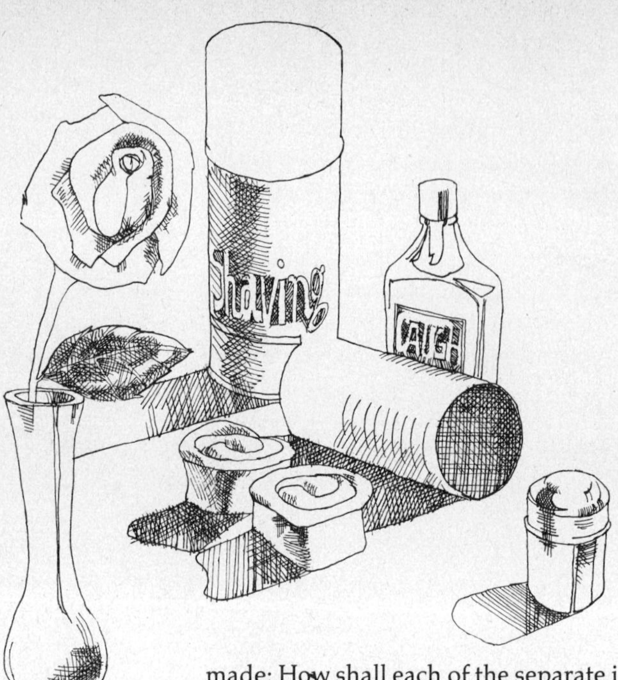

made: How shall each of the separate items be *weighted?* This is the familiar rabbit-and-horse-stew problem. The stew is not half-and-half if it contains one rabbit and one horse. Items on which consumers spend a larger percentage of their income must be weighted more heavily in the index if the composite is truly to reflect changes in the purchasing power of the consumer's dollar.

To illustrate the nature and seriousness of the weighting problem we can compare expenditure patterns in the 1930s with expenditure patterns in the 1960s. In the period 1934–36, according to a BLS survey conducted for the purpose of constructing appropriate weights, 35.4% of total consumer expenditures went for food and 8.2% for transportation. Now if food and transportation prices could be counted on always to go up or down at the same percentage rate, there would be no problem. Indeed, if all prices moved in perfect synchronization, any single item chosen at random could make up the entire price index. But that doesn't happen. So the BLS must sample the prices of many goods and must then weight them appropriately. For example, a 10% increase in food prices and a 2% increase in transportation prices doesn't average out to 6%. Since food expenditures were about 4.3 times as large as transportation expenditures, food had to be counted more than four times as heavily in constructing the average of the two. A more accurate average of the two would therefore be [4.3 (10%) + 1 (2%)] ÷ 5.3, or about 8.5%.

But expenditure patterns change over time with changing tastes, technologies, and incomes. The BLS survey for the years 1960–61 revealed that only 22.4% of consumer expenditures were for food and 13.9% for transportation. The appropriate weights had changed in one generation from approximately 4.3 to 1 to about 1.6 to 1. The same percentage increases of 10% and 2% would have yielded in the early 1960s an average price increase of [1.6 (10%) + 1 (2%)] ÷ 2.6, or only about 6.9%. That's a considerable difference.

And it makes a difference in how we interpret recent changes in the CPI. The weights used in constructing the index are based on surveys like the ones cited above. Since 1964 the BLS has used weights derived from its survey of 1960–61 expenditures. A new survey was made for the years 1972–73, but the BLS will not be able to incorporate the results into its calculation of the CPI until 1977. As a result, the impact of diverse price movements now shows up in the overall index of consumer prices in a way appropriate to the spending patterns of a decade and a half ago.

How much distortion does that introduce into the CPI? It can introduce quite a bit when prices are advancing at markedly diverse rates, as they did, for example, in 1973. Look at table 8F.

Food led the way in pushing or pulling the overall CPI up by 10.8 points, or almost 8½%, in 1973. But that means the CPI overstated actual consumer inflation during this year if consumers were purchasing *relatively* less food in 1973 than they had done in 1960–61. Since food does become a less important item in the average market basket as income rises, and since real per capita disposable income rose by more than 50% from 1960 to 1973, we can be fairly sure that the 1973 increase in the CPI overstated the amount of actual inflation.

The problem is even more difficult than this argument suggests, however. The fixed weights of the CPI are relative *physical quantities* in the base period. That means in effect that the BLS calculates the index by comparing 1967 prices times 1967 quantities-purchased with current prices times *1967 quantities-purchased*. Notice that current prices are not multiplied by current quantities but by the quantities purchased in the base period when relative prices may have been markedly different. That can cause serious distortions when prices change in a highly diverse way because, as the law of demand asserts, consumers alter the quantities of various goods purchased when their relative prices change. The CPI thus reflected the 1973 increase in beef prices as if those increases prompted no reduc-

	All Items	Food	Housing	Apparel and Upkeep	Transportation	Health and Recreation
Table 8F CONSUMER PRICE INDICES (1967 = 100)						
January, 1973	127.7	128.6	131.4	123.0	121.0	127.8
December, 1973	138.5	151.3	140.6	130.5	126.7	133.0

tions at all in the amount of beef purchased. Similarly, fuel oil and coal prices rose 45% in the twelve months following December 1972; but the overall CPI ignored the possibility (certainty?) that people responded to such a dramatic price increase by reducing their consumption of fuel oil and coal.

THE WEIGHTING GAME

The easiest way to see the effect of weighting decisions on a price index (or any index) is to work through an example.

In the year 1710 the typical consumer on Crusoe's Isle consumed 0.8 liters of ale and 1.0 kilo of bread per day. The price of ale was 5 clams per liter and the price of bread was 6 clams per kilo. In 1715 ale sold for 4 clams per liter and bread for 8 clams per kilo. The consumer price index in 1715, with 1710 prices and weights as the base, was

$$\text{CPI} = \left(\frac{(4 \times 0.8) + (8 \times 1.0)}{(5 \times 0.8) + (6 \times 1.0)}\right)100 = \left(\frac{11.2}{10}\right)100 = 112$$

This is the way in which the Bureau of Labor Statistics calculates the Consumer Price Index.

But with ale cheaper and bread more expensive in 1715, consumers would probably substitute ale for bread. Suppose that in 1715 the typical consumer bought 1.0 liter of ale and 0.9 kilos of bread per day. If we use 1715 weights to calculate the price index, we get

$$\text{CPI} = \left(\frac{(4 \times 1.0) + (8 \times 0.9)}{(5 \times 1.0) + (6 \times 0.9)}\right)100 = \left(\frac{11.2}{10.4}\right)100 = 107.7$$

The first index overstates the impact of the price changes because it fails to take account of substitution. A person whose income in 1710 was 100 clams would be *better off* in 1715 with an income of 112 clams. The income of 112 clams would still allow the original purchases of 0.8 liters of ale and 1.0 kilo of bread; but by substituting, the consumer could be better off.

The index with 1715 weights understates the impact. The typical consumer with an income of 107.7 clams in 1715 could have purchased the ale and bread actually bought in 1715 for only 100 clams in 1710. But at 1710 prices he would have chosen a different mix; and 107.7 clams is not enough to make him as well off in 1715 as he would have been with 100 clams in 1710.

The Problem of Quality Changes

The diligent statisticians at the BLS have still other problems to worry about. One is how to take account of *quality* changes. Some are comparatively simple to handle. Specific improvements in the quality of automobiles are treated as increases in quantity and are valued at their estimated cost. That makes sense. A car with an automatic starter is not more expensive than one that has to be cranked just because it costs more; it *is* more; it's a different product. There are plenty of problems even in this to tax the ingenuity of the BLS people. For example, are seat belts an improvement in quality for the person who refuses to wear them? Tastes differ, and quality is inseparable from considerations of taste. But the problems with automobiles at least seem manageable.

Less manageable is a problem like this one: When the cost of a hospital room goes up from $30 to $50 a day, is that a genuine price increase if at the same time improved drugs or other medical procedures reduce the

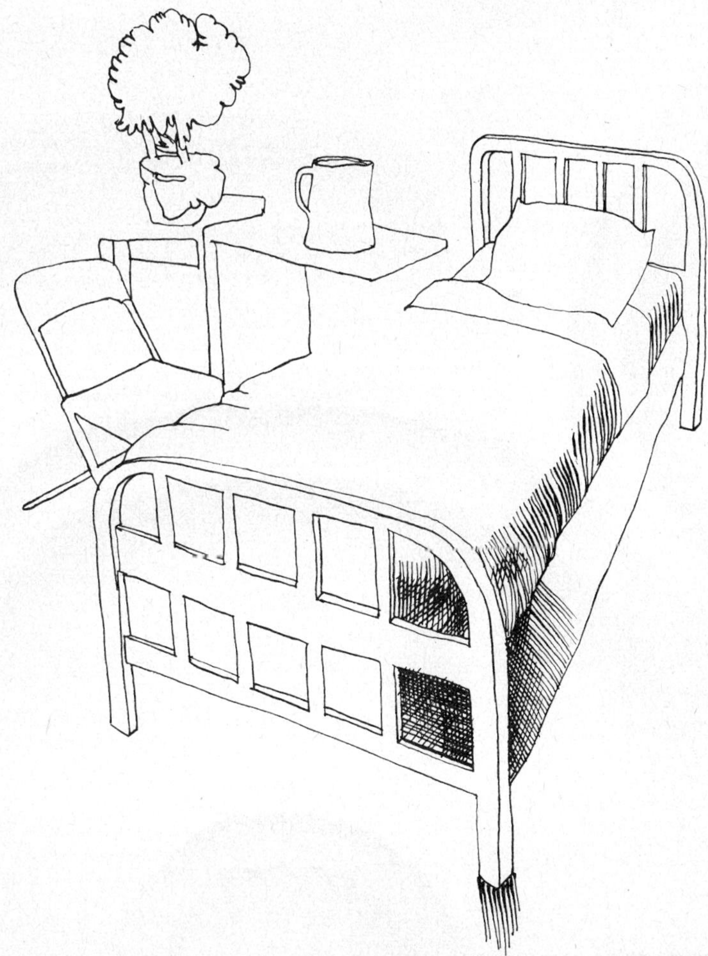

hospital stay from six days to three days? The cost of health (and that's the consumer good most of us are after; few people go to the hospital for a vacation) would have *decreased* in this case from $180 to $150.

Or try this one. One of the authors thinks that the best movies being made today are far more enjoyable than the best movies made a decade ago. The price of movie tickets has also gone up over the decade. But how much more expensive is movie *entertainment?* Three times as much entertainment for twice the money is a price reduction, isn't it? Some economists have argued that the CPI, because of its inability to take quality improvements adequately into account, overstates increases in the price level by 1% to $1\frac{1}{2}$% per year.

Decomposing the GNP Deflator

The Bureau of Economic Analysis confronts most of the same problems in constructing the GNP deflator, and so it is subject to many of the same limitations as the consumer price index. We see how misleading an aggregate index of this type can be if we compare the changes within a set of price indices during the period 1958 to 1964. Contrast the following percentage changes over those years:

7.3%	Consumer price index, all items
8.9	GNP deflator, total
7.4	GNP deflator, personal consumption expenditures
.4	GNP deflator, personal consumption expenditures on durable goods
4.9	GNP deflator, personal consumption expenditures on nondurable goods
13.1	GNP deflator, personal consumption expenditures on services
7.6	GNP deflator, total investment expenditures
15.7	GNP deflator, government purchases of goods
7.1	GNP deflator, total private sector
28.4	GNP deflator, total government sector

It would appear that "the" price level rose from 1958 to 1964 largely because the price of services and of general government operations, which are dominated by services, increased substantially. Does this have any implications for policy? Should we have concluded that the apparent inflation of those years was an illusion? If a family shifts from eating beef to eating lobster, their "cost of living" increases because they are paying higher prices for food; but we would not want to attribute this to inflation. If a large part of the public shifts from beef to lobster, they will similarly pay higher prices for food. But in addition they will do what one family by itself could not do: raise further the price of lobster relative to beef, because the quantity of lobster supplied cannot easily be increased in response to a larger demand. This shift in the public's eating preferences will consequently raise "the" price level.

There just is no satisfactory answer to the question, What is *really* happening to *the* price level? Every price index is a theoretical construct subject to misinterpretation by anyone who doesn't know how it was constructed. We'll provide one further example that will also give us a chance to look briefly at the other price index presented in table 8D, the Wholesale Price Index.

Inflation and the Wholesale Price Index

Suppose we agree that the economy experiences *real* inflation when the total quantity of goods demanded at current prices is greater than the total quantity supplied. That definition is consistent with the analysis of price behavior presented in chapter 3. If the definition is to be empirically useful, however, we must find a gauge which will register any gaps between aggregate demand and aggregate supply. Is the Wholesale Price Index a good candidate for the job? This is an index of changes in the average prices of basic agricultural and industrial commodities. It seems reasonable to assume that these prices will be especially sensitive to changes in the relation between aggregate demand and aggregate supply, because the commodities enter into so many different production processes and because their prices are established by the bids and offers of numerous users and producers. If we accept this hypothesis and look at the behavior of the WPI from 1958 to 1964, we can conclude that there was no genuine inflation during these years. The index varied only within the narrow range of 94.5 to 94.9.

But a sensitive gauge is not always a reliable gauge. The Wholesale Price Index rose 38% from January 1973 to December 1974, almost certainly overstating by a considerable amount the degree of overall inflation during this period. The WPI often magnifies the effects of changes in its components, because they enter as inputs into the production of other components. Consider the effect of fuel prices, for example. The composite index of prices for coal, coke, gas, electricity, crude petroleum, and refined petroleum products increased 87% from January 1973 to December 1974, largely because the Organization of Petroleum Exporting Countries became a successful cartel during this period. That directly raised the price of petroleum, which in turn caused the price of refined petroleum products to increase, which in turn created a greater demand for substitute fuels whose production could not be quickly accelerated so that their prices also rose, which boosted the cost of farm products, chemicals, metal products, and other commodities also entering into the Wholesale Price Index.

Our most sensitive measure of discrepancies between aggregate demand and aggregate supply under some circumstances may become our most unreliable measure under other circumstances, suggesting once again that "hard facts" are not good substitutes for informed judgment. But informed judgment presupposes an ability to see the larger picture and the way in which events relate to one another. That's the job of theory. We must now turn our attention to the theoretical frameworks that economists have constructed for analyzing the phenomena of recession and inflation.

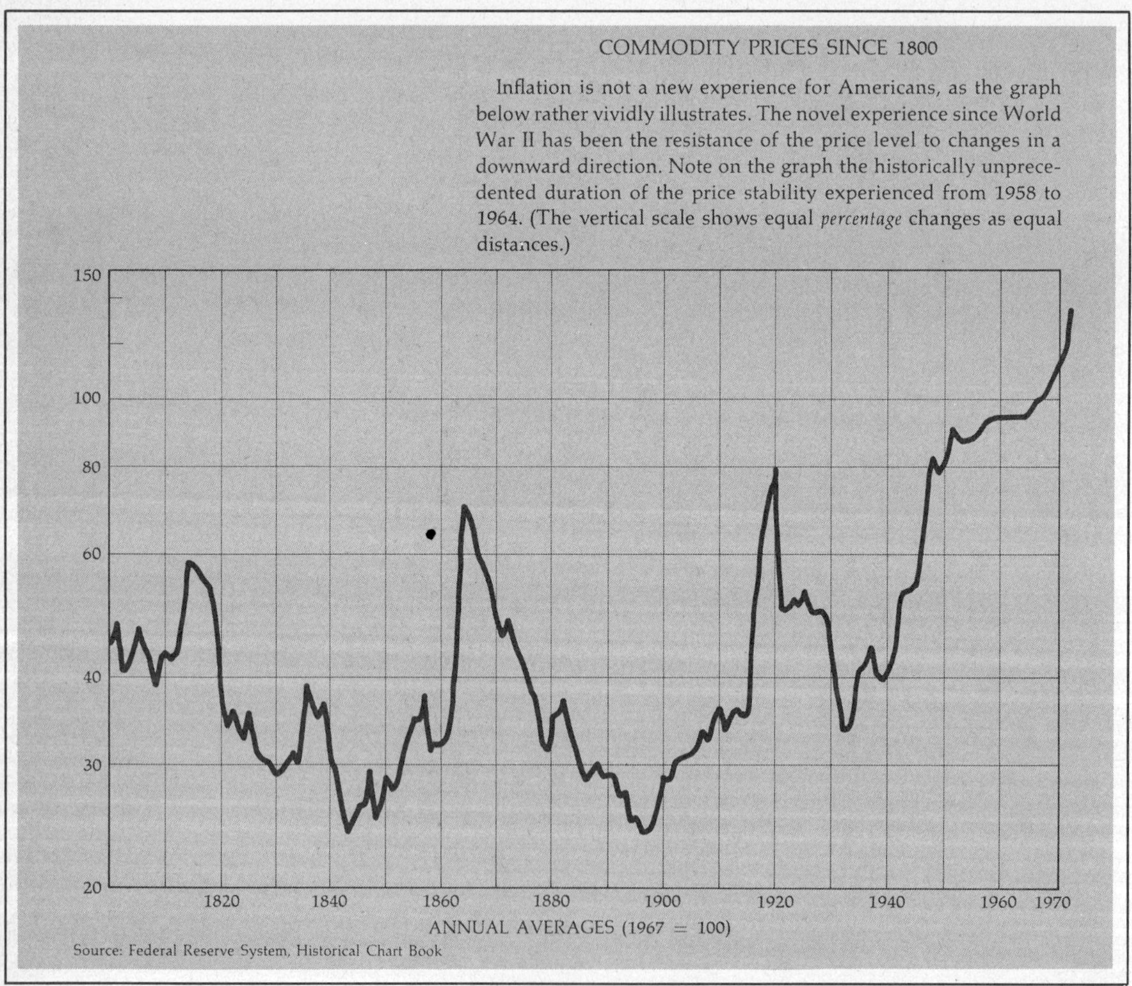

COMMODITY PRICES SINCE 1800

Inflation is not a new experience for Americans, as the graph below rather vividly illustrates. The novel experience since World War II has been the resistance of the price level to changes in a downward direction. Note on the graph the historically unprecedented duration of the price stability experienced from 1958 to 1964. (The vertical scale shows equal *percentage* changes as equal distances.)

Source: Federal Reserve System, Historical Chart Book

Once Over Lightly

The income and product accounts compiled by the Bureau of Economic Analysis are our most comprehensive measure of aggregate economic activity.

Gross national product is the market value of all the final goods produced in a year. It is calculated by adding together the purchases of final goods by domestic consumers, investors, and governments plus the net purchases of foreigners (their purchases of our goods minus our purchases of theirs).

Gross national product can also be calculated by summing the value added to production by each business firm. This will be the total of each firm's before-tax payments to suppliers of labor, land, capital, and risk (*national income* in the narrow sense) plus indirect business taxes and a few other minor items (*net national product*) and capital consumption allowances. The value of gross national product as calculated through value added would equal exactly the value as calculated through total expenditures if it were possible to measure all the components without error.

Final goods produced but not purchased during a year are considered to have been purchased by the firms that produced them; they are additions to inventory, which is one of the components of investment. This seemingly minor point is singled out for review because, as we shall see in chapter 11, many economists believe that unintended changes in business inventories are a key factor in the understanding of aggregate fluctuations.

Disposable personal income can be calculated from national income by subtracting corporate profits taxes, social insurance taxes, personal taxes, and undistributed corporate profits and adding government and business transfer payments to persons, interest paid by government, and the net interest paid by consumers. What the Bureau of Economic Analysis calls *personal income* is disposable income before the subtraction of personal taxes.

The income and product accounts are not intended to be, and should not be, used as a measure of gross national welfare. A great deal of important goods production that contributes to social welfare (home and family production, for example) is not included in gross national product; and many of the costs of production that reduce social welfare (environmental pollution, for example) are also not taken into account.

The principal indices used to measure changes in the price level are the Consumer Price Index and the Wholesale Price Index constructed by the Bureau of Labor Statistics and the Implicit GNP Deflator constructed by the Bureau of Economic Analysis.

Difficult problems of selection, sampling, and weighting must be resolved if an index is to reflect in a reliable way changes in the purchasing power of money or the average money price of goods. It is probably not possible to construct a single index that will satisfactorily measure changes in *the* price level.

Real, as distinct from nominal, changes in income or output are calculated by dividing data on national product in current dollar terms by an index of the price level.

QUESTIONS FOR DISCUSSION

1. Can a society's output increase faster than its income? Can its income increase faster than its output?

2. Suppose that every American family had a counterfeiting operation in the back room and added $40 per week to family income by printing four ten-dollar bills each week. Would this increase national income without a corresponding increase in national output?

3. Why would it be misleading for the Bureau of Economic Analysis to include transfer payments in its calculation of national income? Why would it be misleading for the BEA *not* to include transfer payments in its calculation of personal income? (Hint: Question 3 is related to questions 1 and 2.)

4. BEA statisticians strive to avoid double counting in their calculations of gross national product. Why would there be double counting if the total output of wheat and the total output of bread in a given year were both included in gross national product? Do you understand how double counting is avoided by *not* counting sales of intermediate products *or* by counting only the *value added* by producers?

5. List some ways in which increased *inefficiency* could cause gross national product to rise. Are there any goods contributing to the total of gross national product whose rising output clearly reflects *reduced* welfare?

6. Are government purchases of commodities and services consumption expenditures or investment expenditures? They must be one or the other. Why do you suppose the Bureau of Economic Analysis groups them separately?

7. Why must total expenditures for final goods by consumers, investors, and government and the net purchases of foreigners necessarily equal gross national product? What if some of the year's output is not sold?

8. If it could be shown that a rising gross national product promoted a rising level of anxiety, tension, and conflict in the population, would you favor deducting these psychological costs to obtain the true value of gross national product? How would you do it?

9. Would you favor including the services of housewives in the calculation of gross national product? What arguments could be given for doing so? Are there any good reasons for continuing to exclude these services from the calculation of GNP?

10. As an economy industrializes, a larger percentage of its population tends to enter the labor force as conventionally measured. Less production occurs in the home for family use and a larger proportion of total product passes through the marketplace. What does this imply about the usefulness of GNP data in industrializing societies? Will estimates of per capita income derived from GNP data tend to overstate or understate improvement over time?

11. To be certain that you understand the relation between nominal GNP, real GNP, and the price level, try deriving either the level of GNP in current dollars (table 8A), the level of GNP in 1958 dollars (table 8E), or the Implicit GNP Deflator (table 8D) from the other two for any given year.

12. How much better off financially was a person in 1967 than in 1953 if his income increased over that period by 50%? Use the data of the Consumer Price Index to answer. Do you think your answer overestimates or underestimates the real improvement in the person's living level. Why?

13. Suppose that in 1960 the price of a man's white dress shirt was $5 and the price of a colored dress shirt was $6, and in 1970 the price of a white shirt was $6 and the price of a colored shirt was $8. If 80% of the dress shirts purchased by American males were white and 20% were colored, what was the percentage increase in the price of dress shirts? Would your answer be different if in 1970 80% of the shirts purchased were colored and 20% were white?

14. From 1967 to 1973 the price of cornflakes increased $4\frac{1}{2}$%, the price of refined sugar 25%, milk 27%, eggs 60%, and bacon 61%. What happened over this period to the price of breakfast?

15. From 1967 to 1973 the average price of a visit to a physician's office rose 39.5%. During the same period the average price of prescription antibiotics decreased 28.9%. Did the price of medical care rise or fall? Why might some families find that the net result was a decrease in the price of medical care while others experienced a net increase? What changes in medical care practices might be induced by these divergent price movements?

MONEY AND THE BANKING SYSTEM

The time has come to talk about *money*. You probably didn't even notice that we have come this far without discussing it. The previous chapters, after all, were replete with dollar signs, and dollars are money. But the dollar referred to earlier was simply a conventional unit for discussing relative values, a common denominator that enabled us to compare and add apples and oranges, convenient transportation and unpolluted air, goods in the hand and goods in the bush, the services of engineers and the gains from exchange.

THE USE OF MONEY

One important function of money in a social system is to provide such a unit for accounting. We might have used such other common denominators as bread or human labor. We could have stated the prices of gasoline and sugar in terms of the number of standard loaves for which a gallon of one and a pound of the other would exchange. Or we could have expressed the gross national product as the equivalent of so many hours of "average" labor time. The fact that we don't actually exchange something doesn't prevent us from using it to express comparative or total values. Prices are sometimes expressed in "mills" even though we don't use coins with a value of $\frac{1}{10}$ cent. Similarly British merchants often state prices in "guineas," coins that have not been issued in England since 1813. Both mills and guineas illustrate this accounting function of money.

Chapter Nine

A Medium of Exchange

We're all accustomed to thinking and talking about prices in terms of dollars, because dollars are what we use in the process of exchanging one good for another. We have had a lot of practice in translating the prices of diverse commodities and services into dollar terms. Money functions effectively as a unit of accounting because of all the experience we've had with its function as a medium of exchange.

A "medium of exchange" is just what the words say: a middle-thing used in the process of exchanging one good for another. The alternative to employing a medium of exchange is barter: exchanging the goods at our command directly for the goods we want to obtain.

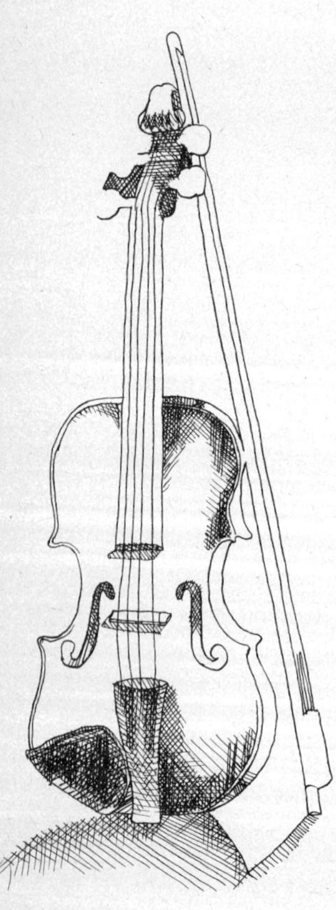

The advantages of using money rather than a barter system are enormous. The cost of exchanging would be far greater, and social wealth as a consequence far less, if there were no money to facilitate the process. In an economic system limited to barter, people would have to spend an inordinate amount of time searching for others with whom they could advantageously exchange. A violin maker would have to find a grocer, a haberdasher, an electrical utility, and a glue supplier, among many others, all willing to accept violins in return for the goods they handle. All that time devoted to searching would be time unavailable for violin making, and the production of violins would fall. Aware of the high costs of exchanging, people would increasingly try to produce goods for their own use to avoid the necessity of searching out others from whom they could buy and to whom they could sell. In a society confined to barter, specialization would decline dramatically. And that means, of course, that people would lose the benefits that accrue from the systematic and widespread exploitation of comparative advantage. The evolution of some kind of money system in almost every known society, even when conditions were extremely unfavorable for it, is eloquent testimony to the advantages of having a generally accepted medium of exchange. When official monetary systems broke down in Western Europe at the end of World War II, cigarettes were widely pressed into service as a substitute medium of exchange.

If money is that important, why hasn't it been introduced earlier? There are several reasons. First of all, we took its existence for granted until now and just assumed you wouldn't notice. Second, the existence or non-existence of money does not, by and large, affect the concepts we were using in the first six chapters. In fact, we usually wanted you to ignore money, to pretend it wasn't there. The important concept of opportunity cost, a major unifying thread in the economic way of thinking, goes beyond the *monetary* notion that first comes to mind when people think about costs. Obsession with money and monetary values can easily obscure understanding of the way the economy functions and of the real costs of economic activities. That's why economists in the nineteenth century sometimes spoke of money as a *veil* that had to be pushed aside before one could see clearly the nature of economic relationships. A vivid illustration of what they meant is provided by the story (perhaps only a legend) of the business executive called to Washington during World War II to help organize military production. Informed one morning that a key defense plant had burned to the ground, he shrugged it off with the comment, "It was insured, wasn't it?" But money from an insurance company does not produce synthetic rubber or "secrete steel rails."[1] Thus a preoccupation with monetary values can sometimes obscure the real forces responsible for the creation of wealth.

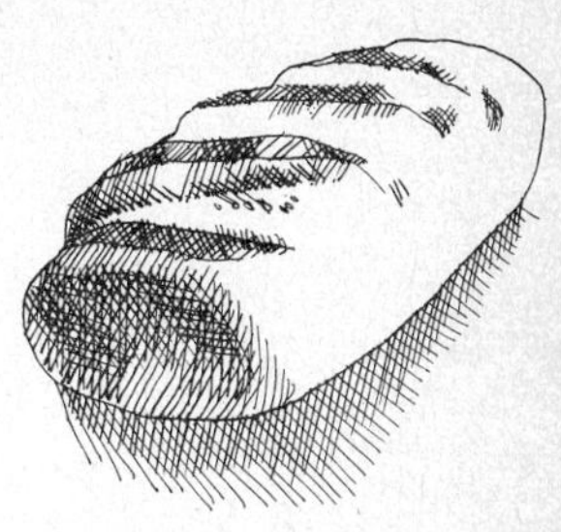

Monetary Complications

We have already encountered one problem, however, that cannot be talked about without introducing money specifically. And that is the problem of inflation. For inflation means a decline in the value of money relative to all other goods or, in more familiar terms, a rise in the money price of goods generally. If you immediately start applying the concepts of economic reasoning to the issue of inflation, you will suspect that a decline in the price (or purchasing power) of money occurs for the same reason that a decline occurs in the price of parsnips or pocket calculators: the supply has increased relative to the demand. And you will be right on target.

But while money is like other goods in many ways, it also has some peculiar characteristics that make it a unique good. Fluctuations in the price of parsnips pose major problems for parsnip growers and minor problems for those who buy them. Fluctuations in the price of money, however, are fluctuations in the measuring rod of economic decision makers that make decisions more difficult and uncertain. Money, as it turns out, is more than the lubricant of the economic system, the coordinator of exchange that adds to our wealth through its power to extend specialization. It can grease the skids as well as oil the economic system.

Many of the difficulties created by money arise from the fact that it is *not* exchanged for goods the moment it's received. If it were, we would in effect have a barter system. The violin maker who wants to eat sells his product to the violinists he can find when he finds them, and *holds* the money he receives—at least until he can get to the grocery store. That might be fifteen minutes later if he's very hungry; or it might be a week later, a month later, a year later. If those nineteenth century economists

1. Clarence E. Ayres relates the story in *The Theory of Economic Progress*, first published in 1944.

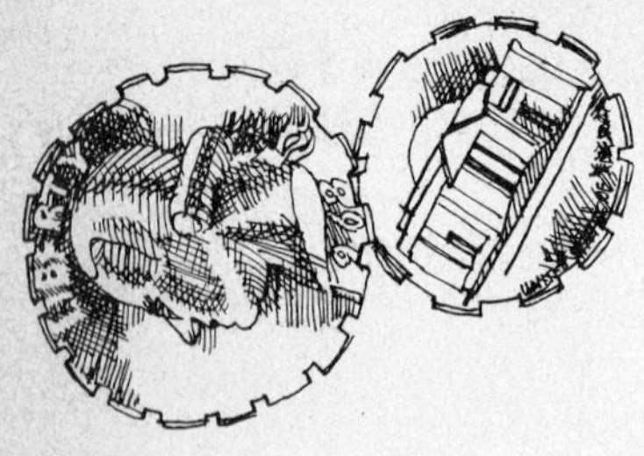

to whom we referred a moment ago had examined more closely the implications of the fact that people do hold money for periods of time before they spend it, they might more easily have seen that money is not a mere veil to be pushed aside if one wishes to view the functioning of the economic system. Money is a part of that functioning, and it can become a cause of its malfunctioning.

Liquidity and the Demand for Money

"Nobody desires money for its own sake," we often say, "but only for the sake of what it can buy." King Midas is supposedly the exception that proves the rule: he was a fool. It's quite true that we accept money in exchange for the goods we have to offer because we intend to use the money to purchase other goods we want. But we do not, as a matter of fact, immediately exchange the money we acquire for some other goods. We hold money, for longer or shorter periods of time, and wait for the right opportunity or for the arrival of some future obligation. If we could not do this, money would actually have no value as a medium of exchange. Money is useful to the violin maker because it enables him to sell his products whenever and wherever he finds a would-be fiddler, and then wait until the opportune occasion to purchase corned beef or pay his electric bill. It follows from this that normal people, and not just King Midas, have a *demand for money.* We want money to hold and not just to spend. The fact is that when we acquire money we rarely know exactly how or when we will spend it. We simply add the money to our stock of assets and wait.

The special advantage of money as an asset to hold, or as one of many forms in which we can store wealth, is its *liquidity.* Money is the most liquid asset. That's what qualifies it to be called money. The more liquid something is, the more moneylike it is. When an asset is completely liquid, it has attained the zenith of moneyness.

What do we mean by liquidity? *The liquidity of an asset depends on the cost of exchanging it for other assets.* An asset that can be exchanged for any other asset at a zero cost is a completely liquid asset. The Federal Reserve note in your wallet is an excellent example. It's an asset you can give in exchange for a great variety of other things you might want because sellers of every sort are willing to accept it without question and at face value. An asset that could not be exchanged at all because no one else would be willing to give anything in exchange for it would be a completely illiquid asset. (Your toothbrush?) In Seattle, a Canadian dollar may be as liquid an asset as a U.S. Federal Reserve note. Farther south, away from the border, its liquidity declines, until merchants refuse to accept Canadian money altogether. If you own a government savings bond, you can exchange it for other assets, but first you'll have to incur the cost of a trip to the bank where you exchange the bond for currency. So government savings bonds are liquid assets, but they're not as liquid as Federal Reserve notes. Are they money? Just how liquid does an asset have to be to qualify as money? That turns out to be a difficult question and competent people disagree on the answer. We'll have to come back to it. In this world of continuous variables and every shade of grey, assets will rarely hit either end of the liquid-illiquid continuum. Most assets are somewhat liquid. The point to remember is that an asset becomes more moneylike, or liquid, as the cost of exchanging it for other assets approaches zero.

The concept of liquidity is important in the economist's way of looking at the world. To be liquid is to have a greater range of choices, better opportunities, and hence more wealth. Your wealth, by which we always mean the range of options available to you, depends (among other things) upon the precise forms in which you're currently holding the goods you own, or, in the useful jargon of finance, upon the *composition of your asset portfolio.* Suppose, for example, that you're in a strange city with a checkbook but no currency and you're hungry. The restaurant signs saying "No Checks Accepted" establish that you are at the moment not as wealthy as you would be with twenty dollars less in your checking account and twenty dollars more in your wallet.

The Cost of Liquidity

Liquidity is valuable and so people have a demand for liquidity. But that's only one part of the picture. In order to possess liquidity you must typically sacrifice other advantages. For example, if you're keeping a sizeable amount in your checking account in order to have it immediately available for purchases you might want to make, you're sacrificing the interest you could earn from having that amount in a savings account. So the opportunity cost of liquidity sets limits to the quantity of liquidity people will demand. The demand curve for liquidity, like all properly behaved demand curves in economics, slopes downward to the right.

The concept of a demand for money often puzzles people; and that, along with the importance of the concept, explains why we're trying to help you think it through carefully. Do not confuse the demand for money with the desire for income. Income is a flow; money is a stock. Your income is the stream of assets coming into your possession, measured per week or month or year, and most people understandably would like it to be larger. Your demand for money expresses the *form* in which you prefer to hold the assets currently in your possession.

Think about it in terms of your own experience. *You* have a demand for liquidity. You probably hold some fraction of your wealth, pitifully small though your total wealth may be, in the form of currency or a checking account. These assets yield you no physiological nutrition, no comfort when reclining, no transportation service, and not even any

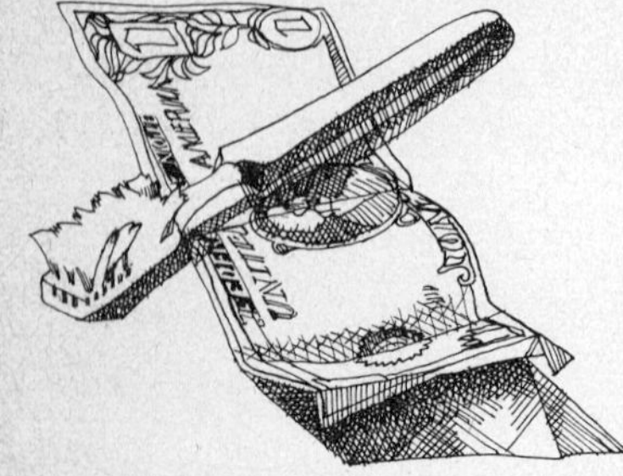

interest income. Why don't you, upon acquiring money, immediately exchange it for something that can minister to your wants? The answer is that one of your wants is for liquidity. Currency in the wallet and a balance in the checking account give you room to maneuver. When you have a supply of these highly liquid assets, you are more free to take advantage of opportunities that present themselves. You are better equipped to handle emergencies, which might take the form of a sudden yen for new bell-bottoms, a threat by the telephone company to cut off your service, or an unexpected chance to attend a concert.

The cost of liquidity is the value of whatever you sacrifice by being liquid. So you don't keep *all* of your monthly allowance in the form of money until the next allowance comes in; but you do try to keep *some*. You are guided in part by the relative liquidity of other assets you possess. If you know that you can sell your record collection in a pinch, you will regard it as a contribution toward your overall liquidity and reduce somewhat your demand to hold money, the almost completely liquid asset. Your ability to borrow is also an important asset and one that may significantly affect your demand for money; if you can exchange your creditworthiness for money at a low cost, your creditworthiness is a highly liquid asset.

Your demand for money and other liquid assets will clearly vary with circumstances. If your monthly income is so small that every dollar you hold in reserve entails the sacrifice of something important to you, you will hold little money on the average. If your immediate future seems secure and well provided for because the college functions capably in loco parentis, you will feel less desire for liquidity. Reckless souls despise liquidity; cautious ones crave it. If the future begins to look more uncertain, then, other things remaining equal, your demand for liquidity will increase. "More uncertain" doesn't necessarily mean more threatening. This uncertainty refers to the good opportunities that may unpredictably come your way as well as to the misfortunes that may strike.

Many economists believe that the public's demand for money or demand for liquidity is an important key to the understanding of aggregate economic stability. We'll be working with the concept in detail in chapter 13, but a brief summary at this point may prove helpful. The quantity of money people will want to hold is going to depend on their current and expected income; the larger their income the more money they will usually want to hold. It will also depend on their reading of the future; the more uncertain the future the more money they will want to hold. And it will depend on the opportunity cost of holding money; the larger the return they can expect from holding alternative assets, such as government bonds or shares in a mutual fund, the smaller the quantity of money they will want to hold.

BANKS AND THE CREATION OF MONEY

Enough of the demand for money. The time has come to talk about the stuff itself. What do we use in the United States as our medium of exchange? Where does it come from? Who decides how much there shall be? Our principal task in the remainder of this chapter and in chapter 10 will be to explain the interactions of private and governmental decision makers that create the supply of money.

When most people think about money they think immediately of green pieces of paper, called Federal Reserve notes, and coins of various sizes and colors. Economists lump these all together and call them *currency*. But what else do we use as a medium of exchange?

Bank Deposits Are Money

The most widely used medium of exchange is not currency but *demand deposit* credits in commercial banks, usually called checking accounts. These are deposits that can be withdrawn or transferred at the pleasure of the depositor or "on demand." Savings accounts are called *time deposits*, because banks may legally require advance notification of withdrawal.

Many students have trouble at first in seeing that demand deposits really are money. They themselves may handle all their transactions by means of currency; when they receive a check, they "cash" it—that is, they obtain currency for the check and spend the currency. But student habits are not typical of the transaction procedures of business firms, government units, and households. The overwhelming majority of exchanges, measured in dollar value, use demand deposits as the medium of exchange. A purchaser instructs his bank to transfer ownership of a portion of his deposit to the seller: he writes a check, in other words. The seller typically deposits the check instead of cashing it: she instructs her own bank to collect the sum whose transfer was ordered by the check writer. No currency at all changes hands. The bank in which the check is deposited makes an entry in its books; the bank on which the check is written makes an equal but opposite entry in its books.

It isn't hard to imagine a situation in which demand deposits are the *only* medium of exchange. As credit cards become more common, people will carry less currency and pay for more of their purchases with monthly checks. Couldn't *all* transactions be handled in this way? It would be possible, although inconvenient in some cases. But currency *could* disappear from existence without any reduction in our use of money as a medium of exchange.[1]

---

1. Credit cards are *not* a medium of exchange but a way of *postponing* payment for a purchase.

Currency plus demand deposits. Is that all? Suppose someone asked, "How much money do you have?" You would calculate the currency in your possession. Having read this far you would then add the balance in your checking account. Should you also add what you have in your savings account? You can get it out quickly or transfer it to your checking account. It's available for spending, even though savings accounts cannot be used directly as a medium of exchange. But then what of the deposit you have in a savings and loan institution? You could also convert that amount into ready cash. And why not also the government bonds you own? They can be cashed too. How far shall we go in calculating how much money you have? Your automobile could also be converted into currency or a demand deposit. Is it, therefore, money?

Notice what we've done now. We have subtly shifted the definition of money from "the commonly employed medium of exchange" to "liquid assets." If we adhered strictly to the definition of money as a medium of exchange, we would want to define the money supply in the United States as the *total of currency in circulation plus demand deposits at commercial banks.* For that is what we use to pay for almost all our purchases. To avoid double counting we must include only the currency that is in circulation and not the amount in bank vaults. Thus when someone deposits a $20 bill in his checking account, the money supply does not change. The demand deposit component rises by $20, but currency in circulation falls by $20. If we continued to count as money the currency now in the bank's possession, we would come to the highly misleading conclusion that deposits or withdrawals of currency from checking accounts change the quantity of the exchange medium held by the community. But they don't; they only change the *form* in which it is held. After you've written a check for "cash," you still have exactly as much money as before, and so does everyone else.

How Do We Want to Define the Money Supply?

But do we want to define money strictly as that which actually functions as the common medium of exchange? What we're really looking for in these chapters is an explanation of aggregate demand or total expenditures. As we shall see, that will depend in part upon the amount of money people are holding relative to the quantities of other assets that they own or would like to acquire. The more money people possess, other things being equal, the more likely they are to surrender some portion of it in exchange for an alternate asset when an attractive opportunity presents itself. Now it is quite clear that most people do not just look at their present stock of currency and demand deposits in deciding how much money they have. Savings held in commercial banks as time deposits

and savings held in such nonbank thrift institutions as savings and loan associations would be regarded by most people as "available cash." So shouldn't we include these deposits in our working definition of the money supply?

There is just no completely satisfactory way to decide what should go into the calculation of the money supply and what should be excluded. The central bankers of the United States, the managers of the Federal Reserve System, calculate the money supply in at least three major ways and publish these sets of figures as M_1, M_2, and M_3.

M_1 is demand deposits plus currency in circulation.

M_2 is M_1 plus time deposits in commercial banks—those banks which provide checking account service as well as accepting the deposits of savers, making loans, selling money orders, and so on.

M_3 is M_2 plus deposits in mutual savings banks and savings and loan associations—sometimes called nonbank thrift institutions.

The table below gives you some notion of the magnitude of the money stock by each of these measures. Since the money supply can and does fluctuate considerably from day to day, figures are usually expressed as averages over such periods of time as a month or a quarter. The numbers below are in billions of dollars and give the average of daily figures throughout the last month of three recent years.

Table 9A	MONEY SUPPLY IN BILLIONS OF DOLLARS		
	M_1	M_2	M_3
1967	186.9	349.6	532.6
1970	221.5	425.3	642.8
1973	271.5	572.2	895.3

Source: Board of Governors, Federal Reserve System

Whichever definition of the money supply we choose, they have all increased significantly since 1967. Moreover, the percentage rates of increase have varied considerably, both among the three measures of the money stock and from year to year within each measure.

But what difference does any of it make? Is there some correct level for the money supply or some ideal rate at which it ought to grow over time? These are important questions. Before you can make sense of the various answers that economists have given to them, however, you must understand something about how money is created and destroyed. What are the forces in both the private and the government sectors of the economy that interact to determine changes in the size of the money stock?

What Determines the Size of the Money Supply?

We can begin with what you know already or can figure out from what has been said. Individuals can directly change the relative sizes of these money stock measures by transferring funds from their checking accounts to their savings accounts or to a savings and loan association and back again. They can also, according to their preferences, hold their share of M_1 in the form of a demand deposit or as currency. The Fed (the common collective term for the Federal Reserve Banks) supplies whatever

amount of currency the public chooses to hold, and takes it back again whenever the public no longer wishes to hold it. Hence an increase in the public's net preference for currency over time deposits, perhaps at Christmas time or during the vacation season, will increase M_1. But since M_1's gain is M_2's loss and M_2 includes M_1, that would not bring about directly a change in the total of M_2.

The reason for mentioning all of this is that such changes in the composition of the public's money holdings have potentially significant indirect effects. Insofar as these preference shifts are seasonal and predictable, they pose no serious problem to the nation's monetary managers. There is mounting evidence, however, that the public is becoming more adept at shifting about among liquid and near-liquid assets and that this is making it more difficult for the Fed to control the supply of money with adequate precision. The issue is one to which we shall return.

The Crucial Role of Bank Loans

But none of this explains how it's possible for M_3 to increase. In December 1973, M_3 was 70% larger than it had been in 1967, as a consequence of a 45% rise in currency and demand deposits, an 85% increase in time deposits, and a 50% jump in deposits with nonbank thrift institutions. Where did all this additional money come from? The basic answer is that it came about through a net expansion of commercial bank loans. For *the money supply increases when commercial banks make loans to their customers and decreases when customers repay the loans they obtained from commercial banks.* That's the short of the story. The long of it is a bit more complicated but not really difficult to grasp.

Suppose your application for a loan of $500 from the First National Bank is approved. The lending officer will make out a deposit slip in your name for $500, initial it in some appropriate way, and hand it to a teller who will then credit your checking account with an additional $500. Demand deposits will have risen by $500. The money supply will be larger by that amount.

Where did the $500 come from? The bank *created* the $500 to lend you. Out of thin air? Not really. But the raw material isn't as important at this point as the fact that the bank really did create new money in making you a loan.

But what if you don't have a checking account at First National? Then the bank can open one and start you off with a $500 balance. But suppose you don't want a demand deposit—you want the money? Slips! A demand deposit *is* money. You can use the demand deposit to buy whatever it is you borrowed for. All right; but what if you decide to withdraw your $500 right away in $20 bills? Fine. The teller will accommodate you. The total of demand deposits will fall by $500, but the total of currency in circulation will increase by $500. The bank takes the currency from its vault, where it is *not* money, and gives it to you, whereupon it becomes currency held by the nonbank public or currency in circulation and hence *is* money.

Does it all seem too simple? Why don't banks keep on doing that indefinitely? It seems just like having your own money machine in the basement. We'll see in a moment that banks are limited in their ability to make loans and thus add to the money supply. But first let's see how the money supply is decreased.

One year later your note comes due. In the interim you've built up your money balance to be able to pay off the loan on time. You have $500 (plus the interest due, which we neglect for present purposes) either in your checking account or in your cookie jar. If it's in the cookie jar, you turn it over to the bank on the due date and money in circulation drops by $500. Note again that currency counts as money when and only when it is held outside the banking system.

If, as is more likely, you have the $500 in your checking account, you write a check for that amount to the bank. The bank subtracts $500 from your demand deposit balance. The money supply goes down by $500.

If you have grasped this simple process, you now understand how money is created and destroyed and the way in which the stock of money expands and contracts. But you must still be wondering what has been left out. Surely private, commercial bankers cannot create money without constraint. And you are right; they cannot. First of all, the bankers must find people willing to borrow on the terms at which the banks are willing to lend. Second, each bank operates within the constraint imposed by its reserves. This is the constraint that banking authorities use to control bank lending and hence the process of money creation. Every bank is legally required to hold reserves in forms specified by law. A bank may make new loans, and thus create money, only when it has reserves greater than the minimum amount it is legally obligated to hold. And the Fed has the power to increase or decrease the reserves of the banking system.

The Central Bank

The Federal Reserve Banks constitute the central bank of the United States, created by an act of Congress in 1913. Although technically owned by the commercial banks that are members of the Federal Reserve System, the Fed is in fact a government agency. Its board of governors in Washington is appointed by the president of the United States with the consent of the Senate. And the board effectively controls the policies of the twelve Federal Reserve Banks. We *seem* to have twelve central banks, but this is only an appearance; it is a legacy from the days when much of the country harbored a populist suspicion of Easterners, Wall Streeters, and men in striped pants with cutaway coats. These suspicions were allayed by scattering Federal Reserve Banks around the country. But the Fed has actually been a single bank (with branches) at least since the legislative changes enacted by Congress in the 1930s. The power of any one of the twelve Banks depends pretty much on the influence it is able to exert, which in turn depends on the quality of its executive officers and its research staff.

Many of the commercial banks in the United States are not subject to the rules of the Federal Reserve System. Banks holding charters from the federal government have the right to put the word "National" in their name and the obligation to join the Federal Reserve System. But many banks hold state government charters; they are permitted but not required to join the Fed. If they choose *not* to join, they operate in accordance with state definitions of reserves and state-established legal reserve minima. Although less than half of all the commercial banks in the United States belong to the Federal Reserve System, member banks have more than three-fourths of the total assets and liabilities of the entire commercial banking system. We're going to simplify this account by pretending that *all* banks are subject to the rules and regulations of the Fed. Since the Fed indirectly but powerfully influences the position of all banks and not just those subject to its direct regulation, this assumption won't give a seriously misleading picture. In the next chapter, when we examine the processes of monetary management, we'll ask about the possible significance of the fact that the percentage of banks holding membership in the Fed has slowly decreased in recent years.

Bank Reserves as Constraints on the Money Supply

Because of its power to fix legal reserve requirements for member banks (within wide limits set by Congress) and its power to expand or contract the dollar volume of reserves, the Fed controls the lending activities of the commercial banking system and thus the process of money creation. Reserve requirements differ for time deposits and demand deposits; moreover, the legal reserve requirement on demand deposits currently varies between 8% and 17½%, depending on the size of a particular bank's total demand deposit liabilities. Under Fed regulations that became effective in 1975, a bank with $500 million in demand deposits must hold reserves equal to 8% of the first $2 million, 10½% of the next $8 million, 12½% of the next $90 million, 13½% of the next $300 million, and 17½% of all demand deposit liabilities over $400 million. (Note that demand deposits are bank *liabilities:* your bank owes you the amount in your checking account.) The Fed also decides what may count as legal reserves. Since 1960 it has been the banks' vault cash plus the deposits the commercial

banks themselves have at the Federal Reserve Bank of their district. To see what all this has to do with changes in the money supply, we'll move in for a close-up look at the First National Bank of Anywhere.

Suppose that the First National Bank has demand deposit liabilities of $90 million and legal reserves of $12 million. (We ignore the complicating but for our purposes irrelevant calculations that would be necessary if we took account of other liabilities and the reserves held against them.) With a little pencil work you can quickly calculate that First National has $1 million of reserves beyond its legal requirements. Against the first $2 million of those deposits it must hold an 8% reserve, or $.16 million; against the next $8 million it must hold a $10\frac{1}{2}$% reserve, or $.84 million; and against the remaining $80 million it must hold a $12\frac{1}{2}$% reserve, or $10 million. With $12 million in actual reserves and only $11 million legally required, First National has excess legal reserves of $1 million. And excess reserves are what banks can lend. So First National will be able to make new loans of $1 million if it can find acceptable borrowers. Let's assume it does so and watch what happens as a result.

First National extends the loans by creating new demand deposits for its borrowers. After the loans have been made, then, First has $91 million in demand deposit liabilities and an unchanged $12 million of reserves. Since with a marginal reserve requirement of $12\frac{1}{2}$% only $.08 million of additional reserves must be held against the additional $1 million in liabilities, the bank will still have excess legal reserves of $.92 million. But the bank cannot expect those new liabilities to remain on deposit. The loans were presumably taken out to finance expenditures. So the borrowers will write checks against the new deposits, payable to customers of other banks for the most part, and First National will lose reserves. To keep the example neat, we'll assume that the $1 million just borrowed is all paid out by the borrowers to people who maintain accounts in other banks. Recipients of the checks deposit them in their own banks; these banks send the checks to the Fed for clearance; the Fed subtracts the amount of the checks from the recipient deposit of First National and adds it to the reserve deposits of the recipient banks; the checks are then forwarded to First National, which deducts the amounts from the demand deposit balance of the payers. At the end of this process, First National will again have $90 million in demand deposit liabilities but now only $11 million in legal reserves.

By this process First National has converted its excess legal reserves into an addition to the stock of money. The new money has left First National and now exists as new demand deposits in other banks. But First National has acquired additional earning assets in the form of new loans, which was its purpose in making the loans.

It should be clear from this brief account that excess reserves and a demand for bank loans on the part of eligible borrowers are the two factors jointly controlling the expansion of the money supply. The Fed can therefore facilitate the growth of the money supply either by reducing the legal reserve requirements or by increasing the dollar volume of reserves. The latter is in fact the Fed's regular operating lever in money management. We'll describe and evaluate the process in the next chapter. Postponing the question of how reserves originate, we now want to trace out what happens when reserves increase.

The Effect of Changes in Bank Reserves

Go back to the case of First National. We started the bank out with $1 million in excess legal reserves. (The word *legal* is important. If a bank's managers want to hold more reserves than the law requires, the entire amount of the legal excess will not in fact be "excess" and will not be available for new loans.) Suppose those reserves had just been created by the Fed because it wanted to expand the supply of money. We traced through the process by which the lending of the reserves added $1 million to the stock of money. But that won't be the end of the matter. A one-dollar change in reserves tends to cause a change in the money stock of *several* dollars. That's why bank reserves are sometimes called "high-power money."

To see why this is so, look at the new position of the banks in which that freshly created money was deposited. They jointly acquired $1 million in additional demand deposits *plus* $1 million in additional reserves. Remember that when the Fed cleared the checks, it transferred $1 million in reserves from the account of First National to the accounts of the recipient banks. So these recipient banks acquired, dollar for dollar, new reserves to match their new demand deposits.

But under a fractional-reserve banking system (where reserves need only be some fraction of deposits), new deposits plus matching new reserves create excess legal reserves. Just to keep matters simple, assume that all the deposits flow to banks in the $10–$100 million deposit category so that they are all subject to a $12\frac{1}{2}\%$ legal reserve requirement. These banks will consequently find themselves with $.875 million in excess legal reserves. If they don't want to hold the reserves and can find acceptable borrowers, they can now make new loans in that amount and thereby create an additional $.875 million of new money. But this still isn't the end, because the banks in which this newly created money is deposited will now acquire excess legal reserves: $.875 million of new demand deposits plus $.875 million of new reserves amounts to a $765,625 addition to excess legal reserves (if the applicable reserve requirement is still $12\frac{1}{2}\%$). The whole process can thus repeat itself again.

CHECK-CLEARING SERVICES

The use of demand deposits as a medium of exchange is greatly facilitated by the check-clearing services the Federal Reserve Banks provide. When an Amarillo, Texas, reader instructs his bank to pay $6.95 to Chess Fanatics Magazine and sends those instructions, in the guise of a check, to the magazine's office in Raleigh, North Carolina, how does the magazine collect? It certainly won't have a representative stop by the Amarillo bank to pick up the amount due. Instead it will deposit the check in its own bank, receive a $6.95 addition to its demand deposits, and let the bank worry about collecting from Amarillo. The Raleigh bank will collect by sending the check to the Federal Reserve Bank of Richmond, Virginia, which will credit it with a $6.95 addition to its reserve account. The Richmond Federal Reserve Bank will in turn send the check to the Federal Reserve Bank of Dallas, which will deduct $6.95 from the reserve account of the Amarillo bank and send it the check. When the check gets back to Amarillo, the chess fanatic will have $6.95 deducted from his account. And the canceled check will be sent to him in his monthly statement. The Federal Reserve Bank of Dallas remits $6.95 to the Federal Reserve Bank of Richmond through the Interdistrict Settlement Fund.

The Fed does not operate the only check-clearing services in the country. Banks often collect local checks through local clearing houses, and sometimes they even collect by sending the check directly to the bank on which it was drawn. The settlement of most checks drawn on member banks, however, is made through the balances the banks maintain with the Federal Reserve Bank of their district.

All checks collected and cleared through the Federal Reserve Banks must be paid in full by the banks on which they were drawn, without deduction of a fee or charge. A handful of banks still collect a fee for clearing checks and are hence ineligible to participate in the Fed's clearing system.

Although the cost of collecting and clearing checks is a substantial part of Fed expenses, the Federal Reserve Banks supply this service at no charge.

The "Money Multiplier"

The essential point is a simple one which should not get lost in the arithmetic. When the Fed (or any other factor) adds one dollar to bank reserves, it enables the commercial banking system to create several dollars of additional money. Exactly how many additional dollars depends on the applicable reserve requirement and the extent to which the newly created money is shifted out of demand deposits. Some portion of newly created demand deposits tends to be withdrawn into circulating currency. Currency in circulation is no longer vault cash and is not included in bank reserves. And this leakage of reserves reduces the value of the "money multiplier."

To illustrate: if all banks were subject to a $12\frac{1}{2}\%$ marginal-reserve requirement, if all legal excess reserves were loaned out, and there were no leakage of currency into circulation (and no transfers from demand deposits into time deposits), then $1 of new reserves would lead to the creation of $8 in additional money. Why exactly $8? Because $1 + (.875) + (.875)(.875) + (.875)^3$ . . . , the expansion path of the money creation process, ultimately approaches $1 \times 1/.125$, or 8.

The actual money multiplier is much less than this, running in recent years between 2 and 3. A multiplier of 2.5 would result from a combination of an average applicable reserve requirement of 15% and a 25% leakage of currency into circulation. The latter would occur if the public withdrew $1 in currency for every $4 added to the money stock, and this is close to actual practice in recent years. Of course, whether the money multiplier is 2 or 8 or anything in between, the expansion process depends on the ability of banks to locate eligible borrowers. So expansion takes time; it doesn't occur instantaneously. That's another point to which we'll return in chapter 10.

This entire discussion has been carried on in terms of excess reserves, additional loans, and more money. It also works in reverse. When reserves are reduced by an action of the Fed (or anyone else), the power of banks to lend is contracted. When a bank's reserves fall below the legal minimum, it reduces its rate of new loans below the rate at which the old loans are being repaid, in order to acquire additional reserves. If the entire banking system is doing this, the result is a net contraction of loans and hence a reduction in the money supply. Eventually, through the acquisition by the commercial banks of additional currency and the reduction of demand deposits as the public repays loans, the legal minimum reserve-to-deposit ratio will be reached. Then the process of contraction will stop.

How We Got This Way

Does it bother you that privately owned banks have the power to create money? A power that the Constitution of the United States assigns to Congress? It all came about because few people understood exactly what was happening when it began. The Constitution speaks only of the power to *coin* money, because almost everyone thought in 1790 that gold and silver coins would be the dominant component of the money supply. By

THE MECHANICS OF MONEY CREATION

The mysterious character of money creation through bank lending diminishes when we describe it in terms of changes in the assets and liabilities of commercial banks. We can more easily focus on the elementary mechanics of the process if we adopt a few simplifying assumptions:

1. The entire commercial banking system is a single bank.
2. The bank maintains only the minimum reserves required by law.
3. There is no leakage of currency from the banks into circulation as demand deposits increase, and no transfer of demand deposits into time deposits.
4. The legal reserve requirement on all demand deposits is 20%.

We assume that Universal Bank has zero excess reserves at the outset and that, in accordance with the conventions of accounting, its total assets are equal to its total liabilities including net worth. To start the process moving, we'll have a prospector walk into one of the branches of Universal Bank with $10,000 worth of gold. He turns the gold over to the bank and receives in return a $10,000 demand deposit. Universal Bank sends the gold to the Federal Reserve Bank of its district and receives in return a $10,000 additional credit to its reserve account. The bank's balance sheet then looks like this:

Assets	Liabilities
Original assets $700,000,000,000	$700,000,000,000 Original liabilities
Reserve account + 10,000	10,000 Prospector's demand deposit

Because Universal Bank need maintain only $2000 in reserves against $10,000 in demand deposits, it now has $8000 in excess reserves. It lends this amount to Avery by creating a demand deposit, and receives in return Avery's IOU. Avery writes a check for $8000 to Barnes, who deposits the check in the bank. The balance sheet will now look like this:

Assets	Liabilities
Original assets $700,000,000,000	$700,000,000,000 Original liabilities
Reserve account + 10,000	10,000 Prospector's demand deposit
Avery's IOU 8,000	8,000 Barnes's demand deposit

Notice that *no reserves have been lost* even though the bank loaned out its excess reserves; the banking *system* does not lose reserves when deposits are transferred from one bank to another. Universal Bank still has the $10,000 in its reserve account; but with $18,000 in additional demand deposits it must now earmark \$3600 as required reserves. That leaves \$6400 in excess reserves which can be loaned to Clyde by giving him a demand deposit in that amount. When Clyde writes a \$6400 check to Darrell and Darrell deposits the check, the balance sheet looks like this:

Assets		Liabilities
Original assets \$700,000,000,000		\$700,000,000,000 Original liabilities
Reserve account + 10,000		10,000 Prospector's demand deposit
Avery's IOU 8,000		8,000 Barnes's demand deposit
Clyde's IOU 6,400		6,400 Darrell's demand deposit

The bank will now have \$24,400 in new demand deposits, against which it is required to hold \$4880 in reserves. So \$5120 in excess reserves will be available for lending.

If we continued to trace out in this way the growth in Universal Bank's assets and liabilities as it acquired additional IOUs and created additional demand deposits, each successive item would be 80% of the preceding item. The cumulative total of $\$10,000 + .8(\$10,000) + .8^2(\$10,000) + .8^3(\$10,000) + \cdots + .8^n(\$10,000)$ approaches \$50,000 as n approaches infinity. The total will get very close to \$50,000 while n is still quite small: ten repetitions of the process described above will bring the total to \$45,705, and when n reaches twenty the total will be over \$49,500.

Each additional dollar of reserves that enters the banking system enables Universal Bank ultimately to add \$5 to the total money supply when the legal reserve requirement is 20%. The legal constraint on the banking system's ability to expand deposits on the basis of new reserves is given by the formula $1/R$, where R is the reserve requirement. Any other factor that also uses reserves, such as currency withdrawals, will reduce the value of the "multiplier" by increasing the denominator in the formula. Thus if the legal reserve requirement were 15% and the public always held \$1 in currency for every \$4 it held in demand deposits, the banking system would be able to create \$2.50 in deposits for every \$1 of new reserves. With the required reserve and currency holdings both stated as a percentage of demand deposits, the formula becomes: $1/(.15 + .25) = 1/.4 = 2.5$.

the time we fully realized that commercial banks could be money creators as important as the Mint or the Bureau of Engraving, we had accumulated enough experience with the system to let it continue. More importantly, perhaps, we weren't at all sure what to put in its place. The complex banking and monetary systems of the industrialized world were not based

BANK CREATION OF CURRENCY

Students are often surprised to learn that commercial banks, which are privately owned institutions operated for profit, create most of the money used as the medium of exchange in the United States. The suspicion that this just cannot be the case may account in part for their resistance to the notion that demand deposits are *really* money.

But for most of our nation's history the federal government has not even been the exclusive supplier of *currency*. Before the Civil War, the principal suppliers of paper money were privately owned banks that printed and distributed their own banknotes. Moreover, these banks were not chartered or controlled by the federal government. They were for the most part chartered by state governments and controlled in their note issues by the willingness of the public to accept the notes. These notes were usually promises to pay gold to the bearer on demand, which the banks issued in the process of extending loans. If the public had confidence in a bank's willingness and ability to redeem its obligations on demand, the notes might circulate indefinitely. If the public lost confidence in a bank, however, note holders would rush to demand redemption. If the bank did not have enough gold to meet its obligations, it would be forced to suspend redemption. Since few people would want to accept the notes of a bank that had suspended redemption, the value of the notes in circulation would fall to a fraction of their face value.

The currency system of the United States before the Civil War was consequently a bewildering variety of banknotes exchanging at uncertain and fluctuating percentages of their face value. In 1863, in an effort to bring greater order out of this chaos, the federal government established a national banking system. National banks were required to invest one-third of their capital in government bonds and were authorized to issue banknotes in an amount up to 90% of the market value of these bonds. (Creating support for the government bond market was probably the government's principal goal at this time.) These notes, called national banknotes, were printed for the banks by the Bureau of Engraving in order to give the currency a uniform appearance. Moreover, each national bank was required to accept the notes issued by other national banks at par. When relatively few banks elected to take out national charters, the federal government in 1865 imposed a 10% tax on state banknotes. This drove state banknotes out of circulation and created a much more uniform currency throughout the nation.

But by the end of the Civil War demand deposits had become more important than currency as a medium of exchange. And so the state banks were not driven out of business. They continued to make loans, but by creating demand deposits rather than by issuing banknotes.

on the principles described in this chapter and the next. On the contrary, these principles were discovered by examination of the processes that had already evolved. Bankers had created the system long before economists, government officials, or *bankers themselves* understood it.

If you wonder how it was possible for a functioning social institution to be created by people who did not understand it, then you're too much a rationalist to be a good historian. Comprehensive social institutions rarely develop in accordance with anyone's plan; they are much more likely to evolve out of step-by-step adjustments to unanticipated changes in circumstances. We must hurry on to add that the banking-monetary system that evolved in the United States often functioned badly, creating speculative booms, inflations, financial panics, bankruptcies, and recessions in a continuing succession, in addition to providing a medium of exchange and a credit mechanism to finance economic expansion.

Do we know enough now to control the banking-monetary system of the country and to ensure that the growth of the money supply keeps in even step with the expanding demand for money and credit, so that money lubricates without disrupting production and exchange? The next chapter carries us into that question.

Once Over Lightly

Money is a social institution that increases wealth by lowering costs of exchange. Low costs of exchange enable people to specialize more fully in accordance with their comparative advantages.

Money is used as the standard unit of accounting in comparing relative values because we have all had experience in using it as a medium of exchange.

Money could not function as a medium of exchange if it did not also function as a store of value over time. People accept money in return for other goods because they know they can hold the money and use it later to obtain the goods they want. But the fact that people can at low cost hold more or less money introduces additional uncertainty and complications into the functioning of an economic system.

An asset is moneylike to the degree that it is liquid. The liquidity of any asset depends on the cost of exchanging it for other assets. An asset that can be exchanged for other assets at zero cost is completely liquid.

The demand for liquidity (or the demand for money to hold) expresses people's desire to have a greater range of choices, more opportunities, and consequently additional wealth. The quantity of money people wish to hold will depend upon their income, their reading of the future, and the opportunity cost of holding money. The opportunity cost of holding money is the value of what is given up by not holding alternative assets.

Because liquidity is a matter of degree, there is no sharp line of distinction between the assets that are money and those that are not. Federal Reserve notes and coins are clearly part of the money supply. Demand deposits are also without any question part of the money supply. Time deposits cannot be used directly as a medium of exchange but are highly liquid; whether or not they should be counted in the money supply is more difficult to determine. Deposits in nonbank thrift institutions raise the same question. Since many other assets are also highly liquid, the decision on exactly what to include in the definition of the money supply must depend on an analysis of current practices and the uses to which the definition will be put.

The money supply increases when commercial banks make loans to their customers and decreases when customers repay the loans.

Banks can make new loans and thereby expand the stock of money when they hold reserves in excess of the minimum amounts established by the banking authorities.

The Federal Reserve Banks attempt to control changes in the stock of money by increasing or decreasing legal reserve minimums and by adding to or subtracting from the total of commercial bank reserves.

Under a system where banks must hold as reserves only a fraction of their total deposits, every one dollar change in reserves leads to a greater than one dollar change in deposits. The relation between changes in reserves and changes in the money supply will be governed primarily by legal reserve ratios, the extent to which the public withdraws additional currency from the banks as bank deposits increase, and the willingness of banks and borrowers to negotiate additional loans.

QUESTIONS FOR DISCUSSION

1. Would your existence be more or less secure if we had a barter economy rather than one using money? Why would we all be poorer if we had to rely exclusively on barter? Is a very poor person subject to 5% fluctuations in his income more or less secure than a wealthy person subject to 50% fluctuations in his income?

2. Can you think of any ways in which emphasis on money obscures the real workings and effects of economic events? What about an argument that the government of India could attack poverty by printing more rupees and distributing them to the poorest people?

3. How much money do you hold, on the average, over the course of a typical month? What would induce you to increase that amount? How could you do this? (Do not confuse money with income.)

4. Name some liquid assets that you own. Rank them in order of liquidity. What criterion are you using to determine relative liquidity?

5. You plan to buy a bicycle this year as soon as you've saved enough money. You have about half the amount saved when you read that bicycle prices are expected to rise considerably in coming months. What might you do? How would this affect your liquidity? Suppose that you have saved the entire purchase price, and then you read that overproduction of bicycles will probably result in large price decreases in coming months. What might you do, and how will your decision affect your liquidity?

6. Shares of common stock listed on a major exchange can be sold quickly— that is, exchanged for other assets. Are shares of stock as liquid as money? Why might a person hold part of his wealth in common stocks and part in money? Why might he shift the composition of his portfolio in order to hold more of one asset and less of the other?

7. Suppose everyone came to believe that prices were going to rise sharply in the next month or so. How would this belief affect their demand for money balances? How would it affect their demand for goods other than money? What effect would this likely have on the prices of goods other than money? What effect would it likely have on the price of money? (The price of money is the rate at which it exchanges for goods, just as the price of other goods is the rate at which they exchange for money.)

8. Money gets a lot of attention but tends to have a bad press. Are the authors of the following statements talking about money as we have defined it, or are they using money as a synonym or symbol for something else? What is that "something else" in each case in which you conclude that money is not really the subject of discussion?

    (*a*) "The love of money is the root of all evil." (Often misquoted as "Money is the root of all evil.")

    (*b*) "Health is . . . a blessing that money cannot buy."

    (*c*) "Don't marry for money."

    (*d*) "Well, fancy giving money to the government! Might as well have put it down the drain."

    (*e*) "Hath a dog money? Is it possible a cur can lend three thousand ducats?"

    (*f*) "If this be not love, it is madness, and then it is pardonable. Nay, yet a more certain sign than all this: I give thee my money."

    (*g*) "Wine maketh merry; but money answereth all things."

    (*h*) "Words are the tokens current and accepted for conceits, as moneys are for values."

    (*i*) "Money speaks a language all nations understand."

9. If you were to ask someone how much money he has in the bank, he might not distinguish in answering between his checking account balance and his savings account balance. Why would economists want to distinguish between the two?

10. At any moment in time, some already printed Federal Reserve notes will be in (*a*) the wallets of the public, (*b*) the vaults and tills of commercial banks, and (*c*) the vaults of Federal Reserve Banks. How does each enter into or otherwise affect the total money supply?

11. People cannot spend the deposits they hold in commercial bank savings accounts or savings and loan institutions without first withdrawing the funds, that is, converting them into currency or demand deposits. But since they are able to do that at almost no cost, these deposits are assets almost as liquid as checking account balances.

    (*a*) Does it follow that total spending ought to be more closely correlated with M_3 than with M_1?

    (*b*) What does a faster rate of increase in M_3 than in M_1 suggest about the public's spending *intentions*?

    (*c*) If electronic funds transfer systems lower the cost of spending savings deposits to the current cost of spending checking deposits, what effect would you expect to observe in the relative sizes of M_1, M_2, and M_3?

12. If bankers can create money, why can't you? Is it against the law for you to create an accepted medium of exchange? Can you think of a situation in which you might succeed in creating a little money? (Hint: Demand deposits, which serve as money, are liabilities of commercial banks; suppose your promissory notes were considered in the community as "good as gold"?)

13. If money is created by bank lending, is it also created by the lending of savings and loan associations, credit unions, and consumer credit companies? What is the difference?

14. Use the information provided in the text to test your understanding of the relationship between bank reserves and money creation.

    (*a*) Fog National Bank has $1 billion in demand deposit liabilities. How many dollars must it legally hold as reserves against these deposits? Do you get an answer of $157.75 million?

    (*b*) Suppose Fog Bank has $160 million in reserves. If we ignore time deposits and the reserves which they require, how large are the bank's excess legal reserves?

    (*c*) If the managers of Fog Bank prefer to maintain $2 million of reserves in addition to the minimum legal requirement, how large are Fog Bank's *excess* reserves?

    (*d*) Fog Bank loans its excess reserves of $250,000 to the Lovers Lanes Company for the purchase of new pin-setting equipment. When the equipment supplier deposits the $250,000 check in the River National Bank, which has total demand deposit liabilities of $200 million, what effect does this have on the River Bank's excess legal reserves?

(*e*) River Bank extends a new loan of $216,250 to a silver processor who uses it to purchase silver from a mine in Two Cushion, Montana. The Two Cushion Bank, where the check is deposited, has total demand deposit liabilities of $7 million. How much will the deposit add to the bank's excess legal reserves?

(*f*) The silver mine in Two Cushion uses all the money received to pay its employees. None of the miners maintains a bank account. They all cash their weekly checks and use currency to handle their purchases. What will happen to the Two Cushion Bank's excess legal reserves right after payday?

(*g*) If all the merchants in Two Cushion use the local bank, what will happen to the bank's liabilities and reserves over the course of the week?

15. How does a withdrawal of currency from checking accounts affect the money supply? How does it affect a bank's reserves? How does it affect excess legal reserves? What effect might this have subsequently on the money supply?

10

THE FEDERAL RESERVE
AND THE MONETARY SYSTEM

The money supply increases as commercial banks acquire new earning assets by lending out their excess reserves. That was the theme of the last half of chapter 9. It raises a long list of questions.

Where do reserves come from? What are the controls on the system? How does the Fed, as the nation's central bank and, by act of Congress, the manager of the monetary system, exercise its authority? How well does it do so? What are its goals? Are the goals it pursues the goals it ought to pursue? Does it have the power to achieve the goals it sets? If you have definitive answers to all those questions when you've read this chapter, you'll know more than the authors or anyone else we're aware of. But at least when you've finished you should have a better idea of where the troublesome questions are and some insight into the interesting life of a central banker.

BANK RESERVES AND THE MONEY SUPPLY

Bank reserves. What are they? Where do they come from? The *Federal Reserve Bulletin*, a monthly publication of the Fed, regularly lists all the Factors Supplying Reserve Funds. But the *Federal Reserve Bulletin* regularly prints more than almost anyone would want to know. The important thing is to understand the principal factors that contribute to *changes* in reserve funds. The best approach is to think it through rather than look it up.

Any one bank can add to its reserves by attracting deposits from other banks. If you want to close your checking account in First National and open an account in Second National, the easiest way is to write a check and deposit it in your new account. When the Fed clearinghouse gets the check, it will subtract the amount of your balance from the reserve account of First and credit it to the reserve account of Second. Similarly, one bank acquires reserves from other banks as its current depositors receive and deposit payments from the customers of other banks. But none of this alters the *total* reserves of the banking system.[1]

The system as a whole will acquire or lose reserves as the public reduces or expands its holdings of currency. Currency that goes into circulation reduces vault cash. If the banks replenish their vault cash by obtaining more Federal Reserve notes, the Fed deducts the value of the notes from the banks' reserve accounts.

Another source of fluctuations in total system reserves is *float*. It takes time for checks to move through the banking system, from the bank of deposit in Des Moines, let us say, to the Federal Reserve Bank in Chicago, then to the Federal Reserve Bank in San Francisco, and finally to the bank in Sacramento on which the check was originally drawn. The Chicago FRB may credit the reserve account of the Des Moines bank before the San Francisco FRB gets around to debiting the reserve account of the Sacramento bank. In the interim, total bank reserves will have grown. *Float* is the term applied to the portion of bank reserves that results from the double counting of uncollected checks. The total can and does vary considerably, due to transportation tie-ups, long holiday weekends, or other seasonal factors. The Fed must estimate and predict the amount of float in bank reserves if it wants to exercise a precise control over those reserves; uncompensated changes in float can lead to sharp expansions and contractions of bank lending.[2]

The United States Treasury is all by itself a potential bull in the china shop. The flow of funds through Treasury hands, as you well know, is enormous; it is also bunchy rather than smooth and steady, with receipts heavily concentrated around tax due dates and those times when the Treasury is selling large issues of government bonds. The Treasury uses the Federal Reserve as its banker, so that a check drawn on a commercial bank and deposited by the Internal Revenue Service draws reserves out of commercial bank reserve accounts. The Treasury tries to compensate by depositing some of the funds received back into its Tax and Loan

---

1. Because bank deposits are subject to different reserve requirements, such a shuffling could alter the pattern of excess reserves and thus expand or contract the banking system's ability to lend.

2. Individuals who write checks on nonexistent balances shortly before payday knowing that the checks will take several days to reach their bank are creating float for their own use

Accounts at major commercial banks. The goal is to keep the bull quiet in the china shop: the Treasury, in consultation with the money managers at the Fed, tries to exert a neutral effect on reserves so that they can be more easily controlled by those who are supposed to be in charge.

Another factor affecting reserves is foreign exchange, an important topic that we'll have to postpone to chapter 14. It's enough for now if you think about what happens when the authors send £40 to the journal *Economica* in England for permission to reprint an article. Their joint bank account falls by about $95 and an English account rises by about £40. Our bank owes us less and some English bank owes *Economica* more. How was the English bank persuaded to add £40 to its obligations? It received compensation. From whom? From our bank, to balance the $95 by which it reduced its liabilities to us. The details don't have to concern us further. But it should be clear that the transaction requires, at some step, the transfer of reserves out of the account of an American bank into the account of a British bank. Foreign exchange, as we'll see later on, can be a highly unsettling force on a domestic monetary system.

Controlling Reserves for Policy Purposes

So far the play has been *Hamlet* without the prince of Denmark. The time has come to introduce the Fed, the central character, and its tools of monetary management. The most powerful tool and the one that sets the stage for the rest is its authority to establish legal reserve requirements. The Fed has been sliding those percentages around quite a bit in recent years; but its aim has been more to adjust certain relationships between banks than to stimulate or contract bank lending.[1] Changes in reserve requirements are generally viewed by Fed officials as blunt weapons, not suitable for the delicate surgery that monetary management usually requires. They prefer to take the reserve requirements as the framework and alter the volume of reserves.

How is that done? The briefest explanation is that the Fed creates and destroys reserves in the same way that commercial banks create and destroy money: by increasing and reducing their loans.

The Fed can extend a loan to a commercial bank directly. This is the second tool it uses to affect bank lending activity. It does so by crediting the bank's reserve account and taking in return the bank's IOU or someone else's IOU (a government bond, for example) that happens to be in

---

1. Recall the paragraphs at the end of chapter 9 on the trial and error evolution of the United States banking system. Variations in reserve requirements for different banks often make sense only if you're familiar with history.

the bank's portfolio—just as a commercial bank lends to its customers by creating a deposit balance in return for an IOU. This directly increases commercial bank reserves. The interest rate at which such loans are made is called the *discount rate.* It's a financial-page celebrity, because many people look upon it as a sign of current Fed policy. It is probably more of a symbol than a genuine rationing device, since the Fed is selective about the banks to which it will loan. Official Fed policy is to accommodate special circumstances rather than loan to any bank willing to pay the rate, and to behave more like a Dutch uncle than a profit-seeking lender. But that's what most people look for from a central bank.

The third and principal technique that the Fed employs to control reserves is the purchase and sale of U.S. government securities. This is also a way of increasing or reducing its loans, either to the United States Treasury when the Fed buys newly issued securities, or to previous purchasers and holders of these securities. The Fed currently holds a portfolio of government securities approaching a value of $100 billion. When it increases its holdings by purchasing securities through dealers in government bonds, it writes checks for the amount of the purchases on its own credit. These checks are deposited in commercial banks. When the banks forward the checks to their Federal Reserve Bank, they are credited with additions to their reserve balances.

In short, the acquisition by the Fed of new earning assets (which is the same thing as the extension of credit to someone, whether commercial banks, the government, or holders of government bonds) tends to increase commercial bank reserves by that amount. And this, as we have seen, enables commercial banks to increase their own loans and thereby the money supply.

The entire process is reversible, of course. The Fed can withdraw credit from member banks or sell some of the government securities already in its asset portfolio. This results in a reduction of commercial bank reserves. For example, when the Fed sells a $1000 government bond, the bond winds up in the hands of someone who pays the bond dealer with a check. But the dealer in turn pays the Fed with a check, and the amount of the check is deducted from the reserve account of the bank on which it is drawn. That wipes out a portion of the total reserves of the banking system.

The Open Market Committee

Federal Reserve purchases and sales of government securities, with the intent of changing commercial bank reserves and thereby affecting the money supply, are called *open market operations.* This is the principal working tool of monetary management. A special committee, made up of the seven members of the board of governors and five of the twelve Reserve Bank presidents, sits as the Open Market Committee and continuously determines the direction of monetary policy. The question of the effectiveness with which the Open Market Committee and the Federal Reserve System manage the money supply has long been debated by both friends and critics of the Fed and by both economists and politicians.

There are two main questions. One concerns the determination of policy. Does the Fed set appropriate goals? The other concerns the execution of policy. Does the Fed do an effective job of achieving the goals it sets for itself? The questions are related, of course, because intelligent policy formulation presupposes a realistic assessment of technical capabilities. The football coach who orders a passing strategy when his team is two touchdowns behind in the fourth quarter is making a poor policy decision if his quarterback has a rubber arm and all his receivers have butterfingers. Textbook accounts are often like football plays on the blackboard; both of them tend to gloss over problems of execution. We must not simply assume that the Open Market Committee automatically does Good, or even that it succeeds all the time in achieving what it sets out to do.

What Can the Fed Actually Control?

In reality, the Fed has no direct control over the money supply. This should be clear from our description of the process by which money is created and destroyed in the United States. The Fed holds the money supply on a leash, and a somewhat elastic leash at that. It can let out the leash—that is, pump additional reserves into the banking system—but exactly how or when this will affect the money supply depends on the responses of the commercial banks and their customers. If they aren't straining at the leash, eager to make new loans, the leash may simply go slack when the Fed extends it: the new reserves will not be fully used to make additional loans and thus create additional money. The years from 1929 to 1939 provide the best example. During that period, the *total* reserves of member banks increased from $2.4 billion to $11.5 billion, while their *required* reserves increased only from $2.35 billion to $6.5 billion. In short, member banks in 1929 tended to hold only the reserves required by law; they turned the rest of their reserves into earning assets, and hence into money, by lending them out. But in 1939, banks retained reserves far beyond the legal requirement. Almost 45% of the reserves held by member banks at the end of 1939 were over and above the minimum requirements set by the rules and regulations of the Fed. From the standpoint of the cautious and conservative banking community, those legally uncommitted reserves were not *excess* reserves. The very low interest rates on low-risk assets gave bankers little incentive to acquire them. They preferred to hold the reserves and hope for better opportunities.

One must be careful about deriving generalizations from the experi-

THROUGH THE BALANCE SHEET LOOKING GLASS

You will acquire a surer grasp of the basic principles of monetary management if you trace through the effects of various actions both on the consolidated balance sheets of the Federal Reserve Banks and on the balance sheet of the Universal Bank (the single bank we introduced in the last chapter to represent the entire commercial banking system).

The number preceding each entry on the balance sheets corresponds to the number assigned to the action as described below. Notice that after each action has been completed the equality between assets and liabilities will have been maintained on each balance sheet.

1. The Fed buys $1000 worth of new securities from the Treasury.
2. The government purchases $1000 worth of rubber cement from the Sanford Ink Company.
3. The Fed sells $500 worth of government bonds, through a bond dealer, to the Sanford Ink Company.
4. Sanford withdraws $100 in currency for the petty cash drawer.
5. Universal Bank replenishes its vault cash by obtaining $100 of additional Federal Reserve notes.
6. The Fed loans Universal Bank $400 and takes as collateral prime commercial paper held by Universal Bank.
7. Universal Bank has acquired through all these steps $800 in additional legal reserves and $400 in additional demand deposits. If the legal reserve requirement is 20%, it has $720 in excess legal reserves. It loans $720 to International Business Machines.
8. IBM pays $720 in taxes due to the federal government.
9. The government transfers $720 from its account at the Fed to its Tax and Loan Account at Universal Bank.
10. The government purchases $720 worth of rubber bands from Elasto, Inc., with a check drawn on its Tax and Loan Account. (We would merely be retracing the preceding step if we had the government transfer the funds back to its Fed account before making the purchase.)
11. Universal Bank repays its $400 loan from the Fed.
12. The Fed lowers the legal reserve requirement to 20%. (There are no entries on the balance sheet corresponding to this action. Why not? What consequences would you predict?)

| FEDERAL RESERVE BANKS | | UNIVERSAL BANK | |
Assets	Liabilities	Assets	Liabilities
(1) + $1000 government bonds	(1) + $1000 Treasury deposits		
	(2) − $1000 Treasury deposits	(2) + $1000 reserve account	(2) + $1000 Sanford demand deposits
	(2) + $1000 UB reserve account		
(3) − $500 government bonds	(3) − $500 UB reserve account	(3) − $500 reserve account	(3) − $500 Sanford demand deposits
		(4) − $100 vault cash	(4) − $100 Sanford demand deposits
	(5) + $100 Federal Reserve notes outstanding	(5) + $100 vault cash	
	(5) − $100 UB reserve account	(5) − $100 reserve account	
(6) + $400 commercial paper	(6) + $400 UB reserve account	(6) + $400 reserve account	
		(6) − $400 commercial paper	
		(7) + $720 IBM IOU	(7) + $720 IBM demand deposits
	(8) + $720 Treasury deposits	(8) − $720 reserve account	(8) − $720 IBM demand deposits
	(8) − $720 UB reserve account		
	(9) − $720 Treasury deposits	(9) + $720 reserve account	(9) + $720 Treasury deposits
	(9) + $720 UB reserve account		
			(10) − $720 Treasury deposits
		(11) − $400 reserve account	(10) + $720 Elasto demand deposits
(11) − $400 commercial paper	(11) − $400 UB reserve account	(11) + $400 commercial paper	

ences of the 1930s. Banks in the Federal Reserve System have not allowed their excess legal reserves to increase beyond 4% of their total reserves since the end of the Korean war. And during the last decade the ratio of excess legal to total reserves has hung in the one-half of 1% to 2% range while trending downward. Since excess legal reserves represent foregone earning opportunities for banks, we should expect the banks to be

straining continuously against the leash—barring the kind of crisis of confidence that seems to have paralyzed a lot of economic activity in the
1930s. But even a little slack and small fluctuations in banks' holdings of
excess reserves are enough to blunt the edge of Fed attempts to control
the money supply with precision.

The leash analogy suggests that reducing the money supply may be
easier than increasing it. After all, you can rein a dog in against his will
(think of a Pekingese, not a Great Dane), even though you can't make him
leave your side just by giving him more rope. There is some validity in the
analogy. But the leash of monetary control is, as we said earlier, a somewhat elastic one, so that even contractionary policy is less precise than
people at the Fed would prefer. By shifting the composition of their assets
and liabilities in response to Fed pressure, the commercial banks can
resist efforts to bring down the money supply. For example, banks might
persuade some of their checking account customers to transfer a portion
of their demand deposit balances into time deposits, on which the legal
reserve requirement is much lower. That wouldn't increase the reserves
of the bank, but it would increase the excess reserves by reducing the
amount of legally required reserves.

The public itself has a large number of ways in which it can frustrate
the intentions of the nation's money managers at the Fed. Of course, no
one sets out obstinately to deflect the course of monetary policy; single
individuals, and even single institutions, probably couldn't succeed in
such an undertaking, anyway. But people do respond to changing circumstances in ways calculated to secure their own best advantage. Suppose,
for example, that interest rates rise rapidly, as they did in 1973 and, after
a brief fall, again in 1974. This could well reduce people's willingness to
hold money in the form of demand deposits, on which banks are legally
prohibited from paying interest. If a substantial quantity of demand
deposits is shifted into savings accounts, M_1 will fall. But that won't be
the end of the matter. Since time deposits are subject to a significantly
lower reserve requirement, the transfer of funds out of demand deposits
will increase the excess reserves and hence the lending power of the commercial banks. As new loans subsequently increase, M_1 will rise once
more. In short, a widespread decision to reduce demand deposits and
build up time deposits is capable of causing the total of demand *and* time
deposits to increase. And such decisions might be made simultaneously
by many people in response to changing conditions that the Fed itself
brought about.

Federal Reserve data reveal clearly that M_1 and M_2 are not rigidly connected. And neither is rigidly connected to the variables over which the
Fed has direct control: reserves and reserve requirements. We really
should not be surprised to discover that the Fed often sets targets for itself
that it subsequently misses by a large margin.

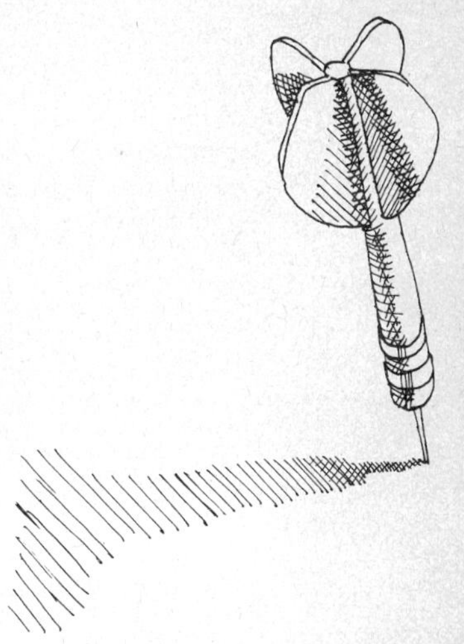

Returning to our leash analogy: Further complications arise from the fact that the dog on one end of the leash isn't always in sight of his master on the other end. The Fed obtains regular and reasonably accurate data on the money supply from member banks, but banks outside the system report much less frequently on the amount of their deposits. The Fed has to make estimates, therefore, and those estimates sometimes turn out to be wrong by a wide margin. The simple way to handle this problem would be to require all commercial banks to join the Federal Reserve System. Officials at the Fed are alarmed by the trend of recent years for state-chartered banks to leave the system and for new banks to enter business without joining. The proportion of total deposits in member banks fell from 86% to 77% between 1947 and 1974 and could go considerably lower if more banks decide that they prefer state to federal reserve requirements.

But the Fed will encounter serious political obstacles if it tries to tighten up its control by getting Congress to require Federal Reserve membership for all commercial banks. The nonmember banks will obviously lobby against such a move, and they can expect support from a number of sources. There are people who think that the Fed is incompetent and should have its power curtailed; others think that the Fed is really controlled by the banking interests it's supposed to regulate and should therefore be given no additional authority. Then there are the state banking officials who don't want to lose their functions or their jobs and can be counted on to employ the rhetoric of states' rights in defense of the present dual system. Whether the United States Constitution settles this question depends on how one interprets the power to "coin money." The authors of the Constitution did not even foresee the importance of banknotes and had no inkling at all of the role that commercial bank deposits would eventually play in the economy as the most important component of the money supply. Had they anticipated this development, they might have reserved to Congress and agencies of its creation the exclusive right to charter and regulate banks. But since they did not, and since the present dual system has a long history, the Fed will not find it easy to persuade Congress that all banks should be required to join the Federal Reserve System or at least be bound by its rules. And so the leash may become even longer and more elastic in the years ahead.

What Is the Target and Where Is It?

The execution of monetary policy is also made difficult by the fact that open market operations are designed to adjust to a moving target when no one can be quite sure at the moment of adjustment exactly where it is or which way it's moving. Worse than that, the target is typically several targets, and they may be moving in different directions. That calls to mind the problem raised earlier: What exactly do we mean by the money

TECHNOLOGY AND THE MONEY SUPPLY

In 1974 First Federal Savings and Loan of Lincoln, Nebraska, concluded an agreement with a local supermarket chain that established the nation's first system of electronic branch banks. Any customer of the Hinky Dinky supermarket chain who also maintained an account with First Federal could pay for his groceries without currency, check, or credit card. The grocery clerk used a small computer terminal to transfer the amount of the purchases from the customer's account into the account that Hinky Dinky maintained at First Federal.

Such electronic branches have been proliferating ever since. A few commercial banks have stepped gingerly into electronic funds transfer systems; but savings and loan associations have been scrambling to get in. The reason is simple. S and L's are not allowed to provide checking account service; electronic funds transfer systems enable them partly to bypass that constraint. By establishing a terminal at the point of sale, they can provide a service much like a checking account, and in some ways even superior. And they can thereby attract a portion of the deposits that now go into checking accounts at commercial banks.

If government regulatory authorities do not intervene (and they are under great pressure to do so), electronic funds transfer might in a few years take over much of the work currently done by demand deposits. If savings and loan associations provide the service, the public will begin to deposit in them a larger percentage of funds that now go into demand deposits. And so deposits in nonbank thrift institutions will increasingly include highly active money. If commercial banks provide the service, they will probably allow consumers to transfer funds from time deposits.

All of this will tend to change the relation between aggregate expenditures and M_1, M_2, and M_3, and will compel economists and monetary officials to reformulate their definitions of the money supply and of the targets at which monetary policy ought to aim.

supply? Should the Fed try to control only M_1, demand deposits and currency held by the nonbank public? Or should the object of its control be M_2 or possibly M_3?[1] The case for concentrating on M_1 is that M_1 is the

---

1. Fed officials have in recent years begun to suggest that still more comprehensive measures of the money supply than M_3 might be the appropriate gauge for policymakers to watch, and two-digit subscripts for M have started to appear in their discussions.

actual medium of exchange in the economy; it is what we use in making expenditures, and aggregate expenditures ought to be the Fed's real concern. If aggregate expenditures exceed the capacity of the economic system to produce goods at the current prices, prices will be bid up and inflation will result. But if aggregate expenditures fall short of productive capacity at current prices, output may fall and the economy may slide into a recession. However, aggregate spending could well be more closely correlated with M_2 or M_3 if spending depends significantly on liquidity and people view *all* deposits in financial institutions as liquid wealth. On which measure should the Fed focus?

One way to answer that question might be to compare each measure of the money stock with the total of expenditures for that year and see which measure is most closely correlated with expenditures. That's what we've done in table 10A.

The dollar figures are the money supply *in December of the preceding year.* Thus money supply data for December 1959 are listed with 1960, on the assumption that the stock of money most likely to influence 1960 spending is the stock at the outset of the year. This seems more plausible than using the average money stock over the course of 1960.

The second column under each measure of the money stock shows the

Table 10A

	M_1			M_2			M_3		
Year	Money stock	% change	GNP/ money stock	Money stock	% change	GNP/ money stock	Money stock	% change	GNP/ money stock
1960	$143.4		3.51	$210.9		2.39	$299.4		1.68
1961	144.2	.56%	3.61	217.1	2.94%	2.40	314.4	5.01%	1.65
1962	148.7	3.12	3.77	228.6	5.30	2.45	336.5	7.03	1.67
1963	150.9	1.48	3.91	242.8	6.21	2.43	362.9	7.85	1.63
1964	156.5	3.71	4.04	258.9	6.63	2.44	393.2	8.35	1.61
1965	163.7	4.60	4.18	277.1	7.03	2.47	426.3	8.42	1.61
1966	171.3	4.64	4.38	301.3	8.73	2.49	462.6	8.52	1.62
1967	175.4	2.39	4.53	317.8	5.48	2.50	485.2	4.89	1.64
1968	186.9	6.56	4.62	349.6	10.01	2.47	532.6	9.77	1.62
1969	201.7	7.92	4.61	382.3	9.35	2.43	576.8	8.30	1.61
1970	208.7	3.47	4.68	392.2	2.59	2.49	593.5	2.90	1.65
1971	221.4	6.09	4.76	425.3	8.44	2.48	642.8	8.31	1.64
1972	235.3	6.28	4.92	473.1	11.24	2.45	727.9	13.24	1.59
1973	255.8	8.71	5.06	525.7	11.12	2.46	823.2	13.09	1.57
1974	271.5	6.14	5.15	572.2	8.85	2.44	895.3	8.76	1.56

Sources: Board of Governors of the Federal Reserve System; Bureau of Economic Analysis

different rates at which each increased, from year to year. The figures show the percentage increase over the preceding year. Thus M_1 increased .56% from 1960 to 1961. (More accurately, as explained in the last paragraph, this was the percentage increase from December 1959 through December 1960.)

The numbers in the third column under each measure show gross national product for the year divided by the money stock. We divided the money supply into GNP to obtain the numbers we're finally after, on the assumption that GNP is a good proxy for total expenditures. There are, as you know from chapter 8, many expenditures that do not enter into the calculation of gross national product, but it's reasonable to suppose that total expenditures from year to year vary proportionately with GNP.

What do the data show? The relation between the stock of money and total expenditures is reasonably stable from year to year, no matter which concept of money we use. The ratio of GNP to M_1 has been rising over time, but it has been rising fairly steadily. The ratio of GNP to M_3 has not moved from year to year by more than 4%, the amount by which it fell from 1971 to 1972. But M_2 shows the most stable relationship to GNP since 1960. The maximum deviations from the average value of 2.45 were a minus 2.5% (1960) and a plus 2% (1967).

The Velocity of Money Circulation

It will be easier to talk about this ratio if we give it a name. Fortunately, it already has a name. Those who study the relationship between the money supply and aggregate spending call it the *velocity of money circulation* or just *velocity.* (It is sometimes called *income velocity,* because it is the velocity with which money circulates relative to expenditures for goods included

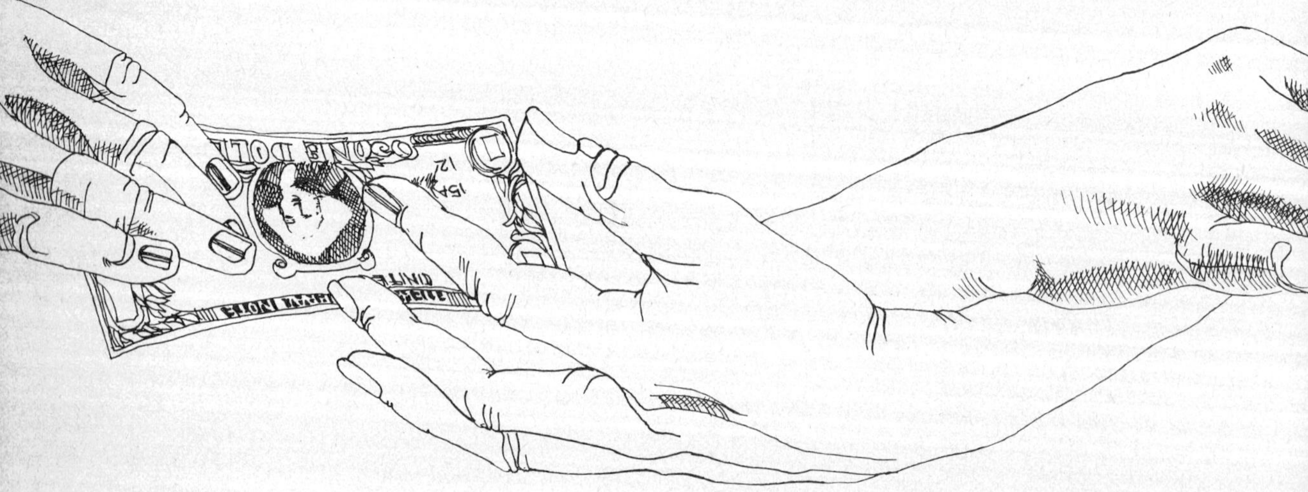

in the calculation of GNP.) It is the average number of times each unit of money changed hands to accommodate total spending on GNP.

The economic meaning of the velocity numbers becomes clearer if we look at them in a slightly different way. In 1972, for example, the public held currency, demand deposits, and time deposits equal in total to $\frac{1}{2.45}$ or 41% of total expenditures on GNP. In 1973, when M_2 was more than $50 billion greater than in the preceding year, it was still about 41% of GNP. Another increase of almost $50 billion in M_2 in 1974 failed to bring any substantial change in that percentage: it continued to be 41% of GNP. It certainly would appear that the public prefers to hold currency plus demand and time deposits equal to about 41% of expenditures on GNP. Despite the sharply different percentage rates at which M_2 has increased from year to year since 1960 (ranging from $2\frac{1}{2}$% to $11\frac{1}{4}$%), the public's holdings of M_2 have varied only between 40% and 42% of GNP.

Does it follow from all of this that the Fed can control the rate at which gross national product grows by controlling the rate of growth in M_2? Have we perhaps found a key to stabilization policy in this stable relationship between M_2 and GNP? Matters are unfortunately not that simple, as later chapters will show. But several questions can be raised at this point even though we are not yet in a position to answer them adequately. In the first place, would M_2 and GNP continue to be so closely correlated if the Fed set out consciously to use one as a means of controlling the other? We could have more confidence in the *future* stability of that relationship if we had a satisfactory theoretical explanation for it. In the absence of such a theoretical explanation we have nothing but an historical correlation; and in human affairs we cannot always be certain that the future will be like the past. One of our subsequent tasks will be to examine a possible reason for the relationship between total expenditures and the stock of

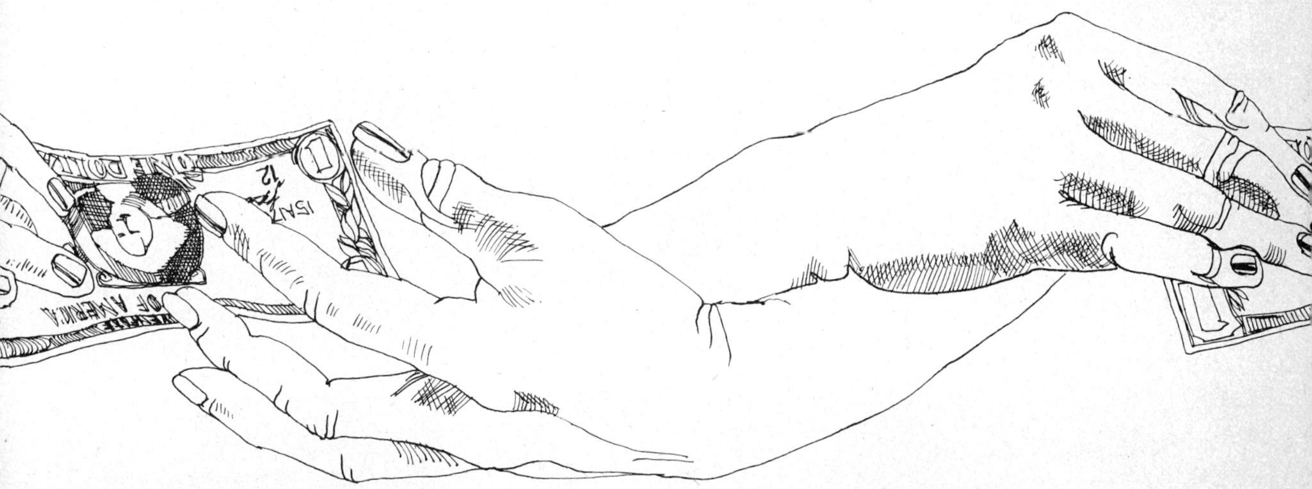

money and to see how much confidence we're entitled to have in the stock of money as an instrument for controlling total spending.

But a more serious dilemma presents itself when we think about the composition of GNP. GNP is equal to real output *times* the price level. An increase in GNP can therefore occur as a result of a decline in the level of production and an increase in prices. That's exactly what did occur from 1973 to 1974. Gross national product rose by 8%, but it did so because a 10.3% increase in prices more than made up for a 2.2% decline in real output. Inflation is hardly compensation for recession. The ability to control the rate of growth in GNP will only be socially useful if it entails the ability to affect *separately* the rate of real growth and the rate of change in the price level.[1]

The third critical question concerns the technical and political constraints on the Fed's ability to manipulate M_2 or any other variable it sets out to control. It's a gross oversimplification to suppose that the Fed has a monetary brake and a monetary accelerator with which it adjusts the money supply as easily and surely as you slow down and speed up your car in traffic. Monetary management may be more like driving a balky mule train which sometimes refuses to go and sometimes won't stop going even when firmly ordered to halt. Let's take a closer look.

FORMULATING AND EXECUTING POLICY

The problems of policy formulation facing the Open Market Committee arise from several sources. The first is uncertainty about the current state of the economy. What's happening to gross national product, employment, prices, exports and imports? It's not enough to have information about what *has* happened—such information is never wholly accurate anyway, and it always arrives with a time lag. If policy is to be effective in countering undesirable trends, policymakers must make good predictions about what *will* happen. The point is obvious and should not have to be mentioned; unfortunately, the obvious is often easy to overlook, and stabilization policy is much too frequently discussed on the assumption that policymakers possess infallible crystal balls.

Political Constraints on Monetary Policy

A second set of problems arises from the fact that the monetary authorities are under continual pressure to pursue goals that may be incompatible

1. Appendix 3 at the end of the book presents a statistical history of the 1974–1975 recession which vividly illustrates this dilemma.

with one another. One such goal is the maintenance of an "orderly market" for government bonds. The phrase is in quotation marks because at times in the past it has really meant making sure that the Treasury can sell new securities when it wants to without depressing the price of government bonds. Deficit spending by the federal government requires the Treasury to bid for funds against other borrowers, often on such a large scale that the borrowing exerts significant upward pressure on interest rates. The Fed, therefore, assumes responsibility for what it calls "even keel" operations whenever the Treasury is engaged in sizeable offerings of new debt. The Fed supplies additional reserves to the banking system at such times to help insure that the Treasury will find purchasers for its bonds without raising interest rates very much and squeezing out other borrowers. This goal can conflict with the Fed's aim of controlling bank reserves to achieve stability of prices and production.

The Fed is also under continual political pressure to keep interest rates down. Down to what? That's rarely made clear. But lower interest rates are better than higher ones in the eyes of a lot of people with considerable political influence. The view persists in some circles that high interest rates benefit bankers at the expense of small business firms, veterans and others who wish to buy homes, and "little people" generally. Who would choose to side with the bankers in such an unequal conflict of interests? Tight money; credit scarcity; bad times for the building industry and the many people (from construction workers, contractors, and materials suppliers through realtors to current and potential homeowners) whose fortunes are tied up with that industry; a falling stock-market average; reduced spending; more unemployment—these are all in the package of associated ills that people point to as evidence that the Fed is pursuing an unduly restrictive monetary policy. And rising interest rates are the most visible indicator, the flashing red light which supposedly signals that the Fed is "putting the economy through the wringer" or creating a "credit crunch." The popularity of such metaphors is itself vivid evidence of the public attitude toward restrictive monetary policy.

Opposition to high interest rates (where "high" often means no more than "higher than they once were") reflects in part an inability to see the necessity of rationing. This is coupled to some extent with hostility toward rationing by means of higher prices, an attitude we've encountered previously. But in the case of interest rates the problem is compounded by the apparently widespread belief that high interest rates arise from a scarcity of money. And money, of course, is only scarce if the monetary authorities decide to make it scarce.

But high interest rates can be attributed to a tight money policy only under special circumstances. In 1973 and 1974, for example, when the prime rate (the rate banks charge on their most secure loans) shot up to

BOND PRICES AND INTEREST RATES

If a bond that will pay $1000 upon maturity ten years from now can be purchased for $558.40, the effective interest rate on that bond is 6%. $1000 to be received in ten years has a present value of $558.40 if the interest rate is 6%.

Suppose that the Fed owns a large number of these bonds and begins to sell heavily. The price of the bonds will fall, just as the price of wheat falls when the supply increases relative to the demand. If the price of the bonds fell all the way to $463.19, the effective interest rate would become 8%. If, on the other hand, the Fed began a large-scale purchasing operation that pulled the price of the bonds up to $613.91, the interest rate would decline to 5%.

Note that the effective interest rate on a marketable security which promises a fixed amount of money does not depend upon what is printed on the bond or what was promised by the original seller. It depends upon the price of the bond in relation to its maturity date.

Does this mean that if you want to buy government bonds but avoid risk you had better purchase nonmarketable securities? Not at all. Suppose you paid $55.84 for a nonmarketable bond which promises to pay $100 in ten years. You will receive 6% interest if you hold the bond to maturity. But if interest rates rise the next day to 8%, you will have lost out on an additional 2% per year by locking yourself in for ten years. If you had purchased a marketable security instead, its price would have fallen to $46.32. The difference of $9.52 is the present value of the additional 2% interest that you just missed out on. Interest is lost in one way, capital value is lost in the other way.

The federal government does allow purchasers of nonmarketable securities to sell their bonds back to the government prior to maturity ("cash" them) for the original principal plus accumulated interest. But the interest accumulates during the first years at less than a 6% rate, so that purchasers of these bonds incur a financial penalty if they fail to hold them to maturity. Bond purchasers can choose their risks, but they cannot avoid them.

record levels, reaching 12% in July of 1974 and staying at that level into October, the cause was definitely *not* tight money. The cause was the experience of inflation and the general expectation of continued inflation. Many financial commentators nevertheless continued to equate high interest rates with tight money and to take the 12% prime rate as incontrovertible evidence that the Fed was "strangling" the economy by "choking off" the supply of money and credit. (Note the metaphors once again.)

Nominal and Real Interest Rates

It may well be that the Fed did not allow sufficient growth in the money stock in 1973 and 1974. The point here is only that interest rates in 1974 were *not* evidence of this fact. We must look closely at the relation between monetary policy and interest rates if we are to avoid the fundamental error that many financial commentators committed in 1974 by using the prime rate (and other interest rates) as evidence of tight money. When the Fed increases the supply of money, the demand remaining constant, elementary supply and demand analysis tells us that the price of money will fall. That's correct. *But interest is not the price of money!* Confusion multiplies like mosquitoes in a mountain thaw when we think of interest as the price of money. Interest rates can be thought of as the price of *credit;* but the price of *money* is the value of money or its purchasing power. Just as the price of strawberries is measured by the amount of money for which strawberries exchange, so the price of money is the amount of strawberries for which money will exchange, or the amount of pipe wrenches, baked beans, book ends, for which it exchanges.

When the Fed increases bank reserves as part of an easier money policy, banks are enabled to expand their lending. Credit becomes easier to obtain and interest rates consequently do tend to move downward. Another way of looking at it is to note that the Fed increases bank reserves by purchasing large quantities of government securities in the bond market. This tends to raise the price of the bonds; and since bond prices are inversely related to their interest yields, we can say that it reduces the interest rate on government bonds. To the extent that government bonds and other interest-paying assets are substitutes, the purchase operations of the Fed push all interest rates down. The two ways of viewing the matter are complementary and lead to the same conclusion: easier money leads to lower interest rates. At least momentarily.

But we must push the analysis further. What happens to the new money created by the Fed when it purchased those bonds and by the commercial banking system when it used the addition to bank reserves to make new loans? The increase in the money supply tends to increase aggregate demand. If the demand for credit from investors, local governments, and consumers expands when aggregate demand grows, that will tend to pull interest rates back up. The net effect after a longer period of time cannot easily be predicted. More importantly, if the expansionary monetary policy leads to an excessive rate of increase in aggregate demand, prices will start to rise. And *the expectation of rising prices will cause interest rates to rise.* Why? Because if prices are expected to increase by 10% per year, lenders will demand an additional 10% in interest as compensation for the anticipated decrease in the value or purchasing power (the *price*) of money. And borrowers with the same expectation of inflation will consent to pay the additional 10% because they anticipate repaying the loan with depreciated dollars. The *nominal* interest rate will then exceed the *real* interest rate by 10%. And it is the nominal rate to which critics were pointing in 1974 when they complained about exorbitant interest rates.

From January 1973 to January 1974, consumer prices rose 9.9% and wholesale prices rose 17.4%. From January 1974 to July 1974, when the prime rate first hit 12%, consumer prices continued to increase at an annual rate of approximately 10% and wholesale prices went up at almost 20% on an annual basis. What would you say were "reasonable" expectations in July of 1974 about the future behavior of prices and the value of money? A 12% prime rate was hardly surprising. The real rate buried at the bottom of that nominal rate may have been as low as 2%.

The irony of all this and the acute policy dilemma it poses for the Fed became exceptionally clear in early 1975, when interest rates were falling but critics complained that they were not falling rapidly enough and called for a faster rate of growth in the money supply to get interest rates down more quickly. The basic facts—the rate of growth in the money supply and the movement of interest rates—were not at issue. The federal funds rate, which is the rate at which banks borrow reserves from one another and a key indicator of interest rate levels in the Fed's thinking, had fallen from 13.5% to 6% between July, 1974 and March, 1975. The total of currency and demand deposits (M_1) had risen at an annual rate of about 2% over this same period. All parties agreed to those facts. Even more interestingly, there was a remarkable consensus among economists inside and outside the Fed that the 2% rate of growth in M_1 was definitely too slow. But the commentators were offering two contradictory analyses in March of 1975. One group was saying that the Fed could and should push interest rates down more rapidly by accelerating the rate of growth in the money supply. The other group maintained that nominal interest rates might in fact rise if the Fed increased the rate of growth in the money supply—even though this group also wanted a faster rate of money growth. In other words, one group was saying to the monetary managers: "Increase the money supply until interest rates go down far enough." And the other was saying: "Increase the money supply but ignore interest rates which might well rise as you do so."

A fuller discussion of exactly how monetary policy affects spending and how both are related to interest rates must be reserved for subsequent chapters. The point here is only that opinions differ and that the Fed is consequently under pressure to control *several* variables whose *joint* control may be beyond its capabilities. The size of the money stock, however defined, is one target at which the Fed is asked to aim; the level and structure of interest rates is an alternative target urged upon the Fed. If changes in interest rates were always tightly correlated with changes in the money stock, it would make little difference at which target the Fed chose to aim. But as we have just seen, the relationship between interest rates and changes in the supply of money is obscure and extremely difficult to predict. By concentrating on the stabilization of interest rates, the Fed may destabilize the rate of growth in the money stock. By concentrating on a stable rate of growth in the money stock, it may allow or even cause fluctuations in interest rates.

The published record of the Open Market Committee's policy directives reveals that through most of the 1960s and to a lesser extent in the 1970s, open market operations were conducted on the assumption that the Fed could and should exercise control over interest rates. Those two convictions began to be less firmly held in the late 1960s, and the focus of the committee's studies and directives came increasingly to be monetary aggregates: bank reserves and outstanding currency, which together are called the *monetary base,* and the stock of money measured by M_1 and M_2. But the published reports of the Committee continue to reveal uncertainty about the most appropriate strategy for economic stabilization.

Steady and Erratic Monetary Growth

Some critics of the Fed believe that this uncertainty is a major cause of the Fed's poor stabilization record over the years. How poor that record has been is, of course, a subject of debate. But one part of the record is clear. The money stock has grown over the years in fits and starts and not in the smooth way recommended by those who believe that fluctuations in the money supply are a major cause of fluctuations in real output. Figure 10A shows what the critics are complaining about. It graphs the annual percentage changes in M_1 and M_2 that were presented in table 10A. To provide a more complete picture, we also show the average federal funds rate in each year as an indicator of the level of interest rates.

Was money a stabilizing or a destabilizing force over this period? Could better monetary policy have produced less inflation over this period? A lower average unemployment rate? Even if the answers to the last two questions are affirmative, does the Fed have the technical capacity and the political independence to design a "better" monetary policy? The issue of political constraints will be considered again after we have examined alternative views of the causes and cures of inflation and recession. But we do want to look more closely at technical problems in monetary management before going on.

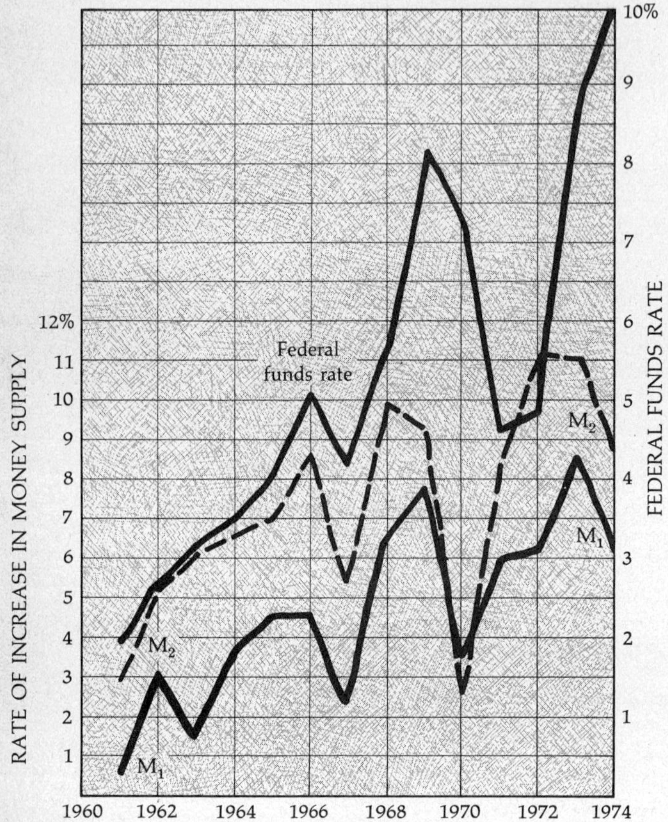

Figure 10A Percentage increase from year to year in M_1 and M_2 and annual average federal funds rate

The Conduct of Open Market Operations

Open market operations are the Fed's day-to-day tool of monetary management. Let's assume that the Open Market Committee has reached a consensus on policy. What happens next?

The real action begins with a domestic policy directive issued to the "Trading Desk" at the New York Federal Reserve Bank. "Trading Desk" is the insiders' jargon for the office of Manager of the System Open Market Account. It is located in the New York Bank because New York City is the center of the country's financial markets. Directives to the Trading Desk are released to the public about 45 days after they're issued, at which time they make extremely dull reading.[1] The assumption behind this procedure is that the public has a right to know what the Fed is up to, but that

1. Prior to April 1975, release was postponed for approximately 90 days.

MONETARY BASE

The *monetary base* is the term used to describe the total of member bank deposits with the Federal Reserve plus currency held by the public and in the vaults of commercial banks (with certain minor adjustments). The monetary base is the variable that the central bankers can most directly affect in their efforts to control the nation's stock of money and, through that, the level of total private spending. As the chart below indicates, however, ability to control the monetary base is not enough to secure accurate control over the money stock, because the relationship between them can and does vary. Note the slight downward drift in the "multiplier" for M_1 and the pronounced upward drift during this period in the "multiplier" for M_2.

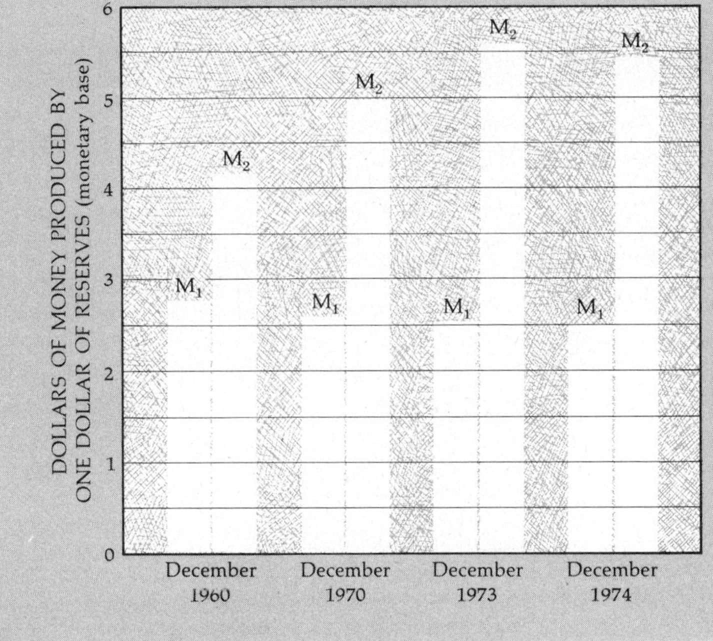

speculation would complicate the Fed's task if the public found out what the Fed was doing before it had finished doing it. Perhaps the Fed prefers not to announce a policy target in advance for fear of embarrassment if it misses.

The directives are drafted by the Open Market Committee at its monthly meeting, after staff reports have been made and the state of the economy, especially of the financial sector, has been discussed. The Trading Desk might be told, for example, to maintain about the prevailing restrictive money market conditions, to keep the annual rate of growth of M_1 between 3% and 7% and M_2 between $4\frac{1}{2}$% and $7\frac{1}{2}$%, to allow the weekly average federal funds rate to vary in an orderly fashion from as low as 7% to as high as $7\frac{1}{2}$%, and to take account all the while of developments in domestic and international financial markets. The Trading Desk may ask for further instructions if these directives turn out to be inconsistent or to raise unforeseen difficulties. The Desk politely does not mention the fact that the directives are always somewhat fuzzy. But monetary management has elements of art as well as science; and this is precisely the point: it may be better to be fuzzy than lucidly wrong.

In executing the directives of the Open Market Committee, the Trading Desk draws upon the voluminous data available to the Fed on monetary aggregates, interest rates of many kinds, bank reserve positions, foreign exchange markets, and the like. But yesterday's data are really useful only insofar as they provide clues to the course of such future events as *tomorrow's* bank reserve positions. So the Trading Desk constructs daily projections and always compares yesterday's forecast of this morning's events with this morning's reality in the hope that this will be a check on the accuracy of this morning's forecast of tomorrow's events that is going to guide this afternoon's open market operations. (The complexity of that sentence is a symbol for the reality it describes.)

Then there are the many factors outside the control of the Trading Desk that affect bank reserves. These factors were discussed at the beginning of this chapter: changes in the public's demand for currency, changes in United States holding of gold and foreign currencies, changes in Treasury balances, changes in float. These must all be countered if the Trading Desk is to exercise control over total bank reserves; but they can only be countered effectively if they are predicted correctly.

So a lot of looking, thinking, conferring, estimating, and projecting goes on each morning before the Trading Desk can transform a policy directive into concrete action for a particular afternoon. The actual open market operations are relatively simple, although they require a fair amount of coordination. Suppose that the Trading Desk decides to sell $200 million in short term government bonds. It contacts the twenty or so government security dealers with which it does business and asks them to obtain bids. Their detailed knowledge of the market enables them to provide within a few minutes firm bids for specific quantities of securities at specific prices. The Trading Desk then chooses the best offers and within half an hour has surrendered title to $200 million of government bonds and received in return checks for $200 million. When the amount of these checks is subtracted from the reserve accounts of the commercial banks on which they are drawn, the Fed will have reduced bank reserves as well as the aggregate stock of money. It will also have applied pressure toward a further reduction in the money supply, since each dollar of reserves under the fractional reserve system is the basis for several dollars of demand deposit liabilities. And all of this will make it a little harder for potential borrowers to obtain bank credit.

But *how much pressure* will this action finally exert on the total banking system and ultimately on the level of spending? That pressure depends on the responses of investors, consumers, local governments, holders of financial assets, and of course commercial bankers. The courses of action they subsequently pursue will be determined by the way they assess the net advantages of many options. Expectations are of crucial importance. A reduction in interest rates will not stimulate spending on capital projects by those who take them as a sign of even lower rates in the near future. Moreover, people are more likely to borrow and spend if their outlook is optimistic. While the actions of the Fed have some effect on private economic forecasts, they hardly control them. In a period of low confidence, a great deal of monetary ease may be unable to induce much additional borrowing and spending. Or the easy money policy may have to be continued for a long time before it counters the prevailing state of pessimism. The danger then is that the ample bank reserves created to spur expansion will be too ample for a period of optimism, and that total spending will generate inflation before the Fed can reverse its policies. A critical question for monetary policy, and one that extensive empirical inquiry has not been able to answer satisfactorily, is the question of the time lag between a monetary action and its effects, from first wave to final ripple.

The design and execution of monetary policy is still a difficult and uncertain art. Scientific knowledge in this area will probably progress slowly enough to keep the life of central bankers interesting for a good while yet.

MUST MONEY HAVE "BACKING"?

Throughout our description of money and the banking system we have treated reserves as constraints upon the power of banks to make loans and thus to expand the money supply. This seems to have little or nothing to do with the concept of a *reserve* fund—something that can be drawn upon in an emergency. But legal reserves do not in fact perform a significant reserve function. The reserve requirement is today primarily a control lever that enables the monetary authorities to adjust the stock of money in the hands of the public.

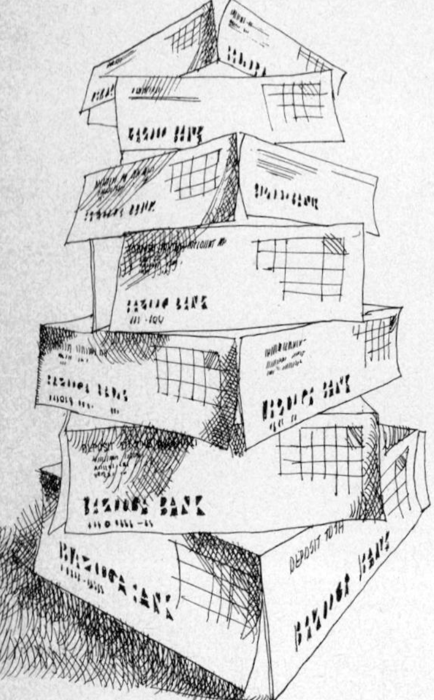

Financial Panics and Monetary Instability

There was a time when bank reserves were thought to be important because they would enable banks to satisfy their depositors' demand for gold or currency. Thus a bank was expected to keep in its vaults gold and currency equal to a certain percent of its liabilities as insurance against the possibility that depositors might suddenly want to make heavy withdrawals. This system did not work well at all. In normal times a bank would be holding large reserves seemingly to no good purpose. But in times of panic, when people began to fear that banks might be unable to meet depositors' demands for cash, even very large reserves were likely to prove inadequate. Banks tried to provide additional protection for themselves without holding a lot of idle, nonearning assets by maintaining deposits in other banks. Interest could be earned on these deposits, but they could also be withdrawn on demand to satisfy an unexpected increase in depositors' demand for gold or currency. However, this was no real solution when the public began to lose confidence in the banking system generally. The New York banks where such interbank deposits were concentrated could not meet the demands on them when these demands started coming in from everywhere simultaneously.

The whole system was like a house of cards. A rumor of trouble at a big bank could create panic among smaller banks holding deposits there. If they rushed to withdraw their deposits, the big bank would find itself with insufficient reserves. If the word spread that some prominent bank might be unable to cover its liabilities, people would become suspicious of other banks and the panic would spread. When banks could not redeem their liabilities, they had to suspend their operations. Each bank closing added to the public's anxiety and made additional runs more likely. Meanwhile, banks would attempt to strengthen their reserve positions in the face of the panic by calling and curtailing loans and by selling liquid assets. At such a time everyone seemed to be demanding gold and currency: depositors who wanted to withdraw their money; banks faced with demands for currency and gold from depositors; business firms called upon to repay promissory notes or denied an extension of existing loans. And as everyone tried to sell off other financial assets to obtain gold or currency, the price of these assets fell. Commercial banks that consequently found the dollar value of the assets they held falling below the value of their liabilities went bankrupt and had to close their doors. This wiped out the money held by customers as deposits in those banks and reduced the money supply. With the stock of money thus reduced and the economy in the throes of a liquidity crisis, the demand for new commodities and services also fell and precipitated a recession.

That pattern of events was repeated for the last time between 1929 and 1933. Currency in circulation rose from $3.6 billion in 1929 to $4.8 billion in 1933, but demand deposits fell from $22.8 billion to $15 billion, reducing the total money supply from $26.4 billion to $19.8 billion: a 25% reduction in the money supply! It isn't surprising that consumer and investor expenditures on new goods was cut almost in half between 1929 and 1933, from $93.4 billion to $47.2 billion.

A More Stable Banking System

But there hasn't been a financial panic in the United States now for more than forty years. Why not? What has changed? The answer has nothing to do with the level of bank reserves. Bank customers no longer rush to withdraw their deposits on every rumor of financial trouble, because their deposits are now insured by the Federal Deposit Insurance Corporation. If a bank closes, for whatever reason, its depositors can expect reimbursement within a few days. When the FDIC was established in 1935, some critics argued that the premiums it charged banks to insure their deposits were far too low, and that it would go broke trying to pay off depositors when banks closed their doors. But the very existence of the FDIC ended the phenomenon of bank runs; and in the absence of runs, banks no longer failed the way they formerly did. The FDIC premiums have thus proved more than adequate. And the institution of the FDIC has turned out to be probably the single most stabilizing reform of the 1930s.

Some credit must also go to improved procedures at the Fed since the 1930s. The Fed now understands clearly that it has the responsibility to provide short term liquidity to the banking system, without regard to the amounts banks happen to be holding as reserves. Thus a bank today can meet any demand for currency, however large, by obtaining additional currency from the Fed. If the bank were to use up its entire reserve balance, the Fed would simply lend the bank additional reserves, taking as collateral some of the IOUs in the asset portfolio of the borrowing bank. Banks are granted access to this "discount privilege" whenever they have a legitimate demand for additional reserves; and this has made the whole banking and monetary system more responsive to changing conditions and more resistant to crises and temporary dislocations.

Every now and then prophets rise up to announce in Sunday supplements and somber tones that the economy is on the verge of another 1929. We don't think you should take them too seriously. Even if the federal government were not as strongly committed as it is to the maintenance of high employment and even if we had learned nothing at all about how to deal with depressions, another collapse like that of the 1930s would be most unlikely. For the banking and monetary system of the United States is today securely buttressed against the kind of collapse that did so much to aggravate fluctuations prior to the thirties and that contributed heavily to the depth and duration of the Great Depression.

What about Gold?

But hasn't something important been left out of all this? If reserves aren't really reserves, what is it that provides *backing* for money? Doesn't money have to have some kind of backing? And where does gold fit into the picture?

The conviction that money must have "backing" if it is to have value raises an interesting question. What stands behind the backing to give *it* value? And behind the backing of the backing? But the whole set of questions is misdirected. In economics, value is the consequence of scarcity. And scarcity is the result of demand plus limited availability. It is clear enough why there exists a demand for money: it can be used to obtain all sorts of other things that people want, which is to say that it is accepted as a medium of exchange. The other part of the picture, limited availability, is taken care of more or less well by the monetary managers.

A commercial bank is solvent not because it has adequate reserves to back up its deposit liabilities, but because it owns assets at least equal in value to its liabilities. When First National makes a $1000 loan by creating a new demand deposit, this $1000 increase in the liabilities of First National is matched by a $1000 increase in its assets. The new asset is the IOU it obtains in return for the loan. A bank stays *solvent* by acquiring good quality assets in return for the loans it makes. Its *liquidity* is protected by the FDIC and by the Fed, which stands ready to discount the bank's eligible assets and provide additional reserves to meet either increased withdrawals of currency or adverse check clearing balances.

But what about the Federal Reserve Banks? We saw that the Fed can create additional money as well as additional bank reserves simply by writing checks on its own credit. Do these checks have any "backing"? Not in the sense most people have in mind when they ask the question. Until rather recently, federal law did require that the Fed maintain reserves equal to a certain percentage of its liabilities. The Fed's liabilities are primarily the sums deposited at the various Reserve Banks by member commercial banks, by foreign institutions, and by the Treasury, plus all outstanding Federal Reserve notes. The old law required the Fed to hold gold or certificates of gold ownership as reserves. But to what purpose? The reserves were not available to anyone on demand, and the statement on old Federal Reserve notes that they could be "redeemed in lawful money" at any Federal Reserve Bank was meaningless: anyone turning notes in for redemption would simply be given new notes. So the statement was finally removed from the face of the notes at about the same time that Congress agreed to drop the pretense that the Fed must itself be required to hold reserves.

The Fed's liabilities, like those of commercial banks, are balanced by

BANK SOLVENCY AND BANK LIQUIDITY

Here is a simplified balance sheet for the Thawville National Bank:

Assets		Liabilities	
Land, buildings, equipment	$300,000	$320,000	Stock shares issued
Vault cash	4,000	160,000	Demand deposits
Reserve account	32,000	200,000	Time deposits
Commercial IOUs	315,000	20,000	Net worth
Government securities	49,000		
Total assets	$700,000	$700,000	Total liabilities plus net worth

The bank is solvent. Its net worth (assets minus liabilities) is $20,000. But is the bank adequately liquid? Suppose that the largest employer in Thawville unexpectedly moves to Eyota and transfers $60,000 in demand deposits to the Eyota Bank. The Thawville Bank will have to meet a sudden $60,000 adverse clearing balance, a sum greater than its entire reserve account. It will find itself insufficiently liquid.

Can the Fed help out? It could loan the Thawville Bank enough reserves to cover its liquidity deficit. Suppose it loaned the $28,000 difference between the Thawville Bank's present reserve account and the demand made on that account by the Eyota Bank. Assets would decline by $32,000 as the bank's reserve account went to zero. But liabilities would also decline by $32,000: a $60,000 decrease in demand deposits minus a $28,000 increase in the Thawville Bank's indebtedness to the Fed. The bank would still be solvent.

The Thawville Bank would find itself in debt to the Fed by more than $28,000, however. The $4000 it still retains as vault cash will not be an adequate legal reserve against its remaining $100,000 in demand deposits and $200,000 in time deposits. Suppose that the minimum reserve requirement on those deposit totals is $25,000; then the Thawville Bank has a reserve deficiency of $21,000. When we add the previous $28,000 to the $21,000 reserve account deficit, the Thawville Bank owes the Fed a total of $49,000. We can think of the Fed as adding $21,000 to the bank's assets by crediting its reserve account with the amount of the deficiency; the Thawville Bank balances this by adding a further $21,000 to its liabilities to the Fed. The bank continues to be both solvent and adequately liquid.

How can the bank eliminate its indebtedness to the Fed? If it sells to other banks its entire holding of government securities, it will acquire from them $49,000 in additional reserves. That will be balanced by a $49,000 loss in earning assets. The bank is still both solvent and liquid.

Now suppose that demand and time deposits in the Thawville Bank fall further as income drops in town and both people and businesses move away. If the Fed refuses to help, the Thawville bank could experience a liquidity problem. It might run out of reserves before it had satisfied depositors' demands for currency and the demands of other banks for reserves to settle negative clearing balances.

If the Thawville Bank tried to maintain its liquidity (satisfy promptly the demands being made upon it for currency and reserves) by selling commercial IOUs to other banks, it might threaten its solvency. If the other banks were unwilling to accept these IOUs except at substantial discounts from the values at which the Thawville Bank is carrying them on its books, the total value of its assets might fall considerably. The bank's liquidity problems would have pushed it toward insolvency.

The Fed protects the solvency of the banking system by helping banks maintain adequate liquidity. If banks are forced to sell earning assets to acquire liquid assets quickly, they may be forced into insolvency through a decline in the value of their asset portfolio. This would be especially likely if an economywide demand for increased liquidity caused the demand for income-earning financial assets to fall just when banks were forced to sell large quantities of these assets.

We have greatly simplified the analysis by ignoring the effect of all this on the largest component of the bank's liabilities, the value of its stock. Net worth and stockholders' equity are in practice inseparable. The market value of the bank's stock could fall all the way to zero as the value of its assets declined, thereby maintaining the balance between assets and liabilities and staving off bankruptcy. Stockholder losses have always been a buffer that partially protected depositors against losses due to bank insolvencies. The risk to bank stockholders is much less now that the Fed works so diligently at maintaining the liquidity of individual banks, even when their problems are attributable to mismanagement.

assets, not by reserves. When the Fed increases its liabilities either by issuing additional Federal Reserve notes or by adding to the amounts in commercial bank accounts, it acquires matching additions to its assets, usually in the form of government securities or high grade commercial IOUs. A commercial bank can become insolvent if the value of the financial assets it owns falls so far that it cannot satisfy the demands for payment of its creditors. Can the Fed become insolvent in the same way? It's hard even to imagine how that might occur. The liabilities of the Fed are the sums on deposit with it and outstanding currency. Suppose these creditors demand payment. What could that even mean? Federal Reserve notes are "legal tender for all debts, public and private"; the Fed can pay off its "debts" by handing the creditor freshly printed "debts," which it can have printed at practically no cost.

A lot of popular thinking on the subject of money is still in the grip of vague notions about "backing" for money, of "ultimate" assets somehow "standing behind" the money we use in everyday transactions. These ideas are probably a heritage from the days of the gold standard. But the United States is not on the gold standard (or any other standard). American citizens have not had the privilege of redeeming their money in gold since the 1930s, and the last vestige of any real gold standard disappeared in the 1970s, when the United States abandoned its commitment to redeem in gold the dollar holdings of foreign central banks. If this fact causes you to doubt the value of your currency or checking account, you can easily shore up your faith by "selling" your money to others. You will find that they are willing to take it and to give you other valuable assets in exchange.

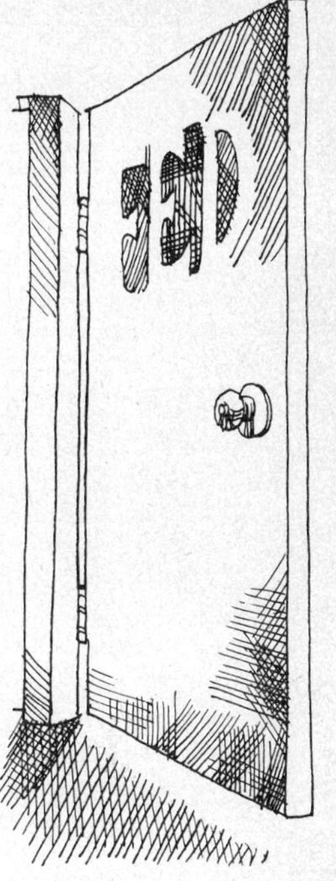

Governments and the Value of Money

The critical factor in preserving the value of money is its limited availability and confidence that the supply will continue to be limited. Nature has made gold relatively rare. It's up to the Fed to keep Federal Reserve notes and demand deposits relatively rare. But some people have more confidence in the reliability of Nature than in the reliability of central bankers and governments. That is why some intelligent and well-informed people would like to see us return to a genuine gold standard, under which currency could be exchanged for gold at some fixed ratio. It is *not* because they think that money must have backing, but because they distrust governmental money managers. If the government were required to maintain the convertibility of demand deposits into currency and currency into gold at predetermined exchange ratios, the limited availability of gold would severely restrict the government's power to increase the money supply.

As a matter of fact, governments have often, especially in wartime, created additional money as a way of financing expenditures without the painful necessity of openly levying taxes. The consequence has usually been inflation, which is a more concealed but hardly a more equitable way for the government to finance its expenditures. Urging a return to the gold standard would seem to be a counsel of despair, however. A government so irresponsible that it must be reined in by gold would be most unlikely to adopt a gold standard or to keep the reins on when they

LESSONS FROM A BANK FAILURE

At the end of 1973 the Franklin National Bank of New York was ranked as the nation's twentieth largest bank and had total deposits of more than $3.7 billion. The spectacular failure of Franklin National in 1974 stirred up memories of the early 1930s, when numerous bank failures contributed to the paralysis of private spending. But the case of Franklin National demonstrates the significant differences between the banking system in the 1930s and in the 1970s.

First, because depositors were insured against loss, they did not initiate a run on the bank when rumors of its mismanagement began to circulate early in 1974. Second, Franklin National *was* mismanaged. Franklin's downfall was not triggered by the state of the economy, something beyond Franklin's control, but by foolish speculation in foreign exchange, apparently motivated by managerial megalomania. Finally, the determination of government monetary managers and banking authorities to assume responsibility was clearly demonstrated. They may even have been *too* eager to assume responsibility and to rescue the bank's owners from the consequences of mismanagement. One could easily infer from the Franklin case that the most rational policy in bank management is a high risk policy, because any profits will go to the bank's owners and drastic losses will be absorbed by protective agencies of the federal government. The Fed ended up lending Franklin $1.7 billion in 1974 to prevent its collapse. And the loan was assumed by the Federal Deposit Insurance Corporation in October 1974, after Franklin had failed. That may have been unwise, but it certainly wasn't a do-nothing policy.

irritated. The problem of irresponsible government is a weighty one; but we cannot believe that the problem could be solved by a return to the gold standard.

Consideration of that issue does, however, raise the question of government spending, taxation, and deficits. The canons of financial orthodoxy long decreed that a government must *balance its budget*. The failure to do so was regarded as a clear sign of irresponsibility, and persistence in such a course was seen as a guarantee of eventual economic disaster. That view was challenged head-on in the 1930s by the argument that government deficits, under the proper circumstances, were a powerful tool for the creation of prosperity. A new way of thinking about the interrelations

GOVERNMENTS OLD AND NEW

Could we solve the problem of irresponsible government management of the money supply by returning to a metallic standard and using as our monetary base some commodity whose quantity is firmly restricted by nature? That was the practice in 1776 when Adam Smith wrote the following:

> In every country of the world, I believe, the avarice and injustice of princes and sovereign states, abusing the confidence of their subjects, have by degrees diminished the real quantity of metal which had been originally contained in their coins. . . . By means of those operations the princes and sovereign states which performed them were enabled, in appearance, to pay their debts and to fulfill their engagements with a smaller quantity of silver than would otherwise have been requisite. It was indeed in appearance only; for their creditors were really defrauded of a part of what was due to them. All other debtors in the state were allowed the same privilege, and might pay with the same nominal sum of the new and debased coin whatever they had borrowed in the old. Such operations, therefore, have always proved favorable to the debtor and ruinous to the creditor, and have sometimes produced a greater and more universal revolution in the fortunes of private persons than could have been occasioned by a very great public calamity.

> Where there is a will on the part of sovereigns, a way is usually found.

between income, expenditure, deficits, money, and interest rates evolved—a way of thinking often referred to as "the Keynesian revolution." That's the subject to which we now turn.

Once Over Lightly

Commercial bank reserves are the primary lever that the Fed uses in its efforts to control the money supply.

The Fed can control bank lending and money creation by altering legal reserve requirements or by altering the dollar volume of bank reserves.

The Fed increases the volume of commercial bank reserves by extending credit. It reduces reserves by withdrawing credit previously supplied.

The Fed extends credit directly to a commercial bank by adding to its reserve account and taking as collateral notes or securities in the bank's asset portfolio. The rate of interest on such loans is called the discount rate.

The Fed changes bank reserves more indirectly by purchasing government securities or by selling securities from its large portfolio. If it purchases newly issued securities, it pays for them by crediting the Treasury's account. When the Treasury draws on this account to make payments to the public, the Fed credit becomes reserves in the commercial banking system. When the Fed purchases previously issued government securities from the public, it pays by means of checks drawn on its own credit, which become bank reserves when deposited.

The purchase and sale by the Fed of government securities as a means of controlling the money supply or otherwise influencing financial markets is called open market operations. Open market operations are the Fed's principal working tool in the conduct of monetary policy.

There are major disagreements among competent authorities about the conduct of open market operations. These disagreements reflect differences of opinion both about the proper goals for monetary policy to pursue and about the targets at which it should aim in pursuit of these goals. Such differences of opinion have been difficult to resolve, because the chain of causal sequences with which the Fed must be concerned is long and uncertain at many points: from data gathering to policy discussions to Trading Desk operations to reserve changes to movements in monetary aggregates and money market conditions to total spending. And at the last there remains uncertainty about the way changes in total spending will separately affect output and the price level.

A key concept for understanding the relation between the money supply and levels of economic activity is the velocity of money circulation. This is the average number of times each unit of money changes hands over a period of time. Velocity declines when the public chooses to hold larger money balances and rises when the public chooses to reduce its money holdings relative to its income or expenditures.

Reserves do not function today as backing for money but as constraints upon bank credit expansion and money creation. The value of money depends not upon its backing, but upon its acceptability as a medium of exchange. The monetary managers maintain the acceptability of money by restricting its quantity.

The Fed contributes to monetary stability by helping the banks maintain liquidity under changing circumstances. Improved Fed procedures for maintaining liquidity at desired levels and the establishment of the Federal Deposit Insurance Corporation have made the banking and monetary system of the United States far more stable than it was prior to the 1930s.

QUESTIONS FOR DISCUSSION

1. To an employee, a bank is a place, people, and activities. But to an economist, banks are often nothing but assets and liabilities in motion. Simplified asset and liability statements are given below for the Federal Reserve System and the Commercial Banking System, each viewed as a single composite bank.

FEDERAL RESERVE SYSTEM		COMMERCIAL BANK SYSTEM	
Assets	Liabilities	Assets	Liabilities
————	————	————	————
————	————	————	————
————	————	————	————
————	————	————	————

(*a*) Insert each of the following dollar amounts (in billions) into the appropriate place or places. (Don't worry about the fact that assets aren't equal to liabilities; these are only partial statements of bank positions.)

$80 U.S. government securities owned by the Fed
 55 U.S. government securities owned by commercial banks
  3 U.S. Treasury deposits with the Fed
215 Demand deposits owned by the public
  8 Federal Reserve notes in commercial bank vaults
200 IOUs of customers who have borrowed from commercial banks
  2 Member bank borrowings from the Fed
 30 Member bank reserves on deposit with the Fed
 65 Federal Reserve notes in the hands of the public
  4 Treasury tax and loan accounts at commercial banks

(*b*) How large is M_1?

(*c*) The public decides to increase its holding of currency to $70 billion by reducing demand deposits to $210 billion. How might this additional currency be supplied, and how would that affect the asset and liability components above?

(*d*) What would be the effects of a Fed purchase of $2 billion in government securities from the commercial banks? What would be the effects of a purchase from the nonbanking public?

(*e*) Trace through the effects on various assets and liabilities if the Treasury borrows an additional $5 billion from the Fed and subsequently spends that amount for goods purchased from the public. What difference would it make if the Treasury borrowed from the commercial banks?

(*f*) What would be the effect if the Treasury borrowed from the Fed and just kept the borrowed funds idle in its account at the Fed? Suppose it kept the borrowed funds idle in its tax and loan accounts with the commercial banks?

(*g*) Where else could the Treasury go to borrow? What effects would you expect on the bank asset and liability statements if the Treasury spent money after borrowing it from the nonbank public?

2. If the Treasury were to sell bonds to the Fed and then purchase goods and services with the proceeds, the money supply would increase. If resources in the economy were already fully employed, where would the goods and services purchased by the government come from? What would happen to prices? Do you agree that "inflation is a tax"?

3. Many people worry about the size of the national debt. (We'll examine that concern in chapter 12.) The marketable debt of the United States government (the savings bonds that many individuals own are not marketable, because they cannot be bought and sold) currently stands at around $300 billion. Suppose the Fed, a government agency, bought up all the outstanding marketable government securities, so that—in a sense—the government owed the debt only to itself. How could this be done? What would happen as a result?

4. You're the manager of a commercial bank, and you want to increase your bank's excess legal reserves. Perhaps you currently have *negative* excess reserves—in which case your bank is borrowing from the Fed, and the Fed may be putting pressure on you to remove that debt. Or you may simply believe that your bank would be in a more advantageous position with a somewhat higher level of reserves. What policies could you pursue to reach your objective? What effects would these policies have on the banking and monetary system?

5. Why does the Fed use open market operations as its principal tool of monetary management rather than changes in legal reserve requirements?

6. Why might the Fed find it easier to expand the money supply in a period of prosperity than in a period of falling output and rising unemployment?

7. There were 14,338 commercial banks in the United States as of June 30, 1974. One-third of these, or 4695, were national banks and therefore required to maintain membership in the Federal Reserve System. Only 1068, or one-ninth, of all state banks chose membership in the System. That was down from one-sixth of all state banks ten years earlier. Do you think membership should be required for all banks? How would you assess the political chances for such a proposal?

8. The only practicable way to calculate the velocity of money circulation is to divide a measure of the money stock into some measure of total expenditures.

(*a*) Test your understanding of the velocity concept by thinking up some way by which it could be measured more directly.

(*b*) Suppose you kept track for one year of your daily holdings of currency and demand deposits. How could you obtain from these data a measure of your own personal contribution to the velocity of money circulation?

9. Examine the data in appendix 3 at the end of the book to see the difference between the rate of change in the money supply and the rate of change in real, as distinct from nominal, output and income. What was the percentage change in M_2 from the first quarter to the fourth quarter of 1974? The percentage change in nominal GNP? The percentage change in GNP when measured in dollars of constant value?

10. When are interest rates "too high"? Why is it difficult for the Fed to control the level of interest rates?

11. The text asserts that in the spring of 1975, most economic commentators were urging the Fed to increase the rate of growth in the money stock. As long as they agreed in this policy recommendation, why would it matter whether they disagreed over the effect this would have on interest rates?

12. Does figure 10A provide any evidence on the question of how interest rates respond to changing rates of increase in the money stock?

13. Why is it important to know not only how large an impact a change in the money stock will have on spending but also *when* this impact will occur?

14. If it is not essential to the value of money that it have "backing" of some kind, why do so many people believe otherwise?

15. What changes in the attitudes of commercial bank managers toward risk and in bank operating procedures would you expect to observe when the government assumes a substantial responsibility for preventing bank failures? Who is likely to gain and who is likely to lose as a result of such changes in bank operations?

16. "Nature has made gold rare but people have made it scarce." Explain.

THE KEYNESIAN REVOLUTION
AND INCOME-EXPENDITURES ANALYSIS

John Maynard Keynes was born in 1883 and died in 1946. In between he made a modest fortune in the stock market, married a prima ballerina, edited the official journal of the Royal Economic Society, composed brilliant biographical sketches, served as a Treasury representative at the Versailles peace conference, resigned that position to write a scathing attack on the treaty and its architects, was raised to the peerage as Lord Keynes, and helped design the international monetary system that was put into effect after World War II. He did a great deal more as well, for he was a brilliant, versatile, and energetic man. Almost twenty years after his death he achieved the cover of *Time* magazine, not for any of these accomplishments but because of a book on money that he had published in 1930 and a second book written out of dissatisfaction with the first one. The second and far more famous book was *The General Theory of Employment, Interest and Money.*

ORIGINS OF THE GENERAL THEORY

The *General Theory*, published in 1936, is by common agreement an obscure and in large part badly written book. The lucid and vivid prose of Keynes's biographical essays breaks through only occasionally in this, his best-known work and probably the single most influential economics book of the century. "What the *General Theory* Means" was a topic for

     Chapter Eleven

numerous essays and symposia after 1936, evidence both that its meaning was deemed important and that few were certain just what the meaning was. Books and articles on what Keynes *really* meant are still appearing four decades after publication of the *General Theory.*

Sometimes we see more readily what a person is trying to assert if we understand what it is he's rejecting. Keynes was convinced that the economic analysis in which he had been trained was incapable of diagnosing and prescribing a cure for depressions because its approach to the question actually assumed the problem away.

Disequilibrium and Equilibrium

What do we observe in a period of depression or recession? Workers are unable to find jobs because employers are not hiring because products cannot be sold. There is an imbalance, it would appear, between quantities demanded and quantities supplied. A surplus exists or, in the language of the nineteenth century economists, an excess of supply.

The economist's solution to a surplus is a lower price. If workers cannot find jobs, it's because they're holding out for a wage that's above their marginal productivity; at some lower wage, all those who want work will be able to find it. If producers cannot sell their entire output, it's again because they're asking too high a price; useful goods can always be sold at a sufficiently low price. It's a matter of supply and demand. A recession is simply a temporary disequilibrium. It will come to an end when prices and wages move to their equilibrium or market-clearing levels.

But there is a difficulty that the traditional curves of supply and demand conceal. They overlook the question of the *path* to equilibrium. Figure 11A shows a supply curve and two demand curves. If for some reason demand falls from D_1 to D_2, the price will presumably move from p_1 to p_2. *But it won't jump there instantaneously.* Not even in the most competitive markets will a new equilibrium price be reached without a *process* requiring time and including step-by-step adjustments.

Through what process will the new equilibrium price of p_2 be reached? Let's make the reasonable assumption that suppliers continue for a while to ask p_1 when the demand falls to D_2. How would they even know the demand had fallen, after all, until they had tried for a time to sell at p_1 and found themselves unable to locate purchasers? But with demand at D_2 and the price still at p_1, the quantity purchased will be q_2. The difference between q_1 and q_2 is the surplus in the hands of sellers and is an unintended and unwanted addition to suppliers' inventories. Eventually this surplus will lead to price cutting and a movement toward the new equilibrium, where the price will be p_2, and the quantity q_3 will be both demanded and supplied. Or will it?

Usually, we just assume in the supply-demand analysis of competitive markets an instantaneous jump to the new equilibrium after a change in one of the curves. But when we do so, we're overlooking the actual process of adjustment and everything that might occur as a consequence of this time-consuming process. What occurs in the case just described? For one thing, the gross income of suppliers is immediately reduced by the difference between $q_1 \times p_1$ and $q_2 \times p_1$. With their incomes unexpectedly reduced, suppliers (who are also demanders) may be compelled to reduce their own demands for goods. As they do so, they shift the demand curves for other products downward to the left, creating for other suppliers the same situation they themselves encountered. Moreover, as producers now find themselves with unintended additions to their inventories, they will curtail production until inventories have been reduced. This reduces the incomes of employees as it increases unemployment. As the adjustment process follows the same course in one market after another, declining incomes and declining demand may spread cumulatively through the economy.

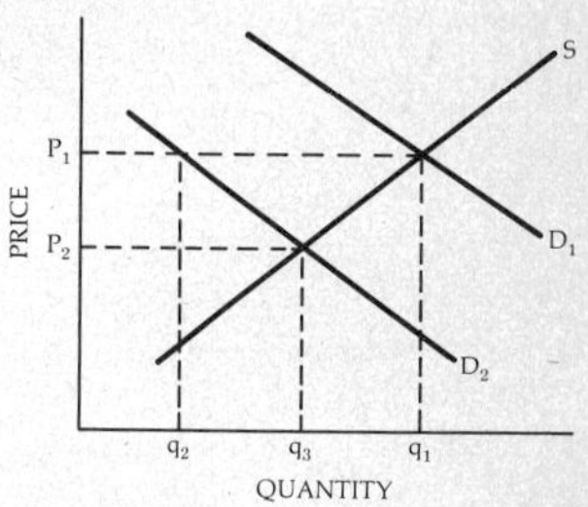

Figure 11A Paths toward equilibrium

Now go back to figure 11A. With demand falling generally, the new equilibrium of p_2 and q_3 *may never be reached.* Before the price can reach p_2, demand may fall even further as a consequence of the general, economy-wide decline in sales, output, employment, and income.

This is all much too simple of course, but it is surely no more so than the assumption that prices shift instantaneously to new market-clearing levels whenever demand falls. The simple description above at least calls attention to the fact that production, marketing, the receipt of income, spending, and price changes all occur in a world characterized by uncertainty, so that buyers and sellers, whether of goods or labor, must *search* for a new equilibrium. This inevitably takes time. And so there will always be a period of disequilibrium before any new equilibrium is reached. And that raises the questions which bothered Keynes.

How long will it take to reach a new equilibrium after the original one has been disturbed by a decline in demand? What prevents the reduced incomes during the disequilibrium period from causing a further and cumulative fall in demand? And why do we assume that the new equilibrium will be unaffected by what happens during the disequilibrium?

Assuming the Problem Away

In the *General Theory*, Keynes wanted to replace the "classical" concept of the equilibrating process because it was not a process at all. Its *assumption* of perfect information guaranteed that all markets would always be in equilibrium *and implied that unemployment or excess supply was impossible.*

No economic theorist prior to Keynes or since his time has actually

SEARCHING FOR "EQUILIBRIUM"

A popular sequence in the old silent comedy films had the hero trying to balance a kitchen table by sawing a little off one leg, then another, then still another, always removing a bit too much and trying to correct it on another leg until he wound up with a coffee table. That's an illustration of how a final equilibrium can be altered by the process of reaching equilibrium.

Here's another simple example drawn from agriculture. The equilibrium price in the graph below would seem to be $3. But planting decisions are made in anticipation of prices that may not be realized. Suppose that the quantity of corn planted depends on *last year's* price, while the quantity demanded depends on *this year's* price. In Year One, drought and blight reduce the intended crop of 5 billion bushels to an actual harvest of 4.5 billion. The price in Year One therefore becomes $3.50. Looking at that price in Year Two, farmers plant for a harvest of 5.5 billion bushels. When they hit their target, the price falls to $2.50. So in Year Three farmers plant less corn (and more soybeans or sorghum). In Year Three, the price rises as a result to $3.50.

In a world of uncertainty, where the "right" decision depends upon correctly guessing what others are doing concurrently, "equilibrium" may never be reached. Or it may only be approached after a long and costly groping process.

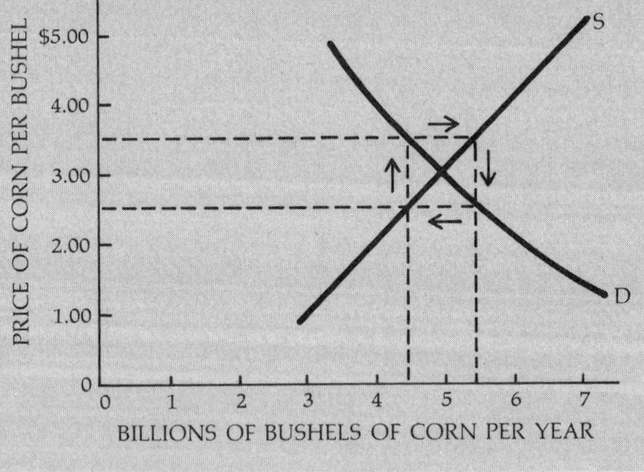

thought that unemployment is impossible or that equilibrium reoccurs instantaneously whenever it's disturbed. But Keynes believed that the equilibrium-oriented and essentially timeless analysis which dominated economists' thinking prevented them from formulating an adequate theory of changes in total output and income. They had no theory of recessions, for the ruling theory assumed them away. The challenge he set himself in the *General Theory* was to "escape from habitual modes of thought and expression" and from old ideas "which ramify, for those brought up as most of us have been, into every corner of our minds." He wanted to construct a theory that would explain the phenomenon of recession by taking into account the consequences of uncertainty and the processes of adjustment over time. That was the origin of *income-expenditures analysis.*

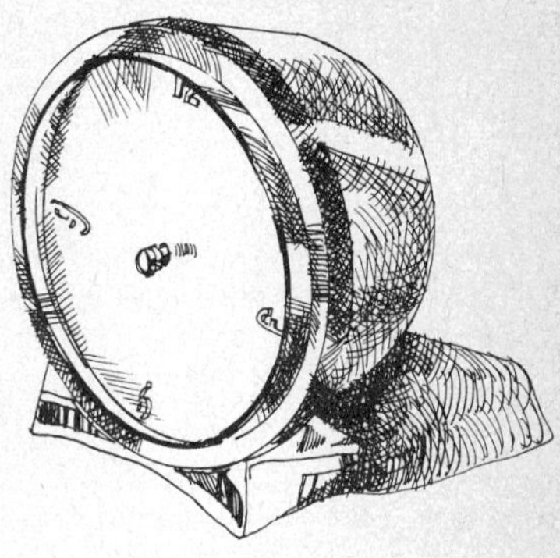

INCOME-EXPENDITURES ANALYSIS: AN INTRODUCTION

Keynes employed two new concepts to express his ideas in simple theoretical form. One was the *propensity to consume* (now more often called the *consumption function*); the other was the *multiplier.*

The Consumption Function

We can best approach income-expenditures analysis by asking what determines consumers' demand for goods. The answer is: far more factors than we can begin to enumerate; but one of these factors is surely consumer income. Keynes maintained that if we deal with *all* consumers together, we can confidently expect to observe a stable relation between aggregate income and aggregate consumption. He called this relation the *propensity to consume.* Moreover, we can confidently state the normal shape of this function, he argued, on the basis of introspection and everyday facts of experience: People increase or decrease their consumption as their income increases or decreases, but not by as much as the change in their income. Let's see to what conclusions this leads.

Picture first a very simple economic system without government, foreign trade, or investment. All demand is therefore consumer demand, and all the income generated by production goes to consumers. Because production responds to demand, consumption expenditure determines output. The economy can be viewed as the simple system of circulation shown in figure 11B. Consumption expenditures are exchanged for consumer goods in the lower loop. In the upper loop, income is provided to consumers in exchange for productive services. The system is in equilibrium when the value of the flows in the top loop equals the value of the flows in the bottom loop. For an inequality in either direction must lead to changes in the rates of flow. If the income that producers pay for productive services exceeds the expenditures consumers make for goods, producers won't be able to pay as much income to consumers in the next round of circulation. If expenditures exceed income, on the other hand, income will increase as

Figure 11B The economy as a circular flow system

producers expand output and purchase more productive services to do so. Only when the flows exactly match each other is there no incentive toward change.

The Multiplier

What happens now if something occurs to jar the system away from equilibrium? Let's suppose that consumption expenditures decline because consumers suddenly decide to hold on to a portion of their income. Fewer goods will now flow to consumers. But producers will subsequently find themselves holding excess inventories of goods and they will curtail production. As a result they will be purchasing fewer productive services from consumers, and so income will decline.

But the concept of the consumption function asserts that consumption expenditure varies in the same direction as income. And so consumption expenditure will experience a further decline. Producers will consequently reduce output again, which will further reduce consumer income; this will again reduce consumption expenditure, and reduced consumption expenditures will again lower production.

Where will the process stop? On the assumption Keynes made about the *shape* of the consumption function, the process will not continue indefinitely. Recall that consumption increases or decreases as income increases or decreases, *but by a smaller amount.* Suppose that for every $1 change in income, consumption demand changes by 75¢. We can then predict that an initial reduction in demand will lead eventually to a reduction in income and consumption *four times as large.* The *multiplier* in this case is four.

The Marginal Propensity to Consume and the Multiplier

The multiplier is the ratio between the eventual change in income and the initial change in demand that caused income to change. How do we know it would have a value of four in the circumstances just described? The logic is exactly the same as that used with the "money multiplier" in chapter 9, relating changes in the money stock to changes in bank reserves. Assume an initial decline in consumption of $64. Income will fall by $64 as a result. Consumption will then fall again by (.75)$64, or $48, reducing income by another $48. This will cause a reduction of consumption by (.75)$48, or $36. The cumulative total of all the successive declines in income will be:

$$\$64 + (.75)\$64 + (.75)^2\$64 + (.75)^3\$64 + (.75)^4\$64 + \cdots + (.75)^n\$64$$

or

$$\$64 + \$48 + \$36 + \$27 + \$20.25 + \$15.1875 + \$11.390625 + \cdots$$

which approaches a total of $\$64[1/(1 - .75)]$ as n becomes infinitely large. Since $1/(1 - .75)$ is 4, the multiplier will be 4 when the marginal propensity to consume is .75. The *marginal propensity to consume* is the term Keynes applied to *the ratio of the change in consumption expenditure to the change in income.*

By means of these two concepts—the propensity to consume and the multiplier—Keynes linked aggregate demand and aggregate supply in a different kind of equilibrium analysis. In doing so he provided a theoretical framework that could explain both (1) the cumulative character of economic downturns and revivals and (2) why a decline or an upturn, once begun, did not continue indefinitely.

SAVING AND INVESTMENT: THE PUZZLE

But hasn't something crucial been overlooked? When income is constant and consumption declines, as we assumed at the beginning in the simple case just described, something else must immediately rise by the same amount. Income not spent for consumption goods is income saved. What happened, we might ask, to that initial increase in unspent income or saving? Did it just sit idly in cookie jars, checking accounts, or savings deposits? Did it have no effect at all on the multiplier process and the movement of the economic system to its new equilibrium between aggregate demand and aggregate supply?

Investment and Saving Before the General Theory

Economists have always known that a portion of consumer income is saved and not spent for consumption goods. But they have also known that consumption is not the total of all expenditures for new goods. Even leaving out, as we shall continue to do in this chapter, government and international trade, the public also purchases *investment* goods. Part of the demand for new production is a demand for capital goods.

As we pointed out in chapter 8, the distinction between capital goods and consumer goods cannot be drawn precisely. Capital goods are defined as produced goods used to produce future goods. But that actually describes every useful good that gets produced. In the national income and product accounts, however, a clear distinction is drawn. Capital goods include (1) producers' durable equipment; (2) producers' buildings; (3) producers' inventories, from stockpiled raw materials through goods in process to goods completed but not yet sold; and (4) residences. The last is added to what is otherwise an exclusively producers' list because the purchase of a house results in a flow of services extending far into the future. The income and product accounts classify government expenditures separately, largely to avoid the difficult problem of distinguishing those government expenditures that are investment from those which should be classified as consumption. However the distinction is finally drawn, it's a useful one. And it's necessary as a complement to the distinction between consumption and saving.

Why, we might ask, would anyone choose to save a portion of his income rather than use it to obtain goods that will provide present satisfaction? The answer is that people are to some extent future-oriented and want to provide for future satisfaction. That can be done by saving: by not consuming the entire amount of current income. If savings are effectively invested, the stream of future satisfactions will be larger than it would be if savings were merely allowed to accumulate in the form of unused money hoards. As long as there are investment opportunities available that offer the prospect of a positive net return, it makes little sense to save and not invest. Many of the "classical" economists whom Keynes criticized were so convinced of the absurdity of saving and not investing that they *identified* saving with investment. "No one saves but to invest." "The portion of income that is saved purchases labor and commodities just as surely as that which is said to be spent." "No one was ever so absurd as to assume that saving will be hoarded." And notice what this implies. A decline in consumption will not trigger any cumulative decline in output and income, because a decline in consumption is a rise in saving, saving is always invested, and investment expenditure must therefore rise by just enough to compensate for the decline in consumption expenditure.

Did the "Classical" Analysis Make Sense?

At first glance all this seems an affront to common sense. People *do* sometimes save without investing, and surely without investing right away. Some saving *does* get hoarded, for short periods of time at least. Income that is saved may be placed in a bank savings account to accumulate interest, but until it is borrowed by someone who wants to spend it, it will *not* purchase "labor and commodities." In what world were the authors of those statements living?

Their problem was the habit of analyzing the phenomena of saving and investment in that timeless world without uncertainty that we criticized earlier, a world in which any imbalance between supply and demand produces an instantaneous change in relative prices and all markets are cleared. They reasoned that if the quantity of savings supplied is greater than the quantity demanded by investors, the two quantities will be brought to equality through some combination of changes in the rate of interest and changes in relative prices.

The following argument tries to present their case in a simple way. Consumption plus saving by definition equals income; and income measures the supply of output at market prices. Consumption plus investment is the demand for output at current prices. If consumption plus saving is greater than consumption plus investment, the quantity of goods being supplied is greater than the quantity being demanded *at current prices;* and so the price level will fall. Not all prices will fall; but the prices of the particular goods in oversupply will fall, causing the average of all prices to decline, until the quantity demanded just equals the quantity supplied.

The trouble with this argument is that it assumes the problem out of existence. It postulates a system of prices so flexible and rapid in its adjustments that everything produced will always be sold. If that were the case, real output and income would never have to make any adjustments in the face of a declining demand. The problem, however, is to understand why real output and income *do* fall; a theory that explains why they will *not* fall is hardly what we're looking for.

When we examine the actual processes of producer adjustment to an inadequate demand, we observe something quite different. Suppose that producers anticipate total sales of $500 billion; they consequently produce $500 billion of goods and generate $500 billion in income. Consumption

EQUALITIES, IDENTITIES, AND
EQUILIBRIUM CONDITIONS

The equality between saving and investment that plays such a central role in income-expenditures analysis can be a source of confusion if the different kinds of equality are not carefully distinguished.

Actual saving and actual investment are equal in our model by definition of the terms we're using:

$$\text{total output} = \text{total income}$$
$$\text{total output} = \text{consumption purchases}$$
$$+ \text{ investment purchases}$$
$$\text{total income} = \text{consumption purchases} + \text{saving}$$

Necessarily, then:

$$\text{investment purchases} = \text{saving}$$

All four of the equalities listed above are identities, which means that the equality is entailed by the definitions of the terms. The equality sign in such cases is often written with three lines rather than two to indicate that the terms are equal by definition. We don't look at any empirical data to see whether total output really does equal total income; if the data we're using provide different totals, we assume that errors occurred in measurement.

The definitions used in the model are not arbitrary, however. They rest upon some real-world relationships. Individuals and societies will either use their current income for current consumption or reserve it for the future, which means that they will either consume their income or save it. They will utilize current output either to provide current services or to provide services in the future, which means that they will either consume it or invest it. The definitional equality or identity between saving and investment rests upon the recognition that saving and investment are different sides of the same phenomenon, namely, the income or output that is not currently consumed but assigned instead to future use.

The classifications used in national income accounting similarly reflect the fact that investment is constrained by the supply of saving and that all saving is invested in some fashion. Even income converted into currency and placed under the mattress has, from the standpoint of the mattress stuffer, been invested. He has refrained from present consumption in order to have money available in the future. He has therefore made an investment, even though it earns a zero rate of return if the purchasing power of money does not change, and a negative rate of return if inflation occurs.

The equality between *intended* saving and *intended* investment is not an identity. It is a *condition of equilibrium*. Think of two wash tubs with a connecting tube at the bottom. Will the water levels in the two tubs necessarily be equal? Not always. If an additional bucket of water is poured quickly into the tub on the right, the water level will be higher there than in the other tub. But water

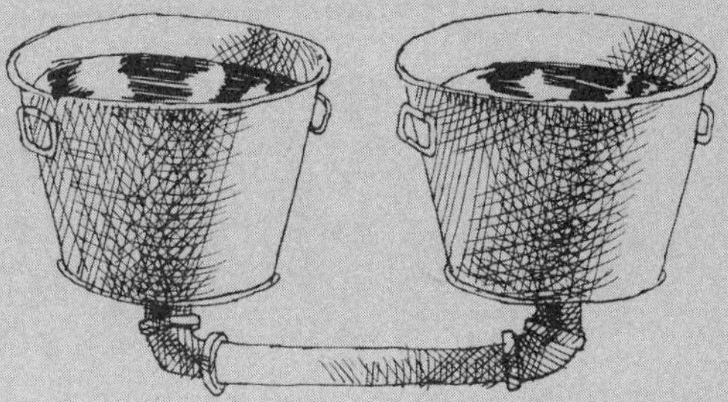

will immediately begin flowing through the tube from the tub on the right to the tub on the left and will continue flowing until the levels are again equal. We can say, then, that equality of the water levels is an equilibrium condition, because if the water levels are not equal they will change in both tubs until they are equal.

The equality between intended saving and intended investment is similarly an equilibrium condition, because if they are not equal intended saving will adjust until it is equal to intended investment. In the case of the tubs, the divergence in pressure is the equalizing or equilibrating mechanism. In the case of intended saving and investment, changes in income push intended saving toward equality with intended investment.

was expected to be $450 billion, and investment expenditures were expected to absorb the remaining $50 billion of output. But consumers for some reason cut back their expenditures to $440 billion and thereby automatically increased their savings to $60 billion. Since it is altogether unlikely that investors will want to purchase those undemanded $10 billion of consumer goods, producers will find themselves holding $10 billion of *unintended inventories*. Additions to inventory are one component of total investment, so total investment will in fact be equal to saving at $60 billion. But $10 billion of that is *unintended investment*. And it will have an effect on future output and income. Producers will curtail production, laying off workers and reducing their demand for other resources, in an effort to bring their inventories down closer to the preferred level.

The classical economists had another argument to fall back upon. The interest rate, as we pointed out in chapter 5, expresses the relative values of present and future goods. At lower interest rates, future goods become

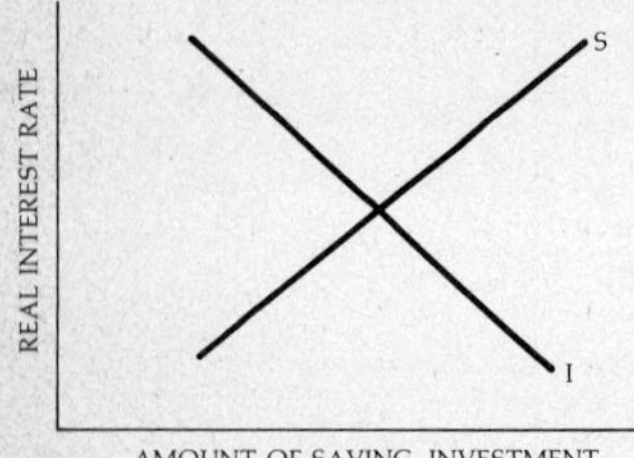

Figure 11C The "classical" theory of interest-rate determination

more valuable relative to goods for present consumption. That's just another way of saying that the demand for capital goods increases as the interest rate falls, or that the rate of investment expenditure varies inversely with the rate of interest. But interest is also the return on saving and the rate of saving varies directly with the rate of interest. If intended saving increases by $10 billion with no increase in intended investment, the interest rate will fall. As it does so, savers will choose to save less, and investors will want to spend more. The interest rate will continue falling until the intentions of savers and investors are brought into balance.

If we reject the hypothesis that the "classical" economists were utterly foolish, we must conclude that when they identified saving with investment they were asserting what would be true *at equilibrium.* By assuming that adjustments from a disequilibrium to an equilibrium position occur through instantaneous price adjustments or, what comes to the same thing, by ignoring the processes of adjustment, they could assert that saving must always equal investment.

An Alternate Perspective

Keynes's attack upon this way of looking at the question took two forms: (1) a different theory of interest, and (2) a different description of the process by which saving and investment are brought into balance. Once again, his attempts at theoretical reformulation stemmed from his recognition of the fundamental importance of uncertainty, of lags and resistances in the processes of adjustment to equilibrium, and of the factors that can intervene to shift an equilibrium position before it is reached.

The Theory of Interest

The preceding discussion of the interest rate was cast in terms of the supply of and demand for *loanable funds.* We can place the interest rate on the vertical axis, the dollar amounts of saving and investment on the horizontal axis. The willingness of income receivers to save, and to save more at higher and less at lower interest rates, yields a supply curve sloping upward to the right. The demand for those funds from potential investors will slope downward to the right, because capital goods are more valuable at lower interest rates. The market interest rate is then determined by the intersection of supply and demand curves.

Keynes had a number of objections to that way of viewing the matter. He doubted that saving depended in any stable or predictable way on the rate of interest. Surely the interest rate was not as important a determinant of the rate of saving as was income. Remember that an increase in people's desire to save is a reduction in consumption, that a decline in consumption reduces income, and that the multiplier process can greatly magnify the effect that such a change will have on income. Any effect that changes in the interest rate might have on saving could easily be swamped by changes in income. And was the level of aggregate saving positively correlated with the interest rate even when considered in isolation? Some might save more at the prospect of a higher return, but others might save less, since at a higher rate of interest a given future income could be obtained from a smaller nest egg. All in all, the interest-saving connection was an extremely weak link in the classical argument.

As for investment, Keynes agreed that it would increase at lower interest rates. But investment also depended, and depended more fundamentally, on the state of investors' expectations. And that, in his judgment, was one of the most volatile and unstable elements in the economic system. It depended not only upon the careful calculation of expected returns from various branches of production, but also upon speculative fancies and the general state of business confidence. "In estimating the prospects of investment," Keynes wrote, "we must have regard, therefore, to the nerves and hysteria and even the digestions and reactions to the weather of those upon whose spontaneous activity it largely depends." In a period of dismal expectations, such as might be brought on by the prospect of recession, even a zero interest rate might not be low enough to maintain an adequate level of investment. Figure 11D expresses the situation Keynes had in mind.

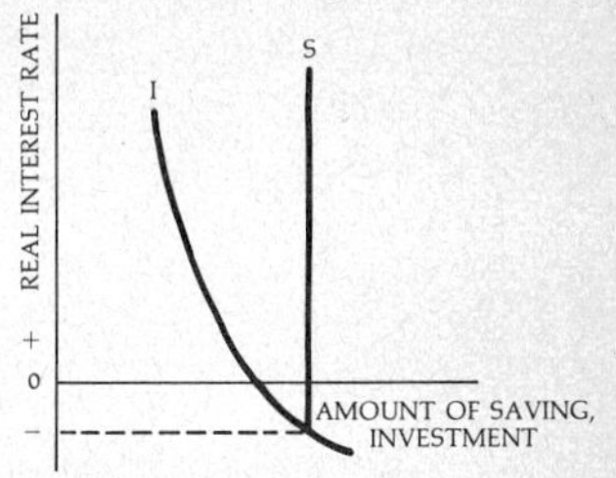

Figure 11D   "Equilibrium" at a *negative* interest rate

A Monetary Theory of Interest

With the link between the interest rate and saving and investment decisions thus radically weakened if not severed altogether, Keynes required an alternate explanation of the forces determining the rate of interest. What he proposed was a monetary theory of interest. The rate of interest was determined by the relationship between the supply of *money* and the demand for *money*. The quantity of money the public wanted to hold varied inversely with the interest rate. Money is demanded, we know, because liquidity is valuable. But at higher interest rates, the opportunity cost of surrendering liquidity tends to be overcome by the opportunity cost of holding onto money (losing the return from ownership of interest-bearing assets). The monetary authorities can control the rate of interest, Keynes argued, by adjusting the stock of money along the public's demand curve for money, as in figure 11E.

Saving and Investment: Intentions versus Outcomes

But the major thrust of Keynes's counterproposal was his alternative explanation of the process by which aggregate saving and investment are equated. His explanation was constructed by means of the two new concepts already introduced: the marginal propensity to consume (along with its complement, the marginal propensity to save) and the multiplier.

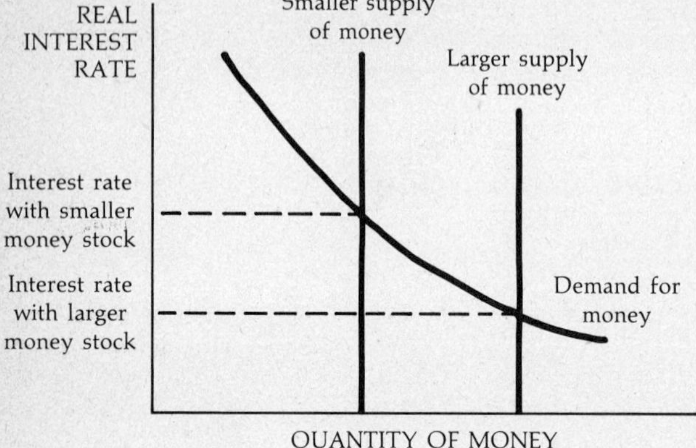

Figure 11E Keynes's "monetary" theory of interest-rate determination

We can visualize the process Keynes had in mind by expanding the circular flow diagram of figure 11B. We'll now ignore the flow of real goods (the productive services and consumer goods) to concentrate on the flow of income and consumption expenditures to which each of the real flows is equivalent. We then add a savings flow and another expenditure flow, the flow of investment spending. Figure 11F presents the expanded model.

Consumption and saving both depend upon income. Investment depends upon expectations and the rate of interest. For the system to be in equilibrium, the flow of intended saving must equal the flow of intended investment. Why? Because if intended investment is more than intended saving, then consumption plus investment (aggregate demand) will be greater than aggregate income (consumption plus saving). That will lead to an increase in production, which will increase income. Income will continue rising in this fashion until the larger income has caused intended saving to increase by enough to match the intentions of investors.

If intended investment were to be less than intended saving initially, then aggregate demand would fall short of current output, and income would decline as production was curtailed. Income would continue falling until the smaller income had caused intended saving to decrease by enough to match intended investment.

It may help if you think of a partially filled bathtub with the drain and the faucet both open. The water level will rise as long as the faucet (intended investment) injects water faster than the drain releases it; the water level will fall as long as the size of the drain opening (intended saving) releases water faster than the faucet injects it. "Equilibrium" (no further change in the water level) will require that the rate of injection be equal to the rate of leakage. A bathtub equilibrium could occur with the water at any level in the tub between empty and overflowing the sides.

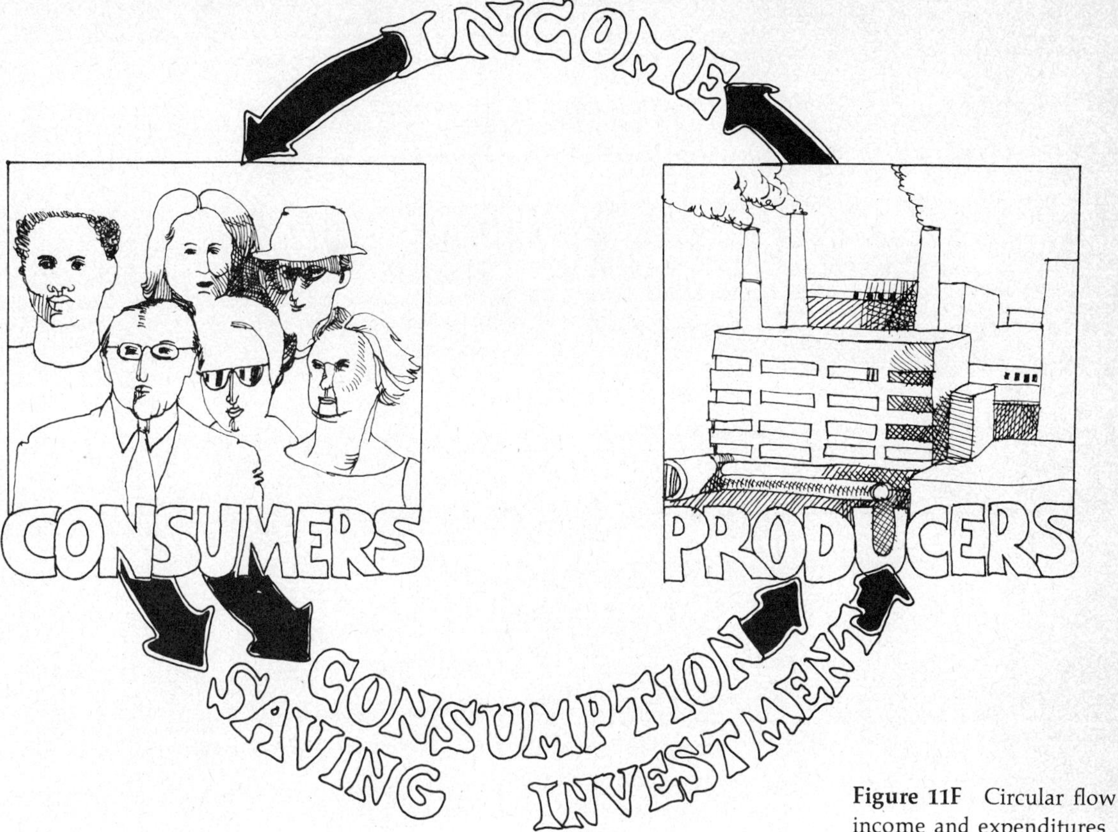

Figure 11F Circular flow of income and expenditures

A Graphic Model of the Saving-Investment-Income Relationship

Perhaps the easiest way to grasp the Keynesian model of the saving-investment-income relationship is by means of a graph like figure 11G. S represents the propensity to save, or savings function. It shows intended saving as a function of income, represented by the letter Y. (Why the letter Y? It's simply a tradition that Keynes originated. The letter I had been appropriated by *investment*.) I represents intended investment, which is assumed in this simple case *not* to vary with income. The equilibrium level of Y will be $800 billion, because that is the only level of Y that allows intended saving to be equal to intended investment.

Let's use figure 11G to calculate the new equilibrium level of Y if intended investment decreases by $20 billion. If line I is redrawn $20 billion lower, it intersects line S where Y is $720 billion. So the equilibrium level of income would be $720 billion rather than $800 billion if intended investment were $80 billion rather than $100 billion.

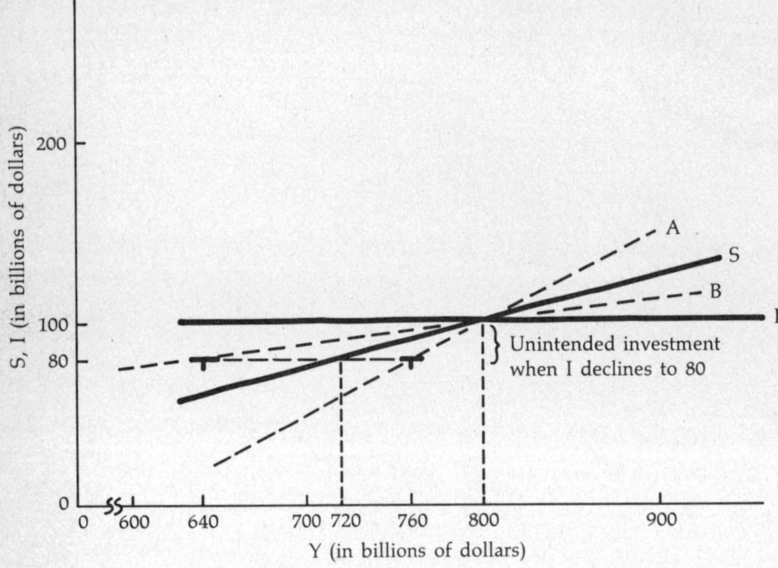

Figure 11G The *intentions* of savers and investors determine Y

The Marginal Propensity to Save and the Multiplier

The multiplier in figure 11G must be 4, because an initial spending change of $20 billion caused an ultimate change in income of $80 billion. The value of the multiplier quite obviously depends on the *slope* of the line S. If S had the steeper slope of the broken line A, Y would fall only to $760 billion in response to a $20 billion decline in intended investment, and the multiplier would be 2. If S had the flatter slope of the broken line B, the multiplier would be 8: a $20 billion decrease in intended investment would cause a $160 billion decline in income.

The slope of the line S is the ratio of the change in saving to the change in income. And this defines the *marginal propensity to save*. We saw earlier that the *marginal propensity to consume* determined the multiplier; the marginal propensity to save is simply its complement. The marginal propensity to save plus the marginal propensity to consume necessarily equals one, because additional income must be either saved or consumed by the definitions we're using. The multiplier will in fact be the inverse of the marginal propensity to save: one divided by the marginal propensity to save.[1]

---

1. Since MPC + MPS = 1, MPS = 1 − MPC. The multiplier is 1/(1 − MPC), which is the same as 1/MPS.

INCOME-EXPENDITURES ANALYSIS
AND THE INCOME AND PRODUCT ACCOUNTS

Which item or items in the income and product accounts, presented in chapter 8, corresponds to Y, which we are calling total income or output? Since we are assuming in this chapter that all saving is done by household consumers, we are ignoring undistributed corporate profits and capital consumption allowances. But if we ignore the setting aside of income to cover depreciation of capital (which is saving), we must also ignore the expenditure of that income to replace or restore capital equipment (which is investment). Investment was defined above as the total of producers' expenditures for new buildings and equipment, expenditures for new residential buildings, and changes in business inventories. That is more accurately known as *gross* investment. *Net* investment is the same total minus capital consumption allowances. Under these assumptions and with government expenditures left out of the picture, the sum of consumption expenditures and net investment is *net national product.*

In the absence of government there are no taxes or transfer payments, and net national product becomes identical with disposable income. Since disposable income is equal to consumption expenditures plus saving, net national product also equals consumption plus saving. In summary:

$$\text{consumption} + \text{(net) investment} = \text{net national product}$$
$$\text{net national product} = \text{disposable income}$$
$$\text{disposable income} = \text{consumption} + \text{saving}$$
$$\text{(net) investment} = \text{saving}$$

Actual saving and *actual* investment must be equal. But *intended* saving and *intended* investment may differ from each other. The income and product accounts do not, of course, register intentions; they only show what has actually occurred. They do, however, measure the variables that form the crucial relationships in income-expenditures analysis: consumption and saving in relation to disposable income, and changes in business inventories in relation to output and expenditures.

Implications of the Keynesian Model

All this is mechanics, however; what we want to understand is the significance of the approach Keynes proposed as an alternative to the saving-investment relationship. He rejected the view that if savers elect to increase their rate of saving or investors decide to reduce their rate of investment, interest rates and other prices will change to bring actual saving and investment into equality and thereby prevent the recession that would have occurred if total demand had fallen short of total output and income.

Instead, Keynes argued, an attempt by savers to save more or by investors to spend less *causes a recession;* and it is the recession that brings the desires of savers and investors into balance. Any gap between savers' plans and investors' plans will translate itself into a cumulative change in income that will continue until saving has been adjusted to investment.

Go back to figure 11G and the original equilibrium with Y at $800 billion. Then assume that income receivers decide to be more thrifty and to save something more than the $100 billion they're currently laying aside out of income. Suppose they collectively decide to save $120 billion. That would be shown on figure 20G by shifting the S curve upward so that saving is $120 billion rather than $100 billion when Y is $800 billion. If we assume that the *marginal* propensity to save (the slope of the savings function) remains unchanged, and draw the new S curve, it will intersect I where Y is $720 billion.

What has happened? The attempt by savers to save more than the $100 billion investors were willing to invest caused a recession. It initially created $20 billion of unintended investment in the form of undesired additions to business inventories. That in turn caused a reduction in output and hence in income. When the recession had reduced income to $720 billion, savers were indeed saving a larger percentage of their income— their original intention. But the income out of which they were saving had fallen by so much that the total amount of saving was no greater than before. It was still equal to the total of original intended investment.

Aggregate Demand and Total Output

All of this can be expressed by means of an alternative statement of the condition for an aggregate equilibrium: consumption expenditures plus intended investment expenditures must equal total output or income.

Consumption plus *actual* investment must always be the same as total output. Consumption plus investment purchases cannot be *less* than output, because any unsold output becomes investment; it is considered to have been purchased by its producer as an addition, willing or unwilling, to inventory. Could consumption plus investment be *greater* than output? There is obviously no way to purchase more of this year's output than was produced this year, but it is certainly possible for consumers and investors to purchase everything produced this year plus some of the output left over from previous years. If this occurs, however, inventories are being reduced, and a decline in inventories is *negative* investment. The amount by which the total of consumer and investor purchases might exceed current output will necessarily be equal to the amount by which net inventories are reduced this year, or the amount of negative investment that occurs. When this negative investment is subtracted from total investor purchases, consumption plus investment will necessarily equal total output.

Intended investment and consumption are another matter, however. If consumption plus intended investment is less than total output, some unintended investment or unintended addition to inventories has occurred. Producers will respond by reducing output, just as they would have wanted to increase output if unexpectedly large purchases had reduced their inventories below desired levels. A reduction in output reduces income and causes consumption to fall. As a result, consumption plus intended investment will once again fall short of total output, and this will prompt further production cutbacks. The multiplier process will continue in this fashion until actual output has fallen to the level of consumption plus intended investment.

We can use the same kind of graphical analysis as in figure 11G to present this version of the equilibrating process. Since income minus saving is by definition equal to consumption, we can derive the corresponding consumption function from the saving function of figure 11G. It is labeled C in figure 11H. We've drawn a line through the graph to mark off all those points at which expenditures on the vertical axis equal income on the horizontal axis. The vertical distance between the consumption function and this reference line shows the level of saving at each level of income.

The investment function has been added to the consumption function to show aggregate demand at various levels of income. It lies $100 billion above the consumption function and is labeled C + I. The equilibrium level of income emerges as $800 billion, because that is the only level at which consumption plus intended investment will equal total output or income.

If consumers now decide to spend $680 billion rather than $700 billion (or to save $120 billion rather than $100 billion), the consumption function and hence the C + I line will shift downward by $20 billion. The result will be a new equilibrium at $720 billion. At this level of income, and only at this level of income, consumption plus intended investment will equal output. The $20 billion change in expenditures causes a change of $80 billion in income; the multiplier is 4. Notice that saving will not be at the originally intended level of $120 billion. The decline in income will have altered the intentions of consumer-savers so that they now want to save only $100 billion.

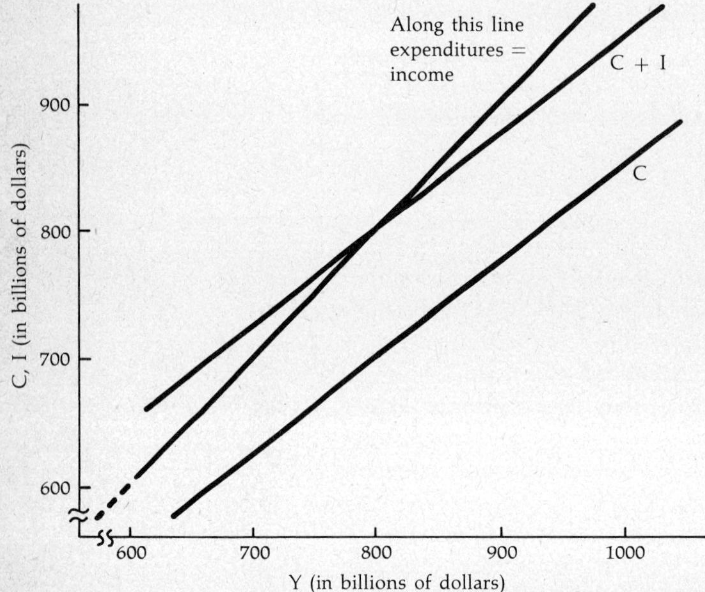

Figure 11H The *intentions* of consumers and investors determine Y

Each way of stating the equilibrium condition, as $S = I$ or as $C + I = Y$, has some advantages. The formula that intended saving must equal intended investment focuses attention on a crucial contention of income-expenditures analysis: equality between intended saving and intended investment will not be brought about by adjustments in interest rates and relative prices, but by changes in total income and output. The fact that any inequality between intended saving and intended investment is evidence of a disequilibrium does not prove, as the classical theorists maintained, that recessions will quickly correct themselves. On the contrary, Keynes argued, it is recession itself that brings about the new equilibrium. We chose this way of introducing income-expenditures analysis in order to focus on the difference between the Keynesian position and the older point of view.

The alternative way of putting it, that consumption plus intended investment must equal total output, has the advantage of being easier to grasp intuitively. Everyone understands that production decisions respond to demand. If buyers do not want to purchase everything that has been produced, producers reduce output; if buyers want to purchase more than has been produced, producers find it in their interest to expand output. Production is undertaken in anticipation of demand, and rises or falls as realized or actual demand exceeds or falls short of expected demand.

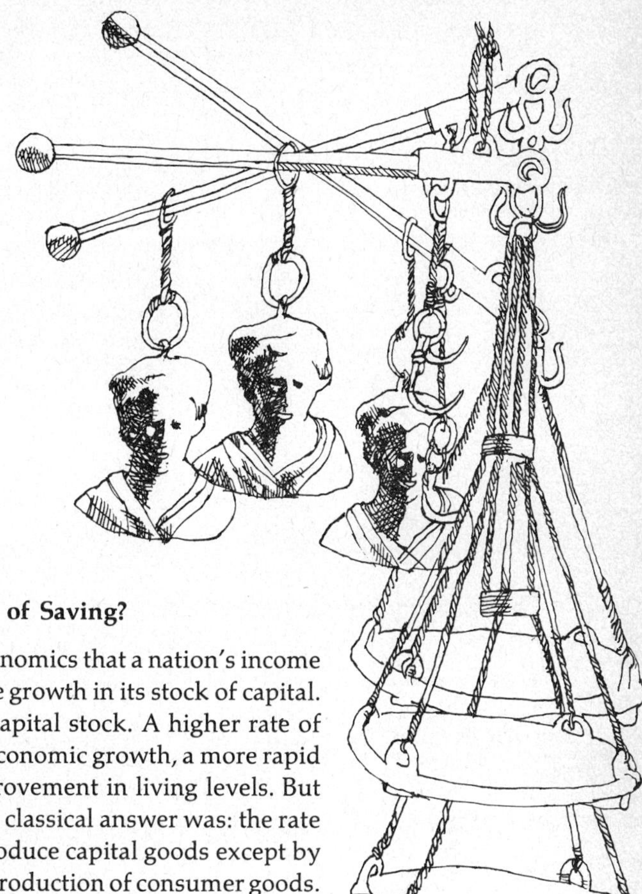

How Valuable Is the Act of Saving?

It has long been a fundamental tenet of economics that a nation's income and wealth grow roughly in proportion to the growth in its stock of capital. Investment is the process that adds to the capital stock. A higher rate of investment therefore means a faster rate of economic growth, a more rapid rise in national income, and a speedier improvement in living levels. But what determines the rate of investment? The classical answer was: the rate of saving. There is no way for a society to produce capital goods except by withdrawing some of its resources from the production of consumer goods. In effect, those who save abstain from current consumption and either purchase capital goods themselves or turn over their income to others who purchase capital goods. Without saving there can be no investment. (If investment is financed by borrowing from abroad, foreigners must do the saving.) The incentive to save must, therefore, be preserved and extended, according to the classical argument, because it is the root cause of social progress.

In the concluding chapter of the *General Theory*, Keynes speculated on the social consequences toward which acceptance of his theory might lead. He thought it might well reduce society's traditional reluctance to interfere with the distribution of income. This reluctance was largely based on the argument of the preceding paragraph plus the assumption that wealthy people save a larger percentage of their income than poor people do. Any attempt to improve the lot of the poor by redistributing income from the rich therefore runs the risk of eventually making the whole society poorer.

The surer route to improving the lot of the poor lay through the encouragement of saving. And that argued against any redistribution of income in the direction of greater equality.

The "Paradox of Thrift"

Keynes's theory cast doubt upon this line of reasoning by suggesting that the desire to save might actually retard investment and economic growth. At least in industrially developed and affluent societies, an increase in "thrift" would reduce aggregate demand and so lower the actual rate of investment and hence the rate of economic growth. This argument came to be known as the "paradox of thrift."

To illustrate the operation of the paradox, let's revise the graph of figure 11G. Instead of assuming that intended investment is constant, let's assume that it varies directly with income. Investment decisions depend upon expectations of profit; these expectations are formed in part by expectations of growth in total income; and changes in current income may be regarded by investors as a clue to future income levels. Let's assume, therefore, that investment spending increases or decreases as income increases or decreases, and by an amount equal to $\frac{1}{8}$ of the change in Y.

In figure 11I, the curves of saving and investment determine the equilibrium level of Y at $800 billion. Note that the marginal propensity to save is still $\frac{1}{4}$, but that the marginal propensity to invest is now $\frac{1}{8}$ rather than zero (as in Figure 11G). Now we introduce an increase in thriftiness, just as we did before: the public decides to save $120 billion rather than just $100 billion out of an income of $800 billion. We show that decision by raising the curve S $20 billion all along its length. The two curves will now intersect where Y is $640 billion. At the new equilibrium level of income, saving and investment will, of course, be equal; but they will have *fallen by $20 billion*. An increase in the desire to save actually caused a decline in both saving and investment. This is the "paradox of thrift."

What happened? The rise in the savings function triggered a cumulative decline in income. But with intended investment spending also dependent upon the level of income, that decline pulled down investment; and the decline in intended investment then added its own impact to the cumulative process that savers had initiated. In this kind of world, a concern for maintaining the incentive to save would seem to be absurd. The situation calls for an increase in spending, not in saving. A higher level of saving will appear of its own accord as income rises if some way can be found to stimulate spending and thus the level of income and output.

But now we've begun to discuss the policy implications of the *General Theory*. Before we can do that, we must introduce government spending and taxes into the income-expenditures model.

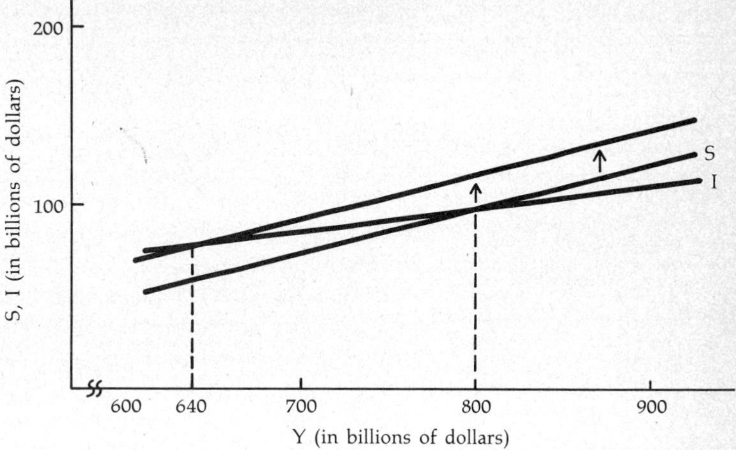

Figure 11I The "paradox of thrift"

Once Over Lightly

When conditions of demand or supply change, business firms and sellers of productive resources do not immediately make perfect adjustments. Because information is a scarce good in an uncertain world, they must search for the pattern of resource allocation that will be most advantageous under the altered circumstances. This takes time and entails learning through mistakes.

Traditional equilibrium analysis has usually abstracted from time and uncertainty by assuming that demanders and suppliers instantly and faultlessly adjust their behavior when change occurs. In such a world, recessions would be impossible. Prices would always be at market clearing levels and all resources would always be employed to their best advantage.

Income-expenditures analysis provides an alternative way of viewing adjustments between aggregate demand and supply, based on the concepts of the consumption function and the multiplier.

If expenditures for new goods unexpectedly decline so that producers are unable to sell at current prices as much as they had planned to sell, producers accumulate unwanted inventories. Their response is not to cut prices but rather to reduce output in an attempt to bring inventories back down to desired levels. But when output is reduced, the incomes of producers fall. Keynes postulated a consumption function according to which consumption changes as income changes but by less than the change in income. And so consumption also declines when output is cut back.

This decline in consumption leads to further disappointments for sellers, who again find themselves with excessive inventories of goods. They reduce production further, which reduces incomes once more, which causes an additional decline in consumption expenditures.

The multiplier in income-expenditures analysis is the ratio between the eventual change in income and the original change in expenditures that triggered it. The value of the multiplier depends upon the rate at which consumption changes as income changes, or upon the marginal propensity to consume (change in consumption divided by change in income). The eventual change in income will be equal to the initial change in expenditures times $1/(1 - MPC)$, where MPC is the marginal propensity to consume. Since the marginal propensity to consume plus the marginal propensity to save equals one, the multiplier can also be stated as $1/MPS$.

In a simple model from which government activities and business saving are excluded, consumption plus (net) investment equals net national product. Consumption plus saving equals disposable income, which, in the absence of business saving, taxes, and government transfer payments, is also equal to net national product. Saving and investment therefore *must be equal.* But this is only true of *actual* or *realized* saving and investment. *Intended* saving can be quite different from *intended* investment.

The "classical" theory assumed that any divergence between intended saving and intended investment would cause changes in the rate of interest and in relative prices that would bring the plans of savers and investors back into balance. The Keynesian theory asserted that, in an uncertain world, interest rates and relative prices would not perform this equilibrating task, or, at least, would not perform it quickly enough to forestall the operation of an alternative equilibrating mechanism. Under this mechanism, the rate of production changes in response to any divergence between intended saving and intended investment. This causes a change in income, which in turn causes savers to revise their intentions. Income and output continue to fall (or rise) until the economy is in aggregate equilibrium, or until intended saving is equal to intended investment.

In the "classical" view of things, saving was what made investment possible. In the Keynesian view, investment also makes saving possible. The critical problem in a developed and affluent economy, Keynes suggested, is not that of providing incentives to savers so that investment can take place and economic growth can continue. The problem is more likely to be one of providing incentives to investors so that the level of output and income can be maintained and recession avoided.

QUESTIONS FOR DISCUSSION

1. Can an economy be at equilibrium if much of its industrial capacity is standing idle and a large percentage of its labor force is unemployed? Is that a question about fact or a disguised argument about the proper way to use the concept of equilibrium?

2. Suppose that demand for the goods listed below turns out to be less than producers anticipated, so that the goods already produced cannot all be sold at current prices. What consequences would you predict in the case of each good? Would prices or production levels be likely to fall first? How long will the sequence of adjustments take?

   (*a*) automobiles

   (*b*) beef cattle

   (*c*) secondary school teachers

3. Is it true, as Keynes assumed in describing the consumption function, that people increase their consumption as their income increases, but not by as much as the increase in their income? Does consumption in one period (a month, for example) depend upon income in that particular period? Would you expect a salesman receiving a highly variable monthly income to vary his consumption as his income varies?

4. Explain in your own words what is meant by the "multiplier." How does the multiplier depend upon the consumption function? If every increase in spending increases income, and every increase in income increases spending, wouldn't the ultimate effect of any initial change in spending be infinitely large? Why not?

5. The text presents two theories of the interest rate. One explains the interest rate as a product of the supply of and the demand for loanable funds, the other as a product of the supply of and the demand for money.

   (*a*) What is the difference between loanable funds and money?

   (*b*) Do the two theories have significantly different implications?

6. If saving suddenly and unexpectedly increases, unintended investment will rise by enough to keep actual saving and investment equal.

   (*a*) What form does this unintended investment take?

   (*b*) What further consequences will this unintended investment have?

   (*c*) Suppose that saving suddenly and unexpectedly *decreased*. Would that be capable of creating a temporary inequality between saving and investment? Explain what might occur.

7. (*a*) How are the marginal propensity to consume and the marginal propensity to save related?

   (*b*) How is each related to the multiplier in income-expenditures analysis?

8. Does investment depend upon saving? Can investment occur if there has been no saving? What are the real differences between the older view that investment could only be maintained by maintaining saving and Keynes's view that a high rate of investment was a precondition for a high rate of saving?

9. Does the "paradox of thrift" imply that saving is an antisocial act and consumption an act that benefits society?

10. Increase your familiarity with the graphic analysis employed in figures 11G, 11H, and 11I and the interrelationships these graphs try to summarize by answering the following questions.

In figure 11G:

(*a*) What would be the new equilibrium level of Y if intended investment increased to $130 billion?

(*b*) What would be the value of the multiplier?

(*c*) If $800 billion is the full employment level of Y, could Y increase by such a large percentage? How?

(*d*) Equilibrium occurs when *intended* saving and *intended* investment are equal. How might such a sudden and unexpected 30% increase in investment force *actual* saving to be larger for a period of time than the amount of income which savers *want* to hold out of consumption? (Hint: How would investors obtain command over the capital goods they want to accumulate?)

In figure 11I:

(*a*) What is the value of the multiplier?

(*b*) Why is it larger than indicated by the formula for deriving the multiplier from the marginal propensity to consume?

In figure 11H:

(*a*) What is the level of saving when income is $640 billion? When it is $800 billion?

(*b*) What is the numerical slope of the consumption function? How is it related to the slope of the saving function graphed in figure 11G?

12

INCOME – EXPENDITURES ANALYSIS
AND FISCAL POLICY

To the classical economists whom Keynes criticized, the ability of an economic system to produce goods and provide jobs was determined by its stock of capital. As saving increased, investment could be increased, the stock of capital enlarged, and employment opportunities expanded. Keynes did not deny that argument, but he did deny its relevance to the economy in which he lived. The modern problem, as he saw it, was to make fuller use of already existing capacity. Increasing the capacity of the economy was a problem of secondary importance. An increased propensity to save would not expand employment. On the contrary, it would be an added threat to full employment because it would be a more difficult challenge for investment to fulfill. The *actual* level of output and employment was determined by the willingness of investors to spend all that the public wanted to save. Recessions came about because the propensity to save in conditions of relatively full employment was greater than the demand for new capital.

Moreover, the demand for capital, Keynes believed, was highly unstable. Some of the arguments he put forward on behalf of that thesis are no longer convincing, but the thesis is inherently plausible and it can be supported with historical data. Investment spending is typically oriented to a more distant future than is consumption spending. Changing expectations about the course of future events will therefore have a larger impact on current investment decisions than on consumption decisions. Investment expenditures also tend to be highly postponable. One can make do with present buildings and equipment for a while *or* take advantage of favorable circumstances to acquire new buildings and equipment ahead of schedule.

Investment spending is therefore more likely to be "bunched" than is spending on consumer goods and especially on nondurable goods.

When the unpredictability and instability of investment spending is inserted into the income-expenditures model of chapter 11, the implica-

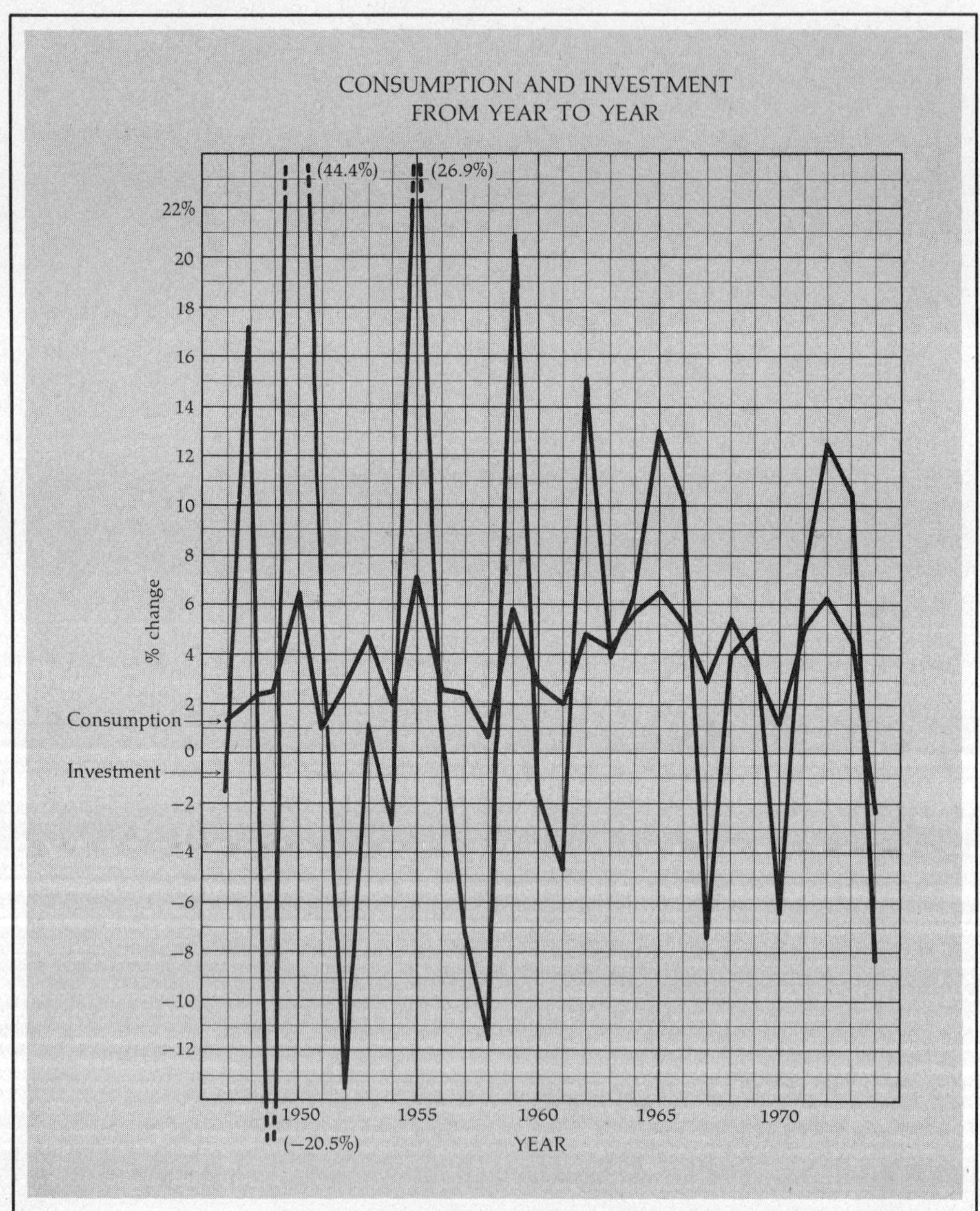

tions are disturbing. Income and output are not likely to increase steadily over time as society adds to its stock of capital equipment. On the contrary, the economy will be exposed to periodic increases and decreases in the rate of investment spending that will be transformed through the multiplier into large fluctuations in the level of income. Moreover, what is lost in the downturns will not be recovered in the upturns. A downturn leads to idle resources—high unemployment in the labor force and unused physical facilities. The output thus lost is gone forever and includes any additions it might have made to future productivity. But the waste of potential output is of lesser importance than the suffering that a downturn imposes upon the workers who lose their jobs and upon new entrants to the labor force who cannot find adequate employment opportunities during a recession. A subsequent upturn will not make up for what has been lost.

Nor may we take for granted that every upturn will be an unmixed blessing. If spurts in investment spending trigger a cumulative expansion that carries aggregate demand beyond the economic system's productive capabilities, prices will rise and the economy will undergo inflation. The policy question to which Keynes was addressing himself—and those who knew him have testified that he never devised a theoretical concept without having in mind a policy application—was whether the economy must submit itself to an endless recurrence of expansions and contractions. Were there ways to correct or compensate for the destabilizing effects of private investment decisions?

The focus in this chapter will be upon fiscal policy and its potential applications to the problem of recessions. Keynes did not believe that fiscal policy was only applicable in periods of recession or that it was the only stabilization tool the government had. But income-expenditures analysis was developed in the depths of the Great Depression and was based largely upon reflections on the problems of recession and unemployment. Its instantaneous success among large numbers of economists was unquestionably related to its apparent applicability to those particular problems, whose urgency in the 1930s would be hard to exaggerate. And it did in fact lead to a preoccupation with fiscal policy, at least among economists, that pushed alternative or supplementary stabilization policies off the stage for almost a quarter century.

THE GOVERNMENT BUDGET
IN AN INCOME-EXPENDITURES MODEL

Fiscal policy is budget policy. Every organization or individual with a budget has a budget policy: a way of managing receipts and disbursements to achieve certain goals. In the narrower sense in which the term is now usually employed, however, *fiscal policy means specifically the employment by the federal government of expenditures and taxes to influence the aggregate level of economic activity.*

We can incorporate the government's budget into income-expenditures analysis in either of two ways. One is to regard taxes as a leakage similar to saving, and disbursements as an injection similar to investment, and rewrite the equilibrium condition as follows: Intended saving plus taxes must equal the total of intended investment plus disbursements by government. (This must include federal, state, and local governments.) Or we can add government purchases of final goods to the purchases of consumers and investors and restate the equilibrium condition: Total output or income must equal the sum of consumption expenditures, intended investment, and government purchases of commodities and services.

A Formal Model

Ordinary language is a very clumsy tool when we try to provide even the simplest summary description of the interrelationships among all our variables once government has been introduced into the picture. Taxes create a difference between net national product and the disposable income on which consumption and saving decisions depend, so that the marginal propensities to consume or save will now have to be expressed as functions of income after taxes. Since taxes will themselves vary with the level of economic activity, they ought to be expressed as a function of income rather than as some constant amount. If we allow investment expenditures to vary with income, as we did in Figure 11I and the accompanying discussion, we have another variable that can't be treated as a constant in our analysis. A further complication arises if we want to treat government transfer payments separately from other expenditures; and we probably

ought to do that because transfer payments do not create a direct demand for output as do government expenditures for commodities and services.

Algebra was created for just such situations. Because the algebra used will be of the most elementary kind, the letters, numbers, and equations which follow should not intimidate anyone. We'll use algebra to put the picture together and to discover the principal implications of the theory. A few minutes spent in mastering the relationships that the equations describe will enable you to think about and discuss the issues of stabilization policy far more surely and confidently.

Step one: Let's define all the symbols we'll be using:

Y = total income or total output
C = the consumption function
S = the saving function
I = the investment function
G = government expenditures for commodities and services (government transfer payments are not included)
Tx = taxes
Tr = government transfer payments (payments not made for services currently being rendered: unemployment compensation, social security benefits, general welfare assistance, veterans' benefits, *etc.*)
$Yd = Y - Tx + Tr$ = disposable income (also $C + S$, by definition)

Step two: We set down the conditions for an equilibrium. What we want to do with all these letters is put them together to see how the equilibrium level of total income is determined and how changes in one variable will change others. We can state the equilibrium condition in either of two ways:

1. $Y = C + I + G$
   (aggregate output or income = aggregate intended expenditures)
2. $S + Tx = I + G + Tr$
   (intended deductions from the income-expenditures flow = intended injections into the income-expenditures flow)

Step three: If we now assign appropriate numerical values, we can solve for the equilibrium value of Y. But we won't want to run through the entire set of equations each time we change a number, so we shall first solve for Y in a general form. Consumption expenditures will be some constant amount plus the marginal propensity to consume times disposable income. We'll treat intended investment, government purchases, and transfer payments as constants. And taxes will be assumed to vary with total income.

Letting c_o represent the constant amount in the consumption function and c_m the marginal propensity to consume, $C = c_o + c_m Yd$. If t stands for the tax rate, $Tx = tY$. We can now proceed as follows:

$$Y = C + I + G$$
$$Y = (c_o + c_m Yd) + I + G$$
$$Y = c_o + c_m(Y - Tx + Tr) + I + G$$
$$Y = c_o + c_m(Y - tY + Tr) + I + G$$
$$Y = c_o + c_m Y - c_m tY + c_m Tr + I + G$$
$$Y - c_m Y + c_m tY = c_o + c_m Tr + I + G$$
$$(1 - c_m + c_m t)Y = c_o + c_m Tr + I + G$$
$$Y = \left(\frac{1}{1 - c_m + c_m t}\right)(c_o + c_m Tr + I + G)$$

Let's try it out with some numerical values, all representing billions of dollars. Assume that investors want to spend 140 while government purchases 300 of commodities and services and disburses 100 in transfer payments. Let taxes be $.25Y$ and let the consumption function be $120 + .8Yd$. Then

$$\frac{1}{1 - c_m + c_m t} = \frac{1}{1 - .8 + .2} = \frac{1}{.4} = 2.5$$

and

$$Y = 2.5(120 + 80 + 140 + 300)$$
$$Y = 2.5(640)$$
$$Y = 1600$$

We can now calculate the equilibrium level of disposable income and of consumption expenditures:

$$Yd = 1600 - 400 + 100 + 1300$$

And so, at equilibrium

$$C = 120 + .8(1300) = 1160$$

Checking our results, we find that Y does equal the total of C, I, and G:

$$1600 = 1160 + 140 + 300$$

Are our results consistent with the alternative equilibrium condition, that saving plus taxes be equal to the total of intended investment, government purchases, and transfers? If

$$C = 120 + .8(1300)$$

then

$$S = -120 + .2(1300)$$
$$S = 140$$

The equilibrium condition is

$$S + Tx = I + G + Tr$$

Inserting the values already obtained, we get

$$140 + 400 = 140 + 300 + 100$$
$$540 = 540$$

There are two ways to get hung up in the mechanics of all these equations. One is to be intimidated by the algebra. The other is to become proficient with the algebra and forget that it is intended as a simplified description of the interactions that determine total output and income. Master the algebra to clear the way. Then you'll be ready to consider the potential implications of all this for policymaking.

The Government Budget and Full Employment

All we know about that $1600 billion income is that it's the equilibrium level under the conditions given. But is that level of income and output consistent with full employment and price stability?

As we know from chapter 7, full employment is extraordinarily hard to define in a way that is neither meaningless nor misleading. As a first approximation, however, let's just assume that we know what we mean by full employment, that we can measure it satisfactorily, and that it's achieved with total income and output at a $1600 billion level. Any increase in aggregate demand that pulled income above that level would therefore cause inflation. The *nominal* value of income—its value measured in current dollars—would increase. But if we assume that *real* output and income cannot be increased beyond the full employment level, any increase in nominal income above $1600 billion would mean that the price level had gone up.[1]

If aggregate demand falls short of $1600 billion, on the other hand, unemployment will appear. What would occur, under these circumstances, if a sudden wave of pessimistic expectations swept the economy and intended investment fell by $16 billion? It isn't necessary to run through all the calculations again. We can see at a glance that with I equal to $124 billion instead of $140 billion

$$Y = 2.5(624)$$

Y will consequently decline from $1600 billion to $1560 billion. How will that affect the other variables that are dependent on the level of income?

---

1. Since full employment, however defined, is a matter of degree, we should not expect the price level to remain completely stable as income approaches the full employment level, or anticipate *no* increases in real output after that point has been reached.

Taxes will decline to $390 billion. Disposable income will therefore decline to $1270 billion. Consumption will fall to $1136 billion, and saving to $134 billion.

Let's compare the original values and the new values of all the variables.

	Original Value	New Value
I	140	124
Y	1600	1560
Yd	1300	1270
C	1160	1136
S	140	134
G	300	300
Tx	400	390
Tr	100	100

Saving, you should notice, is no longer equal to investment. But with government in the picture, it does not have to be equal to investment. The total of saving plus taxes must be equal to the total of investment and government expenditures plus transfer payments. And it is. When $Y = \$1560$ billion the government is running a deficit of $10 billion, and this compensates for the $10 billion by which saving exceeds investment. The total of government expenditures and transfer payments is $10 billion more than tax revenue.

Most of us have learned to think of deficits as Bad Things and evidence that someone is trying to live beyond his means. But note what would happen in our model if the government tried to get rid of the deficit. Any increase in tax rates will reduce disposable income and hence consumption, driving total income even further below the full employment level. A decrease in government expenditures will also reduce aggregate demand and trigger further declines in total income. And as income falls, tax revenues will also decline.

Suppose the government reduced its expenditures by $10 billion in response to the budget deficit. Total income would then fall to $1535. And the budget would still be in deficit, because tax receipts would have fallen to $383.75 billion. The reduction in government spending would only have reduced the deficit from $10 billion to $6.25 billion. The cost of this reduction in the deficit would be a further $25 billion loss in output.

It might be instructive to figure out by how much the government would have to reduce its expenditures to achieve a balanced budget under the circumstances of our model. For the system to be in equilibrium with a balanced budget, saving would have to equal the $124 billion of intended investment. Setting saving equal to investment and solving for the equilibrium value of Y, we obtain the following:

$$S = I$$
$$-120 + .2Yd = 124$$
$$-120 + .2(Y - .25Y + 100) = 124$$
$$-120 + .2Y - .05Y + 20 = 124$$
$$.15Y = 224$$
$$Y = 1493\tfrac{1}{3}$$
$$Yd = 1493\tfrac{1}{3} - 373\tfrac{1}{3} + 100 = 1220$$
$$C = 120 + .8(1220) = 1096$$

Since $I = 124$ and the sum of C, I, and G must be $1493\frac{1}{3}$, the government would have to reduce its expenditures to \$273$\frac{1}{3}$ billion in order to balance the budget. But it would thereby cause a further reduction of \$41$\frac{2}{3}$ billion in output and the increase in unemployment that would go along with it.

Changing Attitudes toward the "Balanced Budget"

Would any government behave in such a fashion? Probably no longer. And that is some evidence of the extent to which the income-expenditures approach to government budgeting has influenced the thinking of contemporary policymakers. Federal government receipts fell by almost a billion dollars between the 1957 and 1959 fiscal years because of the 1958 recession. They had been expected to rise, and expenditures had been budgeted in anticipation of a continuing increase in tax revenues. With expenditures increasing on schedule—even a little ahead of schedule because of the additional outlays for transfer payments that a recession causes—the government budget slipped deeply into the red. The \$13 billion deficit in the 1959 fiscal year was the largest peacetime deficit ever incurred. But despite President Eisenhower's numerous past expressions of devotion to the ideal of a balanced budget, no serious efforts were made by his administration to raise taxes or reduce expenditures.

In 1932, by contrast, in the depths of the Great Depression, Franklin D. Roosevelt campaigned for the presidency by promising to balance the budget. Throughout his first administration, during which unemployment ranged from 17% to 25% of the labor force, he repeatedly tried to reduce government expenditures and persistently proposed new taxes. His primary goal in proposing tax increases may not have been a balanced budget; he seems to have been at least as interested in increasing the taxes on large incomes as in acquiring additional revenue. But the contrast with contemporary practice is striking nonetheless.

In 1975, with the economy again in the throes of recession and the budget deeply in the red, a Republican administration reputed to favor a balanced budget actually called for tax decreases that would add to the size of the deficit.

WHAT DO WE MEAN BY A "BALANCED BUDGET"?

The budget is balanced when expenditures match income. That seems clear enough. But is it really? Think about each of the following cases. In which of them are you engaged in "deficit spending"?

1. You spend $20 per day even though your income on six days of the week is zero and you receive $140 on Friday. Are you running a surplus on Friday and a deficit the other six days of the week? It's obvious that no one balances his budget except with reference to some period of time. But what is the relevant period?

2. You're a salesman whose monthly income fluctuates between $600 and $1000. You nonetheless maintain your expenditures at $800 per month. Are you alternating between deficits and surpluses or are you balancing your budget? Would it make sense to say that you won't know until later whether you've been balancing your budget?

3. You will receive $10,000 next year when the legal formalities are completed on your rich uncle's will. Are you running a deficit if you borrow money in order to increase your expenditures this year? Would your answer change if you aren't certain that his bequest to you will survive a legal test?

4. You borrow money at age twenty-five to buy a house. Are you "living beyond your means"? How would you go about answering that question?

5. By borrowing money now at 6% interest you can purchase an education that will probably double your income for many years in the future. Are you "running in the red"? Is it ever profitable to "run in the red"?

Each of these three administrations displayed a different attitude toward the phenomenon of a budget thrown into deficit by a recession. In the 1930s there was a strong emphasis on bringing the budget back into balance. In the 1950s the approach was to take no action and thus to accept the deficit brought on by recession. In the 1970s the budget was viewed as an active tool for achieving recovery, and an even larger deficit was deliberately courted. In each decade the government had a fiscal policy. But the progression from Roosevelt through Eisenhower to Ford shows the growing influence of income-expenditures analysis on the formulation of that policy.

The Full Employment Budget

Income-expenditures analysis has clearly taught economists and politicians to look at the government budget in a different way. The thought of a deficit is no longer entertained with the same horror it once aroused among students of public finance. And the older definition of a deficit as simply an excess of government expenditures over receipts has lost ground to such newer concepts as the *full employment deficit or surplus.*

The *full employment budget* is the budget that would be in effect if the economy were operating at full employment. The concept is a useful one despite the fact that it rests inevitably on somewhat arbitrary definitions of full employment and on debatable projections of revenue and expenditures. But we do know that tax revenues and, to a lesser extent, transfer payments vary with the level of economic activity. A budget deficit incurred while the economy is operating below capacity might well turn into a surplus at full employment, without any changes at all in tax rates or spending programs.

The only budget that ought to be balanced, many economists now argue, is the full employment budget. In other words, the government should set tax rates that will yield just enough revenue to cover expenditures when the economy is operating at full employment. A downturn will then cause a deficit but the deficit should be ignored. And a boom will yield a surplus, which also ought to be ignored. Such deficits and surpluses will then function as automatic stabilizers. Deficits will compensate in part for declines in private spending, even without deliberate policy actions. And surpluses will serve as an automatic brake on total spending when it rises so rapidly that inflation threatens.

COUNTERCYCLICAL FISCAL POLICY

All of this describes a rather passive use of fiscal policy. Can it be used more aggressively to control or offset fluctuations in aggregate demand? In our model, there is a great difference between the consequences of not taking any action to reduce deficits and the consequences of deliberately creating or adding to a deficit during a recession.

By drawing conclusions from a simple algebraic model we run the risk of slighting the political and technical difficulties that confront budget planners, including all the difficulties associated with uncertainty about the future. But we ought to master the simple mechanics before introducing the qualifications. So let's go back to the model we've developed and ask what size changes in the government budget would restore the economy to full employment.

An Activist Fiscal Policy

The recession was brought on by a \$16 billion decline in investment. A \$16 billion increase in government expenditures in our example would exactly compensate for that decline. At the new equilibrium induced by the expansion of government spending, total income, disposable income, consumption, and saving will all be restored to their previous levels. Saving will therefore be \$16 billion more than investment. But government "saving" will be negative: taxes will be \$400 billion, government outlays for goods and transfer payments will be \$416 billion, and the \$16 billion deficit will compensate for the gap between private saving and investment.

The full employment equilibrium could also be restored by reducing taxes or increasing transfer payments. Suppose the government increases transfer payments by \$16 billion instead of increasing its own purchases of goods by \$16 billion. That won't be enough. By the assumptions of our model, aggregate demand does not increase by the full amount of any increase in transfer payments. Only .8 of any increase in disposable income goes toward increasing expenditures, while the other .2 flows into saving. While a \$16 billion increase in government expenditures *directly* increases the demand for output by that amount, a \$16 billion increase in disposable income leads to only a \$12.8 billion initial increase in demand. And an initial expenditure increase of \$12.8 billion would only bring total income up to \$1592 billion after completion of the multiplier process.[1] To restore Y to its full employment level, the government would have to raise transfer payments by \$20 billion. As .8 of that, or \$16 billion, went toward an increase in consumption, Y would rise via the multiplier process to \$1600 billion. The deficit would therefore be somewhat larger than if the government restored the system to full employment via an increase in its own purchases of goods.

We've been looking at changes in the level of transfer payments as the fiscal policy alternative to changes in government expenditures for commodities and services. The alternative usually talked about, and the one chosen in 1975, was changes in taxes. But the same analysis applies. The government could pay the transfers to taxpayers in the form of a \$16 billion rebate. Taxes would then become 25% of Y minus \$16 billion. It makes a good deal of difference, politically and otherwise, whether the government

---

1. The effective multiplier for any change in expenditures in our model is 2.5. You can see that at once by looking at the solution of the model and noting that Y changes by $\frac{1}{.4}$, or 2.5, dollars for every one-dollar change in I or G. The formal value of the effective multiplier in this model is

$$\frac{1}{1 - c_m + c_m t}$$

This expresses the fact that the impact of a change in income on consumption is reduced in the model by both the marginal tax rate *and* the marginal propensity to save.

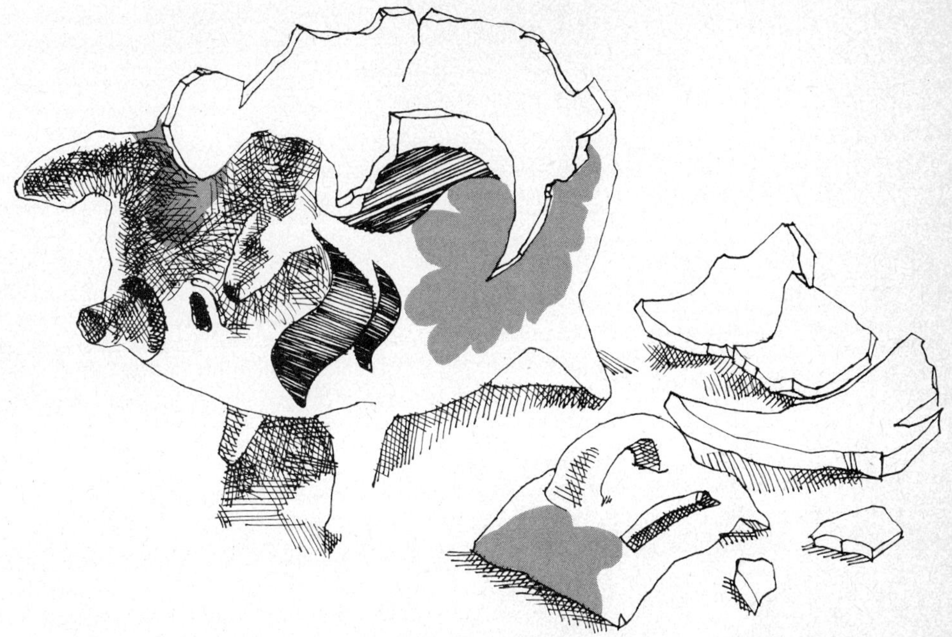

offers rebates to taxpayers or increases its payments to veterans, the unemployed, those on welfare, or retired people receiving social security. But in our simplified model the consequences will be the same either way. And our point here is simply that a change in transfer payments or tax receipts is a less powerful weapon for altering total income than a change in government purchases.[1]

This does not imply that government expenditure increases are preferable to tax cuts when the government wants to expand national income. It implies only that expenditure increases of a given amount are more *powerful* in our model than tax decreases in the same amount. And it explains the objection some economists voiced to President Nixon's 1971 proposal to stimulate the economy by cutting taxes while reducing government expenditures by an equal amount. These economists argued, on the basis of a model similar to the one we're using, that the net effect of the combined actions would be negative. They invoked the concept of the *balanced budget multiplier*. This concept, based on the reasoning we've just gone through, asserts that a change in expenditures coupled with a change in tax receipts of the same amount causes total income to move in the direc-

---

1. We presented the argument in terms of transfer payments because in our model taxes are not a set amount but a function of Y. The analysis would become more complex than seems worthwhile if we tried to determine the tax *rate* change that would yield a specified *receipts* change.

tion of the expenditure change. Thus a $20 billion decrease in tax receipts joined to a $20 billion decrease in government spending would reduce income in our model by $10 billion. For while the tax cut prompts $16 billion of additional consumption, the reduction in government spending lowers demand by $20 billion. The initial impact on aggregate demand is consequently a net decrease of $4 billion. With an effective multiplier of 2.5, as in our model, that becomes a $10 billion reduction in national income when the new equilibrium is reached.

Great Expectations

Income-expenditures analysis achieved rapid acceptance among economists after 1936 largely because it described the dynamics of aggregate fluctuations in a way that also suggested the cure. If recessions are the result of an increased desire to save not matched by a desire to invest, or a fall in investment spending decisions when the public isn't willing to shift its consumption function upward, why not have the government counteract the change through a *compensatory* fiscal policy? It seems quite simple and it would appear to be in everyone's best interest. What stands in the way except the ignorance of the public and politicians? Could more courses in economic principles wipe out recessions the way vaccination has wiped out smallpox? One of the authors grew up during the Great Depression and still remembers vividly the sense of relief with which he discovered fiscal policy in his first economics course. Depressions were not inevitable! The government now knew how to cure them!

But does the economy actually work in the way our model describes it? Or have too many important relationships been omitted? We know, for example, that saving and consumption decisions do not depend exclusively on current income as the consumption function assumes. People often maintain an accustomed level of spending by borrowing when current income declines and by adding to their saving when it rises. Consumption spending can also be affected by expectations of *future* income. How reliable is the multiplier process when we take these factors into account? As for investment spending, it's not only a variable subject to sudden and unexpected changes; it is sometimes fickle enough to respond perversely to the very government actions designed to correct for its misbehavior. To what extent will this invalidate our analysis? And what about the money supply? When we discussed money in chapters 9 and 10, we took for granted that changes in the size of the money stock had some effect on total demand. Can we safely ignore those effects?

We're raising questions now that economists could not even begin to answer until quite recently. And since the answers have only recently begun to be formulated, they're still incomplete and tentative. The problem has been that the effectiveness of fiscal policy as an active tool for economic stabilization could not be tested until those who had political power were willing to try it. That may not have occurred even yet, and it certainly did not occur in this country prior to the 1960s.

Inconclusive Results

Income-expenditures analysis captured the economics profession (or a majority of the profession—some never surrendered) long before it won a sympathetic hearing from any American president or from more than a handful of legislators. Income-expenditures analysis was incorporated into introductory economics texts shortly after World War II, in a move pioneered by the subsequent Nobel prizewinner Paul Samuelson. In his text it became "the modern theory of national income determination." But Keynes didn't make the cover of *Time* that year—or the next. He made it in 1965, one year after Congress enacted and the president signed a tax-reduction bill that had been advocated on the basis of income-expenditures analysis.

Economists don't have an economy of their own to experiment with; they have to rely on the one all the rest of us use. Experiments to test a theory in the social sciences are often not possible until legislators have been persuaded that the theory is a sound one, and it's hard to persuade them in the absence of controlled experiments. Such experiments may never be possible because of our reluctance or inability to employ adequate controls. So it shouldn't surprise you that the reliability of fiscal policy as a stabilization tool is still very much disputed.

In the absence of controlled experiments, economists have fallen back on "thought experiments" and such tests as history happened to provide. The "thought experiments" consisted of thinking through the possibilities and searching for plausible relationships. The *General Theory* was one such grand exercise in experimental thinking.

But an economic theory is better tested by its applicability to events. In the absence of governments willing to run tests, economists interested in the income-expenditures approach looked for verification of its insights in such events as World War II. And many found there a convincing confirmation of the theory.

Empirical Tests?

Throughout the decade of the 1930s the federal government ran deficits that were much too small in the view of those who wanted a major and decisive government stimulus to aggregate demand. But even those modest deficits were largely offset by the surpluses of state and local governments.

World War II changed all that. The total government deficit rose from $.7 billion in 1940 to $3.8 billion in 1941 and then to $31.4, $44.1, $51.8, and $39.5 billion from 1942 through 1945. Real gross national product (in 1958 dollars) rose from $227 billion in 1940 to $361 billion in 1944—a 60% increase in just four years—before declining to $355 billion in 1945. Unemployment in 1940 was 14.6% of the labor force; in subsequent years it fell to 9.9%, 4.7%, 1.9%, and 1.2% in 1944 before rising to 1.9% in 1945.

One of the most interesting pieces of data from this period is the course of personal consumption expenditures. Government purchases expanded enormously during the war, from $36 billion in 1940 to a peak of $182 billion in 1944. But despite this huge government drain on the economy's productive capabilities, personal consumption expenditures also managed to rise between 1940 and 1944. Once the economic system had been prodded into action, it was able to provide 10% more consumer goods while satisfying the extraordinary demands of wartime.

This "experiment in fiscal policy" meant little to those unfamiliar with income-expenditures analysis. Most Americans were convinced in 1945 that the surfeit of jobs was due solely to the huge demand for military goods and the fact that $11\frac{1}{2}$ million workers were in the armed forces (more than $\frac{1}{6}$ of the entire 1944 labor force and 20% of the prewar labor force). They expected the return of unemployment lines and depression when the war ended. But for economists learning to think about the economy in the framework of income-expenditures analysis, the wartime experience demonstrated the effectiveness of fiscal policy. It would have been better, they argued, if the government had paid people during the 1930s to dig holes and fill them in again rather than allow massive unemployment to continue. The income received from such wasted effort would have increased consumption spending, created a larger demand for useful output, and provided additional jobs and income. Of course, it would have been better for the government to pay these people to do useful work. But useless work that stimulated incomes and spending would have been less wasteful in the end than tolerating unemployment and idle resources.

The wartime experience had been a demonstration of the paradox that income-expenditures analysis tried to resolve. The stimulus given to the economy by government deficits had enabled the nation to maintain and even raise real per capita consumption while producing vast amounts of war materials and lending $11\frac{1}{2}$ million members of the labor force to military service.

But the demonstration was most convincing to those who had already been largely persuaded by the logic of the argument. The test was hardly a conclusive proof of the effectiveness of countercyclical fiscal policy. Even if one granted that massive increases in government expenditure, especially when financed by borrowing rather than taxation, were capable of ending a deep and prolonged depression, one might doubt that fiscal policy was in general an effective tool for eliminating aggregate fluctuations.

Many supporters of income-expenditures analysis have therefore appealed to the postwar experience as further evidence in support of their thesis that countercyclical fiscal policy works. It can be shown that recessions have been neither prolonged nor very deep since World War II. The 1974–75 recession broke all postwar records but fell far short of what had happened in the 1930s. But can this record be attributed to the operations of fiscal policy? We would first have to establish that fiscal policy was systematically used as a stabilization tool.

Has Countercyclical Fiscal Policy Really Been Tried?

Neither President Truman nor President Eisenhower seems to have been firmly persuaded that fiscal policy was an appropriate and useful stabilization tool. President Kennedy had studied income-expenditures analysis at Harvard, and he chose as his economic advisers some of the more eminent advocates of that approach to the understanding and control of economic fluctuations. But even Kennedy's public pronouncements on the subject of government expenditures and taxation reveal something less than a total commitment to countercyclical fiscal policy. That may reflect his assessment of popular and Congressional devotion to balanced budgets more than his own views. But if that was the case, then Congressional support for a conscious and deliberate countercyclical use of fiscal policy was not yet present even in the early 1960s. The notion that the federal budget ought to be balanced in each and every fiscal year could hardly be held by someone who accepted countercyclical fiscal policy as an appropriate tool in government efforts at stabilization. The fact that many members of Congress apparently still held this view in the 1960s casts considerable doubt on the argument that the federal government was systematically employing the policy.

Did the tide finally turn in 1964? *Time* magazine obviously thought so. But anyone who looks closely at the Congressional debates preceding the tax cuts and at pollsters' sampling of public opinion in 1964 might retain doubts. The public thought taxes were definitely too high and favored reductions. The argument of the president's economic advisors that high tax rates were imposing "fiscal drag" on the economy was especially appealing. But none of this is convincing evidence that the public or Congress was eager to adopt countercyclical fiscal policy. We know only that they were willing to be told that a tax cut was a good thing for the whole economy and not just for them personally, and a good thing in the long run as well as right now.

The question here is not whether countercyclical fiscal policy *works.* The

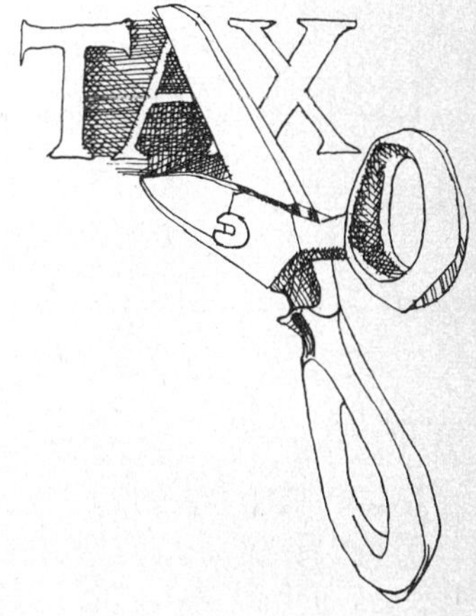

question is whether it has ever been *tried*. If doubt can still remain on the second question it will be very hard indeed to muster convincing empirical evidence for or against the more important first question. The lack of consensus among economists on the effectiveness of fiscal policy as a stabilization tool should not be surprising.

We'll return to the question of fiscal policy and its effects in subsequent chapters, after we've taken another look at the role money might play in determining the level of economic activity, and after we've brought the

PUMP PRIMING

Income-expenditures analysis suggests that the incentives to private investors in the 1930s were not sufficient to secure a level of investment expenditure consistent with high output and employment and that government spending filled the gap in the early 1940s. But why did private investment spending increase after the war and remain high? Why wasn't continued deficit spending by the government necessary to prevent the return of depression?

Income-expenditures analysis does not answer this question, because it offers no explanation for the level of intended investment. Keynes said that investment decisions are based on profit expectations and that these expectations are in large part governed by psychological factors. He provided no systematic theory that would explain why intended investment was so low in the 1930s and so much higher after World War II.

It may be that under appropriate circumstances deficit spending has a "pump priming" effect. By raising the aggregate level of economic activity it may stimulate greater optimism and thereby a revival of investor confidence. Once fiscal policy had primed the pump in this fashion, it might be able to withdraw and again allow private spending decisions to determine the level of output and employment.

Can fiscal policy induce a *self-sustaining* expansion of economic activity? Income-expenditures analysis makes no assertions about the effectiveness or ineffectiveness of pump priming. For that reason it does not explain the marked difference between prewar and postwar investment levels. This is an important issue. But given our enormous ignorance about the way in which mass expectations form and reform, it's an issue on which we can say very little beyond what the "classical" economists said: that a "return of confidence" is essential to economic recovery.

rest of the world into the picture. But all this talk about government surpluses and deficits has brought another issue to the fore.

THE NATIONAL DEBT

Conversations about deficit spending versus balanced budgets always come around eventually to the question of the national debt. This looms so large (if rather vaguely) in the public mind as a serious problem that Congress has placed a legal ceiling on the debt. It's an odd sort of ceiling, much like the ceiling in an elevator going up; the President periodically asks that it be raised and Congress always cooperates. But the existence of a statutory ceiling, even a flexible one, at least persuades people that someone has an eye on the problem.

What kind of problem is it? How large can the debt grow before we encounter disaster? Surely the government can't go on indefinitely living beyond its means, can it? When will the debt have to be repaid? And *how?*

Direct questions deserve direct answers. Very few knowledgeable people worry about the national debt or consider it much of a problem. It could probably grow to several times its present size without presenting any unmanageable difficulties. The federal government can, if it chooses, live beyond its means indefinitely. The debt doesn't ever have to be repaid. The question of how to retire the debt is academic in view of the fact that it will probably never be retired.

Nothing in that paragraph should alarm you or arouse the suspicion that the government is a welsher. No debtor has to pay back his creditors as long as the creditors don't demand repayment. And the individuals and institutions to whom the federal government is indebted are not holding government bonds out of either patriotism or necessity, but out of concern for their own financial welfare. They purchased the bonds because they decided the best thing they could do with their money was to lend it to the government. Moreover, should they change their minds, they would find that the federal government cheerfully redeems certain bonds on demand and that for the remainder there exists an active market through which some other party can easily be found to take the bonds and return the original purchaser's principal.

Refinancing the Debt

Despite the fact that bonds regularly fall due, requiring the federal government to repay the principal, the debt is never retired. For the government secures the funds to repay the principal basically by selling more

bonds. As long as it can find purchasers, the government faces no problems. And finding purchasers isn't difficult. If a particular issue of new bonds doesn't sell, that means the Treasury Department has been stingy in setting the yield. A slightly lower price for the bonds, which comes to the same thing as a slightly higher interest rate, will bring a surge of additional offers to purchase.[1]

You could do the same thing if you enjoyed an adequate credit rating, and many private firms and individuals do. They borrow for a set term and then extend the loan when it falls due. In effect they are paying the interest and borrowing the funds to repay the principal. Lenders are glad to cooperate because they earn their income by lending; the repayment of principal is a nuisance which requires the lender to find a new borrower, and why should the lender want to go to that trouble if the borrower is a good risk and the lender has little fear of default on the loan?

The federal government enjoys a uniquely high credit rating among lenders. Lenders do not request an audit of the government's books, demand collateral, raise embarrassing questions about the efficiency with which the government manages its business, or insist upon evidence that the government is going to start living within its means. For they know that the federal government has the power to collect revenue by coercion and, even more importantly, that it has the power to print money. State and local governments can and do default on their obligations at times; so do some of the largest corporations when their revenues fall short of expectations. But the federal government in such a fix could simply create the money with which to pay its debts. In a pinch it can always count on the cooperation of the Federal Reserve Banks. This power makes the bonds of the federal government uniquely safe and guarantees that buyers can be found at the right price.

Are we to conclude, then, that the national debt is neither a problem nor a burden? That would be going too far. What happens to the debt does make a difference.

Dangers in a Growing Debt

In the first place, *increases* in the debt mean that the government is injecting more into the income stream than it is taking out. If the economy is operating close to capacity, deficit financing may be inflationary. Of course, if the economy is in a depression, an increase in the debt may be the demand stimulus that restores prosperity. It is thus not the absolute size of the debt so much as the direction in which it is changing that ought

1. If a bond maturing one year from now with a value at maturity of $2700 can be purchased for $2500, the yield or effective interest rate on that bond is 8%: a $200 return on $2500. The return is greater than 8% at prices below $2500, less than 8% at prices above $2500.

to be carefully watched. That, of course, is the central argument of fiscal policy advocates.

But the effect of debt increases on aggregate demand is not the only effect. Government borrowing pulls resources away from private into public uses. While taxation has the same effect, taxes have a greater political impact, and expenditures undertaken out of tax revenues therefore tend to be scrutinized more critically than expenditures financed through borrowing. Whether this is a point for or against government borrowing depends upon how one evaluates the relative importance of public and private spending. Some students of American society maintain that we spend far too much on goods for private consumption (automobiles, houses, filet mignon) and far too little on the goods whose provision is largely left to government (education, public parks, national defense). But there are others who maintain just as insistently that government expenditure promotes social welfare less efficiently than private expenditure. However you stand on that issue, the ability to increase expenditures without increasing taxes almost certainly enables governments to spend more than they otherwise would.

The Burden of the Debt

The often heard argument that deficit financing pushes the burden of present expenditures onto our descendants is almost wholly mistaken. The debt we pass on to future generations is for the most part matched by the bonds we bequeath them. If we leave them assets as well as liabilities, we leave them no net burden of indebtedness.

When you stop to think about it, you realize that current expenditures, however they are *financed,* require the use of current real resources. Wars, for example, can be *financed* by borrowing, but they must be *fought* by drawing upon the current population and using the productive capabilities of the current economy. Highways, schools, and dams, regardless of how these projects are financed, all require for their construction the use of current resources that are consequently not available to provide other goods for the current generation. In fact, deficit financing may well make future generations better off. If the borrowed funds are wisely used in the construction of projects that will yield large future services, the current generation is sacrificing the present enjoyment of real resources in order to provide a larger real income to later generations. We are benefiting right now from past government expenditures on schools, roads, public buildings, parks, dams, irrigation projects, and other public investment in the form of a larger output of privately produced commodities and services.

There is one partial exception to all this. If a government borrows from *foreigners* to finance current expenditures, then it is attempting to use the currrent resources of foreigners rather than its own citizens. And future generations will be left with the obligation to repay that borrowing by giving up some of their resources to foreign bondholders. Of course, if the projects for which the government borrows are good investments, they will augment the real income of future generations by more than enough to repay the resources originally borrowed from abroad. We see again that the wisdom of the project for which the borrowing is undertaken is more important than the mere fact that the expenditure is financed by borrowing. And this agrees with everything we know about private spending and borrowing. A business firm or a household will gain from going into debt whenever the project financed by borrowing increases the flow of future goods (income) by more than it increases the stream of future payments on principal and interest.

Numbers and Alarums

This discussion of the national debt has stayed away from actual numbers, because the principles are more important than the numbers, however dramatic the latter can sometimes be made to appear. Some people are apparently thrilled in a terrifying sort of way by the news that if Alexander the Great had started to spend money after the Battle of Issus at the rate of $400 a minute, he would not yet today have spent a sum equal to the total of our public debt. But what does that *mean?* Do we gain a relevant sense of proportion from such numbers? Or are they like estimating the relative importance of mosquitoes and elephants by figuring out how many mosquitoes would have to be put on a scale to balance one elephant?

The interest paid by the federal government annually on the national debt may be a more meaningful measure of its significance, because the interest is the "carrying charge" on the debt. It is currently close to 2% of the gross national product. That's a substantial sum, but it hardly spells fiscal ruin. Another way to put the debt into perspective is to note that in 1945, at the end of World War II, it was approximately equal to the gross national product. Thirty years later the debt was more than twice as large, but it was less than 40% of the value of our annual output.

In short, the national debt is not a major problem. If you've been worrying about it in a vaguely fearful way, we encourage you to discard your anxieties or transfer them to some social problem more deserving of your concern.

Once Over Lightly

Fiscal policy is the use by the federal government of expenditures and taxes to influence the aggregate level of economic activity.

Income-expenditures analysis asserts that government expenditures which exceed or fall short of government income have the same effect on the aggregate economy as gaps between intended investment and intended saving. Aggregate equilibrium exists when intended saving plus tax receipts equals intended investment plus government disbursements for the purchase of goods and for transfer payments. An alternative statement of the equilibrium condition is that intended investment purchases plus consumption and government purchases must equal total output or income.

A change in tax receipts or transfer payments will have a smaller effect on output and income than a change in government goods purchases of the same amount as long as the marginal propensity to consume is less than one.

Insofar as the aggregate level of economic activity affects the balance between government receipts and disbursements, fluctuations in output and income will create deficits and surpluses that will in turn affect the level of income and output. The government could allow recessions to create budget deficits and allow booms to create surpluses without taking any action to close these gaps. That would be one kind of fiscal policy. The government could also move to close these gaps or to widen them in response to recessions and booms. By trying to close the gaps or keep the budget balanced the government would be lending additional impetus to the forces that had generated the recession or boom. By widening the gaps the government would be attempting to introduce a larger counter-force to private spending decisions than will come about automatically as tax receipts and transfer payments change with the level of economic activity.

Economists do not know how powerful or precise an instrument fiscal policy is for the stabilization of economic activity. Part of the reason is the impossibility of adequately controlled experiments. Another reason is the unwillingness of Congress and the president, at least until very recently, to use fiscal policy deliberately and systematically as a stabilization tool.

The size of the national debt is not a good argument against deficit spending. The debt is today a far smaller percentage of the gross national product than it was right after World War II. The government can refinance the debt indefinitely as it falls due and could probably carry a considerably larger debt without serious difficulty.

Changes in the size of the debt are more important than its mere total, because changes represent deficits or surpluses that affect the aggregate level of economic activity.

The wisdom of increasing the national debt should be determined by examining the probable effects on aggregate economic activity and the social productivity of the projects for which borrowing occurs.

An economy viewed as a whole does not shift the burden of current expenditures onto future generations merely by borrowing to finance those expenditures. The real costs of any project are the opportunities foregone by using real resources in one way rather than another. Any expenditure that increases the net value of the future flow of goods benefits those who will live in the future regardless of how that expenditure is financed.

QUESTIONS FOR DISCUSSION

1. When the federal government purchases buildings, airplanes, or the services of economists:

    (*a*) What are the real costs?

    (*b*) How is it determined who will bear the real costs?

    (*c*) If all purchases were financed out of personal income taxes, would the real costs be borne by citizens in proportion to the taxes they pay?

    (*d*) What differences would you predict in the distribution of the real costs if the purchases were financed by borrowing?

2. Will your answers to the questions above depend on whether the economy is at full employment? Will the particular goods the government is purchasing and the level of employment in the industries producing or using those goods make a difference in your answers?

3. The economy moves into a recession and federal government tax revenues fall, creating a budget deficit. The government can raise taxes and/or reduce expenditures to bring the budget back into balance; maintain present tax *rates* and previously planned expenditures and accept the deficit; or reduce taxes and/or increase expenditures, creating an even larger deficit.

    (*a*) Which approach would you recommend, and why?

    (*b*) What arguments might be raised against the approach you recommend?

    (*c*) Which approach would you *least* want to recommend? Why?

4. If the government decreased spending on highways by $5 billion and simultaneously increased spending on energy development by $5 billion, would the equilibrium level of Y be affected? What actual effects on the level of unemployment would you expect?

5. Assume that Congress and the president want to cut taxes by $5 billion to stimulate the economy in a period of recession. Does it matter whether they cut personal income taxes or corporate income taxes? Whether the cuts in personal income taxes are concentrated among low-income groups or more widely distributed? In what ways does it matter?

6. Suppose the unemployment rate is 8% and economic statisticians tell the government that 2 of those 8 percentage points are a direct result of sharply reduced purchases of new automobiles. Discuss the advantages and disadvantages in such a situation of offering a tax rebate to purchasers of new automobiles equal to 10% of the manufacturers' suggested retail price. Is a dollar of tax reduction offered in this way likely to reduce unemployment more than a dollar of personal income tax reduction? Are the longer run effects on unemployment likely to be different from the short run effects?

7. During the depression of the 1930s, increases in federal government expenditures were often accompanied by promises (threats?) of future tax increases to hold down the size of the budget deficit. Do you think this policy had any effect on investment spending?

8. Use the data in table 8A to discuss the real costs of the 300% increase in government purchases from 1941 to 1944.

9. "The size of the national debt is not as important as the size of changes in the debt." Evaluate that assertion.

10. What would be the consequences of a systematic effort by the federal government to retire the national debt over a period of 20 years?

11. Federal government expenditures for national defense, when expressed in dollars of 1975 purchasing power, have averaged just about $100 billion per year from 1966 through 1975. Suppose that world peace were somehow miraculously declared and that the government abolished the national defense budget. What consequences would you predict for the economy? Do you think this would trigger a major depression? Why or why not? What fiscal policies would you recommend to accompany this disappearance of all national defense expenditures?

12. When a corporation successfully sells additional bonds it goes more deeply into debt. Is this evidence that the corporation is failing or succeeding? How well do analogies from the area of business indebtedness apply to questions of government indebtedness? Where do such analogies present a misleading picture, and why?

13

INFLATION AND THE REVIVAL
OF MONETARY POLICY

Ten years after its publication Keynes's *General Theory of Employment, Interest and Money* had become the general theory that interest and money have little to do with employment. We'll sidestep the question of whether this was the intent of Keynes or the work of disciples more Keynesian than their mentor. Either way, it happened. The role that monetary policy might play in preventing undesirable movements in economic aggregates was pushed to the side by economists more interested in the applications of fiscal policy. The United States consistently had a monetary policy during these years, just as it had a fiscal policy long before economists concluded that the government budget might make a contribution toward economic stabilization. But the majority of economists paid little attention to monetary policy in the 1940s and 1950s or assigned it the role of minor assistant to fiscal policy.

MONEY IN INCOME-EXPENDITURES ANALYSIS

The expenditures that make up aggregate demand are almost entirely monetary expenditures. But this does not necessarily mean that the quantity of money affects those expenditures. In the first five chapters of this book we repeatedly examined transactions that involved money without asking whether it made any difference that they occurred through a medium of exchange rather than by barter. The same kind of abstraction from money might work in analyzing aggregate fluctuations.

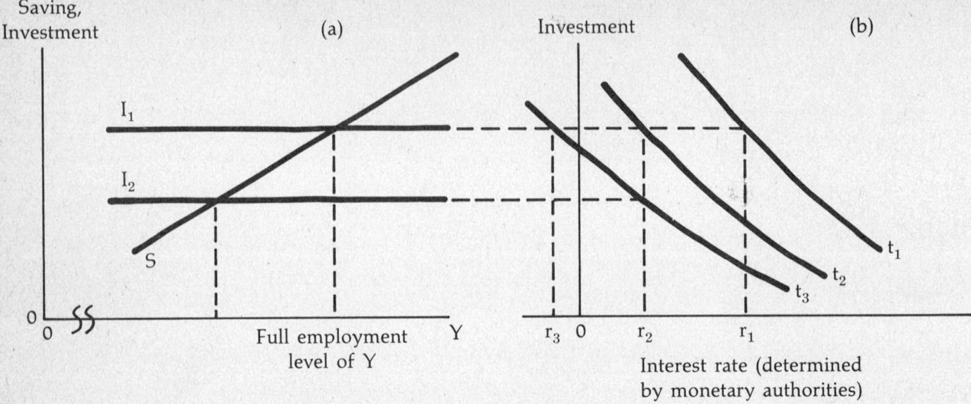

Figure 13A Interest rates and full employment

Keynes was himself extremely interested in the properties of money and the peculiar effects it might have on economic decisions; the title of his book is sufficient evidence of that. But he nonetheless contributed in two ways to the decline of interest in money and monetary policy. First, he constructed an analytical model that *could* be used without necessarily bringing in money. And second, he expressed his skepticism about the effectiveness of monetary policy as an antirecession tool.

Money, Interest Rates, and Investment

How was money incorporated into the *General Theory?* We can answer that question with the help of Figure 13A. Graph (a) presents the aggregate propensity to save (S) and the propensity to invest (I_1, I_2) in a hypothetical economy. The intersection of these curves determines the equilibrium level of total income (Y).

Graph (b) shows the relationship between the quantity of investment and the interest rate with different states of investor confidence. If confidence declines, the curve will shift downward and to the left, from t_1 to t_2 to t_3. Less investment will take place at any particular rate of interest the further "southwest" the curve lies.

According to Keynes, the monetary authorities set the interest rate when they determine the size of the money stock. Suppose they set the interest rate at the level r_1 in graph (b). This will determine how much investment investors are willing to undertake, given their expectations of profit from particular projects and the general state of confidence. The curves $t_1, t_2,$ and t_3 all slope downward to the right because investment opportunities with the prospect of low yields will only be undertaken if the opportunity cost of doing so—the rate of interest—is also low. At higher interest rates, projects promising lower yields are squeezed out. With the interest rate at r_1 and the level of confidence shown by t_1, just the right amount of investment occurs: I_1 and S intersect at the full employment level of Y.

Now suppose a wave of pessimism sweeps over the economy and investors' expectations sink. Each potential investment project is now viewed as offering either the prospect of a lower net return or a smaller probability of the previously expected return. Either way, the curve relating investment and the interest rate will fall downward and to the left. If it falls to the position shown by curve t_2, the monetary authorities might be able to maintain full employment by increasing the money supply enough to reduce the interest rate to r_2.

But if the curve falls to t_3, nothing short of a negative interest rate, r_3, would be able to maintain investment at the level necessary for full employment. If r_2 turns out to be the practical limit below which monetary authorities cannot reduce the interest rate (and Keynes thought there was such a floor under the interest rate), then investment will be at the level shown by I_2, and the economy will move to an equilibrium at less than full employment.

In the analysis of figure 13A, monetary policy does have the power to affect aggregate demand through its effect on interest rates and thus on investment. That power will be limited, however, by the sensitivity of investment to changes in the rate of interest. And it may disappear altogether in the face of a major collapse in investor confidence. In the *General Theory*, Keynes expressed skepticism about monetary policy's usefulness, because he feared that investment was far more responsive to psychological moods and speculative swings than to any practicable changes in the rate of interest. Investment decisions would be dominated by shifts in the curves (t_1, t_2, t_3), with interest rates playing a relatively minor role. Most users of income-expenditures analysis were willing to follow this lead in the years immediately following World War II. And so they looked to fiscal policy as the government's effective weapon in the battle against unemployment.[1]

THE EQUATION OF EXCHANGE

The notion that monetary policy affects total expenditures only through the interest rate was a novel idea in the 1930s. An older tradition in economics, going back at least to the economist-philosophers John Locke and David Hume, asserted a much more direct and powerful influence of money upon total spending. This older theory of money had been used primarily to explain the relationship between the money supply and the price level. It was called the *quantity theory of money.*

---

1. Or did they conclude that monetary policy was ineffective because they were so caught up in the potentialities of fiscal policy? The actual causal connections between policy preferences, choice of theories, and empirical conclusions are not always as clear and straightforward as we would like them to be. We all sometimes reason from conclusions to facts.

The Money Supply and the Price Level

The quantity theory developed out of an interest in the effect that gold imports had on a country's price level in an age when the domestic money supply was closely linked to a nation's monetary gold stock. But the usefulness of the theory does not depend on the particular way in which a country's money supply is determined. In its simplest form, the quantity theory asserts that the price level will vary in proportion to changes in the quantity of money. A doubling of the money supply will double the average of all prices. Halving the money supply will halve the price level. Stated so baldly and boldly, the theory had at least this virtue: it warned statesmen against the folly of supposing that the national income could be increased simply by acquiring more money. The wealth of nations, as Adam Smith pointed out, depended upon their ability to produce want-satisfying goods. A greater quantity of money was of no value to a country if it only altered the rate of exchange between those goods and money, or the price level.

But stated so baldly and boldly, the theory is also wrong. The price level will not always change in direct proportion to changes in the money supply. There are two other possibilities. One is that the change in the money supply will bring about changes in the rate at which real goods are produced. In that case prices will not change by the same percentage as the money supply. The other possibility is that money may be circulated more or less rapidly as its quantity changes. This will again break the direct proportionality of changes in the price level and changes in the money supply.

The possibilities are contained in a simple formula usually known as the *equation of exchange:*

$$MV = PQ$$

M represents the stock of money; V is the velocity of circulation or the average number of times each unit of money changes hands during the period under study; P is the price level; and Q is an index of the real transactions occurring during the period, or the quantity of goods exchanged by means of money.

P times Q is therefore the dollar value of all goods sold for money. M times V is the dollar value of all monetary expenditures for the purchase of goods. And so MV is actually equal to PQ by definition. The equation is an identity and could be written: $MV \equiv PQ$.

You encountered the equation of exchange, even though you weren't introduced at the time, in chapter 10. While discussing the Fed's procedures for exercising control over the money supply, we asked *which measure* of the money stock was the most important one to control. If the goal of the Fed is to control aggregate demand, then the measure on which to focus would be the measure most closely linked to total expenditures. So we ran a little test, the results of which are shown in table 10A. We took gross national product in current dollars as our measure of total expenditures during a year, and let the size of the money stock in the preceding December represent the quantity of money available to finance those expenditures. Dividing GNP by each measure of the money stock gave us a numerical measurement of the relation between changes in each measure of M and changes in total expenditures. And we pointed out at the time that this number had a name: the velocity of money circulation.

Because GNP does not take *all* money-goods exchanges into account, the velocities we calculated were actually the velocities of circulation only for expenditures on goods included in the calculation of the gross national product. But GNP is a good proxy for total expenditures as well as the best measure we have for changes in the value of total output and income. We'll therefore follow the standard practice of using GNP as a synonym for PQ.

By means of these definitions we can now assign an empirical meaning to the four terms in the equation of exchange:

M = the stock of money, measured by M_1, M_2, or M_3

P = the price level, measured by the GNP deflator
(presented in table 8D)

Q = the quantity of goods produced, measured by dividing the
GNP deflator into the value of GNP in current dollars
(presented in table 8E)

V = the velocity of money circulation, measured by dividing the
money stock into PQ, or GNP in current dollars

With the aid of these definitions, let's inquire more closely into the meaning and implications of the quantity theory of money.

What Can Happen When the Stock of Money Changes?

The economists who asserted that the price level would always change in proportion to any change in the quantity of money were implicitly maintaining that V and Q are not affected by changes in the money supply. Money does not circulate more or less rapidly when its quantity alters, they were assuming, and the volume of production does not change when the money supply increases or decreases. No one today defends that simple statement of the quantity theory, and probably no economist ever did mean to defend it as an exact description of reality. But it was useful as a defensive weapon against those who might identify money with wealth and think they could achieve prosperity merely by expanding the supply of money.

An alternative possibility is to hold that V always varies inversely with M so as to maintain a constant volume of money expenditures when the money supply changes. If this were the case, the size of the money stock would be a matter of no consequence at all. The public would simply circulate money more or less rapidly, as its quantity declined or rose, in order to continue spending at its preferred rate. Neither the price level nor the volume of production would respond to changes in the money supply. That proposition is also too extreme ever to have been held as an exact description of a monetary economy. But it was useful to economists who wanted to argue that increases in the money supply were not an effective way to restore prosperity in a recession. In periods of particularly deep or prolonged depression, it might be that any increases in the money stock would simply increase idle money balances. Even that proposition has not been tested, however, because there were no really massive injections of money into the economy in the 1930s.

Let's consider one additional possibility. Suppose that V does not change when M changes, so that increases or decreases in M bring about proportionate increases or decreases in the product of P and Q. How will the effects be distributed between P and Q? This is an extremely important question for anyone who holds that the stock of money does affect the total volume of expenditures. If the economy is already operating at "full employment," then Q cannot increase. If we admit that "full employment" is a somewhat fuzzy concept, we might want to say that Q cannot increase very much or very rapidly when the economy is already operating at high employment. Large increases in the money supply would then have their principal impact on P, and would cause inflation. This is still assuming that V is constant when M increases. The economists who used the simple version of the quantity theory were actually assuming both the constancy of V and an economy operating continuously at "full employment." If, on the other hand, the economy is running well below the "full employment" level, an increase in M when V is constant might cause an increase in Q, and an increase in P, or some combination of the two. If the increase in M primarily affected Q in such a case, "full employment" might be restored in periods of recession through increases in the money supply.

How Stable Is Velocity?

It should be clear from all of this that the importance of money, and hence the potential effectiveness of monetary policy, depends on the actual behavior of V when M changes and the actual separate responses of P and Q under the conditions that exist at the time.

What do we know about the actual behavior of V? One of the factors contributing to the eventual revival of interest in monetary policy after World War II was a wealth of empirical studies demonstrating the relative stability of V. Although those studies were far more comprehensive and detailed than the data presented in table 10A, the velocity numbers in that

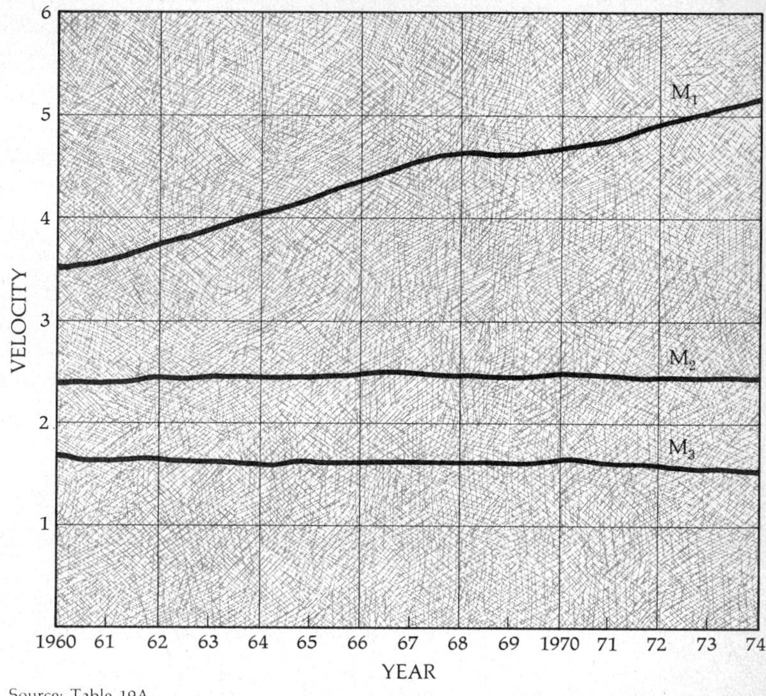

Source: Table 19A

table provide a good enough picture for our purposes. Figure 13B charts the course of velocity from 1960 to 1974. The velocity of M_1 has tended to rise since 1960, but at a fairly steady rate. The velocity of M_2 has fluctuated slightly and shown no long-term tendency to increase or decrease. The velocity of M_3 has fluctuated just a little more than M_2 while drifting almost imperceptibly downward.

If changes in the money stock are in fact closely correlated with changes in PQ, may we conclude the PQ can be controlled by controlling the money supply? We raised the same question briefly in chapter 10 and pointed out three objections to that conclusion. Let's review them. One is the difficulty in separating the effects upon P and upon Q. In a period of inflation we want to restrain P but not Q. In a period of recession we want to expand Q but not P. Can monetary policy do that? The ability to affect the course of P *times* Q is not enough.

Another objection has to do with the difficulties inherent in managing the money supply. We discussed that problem at length in chapter 10. The monetary authorities have not found it easy to select appropriate targets or to hit the targets they choose.

The third objection is the one we want to consider now. In the social sciences a historical correlation is rarely acceptable evidence of a causal

Figure 13B Velocity of money circulation, 1970–74 (GNP ÷ money stock in preceding December)

connection. We might find a strong negative correlation over time between new housing starts and the rate of change in the price of medical services; but we would be reluctant to conclude that the direct manipulation of one will control the other. We would demand a theoretical explanation. If we were then told that general inflation raises the price of medical services and also creates the expectation of continuing inflation, which in turn slows down residential construction by raising interest rates, we might be satisfied that the correlation is not mere coincidence. But we would not then try to stimulate the home building industry by putting price controls on doctors and hospitals.

THE DEMAND FOR MONEY BALANCES

Is there an adequate theoretical explanation for the stability of V? We can best answer that question by using the little device employed in chapter 10 when we first called attention to the velocity concept. Instead of writing the equation of exchange as $MV = PQ$, we write: $M = (1/V)PQ$. While the equations are mathematically equivalent, the latter form makes more behavioral sense. People don't think about the velocity with which they want to circulate money and then take steps to reach their preferred velocity. But people do think about their money balances. They think about them in relation to their anticipated expenditures, and they take actions designed to move their money balances toward the levels they prefer. The public's total stock of money balances is $\frac{1}{V}$ expressed as a fraction of PQ, which is the volume of current expenditures.

It follows that V will be stable if the public does not quickly or easily change its demand for money, or, more specifically, its preferred ratio between money balances and current expenditures.

Actual and Preferred Money Balances

The public as a whole must hold the entire money supply, because it isn't counted as money unless it *is* being held by the public. So total money balances will always be identical to M (regardless of which measure of M we use). But *actual* money balances may not be equal to *preferred* money balances. If the monetary authorities were to increase the money supply at a time when the public was satisfied with its current money holdings, some people would necessarily find themselves holding larger money balances than they preferred to hold. So they would take steps to reduce their money balances back to the preferred level. And if the Fed were to reduce the money supply when people were holding their preferred amounts of money, they would try to raise their balances back up to the previous level.

We issued this caution before, but it may be worth mentioning again: Do not confuse the concepts of money and income. Money is a stock; income is a flow. When we talk about people's preferences for money balances, we are not talking about their attitude toward income. The preference for money balances is the same thing as the demand for money. And the demand for money is the demand for liquidity, not for more income. When someone says that Local 13 of the United Federation of Dingleworkers is "demanding more money," that translates in our terminology into a demand for more income, in the form of higher wages. People can increase their incomes without increasing the amount of their money holdings if they simply step up their spending by the amount of the increase in income. Or they can increase their money holdings in the face of a decreasing income if they are willing to reduce their expenditures by more than the decline in their income. An increase in the demand for money always means an increased desire to hold money balances *in preference to alternative assets.* Thus a person who increases his money balances is not necessarily wealthier than he was before; he simply holds more wealth than before in the form of money rather than in such nonmoney forms as refrigerators or corporate bonds.

Nominal and Real Money Balances

It is the connection between *actual* money balances and *preferred* balances that explains how changes in the money supply affect the economy. But to see how it works you must distinguish between *nominal* and *real* money balances. A person's *real* money balance is the command over other goods that those dollars provide. You might feel secure with $200 in your checking account. But if the price level doubled, that money balance wouldn't be as comfortable. You would have to hold $400 in your *nominal* balance to maintain the level of your *real* balance. People's preferences are for *real* balances; they're concerned, in other words, about the value or purchasing power of those balances. It's true that people may be fooled for a while into supposing that their real balances haven't declined when the price level rises; but they tend to discover the truth and make adjustments. A rising price level, by reducing the purchasing power of money, lowers real balances even though nominal balances haven't changed. On the other hand, a falling price level, other things remaining equal, raises real balances.

Effects of Changes in the Supply of Money

What will happen if the Fed increases the money stock at a time when the public is holding the amount of money it prefers to hold? People will find themselves holding more money than they want to hold. So they will spend some. They will shift the composition of their asset portfolio by exchanging money for other goods. The public *as a whole* cannot get rid of money in this way, because one person's surrender of money for an alternative good must be some other person's acquisition of precisely that amount of money. But the *attempt* on the part of people to reduce their money balances has several kinds of effects that will finally bring actual balances into equality with preferred balances.

One effect will be on the prices of goods. With people more eager than before to acquire goods for money, the price of goods will be bid up. That's inflation: an increase in P.

If the enhanced bidding for goods doesn't raise their price, it must mean that the supply of goods has increased. That's an expansion of production: an increase in Q.

Now if the demand for money balances is a demand for *real* balances, then the rise in P or Q or both will eventually cause the quantity of nominal money balances demanded to increase. It will continue increasing as long as PQ is increasing; PQ will keep increasing as long as the public keeps increasing its demand for goods; and the public will keep increasing its demand for goods as long as its actual money balances are greater than its preferred balances.

Does that seem much too complicated to remember? Then don't try to remember it. Think it through. The average amount of money you want to hold over some period of time will depend on your anticipated expenditures during that time. If the dollar amount of your anticipated expenditures goes up, you will probably want to hold more money on average or to maintain the size of your *real* balances by increasing your *nominal* balances. The point of this whole account is that when the Fed allows more money to be created than the public wants to hold at the time, the attempt to reduce those now excessive balances leads to an increased demand for goods, and hence to either higher prices or expanded output or both. That's an increase in PQ. If you're a representative member of the public, your "share" of PQ will rise, so you'll want to hold more money than you did before. It's all quite logical. PQ rises in response to the increased supply of money until the quantity demanded is equal to the larger quantity now being supplied.

The Demand for Money in the Equation of Exchange

The key to the whole process is the presumed relationship between the quantity of money demanded by the public and PQ. If the public wants to hold money balances equal to $(1/5)$PQ, the public in effect wants V to be 5. Suppose that P is 1.00 (100% of the base year), Q is $1350 billion, the public wants to hold money balances equal to $(1/5)$PQ, and M (we'll use M_1) is $270 billion. The quantity of money being demanded is equal to the quantity supplied. Then the Fed increases M to $300 billion. The public still wants to hold only $270 billion, and so people try to buy more goods with their extra money holdings. This bids up the prices of goods and/or stimulates additional production. Until PQ has increased to $1500 billion, the public will be holding more money than it wants to hold and as a consequence will be taking actions that raise the level of PQ. Equilibrium will be reached when—and this is only one of the many possible combinations, of course—the price level has risen 10% and real GNP has increased to $1364 billion.

Will this same process work in reverse? What would we expect to occur if the Fed decreased the money supply to $250 billion in the initial circumstances described above? With GNP at $1350 and the public demanding money balances equal to $\frac{1}{5}$ of that amount, people will find themselves holding less money than they prefer to hold. And so they will reduce their demand for goods in an effort to restore their money balances. As a consequence, P may fall and Q will probably fall. If PQ falls to $1250 billion, equilibrium will be restored with the quantity of money now available, $250 billion, equal to the quantity demanded, $(\frac{1}{5})$ $1250 billion.

If the demand for money $(\frac{1}{V})$ is constant, changes in the stock of money (M) will lead to proportionate changes in nominal gross national product (PQ). But two qualifications to this analysis must be mentioned.

Hyperinflation and Velocity

If the monetary authorities were to increase the money stock so rapidly that almost everyone came to expect large increases in the price level, the demand for money would almost certainly fall. Money would then be an asset whose future value relative to other assets was expected to decline rapidly. People would therefore want to exchange money for other goods before this happened. Money would become like the Old Maid card that all players try to pass on as soon as they can, and the velocity of circulation would rise. That's what occurred in the German hyperinflation of the 1920s.

A continuing rapid rate of growth in the money supply caused prices to rise; the continuing inflation created expectations of further inflation; these expectations prompted an increase in V and an even more rapid inflation; the falling real value of money induced the monetary authorities to make even more nominal money available; inflationary expectations increased still further and prompted an ever greater reluctance to hold money, until finally people quit work early in the day to spend their money income before it had become almost worthless. In such a situation, *where no one wants to hold money, money is useless;* the monetary system disintegrates, and exchange must occur through the cumbersome processes of barter.

Interest Rates and Velocity

That is one qualification to the generalization that changes in M will induce proportionate changes in PQ. The second qualification is less

PARALLELS AND CONTRASTS

Recall that the equilibrium condition in income expenditures analysis is equality between intended saving and intended investment. In monetary analysis the condition of equilibrium is equality between actual money balances and preferred money balances. We can translate the latter condition as an equality between the quantity of money supplied by the monetary authorities and the quantity of money demanded by the public. The parallel with income-expenditures analysis emerges more clearly if we paraphrase that statement in turn and make it an equality between the quantity of money the monetary authorities intend to supply and the quantity the public intends to hold.

In income-expenditures analysis any divergence between savers' and investors' intentions causes changes in Y, which in turn cause savers to adjust their intentions. In monetary analysis any divergence between the intentions of the monetary authorities and the public causes changes in PQ, which in turn cause the public to adjust the quantity of nominal money it wants to hold.

The equilibrating factors are respectively changes in Y and changes in PQ. Because Y and PQ both represent the level of total output in current dollars or the nominal value of total income, it is changes in the level of the gross or the net national product that bring about equilibrium in both analyses.

But income-expenditures analysis and monetary analysis are not simply alternative ways of saying the same thing. One directs attention to consumer and investor spending intentions and suggests that they are not significantly dependent on the size of the money stock. The other directs attention to changes in the stock of money as the critical factor influencing spending intentions. Income-expenditures analysis assumes the stability of the consumption function. Monetary analysis assumes the stability of velocity. The predictive power and hence the relative usefulness of each theory will depend largely upon the actual stability of these relationships: the relationship between changes in income and changes in consumption in the case of income-expenditures analysis, and the relationship between changes in the money supply and changes in total nominal output in the case of monetary analysis.

drastic. Suppose we ask *why* the public would want to hold money balances equal to $\frac{1}{5}$ of anticipated expenditures rather than, say, $\frac{1}{4}$ or $\frac{1}{6}$. The general answer is that the public is balancing the marginal benefits against the marginal costs of holding additional money. The benefits are the expanded opportunities that liquidity offers. One of the costs is the income foregone by keeping assets in the form of currency or checking deposits rather than in forms that yield interest. It follows, then, that at higher interest rates the quantity of money demanded for any volume of anticipated expenditures would be less than when interest rates are low.

This suggests our second qualification to the assertion that changes in M will induce proportionate changes in PQ. Go back to the numerical example employed a few paragraphs earlier. The public initially wants to hold money balances equal to $(\frac{1}{5})$PQ. If PQ is $1350 billion and M is $270 billion, the quantity of money demanded equals the quantity supplied. When the Fed increases M to $300 billion, the public finds itself holding more money than it wants to hold and consequently begins exchanging money for other assets. But those other assets don't have to be such goods as suitcases and porterhouse steaks, which are included in the gross national product. They could also be financial assets like government bonds or corporate securities.

An increased demand for financial assets will bid up their price and thereby reduce their percentage yield. (A security whose ownership yields $10 per year is returning 8% when its price is $125, but only 6% if its price rises to $167.) Declining rates of return on securities mean declining interest rates and hence a lower opportunity cost of holding money. As a result, the public might now be willing to hold money balances equal to some larger percentage of anticipated expenditures.

Assume just for purposes of illustration that the prevailing rate of return on financial assets does fall as a result of the $30 billion increase in the money supply, and that the public consequently decides it's now willing to hold money balances equal to $\frac{1}{4.8}$ of anticipated expenditures. In that case the new equilibrium would occur with a smaller increase in PQ; PQ would increase to only $1440 billion rather than to $1500 billion. That could be achieved through some such combination as a 6% increase in the price level and a rise in real GNP to about $1358 billion.

The important lesson to be drawn from these qualifications is that we do not have good grounds for concluding that V is a constant or that it will not change in response to changes in M. But the money supply will be an important variable to control, and monetary policy can be effective even if that stringent condition is not satisfied. It is enough for V to be *stable* and *predictable*. Empirical studies of the U.S. economy strongly indicate that the demand for money *is* stable and predictable within the range of economic experiences since World War II.

Summing Up

The thread of the argument has now twisted through some fairly unfamiliar terrain. We hope the thread hasn't broken in your hand and that the unfamiliar now appears less strange than it did when the argument began. What we've been after in this chapter is an answer to the question, *What difference does money make?* How much does money matter when we're concerned with fluctuations in income and output, the level of employment, or the price level? Whatever effects money might have, how do these effects make themselves felt?

The chapter began with a short account of the modest role assigned to money in the framework of income-expenditures analysis. The short account was symbolic of the short shrift usually given to money after World War II, when income-expenditures analysis was riding high and most economists had their eyes fixed hopefully on fiscal policy. But in the 1950s interest in monetary policy and its possible contributions to stabilization efforts began to grow, and economists started to think once more about the role that money played in economic transactions. In the second and third parts of this chapter, we tried to give you a working grasp of contemporary monetary theory by using the equation of exchange and the concept of a demand for money balances. Above all we wanted you to understand the economic meaning of the velocity concept and to see that the way in which money matters is crucially dependent on the stability of money velocity.

THE QUESTION OF INFLATION

The revival of interest in monetary theory that this chapter has reflected came about in part because money *had* been neglected after the 1930s and the Keynesian revolution, and a neglected topic is certain to be cultivated after a while if there are lots of people looking for soil to till. But there was an additional explanation for the renewal of interest in money. The Great Depression failed to return and postwar recessions turned out to be surprisingly mild and shortlived. Instead of the anticipated depression, the United States and most other industrialized nations found themselves battling persistent inflation. And while the impotence of monetary policy against recession was a dogma for many disciples of Keynes, there was much less reason to believe it was powerless to combat inflation.

Monetary policy might also be the only game in town. The low taxes and high expenditures that fiscal policy prescribed against recessions were more feasible politically than the higher taxes and reduced expenditures for which inflation called. If Congress was unwilling or unable to practice enough budgetary restraint to prevent inflation, that task might have to be assigned entirely to monetary policy. As income-expenditures analysis and fiscal policy were developed to deal with depression, so the refurbished quantity theory of money and monetary policy gained adherents partly because it promised it could do something about inflation.

How well monetary policy has done, how well it might do, and the possible costs of using it are questions we'll return to when we try to put all the policy pieces together in chapters 16 and 17. There are important reasons, as we shall see, for deferring those questions until we've brought international exchange into our picture. But if we aren't yet ready to evaluate solutions, we can at least take the time now to look more closely at the nature of the problem.

The Effects of Inflation

Why *is* inflation a social evil? It's hard to get people to take that question seriously in a period of fairly rapid inflation, when every pronouncement by politicians, union leaders, business executives, and television commercials begins with the *assumption* that it's a grave evil and asks only what must be done to stop it.

"In an inflation everything becomes more expensive. And that's obviously bad, isn't it?" It would indeed be bad if it were true; but it isn't true. If the price of *everything* increases in equal proportion, then in *real* terms *nothing* has become more expensive. Note carefully that "everything" includes the services of wage-and-salary workers and every kind of financial asset from mortgages through bank deposits to the "entitlements" of people drawing pensions or social security benefits. Of course, all prices do not increase in equal proportion during an inflation, and so some goods do become more expensive in real terms. But it is a logical corollary that other goods must then become less expensive in real terms. A large part of the social problem, as we shall see, is the tendency of goods to rise in price at different rates during a period of inflation. But unless this has other effects that we haven't yet mentioned, the losses must exactly balance the gains. A pure inflation does not in itself make a society as a whole worse off.

Supply Inflation and Demand Inflation

Pure inflation? The word *pure* should make you suspicious, just as the words *always* and *never* ought to do in questions on a true-false test. By a pure inflation we mean a rise in the average price level not caused by any changes in conditions of supply but brought about entirely by changes in demand. Both kinds of change can cause such an index of the price level as the Consumer or Wholesale Price Index or the GNP deflator to rise. But they ought to be distinguished conceptually. Extensive crop failures will cause food prices to rise. Hurricane damage will raise the price of housing in the affected area. Airplane hijackings will raise the price of air travel if the airlines are compelled to hire security guards. The exhaustion of scarce mineral resources will raise the prices of all goods subsequently produced with resources less suited to the task. Work rules or trade regulations that reduce efficiency will cause higher prices. These are all examples of price increases originating from the supply side. In each case, the ratio of output to input was reduced and there was a consequent reduction in welfare.

When prices rise with the conditions of supply unchanged, however, they can only be rising because the monetary demand has increased. And that is what we mean by a pure inflation. A pure inflation is a decrease in the value of money relative to all other goods, with no change induced by altered supply conditions in the values of those other goods relative to one another.

CHANGES IN THE COMPOSITION OF DEMAND

Even with total monetary demand in an economy constant, the composition of that demand will be changing continually. Tennis will suddenly catch on with the public, for example, and the demand for rackets, balls, nets, and related equipment will rise, while the demand for other goods declines. Will this affect over-all price indices? It may.

If the production of a particular good cannot be increased quickly when the demand for it increases, the good's price will rise. And it may well rise by more than the fall in price of goods whose demand has decreased, resulting in a net increase in the level of measured prices. In general, the more inelastic the supply curves of goods for which demand is increasing, the greater will be the upward pressure exerted on price indices by changes in the composition of demand. Should this be called inflation? Does it qualify as "pure inflation"? There are grounds for answering either way. But however we label it, we will want to distinguish increases in the measured price level due to changes in the composition of demand from changes due to an increase in the total of monetary demand. Their causes are different, their effects are different, and they will yield to different remedies.

From 1958 through 1964, when the Wholesale Price Index was holding steady, the Consumer Price Index was creeping up by about 1% per year. The latter may have been due to the fact that consumers were shifting their expenditures more toward services and other goods whose production could only be increased at sharply higher costs.

We cannot tell merely from looking at a price index to what extent the rise in price of a particular good was due to changes in supply conditions and how much was due to monetary demand. The rise in food prices from 1967 to the present must be attributed in part to each; but sorting out the effect of government acreage restrictions and bad weather from the consequences of an increased money demand is a difficult task. The distinction must be made, however, because the causes and consequences are different. We might say, in fact, that price increases originating on the supply side are evidence of the problem of increased scarcity. There is less of what we want than there was before. But price increases resulting from increased money demand are evidence only of increased money demand. A pure inflation in and of itself makes no one work harder and forces no one to curtail consumption. Its effect is like that of going from measurement in yards to measurement in feet.

The Redistribution of Wealth

How does inflation (and we mean from now on price increases due entirely to increased money demand) create social problems? What problems does it cause? In the first place, it redistributes wealth and income. For when aggregate money demand increases, all prices will not increase in the same proportion and at the same time. Some prices are set for only short periods of time and can move up quickly in response to increased demand: examples are the prices of farm products and many of the raw materials used in industrial production. Other prices, like those at a retail grocery chain, are revised less frequently and so respond less quickly to demand. Commercial and residential rents are usually set by contract and often cannot be changed for long periods; although there are ways for landlords to compel a reopening of the contract and negotiate a higher rental, these procedures entail additional costs to the landlord. Wages and salaries are typically established by agreements that are supposed to extend over longer periods of time; these agreements can also be renegotiated during the contract period, and some will even contain formal clauses calling for renegotiation if certain conditions change. But wages and salaries tend to be less quickly responsive to increased money demand than retail prices and somewhat more responsive than rental prices. There are many prices that cannot be raised quickly, because to raise them requires the consent of a regulatory body that may move with glacial speed: railroads, airlines, gas and electric utilities, and telephone companies all complain of their inability to respond quickly enough to an increased money demand. Then there are creditors who have made long-term loans and cannot raise the payments they regularly receive for that service until the loan matures, perhaps twenty-five years in the future. On the other hand, consider the happy position of the federal government, selling us national defense and a variety of social services and charging a price (the personal income tax) that not only increases, but increases at a progressive rate as monetary demand increases. The net result of all this is that inflation redistributes income.

Prices that respond more slowly to increased demand don't necessarily increase less; sometimes they just take longer to get where they're going. But that still means that income is redistributed during the transitional period. Compare the prices of food and of clothing, relatively quick responders, with the price of rental housing, a slow responder, during and after the sharp inflation at the onset of the Korean War. Table 13A shows the percentage increases from the preceding year for each.

Table 13A	PRICE INCREASES FROM PRECEDING YEAR		
	Food	Rent	Clothing
1951	+11.1%	+4.0%	+9.0%
1952	+1.8%	+4.1%	−0.9%
1953	−1.5%	+5.4%	−0.8%
1954	−0.2%	+3.6%	−0.1%

Source: Bureau of Labor Statistics

But that's ancient history to those who weren't born until after 1954. Let's compare some differential rates of price increase for the protracted inflationary period from 1967 to 1973. (We'll examine inflation since 1973 separately because it tells a somewhat different tale.) Table 13B gives the percentage increases from average price levels in 1967 to average levels in 1973. Plus signs are superfluous in this table: there were no decreases.

Compare these with another significant set of figures. The mean hourly wage of production or nonsupervisory workers in private, nonagricultural industries increased over the same period by 46.5%. Per capita disposable income increased by 52.6%. The statement often made in this period that inflation was eating into the average American's take home pay and reducing his real income is simply untrue. *Real* per capita disposable income rose 20.3% between 1967 and 1973. The mean *real* hourly earnings of production workers rose 10.1% and their *real* spendable weekly earnings rose 4.6%. Part of the difference between these last two figures, by the way, can be attributed to the higher personal income and social security taxes paid in 1973. They averaged 10.7% of gross weekly earnings in 1967 but 12.3% of 1973 earnings.

Who is hurt by inflation, then? Not necessarily the average American worker celebrated in speech and story along every campaign trail in the land.[1] Sharpen up your sense of melodrama on the news that landlords and holders of mortgages are among the chief victims of inflation!

The income redistribution effects of inflation depend heavily, however,

---

1. Remember, though, that the mean, like all averages, conceals differences. All workers did not fare equally well.

Table 13B   PRICE INCREASES FROM 1967 TO 1973

Food	Rent	Clothing	Medical care	Transportation	Fuel oil and coal	Gas and electricity
41.4%	24.2%	26.8%	37.7%	23.8%	36.0%	26.4%

Source: Bureau of Labor Statistics

on how rapidly the inflation occurs and how well it has been anticipated. From January, 1973 to July 1974, the consumer price index rose 16.1%. Over this same period the average hourly wage of production workers increased only 11.9%, and the *real* hourly wage fell by 3.3%. Other available evidence supports the thesis suggested by these data. When prices are increasing slowly, workers can keep pace, but they fall behind when the inflation rate steps up. Landlords also suffered, by the way, as rental rates on housing increased only 7% over this period, or by less than half as much as the average of all items included in the consumer price index. (You're wrong if you think we're ridiculing landlords. Our intention is to call into question the strange but widely shared belief that owners of rental housing are all wealthy, and that they can usually gouge additional rent from tenants at the twirl of a moustache.)

Victims and Beneficiaries

Data on average hourly wages, per capita income, or rental prices conceal a lot of internal differences, of course. And differences are the heart of the problem. Inflation redistributes income because some sellers can raise their prices more quickly in response to a demand increase than can others. During inflationary periods, people whose income derives from prices that increase more slowly than the average surrender purchasing power to people deriving income from prices that increase more rapidly. They quite understandably resent inflation and insist that the government do something about it.

These victims of inflation find political allies, interestingly enough, among many of the beneficiaries of inflation. The political significance of inflation and the strength of popular pressure on government to control it (or at least seem to be controlling it) can only be appreciated if one understands why the beneficiaries of inflation so often join in denouncing it. The principal reason is that they think they too are victims.

Someone who receives a 10% salary increase almost inevitably regards the raise as completely merited, only just, perhaps long overdue. The fact that 8 of those 10 percentage points may reflect nothing but an increase or an anticipated increase in the price of the worker's product is not something that can be readily observed. So it's overlooked. If prices then rise by

FARM PRICES AND FOOD PRICES

The relation between the prices consumers pay for food and
the prices farmers receive for their products has enormous political importance. The public generally regards rising food prices as
a great evil, but farmers and their political allies become deeply
disturbed when prices for agricultural products decline. Over long
periods of time, these two indices do tend to move together. But
over shorter periods, they can and often do move quite diversely,
as the table below shows. And during a period when prices at the
store are rising while prices at the farm are declining, the volume
of political protest rises rapidly. Silence usually reigns, however,
when food prices are lagging behind the rate of increase in farm
prices.

	Food in the Consumer Price Index	Farm Products in the Wholesale Price Index		Food in the Consumer Price Index	Farm Products in the Wholesale Price Index
1960	88.0	97.2	July 1973	140.9	173.3
1961	89.1	96.3	Aug	149.4	213.3
1962	89.9	98.0	Sept	148.3	200.4
1963	91.2	94.6	Oct	148.4	188.4
1964	92.4	94.6	Nov	150.0	184.0
1965	94.4	98.7	Dec	151.3	187.2
1966	99.1	105.9	Jan 1974	153.7	202.6
1967	100.0	100.0	Feb	157.6	205.6
1968	103.6	102.5	Mar	159.1	197.0
1969	108.9	109.1	Apr	158.6	186.2
1970	114.9	111.0	May	159.7	180.8
1971	118.4	112.9	June	160.3	168.6
1972	123.5	125.0			
1973	141.4	176.3			

Notice that over the first six months of 1974, the index of food
prices rose at an *annual* rate of about $8\frac{1}{2}\%$, while the index of farm
product prices fell at an *annual* rate of about 40%. That is a sure
formula for political unrest, despite the fact that farm product
prices in June 1974 were 68.6% above their 1967 level, while food
prices were only 60.3% higher than they had been in the index
base year.

6% during the same period because of the same increase in aggregate demand that accounted for 8 of the 10 percentage points in his last raise, the worker will not rejoice in the fact that he gained from inflation. Instead he will complain that inflation has eaten up 60% of his last raise, and start thinking about ways to restore his loss through another salary increase. We all tend to regard increases in our own money income as our just desert. Increases in the general price level, however, are bad and should be prevented. But prices are not only costs. Looked at from the other side, they're the components of income. We just don't tie the two together.

Inflation is almost universally unpopular, even with the beneficiaries of its redistribution effects, because of the myopia and self-centeredness that causes most of us to regard increases in our own incomes as fully justified and increases in the prices we must pay as a failure in the system. Government will receive no credit, obviously, for getting me what I deserve and have fully earned; but it will be blamed for creating or tolerating a situation in which others are able to rob me of my gains through higher prices.

Effects on Production

Illusion thus plays a major role in making inflation unpopular and creating pressure on governments to do something about it. But the costs of inflation to a society as a whole are not *completely* illusory. Imagine a situation in which the various state governments controlled the standards for weights and measures. Suppose further that the officials in most states had come to the conclusion that the only way to effect a shift to the metric system was to sneak it over on people by gradually expanding the inch until it had become one thirty-sixth of a meter. So at periodic but unpredictable intervals, the officials of various states would announce for their jurisdictions an official increase in the length of the inch—"never enough to notice," as they might say, but enough to push the inch over ten years from its present length of .0254 meters to the desired length of $.027\frac{7}{9}$ meters.

Where would the costs of such a procedure show up? In resources devoted to guessing the timing and rate of changes and insuring against the consequences of mistakes; in resources spent on coordinating decisions among states with inches of temporarily varying length; in resources employed to fit tools conforming to older specifications to products made to newer specifications; in resources wasted on the correction of mistakes arising from the increased uncertainty and the complexity of the coordinating task. The real costs of inflation to a society are like the costs just described.

It is sometimes said that inflation is merely a change in the "length" of

the measuring instrument. Let that be true; it does not follow that inflation has no real costs. An elastic measuring instrument is a serious problem whenever decisions have to be coordinated over space and time. A grave danger arising from the experience of inflation is that people will devote so many resources to dealing with the inflation that production will decline substantially.

PRICES SUBJECT TO CHANGE

When prices are rising rapidly, catalogs quickly become out of date. And companies that sell heavily through catalogs run into problems. Because customers often become angry when told after ordering a good that it is only available at a price higher than the one listed in the catalog, companies prefer to stand by their catalog prices. But if prices rise by 10% per year, a company that issues its catalogs annually may take a severe beating on goods sold shortly before its new catalog is issued. One solution is putting catalogs out more frequently. Another is to issue smaller, special catalogs at various times throughout the year. But either solution raises the firm's cost of doing business.

Acceleration and Hyperinflation

In a hyperinflation, such as some countries have experienced as a result of wars and as Germany experienced in a spectacular way from 1921 to 1923, the measuring instrument becomes worthless. The purchasing power of money becomes so unpredictable that money is no longer useful, barter replaces monetary exchange, inefficiencies multiply, and production finally collapses. But inflation of the kind experienced in recent years in the United States is a much different thing from the German inflation of the 1920s, when prices rose more than *60 billion percent* in a single year. The German experience stands as a warning, however, and raises the question whether inflation can be contained once it gets beyond a certain rate. The economy can adjust to creeping inflation and occasional gallops; we've done it successfully ever since the 1930s. But our past success in containing inflation may have been due in large part to the fact that inflation was not expected to *continue* at any considerable rate. Once inflationary expectations become general, and everyone tries to keep up by getting ahead, won't the rate of inflation tend to increase? And finally reach hyperinflation levels?

That certainly *can* occur. Suppose that everyone anticipates regular and large future price increases. That means they expect the value of money to fall relative to the value of other assets. A rational plan of action for someone with these expectations is to hold money balances to a minimum. But this increases the money demand for goods, raises their prices farther and faster, and creates aggravated expectations of inflation that further reduce the demand to hold money. At the limit, where desired money balances are zero, the velocity of money circulation is infinite. M times V is a very large and inflationary money demand indeed when the value of V is infinity.

Living with Inflation

On the other hand, quite a few countries have lived with rates of inflation in recent years well beyond anything we've experienced and without moving toward hyperinflation and economic collapse. The annual rate of change in the Brazilian price level from 1952 through 1973 was about 30% and went up and down from rates near 10% to rates of almost 100% over the course of a single year. And Brazil has survived. It has done so in part by extensive use of what is called *indexing.* A familiar example of indexing in this country is the escalator clause in wage contracts that calls for automatic wage adjustments when the price index changes. Social security benefits are also indexed by law to prevent their real value from declining as prices rise. We could go much farther in this direction. *All* wages, salaries, rents, and pensions could be indexed. Congress could also adjust the progressive income tax so that higher rates come into play only when *real* income rises. The rate schedules used by public utilities could easily be indexed. So could many kinds of financial assets. The federal government might provide a simple, safe hedge against inflation to the unsophisticated saver of modest means by selling bonds whose value changes with the Consumer Price Index.

The Brazilian indexing system seems at least to have prevented much of the income redistribution that inflation normally causes. And it may have promoted efficiency by reducing uncertainty for investors. But with the gradual extension of the system so that it compensates more fully and more quickly for all increases in the price level, Brazil may now be on the verge of building inflationary expectations so solidly into the economy that inflation will start feeding on itself. For example, an increase in the price level will call for higher wages, the money supply will have to be increased to pay the higher wages, and the larger money supply will pull prices up even faster. It's a way of living with inflation that is full of difficulties and dangers.

Inflation and Social Stability

And how well *has* Brazil survived? Contemporary Brazil is no one's model of a free and democratic society. We can only speculate about the extent to which the social tensions generated by inflation contributed to the social disorder that in turn produced a military dictatorship in 1964. But it is a fact that the annual rate of inflation rose rapidly in the early sixties, from 40% to 55% to 80% per year in 1963, and on up to an annual rate of 150% in March of 1964. Then production collapsed and a military government seized power. And it was this military government that cut through complexities and conflicting interests to establish an indexing system. It is not obvious what the experience of Brazil has to teach us.

Political freedom and democracy rest in any society upon a substantial social consensus. People must believe that they are net beneficiaries of the "system," of the kinds of interaction that the political and social structure allows and encourages. When people come to believe that they are more the victims than the members of a society, they withdraw their allegiance and desert the consensus. And the alternative to government by consensus is government by force. The point of this excursion into political philosophy is that inflation generates a widespread sense of injustice, even—as we argued earlier—among its beneficiaries. If rapid inflation fosters social instability, it may be a serious threat to political freedom and democratic rule.

Once Over Lightly

Economists interested in income-expenditures analysis tended to neglect money and monetary policy after the appearance of Keynes's *General Theory*. They argued that the supply of money affects the level of economic activity primarily through its effect on interest rates and their effect in turn on investment expenditures, and that this effect is of minor importance in countering the impact that expectations have on investment.

Interest in money and monetary policy revived as the fear of depression diminished in the 1950s and concern about inflation increased. New inquiries into the importance of money were grounded in the equation of exchange, $MV = PQ$, which expresses the identity between the stock of money times its velocity of circulation and the average price of goods times the quantity of goods exchanged.

The effect that changes in the supply of money will have on the level of aggregate economic activity depends on the behavior of velocity. The velocity of money circulation when inverted becomes the quantity of money demanded expressed as a fraction of PQ. Changes in M will therefore have predictable effects on PQ insofar as the demand for money is stable and predictable.

If M (the quantity of money supplied) and PQ/V (the quantity of money demanded) are not equal, then the public will want to hold some different quantity of money from the amount the monetary authorities have made available. The public's efforts to increase or decrease its money balances will lead to a decrease or increase in the demand for goods (Q) and a consequent decrease or increase in PQ. This can occur through changes in real output, changes in prices, or both. Since the demand for money balances is a demand for real balances, the quantity of nominal money demanded will increase or decrease with PQ until it equals the quantity of nominal money available to hold. In this way, changes in PQ become the equilibrating mechanism that brings the preferred level of money balances into equality with the actual level of money balances, or M.

Changes in M may themselves cause the quantity of money demanded to change in the same direction and reduce the impact of changes in M on PQ. This occurs through the effect of money-supply changes on interest rates. The opportunity cost of holding money will increase if interest rates rise as a consequence of restrictive monetary policy, and so the public will want to hold somewhat smaller money balances (that is, V will increase). Larger money balances will be desired if interest rates decline in response to an increase in the supply of money (V will decrease).

Inflation should not be thought of as an increase in the price of everything, but rather as an increase in the price of everything *relative to money*. But if *everything* actually increased in price relative to money, inflation would be a very minor problem. Inflation is a social problem in large part because prices of goods rise at different rates and thereby redistribute income and wealth.

Inflation is politically unpopular because those who gain from inflation often mistakenly assume that they have been harmed by it. They blame inflation for increases in the money price of goods they purchase but fail to credit inflation adequately for increases in the money price of goods they sell.

Inflation is capable of reducing aggregate real output by increasing the real costs of coordinating economic decisions.

While there are ways to reduce the wealth-redistributing effects of inflation, there may be none that are both politically feasible and unlikely to accelerate the inflation.

QUESTIONS FOR DISCUSSION

1. How do interest rates affect investment spending?

    (*a*) How do higher interest rates affect residential construction?

    (*b*) "Shall we maintain production and allow our inventories of unsold goods to rise, or should we shut down production until we've managed to sell off most of the finished goods now in the warehouses?" How might the level of interest rates enter into this decision?

(*c*) An electric utility postpones construction of a new generating plant because the market price of its bonds is disappointingly low. How does this illustrate the investment–interest rate relationship?

(*d*) A corporation plans to begin a huge capital expansion program and use proceeds from a sale of new stock to finance the program. But common stock prices decline and the firm postpones the stock sale and the investment program it was intended to finance. Does that have anything to do with interest rates?

(*e*) "Higher interest rates don't deter any business firm that has a profitable use for the money. If we can make 30% on an investment, we're going to invest whether we can borrow at 3% or have to pay 12%." Evaluate.

(*f*) "The higher the interest rate I can get, the more I'm going to invest. Investment increases as interest rates rise." Is that right? Reconcile these sentences with the text's analysis of the investment–interest rate relationship.

2. *Can* the monetary authorities raise or lower interest rates by decreasing or increasing the money supply? What limitations exist on their ability to do this?

3. Is a negative interest rate an absurd conception? Can you cite any negative (real!) interest rates in recent years? What was the real rate of interest earned on $100 in a 5% savings account during 1974, when the price level rose 12%. If you were a business executive able to borrow short term money from the bank at 8%, would your decision on whether or not to go ahead with the loan be affected by your expectations regarding the behavior of prices in the coming year?

4. "A recession occurs when MV is less than PQ." Evaluate that assertion.

5. If V is constant, will an increase in M be more likely to raise P or Q? What are some of the factors that might determine the relative impact on P or Q? Would it make any difference whether the increase in M came about because of Treasury borrowing or because of private borrowing?

6. If P rises while M remains constant, what happens to real money balances? If people were holding their preferred level of real balances prior to the increase in the price level, what actions might they take to restore the level of their real balances? Can inflation occurring simultaneously with a zero rate of growth in the money supply cause a recession?

7. "We cannot predict the effect of a change in the rate of growth in the money stock on the velocity of circulation unless we know how it affects people's expectations regarding *future* changes in the price level." Evaluate that argument.

8. Suppose the Fed substantially increases the reserves of commercial banks and the banks use these additional reserves to add more government securities to their portfolio of earning assets. How will this affect the yield on government securities? Why will it tend also to affect the yield on corporate bonds and mortgages?

9. Numerous public opinion surveys in 1974 and 1975 revealed that the majority of Americans regarded inflation as a more serious threat than unemployment.

   (*a*) Does this imply that the majority of Americans would prefer unemployment with stable prices to being employed in a time of rising prices?

   (*b*) If the management of a firm allowed employees to vote on whether the firm should lay off 10% of the employees or reduce wage rates by 5%, how do you think they would vote? Do you think it would matter whether the workers laid off were to be the ones with the least seniority or were to be chosen by a lottery?

10. If inflation redistributes income and wealth, there will be gainers as well as losers. Which classes and categories of people are most likely to gain from an inflation? Which are most likely to lose? What difference does it make how well the inflation is anticipated?

11. Supply and demand conditions in the market for college professors have changed markedly from the 1960s to the 1970s. Is it easy for college administrators to lower salaries when supply increases and demand decreases? What reaction would you expect from professors who were told that market conditions call for a 7% reduction in their annual salary? What reaction would you expect from them if they were told that the budget will not allow for any salary increases this year although the Consumer Price Index has risen 14% since last year? Does inflation ease the process of making relative price and wage adjustments?

12. Some people argue that the complexity of federal tax laws generates significant social waste. It encourages the extensive use of valuable resources (accountants, lawyers) in searching for loopholes and prompts people toward inefficient activities that are profitable because of tax law quirks. Does inflation generate similar kinds of waste?

13. Secretary of the Treasury William Simon told the House Ways and Means Committee in 1975 that there was no subtler and surer means of overturning the existing basis of society than to "debauch the currency," that is, create continuing inflation. (Mr. Simon cited Keynes and Lenin in support of this position.) Do you agree?

14

10
THE UNITED STATES OF AMERICA
TEN
10
TEN
1000
1000 YEN
BANK OF ENGLAND
BR 7175003
One Pound
BANQUE DE FRANCE

THE ECONOMICS AND POLITICS OF INTERNATIONAL TRADE

No introductory textbook known to us contains a separate chapter on inter*state* economics. But inter*national* economics has its own section in almost every text, its own courses in departmental curricula, and its own specialists working in business, government, and universities. Why is this?

The answer is that specialization and exchange, the social processes that economics attempts to explain, often encounter peculiar difficulties when they are conducted across national boundaries. Unique problems of coordination arise in international exchange. International economics tries to explain the origin of these problems and the consequences of the varied ways in which individuals and national governments deal with them.

NATIONALISM AND INTERNATIONAL TRADE

The statement is often made that nationalism is obsolete in this era of jet planes, space travel, radio-television communication, and nuclear weapons. If obsolete means *no longer appropriate*, the statement may be correct. But if it means *no longer in existence*, the statement is demonstrably false. National governments still erect barriers to trade at their boundaries, still pursue domestic policies that presuppose restrictions on exchange with other nations, and still try to solve domestic problems by treating foreigners as enemies rather than as potential partners in mutually advantageous specialization. We may regret this but we cannot afford to ignore it.

These two chapters on the international economy are inserted here, prior to our final look at the economics and politics of stabilization policies, because to a large and growing extent domestic stabilization policies are not likely to succeed unless they take account of international repercussions. In one sense national governments have always known this. The assumption that domestic prosperity can be achieved by managing foreign trade in appropriate ways is as old as the nation-state itself. In another sense, however, national governments have been insufficiently attentive to international repercussions. They have too frequently assumed that other nations would remain passive in the face of economic aggression, and they have underestimated the ingenuity of those with an interest in circumventing international barriers to voluntary exchange.

An effective stabilization policy for the United States economy today must be constructed in an international context. In the past few chapters we have disregarded the effects of international trade on total output and income, focusing exclusively on the domestic determinants of the money supply and the price level. This was a seriously misleading omission that we must now begin to correct.

How Important Is the International Trade Sector?

In table 8A, we saw that net U.S. exports constituted one of the four components making up the aggregate demand for gross national product. Because the numbers in the net exports column were relatively small, neglecting them may not have seemed a serious omission. But there's a lot of activity hiding behind those small numbers and the activity has been increasing in recent years. The value of United States exports in 1974, as measured by the Bureau of Economic Analysis, was $144.2 billion. By subtracting the $136.5 billion worth of imports, we arrived at the seemingly insignificant total of $7.7 billion for *net* exports. But $144 billion is 10% of the gross national product. A substantial share of domestic production occurs, in other words, in response to foreign demand. And a moment's thought should make it clear that, if all foreign trade suddenly stopped, the decline in our imports would not compensate for the loss of export markets. It's true that $136 billion is almost as much as $144 billion; but the *composition* of our demand for imports is vastly different from the composition of foreign demand for our exports. A disruption of international trade could therefore have disastrous effects on gross national product and employment, even though the little number showing "net exports" hardly budged.

We said that international trade has become increasingly important in recent years. The trend is apparent from table 14A, which shows U.S. exports as a percentage of gross national product in recent years. The increase is partly a statistical illusion. The Bureau of Economic Analysis has improved its procedures for keeping track of exports and imports. But this only means the percentages for earlier years were understated. The important fact is that exports are now about 10% of the entire output of the economy.

Table 14A

Year	U.S. Exports (in billions of dollars)	Exports as % of GNP
1950	$13.8	4.8%
1954	17.8	4.9
1958	23.1	5.2
1962	30.3	5.4
1966	43.4	5.8
1970	62.9	6.4
1974	144.2	10.2

Source: Bureau of Economic Analysis

How Independent Are National Economies?

There is another way to point up the dangers in ignoring international trade. From 1958 to 1964, consumer prices in the United States rose at an average annual rate of 1.2%. From 1971 to 1973, they rose at a rate of 4.8% per year, four times as rapidly as in the 1958–1964 period. What was happening during these same periods in some of the countries with which the United States traded extensively? Table 14B compares the rates of increase in the consumer price level in ten countries.

In each country, consumer prices rose significantly faster in the 1971–73 period than they had in 1958–64. In every case but one, the annual rate of increase was between 3.5 and 5.8 percentage points greater in the later period. That seems odd at first glance. Each country has its own central bank, its own government budget, and its own institutional structures for price and wage setting; yet consumer prices changed in a strikingly similar way. This looks like a remarkable coincidence only until we realize that domestic price levels are affected significantly by international exchange.

Does any other assumption really make sense, though? We don't expect prices in Arizona to diverge significantly from those in Louisiana, despite the considerable geographic and cultural differences between the two states. Paris is closer to Boston than Honolulu is. Why then should we expect the same forces to determine income and price levels in Hawaii and Massachusetts but not in Massachusetts and France?

Table 14B   INCREASES IN CONSUMER PRICES
(annual rates of change)

	1958–64	1971–73
United States	1.2%	4.8%
Canada	1.3	6.2
United Kingdom	2.4	8.2
Germany	2.2	6.3
Japan	4.8	8.3
France	4.3	6.3
Italy	4.2	8.1
Switzerland	2.2	7.7
Netherlands	2.7	7.9
Belgium	1.7	6.2

Sources: Bureau of Labor Statistics, International Monetary Fund, Organization for Economic Cooperation and Development. Data compiled by Research Department, Federal Reserve Bank of St. Louis.

National Currencies and National Interests

One reason to expect differences might be the fact that France and the United States use different currencies. And this does indeed turn out to be a central issue. If every society in the world used the same medium of exchange, the chapters on international exchange in economics textbooks could be very short. They might even be left out altogether. But almost every nation has its own kind of money. As a result, exchanges between the citizens, business firms, or governments of different nations require an extra step: the buyer's money must be exchanged for the seller's money before the transaction can be completed. This gives rise to special problems. More importantly, it provides an opportunity for the *creation* of special problems, with governments usually functioning as the creative agents.

Why don't all nations use the same medium of exchange as the separate states do in this country? How did *national* monetary systems come into existence, and why do they persist?

The ideal would seem to be a single world monetary unit. Is that impossible? The world is presently moving toward universal adoption of the metric system. Why not a universal money as well? Think how inconvenient it would be if every state in this country had its own medium of exchange. Interstate transactions would always require foreign exchange purchases, an added nuisance and an added uncertainty as well. Producers buying or shipping out of state would have to pay attention to fluctuations in exchange rates, since a substantial change that went unnoticed could mean a large loss on a purchase of supplies or a contracted sale. There would probably be far less interstate trade and consequently less opportunity to gain from the varying comparative advantages of each state. One of the reasons economic growth has occurred more rapidly in the United States than in the separate nations of Europe is the larger market in this country to which producers can sell and within which buyers can choose. Adam Smith, perceptive as usual, noted that division of labor—what we would now call the exploitation of comparative advantages—was the principal source of increases in the wealth of nations and that the division of labor was limited by the extent of the market.

But hoping for a unified world monetary system is probably putting the cart in front of the horse. If the peoples of the world woke up tomorrow and found themselves all using the same medium of exchange, they would be no less nationalistic than they are now. They would presumably still want to secure gains for their country at the expense of other countries, and they would still be in the grip of those popular mythologies which insist that buying at home benefits the home economy. Their governments would continue interfering in various ways with international trade. Moreover, policymakers would probably discover before long that having a separate national money makes it easier to interfere with foreign trade and to pursue independent economic policies. And so secessions from the world system would probably begin rather quickly. The point is that, while one money would help to create one world, it also presupposes one world. And that isn't where we are at the three-quarter mark in the twentieth century.

The Evolution of National Monetary Systems

The world has to some extent always had a unified monetary system. Certain metals, especially gold and silver, have functioned for thousands of years as universally accepted mediums of exchange. How did they come to acquire such wide acceptance? The answer lies in some combination of rareness, distinctiveness, beauty, malleability, and high ratio of weight to volume. These characteristics helped assure that the medium of exchange would be scarce, easily recognized, divisible into convenient units, portable, and hard to counterfeit, all of which are characteristics of a successful money. Contemporary national monetary units evolved from gold and silver, or *specie* money.

There were many reasons for this evolution. To begin with, specie provides a much more convenient money when it has been minted into coins of a certified weight. And government was a logical candidate for the job of minting and certifying. By putting a little less metal into the coin than was indicated by its stamped value, the government could even earn revenue from this service. The term for the difference between the coined value of the metal and its bullion value is *seigniorage*. As long as the seigniorage did not exceed the additional convenience value of having coins rather than bullion, the coins would circulate at their stamped value rather than their lower bullion value.

Governments pressed for revenue often yielded to the temptation to reduce the amount of metal in their coins beyond this limit. (We quoted Adam Smith on the subject in chapter 10.) This policy worked most effectively as a revenue-gathering device when coins minted elsewhere and offering a higher ratio of bullion value to stamped value could be excluded or otherwise discriminated against.[1] And so national governments acquired a special interest in coins of their own minting and gradually assumed for themselves the exclusive legal right to coin specie within their own borders. This created a system of predominantly national coins and was a significant step toward separate national monetary systems.

Another major step was taken with the evolution of paper money. Paper money originated as receipts for specie in storage. People owning large quantities of gold, for example, might want to store it with the local goldsmith, who had facilities for keeping gold secure. Later on, when they wanted to make a payment, they could hand over the receipt rather than go to the trouble of withdrawing the actual gold. If the goldsmith who had issued the receipt was thoroughly reliable, his receipt might be retained by the new holder and used again by him as a means of payment. When goldsmiths discovered that their receipts were circulating as money so that only a fraction of the gold in their vaults would ever be needed at one time to redeem outstanding receipts, they began to lend some of the gold left in their care. The easiest way to lend was by giving the borrower a receipt rather than the actual gold. If the receipt circulated and was not presented for redemption, the gold remained on deposit and might be loaned again. And now we have described the origin of money creation through the lending of reserves, as well as the origin of paper money.

As goldsmiths turned into banks and gold receipts into banknotes promising to pay specie on demand, paper money came to be denominated in national monetary units rather than in specie weight: 50 *dollars* of gold, for example, rather than 2.5 *ounces* of gold. This step toward the nationalization of paper money was carried further as national governments first tried to

---

1. One way for a government to discriminate in favor of its own coinage is to make it *legal tender* and to accept no other coins in payment of taxes. Money is legal tender whenever creditors must accept it in payment of debts or lose any further legal claim on the debtor who "tenders" (offers) it. Federal Reserve notes display the sentence, "This note is legal tender for all debts, public and private." A loan company might refuse to accept your check when your loan falls due and continue charging you interest. But the company could not refuse your tender of Federal Reserve notes and legally collect further interest.

regulate, then began to issue, and finally claimed the exclusive right to print paper money.

As long as all paper money was redeemable in gold at a fixed rate, each nation's paper money had a fixed value relative to that of every other nation. If a twenty-dollar Federal Reserve note can be exchanged for 1 ounce of gold and a twenty-pound Bank of England note for 5 ounces of gold, then 1 British pound will exchange for 5 American dollars. Banknotes that promised to pay gold to the bearer on demand did not always fulfill their promises, of course. We described briefly in chapter 9 the vicissitudes of privately issued banknotes in this country. Government-issued notes that were not redeemable in specie would also fluctuate in value, introducing shifting and uncertain disparities between the price of goods in *gold* dollars and the price of the same goods in *paper* dollars. When governments obtained effective control of paper-money issue, however, a new possibility appeared. A note that promised 20 dollars in gold promised 1 ounce of gold *only if the value of a dollar was* $\frac{1}{20}$ *ounce of gold.* Could governments possibly change the gold value of the dollar (or the pound or the franc) to achieve certain policy objectives?

The fact is that anyone with sufficient control over supplies of gold and paper dollars can set the value of each in terms of the other through buying gold with dollars whenever the price of gold falls and selling gold for dollars whenever it rises. This is called *pegging* the dollar to gold or, alternatively, pegging gold to the dollar. National governments concluded in this century that they did have the power to peg their currencies and thereby to fix the rate at which their monetary units exchanged for the monetary units of other nations. And that conclusion was another major step toward the nationalization of the international economy.

EXCHANGE RATES: CAUSES AND CONSEQUENCES

Any description of the evolution of national monetary systems runs the risk of exaggerating the power of national governments. We noted at the beginning of this chapter that governments have persistently underestimated the ingenuity of those whose interests conflicted with the goals the government was pursuing through its international policies. No government has ever been able to peg its monetary unit to gold or to anything else in an arbitrary way. The dollar value of gold and the gold value of the dollar are prices; and prices affect behavior, which in turn affects prices.

Let's suppose that the U.S. government pegs the dollar at $\frac{1}{35}$ ounce of gold and the German government pegs the mark at $\frac{1}{140}$ ounce of gold.

(The exposition will be much simpler if we assume there are only two nations in the world; the principles are the same for any number of nations.) What will now occur?

To begin with, Americans will now be able to purchase 4 marks for 1 dollar and Germans will be able to purchase 1 dollar for 4 marks. The two currencies are linked to each other through their common link to gold. The exchange rate between dollars and marks is 1 dollar = 4 marks.[1]

The important fact is that this exchange rate determines the price to Americans of German goods and the price to Germans of American goods. A Volkswagen, for example, that carries a factory price tag of 10,000 marks will carry also an implicit price of 2500 dollars. If the exchange rate were 1 dollar for 5 marks, a 10,000-mark price would be a 2000-dollar price. Meanwhile, a factory price tag of 3000 dollars on a Chevrolet would be read by Germans as 12,000 marks if the exchange rate is 1 dollar for 4 marks. At a rate of 1 for 5, the Chevrolet, though its factory price remained unchanged, would seem to a German to have gone up in price to 15,000 marks.

Demand and Supply

It follows that the attractiveness of foreign goods will depend on the exchange rate and on the price levels in each country. A devaluation of the dollar relative to gold will raise the dollar price of the mark, lower the mark price of the dollar, cause German goods to look less attractive to Americans, and cause American goods to look more attractive to Germans.[2] German imports (equals American exports) would consequently tend to increase and American imports (equals German exports) would tend to decrease.

The "demand for marks" curve in figure 14A says that, at prevailing price levels in the two countries, Americans will demand 12 million marks to purchase 12 million marks worth of German goods. At 40¢ per mark they will demand 10 million marks, at 50¢ they will demand 8 million, at 25¢ they will demand 16 million. It just so happens that in each case Americans will be supplying 4 million dollars: $33\frac{1}{3}$¢ $\times$ 12 million, 40¢ $\times$ 10 million, 50¢ $\times$ 8 million, 25¢ $\times$ 16 million all equal 4 million dollars. (The

---

1. The post–World War II system under which the mark was pegged directly to the dollar will be discussed in the next chapter.

2. Students are often confused by the fact that a devaluation sometimes looks at first glance like a revaluation (the word always implies an *upward* revaluation). You have to think about it for a moment to see that, when the mark goes from 25 cents to 30 cents, this is a decline in the value of the dollar and an increase in the value of the mark. The British pound was *devalued* in 1967 when it was changed from $2.80 to $2.40. The value of the dollar *increased*, relative to the pound.

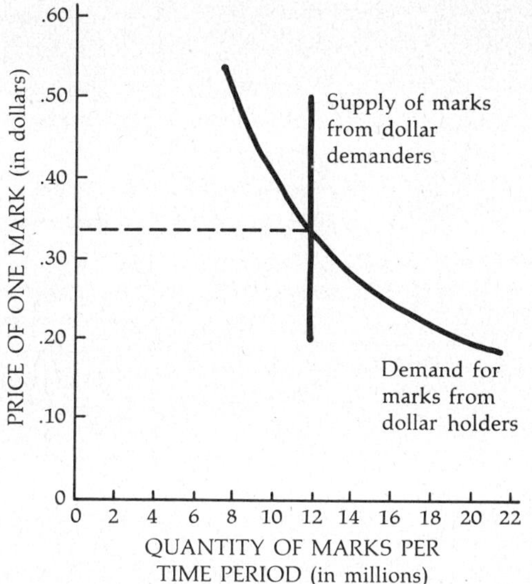

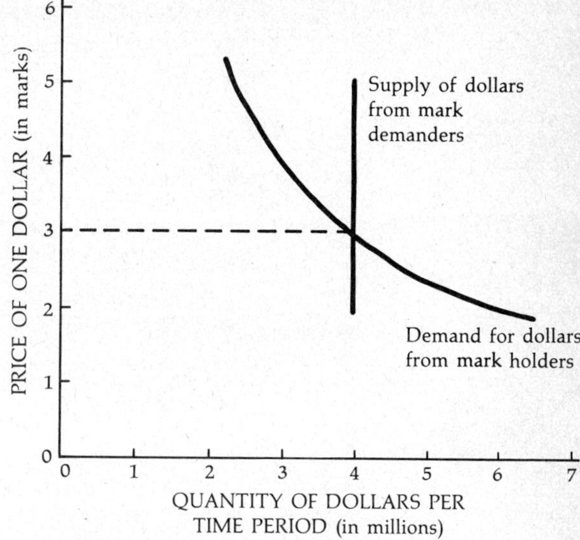

demand for marks is *unit elastic*.) On the right side of figure 14A we have drawn the supply curve of dollars, consistently with the demand curve for dollars, as a vertical line at 4 million dollars.

Figure 14A At any exchange rate other than 3 marks = 1 dollar, there will be either a surplus of dollars (= shortage of marks) or a shortage of dollars (= surplus of marks)

The supply curve for marks (on the left graph) shows that Germans will offer 12 million marks to obtain dollars at every price of marks within the range shown. That translates into the "demand for dollars" curve shown on the right graph: 3 million dollars demanded at a price of 4 marks per dollar, 4 million dollars at a price of 3 marks, 6 million dollars at a price of 2 marks. (The unit elasticity of the two demand curves, which yields vertical supply curves in each case, is another expositional simplification and not an empirical assertion.)

The same conclusion emerges from either graph. The gold price of the dollar and of the mark must be set so that 1 dollar exchanges for 3 marks. At any other exchange rate, given the price levels in each country, the quantities of each currency demanded and supplied will not match.

Undervalued and Overvalued Currencies

What will happen if the German government nonetheless pegs the gold price of the mark at $\frac{1}{140}$ ounce of gold while the dollar is pegged at $\frac{1}{35}$ ounce of gold, so that the exchange rate is 4 marks for 1 dollar? Figure 14A tells us that 16 million marks will be demanded while only 12 million marks are supplied, which is equivalent to saying that 3 million dollars will be demanded and 4 million dollars supplied.

The American banks that handle foreign-exchange transactions will consequently find themselves running out of marks and the German banks will find themselves accumulating mounting quantities of dollars. The American banks will replenish their stock of marks by selling dollars to the government for gold and using the gold to buy marks from the German government. The German banks will reduce their unwanted dollar accumulations by selling the dollars to the American government for gold and selling the gold to the German government for marks. As long as Americans can keep acquiring marks in this way and Germans can continue to sell unwanted dollar accumulations, the exchange rate will remain at 1 dollar = 4 marks and the dollar-mark market will be in disequilibrium.

A "disequilibrium" implies that something now happening cannot continue indefinitely. The critical factor is the gold flow.

1. The United States will be continuously selling gold to Germany and reducing its stock of monetary gold.
2. The U.S. government (or the central bank) will be draining dollars out of private holdings and reducing the size of the money stock in the United States.
3. The German government will be continuously accumulating gold and adding to its monetary gold stock.
4. The German government will be pouring marks into private holdings and increasing the size of the money stock in Germany.
5. Because the dollars lost in the United States and the marks created in Germany respectively reduce and increase commercial bank reserves, a further contraction of the U.S. money supply and expansion of the German money supply will ensue.

What happens next cannot be predicted unless we know what policies the U.S. and German governments choose to follow in such a situation. One prediction can be made with confidence, however: people in the United States will begin talking about the "balance of payments deficit." For rather odd reasons to which we'll come, people in Germany are less likely to begin talking about a "balance of payments surplus."

THE BALANCE OF PAYMENTS

Any price that fails to equate the quantity demanded with the quantity supplied will result in either shortages or surpluses. Where will shortages or surpluses in international exchange show up? According to the conventional wisdom they reveal themselves in the *balance of payments*. But it would be far more accurate to say that they are *concealed* by the balance of payments. To understand why this is so, you must first acquire a little knowledge about balance of payments accounting.

Credits and Debits

Balance of payments accounting is an attempt to keep track of one country's international transactions by dividing them into transactions that earn foreign exchange, called credits, and transactions that use up foreign exchange, called debits. If you keep this basic definition in mind you should have no trouble deciding under which column to list a particular item.

Exports are credit items in the balance of payments. Foreigners who want to purchase our products must ultimately pay dollars to the American sellers. This results either in the reacquisition by Americans of dollars previously held by foreigners, in the acquisition of foreign currency that is used to purchase dollars, or in the acquisition of some other medium of international exchange that can be used to purchase dollars. U.S. imports simply reverse this flow. To purchase the products of some other country, we must either turn over previously acquired holdings of that country's currency, obtain some by giving up dollars in exchange, or use up our stocks of some other accepted international exchange medium to obtain the required currency.

That's all there is to the balance of payments if we define exports and imports broadly enough. Imports, for example, must include not only commodities like magnesium and tape recorders, but also services like the Geneva hotel room used by an American tourist or the entertainment provided in Fort Worth by an English rock group. Payment for these services entails the using up of foreign exchange and so they are debit items in the U.S. balance of payments.

What about gold? Gold sales or exports are credit items, just like any other exports; gold purchases or imports are debit items. Gold sales are a way of acquiring foreign exchange just as are sales of wheat. Momentary confusion may arise from the fact that gold is itself considered a medium of international exchange. Treat it like any other commodity, however, and you'll get it into the correct column.

We must also include under imports the "purchase" of whatever it is we obtain when our government extends foreign aid, or when Americans send money to relatives in Europe. If it seems inappropriate to think of either activity as "importing," the fact remains that any payments made to foreigners by the United States government, private organizations, or individuals use up foreign exchange and must therefore be classified as debits. These payments may in turn be used to purchase American exports (sometimes that's a condition of the grant); if so, the export is a credit item, but the gift, grant, pension, or other remittance that made it possible goes under the debit column. By the same token, gifts to us by foreigners or payments made to Americans by Lloyds of London in settlement of insurance claims are credit items in our balance of payments. And the sizable income we receive each year as a return on our overseas investments goes into the credit column, because it is a source of foreign exchange earnings for the United States.

Accounting for Foreign Investment

What about the original acts of investing? Capital flows can be treated like commodities and services if attention is focused on the stock, bond, or other evidence of indebtedness that changes hands. Thus foreign investment by Americans amounts to importing IOUs, and investment by foreigners in the United States is a U.S. export of IOUs. If this way of describing the matter strikes you as strained, you can keep the effects of foreign investment clear by concentrating on the definition of credits and debits. Investment by Americans in the French economy is a debit item in our balance of payments, because Americans must purchase French francs to buy an interest in French companies. And Britons buying shares of General Motors contribute to the credit side of our balance of payments, because they must obtain dollars to complete the purchase.

There is an alternative way of looking at foreign investment that sometimes proves useful. We can regard international investment as the acquisition of *claims.* Anything that increases our claims on foreigners or decreases their claims on us is a debit item in our balance of payments. Anything that decreases our claims on foreigners or increases their claims on us is a credit item. Don't try to memorize that; just use the definition of credits and debits: We acquire claims on foreigners by extending them loans, whether long-term or short-term. That requires us to use up foreign exchange, so it's a debit item. When such loans are repaid, foreigners reduce our claims on them by giving us foreign exchange and this is a credit in our balance of payments. The usefulness of this somewhat strange way of describing the matter will emerge when we try to puzzle out the meaning of a balance of payments deficit or surplus. The point is that if a substantial part of our credit items consists of loans from foreigners, we are enlarging the total of foreign claims against us; we are going more deeply into debt. That isn't necessarily bad. But short-term debts that might have to be repaid suddenly are a cause of concern to some students of the balance of payments.

The pieces of the puzzle have all been laid out. Suppose that we now sum the values of all the debits in the course of a year, then of all the credits, and find that they are not equal. We conclude in such a case that we made a mistake in record keeping. Errors and omissions are inevitable, of course, when one is trying to keep track of *all* international transactions.

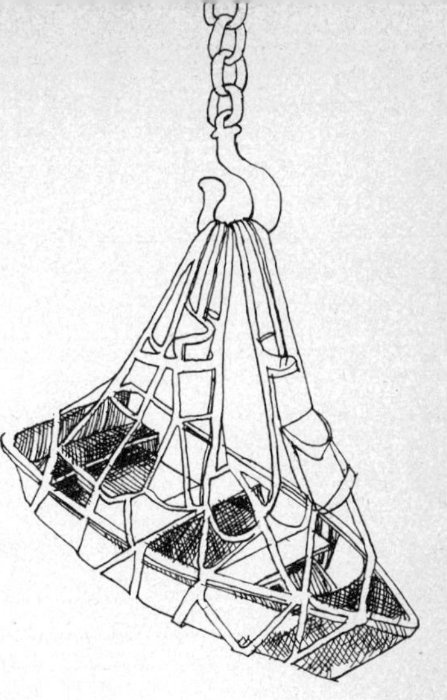

The value of some transactions can only be guessed at (as when the balance of payments accountants tacked on $40 million in the 1920s for imports of bootleg liquor). And the value of many perfectly legal transactions is estimated from incomplete records, inaccurate data, and partial samples. So measured credits and debits never do turn out to be precisely equal in balance of payments statements. The keepers of the accounts rise to the occasion by adding the difference to the smaller of the two totals and labeling it Net Errors and Omissions.

Credits Always Equal Debits

The Errors and Omissions component in the balance of payments has been embarrassingly large in recent years, hitting a record $10 billion in 1971—one-quarter the size of all our measured merchandise exports. But that isn't our concern at the moment. The significant fact for our purposes is that the Bureau of Economic Analysis always inserts whatever fudge factor is required to make the credits and the debits equal. *For the balance of payments always and necessarily balances.* It is constructed in accordance with the rules of double-entry bookkeeping, which specify that each transaction must be entered on the ledger twice, once as a debit and once as a credit. Let's see how this works out.

Suppose that Germany exported 100 boats to America, and that this was the only international transaction of the year by either country. The German accountants would enter the value of the boats as a credit in their balance of payments because it's a merchandise export. The American accountants would enter it as a debit under merchandise imports. It appears at first that, in both countries, the balance of payments is out of balance for the year; Germany will have a credit surplus, America a debit surplus. But not actually. The rules of double-entry bookkeeping decree that the boats must be "paid for" in some fashion. In the unlikely event that Germany gave them away, the German accountants would balance the credit item (so many marks worth of boats) with a debit item: a gift, or grant, or unilateral transfer of the same mark value as the boats. If, as usually occurs in such cases, Germany sold the boats but America hasn't yet paid for them, the German accountants balance the credit with a debit item called foreign loans: Germany imported IOUs to balance the export of boats. And in America the accountants balance the debit item created by importing boats with a credit item reflecting an export of IOUs just sufficient to purchase the boats. That makes excellent sense. Anything that hasn't yet been paid for (and wasn't a gift) has been sold on credit. The seller has in effect made a loan to the buyer; the seller has imported an IOU, or acquired a new claim on the importing country.

You might be a little surprised to discover that the balance of payments

U.S. BALANCE OF PAYMENTS SUMMARY

Balance of payments accounting is a complex and continuously changing science. You won't understand everything in this summary. But the authors don't, either, so you probably shouldn't worry about it. All figures are in millions of dollars.

Line	Credits (+), debits (−)	1971	1972	1973
1	Merchandise trade balance[1]	−2,722	−6,986	471
2	Exports	42,754	48,768	70,277
3	Imports	−45,476	−55,754	−69,806
4	Military transactions, net	−2,908	−3,604	−2,266
5	Travel and transportation, net	−2,341	−3,055	−2,710
6	Investment income, net[2]	5,021	4,526	5,291
7	U.S. direct investments abroad[2]	6,385	6,925	9,415
8	Other U.S. investments abroad	3,444	3,494	4,569
9	Foreign investments in the United States[2]	−4,809	−5,893	−8,693
10	Other services net[2]	2,781	3,110	3,540
11	**Balance on goods and services[3]**	**−170**	**−6,009**	**4,327**
12	Remittances, pensions, and other transfers	−1,604	−1,624	−1,943
13	**Balance on goods, services, and remittances**	**−1,774**	**−7,634**	**2,383**
14	U.S. Government grants (excluding military)	−2,043	−2,173	−1,933
15	**Balance on current account**	**−3,817**	**−9,807**	**450**
16	U.S. Government capital flows excluding nonscheduled repayments, net[4]	−2,111	−1,705	−2,938
17	Nonscheduled repayments of U.S. Government assets	227	137	289
18	U.S. Government nonliquid liabilities to other than foreign official reserve agencies	−478	238	1,111
19	Long-term private capital flows, net	−4,381	−98	62
20	U.S. direct investments abroad	−4,943	−3,517	−4,872
21	Foreign direct investments in the United States	−115	383	2,537
22	Foreign securities	−966	−654	−807
23	U.S. securities other than Treasury issues	2,289	4,507	4,051
24	Other, reported by U.S. banks	−862	−1,158	−647
25	Other, reported by U.S. nonbanking concerns	216	341	−200
26	**Balance on current account and long-term capital[4]**	**−10,559**	**−11,235**	**−1,026**
27	Nonliquid short-term private capital flows, net	−2,347	−1,541	−4,276
28	Claims reported by U.S. banks	−1,802	−1,457	−3,940
29	Claims reported by U.S. nonbanking concerns	−530	−305	−1,240
30	Liabilities reported by U.S. nonbanking concerns	−15	221	904
31	Allocation of Special Drawing Rights (SDR's)	717	710	....
32	Errors and omissions, net	−9,776	−1,790	−2,303

Line	Credits (+), debits (−)	1971	1972	1973
33	**Net liquidity balance**	−21,965	−13,856	−7,606
34	Liquid private capital flows, net	−7,788	3,502	2,302
35	Liquid claims	−1,097	−1,247	−1,944
36	Reported by U.S. banks	−566	−742	−1,103
37	Reported by U.S. nonbanking concerns	−531	−505	−841
38	Liquid liabilities—	−6,691	4,749	4,246
39	Foreign commercial banks	−6,908	3,716	2,952
40	International and regional organizations	682	104	377
41	Other foreigners	−465	929	887
42	**Official reserve transactions balance, financed by changes in—**	−29,753	−10,354	−5,304
43	Liquid liabilities to foreign official agencies	27,615	9,734	4,452
44	Other readily marketable liabilities to foreign official agencies[5]	−551	399	1,118
45	Nonliquid liabilities to foreign official reserve agencies reported by U.S. Govt.	341	189	−475
46	U.S. official reserve assets, net	2,348	32	209
47	Gold	866	547	....
48	SDR's	−249	−703	9
49	Convertible currencies	381	35	233
50	Gold tranche position in IMF	1,350	153	−33
	Memoranda:			
51	Transfers under military grant programs (excluded from lines 2, 4, and 14)	3,204	4,189	2,772
52	Reinvested earnings of foreign incorporated affiliates of U.S. firms (excluded from lines 7 and 20)	3,157	4,521	....
53	Reinvested earnings of U.S. incorporated affiliates of foreign firms (excluded from lines 9 and 21)	498	548	....
	Balances excluding allocations of SDR's:			
54	Net liquidity	−22,682	−14,566	−7,606
55	Official reserve transactions	−30,470	−11,064	−5,304

Notes to table

1. Adjusted to balance of payments basis; excludes exports under U.S. military agency sales contracts, and imports of U.S. military agencies.

2. Fees and royalties from U.S. direct investments abroad or from foreign direct investments in the United States are excluded from investment income and included in "Other services."

3. Includes special military shipments to Israel that are excluded from the "net exports of goods and services" in the national income and product (GNP) accounts of the United States.

4. Includes some short-term U.S. Govt. assets.

5. Includes changes in long-term liabilities reported by banks in the United States and in investments by foreign official agencies in debt securities of U.S. federally sponsored agencies and U.S. corporations.

Note.—Data are from U.S. Department of Commerce, Bureau of Economic Analysis. Details may not add to totals because of rounding.

always and necessarily balances. Time and again one hears that we *must* do this, or we *cannot* do that, "because of the balance of payments." The implication is that its balance is precarious, and that we are in danger of disastrously losing our equilibrium. But patriotism is the last refuge of a scoundrel, as Samuel Johnson suggested; and the balance of payments has often been the last refuge of Dr. Johnson's patriots. Special-interest groups looking for favors look also for a way to wrap themselves in the balance of payments. A little clarity on the significance of the balance of payments can therefore go a long way toward locating the public interest amid the confusing claims of competing partial interests.

The Ambiguity of Equilibrium

No one who understands balance of payments accounting is ever worried that the balance of payments won't balance. But many people do worry about the *way* it balances. In essence, they disapprove of some events that contributed to the balance. It isn't always easy to determine *why* they disapprove. An extraordinary amount of foggy rhetoric surrounds most discussions of the balance of payments. Some of the rhetoric is disguised political pleading and is therefore purposely foggy. But what one person fears and calls a disequilibrium in the balance of payments will often be recommended by another as a good policy for avoiding or curing a disequilibrium.

What was it that informed people had in mind in the 1960s when they started to worry about America's continuing balance of payments "deficits"? Where did such deficits show up? We know they could not appear as an excess of debits over credits; that would be Errors and Omissions and not a deficit. Where did they appear? One place was in the item for gold exports. Net sales of gold by the United States steadily reduced the Treasury's gold stock from $22.86 billion in 1957 to $10.89 billion in 1968. But why call that a deficit? Because, according to those who saw gold exports as evidence of disequilibrium in the balance of payments, a country cannot continue indefinitely to pay for its imports by drawing down its gold stock.

That's true, of course. But neither can a country continue indefinitely to pay for its imports by drawing down its stock of mineral resources. Nonetheless, no one regards Venezuelan oil exports or Rhodesian chrome exports as evidence of a deficit in those countries' balance of payments. Why single out gold for special treatment? We'll return to that question.

The other major piece of evidence pointed to by those who argued that the United States was running a deficit in its balance of payments was the rising total of short-term claims on the United States in the hands of foreigners. This large and growing total was evidence, they said, that we

were paying for our imports by persuading foreigners to extend us short-term loans. That was also true. But why was it evidence of a deficit? Why wasn't it simply viewed as part of the exchange-obtaining or credit transactions that balanced our exchange-using or debit transactions? The answer, once again, was that we could not expect to continue on such a course indefinitely. Sooner or later foreigners would presumably decide that they held enough claims against us, refuse to extend further credit, and start calling for payment on the claims already held.

One response to this argument is, So what? If foreigners won't lend us the means to buy their goods, we'll either find other means or stop buying. The United States imported a lot of IOUs in the 1950s in payment for our merchandise exports. When we were no longer willing to lend, we reduced our exports. And if foreigners decide to reduce their holdings of claims on the United States, we'll simply pay them off when the claims come due.

But could we do this? By what means can we pay off foreign claims on the United States? Suppose German commercial banks are holding $10 billion on deposit in New York banks or as dollar deposits in foreign branches of U.S. banks. These are claims on the United States; they are liabilities owed to German banks by U.S. banks. How were they acquired? Let's assume that the deposits were accumulated as Americans purchased Volkswagens and other imports from Germany. To buy German goods, we must pay with marks. The German banks made this possible by accepting the dollars from Americans and turning over an equivalent value in marks to the German exporters. By hanging on to those dollars and not asking the United States to redeem them with marks, gold, or some other acceptable foreign currency (or wheat, computers, or Chevrolets), the German banks were lending us the foreign exchange with which to import German goods.

Suppose now that they want to "liquidate" these claims. The deposits are payable on demand, and the German banks demand payment, just as you do when you write a check against your account in a commercial bank. The U.S. banks will meet the demand—but with *dollars*, of course, since their liabilities are denominated in dollars and not in marks, gold, or Chevrolets. The German banks will have to obtain the marks they want in exchange for dollars by turning the dollars over to the Central Bank of Germany. The net result of these transactions from the U.S. point of view is that the $10 billion formerly owed by U.S. banks to German commercial banks is now owed to the German Central Bank. If it's willing to hold the dollars, all is well. But if it's not, it had the right until recently to ask the U.S. Treasury to take the dollars off its hands for an equivalent value in gold. Until 1971, the Treasury Department was committed to redeeming dollars in gold at $35 an ounce for any central bank holding dollars but preferring gold.

That brings us back to the first symptom of a "deficit": gold sales. An increase in short-term foreign claims on the United States could not continue indefinitely, because they were potential claims on our stock of gold. Not only is that stock finite; in the 1960s it shrank while the total of potential claims against it swelled, so that the U.S. Treasury could no longer exchange gold for all the foreign-owned dollars. A disastrous run on U.S. gold reserves seemed imminent.

But why would that be "disastrous"? Suppose we simply paid gold to the official agencies authorized to exchange dollars for gold until our gold stock was exhausted and then announced that we had no more to sell. That wouldn't be dishonest; we would have honored our commitment as long as we could and quit only when there was no longer any way to continue. Unsatisfied holders of dollars could then choose either to continue holding the dollars or to exchange them for some other asset: commodities and services produced in the United States, for example, or income-earning securities such as U.S. government bonds or shares in American corporations. Where is the "disaster" in any of this?

We must push the analysis one step farther. The willingness of German banks to accept dollars (from American importers) and pay out marks (to German exporters) maintained a balance between the quantities of each currency demanded and supplied. If they had not acted in this way, the efforts of Americans to purchase a greater value of marks than Germans were willing to purchase of dollars would have led to further U.S. gold exports to Germany.

The Hidden Agenda: No Change in the Exchange Rate

Why were the German commercial banks willing to go on accepting dollars at the official rate of exchange even though supply and demand were calling for a lower exchange rate for dollars? The answer is that they knew they could obtain marks for the dollars at the official rate from their own Central Bank. The Central Bank, in turn, continued paying at this rate because that was the rate at which its dollar holdings would be converted by the U.S. Treasury, into either marks or an equivalent value in gold. The linchpin of the system was the willingness and ability of the U.S. Treasury to continue paying gold for dollars at the predetermined rate. If it stopped doing that, supply and demand would take over. The dollar would presumably depreciate and the mark would appreciate. And that was the "disastrous" consequence that so many feared and for which we've been searching in the last few paragraphs.

The whole business is complicated by the fact that the German Central Bank (and some other central banks) went on accumulating dollars even after they knew that the U.S. Treasury could not redeem them in gold. They cooperated by not exercising an option they had, because they did not want to precipitate "disaster."

Is there a voice from the back of the room willing to wonder out loud what's so "disastrous" about a change in the dollar-mark exchange rate? If relative prices, including exchange rates, do not reflect conditions of demand and supply, shouldn't we expect them to change? Aren't price changes the way to correct a disequilibrium?

When Is the Solution the Problem?

Those who believe that exchange rates should be fixed and unvarying will naturally reject the argument that a new rate of exchange can be a solution to the *disequilibrium.* As far as they're concerned it's like calling the death of the patient a cure for cancer. They will rather urge special government policies to reduce the pressure. They might point out that the supply of dollars is something the U.S. government controls, and that the simplest way for any supplier to keep the price of his product from depreciating is to stop supplying so much. That makes excellent sense, but it is often a difficult counsel for governments to accept. The U.S. government chose instead to impose additional taxes on imports, create new restrictions on the travel of Americans abroad, enact legal limitations on foreign investment by Americans, and utter all sorts of threats and promises to American corporations doing business abroad. The aim of each such policy was to deter people from engaging in activities that increase the demand for marks and thereby increase the pressure for an appreciation in the mark's value (which equals a depreciation of the dollar.)

But could any or all of these policies eliminate the disequilibrium? Those who see such government interference with voluntary international exchange as *evidence* of disequilibrium will certainly not agree that controls can *end* the disequilibrium. Consider an example from earlier chapters. If a city imposes rent controls because municipal officials believe that rising rents mean disequilibrium in the rental housing market, these officials will soon find themselves compelled to write and administer detailed codes of conduct governing landlord-tenant relations. They will regard such codes and other accompaniments of rent control, like long waiting lists, as necessary to achieve equilibrium. Opponents of rent control, who define equilibrium as rough equality between quantity demanded and quantity supplied *without* codes or waiting lists will point to the queues and codes as evidence of disequilibrium and to rising rents as the solution. The fascinating part of all this is that one group's solution is the other group's evidence of disequilibrium. That happens in many areas of economic life, but it happens most frequently and confusingly in the area of international exchange, where the concept of a balance of payments equilibrium is widely used but extraordinarily difficult to define in a satisfactory way.

Equilibrium always turns out to mean a balance among the *appropriate* factors. The concept is therefore a source of confusion whenever the criteria

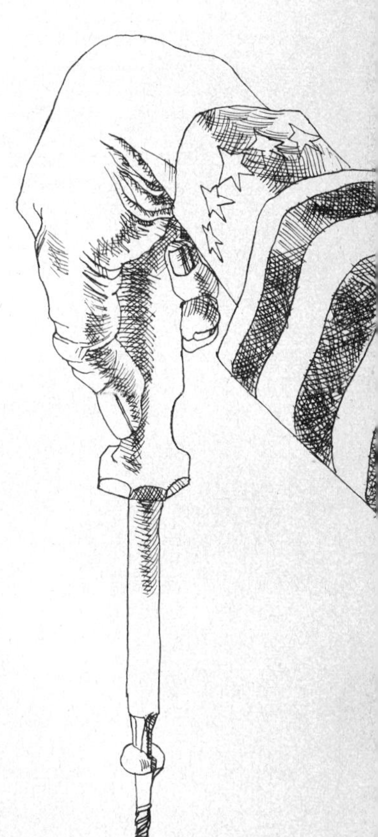

of appropriateness cannot be agreed upon. In the rent-control case, for example, the controlled price becomes an equilibrium price as soon as one includes in the total price such nonmonetary costs as the inconveniences of queuing up. But economists usually agree in such cases to exclude non-monetary costs as "inappropriate" to their concept of equilibrium. When we apply the concept, however, to the sum of all the international trans-actions engaged in by a nation's inhabitants, we run the risk of obscuring more than we clarify. Experts simply do not agree on how to measure the deficit or surplus in a nation's balance of payments, or even whether *any* definition can be adequately defended. The consequence is a variety of definitions with *disguised political intent.* We're not implying any malice or attempt to deceive on the part of those who define the balance in a particu-lar way. But the fact remains that by defining the balance on the hidden assumption that particular objectives must be achieved, one can too easily sidestep the task of defending the appropriateness of those objectives.

Remember the warning at the outset of this chapter. International eco-nomic policies often pursue poorly defined and inconsistent goals. A con-cept as vague and ambiguous as "balance of payments equilibrium" makes it all the harder to decide what we're actually doing and what we really want to achieve.

NATIONAL GOALS AND FOREIGN TRADE POLICY

We're ready now to return to the question we left unanswered at the end of the section on Undervalued and Overvalued Currencies in order to discuss the uses and abuses of the balance of payments concept. What will happen when the exchange rate between two currencies is inconsistent with the demand for each currency? It depends upon the policies the gov-ernments are pursuing.

The Rules of the International Gold Standard

It was the task of the monetary authorities under the gold standard system to choose an initial gold value for their currency that would reflect the currency's actual purchasing power relative to other currencies. This, it was assumed, would balance the international demands for each cur-rency and prevent the consequences enumerated at the end of the section on Exchange Rates.

But the purchasing power of a currency depends on price levels at home and abroad, and price levels change. Varying rates of inflation or deflation as well as differing rates of economic growth continuously threatened to

ON THE IDENTIFICATION OF DEFICITS

The *Survey of Current Business* celebrated its fiftieth birthday in 1971 with a special anniversary issue. A long list of distinguished economists was invited to submit papers commenting on the contributions to knowledge made over the years by the *Survey's* various statistical series (*The Economic Accounts of the United States: Retrospect and Prospect,* July 1971). A number chose to focus on balance of payments data and the meaning of a "deficit." The director of the Bureau of Economic Analysis, George Jaszi, reviewed the reviews at the end of the volume. He had this to say about the problem of defining a balance of payments deficit:

> With differences only in their degree of emphasis, our contributors point out that the payments balance cannot be represented by a single figure and that the presentation of a wide variety of balances is more conducive to the analysis of our balance of payments position. Ideally, perhaps no balance should be published at all. . . .
>
> Several factors seem to conspire to make the definition of payments balance an impossible task. The very notion of a dynamic balance of payments equilibrium is elusive, and balance of payments adjustment theory is torn by internal dissent. To make matters worse, even the view that ex post [actual] magnitudes can be used as though they were ex ante [intended] is allowed to infiltrate. In the realm of the GNP accounts, short shrift would be given to a fifth column which spread the view that the presence of expansionary or deflationary tendencies would be visible in an imbalance between [actual] saving and investment in the saving-investment account.
>
> Having witnessed over the years many attempts to define and redefine a payments balance—attempts whose only visible progression was circular—I have often felt that all definitions of a payments balance should be abolished, with a fine shout of "a plague on all your houses."

create over- or undervalued currencies and thus to trigger the kind of gold flow described above. The easy solution would seem to be regular adjustments in the price at which the various monetary authorities exchanged their currencies for gold. The "rules of the game" under the old gold standard frowned on that method of adjustment, however. For a country experiencing inflation relative to other countries to devalue its currency by raising the price of gold was to endorse that inflation. The sound, orthodox procedure called for the monetary authorities to resist the inflation by maintaining the price of gold. What was then supposed to occur?

Changes in the Domestic Price Level

When gold began to be exported from a country because inflation had caused its currency to be overvalued, that country's money supply and commercial bank reserves would decline. As the reserve losses forced banks to reduce their lending, the money supply would contract still further. The countries with undervalued currencies would import gold and their bank reserves and money supply would consequently rise. The price level was assumed to be a function of the money supply. In terms of the equation of exchange in chapter 13, P was thought to be determined by M, because V and Q were assumed to be fixed by nonmonetary forces or, at the very least, to be relatively stable. Deflation would consequently occur in countries with overvalued currencies, inflation in those with undervalued currencies, and both would continue until purchasing powers were again at parity. Thus domestic price level changes that were out of step with price level changes in other countries were supposed to be self-correcting. If all nations followed the rules of the game, gold flows and consequent changes in the size of money stocks would continuously adjust each price level to all others. Despite the use of different currencies, then, the economic systems of nations on the gold standard would be closely linked in a unified international economy.

In actual practice the system never worked that smoothly or automatically. Monetary authorities could and did intervene, either to aid or to inhibit the working of the adjustment mechanism. They might aid it by taking independent action to restrict bank lending and raise interest rates as soon as they detected a decline in the nation's gold reserves. On the other hand, they might choose to neutralize the gold outflow by supplying new reserves to the banking system to compensate for the reserves lost when gold was exported. The domestic money supply and price level would not decline in that case. *Supportive* actions by domestic monetary authorities presumably improved the functioning of the adjustment mechanism. But there were often good reasons, as they saw it, to *counter* the adjustment mechanism by supplying new reserves to the banking system when gold was exported, and by siphoning off the additions to reserves that came with gold imports. Nations were reluctant to accept the domestic inflation that was called for to correct an international under-valuation of their currencies. And they were even more reluctant to accept deflation as a cure for an overvalued currency when deflation turned out to be associated with falling output and rising unemployment.

Changes in Output and Employment

The theory of the international gold standard prescribed painless adjustments in domestic price levels as the cure for inappropriate rates of exchange between different currencies. But the adjustments were not in fact painless. Changes in M were not confined in their effects to changes in P; they also affected Q. The international gold standard collapsed in the 1930s, after stumbling attempts to restore it following World War I, because governments were not willing to subject their economies to disruptions originating in the rest of the world. In fact, they began to look upon exports and imports as variables that could be adjusted to achieve national goals rather than as autonomous forces to which domestic policy must conform.

The policies of the 1930s can be explained with the aid of the income-expenditures model. That model makes national income and output dependent on aggregate demand, defined now as the sum of consumption, investment, and government expenditures *plus* net exports (exports minus imports). We'll use PQ rather than Y in the model so that we can distinguish price level changes from changes in real output and associated changes in employment. The basic equation is

$$PQ = C + I + G + Ex - Im$$

A decline in aggregate demand, whatever its source, need not cause a fall in real output and employment if prices are sufficiently flexible. And price flexibility was widely assumed by economic analysts prior to the 1930s. But prices do not in fact adjust all that easily and quickly to decreases in demand. Firms that are not price takers as defined in chapter 5 (and most are not) set their prices initially on the basis of money costs previously incurred and anticipated demand; they tend to resist price reductions when demand falls short of expectations. At best, therefore, prices will fall only after some time has elapsed; and during that time unsold inventories will mount and production will be curtailed. This is the essence of a recession when it occurs in many industries simultaneously.

A government facing the onset of a recession and looking at this model might choose to counter the decline in aggregate demand with actions designed to increase exports or decrease imports. Policymakers in the early 1930s were not thinking in terms of this model because it hadn't yet been developed. But they didn't have to. There was a more immediate force that impelled them to look at the international sector for a possible policy tool: the interests of particular producers who could marshall strong political support. "Everybody knows" that imports destroy the jobs of American workers. In a period of high unemployment, therefore, producer lobbying for protection against foreign competition becomes almost impossible for politicians to resist. Taxes on imports are consequently raised and quotas are imposed. There are also many ways in which a government can subsidize exports and many arguments by which sellers seek to justify such subsidies. All those arguments become more persuasive in a recession.

In terms of the model, each nation tried to increase exports and decrease imports in order to raise PQ and reduce unemployment. In effect, each nation wanted to cut back on its employment of foreign workers and get other nations to hire more of its own labor force. There was obviously no way such a policy could work for every country. Exports as well as imports consequently declined for everyone. Each country was in effect trying to "export" its unemployment problem. But the principal result was a decline in the total of international trade, further economic disruption, and a loss of the gains from specialization.

Tariffs or quotas on imports and subsidies to exporters were one set of techniques in this abortive policy. Another was deliberate devaluation. Recall the way in which exchange rates between currencies affect the prices perceived by foreigners. The prices of exports become more attractive when a country's currency depreciates, while the prices of imports rise to discourage import purchases. A single country or a few countries can at least temporarily increase net exports in this way; but they cannot all do so simultaneously. The international monetary system turned chaotic as governments competed to manipulate the links among currencies in the hope of stimulating their net exports. The gold standard broke down and international trade increasingly had to be conducted through clumsy and inefficient barter negotiations.

It is obvious in retrospect that these policies were ineffective and even perverse. They could not stimulate aggregate demand in one country without depressing it in another. But they could and did reduce real income by inhibiting the gains from international specialization and trade during the 1930s. One source of the problem was a worldwide depression for which governments were desperately seeking remedies. Since the use of fiscal or monetary policy as correctives was not well understood, governments grasped at whatever straws they found. And in a depression, as we have seen, special interests will make the straws of trade intervention look politically attractive.

But another source of the problem seemed to be the international monetary system itself. The gold standard appeared to be too rigid in a period of major economic distrubances. When countries tried to make it more flexible by altering the gold price of their currencies, the system broke down completely.

This background enables us better to understand the directions in which the international monetary system evolved after World War II. We'll examine the rise of that system and the causes of its decline in the next chapter. Before we do so, however, let's take a look at some of the popular misconceptions about international trade that helped shape the self-defeating policies of the 1930s and that, unfortunately, still command wide allegiance today.

COMPARATIVE ADVANTAGE AND INTERNATIONAL TRADE

Popular thinking hangs on tenaciously to the notion that some countries may be able to produce almost everything at a lower cost. If wages in Japan or Mexico or Italy are lower than in the United States, won't Japanese, Mexican, and Italian manufacturers be able to produce just about anything more cheaply than U.S. manufacturers can do it? How can the United States compete with countries that tolerate wage rates, even for skilled workers, below our legal minimum? In Japan, Mexico, and Italy, however, you could find workers arguing that they can't compete with America's low cost techniques of mass production. And the suspicion arises that something is wrong with the argument.

Opportunity Cost and Comparative Advantage

The basic flaw in such arguments is the neglect of opportunity cost. It is *logically* impossible for one country to be more efficient than another in the production of everything. And that becomes apparent as soon as you remember to calculate efficiency as a ratio between what is produced and what is consequently *not* produced. The real cost of producing anything is the value of what is given up in order to produce it. Calculations in dollars, yen, pesos, and lira all too easily obscure these real costs of production.

The fundamental principle guiding international trade is the familiar principle of comparative advantage, first stated explicitly in chapter 4: Don't do anything yourself if you can persuade someone else to do it for you at a lower cost. To be persuasive, simply offer in exchange something that you can in turn produce at a lower cost. But that refers to *opportunity costs.*

Suppose that two television sets of identical quality cost respectively $300 and 90,000 yen to produce in the United States and Japan. Which cost is lower? We obviously can't know until we find out the relative value of dollars and yen. If 300 yen exchange for $1, then the costs of production are the same. If $1 will buy 310 yen, then the Japanese set is cheaper, because the cost of the Japanese set would be about $290, or 90,000 divided by 310. If we make the comparison in Japanese currency, the U.S. set would cost 93,000 yen. The U.S. sets would be cheaper, on the other hand, if $1 were worth anything less than 300 yen.

During 1971 the average price of a yen to Americans was about .29 cents ($.0029). In 1973, however, a yen cost .37 cents. That's a substantial difference. A Japanese television set costing 90,000 yen would have cost $261 dollars in 1971 but $333 in 1973. We obviously can't make meaningful cost comparisons between countries unless we know the rates of exchange between their currencies. At *some* exchange rate, all prices in one country could indeed be higher or lower than in some other country. But the problem then would not be rooted in low wage rates or efficient techniques of mass production. It would simply reflect an inappropriate exchange rate.

But what is an *appropriate* exchange rate? We argued earlier that it's a rate which equates the quantities of a country's currency that are internationally demanded and supplied. Let's try to tie that in now with the important principle of comparative advantage. We'll work with a simple problem involving two countries which each produce only four goods. Once the basic principles are clear, the conclusions can be applied to as many countries and goods as you please. The table below lists the domestic prices for all four goods in the United States and in Japan. We'll assume that those relative prices reflect opportunity costs within each country, and that the units refer to goods of identical quality.

Prices per Unit
(identical quantity and quality)

	United States	Japan
textiles (x yards)	$20	4,500 yen
meat (y pounds)	40	13,500
grain (z bushels)	30	10,500
radios (one set)	50	14,400

Forget about the exchange rate between dollars and yen. Assume, if you wish, that the United States and Japan do not yet trade. The question we want to ask is: Which country produces which goods at a lower cost than the other? If those are the only goods produced in each country and their relative prices reflect relative opportunity costs, can you decide which country is the more efficient (lower-cost) producer of each good?

All we can do with the data we have is determine the *relative* costs of any two goods in one country *relative* to the other country. But we require no more, because that is the meaning of comparative advantage.

Because meat costs 3 times as much to produce as textiles cost to produce in Japan but only 2 times as much in the United States, Japan has a comparative advantage over the United States in the production of textiles relative to meat. It follows logically that the United States then has a comparative advantage over Japan in meat production relative to textiles.

Between textiles and grain, the comparative advantage in textiles lies with Japan and so the comparative advantage in grain must lie with the

United States. The proof again is the fact that in Japan grain costs $2\frac{1}{3}$ times as much to produce as textiles and in the United States only $1\frac{1}{2}$ times as much.

Between textiles and radios, Japan again has a comparative advantage in the production of textiles and so the United States must have the comparative advantage in radio production.

How about meat and radios? The United States produces radios at $1\frac{1}{4}$ times the cost of meat and Japan at only $1\frac{1}{15}$ times the cost of meat. So Japan has the comparative advantage in radios and the United States in meat. Contrast this with the preceding case to be sure you grasp the point. Japan has a comparative advantage relative to the United States in radios *if the comparison is with meat*. If the comparison is with textiles, the United States has the comparative advantage in radio production.

To finish off the list of possible comparisons: Between meat and grain, Japan has the comparative advantage in meat and so the United States has the comparative advantage in grain. Between grain and radios, the United States has the comparative advantage in grain, which means that Japan has the comparative advantage in radios.

Prices as Indices of Comparative Advantage

A student could lose his mind doing this. The data are hard to keep straight and the conclusions are even harder to express verbally in any simple way. If this is the meaning of comparative advantage, how could it possibly guide efficient decision making? It takes an advanced degree in crossword puzzles just to figure out who has a comparative advantage in what relative to which relative to whom. Fortunately for us all, prices very neatly sum up all the information any decision maker has to have. By looking at relative prices and the exchange rate, any producer or purchaser can obtain at a single glance the essence of the results that we just ground out so laboriously.

If the exchange rate is 300 yen = \$1, textiles and radios are cheaper in Japan and meat and grain are cheaper in the United States. The table below shows all prices in yen.

Prices in Yen
(300 yen = \$1)

	United States	Japan
textiles (x yards)	6,000	4,500
meat (y pounds)	12,000	13,500
grain (z bushels)	9,000	10,500
radios (one set)	15,000	14,400

If the exchange rate is 280 yen = \$1, only textiles are cheaper in Japan. The table again shows all prices in yen.

Prices in Yen
(280 yen = $1)

	United States	Japan
textiles (x yards)	5,600	4,500
meat (y pounds)	11,200	13,500
grain (z bushels)	8,400	10,500
radios (one set)	14,000	14,400

The yen price of a dollar would have to fall below 225 yen to make even textiles cheaper in the United States. *But then Japan and the United States could not trade at all.* The yen would be so overvalued at that rate that there would be no dollar demand for yen and hence no dollars available for Japanese to use in purchasing the cheaper American goods. That exchange rate would turn the United States and Japan into isolated economies unable to take advantage of one another's relative efficiencies. Japanese consumers could not benefit from the relatively abundant supply of land in the United States that is presumably the explanation for America's comparative advantage in meat and grain production; and American consumers could not benefit from the relatively abundant supply of labor that makes textiles and radios cheaper to produce in Japan.

If any trade at all is to occur, the exchange rate must be between 225 yen = $1 and 350 yen = $1. (We're ignoring the effect of transportation costs, which would further narrow the permissible range.) Exactly where it settles down within that range will depend upon the strength of the demands for each good, the ability of each country to expand production, and what happens to relative opportunity costs as production patterns change in response to international trade.

One illustration will be enough to make the point. Suppose the rate starts out at 300 yen = $1. Americans then find Japanese radios cheaper than domestically produced radios ($48 versus $50). If a huge American demand for radios causes an expansion of the radio industry in Japan, and that expansion requires the use of resources not as well suited to radio production, the marginal opportunity cost and hence the price of Japanese radios will rise. It couldn't rise above 15,000 yen, because at that price the U.S. demand would disappear. But the prices of other goods in both countries would also be changing in response to the reallocation of productive resources that trade had brought about and the consequent changes in marginal costs. The possibilities are endless.

Perhaps you were beginning to fear that this example would be endless too. But it's important to see how *relative prices reveal comparative advantages* in international trade and what real opportunity costs of production lie behind those prices.

The Fear of Imports

The principle of comparative advantage took a distant back seat in the early 1930s, when the industrial countries of the world watched domestic production and employment tumble. Everyone knew that imports replaced domestically produced goods and that domestic production increased when exports increased. Reversing the decline in domestic production was the priority item on each country's agenda. Restricting imports while subsidizing exports seemed a straightforward approach toward that goal. And for reasons that we have examined, it was an approach with political appeal.

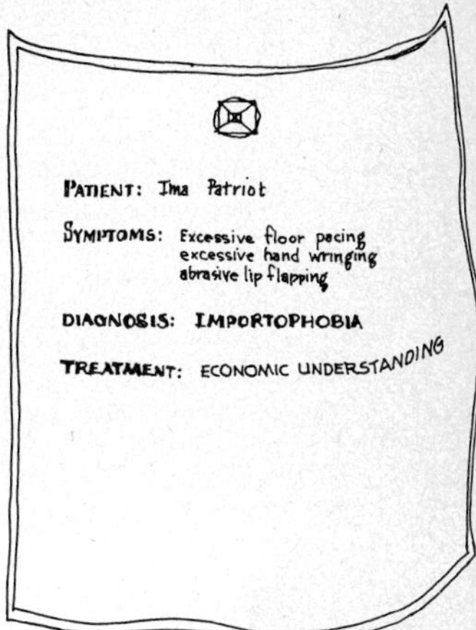

The argument that imports destroy jobs has the seductive appeal of a half-truth. When Americans buy Japanese radios they do not buy as many domestically made radios. An increase in radio imports can therefore lead to production cutbacks and layoffs in the domestic radio industry. So the owners and employees of radio manufacturing firms have an obvious interest in restricting imports. And when they go to Congress to request taxes or quotas on radio imports, they have a handy slogan with which to claim that such protection is good for the country: It protects American jobs. The popular appeal of that slogan will be especially strong in any period when unemployment is increasing and there is a recession in the economy.

But the argument is highly misleading. In the first place, jobs are created by the production of exports as well as by the production of goods that compete with imports. And how can American firms continue to sell abroad if foreign firms are not allowed to sell in the United States?

Secondly, jobs should not automatically be treated as goods. Some jobs no doubt are intrinsically satisfying and worth doing for themselves without regard to the commodities or services that result. But that's certainly rare. The justification for jobs is generally the income they provide for workers and the corresponding benefit to others in the form of useful goods. The "protect American jobs" argument ignores the gains in real income that come from specialization. If the Japanese can make better radios and sell them at lower prices than American manufacturers can do, Americans ought to produce other products and buy their radios from Japan. The attempt to justify the protection of less efficient producers on the grounds that this will preserve jobs runs quickly into absurdity. Why not push the argument further and produce domestically all the coffee we consume? American soil, climate, and geography are not as well suited for the production of coffee trees as are large areas of Brazil and Colombia; but think of all the jobs we could create by building and operating huge greenhouses in which we try to duplicate the favorable growing conditions in those countries. And why stop with goods currently imported? Think of how many new jobs we could create by outlawing the use of automated equipment in the telephone industry or by requiring street sweepers to use toothbrushes in their work.

Producer Interests and the National Interest

For two centuries economists have argued along these lines against the proponents of restrictions on imports, but they have not had much success. A French pamphleteer-economist named Frédéric Bastiat (1801–1850) wrote a witty satire in 1845 in the form of a petition by the French candlemakers for protection against the unfair competition of the sun. Their request to the Chamber of Deputies for legislation that would protect the jobs of candlemakers by prohibiting windows brilliantly exposes the absurdity of protectionist logic. Bastiat's satire has been reprinted numerous times, but the arguments he ridiculed do not disappear.

Part of the explanation must be found in the resistance of special-interest groups to mere logic. People are readily persuaded by arguments in which they want to believe, but have difficulty understanding arguments that run counter to their interests. And the political process almost guarantees that the group that stands to benefit from restrictions on international trade will have a louder voice in policy formation than the larger group that stands to lose.

The beneficiaries of tariffs or quotas on radio imports are the owners and employees of American firms manufacturing radios. They know precisely what their interest requires; they keep themselves informed about changes and prospective changes in economic or political circumstances that might affect their interests in any way; and their interest in the specific issue of U.S. importation of Japanese radios is substantial enough to justify lobbying for their cause.

Those who are harmed by restrictions are potential purchasers of radios, the owners and employees of firms producing goods for export, and the owners and employees of the Japanese radio firms. Each individual in the first two groups has such a small interest in the outcome of policy discussions regarding radio imports that he isn't likely even to notice that such discussions are taking place, and he is even less likely to invest his time or energy in lobbying for that interest. It's not that domestic radio buyers lose less than the domestic radio producers gain but rather that the losses are spread over many millions of people while the gains are concentrated among relatively few. The larger interest does not acquire proportionate political influence because it costs too much to organize that interest and give it effective expression. This is the main reason why special interests so often defeat the "public interest."

The third group harmed by import restrictions—the Japanese producers—have a sufficiently concentrated interest; but as foreigners, they lack political influence. The upshot of the matter is that the jobs and income of people producing import-competitive goods are often protected by their governments despite the fact that their gains are less than the losses incurred by those who are less effectively represented in the political process.

This explanation for the popularity of governmental restrictions on imports may be unduly cynical. There can be little doubt that many Americans, including some who are actually harmed by protective tariffs and import quotas, genuinely believe that this country can, at least under certain circumstances, be damaged by imports. Let's examine the arguments they use.

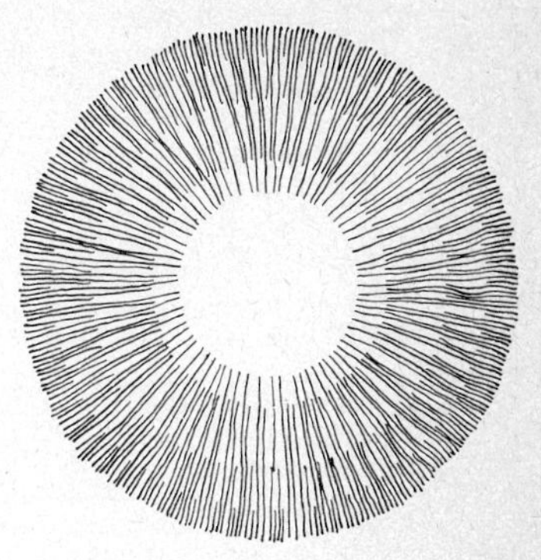

Arguments for Protection

The national security argument comes first. If we don't restrict the import of Japanese radios, our radio making industry may be destroyed. Then what would we do for radios in the event of war with Japan or even war with some other country that results in a cutoff of our Japanese trade? Maybe we could do without radios for the duration. But don't radio makers possess special skills that might be essential in wartime? Can we afford not to have an available pool of human skills and specialized equipment that can readily be adapted in a national emergency to the production of sophisticated military hardware? The basic argument can be applied with modest changes to almost any industry one might mention. Even the candle manufacturing industry included "high essentiality of labor and materials under war conditions" in a 1951 brief filed with the Senate Finance Committee on behalf of protection against candle imports. (What would we do, after all, if the lights went out in wartime?) The national security argument is not *logically* fallacious. But the fact that the argument can so easily be extended to any imports whatsoever should at least make us wary. How large a price should we be willing to pay in reduced real income for how large a gain in military self-sufficiency? And is this a genuine gain in national security? Can't the economic strength and hence the military security of a country actually be reduced by excessive efforts toward self-sufficiency? How often are these questions seriously asked before the national security is invoked to justify a new tariff or quota?

Another logically valid argument for protection goes by the name of the "infant industry" argument. It may take some time for an industry to develop the special skills, experience, and other resources that would make it efficient. If established foreign producers are allowed to sell freely in the American market, they may be able to keep domestic firms from developing. The argument assumes that American firms are less efficient

ENERGY INDEPENDENCE

Should the United States try to become independent of all foreign energy sources by 1980?

Both independence and interdependence have real costs, but in a period of national alarm about the threats other nations might pose to our security and well-being we are likely to underestimate the cost of independence.

Any and every import creates a degree of dependence on foreign suppliers, and dependence entails increased vulnerability. There is more to the matter than this, however. The dependence runs both ways, since those from whom we import also import from us. So long as it is in their interest to buy from us, it will be in their interest to sell to us.

Moreover, the pursuit of invulnerability through independence is a costly route to take. No one can predict with confidence how much more we will pay for energy between now and 1980 and afterward, because the cost will depend, to mention just some obvious factors, upon technological developments, the amount of attention given to environmental concerns, and the encouragement or discouragement that nuclear power receives. But the costs will be considerable, and the political difficulties that President Ford's energy independence program was encountering in 1975 suggest the public may find the price too high.

Is the public too nearsighted to discern the genuine public interest? If direct costs are the only consideration, the public's alleged myopia may actually be the better long-run perspective. A *certain* increase in *present and future* costs to preclude a *possible* increase in *future* costs does not automatically sound like a good bargain.

How much would we save in future costs after 1980 if we went ahead with our energy independence program and our worst fears were realized? What is the probability that our worst fears will in fact be realized? What is the present value of these additional costs multiplied by their probability when discounted at an appropriate rate of interest? And is that sum greater than the sum of the discounted costs we will incur by pushing ahead toward energy independence?

But there are also indirect costs that ought to enter the calculations. What will be the effect on the environment, on life styles, or on other nations through the example we set if the United States does or does not increase present energy costs and reduce energy consumption? The economic calculus can help us find the answers, but it is no substitute for hard thought and informed discussion about the goals we want to pursue.

in their infancy but would become more efficient than foreign competitors if they were given protection while they matured. Alexander Hamilton, the first U.S. Secretary of the Treasury, used this argument in an effort to persuade Congress that some protection against imports was in the national interest. He also argued, though, that outright subsidies were preferable to other forms of protection, because subsidies were clearly visible and could more easily be removed once they had served their purpose. That part of Hamilton's argument has not been popular with the advocates of protection, who understandably prefer a subsidy disguised as a tax on imports. But it's hard to imagine how the infant-industry argument could possibly be appropriate in the United States today. Do we have any infant industries? We have *new* industries appearing all the time. But for the purposes of this argument an infant industry is a new domestic industry competing for survival among *well-established* foreign industries. Examples are hard to find. And even if examples can be located, the argument will only apply if the infant shows promise of maturing quickly into an adolescent who can more than make it on his own. He must *more* than make it if he is to compensate society for the cost of supporting him during his infancy. All things considered, the infant-industry argument probably has no applicability to the United States today. It is an intellectual curiosity that probably hangs around only as a strategic diaper for gray-bearded but anemic "infants."

Are there other good arguments for protection? A legitimate but limited argument can be constructed from the costs of change. The closing or curtailment of an industry unable to meet foreign competition entails losses for its owners and employees. The losses will be greater the more narrowly specialized are the human and property resources displaced by competition. Is there a case for protection under such circumstances? Notice that the argument can be applied to the case of an industry hurt by domestic as well as foreign competition. Domestic competitors have political influence, of course, and are therefore harder to exclude by special legislation. Nonetheless, if resources were attracted into an industry because of existing tariff protection, it may be unfair to jerk that protection away suddenly. So there is a case for the maintenance of prior and long-continued restrictions on imports, or at least a case for their reduction (in the interest of efficiency) at a slow rate (in the interest of equity). Equity considerations, along with political realities, may also suggest a policy of transitional subsidies designed to reduce the loss to workers and owners or to help them move into new opportunities. But this argument cannot support the introduction of new or additional restrictions against imports.

Uncommon Sense: Comparative Advantage

Since there is no limit to the number of bad arguments that can be constructed in support of restrictions on imports, it would be an exercise in futility to attempt to anticipate and refute each one. The fact that there is at least a kernel of truth in most such arguments complicates the task of analyzing them. The truth must be winnowed from the chaff which surrounds it before the limitations of its applicability can be discussed. Nothing would contribute more toward raising the quality of public discussion in this area than a firm grasp of the principle of comparative advantage.

The principle of comparative advantage shows why and how exchange creates wealth. It keeps insisting that the cost of a transaction is the value of what is given up and the benefit is the value of what is obtained, and that it is nonsense to suppose a country can grow wealthy by exporting more than it imports. The principle of comparative advantage destroys the claim that one country may be more efficient than another in the production of *everything.* The logical impossibility of this premise is apparent from the very definition of efficiency as a ratio between the value of what is produced and the value of what is consequently *not* produced, or between the value of the goods obtained and the value of the goods that had to be sacrificed to obtain them. By focusing on the real factors involved in production and trade, the principle of comparative advantage disperses the fog that creeps in when trade policy is discussed exclusively in monetary terms.

"But then we'd be losing dollars!" So? Dollars cost almost nothing to produce. If other countries want to trade transistor radios for dollars, that's a marvelous swap from our point of view. And that's actually what occurred for about fifteen years under the new international monetary system created after World War II..

Once Over Lightly

As long as goods and financial assets can be exchanged across national boundaries, international trade will affect national levels and patterns of output, employment, prices, and income distribution. Increasing international trade makes the coordination of domestic and international policies more urgent. The increasing determination of national governments to manage their domestic economies may simultaneously make it more difficult.

An international monetary system, like any monetary system, reduces the cost of transactions and so facilitates specialization and improves efficiency. But the world money supply is composed of many different moneys, often exchanging for one another at uncertain and unpredictable rates.

The exchange rates between currencies and domestic prices in each country are variables that mutually determine one another. The reduction of a currency's price in foreign exchange will increase the total quantity of domestic goods demanded, both by making that country's exports cheaper to foreigners and by making imports more expensive to its own residents.

A government that pegs the rate of exchange for its currency at a level that does not equate the quantity of its currency demanded with the quantity supplied will lose or accumulate international reserve assets. The government will call this a disequilibrium in its balance of payments only if it does not *want* to lose or accumulate such assets.

The balance of payments must always balance, because it measures international transactions that are always assumed to entail something of value received for anything given up. The term *deficit* or *surplus* is applied to balancing items of which someone disapproves or to actions affecting the composition of the accounts of which someone disapproves. The disapproval rests upon predictions of undesired consequences.

The loss or accumulation of international reserve assets affects the level of domestic bank reserves and the money supply. This in turn may affect price levels, or levels of output and employment or both.

Governments that try simultaneously to manage their foreign exports and imports and their domestic price and output levels often find this to be a difficult balancing act. Harmonizing such policies is especially difficult when other governments are pursuing parallel but conflicting policies.

A major source of inconsistency in national policies is the desire of governments to satisfy political pressures from producers who want both an expansion of export markets and protection against import competition.

International efficiency is promoted when international exchange is governed by relative opportunity costs or the principle of comparative advantage. Inappropriate exchange rates, import tariffs or quotas, and export subsidies can conceal or distort relative opportunity costs. Nationalist sentiment and the disproportionate political influence of producers tend to keep the principle of comparative advantage from regulating international trade as effectively as it regulates domestic trade.

QUESTIONS FOR DISCUSSION

1. In order to take advantage of lower production costs, a Massachusetts textile manufacturer builds a factory in North Carolina and a United States television maker opens an assembly plant in Mexico.

   (*a*) In what ways is the action by the television firm different from the action by the textile firm?

   (*b*) Is either action contrary to the national interest?

   (*c*) Is either action likely to encounter effective political opposition?

2. The table below shows consumer price indices for four countries from 1970
    to 1974.

Year	United States	Canada	France	Germany
1970	100.0	100.0	100.0	100.0
1971	104.3	102.9	105.5	105.3
1972	107.7	107.8	111.7	111.1
1973	114.4	116.0	119.9	118.8
1974	127.0	127.9	135.5	126.8

    Do you think the similar patterns between the United States and Canada
    and between France and Germany are mere coincidence?

3. What would be the consequence for Volkswagen sales in the United States
    of a depreciation in the mark relative to the dollar? How would this affect the
    profitability of sales to the United States by the Volkswagen Company?
    Would you expect the longer term effects to differ from the short run effects?

4. How are the supply curves of figure 14A related to the demand curves?
    What would the supply curves look like if the demand curves fell more
    steeply? If they fell less steeply?

5. 1971 and 1972 were years in which there was widespread concern about the
    "deficit" in the U.S. balance of payments. Where would you locate the "defi-
    cits" in the balance of payments summaries for those years?

6. One of the steps taken by the U.S. government in the 1960s to correct the
    "balance of payments problem" was to restrict foreign investment by U.S.
    firms and banks. How would such a program, if it had been effective, have
    influenced U.S. debits and credits? Would the longer term consequences be
    different from the short run consequences?

7. If the value of Iran's merchandise imports is 20% greater than the value of
    its merchandise exports, does Iran have a deficit in its balance of payments—

    (*a*) If the difference is covered by twenty-year loans?

    (*b*) If the difference is covered by one-year loans?

    (*c*) If the difference is covered by selling gold from the national treasury?

    (*d*) If the difference is covered by selling newly mined gold?

    (*e*) If merchandise imports are 400% greater than merchandise exports
    excluding petroleum, and the difference is made up by selling newly extracted
    "black gold"?

8. Why do so many Americans believe that this country would be endangered
    by Arab ownership of "essential" U.S. industries and also believe that
    American owners of foreign industries pose no threat to the national secu-
    rity of those countries? Why are U.S.-owned foreign enterprises thought to
    be at the mercy of foreign governments, while the United States is at the
    mercy of foreigners owning U.S. enterprises?

9. How do U.S. imports reduce the domestic money supply? How can the Fed prevent this from occurring? What would be the consequences of such "neutralization" actions by the monetary authorities?

10. Why cannot one country have a comparative advantage over another country in the production of everything if the first country has excellent natural resources, a huge capital stock, a highly skilled labor force, and ingenious technicians and managers, while the second country is poor in all four areas?

11. What evidence exists to support the view that Japan has a comparative advantage over against the United States in the production of small automobiles? How would you account for this comparative advantage? How would you explain the fact that the United States seems in general to have a comparative advantage in the production of large automobiles but a comparative disadvantage in the production of smaller ones?

12. Suppose that a Canadian firm appeals for protection against imports from the United States using the infant industry argument. It offers data showing that it can currently produce and sell widgets for $10, that American producers can sell them in Canada for $8, and that if American competitors are excluded from the Canadian market, the firm will develop greater efficiency and after ten years of protection be able to sell widgets for $7. It therefore proposes what is in effect a $2 per widget tax on Canadian consumers for ten years in return for a $1 benefit in perpetuity.

   (*a*) Would that be a good bargain for Canadian consumers if the facts are as stated? (Don't forget that future benefits must be discounted before they can be compared with present costs.)

   (*b*) How would you choose the discount rate to use in calculating your answer?

   (*c*) If the protection were granted, do you think it would be eliminated at the end of ten years? What arguments would be used to support its continuance?

   (*d*) Do you think the efficiency of the Canadian firm is as likely to increase when it is protected from foreign competition as when it is not?

   (*e*) Why do so many Americans believe that competition is not altogether desirable when it comes from foreign producers?

15

1
UNI~DOLLAR
ONE
EARTH
EARTH
ONE
ONE
UNIVERSAL MONEY
ONE

ONE
ONE
OPEC
OPEC
ONE
ONE
One Petro Dollar

ONE EURODOLLAR
EINS
ONE
9
9
9
9
UN
UNO

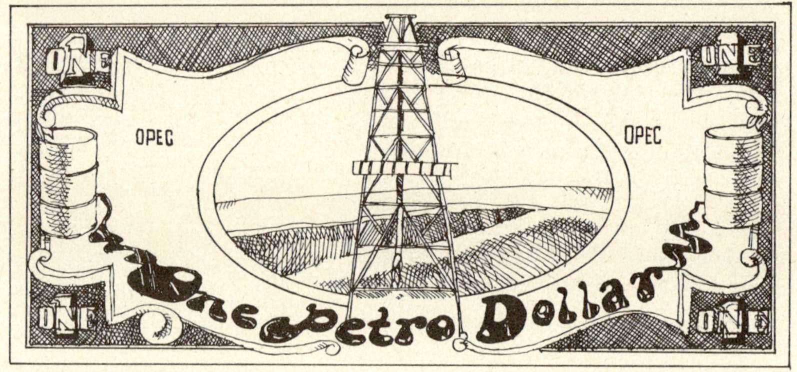

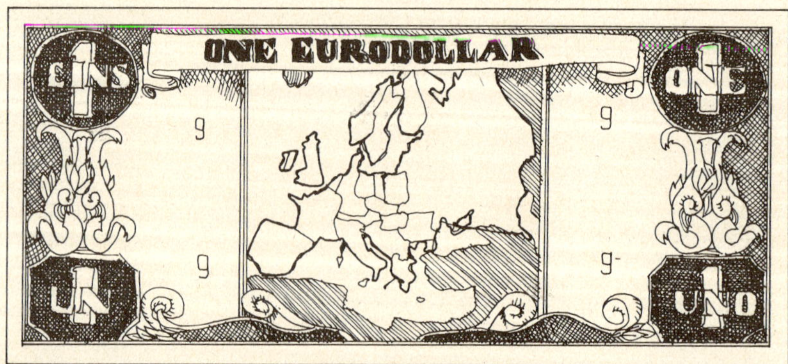

THE CHANGING
INTERNATIONAL MONETARY SYSTEM

The principles of the international monetary system and the prerequisites for international monetary order may have been better understood a decade ago than they are now. Events have moved faster than theories in recent years, and new truths have not yet firmly established themselves as successors to the old truths that practice has called into question.

THE SYSTEM OF BRETTON WOODS

The statesmen who gathered at Bretton Woods, New Hampshire, in 1944 to design a new system for linking the world's currencies could hardly doubt the power of nationalism. They knew that a successful world monetary system would have to leave each government free, within wide limits, to pursue its own chosen domestic policies. But the participants in the Bretton Woods monetary conferences were also internationalists, and they hoped to devise a system under which national sovereignty could coexist with international cooperation.

John Maynard Keynes was a leading participant in those conferences. He was convinced, as were most other participants in the negotiations, that national governments had the power to influence domestic levels of income and employment. They expected that power to be used against any recurrence of depression. Their task, therefore, was to devise a system of international currency links that could maintain itself and function effectively in the face of divergent national economic policies.

The twin concepts of *links* and *liquidity* will help us appreciate the nature of the problems they saw themselves facing.

Maintaining Fixed Exchange Rates

The demand for particular currencies from holders of other currencies varies continuously, even over short periods of time, in response to continuously shifting patterns of relative prices and production within countries. Moreover, levels of prices and production will shift over time as a result of changes in demand, in technology, in resource availability, and also in government fiscal and monetary policies. It was feared that if supply and demand were allowed to determine exchange rates without any official intervention, the rates would fluctuate unpredictably and seriously hamper international exchange by making it too uncertain and risky. Fluctuating exchange rates were regarded as unsatisfactory international monetary links.

If official monetary institutions, such as central banks, are to peg exchange rates at a steady level, they must possess an adequate stock of acceptable international reserves. An exchange rate is pegged by selling a currency when its value starts to rise and buying when it starts to decline. But what could a central bank use to buy its own currency? It would have to be an asset that was acceptable to the other countries from whom the currency was being purchased. Gold was one such reserve asset. A stock of monetary gold would give a central bank liquidity with which to maintain a stable price for its currency in the face of temporary downward pressure. Was there enough monetary gold around to provide every central bank with sufficient liquidity to prevent its currency from fluctuating in value? Perhaps there was not. Of course, the value of the physical gold stock could have been increased simply by raising the price of gold in terms of the dollar and other currencies. As we shall see, however, there was strong resistance to taking that step. Moreover, the bulk of the world's monetary gold stock was in the United States by the end of World War II, so that the gold in other nations seemed to many clearly insufficient to permit monetary authorities to maintain their currency's price by pegging.

International Reserve Currencies

But gold is not the only reserve asset that might be used. The international reserves available to a central bank for pegging operations will include, besides its monetary gold stock, its holdings of "sound" foreign currencies. When is a foreign currency "sound"? It is sound when everyone believes that the currency is not going to depreciate in the foreseeable future. And why would they believe that? They would believe it if they were convinced that the country issuing the currency was willing and able to pursue policies that would prevent depreciation. And what causes or prevents depreciation? Depreciation results from a country's inability to export at prevailing exchange rates as much as it wants to import, and from its inability in such a situation to stem the depreciation by selling gold or other reserve assets. A country currently balancing its trade accounts by importing short-term liquid assets and also holding a huge stock of reserve assets therefore possesses a sound currency par excellence.

Sound as a Dollar

And now we have described the U.S. dollar as it appeared at the end of World War II. The U.S. gold stock was over $20 billion in 1946 and had climbed to almost $25 billion by 1949—certainly enough, it seemed, to maintain the price of the dollar even in the face of prolonged pressures toward depreciation. But no pressure appeared imminent. U.S. exports were in heavy demand and the war-ravaged economies of Europe seemingly would, for some time, have little to offer in return. Inflation in the United States could alter this picture; but there was no reason to believe this country would experience inflation at a greater rate than the rest of the world, and substantial reason to believe its productive capacity would do a better job than anyone else's of keeping the supply of goods in step with the demand. So the dollar after World War II was "as good as gold." It was *better* than gold, in fact, because a nation's gold reserves earned no interest. But a country that chose to hold its international reserves in the form of dollars could earn a return on those reserves by depositing them in U.S. banks or by purchasing U.S. government securities that could be quickly and costlessly converted into dollar deposits.

The Dollar as International Currency

That's how it came about that the Western world moved toward a dollar-gold standard after World War II. The United States pegged the dollar to gold at a price of $35 per ounce. Other countries then pegged their currency to the dollar. The United States held its international reserves primarily in the form of gold. Other countries might hold gold too; but they could also hold as reserves dollar deposits and assets such as U.S. government securities that were convertible into dollar deposits. These deposits were in turn convertible into gold on demand by foreign monetary authorities.[1]

1. We are unjustly ignoring in this discussion the pound sterling. During the era of the classical gold standard, London was the financial center of the world. The Bank of England maintained pound-gold convertibility, and the pound was the major international reserve asset. After World War II, nations that maintained close and extensive trading relations with the United Kingdom resumed the practice of holding sterling balances as reserves. Not until 1954 did the total of sterling in international reserves fall below the total of dollars. But the decline of sterling as an international reserve occurred steadily; it fell from 40% of all official reserves in 1948 to a little more than 5% by 1971.

Under this system the dollar performed on the international level all the functions typically performed by a domestic currency. It was an international medium of exchange: French imports from Sweden, for example, could be paid for by transferring ownership of dollar deposits. Dollars were held not only by central banks that wanted international reserves, but also by private citizens of foreign countries. They often preferred to accumulate dollar assets rather than their own currency, because they believed that the dollar was less likely to depreciate through inflation. It was also the international unit of accounting and was employed in practice to measure the value of international transactions. And the dollar was the world's intervention currency, because the monetary authorities of different nations purchased and sold dollars in order to maintain the value of their currencies in the foreign exchange market.

How Much Liquidity?

A major difference between such a dollar-gold system and a gold-only system is the larger stock of international reserve assets that the former provides. Why is that important? The monetary authorities of any country want liquidity for reasons similar to those discussed in chapter 9, where we described the demand for liquidity. The future is uncertain. They want to be able to handle unforeseen contingencies. Unexpected developments might push a country's imports far beyond its exports for a temporary but protracted period. This could be handled without depreciation by dipping into the reserves. With inadequate reserves, depreciation might be avoidable only by curtailing imports that were important to that country's economic development, military security, or political stability. How much liquidity was desirable?

Just as there's no rule of thumb for deciding how large any individual's money balances ought to be, there's no rule of thumb for choosing the appropriate amount of international liquidity. But the world's monetary gold stock was relatively fixed.[1] And there seemed to be no law of nature decreeing that the amount of heavy yellow metal in the world, at its current price, had to be equal to the amount that all countries collectively wanted to hold as reserves. The supply of monetary gold, at the fixed rates of exchange between gold and various currencies, might be insufficient to satisfy the international demand for liquidity. Wasn't that likely, in fact? Just as an individual's preferred level of money holdings is a function of his regular income and expenditures, so a nation's preferred level of reserve holdings could be expected to depend on the total of its imports and exports. An expansion of world trade would presumably require an

---

1. It was *relatively* fixed because gold could be attracted from the ground or private hoards, and could also disappear into private hoards or into industrial and ornamental uses.

expansion of reserve assets if the trading world was not to encounter a persistent liquidity shortage. And liquidity shortages threatened free trade and stable exchange rates.

How so? A nation with inadequate reserves could not weather temporary import surpluses. Even minor dislocations, due perhaps to a poor harvest or a development boom, could quickly deplete the reserves and compel a choice between accepting a lower exchange rate or some combination of import restrictions and export subsidies. Either choice conjured up memories of the 1930s. Adequate reserves were therefore desirable as insurance against a return to the thoroughly discredited policies of the thirties. The dollar-gold system met the demand for an increased supply of international reserves and pleased those who thought that gold by itself provided insufficient international liquidity.

The International Monetary Fund

The architects of the postwar international monetary system designed an additional stabilizing feature for the system in the form of the International Monetary Fund. The IMF was designed to be the central bank of the central banks, or the monetary authorities' monetary authority. Assigned to headquarters in Washington, D.C., in deference to the dominant position of the United States in international finance, the IMF was supposed to increase the liquidity of the international monetary system by lending reserves to countries that were experiencing temporary pressures toward depreciation. The IMF would tide them over until the emergency had passed and they could again begin earning through exports enough foreign exchange to pay for their imports. The loans were made out of sums deposited with the IMF for that purpose by member countries, but principally by the United States. The loans were for short periods and were intended to cover only temporary exchange shortages. A nation was expected to get its affairs in order during this period of grace, and the IMF was not above nagging when it thought a government might be abusing the grace it had received.

What Is "Irresponsible"?

Let's pause for breath. You can test your comprehension at this point by thinking about ways in which such grace could be abused. To begin with, we know that a country runs into trouble when it can't export enough IOUs (that is, borrow enough) to make up the difference between its merchandise and service exports and everything it's trying to import. Why might that be occurring?

A government could be purchasing goods from abroad in blithe disregard of its eventual ability to produce enough goods to pay for them. It could be doing that to build up its military strength, to promote an economic development program, or in response to any of the innumerable pressures toward increased expenditures experienced by governments subject to popular will. It's analogous to a consumer on a credit binge, who prefers not to think about the relation between his future income and his coming monthly payments.

Or a government might be spending more than it's collecting in taxes and financing the deficit by adding to the money supply. This causes domestic inflation, and inflation makes foreign goods look more attractive to importers and exports less attractive to foreigners.

Both examples show a government trying to live beyond its means—that is, beyond its ability to finance current expenditures out of current taxes or domestic borrowing. And that's what the IMF would complain about when warning that its line of credit was temporary and nagging a country to set its house in order. Nagging, as you might suspect, has never been an effective tool of international diplomacy. But nagging by a banker carries a sanction: the possibility of no more credit. And without IMF credit, the country would be unable to continue living beyond its means. It would be forced to change its ways.

Or would it? The offending government sometimes responded by imposing import restrictions or interfering in other ways with the free flow of international trade, the very event the IMF was supposed to make unnecessary. Or it suddenly devalued its currency, another violation of the IMF's code of good conduct. It would announce one morning that the pound sterling (or franc, lira, escudo, peseta) would now be exchanged for $2\frac{2}{5}$ dollars rather than the $2\frac{4}{5}$ dollars offered yesterday. With this one move it could make its exports cheaper to foreigners and imports more expensive to its own citizens—*if* other countries did not respond by devaluing their own currencies proportionately. This last possibility was the one that made the IMF nervous. Devaluations to promote exports and curtail imports were reminiscent of the 1930s. Moreover, they broke the link among currencies whose maintenance was the primary goal of the entire system. A wave of devaluations, or even the fear of a wave of devaluations, would introduce all the uncertainties of freely fluctuating rates. They would upset the planning of exporters and importers, encourage purely speculative purchases and sales, and generally interfere with the development of stable patterns of trade and specialization. What could be done?

The Best Laid Schemes

The inevitability of *some* devaluations and revaluations (remember that the term *revaluation* is reserved for *upward* revaluations) was generally recognized. The rules of the IMF therefore provided for limited exchange-rate adjustments, after consultation with the IMF, when the international value of a country's currency was seriously out of line with its domestic value. And this procedure, the Bretton Woods conferees hoped, would correct the excessive rigidity of the old gold standard. The new system was built to bend so that it would not break.

But the system never worked as it had been designed to do. The tendency for currencies to appreciate or depreciate away from the official rates proved the rule rather than the exception in the quarter century after World War II. Economic development moved in many different directions, at vastly different speeds, and with diverse and unpredictable effects on production and price levels. Governments were simply not willing to let their domestic policies be dictated by the need to maintain a fixed rate of exchange between their currency, the dollar, and the other currencies pegged to the dollar. The flexibility of the new system still wasn't sufficient, because the world itself was changing rapidly and because national governments insisted upon far more freedom to maneuver than most observers had anticipated.

England probably tried harder than any other nation to follow the rules of international responsibility. She wanted the pound sterling to be a sound currency and not one that fluctuated in value or displayed a persistent tendency to depreciate. And so England pursued contractionary monetary and fiscal policies whenever the pound started to depreciate because Britons were trying to purchase abroad more than they were selling. The results, in the opinion of critical observers, were "stop-and-go policies" that disrupted domestic production but could not prevent depreciation of the pound. Evidence mounted steadily that stop-and-go policies designed to secure exchange rate stability reduced real incomes, added to unemployment, slowed down economic growth, aggravated social conflicts of interest, and ultimately failed to prevent domestic inflation.

Recall the "classical" mechanism by which a balance was supposed to be maintained by each nation between its credits and debits. Rising debits would reduce the domestic money supply, pull down domestic prices, stimulate exports, and discourage imports. Nations with rising credits would experience domestic inflation and its twin consequences of expanding imports and shrinking exports. In this manner a balance was supposed to be automatically maintained. There is surprisingly little evidence, however, that prices actually moved enough to achieve the desired results. The results may have appeared nonetheless because a different mechanism was at work. Nations losing international reserves would indeed experience a monetary contraction, often because the monetary authorities induced it as a way of raising interest rates and encouraging foreign deposits in domestic banks to build up international reserves. But all this was more likely, as it turned out, to cause recession than deflation. The nation would experience a fall in Q rather than P. In a recession, however, imports fall sharply. And they rise sharply in nations experiencing an

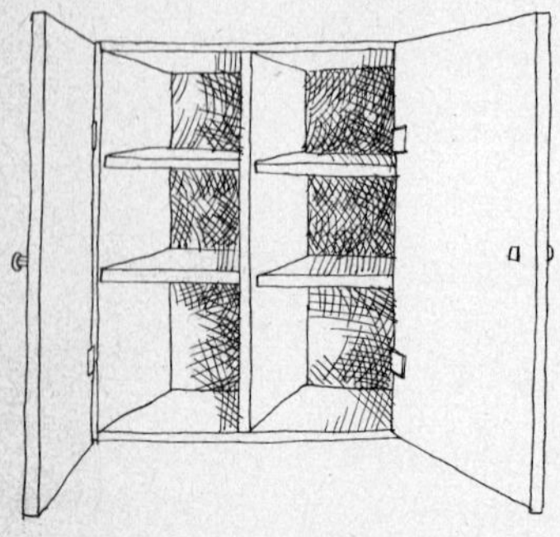

economic boom brought about by the easy money and low interest rates that an inflow of international reserves either causes or permits. So the cure largely worked, to the extent it worked at all, by giving the patient a disease (recession or inflation) worse than the one for which the cure was designed (balance of payments "disequilibrium").

On top of all this, it is not universally conceded that the new flexible-fixed exchange rate system actually succeeded in reducing uncertainty and promoting a more efficient international allocation of resources. The exchange rates were not in fact fixed, as proved by periodic devaluations and revaluations. They did not, it is true, fluctuate from week to week except within the very narrow limits permitted by the peg. But because they were not free to move regularly in response to changing conditions of supply and demand, their movements were large and abrupt when they finally did occur. The certainty of international traders and investors regarding day-to-day exchange rates was accompanied by longer term uncertainty. It is not clear that the former certainty did more to promote trade than the latter uncertainty did to inhibit and distort it. On the other hand, it isn't clear that either form of uncertainty had significant effects. The largest impact of the "flexibly fixed" exchange rate system may have been on the domestic policies of the countries that more or less faithfully paid homage to it.

THE ROLE AND FATE OF THE DOLLAR

This description and evaluation of the dollar-gold standard in the quarter century following World War II has so far slighted the principal actor in the drama, the dollar. It was the dollar and U.S. policy that sustained the Bretton Woods system in its early years and finally brought about its disintegration in 1971. The international monetary system at this writing and the direction of its probable evolution can best be understood by looking at the history of the dollar as the world's reserve currency.

The "Dollar Shortage"

A nation obviously cannot build up and hold dollar reserves unless it finds ways to acquire dollars. How *did* the countries on the dollar-gold standard acquire supplies of dollars after 1945? Since dollars originate in the United States, they can only be obtained through direct or indirect transactions with the United States. Let's review the kinds of transactions that supply dollars to the rest of the world.

United States imports are one. But U.S. exports exceeded imports in every year from 1946 to 1970 by amounts ranging from $310 million in 1959 to $11.6 billion in the reconstruction year of 1947. And exports use

up the dollars that our imports supply. So the exchange of merchandise and services made a negative net contribution toward supplying the world with dollar reserves.

Another source of dollars was U.S. government grants, pension payments, private gifts, and other "unilateral transfers." From 1946 to 1970 the annual total of such transfers never fell below $2.2 billion and in 1949 hit a peak of $5.6 billion. To this total can be added the expenditures made abroad by the government for military purposes. After the Korean war these expenditures climbed from $2 billion in 1952 to almost $5 billion at the end of the 1960s.

But against all this must be set the payments other countries made to the United States as a return on its foreign investments. The income-earning foreign investments of American citizens and corporations grew rapidly during the quarter century we're examining and by the late 1960s they were receiving net investment income of around $6 billion a year.

From 1946 to 1957, the net outflow of U.S. dollars from all the transactions we have mentioned was *negative*. Over $17 billion more dollars were *earned* for the United States through all these transactions than were *supplied*. This was made up by extensive foreign investment, both by the U.S. government and by private organizations and individuals, short term and long term, direct and portfolio.[1] But the net amount was not enough, from the standpoint of some critics, to provide adequate international reserves and liquidity for the nations on the gold-dollar standard. That was what lay behind much of the talk (up to 1957) about "the dollar shortage." Unable to earn enough dollars to build up their reserves to a satisfactory level, other countries found themselves quickly in a bind whenever their export earnings dipped or their import payments rose. Without a supply of dollars, monetary authorities in other countries could not maintain their currencies at the established exchange ratios. They had no choice then, unless they wanted to swallow the bitter medicine of deflation or, more probably, recession, except to impose controls on international transactions or to devalue. And either course was contrary to the intent of the system.

Not Enough Liquidity?

Some students of the problem came to the conclusion that the periodic devaluations, controls, and half-hearted attempts to take the classical "cure" which plagued the world economy after World War II could only be eliminated by finding an additional source of international liquidity. One way to do that would be to increase the price of gold. The stock of

---

1. Direct investment occurs when a U.S. company expands the capital invested in overseas operations that it controls. Portfolio investment is the purchase of securities in foreign firms that are not controlled, simply as a way of acquiring additional income-earning assets. The distinction is fuzzy at the edges.

gold, though relatively constant in physical terms, could easily be increased in value terms through a decision by the United States to raise its dollar price. If the United States had announced in the late 1940s that it would henceforth pay $70 rather than $35 for an ounce of gold, the world's stock of monetary gold would have been doubled by a stroke of the pen. It would probably have more than doubled, since the higher price would have stimulated additional gold production and persuaded private holders to sell at least a portion of their hoards to the monetary authorities.

Or Not Enough Self-Discipline?

Why wasn't this recommendation adopted? The primary reason was probably the belief that a shortage of liquidity was not the actual problem. Particular countries were chronically running out of reserves because they were unwilling to discipline themselves and live within their means. There was no dollar shortage; there was only a widespread desire by countries to spend more than they earned. An increase in the overall supply of reserves would have alleviated their problems only temporarily and given them an excuse to continue on their undisciplined courses. The danger of any rise in the price of gold was the additional latitude and incentive it provided for inflation. The same reasoning was applied to the proposal put forward in the 1950s that the IMF act as a genuine central bank and create new international reserves on its own credit, much as the Fed creates reserves for commercial banks in the United States. The objections to these proposals go to the heart of the perplexing issue that has dogged our steps throughout these past two chapters. Let's deal with it through a series of questions.

The Fundamental Questions

1. When a government incurs a budget deficit, is it doing so to stimulate output and employment? Or is it doing so because it cannot or will not collect the taxes required to support its expenditures?

2. Does the deficit stimulate real output, or does it pull up the price level? If it does both, when does it do which? Are the effects even separable? If they're separable in principle, are they separable in actual practice? Do we know enough to be able to cut off stimulus after it has had its major effect on output and employment, and before it starts to cause inflation? Is it possible, given institutional and political realities, that fiscal or monetary stimulus is regularly required for "full" employment *and* that it inevitably causes some inflation?

3. If the last question is answered affirmatively, a critical question arises: What is the desirable tradeoff between high employment and price stability? How much of one ought to be sacrificed for the sake of the other?

SHORTAGES OF MONEY

Complaints about a shortage of money go as far back into history as commerce itself. Seventeenth and eighteenth century thinking about the sources of national prosperity frequently focused on the importance of an ample money supply and ways to secure it. An obsession with money was perhaps the chief characteristic of economics in the "age of mercantilism." One of the American colonists' objections to British economic policy was its alleged tendency to drain specie from the colonies and leave them with an inadequate money supply. William Jennings Bryan campaigned for president in the 1890s proclaiming, "You shall not crucify mankind upon a cross of gold"; he and his followers demanded the monetization of silver because they wanted a larger supply of money.

Those whose livelihood depends upon their ability to sell goods for money are understandably tempted to identify hard times with a shortage of money. But a shortage can always be eliminated, as we saw in chapter 3, by an increase in price. Why weren't shortages of money handled in this way?

The problem is that the price of money is its general purchasing power. An increase in the price of money is therefore a fall in the general price level. And to many people that was the problem, not the solution. They did not want to see the prices of the goods they sold fall. Falling prices were to them evidence of the problem: a shortage of money.

Deflation, like inflation, redistributes income and wealth and antagonizes those it harms. But it is also associated with recession and rising unemployment if prices resist the downward push of a declining monetary demand. The "hard times" that popular thinking identified with "money shortage" were therefore not entirely a product of the merchant's obsession with monetary demand; people were correctly associating money shortage with deteriorating economic opportunities.

4. And this question leads in turn to another: how much attention should governments pay to the international repercussions of domestic policies? Is it irresponsible or is it sensible for a government to select its policies with attention to the domestic economy and let the exchange rate fend for itself? And if a government does accept an obligation to maintain the international value of its currency, to whom is that obligation owed? Is it owed to other countries? To its own exporters, importers, and investors

in foreign enterprises? To its own citizens who dislike inflation and for whom government attention to the exchange rate is a discipline against the chronic temptations of governments to follow inflationary policies?

These questions were not answered during the discussions of the 1950s and they have still not been answered conclusively to this day. The quest for an international monetary system that will enable nations to behave responsibly toward one another is still impeded by disagreements regarding the wisdom of particular domestic policies.

But the United States had its own reasons for not wanting to increase the price of gold in the 1950s and they probably tipped the scale. In the first place, an increase in the dollar price of gold is a devaluation of the dollar, at least with respect to gold. And a devaluation of the dollar seemed to be an abandonment of the U.S. commitment to maintain a constant value for the dollar in terms of gold. Nations that were holding dollars rather than gold reserves would be penalized for their participation in the dollar reserve system. The beneficiaries would be individuals hoarding gold (illegal for Americans from the 1930s until 1975, but not illegal in other countries); nations that had turned up their noses at the dollar by exchanging dollars for gold; the Soviet Union, which had a gold stock of unknown but considerable size; and the Union of South Africa, which was the world's leading gold producer. None of these was thought to be a particularly worthy recipient of the windfall gains that would accrue from an increase in the price of gold. To increase the dollar price of gold in the absence of urgent reasons seemed like raising the wages of wickedness.

From Shortage to Surplus

As so often happens, however, events outran discussion. The problem changed while everyone was still arguing about its nature and solution. In the late 1950s the U.S. gold stock began to flow overseas into the reserves of other nations and foreign holdings of dollars steadily increased. Conferences on the dollar shortage had not yet adjourned before some began to worry about the threat of a dollar surplus. What had happened?

In the first place, the nations of Western Europe and Japan had largely recovered from the devastation of World War II. They were increasingly able to do without imports from the United States and to compete with the United States for export markets.

Moreover, some of them—most notably France—resented the privileged position of the dollar in the international monetary system and saw no reason, now that they were again economically strong, why they ought to accept the dollar as an international reserve asset. Certain economic advantages accrue to a country able to get its currency accepted as an international reserve asset. In effect it is able to purchase goods from abroad on credit at low or even zero interest rates. The exporting nation holds the payment received as a reserve instead of using it to claim in turn commodities and services from the importing nation.

There was a great deal of American resentment against France when the French monetary authorities under de Gaulle began purchasing gold from the United States with the dollars they acquired. But France had a special incentive to redeem dollars in gold: some of those dollars had been acquired through the purchase by U.S. corporations of controlling interests in French firms. The French resented that and doubly resented the suggestion that they should themselves finance the takeovers by agreeing to hold the dollars spent for the purchase of their own corporations.

Whatever the root causes, the mounting dollar "surplus" reflected an attempt on the part of the United States to import more from other nations than we were exporting to them. Our merchandise and service exports continued to exceed imports until 1971, and our net income from foreign investments continued to grow; but the margin was not large enough to cover net new foreign investment by the United States (imports of securities) plus the total of our foreign grants and overseas military expenditures. And so the dollar came to be viewed as an *overvalued* currency. This means that the quantity of dollars demanded at existing rates of exchange fell short of the quantity we were supplying in the absence of continuing intervention by monetary authorities to shore up the demand.

The Unique Status of the Dollar

Other countries in such a situation could and did devalue their currencies to make their exports temporarily more attractive to others and imports less attractive to their own citizens. But that wasn't a readily available option for the United States, because we did not control the rate of exchange between the dollar and other currencies. The dollar was pegged only to gold; the rate at which it exchanged *for other currencies* was determined by the rate at which those currencies were pegged by their governments to the dollar. All we could have done, then, was devalue the dollar relative to gold. Unless this prompted other countries to revalue their currencies with respect to the dollar, such a devaluation would have no effect. One of the costs associated with being the issuer of a reserve currency is that the issuing nation gives up a large measure of control over the rate at which its currency will exchange for others.

If the dollar was overvalued, some other currencies had to be undervalued. Why weren't the monetary authorities in those countries willing to revalue their currencies upward and thus accomplish the dollar devaluation we could not effect on our own? Part of the answer is contained in the politics of protection discussed in the last chapter. The undervaluation of the German mark and the Japanese yen meant that producers in these countries had a competitive advantage in selling their goods abroad. It also

meant that German and Japanese consumers paid higher prices for the goods they imported, but the voice of consumers is rarely as influential as that of producers in shaping a government's international trade policy. The German and Japanese governments "cooperated" diligently to maintain the value of the dollar by accumulating and holding short-term claims against the United States. Thus they kept their own currencies undervalued and maintained their competitive advantage in exports.

With the burden of adjusting to the "disequilibrium" thus thrown back upon the United States, we tried a variety of measures to reduce the flow of dollars abroad. At one time or another we raised the cost to American tourists of bringing back foreign merchandise, placed a tax on borrowing by foreign corporations in the United States, restricted foreign lending by U.S. banks, imposed first voluntary and later mandatory controls on direct investment abroad by U.S. corporations, recalled the dependents of American servicemen stationed overseas, threatened to impose quotas unless particular countries "voluntarily" curtailed their exports to us, and in a variety of smaller ways tried to discourage imports and encourage exports. Meanwhile we began lecturing other nations on their obligation to assume a fair share of the expenditures we were making abroad for military security in Europe and economic development in poor countries.

Away from Gold

In 1968, with the outward flow of dollars continuing, we announced to the world that we would henceforth redeem dollars in gold *only* for foreign central banks. The real significance of this declaration was its clear implication that our continued readiness to redeem dollars for central banks depended on their sparing use of the privilege. So a "two-tier" market for gold was officially established. The United States bought from and sold (very little!) gold to central banks at $35, and private purchasers paid whatever supply and demand might dictate. The subsequent rise in the free market price of gold, to almost $200 an ounce at one point, excited speculators, grabbed headlines, displeased jewelers, delighted gold producers and owners of stock in gold companies, troubled dentists and their patients, and confirmed prophecies of all those who had said that gold was grossly undervalued at $35 an ounce. But it did not seriously affect the world monetary system. The world monetary system had moved farther from any meaningful kind of gold standard than most people suspected. Gold was on its way to becoming just another good.

In August of 1971, by presidential decree, the Treasury Department suspended "temporarily" the convertibility of dollars into gold "except in amounts and conditions determined to be in the interest of monetary stability, and in the best interests of the United States." The world was officially off the dollar-gold standard. The president's speech announcing this policy indicated that it was a response to "speculators" who were "attacking" the dollar. But that's a lot like saying that a divorce is caused by the judge who enters the decree. The plain fact was that the United States no longer wished to live with the situation in which it found itself.

THE FUTURE OF THE INTERNATIONAL MONETARY SYSTEM

If the world was off the dollar-gold standard after 1971, what standard was it on? For awhile after the suspension of the dollar's convertibility into gold, no one was quite sure. Foreign countries continued to peg their currencies to the dollar at the previous rates. But they now knew that if these rates resulted in a net inflow of dollars, they could not count on the United States to convert the dollars into gold. Two of their options were to continue pegging their currencies at the old rate and accumulate undesired dollar balances that were likely to decline in value, or to revalue their currencies by paying less for dollars, thus making their own goods more expensive and American goods less expensive.

Floating Exchange Rates

There was a third option. The monetary authorities in those countries could simply stop purchasing dollars. When their citizens acquired dollars in international exchange, they would have to turn elsewhere than to the central bank in order to turn those dollars into domestic currency. By taking that option, monetary authorities would give up the attempt to peg the rate of exchange between their currencies and the dollar, and allow it to find its own level in the market. The ideal of fixed exchange rates yields to a system of *free* or *flexible* or *floating* exchange rates. Apparently any label will do as long as it begins with the letter *f*, but *floating* has come to be the preferred term. It has also since 1971 come to be the preferred option.

When the United States suspended the convertibility of the dollar and other countries more or less reluctantly gave up the effort to maintain an established rate of exchange between their currencies and the dollar, some experts announced the breakdown of the international monetary system and the appearance of a world monetary crisis. They called for emergency conferences to create a new system that would restore order before the flow of trade and exchange broke down in chaos.

But other experts rejoiced in the disappearance of the old system. The first group's crisis was the second group's solution. Those who held the

latter view had long argued that the real problems in the international monetary system arose from that system itself and specifically from the attempt to maintain fixed exchange rates. The chronic balance-of-payments deficits and surpluses that worried so many governments were simply the consequence of their refusal to let exchange rates float with changing conditions of supply and demand. It was not a problem to be managed but a problem arising out of the attempt to manage. In international economics, as we commented earlier, solutions are often problems and problems are solutions, depending upon one's perspective and objectives.

Prior to 1971 there was extensive support among academic economists for a movement toward floating exchange rates. These economists argued that government attempts to fix the rates had demonstrably failed. Such attempts did not in fact make it easier for international traders and investors to predict the future. On the contrary, as price controls of any sort inevitably do, they led governments into all sorts of trade and exchange restrictions. And they did not subject domestic policy to any "balance of payments discipline," because countries were always willing to devalue anyway when attention to the balance of payments might threaten cherished domestic objectives. In short, fixed exchange rates offered the worst of all possible worlds: increased uncertainty in the name of greater stability, restrictions on trade for the sake of free trade, and a "discipline" that inhibited flexibility and allowed irresponsibility.

Outside of academic circles, however, and especially among the economists working for central banks, floating exchange rates were regarded as unworkable if desirable and undesirable even if workable. They would indeed increase uncertainty for foreign traders and investors, it was argued. But they would also create additional uncertainty for domestic producers and investors because a change in exchange rates could quickly and radically change the potential profitability of industries producing exports or goods that competed with imports. Moreover, governments were not likely to remain passive when a sudden depreciation in the currency of a major trading country led to an unexpected surge of imports or threatened established export markets. They were far more likely to retaliate with trade and exchange controls that would eventually lead to a breakdown of international exchange similar to the one that occurred in in the 1930s. And though the discipline of the balance of payments had not compelled governments to pursue noninflationary policies, their fiscal and monetary policies had generally been less expansionary and inflationary than they would have been under a system where floating exchange rates removed any reason to be concerned with the balance of payments.

It may be worth observing that the proponents of fixed rates often spoke about the "academic" (that is, unrealistic) nature of the floating rate proposals offered from the ivory tower vantage point of a university setting.

THE "PETRODOLLAR CRISIS"

There are fads and fashions in popular crises, and 1975 was a banner year for the "petrodollar crisis." *Petrodollar* was the new word coined in 1974 for the monetary payments made by oil-importing countries to the members of the Organization of Petroleum Exporting Countries. Why were petrodollars an object of concern?

The export earnings of OPEC countries more than quadrupled from 1973 to 1974 because of higher oil prices. There was obviously no way in which these countries, most of them with quite small populations, could increase their imports proportionately in a short period of time. That meant they were going to accumulate large and growing stocks of such monetary assets as marks, pounds, yen, francs, gold, and dollars, which were the preferred medium of exchange for oil imports. The Banque de Bruxelles estimated, for example, that Saudi Arabia and Iran collectively increased their oil revenues from $8.8 billion in 1973 to $47.6 billion in 1974. But their combined international spending in 1974 was only $16.1 billion. (The data were reported in the *Wall Street Journal* of December 30, 1974.) The total OPEC surplus for 1974 was estimated at $60 billion. What was going to happen to that surplus or to the "overhang of petrodollars" as some ominously called it?

Well, what *could* happen? The OPEC countries will presumably want to loan their surplus. But to whom, on what terms, and for what purposes? Financial transactions by OPEC countries have so far been veiled in just enough secrecy to aggravate the anxiety of those who fear that petrodollars will soon disrupt the whole international monetary system. One fear is that the substantial funds deposited in international banks (and subsequently loaned to borrowers) might be recalled suddenly. Banks cannot pay interest on deposits unless they can lend on the basis of those deposits. But they cannot grant borrowers the long-term loans they want if OPEC countries insist that their deposits always be available on short notice.

One solution is for potential borrowers of the surplus to seduce OPEC countries into long-term commitments by offering a higher rate of return. That has clearly been happening. But long-term investments encounter another problem: the suspicion of foreign investment. Americans for some reason don't like the idea of Arabs buying (that is, investing in) Miami hotels, Iowa farms, or Lockheed Aircraft, and Germans are upset to learn that Kuwait has purchased a piece of Daimler-Benz, the manufacturer of Mercedes automobiles.

There is a fine irony in the thought of Saudi Arabian owners of

> American hotels worrying about shrinking profit margins caused
> by rising utility bills that result from the higher price of Arab oil,
> or of Kuwaiti investors lamenting Daimler-Benz losses attribu-
> table to the reduced demand for automobiles brought about by
> rising gasoline prices.
>
> We might do well to remember that international investment
> creates international communities of interest. That can't be alto-
> gether bad in a world threatened by international suspicion and
> hostility. What better way is there to persuade the Arab nations
> to understand and sympathize with our interests than to have
> them purchase a large piece of those interests?

And the academic economists occasionally noted that the fixed rate system
provided a lot of gainful employment for central bank economists and
required them to attend frequent conferences in such pleasant or exotic
places as Geneva and Nairobi.

Some of the evidence is now in. Floating rates *do* work. The majority of
the world's countries, however, do not let their currencies float freely. They
try to keep them more or less closely related to some other, major currency.
The dollar is only one such currency; the pound sterling, the French franc,
and the mark have their own set of satellite currencies. Even the major currencies are not always allowed to float freely. Governments intervene to
practice what has come to be called a "dirty float" and do not keep their
hands off to achieve a "clean float." Don't conclude that "dirty" necessarily
means naughty. The new head of the International Monetary Fund, presumably a spokesman for virtue, told an IMF conference in Nairobi in
September of 1973 that he welcomed central bank intervention in currency
markets as a way of reducing "gyrations" and pushing currencies toward
their true "underlying value."

Where Are We Headed?

How can the beginning student of economics hope to decide which is
the best monetary system for the world when the experts disagree? Perhaps
it isn't that important to decide. This chapter has tried to show that events
have their own logic in international economics. We shall nonetheless
attempt a concluding summary and a timorous glance into the future.

Gold is gone as *the* international reserve asset. It will always have value
because it has other uses than as a medium of exchange. And as long as
people "believe in gold" or think of it as the safest investment in a period

FOREIGN EXCHANGE RATES IN RECENT YEARS

(In cents per unit of foreign currency)

Period	Australia (dollar)	Austria (schilling)	Belgium (franc)	Canada (dollar)	Denmark (krone)	France (franc)	Germany (Deutsche mark)	India (rupee)	Ireland (pound)	Italy (lira)	Japan (yen)
1971	113.61	4.0009	2.0598	99.021	13.508	18.148	28.768	13.338	244.42	.16174	.28779
1972	119.23	4.3228	2.2716	100.937	14.384	19.825	31.364	13.246	250.08	.17132	.32995
1973	141.94	5.1649	2.5761	99.977	16.603	22.536	37.758	12.071	245.10	.17192	.36915
1974	143.89	5.3564	2.5713	102.257	16.442	20.805	38.723	12.460	234.03	.15372	.34302
1974—Jan	148.23	4.8318	2.3329	100.859	14.981	19.905	35.529	11.854	222.40	.15433	.33559
Feb	148.50	5.0022	2.4358	102.398	15.570	20.187	36.844	12.131	227.49	.15275	.34367
Mar	148.55	5.1605	2.5040	102.877	16.031	20.742	38.211	12.415	234.06	.15687	.35454
Apr	148.41	5.3345	2.5686	103.356	16.496	20.541	39.594	12.711	238.86	.15720	.36001
May	148.44	5.5655	2.6559	103.916	17.012	20.540	40.635	12.841	241.37	.15808	.35847
June	148.34	5.5085	2.6366	103.481	16.754	20.408	39.603	12.735	239.02	.15379	.35340
July	147.99	5.4973	2.6378	102.424	16.858	20.984	39.174	12.759	238.96	.15522	.34372
Aug	148.24	5.3909	2.5815	102.053	16.547	20.912	38.197	12.525	234.56	.15269	.33082
Sept	144.87	5.2975	2.5364	101.384	16.111	20.831	37.580	12.316	231.65	.15103	.33439
Oct	130.92	5.4068	2.5939	101.727	16.592	21.131	38.571	12.416	233.30	.14992	.33404
Nov	131.10	5.5511	2.6529	101.280	16.997	21.384	39.836	12.397	232.50	.14996	.33325
Dec	131.72	5.7176	2.7158	101.192	17.315	22.109	40.816	12.352	232.94	.15179	.33288

Period	Malaysia (dollar)	Mexico (peso)	Netherlands (guilder)	New Zealand (dollar)	Norway (krone)	Portugal (escudo)	South Africa (rand)	Spain (peseta)	Sweden (krona)	Switzerland (franc)	United Kingdom (pound)
1971	32.989	8.0056	28.650	113.71	14.205	3.5456	140.29	1.4383	19.592	24.325	244.42
1972	35.610	8.0000	31.153	119.35	15.180	3.7023	129.43	1.5559	21.022	26.193	250.08
1973	40.988	8.0000	35.977	136.04	17.406	4.1080	143.88	1.7178	22.970	31.700	245.10
1974	41.682	8.0000	37.267	140.02	18.119	3.9506	146.98	1.7337	22.563	33.688	234.03
1974—Jan	40.094	8.0000	34.009	139.08	16.739	3.7195	148.66	1.7205	20.781	29.727	222.40
Feb	40.489	8.0000	35.349	140.31	17.351	3.8567	148.76	1.6933	21.373	31.494	227.49
Mar	41.152	8.0000	36.354	143.40	17.734	3.9519	148.88	1.6927	21.915	32.490	234.06
Apr	41.959	8.0000	37.416	145.12	18.170	4.0232	148.85	1.7080	22.730	33.044	238.86
May	42.155	8.0000	38.509	146.07	18.771	4.1036	148.78	1.7409	23.388	34.288	241.37
June	41.586	8.0000	37.757	145.29	18.410	4.0160	148.86	1.7450	22.885	33.449	239.02
July	41.471	8.0000	38.043	145.15	18.519	3.9886	149.73	1.7525	22.861	33.739	238.96
Aug	42.780	8.0000	37.419	143.73	18.246	3.9277	146.83	1.7466	22.597	33.509	234.56
Sept	41.443	8.0000	36.870	139.64	17.993	3.8565	142.69	1.7339	22.333	33.371	231.65
Oct	41.560	8.0000	37.639	129.95	18.165	3.9246	142.75	1.7422	22.683	34.528	233.29
Nov	43.075	8.0000	38.438	130.42	18.404	3.9911	143.88	1.7522	23.175	36.384	232.52
Dec	42.431	8.0000	39.331	130.56	18.873	4.0400	144.70	1.7716	23.897	38.442	232.94

Source: *Federal Reserve Bulletin*

of inflation or uncertainty, the demand for it and consequently its price may remain near current levels. (The policy of South Africa toward gold production will have a lot to do with the future price of gold.) And gold will probably continue to serve as a benchmark of some sort in international exchange. The values of at least some assets will continue to be stated in a particular weight of gold even though the assets are not freely convertible into gold. But the world will not return to a real gold standard in which the value of currencies is maintained by keeping them directly or indirectly convertible into gold.

Neither are we likely to see a return to the dollar-gold standard or to a system where any single currency functions as the dominant medium of international exchange, principal reserve asset, universal unit of international accounting, and pivot to which other currencies are pegged. Countries whose currencies might be candidates for the role will likely decline such an extensive honor to avoid the limitations that the role imposes on independent policy formation. And other countries will be reluctant to concede the honor, because they regard it more as a privilege than a burden.

The Social Character of Money

What kind of system might evolve, then, to provide links between separate monetary systems and adequate international liquidity? The safest prediction is that it will indeed evolve, and not be created by a conference either of world bankers or academic economists. For money is a social phenomenon, not just an artifact of commercial banks, monetary authorities, and financial experts. The indispensable prerequisite for an international money is that it be almost universally accepted throughout the world as a medium of exchange. What gives money universal acceptability? Nothing other than the fact that it is universally accepted! Acceptability requires use, in other words, and use presupposes acceptability. This isn't arguing in a circle. It is simply taking note of the fact that nothing has ever come to function successfully as money except by coming gradually to be used and accepted in a particular society. Social use and not legal declarations creates a monetary system. Consider the easygoing acceptance of Canadian money in northern border areas of the United States. Or ask yourself how checking accounts came to be the major component of the money supply in this country.

This analysis rules out, at least for the foreseeable future, a single world currency used in all countries alike. That's the system used to facilitate "international" exchange among the fifty states. But the social foundation for such a reform does not exist throughout the world. Even Canada and the United States have separate (though strikingly similar) currencies, evidence that Canadians and Canadian interests are at least somewhat different from the people and interests to the south. Separate currencies reflect both a measure of social distance and a determination to preserve that distance. The United States could easily supply a stock of money adequate for all of North America. But Canadians and Mexicans would see in such a move evidence of a U.S. desire to take them over and destroy their separate identities. A single monetary system promotes economic integration. The governments of Canada and Mexico would probably be reluctant to sacrifice the additional bit of independence that the *absence* of a common money provides.

Special Drawing Rights

The future of SDRs should be viewed in this light. SDR stands for Special Drawing Rights on the International Monetary Fund, sometimes referred to as "paper gold." We mentioned earlier, in discussing the international demand for liquidity, the proposal that the IMF create international money in the way that national central banks create domestic money. There is no logical reason why this could not be done. And SDRs currently exist, in quite limited quantities. They are credits that nations have with the IMF that can be transferred to other nations in settlement of international claims. But the total value of SDRs is fairly small at the present time and cannot be expanded in the absence of international agreement on the method of expansion. Anything more than a limited agreement for a limited expansion of SDRs will be difficult to achieve. If the IMF functions successfully in the years ahead and gains increasing trust and cooperation from member nations, it will increasingly be regarded as "everybody's" central bank and may be authorized to issue large quantities of additional SDRs. But for the IMF to function successfully and acquire that kind of trust and cooperation, it will first have to be viewed as "everybody's" central bank and not as the creature of the developed Western nations or of the United States. That in turn presupposes an evolution toward internationalist attitudes and sentiment far beyond what we currently observe.

No gold standard. No dollar or sterling standard. No SDR standard. No single currency for the world. Toward what system *are* we likely to move, then? Probably toward one not very different from the system which evolved after 1971. The rates at which currencies exchange for one another will be set by underlying forces of supply and demand with regular nudges in this direction or that from the monetary authorities and an occasional sharp jolt. Now that the pins have fallen out of the old fixed exchange rate system, it will be extraordinarily difficult to reconstruct it or build a new one. Governments have come to prize their freedom to cut the cloth of domestic economic policy to the pattern they choose; the system of fixed exchange rates required that governments tailor domestic policy to fit the shape of the international economy. That may or may not have been a valuable discipline; but external discipline is no more appreciated by governments than it is by college students.

A second reason why we should not expect to see the reemergence of a fixed exchange rate system is that its construction would require extensive international cooperation. Sufficiently close cooperation among the nations of the world is unlikely at the present time. Not only are there conflicting interests that would have to be resolved before a working agreement could be reached; there is also no consensus on what went wrong with the old system and what should have or even could have been done to save it. The

SDRs: SPECIAL DRAWING RIGHTS

The International Monetary Fund created Special Drawing Rights (SDRs) in 1969 as a new international reserve asset that the IMF could issue whenever it thought a growth in global reserves was desirable. Countries were obligated to supply their own currencies, up to a certain limit, in return for SDRs tendered by other countries—although this requirement was only imposed on countries with strong reserve positions. The IMF intended to create SDRs and credit them to the account of a country with a serious reserve shortage; that country would then use them to obtain a defined amount of currency from other participating countries. By imposing *obligations* to accept SDRs, the IMF itself designated them as inferior reserve assets.

What is the value of one SDR? It was set originally at the dollar's par value in gold: 1 SDR $=$ 1 dollar $= \frac{1}{35}$ ounce of gold. But the United States subsequently devalued the dollar relative to gold, and 1 SDR rose to \$1.08571; 1 SDR rose to \$1.20635 with the second devaluation of the dollar.

Since July 1974, the value of the SDR has rested on a weighted average of the exchange rates of 16 IMF member countries. The weights vary from 33% for the U.S. dollar and 12.5% for the German mark down to 1% each for the Austrian schilling and South African rand. That makes the SDR a highly stable reserve asset. Its value will rise or fall roughly in proportion to the average rise or fall in the prices of the principal currencies for which it exchanges. It was this stability that prompted OPEC nations in 1975 to shift from the dollar to the SDR in quoting oil prices.

During the single month of February 1975, the average daily value of the SDR fluctuated between \$1.231342 and \$1.2613187. That's a $2\frac{1}{2}$% variation within just a few weeks and the SDR doesn't seem to be very stable. But think about it again. Was it the SDR or the dollar that was fluctuating in value? If the yardstick is continually varying in length, the item being measured will *seem* to change its length.

Since the SDR's value is now a weighted average of the value of the principal international currencies against which SDRs exchange, it makes more sense to think of the SDR as the yardstick and assign the variation to the dollar. There is, of course, no absolute standard of value in economics. But SDRs may be the most satisfactory yardstick we have. They are certainly more satisfactory than gold, whose purchasing power in terms of national currencies or real goods has varied enormously in recent years. The notion that gold is *the* standard is a powerful prejudice that is difficult to shake, despite the fact that the purchasing power of gold can easily be manipulated by the governments of the Soviet Union and South Africa.

United States has blamed the nations that deliberately maintained under-valued currencies, discriminated against our exports, and refused in general to shoulder their share of the world's burdens. Other nations have blamed the United States for trying to hang on to the benefits of having the world's key reserve currency without being willing to accept the costs. Those costs are primarily the acceptance of fiscal and monetary restraint to staunch an outward flow of international reserves even when such restraint threatens to reduce domestic output and employment.

Both criticisms overlook a major dilemma confronting any reserve currency. There is a slippery relationship between its supply and its demand. Supply and demand analysis would yield few useful predictions if changes in the supply of some commodity regularly triggered changes in the demand for it. But that happens with reserve currencies. The United States supplied dollars to the world by making expenditures abroad. Those dollars became international reserves insofar as countries retained some portion of the expenditures in the form of short-term claims on the United States. But by the conventional measure, this is a *deficit* in the U.S. balance of payments. And deficits are signs of economic weakness. Here is the paradox: The dollar is in strong demand when it is regarded as sound. An increased supply of dollars to meet a strong demand is interpreted, however, as a sign of weakness, and reduces the foreign demand to hold dollars. Perhaps this is why the dollar shortage turned so suddenly to a dollar surplus in the late fifties. The line between shortage and surplus may be a razor's edge on which a currency can only be balanced by skilled and strenuous acrobatics.

International Policies in National Contexts

If the requisite skill coupled with the requisite will to recreate and maintain a world system of fixed exchange rates does not exist, a system of floating rates, either dirty or clean, is the alternative. We have already noted the alleged advantage of such a system: It puts the burden of adjustment to changing international trade patterns upon international exchange rates, thereby insulates the domestic economy from the effects of international disturbances, and enables domestic policymakers to ignore the balance of payments. That sounds good, but it may be neither wholly true nor wholly a blessing.

A change in a country's foreign exchange rate *does* affect the domestic economy. A depreciation, for example, makes imports more expensive and so drives up the prices people must pay. It also increases the foreign demand for exports, which pulls up prices and puts additional upward pressure on the domestic price level. Since depreciation is usually the consequence of *prior* inflation, the fact that it causes *further* inflation should at least be grounds for caution. If prices were as flexible downward as they are upward, the inflationary pressures in the countries with depreciating currencies might be countered by deflationary pressures in the countries whose currencies are appreciating. But if most prices are strongly resistant to downward pressure, as many insist they are, all relative price adjustments must be upward adjustments. Floating exchange rates could then be a system for the international transmission of inflation. To what extent have floating exchange rates been responsible for the worldwide inflation of the past few years? Some critics have assigned them a major share of the blame.

In addition to the inflationary threat they pose, they create substantial price uncertainty for exporting industries and industries that compete extensively with imports. This increases investor and producer uncertainty and may aggravate income and employment instability. An American firm that had just invested heavily in a new bicycle-manufacturing plant could be badly hurt by a sudden depreciation of the pound that made British bicycles temporarily much cheaper than its own. If this starts to occur, will nations be willing to let the international economy run itself? Or will they once again pick up the weapons of import restrictions, export subsidies, and controls on capital movements? The use of these weapons reduces global welfare by preventing resources from being allocated in accord with comparative advantage. But neither the principle of comparative advantage nor the concept of global welfare has ever won a national election. The international economy, and consequently the international monetary system, will continue to be subservient to national economic goals as long as nationalism controls the policies of governments.

Perhaps the difficult questions are finally not questions of the best institutional arrangements for ordering an international economic system. These may be mere technical questions that reasonably intelligent and informed people could answer to almost everyone's satisfaction *if* national governments stopped pursuing domestic policies that interfere with *any* international order. This last statement doesn't necessarily imply that national governments are villainous. But the overriding fact is that international policies are developed in the context of national economic policies. Governments today have programs by means of which they try to control economic growth, fluctuations in production, unemployment, price levels, and the distribution of income. And the realities of democratic politics decree that those programs take precedence over the maintenance of a stable international economic system. Four passengers in a single automobile will never agree on the best way to get where they're going if they disagree about where they ought to be going.

Perhaps when we acquire a better understanding of the effects of fiscal

EURO-DOLLARS AND OTHER STRANGE BEASTS

Some of the most complex issues in international monetary economics are issues created by the use of bank deposits denominated in foreign currencies. No one is quite sure about the size of these deposits, the way in which they expand or shrink, or how they can be controlled in the interest of domestic and international monetary stability.

Suppose that a German citizen purchased a painting by Jasper Johns from a New York dealer and paid for it with a check for 180,000 marks drawn on a Hamburg bank. If the dealer then deposited the check in First National City Bank, his balance would rise by about $75,000. (The exchange rate is assumed to be 2.4 marks to the dollar.) First National could offset the $75,000 increase in its liabilities if it sold the marks for that amount of dollars.

But suppose that the dealer prefers to hold marks because he thinks marks are less likely to depreciate than dollars. And he persuades First National to maintain its liability to him *in marks.* He would then be the owner of a checking account denominated in a foreign currency. He could spend those marks by writing checks against that account. If there are other Americans who would prefer marks to dollars, these "Americo-marks" could function as money in the United States. They would constitute a genuine addition to the stock of assets that can be used directly as a medium of exchange.

"Americo-marks" are not in fact a medium of exchange in the United States. But Euro-dollars *are* an important component of the money supply in Europe. Some of those European bank deposits denominated in dollars did not even originate in U.S. payments to Europeans. They were created by the same kind of money-creation-through-lending that we described in chapter 9. Insofar as dollar loans by European banks to Europeans are redeposited in European banks that offer dollar-denominated accounts to their customers, the only limit on the Euro-dollar "money multiplier" will be the reserve ratio the banks collectively wish to, or are required to, maintain.

The Euro-dollar is a vivid symbol of the international nature of the monetary economy and one more reminder of the dangers and difficulties inherent in managing a national economy as if it were isolated from the rest of the world.

and monetary policies and of other government techniques for influencing economic activity, we shall be in a better position to construct a satisfactory international system. But that may require a more comprehensive understanding of economic systems than the science of economics by itself can provide. Some even argue that it would require a reorientation of our basic approach to the organization of economic systems. Those are some of the issues with which we'll be wrestling in the concluding chapters of this book.

Once Over Lightly

The new international monetary system that was formulated at Bretton Woods in 1944 and that survived roughly (in both senses) until 1971 was designed to secure both flexibility and stability in international exchange and to harmonize national independence with international interdependence.

Fixed exchange rates were the goal. Other nations pegged their currencies to the dollar and the United States pegged the dollar to gold.

Divergent rates of inflation and economic growth, shifts in demand and technological change, and differences in policy targets and procedures for hitting those targets created constant pressure for exchange-rate adjustments under the Bretton Woods system. Insofar as nations altered their exchange rates, the system failed to provide stability. Insofar as they imposed restrictions on international trade or domestic production to maintain their exchange rates, the system failed to provide adequate flexibility.

The system invited extensive recriminations. The United States was blamed first for importing too little and creating a dollar shortage, then for importing too much and cheapening the principal international reserve currency. Other countries were blamed for irresponsibly trying to live beyond their means or for irresponsibly seeking competitive export advantages by maintaining undervalued currencies. Through all of this, people nonetheless found ways to expand the volume of international trade.

The system collapsed when neither the United States nor other countries could or would take steps to achieve a balance between the quantity of dollars demanded and the quantity of dollars supplied internationally. The United States severed the last official gold-dollar link in 1971 and other countries reclaimed their right to peg or not peg their currencies as they saw fit.

The system of floating exchange rates that ensued has apparently not yet introduced so much uncertainty as to create new restrictions, legal or voluntary, on trade. It has reduced the frequency of "balance of payments crises" by making nations, and especially central bankers, less anxious (or at least less vociferously anxious) about movements in exchange rates.

The system may also have contributed to the international transmission of inflation by removing an incentive for national governments to practice monetary restraint.

It will be difficult and perhaps impossible in the foreseeable future to create a new international monetary system because of the difficulties in the way of achieving consensus among national governments. But so long as international trade in goods and securities continues, and even continues to grow, a functioning international monetary system exists.

The most serious problem facing national governments today may not be the creation of an international exchange system, but the reconciliation of inconsistent domestic and international policy objectives.

QUESTIONS FOR DISCUSSION

1. Does the United States today have a single currency and a completely unified monetary system? Are exchange rates between Georgia and Alabama fixed or floating? Can you think of circumstances where money acceptable as a medium of exchange in one geographic region must be converted into another form of money (at some cost) before it can be used in other regions? How do people who travel extensively in the United States avoid both the risk of carrying large quantities of universally accepted money and the inconvenience of not having a money that is generally acceptable where they're traveling?

2. In 1860, there were about 1500 state chartered banks in the United States, each issuing its own paper money in a variety of different types. These bank notes were promises to pay specie on demand to the bearer of the note; they were therefore liabilities of the issuing banks. There was no homogeneous paper money that was accepted everywhere.

    (*a*) What kinds of problems would you expect to find under such a system?

    (*b*) Did the different regions of the country have fixed exchange rates?

    (*c*) Could "balance of payments deficits" occur under such a system?

    (*d*) Would you expect such a system to reduce or intensify interregional conflicts of interest?

3. As one way of paying for the Civil War, the federal government in 1862 began issuing non-interest-bearing notes that were not redeemable in specie. The federal government simultaneously refused to accept "greenbacks," as they came to be called, in payment of taxes.

    (*a*) What would you expect to occur in such a situation?

    (*b*) In July 1864, the New York money market was offering about $40 in gold for $100 in greenbacks. What does this imply about prices of goods in the United States at the time? If you were to ask a seller of clothing what price he was charging, how would he answer?

4. Per capita currency in circulation in the United States increased by almost 20% from 1870 to 1895. Does this prove that the claims of a money shortage made by William Jennings Bryan and his followers in the 1896 presidential campaign were mistaken?

5. A farmer plants corn in May expecting to purchase dollars in October when he harvests his crop. How does he protect himself against an unanticipated increase in the price of dollars (equals depreciation in the price of corn)? Is the same kind of protection possible for British producers of Scotch whiskey who contract to sell a certain quantity to the United States for a certain number of future dollars and want to protect themselves against a depreciation of the dollar relative to the pound?

6. If someone bought gold in 1944 at $35 an ounce and sold it in 1974 at $175 an ounce, how much "profit" did he earn? What was the annual percentage return on his investment over this period? (You must find out approximately what interest rate equates $35 now with $175 available 30 years in the future.) Would he have done better by purchasing shares in a mutual fund that paid 8% compound interest in dividends plus appreciated value? (Hint: At 8%, a dollar 30 years from now has a present value of less than 10¢.)

7. In the late 1960s, the Fed tried to keep short-term interest rates up in order to "protect the U.S. balance of payments." How could this affect the balance of payments? The Fed simultaneously tried to keep long term interest rates low to encourage investment and economic growth. Where is the line between the short term and the long term? Can the "line" be crossed?

8. How would you expect a recession to affect a country's imports of merchandise, services, and securities?

9. Explain what Charles de Gaulle meant when he rejected U.S. complaints about French purchases of gold in the 1960s by stating that France could not be expected to finance an American takeover of French industry.

10. "Floating exchange rates free a nation to pursue the domestic policies it prefers." Is that true?

11. "Money is accepted because it's acceptable." Is that an empty platitude or an important truth?

12. How will the acceptability of SDRs be affected by the decision of OPEC governments to quote petroleum prices in SDRs rather than dollars? Will this make petroleum more expensive or less expensive to United States buyers? Explain your answer.

13. SDRs are credits created by the International Monetary Fund. How should the IMF decide how many such credits to create and to which countries' accounts they ought to be credited? Some people have suggested that since SDRs are new money, they should be given initially to the poorer countries.

Do you agree? Would this be a costless way of aiding less developed countries?

14. Is it harmful to U.S. prestige when the dollar depreciates? Why do you suppose that governments usually express more official alarm over depreciation than over appreciation of their currencies?

15. Assume that you are the manager of the German Central Bank and that you are confronted with the problem presented at the end of the section on Exchange Rates in chapter 14. The mark is undervalued relative to the dollar so that your bank is continuously acquiring additions to its gold stock and adding marks to the domestic money supply.

   (*a*) Why will this tend to cause domestic inflation?

   (*b*) What effect will the domestic inflation have on the flow of gold?

   (*c*) What steps might you take (other than revaluing the mark) to prevent the undervaluation of the mark from causing inflation?

   (*d*) If you call in the owners of the Volkswagen Corporation and ask them whether you should revalue the mark, what do you think they would say?

   (*e*) If a Chevrolet costs 4000 dollars, a Volkswagen costs 12,000 marks, and the dollar-mark exchange rate is 1 for 4, what is the Chevrolet-Volkswagen exchange rate? (What percentage of a Chevrolet will a Volkswagen purchase and how many Volkswagens will a Chevrolet purchase?) Who would gain from a revaluation of the mark? Who would lose?

   (*f*) What might the elasticities of demand for internationally traded goods have to do with your answer to the last question?

16. The governments of Lower Slobbovia and Upper Elysium each ran $5-billion budget deficits last year, which they financed by selling bonds to their central banks. Imagine that you are the IMF representative assigned to deal with each country and that they appeal to you for a loan to help them with balance-of-payments difficulties they're beginning to encounter. Construct some plausible dialogues that might ensue.

17. Every Federal Reserve note shows the name of the Federal Reserve Bank that issued it. Check the notes in the possession of members of the class to see where they were issued.

   (*a*) How did notes from outside the Federal Reserve district in which you live come into the possession of people in the class?

   (*b*) What would occur if the Federal Reserve Bank of Boston drastically curtailed its issue of Federal Reserve notes and the Bank of San Francisco substantially increased its issue while all other Reserve Banks maintained their present policies? How would you expect this to affect the distribution of Federal Reserve notes by the bank of issue? How do you think this policy would change the pattern of notes held by students in your class after a period of one year? (The little map which follows may help you make reasonable guesses.)

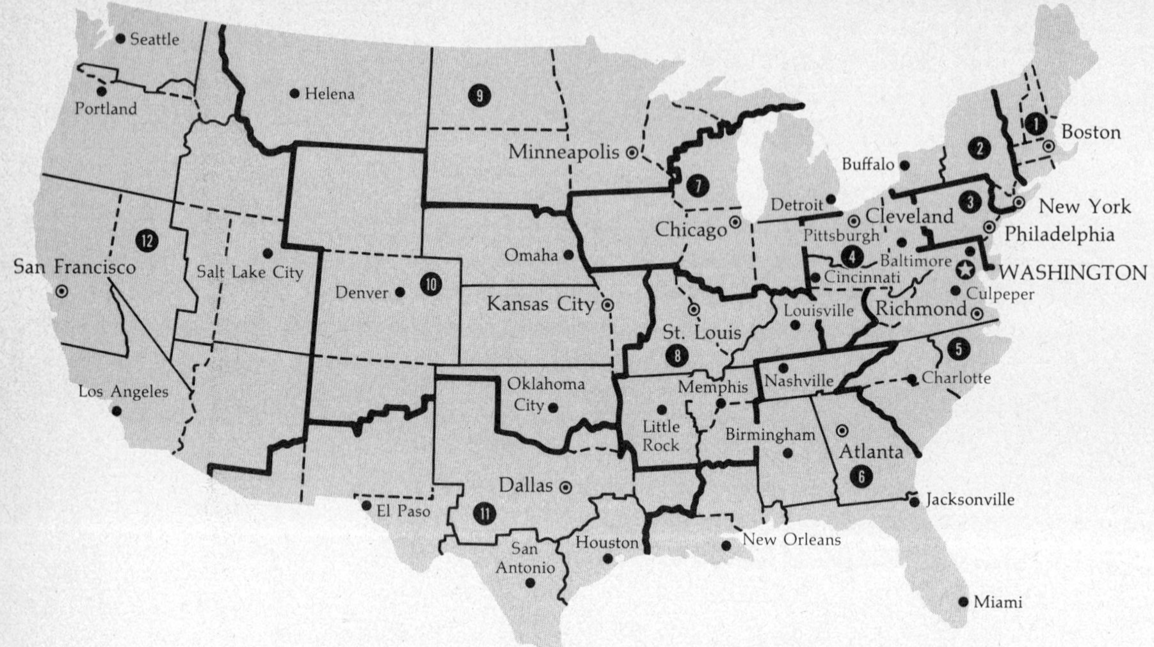

(*c*) What would occur if the monetary authorities in the United States sharply increased the rate of money production while monetary authorities in Germany sharply decreased the rate of money production? Would you expect the same consequences as in part *b* of this question? Why or why not?

(*d*) The data below show the compounded annual rates of change in the money supply of ten industrialized countries on which the Federal Reserve Bank of St. Louis publishes a quarterly scorecard.

	% change, 1st quarter 1970 to 4th quarter 1972	% change, 4th quarter 1972 to 4th quarter 1974
Belgium	10.9%	9.6%
Canada	12.5	9.3
France	12.2	11.0
Germany	12.2	5.7
Italy	21.8	18.2*
Japan	24.6	14.4
Netherlands	16.2	4.8
Switzerland	12.8	−0.9
United Kingdom	14.2	5.2*
United States	6.9	5.8

(*through 3d quarter 1974)

Those data certainly do not provide a definitive answer to part *c* of this question. But they do provide a license to speculate. What do they suggest to you?

(*e*) If U.S. monetary authorities create new money at a faster rate than Americans want to add to their money holdings, by what processes might some of that money flow to other countries? How might we manage to make use of money created in other countries if U.S. monetary authorities increased the domestic supply less rapidly than the demand was growing?

16

FISCAL AND MONETARY POLICY
The management of aggregate demand

Beginning students of economics sometimes get the impression that fluctuations in the aggregate level of economic activity could be easily controlled if we simply made up our minds to do so. Unemployment and inflation both *seem* to be consequences of inappropriate levels of aggregate demand. Since the government can change the level of aggregate demand by means of fiscal or monetary policy, it would appear that government has the power to stop inflation and reduce unemployment. Some therefore conclude that the failure to control aggregate fluctuations is evidence of the stupidity or wickedness of politicians or of the political influence wielded by reactionary special-interest groups.

THE GENIE CONCEPTION OF GOVERNMENT

"If current demand is inadequate or excessive, let the government use its powers to alter aggregate demand and bring it to the appropriate level." It sounds so simple and sensible. But it isn't necessarily sensible, because it isn't simple at all. Who knows the current level of aggregate demand, the appropriate level, and the actions that will move aggregate demand from the wrong to the right level? Who knows all the unintended side effects of such actions, and how to prevent the undesirable and bring about all the desired side effects? Who knows the length of the time lags between a fiscal or monetary policy action and its impact on spending, prices, output, and employment? And what good will it do to know if one lacks the power to compel action? In a democracy power is shared by many people with different perspectives and ideals and conflicting interests. Among these human beings who are neither omniscient, omnipotent, nor wholly impartial we must regrettably include Federal Reserve officials, members of the House and Senate, officers of the federal administration up to and including the chief executive, and even the professional economists who serve on their research staffs, function as their council of advisers, or offer outside criticism.

Solutions by Assumption

A strange thing often happens when social scientists try to construct policy proposals. They suggest a solution to problems in their area of competence and assume that problems in other areas either don't exist or can be resolved with no difficulty. A psychologist, for example, may look at the growing incidence of "mental illness," attribute it to the way children are reared in our society, and recommend new socialization patterns as the solution. But a sociologist disturbed by some of the consequences of the ways Americans rear their children will attribute our patterns of socialization to psychological problems and urge us to adjust our attitudes. The psychologist ignores the problems of social interaction and the sociologist ignores the problems of motivation and character structure.

Economic reformers make this mistake when they assume that government is a *deus ex machina:* that it need only be invoked and instructed and, like Aladdin's marvelous genie, it will faithfully do as it is told. They are assuming in such cases that the problem the political scientist wrestles with —getting governments to behave efficiently and equitably—has already been solved. This Genie Conception of government enables economists to get around the difficulties arising from the fact that political institutions are controlled by people. And that doesn't mean The People—another dangerous abstraction—but people like us, who are often ignorant and shortsighted and sometimes even guilty of defining the public interest in suspiciously self-serving ways.

No economist would construct policy proposals on the assumptions that producers and sellers put the public interest ahead of their own interests, have all the information they want, and cannot be prevented by their suppliers, employers, or customers from doing whatever they deem best. To do that would be to ignore the very questions economists try to answer. Noneconomists frequently argue today that pressing social problems like pollution should be handled through the acceptance by business firms of their "social responsibilities." It's undoubtedly true that a lot of problems would diminish or disappear if business executives always acted in the public interest. But will they *want to,* will they *know how to,* and will they *be able to?* Economists realize that to assume an affirmative answer in each case is to ignore the problems of the economic order. We must be careful not to adopt in the political sphere a conception of human interests and capabilities that we would recognize as absurd if adopted in the economic sphere. In short, we must be on our guard throughout this chapter against the Genie Conception of government.

FISCAL AND MONETARY POLICY IN USE

The preceding chapters have introduced you to two tools for the management of aggregate demand: fiscal policy and monetary policy. How much difference does it make which one is chosen? Is one more effective than the other? Do they have different side effects that make one a more appropriate tool than the other? Or does it depend on the circumstances? Is there a proper mix of the two or different mixes appropriate for different circumstances? While there is a considerable consensus among economists today on these questions, major areas of disagreement still remain. More importantly, perhaps, the debate between advocates of fiscal policy and advocates of monetary policy has been joined by those who believe that either policy is likely to be too much and by a growing number who find both together inadequate. The making of stabilization policy is still far from a settled science.

The Rise of Eclecticism

It has only been within the last decade that monetary policy has achieved anything like equal status with fiscal policy in the thinking of economists. The impotence of monetary policy as a means of restoring prosperity seemed to many to have been adequately demonstrated in the Great Depression when the Fed relaxed the controls over money creation but could not stir a revival of bank lending and private spending. The power of fiscal policy had seemingly been just as clearly demonstrated by the "fiscal experiment" of 1940–44. When the urgencies of war finally overcame concern for a balanced budget and the federal government began spending profusely, private spending also revived. For reasons that are not altogether clear, private consumption and investment were able to take up the slack when government expenditures fell sharply after the war.

Monetary policy inched its way back into esteem through a concurrence of events that we've already mentioned. One was the unexpected mildness of recessions in the postwar period and the persistence of inflation. Inflation was a problem against which monetary policy was *not* considered powerless and on which the monetary managers were able to practice their stabilization skills. Related to this was increasing recognition of the possibility that monetary policy, though perhaps impotent at the depth of a severe depression, might well be effective as an expansionary tool in mild recessions. Another reason for the revival of monetary policy was the research done during this period by economists convinced that changes in the money supply had a more predictable impact on total spending than the advocates of fiscal policy believed.

Today most economists prefer to think of themselves as eclectics, willing to use fiscal *or* monetary policy rather than debate their respective merits. This may be evidence of an admirable open-mindedness. It may also be simple prudence in the face of the difficulties encountered when one tries to measure the effects of either policy. These difficulties are compounded by the fact that fiscal policies will usually have monetary repercussions whether or not they're intended. A fan of fiscal policy can then credit his preferred tools, while the fan of monetary policy attributes the effects to the changes that the fiscal action induced in monetary conditions.

Monetary Responses to Fiscal Policies

Why does fiscal policy inevitably have an impact on the monetary sector? Consider the case of a government decision to provide a fiscal stimulus by cutting taxes while increasing expenditures. The Treasury must obtain money in order to spend. There are basically two ways to get it. The Treasury can either have new money created, or it can borrow from the stock of already existing money. Whichever course is chosen, the fiscal actions will have monetary effects. Let's try to sort out the possibilities.

The Treasury does not create new money on its own. As we saw in chapters 9 and 10, the creation of additional money comes about through credit expansion by commercial banks and the Fed. We can therefore set the problem up in terms of the three sources from which the Treasury may borrow: the Fed, commercial banks, or the nonbank public.

Suppose the Treasury borrows from the Fed in order to secure the funds to finance expenditures not covered by taxes. The Fed in effect gives the Treasury additional deposits in exchange for government securities. When the Treasury then spends these deposits, they flow into the bank accounts or currency holdings of defense contractors, welfare recipients, military personnel, or whoever is on the receiving end of the expenditures. The money supply consequently increases.

These new deposits are also new reserves for the commercial banking system. Banks will therefore find their lending power increased. If they can locate eligible borrowers, the commercial banks will, by expanding their loans, create a further addition to the money supply.

It follows that the money supply could increase by the entire amount of the deficit, even though the Fed directly financed only a portion of the deficit. A $50-billion deficit, for example, could be handled through some combination like a Fed purchase of $15 billion in new government securities and commercial bank purchases of $35 billion. The Fed purchase, by supplying new reserves to the banking system, enables the commercial banks to acquire additional government securities by creating new demand deposits.

Now suppose that the Fed wants to prevent the growth in the money supply that would result from increased Treasury borrowing. Insofar as the Fed is successful, the Treasury will be forced to compete with other borrowers for use of the existing money stock. Unless there are idle funds around, interest rates will consequently rise until the higher cost of borrowing squeezes out the excess demand. The net effect, then, will be an expansion of government spending and a compensating reduction of private spending. But this defeats the original purpose of the government's policy; an increase in government spending that is exactly matched by a decrease in private spending provides no stimulus to *total* expenditures.

There's one other possibility. Suppose the public is holding large money balances because consumers and investors are fearful of the future. They might be persuaded to exchange those balances for government securities. That would give the Treasury the money it wants without an increase in the measured money stock. More spending would then occur with no increase in M because the public had been persuaded to exchange money for government bonds and the government then spent the money. In effect,

V would have increased. But is any of this very likely except in a period of deep depression? Perhaps in the 1930s public confidence was so low that deficit spending could tap large idle money balances. But that doesn't seem to describe the situation at any time in the past three decades.

The conclusion is a simple one. Deficit spending by the government affects the monetary sector. It results in some combination of an enlarged money stock and higher interest rates. If the Fed tries to prevent public expenditures from crowding out private expenditures by making more credit available when the Treasury is borrowing, it causes a growth in the money supply. But if the Fed tries to prevent an increase in the money supply, it will force private borrowers to bid against the Treasury for the limited supply of credit. Fiscal policy is inseparable from monetary policy.

Is monetary policy equally inseparable from fiscal policy? The link is not as close in the other direction. Government spending uses money but more money can be created and spent independently of any changes in the government budget. It doesn't follow, however, that fiscal policy cannot be a useful aid to monetary policy. Remember that the Fed does not directly control the size of the money stock. It can increase the available reserves of the banking system, but it cannot force anyone to borrow and thereby convert free reserves into money. Government borrowing and expenditure is one way to increase the money supply. And in a period of low confidence, when consumers and investors don't want to borrow, fiscal policy might be the only practical way to make monetary policy effective.

All of this has one very important implication. The sometimes vehement debate in recent years over the respective roles of fiscal and monetary policy in causing inflation was largely a debate over a non-issue. The federal government ran very large deficits in the 1968, 1971, 1972, and 1973 fiscal years, spending about $85 billion altogether in these four years beyond what it collected in taxes. To ask whether this would have caused inflation if the Fed had not simultaneously allowed a rapid expansion in the money supply is a pointless question. An expansion of the money supply was necessary if the mounting federal expenditures were not to crowd out private spending.

Fiscal Policy: Scalpel or Axe?

It is more useful to ask why the federal government ran such large deficits. And the answer isn't hard to find. The government was committed to military and domestic programs that entailed an expansion of budget outlays beyond the rate at which Congress was willing to raise taxes. But it's a bit more complicated than this suggests. Tax rates were in fact increased in 1968 as a result of which federal government budget receipts rose 30% from 1967 to 1969. Expenditures increased by only 15% over this period, and the federal budget, measured through the income and product accounts, showed an $8 billion surplus in 1969. But something unexpected happened. The percentage of disposable income that consumers saved fell from 7.4% in 1967 to only 6% in 1969. Consumers were apparently unwilling to reduce their expenditures in the face of what they saw as a temporary increase in taxes. They cut their saving instead, so aggregate private demand did not fall as much as Congress had anticipated. Investment spending also failed to slow down. It increased by 8% in 1968 and 10% in 1969. (From 1966 to 1967 it had *declined* by 4%, and it fell by 2% from 1969 to 1970). In short, we cannot simply blame Congress and the president for a cowardly refusal to raise taxes to match mounting expenditures. Private spending didn't respond as sensitively to tax rate changes as many had expected.

In defending our political leaders against the charge of fiscal irresponsibility, we have also called attention to a potential weakness in fiscal policy as a tool for aggregate demand management. In the income-expenditures model of chapter 12, consumption expenditures were treated as a stable function of after-tax income. We could also have made investment depend on tax rates, because it undoubtedly does; but we took the simpler route and assumed that changes in taxes had no effect on investment expenditures. The crucial question, however, is whether investment spending is a stable and predictable function of tax rates. The evidence strongly suggests that we do not know how to predict the short term effect of changes in taxes on private spending. A large enough increase in taxes will certainly reduce private spending, and a sufficiently large tax reduction is bound to increase it. But we'll have to have a far more precise knowledge than that if we hope to use tax changes as a way of preventing undesired movements in aggregate demand.

The Importance Once Again of Uncertainty

Perhaps we must go back to Keynes and his reminder that economic decisions are made over time and in the presence of uncertainty. Substantial unemployment could arise and persist, Keynes argued, because changed conditions do not immediately create a new equilibrium. Consumer and producer responses to one another are hesitant, groping, and often erroneous. They don't cease to be hesitant, groping, and erroneous simply because the government is trying to control aggregate demand. The unpredictability of the government's actions may even increase the frequency and severity of errors in the private sector.

One of the small group of people who discussed the ideas of the *General Theory* prior to their publication, the distinguished British economist Joan Robinson, has protested vigorously in recent years against the tendency to use Keynesian notions and to forget the insight on which they were based. The essence of Keynes's problem, she has pointed out, was uncertainty.

"The main point of the *General Theory* was to break out of the cocoon of equilibrium and consider the nature of life lived in time—the difference between yesterday and tomorrow. Here and now, the past is irrevocable and the future is unknown." But this was apparently "too great a shock," she added sarcastically, and "orthodoxy managed to wind it up in a cocoon again."[1] It would certainly be a very unKeynesian use of Keynes to substitute our equilibrium models for reality and assume that the effects of fiscal policy *or* monetary policy can be predicted with precision.

Let's take a systematic look at the information problems any successful program of aggregate demand management must solve. Policy making today can take advantage of the vast strides we have made in recent years in the accumulation of statistical data on the economy's performance. But information of this sort will always be approximate. It just isn't possible to summarize in both an accurate and a useful way a diverse and multi-faceted economic system the size of ours. When we say, then, that "unemployment has risen from 5.2% to 5.4%," we mean that the summary indicator constructed by the Bureau of Labor Statistics from sample data shows a rise *last month* in measured unemployment. By itself that indicator does not tell us who the unemployed are, why they've become unemployed, what the net costs to them of unemployment are, where unemployment is rising and where it's declining, how many people have left the labor force as a result of discouragement, how many have entered to compensate for family income lost through another person's unemployment, or the distribution of unemployment by duration. Additional information is available on each of these questions. But where is the line between too little information to tell us what's happening and too much information for us to see what's going on?[2] New techniques for gathering and processing information can help, but they aren't the complete answer. The first rule for computer-assisted analysts is still the GIGO principle: Garbage In, Garbage Out.

Moreover, all the information available will be dated. It will summarize the situation in the past. That past will be a more-or-less recent past depending upon the speed with which accurate data can be assembled. It's quite fast for data on the monetary system because of legal requirements for regular and accurate reporting by banks, but it is much slower and more inaccurate for data on gross national product or international trade. But even very recent and reliable data aren't enough. Since any policy

---

1. The quotations are from a lecture delivered by Joan Robinson before the American Economic Association and printed in the *American Economic Review,* May 1972, pp. 1–10.

2. Executives in large organizations are dependent upon subordinates to feed them adequate information. It isn't as often recognized, however, that an executive's power to make effective decisions also depends upon the willingness and ability of subordinates to *screen out* less useful data.

actions will impinge on future situations, the challenge is to obtain estimates on future data by extrapolating from the past. And this requires that theorizing accompany the data. If unemployment has gone up by two-tenths of one per cent in each of the last three months, shall we choose a policy on the assumption that it's bound to continue? Or shall we assume that what goes up must come down? Either assumption would be naive; theorizing of considerable sophistication is required to extrapolate economic data effectively.

Predicting the Consequences of Policy Actions

What we really want to know, however, is what will happen *if various policy actions are taken.* What will be the direct and indirect effects of the actions, and how long will they take to make themselves felt? How long does it take for a purchase of government securities by the Fed to result in an increased demand for consumption and investment goods? How much of the impact will come almost at once, perhaps as a reaction to the mere news of an easier monetary policy? How will the rest of the impact be distributed over time? Fiscal actions raise the same questions. The actual multiplier effect of a change in government expenditures or taxes can't be determined by arithmetic manipulations of various marginal propensities, because we don't really know the future values of those propensities. Public attitudes toward tax and expenditure changes may bring about a shift in spending or saving plans and the size of the relevant multiplier when the policy action is announced. And the distribution of the multiplier effects over time is a crucial piece of information if stabilization policy is not to become destabilization policy.

Knowledge about the time lags between monetary or fiscal actions and their effects has been extremely hard to obtain. There is no way to deduce the distribution of lags from pure theory; we have to rely on empirical measurements. But how are we going to sort out the effects of a particular fiscal or monetary stimulus from the effects of all the other forces at work in the economy? Perhaps we could sort them out if we could run a dozen experiments over the course of a quarter century, or divide the economy at the Mississippi River, set up a blockade to keep the effects from leaking back and forth, and then give the injection to the West while using the East as the control group. Even these heroic measures would yield unreliable knowledge, however, because the lags might well be growing longer or shorter over the years. It's quite possible that in trying to measure the time lag between a fiscal or monetary action and its effects we're trying to measure the length of something that has no standard length. At best it's like trying to measure the length of an earthworm. Unless you kill it, how do you measure the length of a wiggling worm that makes itself longer and shorter in response to your measurement efforts?

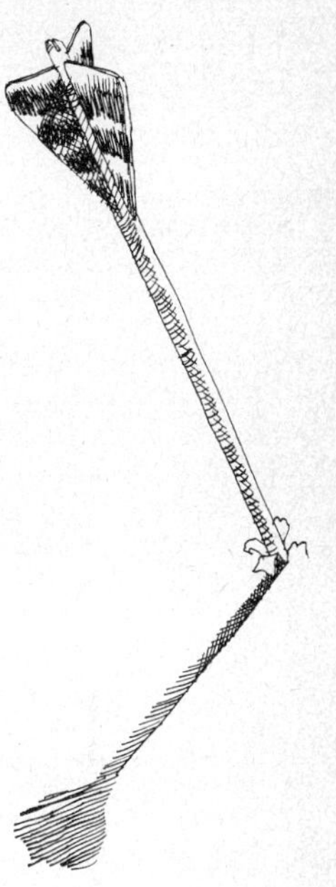

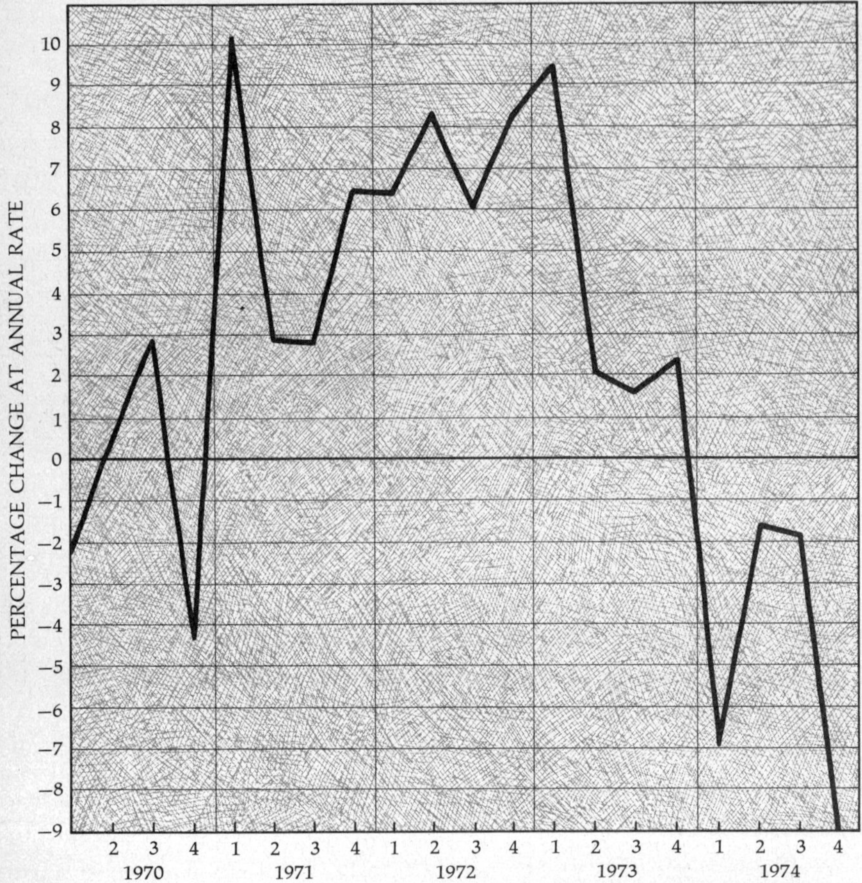

Figure 16A Quarterly changes in real gross national product

How much difference does all this make? Try your hand with figure 16A to see how much difference it *might* make. The graph shows percentage changes (at an annual rate) from quarter to quarter in real gross national product from the first quarter of 1970 to the final quarter of 1974. The average annual growth rate for real GNP over the past twenty years has been close to 4%, so you may use 4% as a benchmark.

If you had been National Stabilization Czar in the third quarter of 1970, would you have wanted to step on the fiscal-monetary brake, press on the accelerator, or just coast? (Remember that you can't see ahead!) Would you have changed your mind when the fourth quarter data came in? How would you have felt about your fourth quarter stabilization actions when you finally saw the data for the first quarter of 1971?

Or look at the record of real GNP from the third quarter of 1971 through the first quarter of 1973. Would you have been worrying at the start of 1973 about an unsustainable boom and the danger of future inflation? Especially if you also saw that the implicit price deflator had risen 5% on an annual basis since the last quarter of 1972? If you came to the reasonable conclusion that some restraint was in order at this time and stepped on the fiscal-monetary brake, you might have been encouraging contraction in a period when private spending was undergoing its own contraction. And if there is a 15 month time lag before the principal effects of fiscal-monetary actions are absorbed, you might have guaranteed a sharp and prolonged recession.

Fiscal or Monetary Policy

In order to focus on some of the problems that must be faced in any attempt at demand management, we have been looking at fiscal and monetary policy as if they were simply alternative ways of accomplishing the same ends. But fiscal and monetary policy are by no means perfect substitutes, and many economists doubt that they are really close substitutes at all. The differences, real or alleged, have to do with direct effects, indirect or side effects, and political constraints.

Direct Effects

We have already encountered the argument that monetary policy is of little use in combating a recession. That argument is less widely held today than it once was. It stays around largely as a result of the belief that in a deep and prolonged depression an expansion of bank reserves would probably not increase private spending significantly. Fiscal policy would have to be employed under those circumstances to turn the reserves into money and get the money into circulation. The effectiveness of monetary policy in *holding down* aggregate demand during a period of inflation is generally accepted, however.

What about the direct effects of fiscal policy? Here there is considerable disagreement among economists. The argument has been advanced in recent years that the level of real income and output is not significantly affected by increases in government expenditure. This represents a dramatic dissent from what was generally accepted only ten years ago and it is even now a minority position. Those who argue this position maintain that if the government increases expenditures relative to taxes without simultaneously increasing the money supply, the primary effect will be to crowd out private spending. The government will have to reduce the money holdings of the public in order to obtain the funds for its expenditures, and the public will respond by reducing expenditures relative to income in an effort to restore its money balances.

Another way of looking at the matter is to note that when the government tries to increase expenditures relative to tax receipts, it will be increasing the demand for a fixed supply of loanable funds. This will raise interest rates, and less private spending will occur when interest rates rise.

Two arguments may be weaker than one, however. If interest rates rise in response to increased government borrowing, the quantity of money the public wants to hold will decrease. Recall from chapter 13 that the demand for money balances is a negative function of the interest rate, because the interest rate is part of the opportunity cost of holding money. Some net increase in total spending should probably be expected, then, when the government borrows from the nonbank public in order to spend.

But this probably doesn't get at the important issues. The advocates of fiscal policy can point out that deficit spending is called for at times when the reluctance of the public to borrow and spend is keeping the money supply too low. It is therefore unrealistic to analyze the effects of fiscal policy on the assumption that no increase occurs in the stock of money. Those who question the effectiveness of fiscal policy, on the other hand, may be making an equally important but quite different point. Deficit spending in recent years has not in fact been financed to any significant extent out of bank reserves that were legally available for money creation but could not actually be loaned because the private demand for credit had collapsed. And when there are no excess bank reserves for the Treasury to tap, then an increase in government expenditure (relative to taxation) will either crowd out private spending *or* cause an inflationary increase in the money supply. Total money demand may rise in such a case, but without a corresponding increase in real output. That results in inflation.

If this is an accurate representation of the argument, the competing claims are compatible. One side is pointing to the effectiveness of fiscal policy in a major recession; the opposite side is warning against the inflationary potential of deficit spending at all other times.

Indirect Effects

What about the indirect effects of fiscal and monetary policy? Assume that either one is capable of providing a sedative or a stimulus to economic activity when sedative or stimulus is the appropriate medicine. Are there side effects that might incline us to choose one over the other?

A lot of attention has been directed to the effect of monetary policy on interest rates and to the consequences of interest rate changes. We must be careful about the assertions we make here, for it is not simply true that easier money means lower interest rates and tighter money means higher rates. The immediate effects and the later effects of monetary policy on interest rates, especially if we're looking at nominal rates, tend to be in opposite directions. But it's nonetheless true that an active monetary policy can cause interest rates to change. And that can have unsettling and inequitable effects.

Discriminatory Effects of Monetary Policy

Some sectors of the economy are unusually sensitive to interest rate changes. State and local government capital projects may have to be halted when interest rates rise. But the standard example is residential construction. Fluctuating interest rates can cause alternating boom and recession in the construction industry and impose large costs on the people who work in that industry.

Another way in which monetary policy may create inequities is through its effects on bond prices. A rise in interest rates causes a fall in the market price of bonds. Suppose that a university has invested its September tuition receipts in government bonds and intends to sell the bonds as it requires cash to finance expenditures. It would sustain a loss if Fed policy caused short term rates to rise sharply just before the university had to sell its securities to obtain cash.

Some have also argued that tight money discriminates against small business firms because larger firms get preferred treatment from banks when credit is tight, can more easily raise money from nonbank sources, and are able to generate funds internally.

A great deal of concern was expressed in the 1960s about the effects of interest rates on the U.S. balance of payments. The foreign demand for dollars depends in part on the interest rate foreigners can obtain by holding dollars, relative to what they can obtain from holding other currencies. Higher interest rates in the United States therefore attract an additional supply of foreign exchange (or, what comes to the same thing, they maintain the foreign demand for dollars). The Fed was consequently under pressure in the 1960s to keep interest rates high as a way of "protecting the balance of payments." This restricted the Fed's ability to pursue other objectives through monetary policy. The movement to floating exchange rates described in the last chapter has enabled the Fed to pay less attention to the international repercussions of its actions.

Another argument asserts that economic growth depends in the long run on the rate of investment and that the rate of investment varies inversely with the average level of interest rates. Suppose that the government uses monetary policy as the preferred instrument for contracting aggregate demand and fiscal policy when it wants to provide a stimulus to output and employment. A side effect would supposedly be higher average interest rates, less investment, smaller increases in the capital stock, and less growth in the productive potential of the economy.

Effects of Government Spending

The argument that by using fiscal policy to stimulate spending and monetary policy to restrain spending we are reducing the rate of investment rests, however, upon the questionable assumption that the government is not purchasing capital goods when it spends. A sizable percentage of total government spending does go, however, toward the purchase of capital. Schools, dams, highways, and public buildings of many kinds are all capital. By allowing the government to control a larger portion of total spending, we may in fact be *increasing* the investment-to-consumption ratio and thus increasing the rate at which the nation's productive potential expands. Since government investment decisions are not based on the same criteria as private investment decisions, we have no good way to decide whether the rate at which future output expands is increased or decreased by more government spending and less private spending. How do we compare the additional services produced by an expanded Smithsonian Institution with the services that would have been produced if the funds had gone instead to residential construction? And who will be courageous enough to divide military expenditures into consumption and investment and to estimate what part of the latter is profitable rather than wasteful investment?

Some people think our inability to answer questions like these is in itself a strong argument against growth of the government sector. And one side effect of fiscal policy is certainly its tendency to promote such growth. Fiscal policy is in theory a contractionary or expansionary tool. In practice, however, it is primarily a weapon for promoting expansion, because it's so much easier politically to reduce taxes and raise expenditures than to reverse the procedure. A society committed to the use of fiscal policy will consequently tend to find itself steadily enlarging the government sector of the economy.

Has that been happening in recent years? Table 16A provides some data on the relative size of the government sector. The first column in table 16A shows *total government* purchases of commodities and services as a percentage of gross national product. The second column shows *federal* government purchases as a percentage of GNP. The third column takes account of the increasing importance of transfer payments by presenting total government *receipts* as a percentage of GNP.

Table 16A GOVERNMENT ACTIVITIES
AS A PERCENTAGE OF GNP

Year	Total government purchases	Federal government purchases	Total government receipts
1929	8.2%	1.3%	11.0%
1939	14.7	5.6	17.0
1949	14.7	7.8	21.8
1959	20.0	11.1	26.8
1969	22.6	10.6	31.9

Source: Bureau of Economic Analysis

THE PERILS OF FINE-TUNING

There is something slightly absurd about the belief that the federal government can use its budget as a stabilization tool when almost all observers agree that Congress no longer has effective control over the budget. The spending programs of the federal government are so many and so complex that no one in Congress or the Executive Branch can even begin to evaluate all of them for the purpose of determining annual appropriations. Next year's budget begins, as a result, by taking this year's budget for granted and adding on. Once a program finds a home in the budget, it is almost impossible to evict. Its beneficiaries form a knowledgeable and determined lobby for its continuance and no one on Capitol Hill will have the time, energy, or interest to accumulate the evidence that could justify its removal. What's the use of knocking yourself out just to cut $3 million from the budget when $3 million is only .001% of the total? And why make the effort when the only certain outcome for the legislator who does is the perpetual enmity of those whose appropriations are challenged?

Grand Designs

The emphasis on side effects serves as a useful reminder that "aggregate demand" is a broad abstraction. The social impact of any expansion or contraction on total spending depends upon what is being purchased or not purchased. Government expenditures stimulate the production of particular goods, not goods in general, and any expansion of government spending relative to private spending increases the relative size of the

public sector. Demand can be expanded through fiscal policy without enlarging the public sector if taxes are cut; but this, too, will affect the *composition* of output in a manner dependent upon which taxes are reduced. A tax credit given to businesses for investment in plant and equipment will increase the rate of capital formation more than will a reduction in the personal income tax. One of the practical difficulties confronted by fiscal policy is precisely this need to choose from among competing claimants. Any change in the pattern of taxes or government expenditures will be a matter for political bargaining, because it will inevitably affect the distribution of income. It will also affect future economic development because it alters the ratio of consumption to investment.

Some economists have viewed these side effects as more of an opportunity than a difficulty. Since either fiscal policy or monetary policy is capable of providing as much expansion or contraction in aggregate demand as we're likely to want, they argue that we should choose our mix by first choosing the side effects we prefer. It has been suggested, for example, that if we want rapid economic growth, we could pursue an easy money policy with plenty of credit at low interest rates for potential investors, and counter the inflationary consequences with a high rate of taxation on consumption expenditures. There was a period in the 1960s when the more enthusiastic students of aggregate demand management were cheering a three-cornered dance. The Fed was to keep short term interest rates high to attract foreign bank deposits and protect the balance of payments and to keep long term rates low to encourage investment. Meanwhile recession and inflation would be prevented by deft manipulation of the federal budget.

Scanty Information

The truth is, however, that we don't begin to have the detailed knowledge that such delicate operations would require. How long could investment and consumption expenditures be "twisted" in the manner just described before reduced consumer spending brought a halt to further investment? How would different industries be affected, and with what consequences? Presumably such an approach would reduce output in consumer goods industries and expand it in investment goods industries. How quickly would workers released from automobile assembly lines find jobs producing machine tools? When the policy changed again, would they find their way back? How much would unemployment increase and for how long in response to these policy-initiated changes in the composition of aggregate demand? It's all slightly reminiscent of the tenth grader who just dissected his first crayfish and wants to move right on to heart transplants.

WHAT DO AVERAGES AND AGGREGATES CONCEAL?

The graph below provides a picture of the diversity contained within the movement of economic aggregates. The lines graph selected components of the Federal Reserve Board of Governors' Index of Industrial Production. The average level of production in each industrial category is stated as a percentage of 1967 production levels. The heavy line charts the *total* index of industrial production. (The monthly data given for 1974 are seasonally adjusted.)

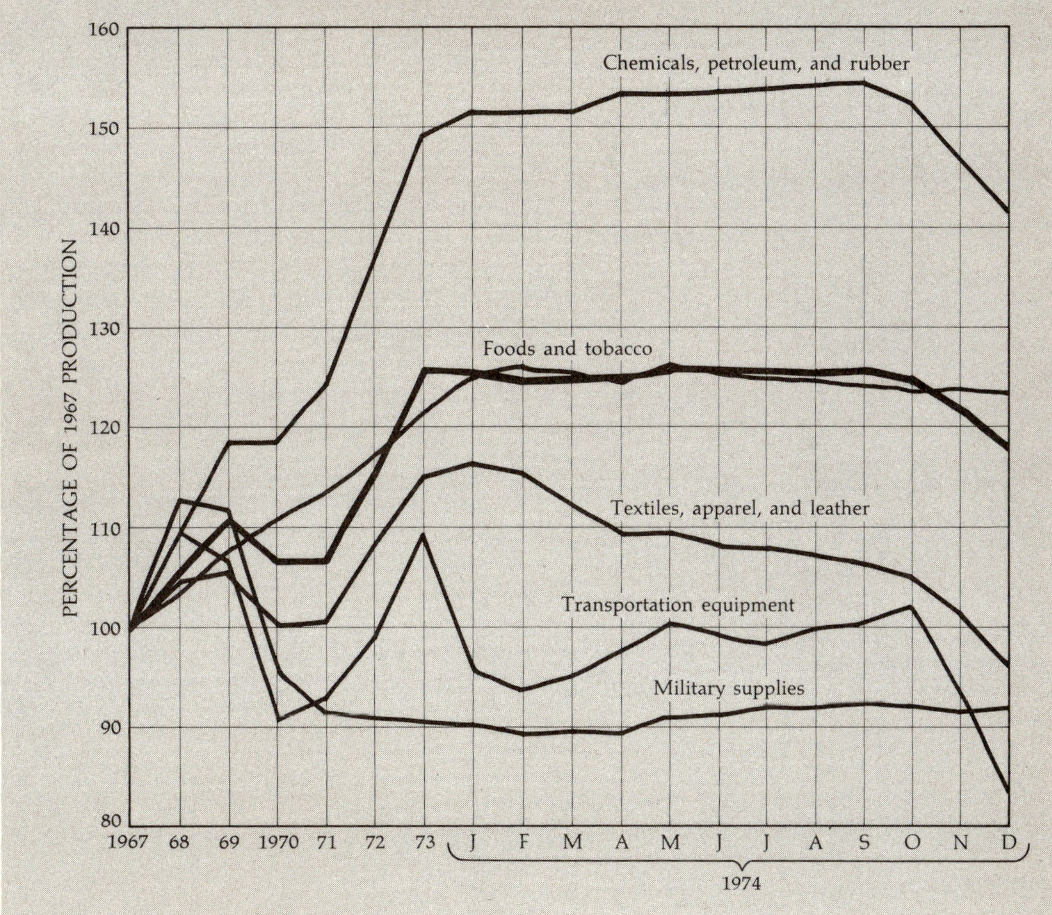

Political Constraints and Problems of Timing

Much of the optimism of the 1960s with regard to the potentialities of demand management stemmed from a failure to give proper weight to political constraints. The Genie Conception of government entered into the recommendations of economists when they assumed that nothing was required to improve policy except further economic research. Once the experts had found the best policy, putting it into effect would be no problem at all.

But fiscal policy in particular is clearly subject to major constraints imposed by the political process. A change in federal government expenditures or taxes requires action by the House of Representatives and the Senate, with committee meetings before and often after, and a presidential signature at the end. That takes *time* and timing is crucial in effective countercyclical policy. The discussions will be complicated and prolonged by the fact that, even if Congress agrees quickly on the desirability of changing expenditures or taxes by a particular amount, it would still have to decide *whose* taxes and *which* expenditures will be changed. Conflicting interests will be involved and alternative theories about the expansionary or contractionary effects of a particular action will enter the debate. Meanwhile some members of Congress will certainly decide that an important tax or expenditure bill provides an opportunity to eliminate the depletion allowance for oil producers, give a bonus to retired people on social security, prop up the housing industry with a special subsidy, or take a slap at multinational corporations—to mention only those concerns that managed to achieve expression in the March 1975 "antirecessionary" tax bill.

The more in a hurry Congress and the president are, the more likely they are to produce fiscal policy actions that no competent and impartial observer will be able to defend. The imperative of haste tends to enhance the power of the less responsible elements who are willing to enforce their demands by threatening to block any action at all. But due deliberation, the careful assessment of alternatives, and the weighing of probable short- and long-term outcomes may require so much time that the moment for action passes before any action is taken. The 1974–75 recession probably began late in 1973. Congress passed an antirecessionary tax cut at the end of March in 1975, and it was even at that late date a tax bill filled with evidence of undue haste. Only six months prior to the tax cut, the word from the White House was still WIN (Whip *Inflation* Now). Could we find better evidence of the lag between the appearance and the recognition of a problem?

Advocates of stabilization through fiscal policy who are not mesmerized by the Genie Conception of government have long been aware of these difficulties. They know that the protracted discussions that precede any

Congressional action on taxes and expenditures can easily make fiscal policy unworkable: action may not be possible until the time for it has passed. They have consequently looked around for ways to speed up the process. One proposal recommended by some economists and urged by President Kennedy was that Congress authorize unilateral action by the president. Appropriations for particular projects could be approved by Congress, put on the shelf, and taken off whenever the president and his advisers decided that the stimulus of increased government expenditures was called for. Congress could also authorize the president to increase or decrease tax rates within narrow limits when aggregate demand seemed excessive or inadequate.

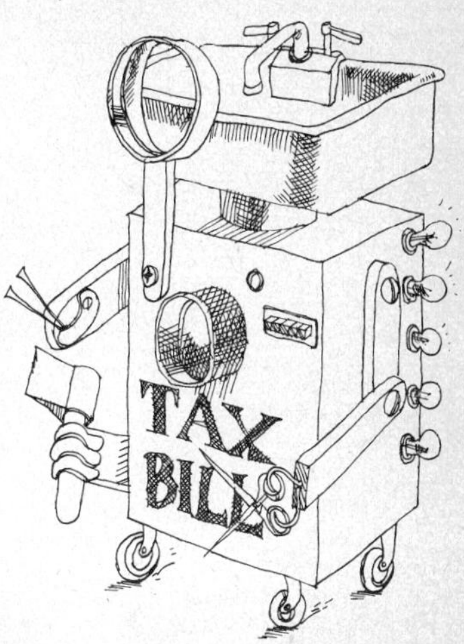

This proposal doesn't exactly assume a genie; it's more like trying to create one. If you're wondering why Congress never acted on such a "sensible" recommendation, think for a moment about the political power that a president would command if he could unilaterally determine the timing of tax decreases and the placement of expenditure projects. Do you recall the furor that erupted in the early 1970s when a president tried to "impound" appropriations on the grounds that they would add to the deficit and increase the rate of inflation? We are not likely soon to sanction such actions by even the most trusted of leaders. And that means discretionary fiscal policy will continue to be a largely unusable weapon against fluctuations in total spending.

Democratic Monetary Policy?

If fiscal policy is subject to such stringent political constraints and if monetary policy is an alternate way to bring about changes in aggregate demand, should the government rely on monetary policy to promote stabilization? The question raises important issues in political philosophy. Isn't it a virtue of fiscal policy in a democratic society that it requires political consent and cannot be practiced, as monetary policy can, by a small group of experts insulated from the pressures of public opinion? On the other hand, might it not be a good thing to insulate aggregate demand management from irrelevant and uninformed pressures? Still, who is to say which pressures are irrelevant? And what are the implications for democracy of policies that take advantage of public ignorance? Wouldn't it be better in the long run to educate the public than to run policies behind the back of Congress?

You can't expect educators to take a stand against education and we won't. But the educational task, difficult enough already, will be even more difficult if the experts themselves don't know exactly *how* fiscal policy and monetary policy work, singly as well as jointly, to affect aggregate demand.

Is It Better to Have Tried and Failed?

It has become increasingly obvious in recent years that we do not have the knowledge that would be required to steer the economy on a steady course of full employment and price stability. But are we better off than we would have been if we hadn't tried? Many economists now agree that *fine-tuning,* as it is called, has been oversold, that we have been much too optimistic about our ability to reduce aggregate fluctuations through demand management. A smaller number go farther and argue that the attempt to stabilize has actually increased both unemployment and inflation.

How could this occur? The key element in their argument is the relation between unemployment and uncertainty. Unemployment occurs largely because mistakes have been made that must subsequently be acknowledged and corrected. Anything that increases uncertainty for economic decision makers increases the probability of mistakes and hence the frequency with which resources must be reallocated. And that will increase the average level of unemployment. The question then becomes: Have the behavior of the federal budget and the behavior of the money supply in recent years made the future more predictable? Or have they increased the uncertainties confronting economic decision makers?

Stabilizing Factors

We cannot jump from the fact that there have been no major recessions since the 1930s to the conclusion that the net effect of government stabilization efforts was greater stability. Other factors have been at work. We earlier discussed the importance of the Federal Deposit Insurance Corporation in eliminating the phenomenon of bank runs and the supporting role of the Fed as the guarantor of short-run liquidity to the banking system. Between them they have eliminated the panics that once swept regularly through the financial sector; and with financial panics a thing of the past, the economy has not again had to go through anything even remotely approaching the 25% contraction in the money supply experienced between 1929 and 1933.

Another stabilizing factor seems to have been the tendency for personal consumption expenditures since World War II to maintain their own steady rate of increase despite fluctuations in GNP. From 1948 to the recession year of 1949, for example, real GNP remained nearly constant, but personal consumption expenditures increased 2.7%. From 1953 to 1954, while GNP was falling 1.4%, consumption was rising 2%. From 1957 to 1958, GNP fell 1.1%, but consumption increased .7%. Some of this can be credited to the partial insulation of disposable personal income from fluctuations in GNP. In the three years cited above, disposable personal income (in real terms once more) increased more rapidly than GNP, rising

.4%, 1%, and .9%. One insulator is our system of progressive taxes on personal and corporate income, which automatically reduces tax receipts as GNP falls and reduces those receipts by more than the percentage fall in GNP. Another insulator is the fact that government transfer payments rise when GNP falls and fall when it rises. We spoke of these earlier as automatic fiscal stabilizers. The point here is that they operated even in the absence of efforts to fine-tune the economy, and might well have been responsible for the mildness of postwar recessions.

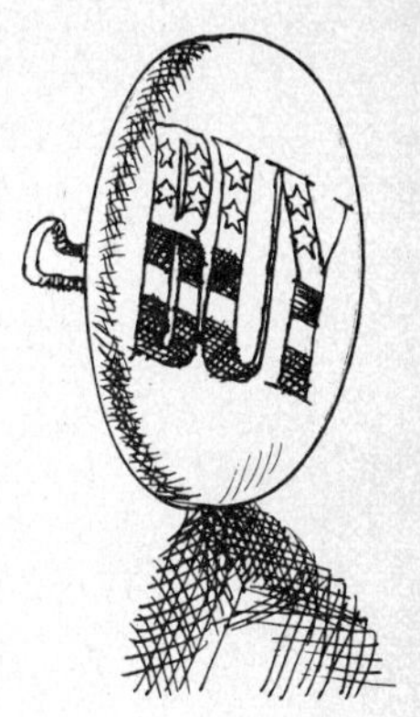

Destabilizing Factors

If personal consumption expenditures have been a steady and stabilizing component of aggregate demand, investment expenditures have not. You can go back to table 8A or, even better, to the graph on page 270, to see just how unstable private investment spending has been. But how much of this was due to changes originating in the government sector? Changing tax regulations, especially those affecting investment, shifts in the degree of monetary ease or tightness, and huge swings in the government budget from deficit to surplus and back to deficit *may* have been compensatory forces. But they may also have caused some of the fluctuations in investment. We've already mentioned the way in which money market conditions, affected by fiscal and monetary actions, tend to destabilize the housing industry. What about the policy of shifting between tax surcharges to dampen inflation and special tax credits for investment spending to promote employment? Since there is usually considerable discretion about the timing of investment expenditures, government policy reversals may themselves be largely responsible for the large fluctuations in private investment from year to year.

But it's most important that we probe beneath the surface of such aggregates as consumption, investment, and government purchases. For the changing composition as well as the changing level of these totals affects the unemployment rate. A very large part of the 1974 unemployment was the consequence of changes in the demand for automobiles. And a rise in consumer spending is not certain to return that demand to earlier levels. There is something disturbing about a government that officially encourages us to burn less gasoline (to conserve energy) and to buy more cars (to restore prosperity) and simultaneously claims to be responsible for *stabilizing* employment. Can we really depend on the stabilization skills of an agent so adept at keeping its right hand from finding out what its left hand is doing?

Before asking what the government might do to *reduce* unemployment in a particular industry, we might want to ask whether the government has done anything to *raise* unemployment. The supply of people with doctoral degrees in the sciences is today greater than the number of available jobs in large part because the government began subsidizing the education of scientists fifteen years ago and continued to do so even after surpluses had started to appear. When the government makes a decision to send men to the moon, to produce a particular military plane, to restrict oil imports, to subsidize a giant railroad system, to enforce high standards of job safety in industry, to become self-sufficient in energy by 1980, to encourage home ownership with government subsidized loans, to enlarge steel-making capacity by granting special tax refunds for investment—all examples are actual decisions the federal government has made—it signals labor and other resources to move in specific directions. It tells people to change their places of residence, to acquire certain knowledge and skills, and to sink resources into particular projects. Any subsequent slackening of government intentions or shift in emphasis announces that these resource movements were partly mistaken and creates unemployment.

Good timing is at the heart of effective countercyclical policy and good timing is difficult to achieve for all the reasons we've mentioned. Moreover, the mere probability of government intervention coupled with uncertainty about the nature and timing of that intervention makes the future more difficult to predict. And any sudden change in government policy, even though it may stabilize *aggregate* demand, will create additional unemployment for a period of time while particular industries are adjusting to the change. We certainly know now in the mid-seventies that a high and rising level of aggregate demand is consistent with falling demand in particular areas and temporary increases in unemployment.

The Case for an Automatic Pilot

Increases in the unemployment rate are political signals, however, for an expansion of aggregate demand. But that expansion may well be inflationary if the unemployment is due to something other than a deficiency of aggregate demand. We can sketch an instructive scenario in which the government's attempts to fine-tune the economy upset a lot of private economic calculations, the adjustments people make add to the official unemployment rate, government responds by increasing aggregate demand, this causes the price level to begin rising, and attempts to stop the inflation aggravate unemployment. Some economists are today persuaded that this has in fact occurred and that government could consequently make its most effective contribution toward eliminating aggregate fluctuations by not trying so hard to eliminate all fluctuations. A graceful elephant *could* succeed in stabilizing a small boat on a rough sea by shifting its weight with delicacy and perfect timing. Some of the passengers might nonetheless prefer that the elephant sit as still as possible.

"Automaticity" is the policy goal of economists who doubt the practicality of discretionary demand management. They want the Fed to maintain a steady hand on the money stock and either hold it constant or cause it to increase by some definite, known, and uniform rate. As for fiscal policy, they want only as much of it as comes about automatically, without the discretionary intervention of Congress or the Executive Branch. When an economic downturn begins, tax receipts will automatically fall because corporate and personal incomes are declining and government outlays will increase because government transfer payments rise when the aggregate level of economic activity declines. These automatic stabilizers presumably function in the manner of mechanical governors and dampen oscillations in the economy. The proponents of automaticity argue that any additional discretionary policy actions are more likely to aggravate than reduce instability because discretionary actions are so hard to time appropriately and because anticipation of them creates additional uncertainty for private decision makers.

The contemporary case for an automatic pilot is not identical with the view that dominated economic thinking prior to the 1930s and the publication of Keynes's *General Theory.* The older view was that government should actually retrench in a recession and cut its expenditures and increase tax rates if that was necessary to preserve a balanced budget. A balanced budget, in turn, was viewed as the test of responsible government and the one surest indicator to the business community of the government's determination to maintain or restore "confidence." And confidence was seen as the key to recovery. That view, though still influential in the 1930s, has very few supporters today. But note that such a policy, if adopted, would also be a discretionary policy, not an automatic one. It would be equally capable of aggravating instability because of faulty estimates, errors in timing, and the additional uncertainties created for decision makers.

Automatic versus Discretionary Policy

There are automatic monetary stabilizers as well as automatic fiscal stabilizers in the economic system. A boom will eventually run against rising interest rates and credit rationing if the monetary managers don't feed the boom by pumping new reserves into the banking system. During a period of economic decline, lending terms tend to improve and this will encourage some potential investors. But the monetary managers have in fact behaved perversely a good part of the time, the leading opponents of monetary fine-tuning argue. For one thing, they have paid too much attention to interest rates and, by attempting to stabilize interest rates, they have caused the money supply to grow erratically. This in turn has fostered an irregular rate of growth in gross national product, higher unemployment, and then inflationary rates of expansion in the money stock in response to the rise in unemployment.

THE DANGERS IN PICTURESQUE ARGUMENTS

Debates between the proponents of discretionary stabilization policy and purely automatic policy are often conducted by means of analogies and metaphors. The elephant-in-the-boat example used in the text is an argument by analogy and, like all such arguments, can provide only an illustration and never a proof. Here is an analogy commonly used by the advocates of discretionary policy:

> It's true that automobile accidents are occasionally caused by a driver's misguided efforts to avoid an accident. But will anyone seriously claim that we would have fewer accidents if drivers were forbidden to engage in defensive maneuvering?

But is driving an automobile really analogous to fine-tuning an economy? Or is it an altogether different kind of task? The argument by analogy begs that question.

Sometimes the analogy is less clearly stated and hence the extent to which the argument rests upon analogy is harder to recognize.

Consider this statement: "History provides no support for the notion that our economy is inherently stable. On the contrary, experience shows that blind reliance on self-correcting tendencies leads to serious trouble."

Hidden in that line of reasoning is the assumption that the economy is like an object without eyes. But economic decisions are made by human beings who do have eyes and who make conscious decisions. Isn't the real question one of *whose* eyes and *whose* decisions can best be relied upon? Do the many eyes of individual consumers, investors, and producers enable them to make better decisions than will be made by government economic managers who will necessarily have less information? The metaphor begs that question.

The argument against discretionary fiscal and monetary policy is hard to evaluate because of the difficulties in devising experimental tests. In the absence of convincing empirical evidence, economists behave like anyone else and take their positions on the basis of theoretical predilections and political preferences. General skepticism about the ability of government to solve social problems and admiration for the way in which free-market processes do the job make an economist more receptive to evidence that discretionary demand management has done more harm than good. Those who are less satisfied with the performance of the market system find a touch of absurdity in the notion that policymakers should have their hands tied, and are quite unimpressed by the evidence that discretionary policy has been destabilizing in its net effects.

Suppose we were to ask both the advocates and the opponents of discretionary demand management how their views had been affected by international economic developments in the 1970s. We could single out, as international developments that might have compelled changes in their thinking about stabilization policies, the unanticipated shortfalls in world grain production that boosted average crop prices more than 100% from 1970 to 1974; the equally unexpected successes of the OPEC cartel that had so much to do with the doubling of fuel prices over the same period; revolutions and counterrevolutions in Chile, Southeast Asia, and elsewhere; the breakdown of the fixed exchange rate system; and the simultaneous acceleration of money stock growth rates and inflation rates in industrialized countries. A much more chaotic world economy now seems to be intruding consistently upon the relatively stable and predictable economic universe to which business decision makers in the United States had become accustomed. Drought, revolution, industrial development, or shifts in the direction of economic planning anywhere in the world will in the future much more than in the past affect the demand for U.S. goods and the availability of the imports upon which our gross national product increasingly depends. What does all this imply for domestic policymakers charged with pursuing full employment and price stability?

The advocates of discretionary fiscal-monetary policy might reply that aggregate demand managers will have to play a major role in cushioning the effects of such external disturbances. Stable growth for the U.S. economy in a highly unstable world will require frequent monetary and fiscal actions of a compensatory nature. The economy may have been able to stay on a fairly steady course in the 1950s and 1960s without a great deal of active assistance from fiscal or monetary policy. But, as the inflations and recessions of the 1970s have already demonstrated, that is far less likely in the future.

What might the opponents of discretionary stabilization policy say in response to the same question? They might reply that international developments in this decade have further demonstrated the impossibility of achieving economic stability by manipulating aggregate demand. Increasing interdependence among national economies means that effective economic decision making now requires more information of a broader nature than it has ever required before and increased flexibility of response. Statistical data on economic aggregates are the kind of information available to fiscal and monetary managers, but are not the kind of information that successful economic coordination requires. If we did not know how to stabilize the economy in the relatively placid context of the 1950s and 1960s, we certainly do not know how to stabilize it now. The most important task for government may be to avoid throwing its considerable weight around in ways that increase uncertainty and aggravate instability.

What Are the Unanswered Questions?

Disagreement among economists about the relative effectiveness of fiscal and of monetary policy or about the desirability and dangers of attempting to fine-tune the economy with the tools of demand management is evidence of the unsettled state of economic knowledge. While much has been learned since the 1930s, many fundamental questions are still unresolved.

One such question is the relative utility of income-expenditures and monetary analyses. $Y = C + I + G$ and $MV = PQ$ aren't contradictory theories, of course; they both assert that aggregate demand determines the nominal level of total income or the national product measured in current dollars. Both theories can be extended, and have been extended, to take account of variables that the other theory deems important. But they are competitive theories nonetheless. One theory calls attention to consumption and investment as the components of private demand; the other passes over these components to focus on money as the medium of demand. Implicit in any economist's choice of one equation over the other as an analytical framework are judgments on unsettled questions such as these:

1. How stable is the demand for money in the short run and in the long run?
2. How stable is the relation between consumption and disposable income?
3. How does monetary policy affect the nominal interest rate quoted by lenders and the real interest rate that results from subtracting expectations of future inflation?
4. How do interest rates affect consumption and investment spending?
5. How do increased government expenditures affect consumption and investment spending directly (by perhaps displacing them) and indirectly (by stimulating them)?
6. What are the principal factors responsible for fluctuations in aggregate investment?
7. How long are the lags between policy actions and their effect on spending decisions?
8. How closely are unemployment rates and rates of inflation linked to changes in aggregate demand?
9. How are output and employment fluctuations in one country transmitted to other countries?

10. How much control do monetary managers have over the money supply when banks, corporations, and individual citizens have learned how to transfer financial assets and liabilities so quickly and almost costlessly from one nation to another?

One can hope that further empirical inquiry and theoretical discussion will eventually resolve these questions and others that may prove equally important. But that would not necessarily end all controversy. Underneath these and, indeed, *most* significant controversies in economics lies a much broader question and one far more difficult to answer: *How effectively does the market function to allocate resources?* How flexible are prices and how quickly do resources move in response to a decrease in demand in one area and an increase in another? If prices are inflexible and especially if they are inflexible in a downward direction, if resources respond sluggishly to changes in demand conditions, or if powerful economic interests are more *controlling of* than *controlled by* supply and demand, then even the most adroit management of aggregate demand will have little chance of promoting full employment and price stability.

Does the market work well enough to give fiscal policy *or* monetary policy a reasonable chance to succeed? We'll examine that question in the next chapter and discover how very far it takes us beyond the questions for which economists have any satisfactory answers.

FLEXIBILITY AND FINE-TUNING: A LOGICAL PUZZLE

Is there an inconsistency in the argument for fine-tuning?

The case for fine-tuning assumes that the economy is flexible enough to channel a dose of stimulus into slack sectors without unduly expanding demand in those sectors that are already operating close to capacity. It assumes, for example, that a tax cut or an increase in the money stock to counter the recession developing in 1974 would have had much greater effects on the automobile and housing industries than on nondurable consumer goods industries, and that its impact on construction activity would be greatest in those geographic areas where building trades unemployment was highest.

But if the economy was not flexible enough to prevent the unemployment level from rising to 9% in the spring of 1975, would it have been flexible enough to channel aggregate demand stimulus into those sectors where it's most wanted?

Once Over Lightly

The potential effectiveness of fiscal or monetary policy as tools by which government might stabilize the aggregate level of economic activity depends on the effectiveness of political processes as well as the knowledge and skills of economic advisers.

The separate impacts of fiscal policy and monetary policy are very difficult to determine, because fiscal policy inevitably affects the monetary sector and monetary policy actions are often accompanied by fiscal policy actions.

Because government deficits must be financed in some way, they will tend to cause either an increase in the money stock or increased competition for available funds, higher interest rates, and a partial displacement of private spending. The latter is the potential "crowding out" of private expenditures by government expenditures.

Fiscal policy depends on changes in federal government expenditures and tax receipts, and both of these are subject to major political constraints. Proposals for making fiscal policy a more flexible tool by granting to the president a limited authority to alter expenditures and taxes will encounter political resistance to any reduction in the power of Congress over the budget.

The tidy equilibrium models of economists in which there are no data problems and no time lags of uncertain length present a misleadingly simple picture of the difficulties that fiscal or monetary policy encounter in practice. The information that policymakers can have will be both dated and inaccurate.

One of the most important obstacles to the use of fiscal or monetary policy as stabilization tools is our lack of reliable information on the time lag between a policy action and its consequences.

Neither fiscal policy nor monetary policy is neutral in its effects on the composition of output and the distribution of income. These side effects may become reasons for choosing or not choosing a particular policy.

Fiscal or monetary policy may be able to alter the level of aggregate demand but nonetheless be unable to alter it with sufficient precision to reduce aggregate fluctuations.

Attempts to stabilize could actually be destabilizing. The greater our ignorance or misinformation about the time lags inherent in aggregate demand management, the greater is the probability that stabilization policy will be destabilizing.

The economic system contains a number of automatic stabilizers that come into operation in the absence of any decisions by government and partially offset expansions and contractions in aggregate demand. The effectiveness of these stabilizers is a disputed issue. The stabilizers range from automatic changes in tax receipts as GNP changes, through movements in interest rates as private demand for credit changes, to movements in prices and wages in response to conditions of excess or inadequate demand.

Some economists are sufficiently impressed by the destabilizing potential of discretionary policy to argue that exclusive reliance on automatic stabilizers will yield better results than will attempts to fine-tune the economy.

Inadequate knowledge about important behavioral relationships and continuing theoretical disagreements continue to impede the development of a consensus among economists on the effectiveness of aggregate demand management. A good deal of controversy is rooted in disagreement about how effectively the market system allocates resources.

QUESTIONS FOR DISCUSSION

1. What gives rise to "social problems"? What special advantages might government have for dealing with "social problems"? Choose some particular social problem that you think government is uniquely qualified to solve, and then reflect on the assumptions you're making about the workings of government.

2. Some observers claim to find evidence that from the 1930s to the 1960s Americans believed strongly in the ability of government to solve social problems (poverty, crime, urban decay, mental health, unequal education, racial and sexual discrimination, health care), but that the late 1960s and the 1970s have seen a growing disillusionment in this area. What evidence can you present for or against this thesis?

3. Would most of our economic problems disappear if business firms operated more on the basis of the public interest rather than private interests? Is the proposal that business behave in a more socially responsible way a useful proposal? Substitute "government officials" for "business firms" and examine the same question.

4. When did the Great Depression end? Why did it end? How do you know?

5. Examine the thesis that the federal budget deficits for the 1976 and 1977 fiscal years did or did not significantly "crowd out" private expenditures.

6. Senator Hubert Humphrey said shortly after the March 1975 tax cuts that "common sense" told him federal borrowing would not raise interest rates and crowd out private borrowers. "To a large extent this credit market question takes care of itself," he said. "Private demands for credit go down when unemployment is high. This makes room in the credit market for government demand, which goes up." Do you agree?

7. Can you think of any experiment by which we might test the proposition that fiscal policy affects total spending regardless of what is happening to the money supply?

8. Does monetary policy require assistance from fiscal policy to be effective?

9. Suppose we knew that an increase in the budget deficit or in the growth rate of the money stock would have 95% of its impact by the end of two years, 55% of its impact within one year, and 20% within six months. Would that knowledge solve the timing problems associated with aggregate demand management?

10. "An increase or decrease in government spending will usually entail an offsetting decrease or increase in private spending." Under what circumstances would you expect that statement to be true? Why? Under what circumstances would you expect that statement to be false? Why?

11. "An easy money policy is good for the housing industry in the short run but bad in the long run." Evaluate that argument.

12. What are some of the ways in which monetary policy can affect the flow of international payments?

13. In 1974, government purchased 22% of the goods in the gross national product, and the private sector purchased the other 78%. The 78% that went to the private sector was divided between consumption and investment expenditures; consumption took 81% and investment 19%.

    (*a*) Do you think the government spent more than 19% of its share on investment goods?

    (*b*) State and local governments purchased 62% of the goods absorbed by the government sector, and the federal government 38%. Would you classify the $70 billion spent by state and local governments on education as a consumption or an investment expenditure?

14. Would you favor the proposal, mentioned in the text, to give the president authority to change tax rates or to authorize expenditures on his own (within Congressionally designated limits) as a way of making fiscal policy more flexible? Why or why not?

15. Can discretionary monetary policy improve upon the automatic monetary stabilizers that would be operative if the Fed simply increased bank reserves at a steady rate? Under what circumstances would discretionary policy be destabilizing in its effects? Under what circumstances would it reenforce the operation of the automatic stabilizers?

16. Would you expect to find a relationship between an informed person's attitude toward attempts at fine-tuning and his reactions to the following judgments? Explain why.

(*a*) "The article by Hayek in the appendix on the problem of knowledge exaggerates both the difficulty of obtaining useful information and the effectiveness of the market in generating and disseminating such information."

(*b*) "The government must establish procedures for national economic planning if we are to avoid the kinds of economic crises experienced in the early 1970s."

(*c*) "The market does not work as it used to. Competition no longer sets prices or allocates resources in the U.S. economy. Most of that is done by organized interest groups with substantial market power."

(*d*) "The U.S. economy displays an absurd social imbalance. Privately purchased goods are produced in abundance, while public sector goods such as education must be content with the leavings."

(*e*) "Power tends to corrupt and absolute power corrupts absolutely."

17

INFLATION, UNEMPLOYMENT, AND THE POLITICALIZATION OF THE ECONOMY

Nothing contributed as much to the public's sudden disillusionment with economists in the early 1970s as the appearance of rapid inflation combined with high and rising unemployment. This wasn't supposed to happen, according to the public's notion of what economists were teaching, because inflation and recession are opposites.

INFLATION *VERSUS* UNEMPLOYMENT

Inflation and recession are not actually opposites, of course. The opposite of inflation is deflation, which is a falling rather than a rising price level. There is no generally accepted term for the opposite of recession, but *boom* comes close. It is a period of increasing output and employment mixed possibly, but not necessarily, with rising prices. But if inflation and recession aren't opposite in the strict sense, they have been considered opposites in the sense of sunshine and rain: the two are not expected to occur at the same time.

It's clear that the general public was surprised in 1970 when unemployment rose to 6.2% in the month of December, despite the fact that the consumer price index had gone up throughout the year at an average annual rate of 7%. The spectacular show was still to come, however. Unemployment rose during 1974 from 5.2% in January to 7.2% in December, while the Consumer Price Index added the phrase "double-digit inflation" to our vocabulary of jargon by rising 11%.

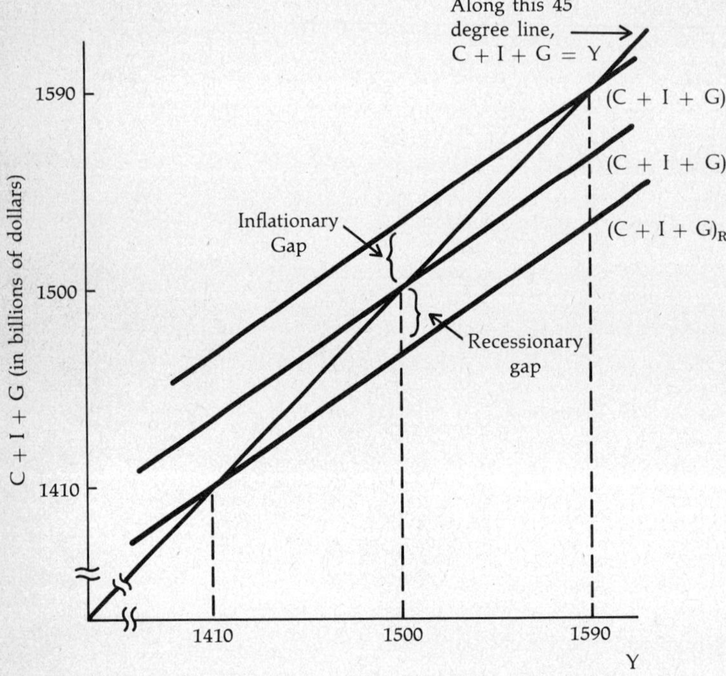

Figure 17A　Implications of
income-expenditures analysis

Inflationary and Recessionary Gaps

Professional economists weren't as embarrassed by all this as some journalists and television commentators, perhaps too eager to proclaim a crisis, claimed they were. But it is true that the economics textbooks had for some years been analyzing inflation and recession as if they resulted from opposite forces and therefore could not occur simultaneously. Income-expenditures analysis was especially vulnerable on this score, with its concept of a full employment level of aggregate demand below which involuntary unemployment appeared and above which the price level rose. Graphs like the one in figure 17A were often used by economists to present the implications of income-expenditures analysis.

The sum of the components of aggregate demand is on the vertical axis and total income or output is on the horizontal axis. At equilibrium, C + I + G will be equal to Y. The 45 degree line, because it marks off all the points in the graph at which C + I + G does equal Y, shows all possible equilibrium positions. Since consumption increases as income increases, on Keynes's assumptions, but by less than the increase in income, the total of C, I, and G will increase as Y increases, but at a slower rate. The three aggregate demand curves are drawn with a slope of less than one (actually $\frac{2}{3}$) in order to show this relation between total expenditure and income. All this is merely an extension of the graphical analysis introduced in chapter 11 (see especially figure 11H on page 260).

If the intentions of consumers, investors, and the government are as shown by $(C + I + G)_F$ in figure 17A, the equilibrium level of Y will be $1500 billion. You can readily see from the graph that, at any higher level of Y, $(C + I + G)_F$ would be less than Y and so, by the logic of the process described in chapter 11, Y would fall. At any lower level of Y, $C + I + G$ would be greater than Y, and Y would rise.

Assume that $1500 is the full employment level of Y. Then, by definition, there will be excessive unemployment if aggregate demand generates only a $1410 billion level of Y. This would occur if the intentions of consumers, investors, and the government were as shown by $(C + I + G)_R$. If, on the other hand, aggregate spending plans were as shown by $(C + I + G)_I$, so that Y rose to $1590 billion, the economy would undergo inflation.

The vertical difference between $(C + I + G)_F$ and $(C + I + G)_R$ was called a recessionary gap; it's the amount by which aggregate demand falls short of what it would have to be to get the economy to full employment. The vertical difference between $(C + I + G)_F$ and $(C + I + G)_I$ is an inflationary gap; it's the amount by which aggregate demand exceeds the ability of the economy to supply new goods at stable prices.

INFLATION *WITH* UNEMPLOYMENT

This way of setting up the problem leaves the impression that inflation cannot occur when a recessionary gap exists and recession cannot occur in the presence of an inflationary gap. Inflation and unemployment in this analysis are opposites. They are caused, respectively, by an excessive level or an inadequate level of aggregate demand, and we should not expect to observe both at the same time. Moreover, the way to deal with inflation is to "close" the inflationary gap. Recession calls for closing the recessionary gap. Inflation *plus* recession then calls for . . . some other way of looking at the problem.

Bottlenecks, Full Employment, and Inflation

The standard textbook analysis that we've been summarizing actually did allow for the possibility of *some* inflation before a recessionary gap had been fully closed (or before full employment was reached) and the appearance of *some* unemployment before an inflationary gap had been completely closed (or increases in the price level brought to a halt). Figure 17B presents that analysis by extending figure 17A.

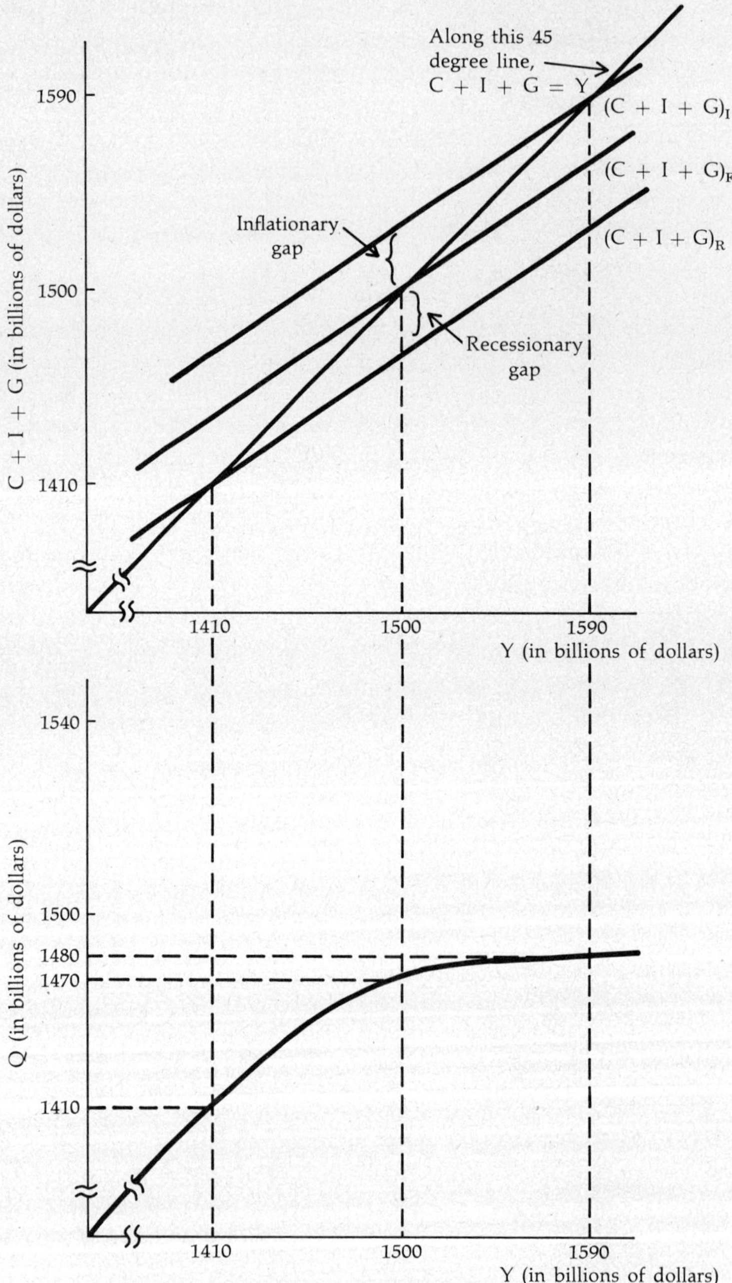

Figure 17B Extension of figure 17A

The level of employment actually depends on real output Q rather than nominal output or income Y (which equals P $\times$ Q). Increases or decreases in Y ordinarily entail increases or decreases in Q. But when the economy is operating near the full employment level, increases in Q (real output) are hard to obtain. Bottlenecks of various sorts appear, and some prices rise even though resources are not fully employed. This is shown on the lower graph of figure 17B by the curve, the slope of which increases at a decreasing rate as Y gets close to $1500 billion. Beyond the full employent level of Y, Q can be increased only with great difficulty, and increases in Y result in very small increases in Q.

Since Y = PQ, P = Y/Q. The price level, in other words, is the ratio of nominal to real income. The economy cannot be brought from a $1410 billion level to the full employment equilibrium of $1500 billion without some increase in the price level. On the graph, this is an increase from the price level 1410/1410 to the price level 1500/1470 or a 2% increase in the price level. If aggregate demand rose to (C + I + G)$_\mathrm{I}$, the equilibrium level of Y would be $1590 billion but real income would only be $1480 billion. This would entail an additional 5% increase in the price level.

This, in outline, is the analysis behind the argument, familiar long before 1970, that inflation and unemployment not only *could* coexist but were even *likely* to be found together. The conclusion of this exercise was that acceptance of a certain amount of inflation is the price society must pay to achieve "full employment." If the economy depicted in figure 17B is to be spared *completely* from inflation, then Y cannot be allowed to increase beyond about $1425 billion. Above that level, Q cannot keep pace with Y and inflation begins. But unemployment will be high—the graph doesn't tell us *how* high—if Y is only $1425 billion. Society must therefore choose between less unemployment and less inflation; within a certain range, at least, one cannot be reduced without increasing the other.

This line of analysis has considerable political importance. If the zealous pursuit of full employment causes inflation and if inflation cannot be stopped without creating unemployment, policymakers face a dilemma. But the dilemma is more complex than this simplified analysis suggests. Let's look at the matter more closely.

Full Employment, Search Costs, and Inflation

It's plausible to assume that when expansionary fiscal policy or monetary policy increases aggregate demand from (C + I + G)$_\mathrm{R}$ to (C + I + G)$_\mathrm{F}$, some inflation will occur before equilibrium is reached at $1500 billion. Resources must be *attracted* back into employment by a bidding process that is quite likely to mean some increase in the average of all prices. But

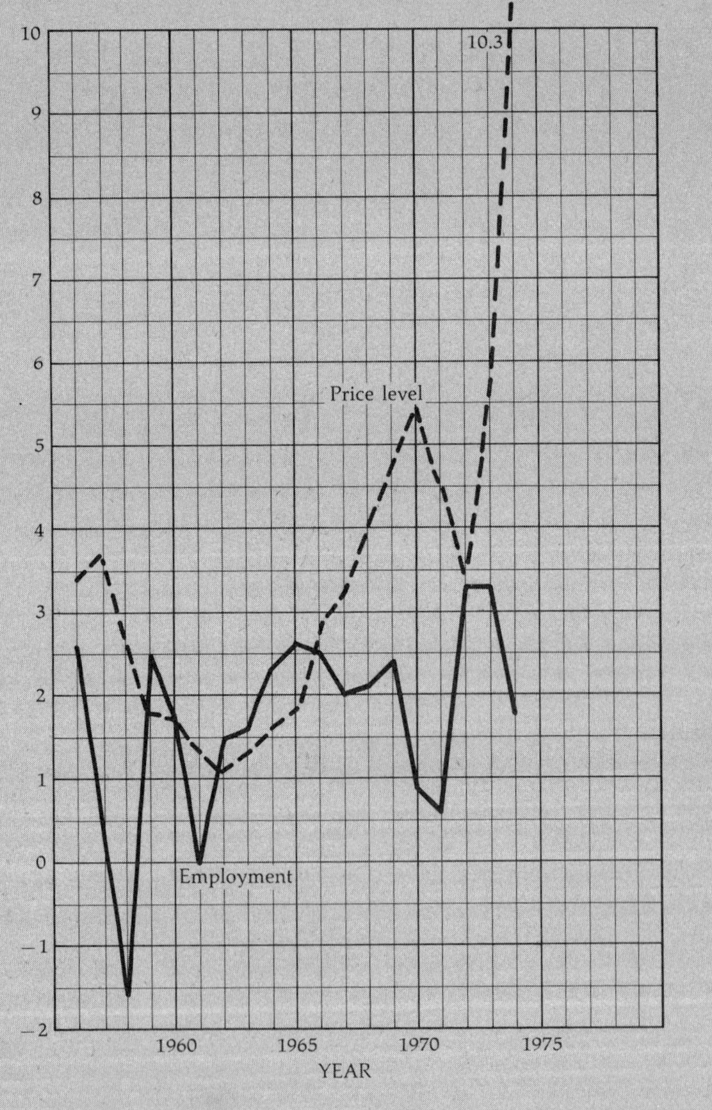

EMPLOYMENT AND INFLATION
Percentage change from year to year in total civilian employment and in the implicit price deflator for gross national product.
10.3
Price level
Employment
10
9
8
7
6
5
4
3
2
1
0
−1
−2
1960
1965
1970
1975
YEAR

will the price level *continue* rising after the new equilibrium has been reached? Once resources are again fully employed, no further bidding up of prices or wages would seem to be required. The inflation associated with the movement to full employment could be a consequence of this *movement* and not of the full employment. An increase in the price level may have to be accepted to *restore* full employment, but once full employment has been reached, there is less reason to expect prices to continue rising.

But that is too simple a view of the matter. An economy "in aggregate equilibrium" will still contain a great deal of internal movement. Some industries will be growing and others declining. New production techniques, changes in the composition of demand, and entry into and exit from the labor force continue even when the economy is at a "full employment equilibrium." Resources will still have to be attracted into the expanding sectors through the offer of better employment terms. If prices and wages would fall slightly in declining industries and rise slightly in expanding industries, this continual reallocation of resources could take place with no increase in the average level of prices. If, however, prices and wages are quite rigid in a downward direction, all the price-wage adjustments needed to secure a reallocation of resources will have to be upward adjustments. Prices will then rise in expanding industries while remaining constant in declining industries, and the net effect will be an increase in the price level.

Downward adjustments of prices and wages are less likely to occur the closer the economy is to full employment. Why is this? Suppose that a college faced with declining enrollments tries to reduce faculty salaries. If the faculty members who are offered lower salaries believe that they can easily find other jobs that are just as good, they aren't likely to accept the reductions. If, on the other hand, they suspect that alternative employment opportunities will be hard to find, they will at least think twice before turning down the college's offer and looking for a different job. Anyone who followed the news closely during the 1974–75 recession could read about many cases where employees accepted wage reductions as an alternative to employment cutbacks. The employees would surely have been more reluctant to accept reductions (in some cases employees even initiated them) if they had thought that there were good employment opportunities elsewhere.

Remember that employers and employees do not have perfect information. They must search for what they want and incur the costs of that search. In a period of high employment, the cost of finding a new job will on average be lower for employees; they will therefore be more ready to give up a job when they think the wage is unsatisfactory and begin searching for another. So employers will find it more difficult to reduce wages.

Search costs for employers, however, are higher in periods of full employment. And so employers will offer wages higher than they might otherwise be willing to offer in order to avoid extending the costly search for the new employees they want.

The same argument applies to prices in product markets. When the economy is operating close to its capacity, excess supplies are generally hard to find and buyers will pay higher prices rather than search for alternative sources of supply. In a period of high unemployment and substantial excess capacity, sellers will be shaving prices because buyers are hard to find.

The identical conclusion emerges however we look at it. Full employment fosters an upward creep in prices and wages; substantial unemployment and excess capacity encourages a downward drift in prices and wages.

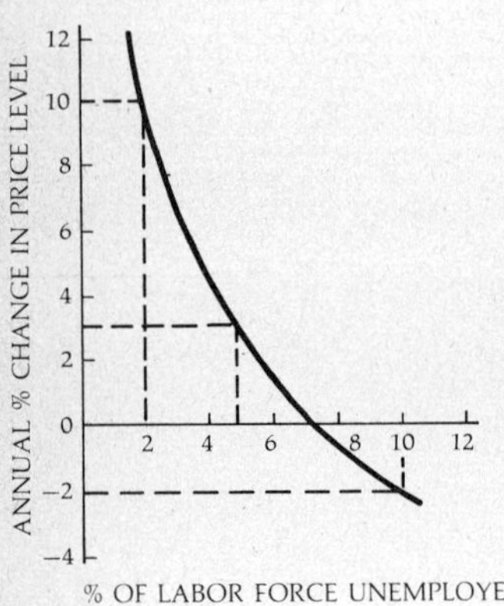

Figure 17C Phillips curve

The Phillips Curve: Use and Abuse

In 1958 a British economist named A. W. Phillips published a study on "The Relationship between Unemployment and the Rate of Change of Money Wage Rates in the United Kingdom, 1861–1957" and invented the "Phillips curve." Phillips showed that there was a stable relation during the period he studied between the unemployment rate and the rate at which the average money wage increased. Unemployment was greater when money wage rates were increasing more slowly and fell in periods when money wage rates were rising rapidly. That seems thoroughly plausible. During periods of high demand for labor, employers will tend to bid up wage rates to obtain and keep the employees they want. In periods of high unemployment, employers will not have to bid so energetically for labor, and wage rates will increase less. But the argument was subsequently extended by others to suggest that unemployment might be reduced by allowing an inflationary rate of increase in money wages and, by extension, in the average of all prices. The Phillips curve of this latter argument purports to show that there is a trade-off between inflation and unemployment, so that less of one can be obtained by accepting more of the other. Figure 17C offers an illustration.

The Phillips curve as drawn above suggests that unemployment can be lowered to 2% of the labor force by accepting 10% inflation per year; that 2% annual *deflation* can be achieved by accepting a 10% unemployment rate; and that 5% unemployment can be obtained with 3% annual inflation.

At first glance this may seem to be only an illustration of the argument we've been making about the relation between upward creeping prices and wages and the level at which the economy is operating. But it actually implies much more than we've contended, and its implications may be seriously misleading. It does *not* follow either from the argument we've presented or from A. W. Phillips' data that policymakers have a menu like the one in figure 17C from which they can simply choose their preferred combination of inflation and unemployment.

The problem is that an attempt on the part of fiscal and monetary authorities to *use* the curve will cause it to *shift.* Suppose that the unemployment rate has been 5% for some time and that prices have been rising at an annual rate of 3%. The government consults the Phillips curve and decides to reduce unemployment to 3% by raising the inflation rate to 7%. It adopts a more expansionary fiscal or monetary policy, prices and wages rise at a faster rate, and unemployment falls toward 3%. The key question now is whether unemployment can be *maintained* at this lower level without *further* accelerating the rate of inflation.

Can Inflation Lower the Unemployment Rate Permanently?

To answer this question we must ask *why* unemployment would decline in the first place. In reasoning through the unemployment-inflation relationship, we argued that price and wage movements were a response to tightness or slackness in markets. In other words, the level of employment was the cause and price-wage movement the effect. We cannot simply assume that because full employment causes inflation, inflation will bring about full employment. When there is a big crowd at the basketball game, the gymnasium temperature rises because of the body heat; but the athletic department cannot make a crowd come to watch a losing basketball team by overheating the gymnasium.

Nonetheless, the policy of deliberately stepping up inflation probably would lower the unemployment rate—temporarily. People are unemployed because they don't find the job opportunities of which they're aware sufficiently attractive. If the level of real wages could somehow be increased across the board, all employment opportunities would become more attractive. Employment would therefore increase *except* for the fact that employers will demand less labor at higher real wage rates. However, when money wages and prices advance together, as they do in a general inflation, real wages don't actually increase. But *workers think they have increased,* and that will be enough to lower the unemployment rate.

A policy of deliberate inflation makes job opportunities *seem* more attractive by raising the *money* wage rate offers of employers. And this is how inflation reduces unemployment. But the higher wage rate offers are only *seemingly* more attractive. *Real* wage rates do not rise; only money wage rates rise. As long as potential employees don't realize that the job opportunities they're now accepting are in reality no better than the opportunities they previously rejected, employment will indeed rise. Employment will fall back down to its previous level, however, when employees discover what's happening and realize that inflation is creating the illusion of more attractive wage offers. As they discover that they've been "tricked,"

employment will decline again and the Phillips curve will now pass through the point of 7% inflation, but with unemployment back at its previous level of 5%. The curve will have shifted upward. No permanent reduction in unemployment will have occurred, but the economy will be undergoing more rapid inflation.

A deliberate policy of pursuing lower unemployment by creating a higher rate of inflation calls for *continually increasing* the inflation rate so that workers continually *expect* less than the actual rate of inflation. In this way they can be made continually to overestimate the real value of the money wages they are being offered. We must either continually increase the rate of inflation or assume that employees pay exclusive attention to money wage rates and never consider real wage rates. This is a superficially plausible assumption; we know that few employees consult the most recent changes in the Consumer Price Index before deciding whether a wage offer is adequate. They look at *money* wage rates, in other words. But they also learn after a while that their wages buy less and adjust their perception of the wage rate's real value. An extreme example will make the point. In 1956, workers stood in line for jobs at manufacturing firms offering $2 an hour. In 1976, manufacturers can find almost no one who will accept employment at that wage. Employees *do* know, even if they've never heard of price indices, that $2 is a much lower hourly wage today than it was twenty years ago.

Policy cannot be constructed on the assumption that workers will be permanently fooled; people do learn from experience. And the simultaneous existence of high unemployment with very rapid inflation in the early 1970s ought to be sufficient evidence that people *have* learned. When they begin to assume continued inflation, they no longer suffer from the illusion that money wages and real wages are the same thing.

But now suppose that the government discerns the error of its ways and regrets its policy initiative. Unemployment is back at the old 5% level but inflation is now progressing at 7% per year. The government therefore decides to reverse its policy and get inflation down to 3% again. So it eases up on the fiscal-monetary stimulus it's been applying. Monetary demand will now stop increasing so rapidly, producers will be unable to sell at the prices they had anticipated, inventories will mount, production will be curtailed, and unemployment will rise. Eventually sellers will learn not to expect such a rapid rise in prices, they will adjust downward the prices they ask and the prices they offer to pay for inputs, sales will revive, inventories will decline, production will start up again, and unemployment will fall. But that won't all happen within a week or even a month. The higher unemployment that will result from an attempt to slow down the rate of inflation will be temporary; but temporary can be a long time. The cost of letting inflation get out of hand may be very high indeed.

Conclusions and Implications

Let's try to summarize the conclusions that have emerged so far from our examination of the relationship between inflation and unemployment.

1. A movement from a situation of low employment to one of high or "full" employment will generally be accompanied by a rising price level. Increased demand will bid up some prices and wages even before "full" employment is achieved.
2. Increases in aggregate demand when the economy is already operating in the vicinity of "full" employment will have their principal impact on the price-wage level. Modest and temporary increases in real output and employment may result, but most of the rise in Y will be in P rather than in Q.
3. An economy operating in the vicinity of "full" employment tends to experience creeping inflation. By lowering search costs for sellers of both products and labor and raising search costs for buyers, "full" employment promotes an upward drift in the terms of price and wage bargains.
4. The unemployment rate is affected by *changes* in the rate of inflation. An unanticipated increase in the inflation rate tends to reduce unemployment; and an unanticipated decrease in the inflation rate tends to increase unemployment. But a constant rate of inflation, because it's presumably fully anticipated, probably has no effect on the unemployment rate.

There are some important policy lessons tucked away in those four conclusions for anyone who dislikes both high unemployment rates *and* inflation.

1. Avoid recessions if you want to avoid inflation because the process of recovery from a recession usually entails inflation.
2. Try not to let inflation get started if you want to prevent high unemployment because slowing down the rate of inflation will ordinarily cause unemployment to increase.
3. Creeping inflation is probably the price that a society must pay for all the gains that accrue from continuous operation at or near the economy's capacity.
4. The Phillips curve is a dangerous concept if it encourages the illusion that a permanently lower unemployment rate can be "purchased" by accepting a higher rate of inflation.

Lessons 3 and 4 are not contradictory. Lesson 3 merely acknowledges the fact that upward price adjustments will dominate downward adjustments and lead to a slow upward drift in the price level when the economic system is operating with very little slack. It warns, you might say, against the pursuit of perfection. Lesson 4 warns against confusing cause and effect and assuming that since high employment generates inflation, more inflation will generate higher employment.

WHAT UNEMPLOYMENT RATE IS ACCEPTABLE?

When is the unemployment rate "too high"? If there is an unavoidable minimum of "frictional" unemployment, how can we decide whether it is 2%, 6%, or something else? Is there a *natural* rate of unemployment?

Let's reflect on the problem of office space in New York City to see if it suggests a way of thinking about this question. There will always be *some* vacant office space in New York. A zero vacancy rate is neither possible nor desirable. Firms will continually be moving into and out of the city or looking for office space more suitable to their changed circumstances. Newly constructed space will not be rented immediately and vacated space will stand empty for at least a short interval. If the vacancy rate were to fall to 1%, firms looking for space would have difficulty finding it. We would expect to hear complaints about the "tightness" of the market, to observe rising rents as firms competed for the office space they wanted, and to see an increase in the rate of office building construction as developers came to anticipate larger profits providing new space.

A 10% vacancy rate would produce the opposite results. Owners of office buildings would complain about the "glutted" market, rents would decline as owners competed for occupants, and the rate of new construction would slow down.

If we were to observe no net tendency for rents to rise or decline, no tendency for the rate of new construction to accelerate or slow down, and no greater incidence of complaints from owners about "gluts" than from tenants about the "tight" market, we could conclude that the vacancy rate was at its "natural" level.

Could we argue in an analogous way that the unemployment rate is at its "natural" level when we observe no net tendency for wage rates to rise or decline, no tendency for the rate of labor-force participation to increase or decrease, and about as many complaints from workers that "there are no jobs" as complaints from employers that "you can't get help"? Since the volume of complaints would be hard to tabulate, we might substitute something like the number of job seekers registered with state employment agencies and the number of job vacancies listed by employers.

This approach will unfortunately not enable us to decide with confidence whether the unemployment rate at any time is excessive or merely at its "natural" and acceptable level. But it does clarify the problem somewhat and indicate the kind of data at which we might look to decide whether or not the current unemployment rate should be a matter for concern.

The Bureau of Labor Statistics divides the unemployed into job losers, job leavers, those who are reentering the labor force after an absence, and new entrants into the labor force. We can compare each with a category of office space. Job losers correspond to offices that are empty because tenants choose to leave. Job leavers correspond to offices that are empty because tenants have been evicted. (Note that landlords often "evict" tenants by demanding a higher rent.) Reentrants correspond to offices that had previously been withdrawn from the market because the owners did not expect to receive rental income equal to maintenance costs but are now again being offered for rent. New entrants can be divided into two groups. Young people entering the labor force for the first time correspond to newly constructed space. Older people who have not previously held jobs because other family members earned an adequate income but who have now been pulled into the labor force either by declining family income or by more attractive job offers correspond to older space being offered for rent for the first time. A firm may decide, for example, to sublet a portion of the space it had previously reserved for its own purposes, either because business has fallen off or because high rental prices have persuaded its managers that more can be earned by renting out the space than by using it for the firm's own operations.

All of this suggests that a wide variety of economic, political, or cultural changes could cause the "natural" unemployment rate to increase or decrease. Do you agree that each of the following would *increase* the "natural" rate of unemployment?

(*a*) Employer discrimination against women diminishes and more women consequently begin looking for jobs in the labor market.

(*b*) Blacks come to believe that job prospects have improved, perhaps as a result of antidiscrimination legislation, and some who had stopped looking for work out of discouragement reenter the labor force.

(*c*) Unemployment compensation benefits are increased and extended so that the cost of remaining unemployed while searching for a better job declines.

(*d*) Young people come to believe that they should not select a career course until they have experimented with a variety of jobs.

(*e*) Family incomes rise significantly faster than per capita incomes.

Lessons 1 and 2 are of doubtful value if we don't know *how* to avoid recessions or increases in the rate of inflation. A fiscal-monetary activist might extract from them a recommendation for fine-tuning. A fiscal-monetary passivist, on the other hand, will argue that the attempt to fine-tune is a principal cause of recession and inflation, and will see in these lessons a case for restraint in the practice of demand management. The issue of fine-tuning versus automatic controls was discussed in chapter 16. One conclusion to which we came then was that a satisfactory conclusion is unlikely until we know a great deal more about the way individual decision makers adjust to change when the future is uncertain.

Would a sure recipe for rapid inflation coupled with high unemployment be of any use? Could it serve as a warning to policymakers? Let the government run continual large deficits and finance them by creating new money with Fed purchases of government securities. The accompanying expenditure programs should change often and unpredictably. Tax policy should also change often and unpredictably. Credits granted for new investment should be followed by surtaxes on capital purchases. Then policy should move back to investment tax credits. Periodic threats to raise corporate income taxes will also help if the threats can be made credible. Price controls should be imposed to create shortages that may compel some firms to shut down; the controls should be removed before the public learns to adjust to them, however, and then reimposed after a while. The government should also pass legislation imposing detailed but unenforceable controls on job safety procedures and emission of pollutants and then rescind the legislation long after its unworkability has become apparent. Impose and remove, in as unpredictable a way as possible, import quotas, tariffs, taxes, other controls on foreign investment, and export subsidies. (Anyone can add his own ingredients as soon as he understands the formula.) Increase monetary demand well beyond the rate at which real output can increase while introducing as much uncertainty as possible into the situations confronted by consumers, investors, employees, and employers. Rapid inflation and high unemployment are guaranteed to occur simultaneously.

PRICE AND WAGE CONTROLS

Arthur F. Burns is a distinguished economist who became chairman of the board of governors of the Federal Reserve System in 1970. Along with most other economists, Burns had long maintained that the key to a stable price level is monetary and fiscal restraint on the part of government and not wage or price controls. But when he found himself in charge of imposing an important part of that restraint, Burns changed the direction of his thinking. His public speeches reveal the evolution of his thought.[1] Burns reluctantly concluded that labor and product markets did not function well enough for fiscal and monetary policy to be effective. Strong unions and business firms with substantial market power were able to raise wages and prices in the absence of any increases in demand. Confronted with this situation, monetary and fiscal authorities had to choose between causing unemployment by refusing to expand total demand or increasing the rate of inflation by underwriting the wage and price increases.

Market Power, Unemployment, and Inflation

To understand Burns's reasoning, suppose that a significant number of wage rates are set by collective bargaining, and that unions have the ability to obtain money wage increases in excess of productivity increases. This would mean that unions (or some unions) can obtain for their members a money wage that is above the value of labor's marginal productivity. Another way of putting it is to say that the unions can persuade some employers to pay workers a money wage greater than the current value of the marginal worker's *net* contribution to the firm's revenue.

Because marginal workers now add more to the costs than to the revenue of the firm, employers adjust by reducing the number of workers they hire. They may not actually lay anyone off; instead they will just refrain from replacing workers as they retire or quit. The result is a reduction in the number of jobs available and an increase in measured unemployment. If employers raise their prices to recover the higher labor costs, they won't be able to sell as much at higher prices and the reduced sales will eventually lead to employment cutbacks. Even if union members realize that higher money wages mean fewer jobs, a majority may vote for the wage increase in the belief that they themselves will be protected by seniority; they risk the jobs of *other* employees who have less seniority.

---

1. A comprehensive but succinct summary of Burns's opinions on the possibilities and difficulties of demand management is contained in the appendix. It's valuable to study the views of a powerful policymaker who has substantial freedom from political constraints and is an excellent economist and a lucid writer.

Rising unemployment caused by this kind of market power puts the government under pressure to adopt an expansionary fiscal or monetary policy. When it does so, the price level rises. The rise in the price of everything else will reduce the *relative* price of the good whose sales had fallen, its sales will expand once more, and employment in that industry will be restored. In the event that employers are price takers and lack the market power to pass the wage increase along to buyers, the increase in the price of *all* goods does the job for them. The real wage is consequently reduced and employment is restored to its initial level. The upshot of the matter is that the use of excessive market power creates unemployment problems and that the government is forced to cause inflation to deal with the unemployment problems.

How did we get into such a bind? Is there a way out? Burns has pointed to three principal causes of the problem. They are strong unions; business firms selling in insufficiently competitive markets; and innumerable government regulations that tolerate, encourage, and even require practices that raise costs and reduce efficiency. In the last category Burns includes subsidies to farmers, legal restrictions on entry into various trades or professions, import quotas and tariffs, the federal minimum wage law (especially in its application to teenagers), aspects of our welfare programs, price maintenance laws, and the failure to enforce antitrust legislation. The solution is structural reforms directed toward increasing competition and thereby making wages and prices more responsive to forces of supply and demand.[1]

But reforms of that sort can't be implemented quickly. The active participation of government in the creation of the problems suggests that such reforms will only be possible, if they're possible at all, after a long campaign of public education. In the meantime we shall have to make do with second-best policies. Some legal controls on prices and wages may be necessary if we are to avoid confronting the nation's fiscal-monetary managers with the unpleasant choice between accepting unemployment of causing inflation.

Defensible and Indefensible Arguments for Controls

The general public has never had much trouble believing that inflation is the result of irresponsible behavior on the part of sellers, whether of products or of labor services. The public looks for villains when things go wrong and seems to find them among the business firms that announce price increases and the union leaders who call for wage hikes. An excessive rate of increase in monetary demand is a force too abstract and impersonal

---

1. Keep in mind that union strength, corporate market power, and anticompetitive government regulations *must be increasing* if the problem to which Burns calls attention is growing worse.

"DEMAND-PULL" AND "COST-PUSH" INFLATION

If the monetary demand for goods increases faster than additional goods can be produced, prices will be bid up. This is the usual way in which inflation occurs. But the average of all prices might also rise because some sellers are able to raise their prices in the absence of any increase in demand. This is sometimes called *cost-push* inflation to distinguish it from the traditional *demand-pull* inflation. But cost-push inflation usually requires assistance from demand-pull. The market power of sellers is unlikely to cause persistent inflation unless the monetary managers cooperate.

We can use the equation of exchange, $MV = PQ$, to consider the possibilities. Let's suppose that there is a competitive sector of the economy where individual sellers of products and of labor have no power to raise their prices or wages and where they do not combine to achieve this power. And let's suppose that the remainder of the economy is a "monopolistic" sector (with "monopolistic" enclosed in quotation marks to remind you that it's a word with almost as many meanings as it has users). Goods produced in the competitive sector are represented by Q_c, goods produced in the "monopolistic" sector by Q_m. Now $Q_c + Q_m = Q$, and if P_c and P_m represent respectively the average prices of goods produced in each sector, then $P_cQ_c + P_mQ_m = PQ$. We rewrite the equation of exchange as

$$MV = P_cQ_c + P_mQ_m$$

What will occur if the government regulators, powerful labor unions, or giant corporations allegedly responsible for the existence of a "monopolistic" sector raise P_m in the absence of any increase in the demand for Q_m?

The law of demand tells us that when P_m rises, Q_m will fall. The more elastic the demand for Q_m, the larger will be the decline in Q_m and the consequent increase in unemployment in the "monopolistic" sector. But output and employment might also decrease in the competitive sector. If the demand for Q_m is inelastic, people will spend more income than before in purchasing a smaller quantity of these higher-priced goods, less income will consequently be left for the purchase of competitively produced goods, and so the demand for Q_c will decrease. The more resistant prices in the competitive sector are to downward pressure, the larger will be the resulting decline in Q_c and decline in employment in the competitive sector.

The maintenance of previous levels of output and employment in the face of a rise in P_m requires, therefore, an increase in MV. V would increase when the "monopolistic" sector raises its prices only if the increase in P_m somehow induced the public to prefer smaller money balances. It is difficult to imagine why or how that would occur. If the demand for money balances does *not* decrease, an increase in MV requires a larger stock of money. And so the responsibility passes to the monetary managers. M will have to be increased if a rise in the unemployment rate is to be prevented.

Whether we choose to call the resulting rise in the average of all prices a cost-push or a demand-pull inflation and whether we put the blame on the "monopolists" or the money managers is less important than that we understand the process by which this kind of inflation might occur. Of course, a model of how it *might* occur is no evidence that it *has* occurred. How much power "monopolists"—unions, corporations, or government agencies—actually have to raise prices in this manner is a difficult empirical question. And regardless of how much power they have, the problem will not have grown worse in recent years unless their power has been increasing. That, too, is a disputed empirical question.

to be a good candidate for villain, and so corporations and unions tend to be blamed for inflation even when wages and prices are clearly being pulled up by excess demand and not being pushed up by market power. That's why the imposition of wage and price controls during a period of inflation usually encounters, at least initially, an overwhelmingly favorable response from the public. A case in point is the wage-price freeze announced in August 1971.

The popularity of wage and price controls as a way of dealing with inflation makes it all the more urgent that the public understand the mechanisms of inflation. The argument made by Arthur Burns and many other economists is a defensible one. It calls for controls on those wages and prices that are not adequately controlled by competition, so that the fiscal and monetary authorities can pursue noninflationary policies. And it looks forward to structural reforms that would eliminate the restrictive practices that made the controls necessary.

This is an argument vastly different from the one that calls for controls to keep wages and prices from rising *after* the fiscal or monetary authorities have expanded aggregate demand at a more rapid rate than the rate at which real output can be increased, or after some disaster (war, oil embargoes, crop failures) has reduced the level of real output. In such circumstances, controls are worse than useless. They suspend the rationing system by which scarce goods are allocated among competing claimants. This means that the goods have to be allocated by other criteria. Buyers will get in line early, cultivate contacts, try to negotiate special agreements, or offer illegal monetary inducements to get around the maximum price.

The incentive to hoard goods increases, because goods are undervalued at their legal prices and because buyers cannot be sure of obtaining supplies in the future. This further aggravates the scarcity. Producers have less incentive to expand output and maintain quality. Production will fall further as manufacturers find themselves unable to obtain particular inputs that have disappeared from suppliers' inventories. They may even have to suspend production and lay workers off. Export controls will be instituted to keep other countries from taking advantage of the controlled prices. Bartering will creep into the supply system and not only decrease efficiency but also raise cries of inequity from those producers who have nothing of value to offer their suppliers. Items such as paper bags, shoe heels, plastic syringes, and lawn fertilizer will unexpectedly disappear from retail shelves as shortages multiply and breed further shortages. Relative prices will not be able to change in response to changing relative scarcities, and the structure of prices will start to give misleading signals to resource users. In short, suppression of the price system suspends the mechanism of economic coordination and leads to inequities, inefficiencies, and disruptions of production that only worsen the imbalance between demand and supply.

Imposing price controls in the face of an inflation caused by too many dollars chasing too few goods aggravates the problem by reducing the supply of goods and diminishing the incentive of demanders to economize in their use. And this is true whether the imbalance was caused by an excessive creation of dollars or a deficient creation of goods. Moreover, it diverts the attention of the public from the actual causes of the inflation and the proper remedies. Of course, a government whose fiscal and monetary policies have fueled an inflation will be only too happy to encourage the public's belief that private avarice is the root of the problem, that public-spirited self-restraint on the part of citizens is the ultimate answer, and that the rascals who have no public spirit must be controlled by law. Congress will rarely admit that its own spending habits are the cause of any ills.

What Can We Learn from Wartime Price and Wage Controls?

The wage and price controls of World War II are sometimes brought forward as evidence that controls can in fact be effective in preventing excess demand from pulling up prices. But this argument ignores some important facts. For one, it overlooks the public's willingness to put up with shortages and tolerate inequities when they are viewed as temporary necessities. Above all, it overlooks the alternative rationing system created by the federal government during World War II to allocate scarce goods among competing claimants. It ignores the complex point system, the books of ration stamps, the special gasoline coupons, the priority allocations, and the army of controllers that were all required to make the system work as well as it did. It overlooks the role of wartime patriotism in securing the voluntary cooperation that kept the system functioning for several years and closes its eyes to the illegal and semilegal evasions that sometimes helped the system work by enabling people to circumvent it. And when the controls were removed after the war, the excess demand dammed up behind them poured out to raise prices 33% between 1945 and 1948.

The public must learn to distinguish carefully between arguments for limited controls in selected situations where competition is an ineffective regulating force and across-the-board controls imposed to prevent excess money demand from raising prices. The latter is a recipe for disaster. The former may be an effective way to deal with a difficult economic and political problem.

But even limited wage and price controls are going to pose major difficulties. On whom will they be imposed, and how will this be determined? Who will decide when adjustments are called for and what criteria will they employ? Whatever the economic rationale, will the political system be adequate to such a task? It is essential to note that Arthur Burns assigns much of the blame for the decline of competition to government policies. Is it realistic to expect the same government to undo its own work? Regulatory agencies like the Interstate Commerce Commission and the Civil Aeronautics Board that have long taken their function to be the prevention of competition will not suddenly revise their thinking and procedures. State legislators who bow to industry lobbies and create legal cartel arrangements aren't likely to acquire new wisdom or courage any time soon. Anticompetitive laws in the areas of agriculture, labor, and international trade continue to command a Congressional majority. Who will mind the sheep when the shepherds have such a taste for mutton?

INCOMES POLICY

A phrase sometimes used in place of "wage and price controls" to describe the kind of approach recommended by Burns is *incomes policy*. It's an apt phrase, because it calls attention to the origins of the problem and the inherent difficulty of resolving it. If costs are in fact pushed up in the absence of demand increases, it is the result of people's pursuit of higher incomes. They want a larger share. Workers want higher wages, property owners want larger returns on their investment, and business executives want larger rewards for making their firms' revenues increase faster than costs. They all pursue their objectives by trying to raise certain prices relative to others. This poses no problem if competition adequately constrains them. But where economic interests are able to combine or collude, they may be successful in enlarging their share of the pie. Or they may simply offset one another and leave everyone's share unchanged while jacking up the price level in the course of the struggle.

Controls and Income Distribution

If the government tries to control the prices that these groups are able to set it implicitly makes a judgment on *how income ought to be distributed.* By referring to such a program as an incomes policy we are at least calling attention to the scope and importance of the problem being tackled. And it's a problem that looks more formidable the longer it's examined.

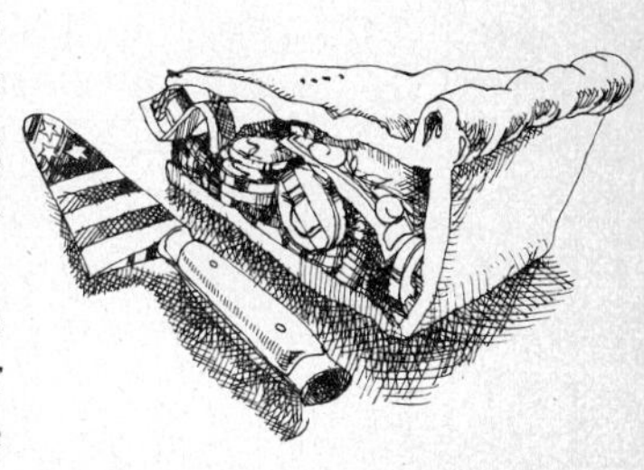

The problem is that the sum of the dollar claims people make on the national income invariably comes to much more than 100% of the dollar value of the national income. To put it crudely, there aren't many people who believe they deserve less than the average and a lot of people who claim more than the average. So what's new? There may be nothing new in the situation if you confine your attention to Western nations and the other nations and cultures descended from Europe. But within these societies the demand by individuals and groups for a larger share of the social product has generally been kept in check by the similar demands of others, and the market has functioned as the adjudicator of competing claims. The market was never a completely "free" market; groups that were able to use political processes to influence market outcomes did so. Two hundred years ago the American Revolution came about in part as the consequence of conflict among such powerful economic interests; each was bent on using the state to improve and protect its own economic opportunities.

The Organizational Revolution

But in the twentieth century two new elements may have appeared. Interest groups are now more effectively organized into labor unions, farm federations, corporations, and professional and trade associations. They are consequently better able to protect their members against the adverse consequences of competition. The economist Kenneth Boulding has called this "the organizational revolution" in a book with that title. As each group pursues its own interests by reducing competition, the market ceases to be an effective regulator of economic activity. The invisible hand that Adam Smith saw leading people to promote the public interest while intending only to pursue their private interests depends upon the existence of competition. In an economy dominated by power blocs, the pursuit of private interests may destroy the public interest.

Rejection of the Market

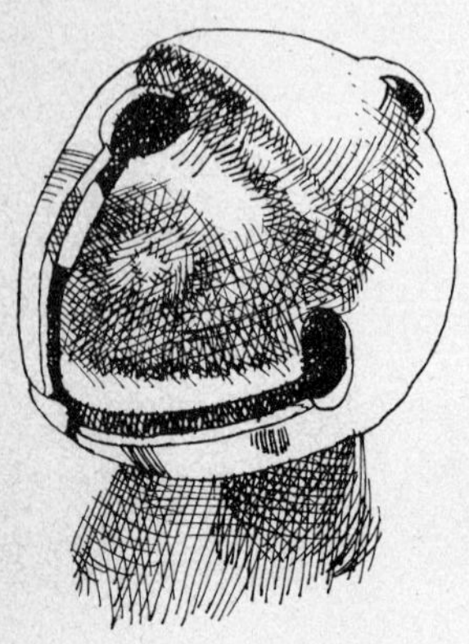

A second development that some observers see is a decline in the perceived legitimacy of market outcomes. By this we mean that fewer people are now prepared to accept market processes as fundamentally just. Perhaps this is related to the first factor mentioned. If people believe that the economy is not governed by "fair competition" but by "special interests," they will not give their consent to the way income is distributed. They will rather try to use the political process to shape the economic process more into line with their own perceptions of fairness.

If this analysis is correct, then governments will not be able to use incomes policy to rein in conflicting interests because *it is incomes policy over which the interests are conflicting.* A particular criterion of fairness cannot be used to settle a dispute over the appropriateness of that criterion. The Genie Conception of government conceals this dilemma. We may be able to see that the economic system does not work as it should and to outline government policies that would improve its performance. But the same forces responsible for the unsatisfactory performance of the economy will block the adoption of the political policies being recommended. It is painfully reminiscent of the fable about the mice who wanted to protect themselves against cats by putting a bell on each cat. If cats let themselves be belled by mice, however, mice would have no reason to want bells on cats.

THE POLITICALIZATION OF THE ECONOMY

Throughout most of this book we have assumed that people want for themselves more of the commodities and services that the economy can provide. From chapter 7 on we have supposed that everyone prefers higher to lower unemployment rates and price stability to inflation. The analysis of economic practices and policies is much easier when we know what the goals are and can take certain shared social purposes for granted. When the goals themselves are in dispute, however, it is difficult to find a vantage point from which to gain perspective.

Economists are no more adept than anyone else at resolving disagreements that involve conflicting goals. The science of economics has nonetheless been able to make analytical advances in the face of conflicting social interests by tying itself closely to the analysis of market processses and outcomes. Markets are just exchange networks. And voluntary exchange is a process by which people who have conflicting interests achieve agreement. It's a limited agreement; but it's enough to enable people with conflicting interests to cooperate in ways that make each participant better off. Anyone who is not made better off simply doesn't exchange. To secure the cooperation of others in improving our own positions, we must find ways to improve their positions, too. Economists view the market as a vast computer into which all preferences are registered, in which all contradictory intentions are accommodated, and from which a particular mixture of output emerges and is distributed. By sticking closely to the analysis of market processes, economists have been able to incorporate conflicting goals and interests into their analyses *without judging among them.* No vantage point above the fray is required to interpret what's going on.

Economic Decisions and Political Judgments

When the members of a society begin to object to the market process itself, however, and when one of the goals becomes the transformation of the system for accommodating conflicting purposes, the economist's task grows immensely more difficult. And that is the situation we have today. What we have called the politicalization of the economy is in large part an attempt to change the rules of the game. The market system itself is in question.

The most fundamental objection to the market process is that, while it may enable all participants to better their conditions, it takes for granted the initial distribution of the resources on the basis of which people exchange. The justice and therefore the political acceptability of market outcomes depends on the justice of the positions from which everyone begins. In very poor societies it makes a great deal of sense to ignore the distribution of wealth in order to concentrate on increasing the total amount available. This is especially sensible if the growth of national income entails increases in income for those at the bottom of the ladder. And this has in fact been the historical tendency in market-organized economies. But more total income becomes relatively less important as a society becomes more affluent, and questions about the way the income is distributed start to take on increasing significance.

A closely related objection to the market process has to do with the appropriate tradeoff between marketable commodities and services on the one hand and less tangible goods such as serenity, beauty, or community on the other. In a society with an abundance of marketable goods, the marginal cost of paying attention to their marginal cost may seem too high to justify the effort. And an economic system that works by focusing attention on these costs may increasingly seem to reflect an irrational attachment to rationality.

The link between all this and the pursuit of full employment and price stability should be obvious. Economic policymakers will be hard-pressed to achieve these goals, not only because we lack an adequate knowledge of money velocities, expenditure multipliers, and time lags, but also because full employment and price stability are not the only goals we're pursuing. We have turned increasingly in this century to government as the appropriate agency to regulate the economy in the interest of a better society. If the results have often been disappointing, it may be because we have thoughtlessly adopted the Genie Conception of government and have paid too little attention to the actual consequences of well-intentioned proposals. But it may also be because we have given too little thought to the question of what we mean by "a better society."

Once Over Lightly

Recession and inflation are not simple alternatives between which policymakers can choose. The fact that low rates of unemployment are historically associated with periods of rising prices does not mean that policymakers can always reduce unemployment by causing or tolerating inflation.

In a period of recovery from a recession, the price level may begin rising before total output and employment regain prerecession levels. This is especially likely if increased demand raises some wages and prices and others are resistant to downward pressure.

Halting or slowing down the rate of inflation may cause a recession. If sellers of products and labor anticipate continued inflation, they will hold out for higher prices and wages than they would otherwise ask. If the expected inflation does not materialize, they will be unable to sell as much as they had anticipated selling. High unemployment rates and accumulations of unwanted inventories will continue until events have taught sellers to revise their expectations and lower their price and wage demands.

An economy that is continuously operating close to capacity tends to create sellers' markets. In such markets, search costs are low for sellers and high for buyers. Sellers consequently tend to hold out longer against lowering their prices, buyers tend more quickly to accept prices higher than they had anticipated, and price and wage levels creep upward.

Unemployment levels might be lowered temporarily and output levels temporarily increased by an acceleration in the rate of inflation. This will occur if sellers of labor and products mistakenly assume that they are being offered better terms. But employment and output levels will decline again as sellers of labor learn that *real* wages have not increased and sellers of products learn that costs have increased along with prices. Only a constantly accelerating inflation can maintain the illusion of better terms and keep employment and output at these higher levels.

Price and wage controls that are imposed when aggregate demand exceeds the ability of the economy to produce at current prices create shortages, inefficient resource allocation, and disruptions in production.

They cannot solve the problem of inflation caused by excessive monetary demand, but they can make the problem worse.

Sellers of labor and products who are sufficiently well organized to raise wages and prices in the absence of any increase in monetary demand will reduce the quantity of labor demanded and increase unemployment. If the government responds by increasing monetary demand, it will be able to prevent the increase in unemployment by causing inflation. Some economists believe that labor unions, large corporations, and government regulations are reducing competition in many sectors of the economy and thereby confronting aggregate demand managers with the unpleasant necessity of choosing between the acceptance of unemployment and the acceptance of inflation. They therefore argue for controls on those wages and prices that are not, in their estimation, adequately controlled by competition.

The imposition of such controls entails a prior decision by government as to which groups will not be allowed to use their political or market power to increase their incomes. In the absence of a political consensus on how income *ought* to be distributed, the government will probably be unable to formulate and enforce such an incomes policy.

Most goods are scarce; they can only be obtained by sacrificing other goods. This may also be true for the goods of high employment and stable prices. It is possible that some of the goals we are pursuing through political processes will make high employment and price stability impossible to achieve.

QUESTIONS FOR DISCUSSION

1. (*a*) Why is the price level likely to rise faster the lower the level of unemployment in the economy?

    (*b*) Does raising the unemployment rate slow down inflation? How so? How long does it take?

2. (*a*) Is aggregate demand inadequate if there is a shortage of automotive mechanics and a surplus of secondary school teachers?

    (*b*) Can substantial unemployment exist at a time when listed job vacancies exceed total unemployment?

3. "There is no danger that a government deficit will cause inflation when unemployment stands at 8% of the civilian labor force." Do you agree?

4. How and why does the attempt to lower the permanent rate of unemployment by deliberately causing inflation depend upon an illusion?

5. "The basic cause of an excessively high unemployment rate is uncertainty." Explain whether you agree or disagree with this statement and why.

6. Would you expect a different effect on employment from the imposition of a temporary quota against imports than from the imposition of a quota that is expected to be permanent? Why?

7. If union-won wage increases add to unemployment and the Fed then expands the money supply to reduce the unemployment rate, who is the villain responsible for inflation?

8. If it is socially irresponsible for sellers to raise their prices in periods of inflation, why did the government raise the price of the annual *Economic Report of the President* from $3.05 in 1974 to $3.25 in 1975?

9. Is it socially responsible for the Civil Aeronautics Board to raise the prices of airline travel but socially irresponsible for food processors to raise the prices of frozen vegetables?

10. Make up two lists of prices and wages. One should contain specific prices and wages that in your judgment *are not* adequately controlled by competition and the other should contain specific wages and prices that you think *are* adequately controlled by competition. What criteria will you use? What evidence do you have to support your lists?

11. Is it unjust for money wage rates to rise less rapidly than prices? Is it unjust for some money wage rates to rise faster and others more slowly than prices? Can you think of some wage and salary rates that *ought to* rise less rapidly than prices? On what basis would you answer this question?

12. "A teacher of chemistry should not be paid more than a teacher of history simply because the demand for chemistry teachers is greater relative to the supply. Teachers are not commodities. They are professional persons with family responsibilities who are providing essential public services." Do you agree with that statement? Under what circumstances do you think its principles are most likely to find acceptance?

13. Why does it take so much more effort and involve so much more conflict for the faculty of a college to agree on a revision of the curriculum they are "selling" to students than for the managers of department stores to decide on the mixture of goods they will offer for sale?

14. Is it possible to control inflation by having a panel of experts pass on all proposed wage and price increases? Should such panels include an equal number of business, labor, and consumer representatives.

15. "Because government is not limited by private profit, it can often accomplish what private interests cannot accomplish." Discuss.

18

ECONOMICS AND THE GOOD SOCIETY

Why is there so much disagreement about economic policies among intelligent and well-informed people who are genuinely looking for the public interest and not simply advocating their own narrow interests? Why is it so much more difficult to achieve consensus on the best way to manage the economy than on the best way to put people on the moon? Are economic interrelationships that much more complex than the relationships that had to be mastered to achieve a successful lunar landing?

FACTS AND VALUES

Economists have often pointed out, as a way of answering these questions, that disagreements over economic policy stem from two different kinds of disagreement. There is disagreement about *what is* and disagreement about *what ought to be.* Science can supposedly answer questions of the first type, because they only require attention to facts and logical reasoning. But when we disagree about what ought to be or about the goals of economic policy, we are in the realm of ethics. And we do not have any way of resolving ethical disagreements. They are ultimately judgments of value; and ultimate value judgments cannot finally be proved or disproved.

There is something unsatisfactory about this way of setting up the problem, however. In the first place, the science of economics is not completely independent of economists' value judgments. Our theories are not

based exclusively on observation and the rules of logic; the value judgments of scientists often shape their choice of theories, both in the physical sciences and more obviously in the social sciences. In the second place, disagreements about what ought to be often *can* be resolved by closer attention to fact and logic. Perhaps there is no way of resolving disagreement on *ultimate* values. But when is a value ultimate? How many of our important ethical disagreements are actually rooted in ultimate and therefore unresolvable differences?

One very important reason why people disagree about goals is that they disagree on what is possible. One group may recommend a policy because its members assign a high priority to achieving greater economic equality. Another group may oppose the policy because its members place a high value on individual freedom of choice. But each group may believe that its goal can be achieved without any substantial sacrifice of the other goal and make its policy recommendations on this assumption. For example, people who want laws against racial and sexual discrimination by employers rarely believe that the administration of these laws will infringe in any significant way on individual freedom. Opponents of such legislation, on the other hand, often do not see how it can be made effective unless those charged with administering the law are granted the power to make essentially arbitrary decisions. The real disagreement may consequently not be about the relative importance of equality and freedom but about the problems likely to be encountered in administering ambiguous laws. Even the fundamental (or seemingly fundamental) disagreements that characterize debates between "capitalists" and "socialists" may be largely of this kind.

Surprisingly little of the disagreement over economic policy turns out to be purely disagreement about goals. Far more commonly, a policy will be recommended by one group but opposed by another because the two groups expect different consequences from its adoption. This does not mean that we could easily reach consensus if we all looked at the consequences of the proposals we're recommending. It does mean, however, that we have much to learn by paying closer attention to the criticisms of others. Every action has unintended and often undesirable consequences. But someone strongly committed to the goal an action is designed to achieve will be less capable of perceiving or appreciating these consequences than someone else whose primary commitment is to different goals.

The authors of this book do not believe, therefore, that strong convictions have no proper role in economic policy discussions or that economists ought to or even can keep value judgments out of their analysis. But this danger is much less than the danger that people will refuse to let their goals be affected by criticism. It is much too easy to become totally convinced of the justice of one's goals and to treat all criticism as evidence of bad faith. But the best and the worst social goals can only be sought by employing fallible policies that may in the end do more harm than good despite the purity of intention behind them. The full consequences of the economic policies we adopt will never be known with certainty. But economics can suggest answers even for a society beginning to question its goals, because economics is a way of thinking that clarifies the consequences of social action.

THE ECONOMIST'S PERSPECTIVE

An answer presupposes a question, however, and the answers we discover are products of the questions we ask. A great deal therefore depends on where we begin, the point of view we adopt, what we assume before we start, and the concepts that we use to organize our thinking and questioning. Thomas Kuhn, an influential philosopher of science, has argued that all scientific activity is rooted in some *paradigm.* By this he means a set of working assumptions that guide inquiry by posing certain questions and ignoring others. Every scientific theory reveals something at the same time that it conceals something else. What does the economic way of thinking reveal? And what does it conceal?

The economic way of thinking employs such concepts as demand, opportunity cost, marginal effects, and comparative advantage to *order* familiar phenomena. The economist knows very little about the real world that is not better known by businessmen, engineers, and others who make things happen. What he does know *is how things fit together.* The concepts of economics enable us to make better sense out of what we observe and to think more consistently and coherently about a wide range of interrelated phenomena.

This turns out in practice to be a largely negative kind of knowledge. Perhaps you detected, as you read through the chapters of this book, a greater emphasis on what *should not* than on what *should* be done. But negative conclusions are important, and they may be especially important in an area like economics. The economist Frank Knight used to defend the heavily negative character of economic reasoning with a quotation: "It ain't ignorance that does the most damage; it's knowin' so derned much that ain't so."

Too many people "know" how to solve pressing social problems. Their mental picture of the economic universe is a simple one in which intentions can easily be realized and the only obstacle to a better society is therefore a lack of good intentions. How many times have we encountered grand solutions to vexing social problems prefaced with the words "All we need to do is . . ."? But social actions have consequences that run far beyond those that can be easily predicted or foreseen. Restricting textile imports into the United States, for example, does, for the present at least, protect the jobs and income of textile producers; that's clear enough. But it takes a tutored eye to notice that this will shift even more income away from other Americans by raising textile prices, reducing American export opportunities, and in general inhibiting the exploitation of comparative advantage. Again, it is easy to see that rent controls hold down the money payments that tenants must make to landlords. But how many advocates of such controls are aware of the alternative payments that tenants will have to make, of the new forms of discrimination that will replace discrimination on the basis of money price, and of the short- and long-run effects upon the supply of rental housing?

Nonetheless, people easily become impatient with those who warn against the inadvisability of actions that will make matters worse and propose no solutions of their own. In a society such as ours, accustomed to the almost miraculous accomplishments of science and technology, the demand for "doing something" tends to exceed by a wide margin the supply of genuine solutions to social problems. We have probably erred in assuming that social problems can be handled in the same way that we manage technological problems. We know that conflicting interests create hard problems for social policymakers. We still underestimate the difficulties in the way of bringing about planned social change because we underestimate the complexity of social systems, of the networks of interaction through which behavior is coordinated in a society and people are induced to cooperate in the achievement of their goals.

Economists and the Market System

This argument is closely related to the accusation that the economic way of thinking contains an implicit bias in favor of capitalism, competition, and free exchange. The accusation is substantially true. Many economists have been and are socialists, of course; many have had serious misgivings about the consequences of unrestricted competition; and economists are by no means unanimously in favor of completely free exchange. But the critics who accuse economics of this kind of ideological bias are really talking about a predisposition of thought; they are not denying that there are exceptions. And they have a point.

Economics developed in the late eighteenth and early nineteenth centuries largely out of efforts to understand the self-regulating aspects of economic systems. In the face of a widespread belief, amounting almost to a commonsense conviction, that political regulation was indispensable to an adequately functioning economy, economists assumed the task of expounding the alternative thesis. As they examined in ever greater detail and depth the interactions among the innumerable decisions that make up an economic system, they evolved a body of theory stressing the cooperative aspects of free exchange. The economist's way of thinking has tended to reveal the order and the coordination that lie beneath the seeming chaos of an unplanned and unregulated economy. The elements of conflict, disorder, and disruption that are also found in every economic system have tended to be regarded by the economist more as disturbing factors than as objects of his primary interest.

On top of all this, economic theory often treats proposals for reform of the economic system rather unkindly. It is not that economists are themselves uninterested in reform or that they are the paid lackeys of the privileged classes. But economic theory, by revealing the inter-dependence of decisions, calls attention to the unexamined consequences of proposals for change. "It won't work out that way" is the economist's standard response to many well-intentioned policy proposals. Realism is not necessarily conservatism, but it often appears to be quite similar. And there *is* a sense in which knowledge does promote conservatism. Even physicists have been accused of hopeless conservatism by would-be inventors of perpetual-motion machines.

Individualism and Economic Analysis

Another indictment frequently leveled against economics accuses it of an excessively individualistic point of view. The critics object that econo-mists conceive of society as nothing but a collection of individuals pur-suing their own interests. And that's quite true in one sense. The funda-mental concepts of economics refer to choice as the basis of all economizing activity; and the only choices about which we can think and talk meaning-fully are the subjective evaluations of individuals. So the economic way of thinking is deeply colored by "methodological individualism," a pro-cedure that makes individual choice the basic unit of analysis and tries to explain all social occurrences by reference to the preferences of individuals.

But is this a flaw or a strength? No one seriously believes that "the good" can be simply identified with "what individuals happen to prefer." As a working assumption, however, this may be less dangerous than unexam-ined concepts of the social welfare, the national interest, or the good of society. The economist is occupationally conditioned to wonder about the composition of such aggregates as "social," "national," and "public" and to suspect all aggregates until they have been broken down into the costs and benefits that individuals experience. That's a healthy suspicion, and probably a strength rather than a limitation of the economic way of thinking.

It's associated, however, with some additional modes of thinking that may not be equally defensible. One is a reluctance to inquire into the origins of the values that individuals happen to hold. Our choices as individuals are certainly conditioned by our socialization, and no one who has given serious attention to the question will deny that our socialization sometimes serves us badly. There is consequently much to be said for looking critically at the way in which values are formed in our society and at how and why individuals come to hold the preferences that guide their choices. Since the tools of economic analysis are not well suited for this kind of inquiry, the writings of economists contain almost nothing on the origin of preferences. And that often leaves the impression, whether intended or not, that economists consider the preferences of individuals to be *beyond criticism.*

Consensus and Cooperation

There is an additional reason why economists may be relatively disinterested in the criticism of individual values. They know that social cooperation is often possible among people even when their values diverge widely. The economic way of thinking spells out the workings of the market system, a remarkably effective means of securing cooperation without agreement. This may well be the most important difference between economic and political processes. While the political process works through the establishment of consensus, the economic or market process allows more room for individuals to go their own separate ways and even to help one another attain goals of which they mutually disapprove.

Think for a moment about *books.* Books not only reflect particular values; they also *teach* values. Sometimes openly, sometimes covertly, sometimes without the authors even being aware of it, books inculcate attitudes toward family, sex, religion, politics, or authority. Even a determined effort to avoid value judgments teaches values; although the authors may claim that it teaches openness and tolerance, their critics can often justifiably claim that it teaches skepticism and ethical relativism. *Books are controversial.* But with the market controlling the publication of books, everyone can be relatively satisfied. People will buy and read what they prefer and largely ignore the rest. Moreover, the lumberjack who belongs to the John Birch Society will cut down trees to make paper for the printing of communist pamphlets and the militant trade unionist will set type for a book attacking labor unions. When the production and distribution of books becomes subject to the political process, however, this easy method of accommodation is not available. A consensus on values must be reached before decisions can be made. Bitter, violent, and prolonged controversy erupted in Kanawha County, West Virginia, in 1974 when people began to criticize the textbooks used in elementary and secondary public schools. They claimed that their children were being indoctrinated in alien

values. The Kanawha County case showed both how difficult it may be to reach a consensus on values and what can occur when political decisions are made in the absence of consensus.

The questions raised in West Virginia proved bitterly divisive not because they touched upon ultimate human concerns but because these concerns had to be reconciled through the political process. The differences in value and belief were surely no broader or deeper than some of the differences among people of various religious persuasions; the former might even be viewed as an aspect of the latter differences as they existed in West Virginia in 1974. But we do not have public churches in this country and we do have public schools. People can choose the church they prefer and ignore the rest; they cannot easily choose for their children the kind of public school they prefer. The point is that conflicting values can peaceably coexist within a market or economic system and they cannot peaceably coexist within a political system.

This does not prove that we should prohibit public schools as we have prohibited state churches. Some disagreements on value questions may have to be faced and a resolution attempted despite the difficulty of the task. The 1954 Supreme Court decision on racial segregation forced this nation into a discussion of values that still continues and from which we have learned a great deal and grown in ways that no one could have predicted a quarter century ago. That decision also opened the way to greater discord and violence, however; and these are signs of the distance we must still traverse in reaching a consensus on the ethical significance of racial differences.

"Basic Values" or "Mere Tastes"?

But could a society such as ours hold together if value consensus were the precondition for *all* social cooperation? Is it not one of the strengths of the market system that it can tolerate an extraordinary range of value differences? To put it bluntly, the market system permits individuals to pursue all kinds of tasteless, inane, elitist, immoral, and useless goals and to do so with the cooperation of some of the very people who think those goals are contemptible.

Economists, as analysts of the market system, object only to the use of such adjectives as tasteless or contemptible. In the market system and in economic analysis, all judgments, from the most thoroughly reasoned and deeply felt to the most capricious and trivial, become "tastes and preferences." And *de gustibus non est disputandum:* one does not argue about tastes. Or is it that one *should* not argue about tastes? At least one does not *have to* argue about tastes under a market system. So why go looking for trouble?

"Quantity of pleasure being equal," the utilitarian philosopher Jeremy

Bentham once asserted, "pushpin [a children's game] is as good as poetry."
While economists have often felt repelled by the philistinism of that
remark, they have also tended to view it as a position preferable to most
efforts to impose one's preferences upon others. And they have supported
the market system in part because it offers a way by which society can
minimize the need to legislate values.

Economics and Ethics

There is another sense in which economics has been accused of excessive individualism. The economic way of thinking is often said to *endorse*
self-seeking activities and to place a stamp of approval upon the pursuit
of one's own interests and the neglect of the public interest. The basic
assumption of economic theory—that individuals do in fact pursue their
own interests in a rational way—is sometimes hard to distinguish from
the belief that everyone *ought* to look out for himself first and foremost.
Adam Smith said that an individual who pursued his own interest frequently promoted the interests of society more effectively than when he
consciously aimed at the public good. This may be true. But it is dangerous
as a principle of ethics and this is what it has sometimes become in the
hands of Adam Smith's descendants. In a subtle way it suggests that the
person who tends most narrowly to his own business and never thinks
about anyone's welfare but his own is really more ethical than the person
who occupies himself with social causes.

But Adam Smith wrote a book entitled *The Theory of Moral Sentiments*
before he wrote *The Wealth of Nations.* In the earlier book he maintained
that sympathy, a feeling for others through "putting ourselves in their
situations," was the effective cement of society. The ideas in *The Wealth of
Nations* presuppose the ideas in *The Theory of Moral Sentiments.* Economic
theory presupposes a social bond. The pursuit of one's own interests that
Adam Smith recommended presupposes at least some sympathetic inclu-
sion of the welfare of others in one's own interests. In short, a free society,
in which people may behave as they please, is only possible if there are
some ways in which it does not in fact please people to behave. The economic way of thinking can ignore the important role that consideration for
others plays in the functioning of an economic system only if such consideration is a dominant feature of social life.

Economics and Rationality

Economic theory is to some extent capable of explaining or predicting
the social consequences flowing from the pursuit of *every kind* of human
interest as long as people are rational. If people are not interested in rationality, the predictive power of economics diminishes rapidly. Rationality

here means concern for the relationship between ends and means, the attitude of calculation and planning, and purposive behavior. Frank Knight once described economic theory as "an abstract rationale of all conduct which is rational at all, and a rationale of all social relations arising through the organization of rational activity." Rationality in this sense is what Wordsworth had in mind when he wrote:

> . . . high Heaven rejects the lore
> Of nicely-calculated less or more.

Wordsworth could speak for "high Heaven" only by virtue of his poetic license. But he gave effective expression to the feelings that many people have toward a social order in which cost-benefit analysis is the ruling principle, and toward a science of society that explains all behavior in terms of marginal costs and benefits. The romantic doctrine of Wordsworth is dangerous. It too easily becomes a glorification of impulse and a rejection of intelligence, and leads to attitudes that will not create great poetry *or* engineering triumphs. But it is possible that we have become so preoccupied with technique and with means toward ends that we have lost our capacity to discover and nurture worthwhile goals. Perhaps we do tend to view everything as a potential input, a mere means to an end, and to treat other people and finally ourselves as no more than economic resources. Has a too narrowly conceived rationality become an obsession in our society and crowded out such alternative perspectives on life as the contemplative, the aesthetic, and the playful? Some critics maintain that the economic way of thinking encourages our already excessive compulsion to use, control, and dominate in a society that would gain far more from learning to be open, nonmanipulative, and receptive toward the surrounding world.

The sociologist Daniel Bell, who is an opponent neither of rationality nor of economics, has written: "The economizing mode—the exact calculation of monetary costs and returns—has been an efficient organizer of production, but at the expense of . . . the treating of men as 'things' within the sphere of production." Economists use two defenses against this argument. One is that they only describe; they do not prescribe. The other is that the economic way of thinking only treats people as things in the hands of those who are unwilling to view them as anything more. A good example is the economic valuation of human life. Who can place a money value on a life? But if the economist can show that certain social policies implicitly value human life at *less than* its worth as a productive machine, then surely those policies ought to be changed.

But to escape from tradition is never easy. And the tradition in which economists were reared does tend to regard consumable things as "goods" and all else as resources, things that can be used in the production of goods. Thus labor becomes a resource and abilities become human capital. There is nothing in the *logic* of economics that precludes us from viewing work as a social activity that can and should have value for itself. But there is a great deal in the *history* of economics that makes it difficult for economists to do so. This may be a very important limitation in a world where more things yield progressively less additional satisfaction as they simultaneously become more difficult to produce, and where the process of creating may soon be more valuable than its product.

Economics and Civilization

John Maynard Keynes once proposed a toast to economists, "the keepers of the possibility of civilization." The possibility of civilization—that is all. The efficient allocation of resources enlarges the realm of possibility; but it does not by itself guarantee the progress of civilization. A well-coordinated and smoothly functioning economic system gives individuals more opportunity to choose; it does not guarantee that they will choose well. The economic way of thinking, especially in a democracy, is an important preliminary. It is extremely important; but it is only preliminary.

Economists are for the most part ready to admit that the concepts they employ sometimes distort the reality they study. And they are willing to submit their analyses and conclusions to the test of rational criticism. But some point of view is indispensable to any inquiry, in the physical sciences as well as the social sciences. A completely open mind is a completely empty mind, and empty minds learn nothing. If the economic way of thinking sometimes leads to distortions, to misplaced emphasis, or even to outright error, the appropriate corrective is rational criticism. The application of that corrective has frequently altered the conclusions of economic science in the past. It will probably continue to do so in the future.

THE USE OF KNOWLEDGE IN SOCIETY

appendix 1

F. A. HAYEK

I

What is the problem we wish to solve when we try to construct a rational economic order?

On certain familiar assumptions the answer is simple enough. *If* we possess all the relevant information, *if* we can start out from a given system of preferences and *if* we command complete knowledge of available means, the problem which remains is purely one of logic. That is, the answer to the question of what is the best use of the available means is implicit in our assumptions. The conditions which the solution of this optimum problem must satisfy have been fully worked out and can be stated best in mathematical form: put at their briefest, they are that the marginal rates of substitution between any two commodities or factors must be the same in all their different uses.

This, however, is emphatically *not* the economic problem which society faces. And the economic calculus which we have developed to solve this logical problem, though an important step toward the solution of the economic problem of society, does not yet provide an answer to it. The reason for this is that the "data" from which the economic calculus starts are never for the whole society "given" to a single mind which could work out the implications, and can never be so given.

The peculiar character of the problem of a rational economic order is determined precisely by the fact that the knowledge of the circumstances of which we must make use never exists in concentrated or integrated form, but solely as the dispersed bits of incomplete and frequently contradictory knowledge which all the separate individuals possess. The economic problem of society is thus not merely a problem of how to allocate "given" resources—if "given" is taken to mean given to a single mind which deliberately solves the problem set by the "data." It is rather a problem of how to secure the best use of resources known to any of the members of society, for ends whose relative importance only these individuals know. Or, to put it briefly, it is a problem of the utilization of knowledge not given to anyone in its totality.

This character of the fundamental problem has, I am afraid, been rather obscured than illuminated by many of the recent refinements of economic theory, particularly by many of the uses made of mathematics. Though the problem with which I want primarily to deal in this paper is the problem of a rational economic organization, I shall in its course be led again

Reprinted by permission of the author and the American Economic Association from *American Economic Review,* September 1945.

463

and again to point to its close connections with certain methodological questions. Many of the points I wish to make are indeed conclusions toward which diverse paths of reasoning have unexpectedly converged. But as I now see these problems, this is no accident. It seems to me that many of the current disputes with regard to both economic theory and economic policy have their common origin in a misconception about the nature of the economic problem of society. This misconception in turn is due to an erroneous transfer to social phenomena of the habits of thought we have developed in dealing with the phenomena of nature.

II

In ordinary language we describe by the word "planning" the complex of interrelated decisions about the allocation of our available resources. All economic activity is in this sense planning; and in any society in which many people collaborate, this planning, whoever does it, will in some measure have to be based on knowledge which, in the first instance, is not given to the planner but to somebody else, which somehow will have to be conveyed to the planner. The various ways in which the knowledge on which people base their plans is communicated to them is the crucial problem for any theory explaining the economic process. And the problem of what is the best way of utilizing knowledge initially dispersed among all the people is at least one of the main problems of economic policy—or of designing an efficient economic system.

The answer to this question is closely connected with that other question which arises here, that of *who* is to do the planning. It is about this question that all the dispute about "economic planning" centers. This is not a dispute about whether planning is to be done or not. It is a dispute as to whether planning is to be done centrally, by one authority for the whole economic system, or is to be divided among many individuals. Planning in the specific sense in which the term is used in contemporary controversy necessarily means central planning—direction of the whole economic system according to one unified plan. Competition, on the other hand, means decentralized planning by many separate persons. The half-way house between the two, about which many people talk but which few like when they see it, is the delegation of planning to organized industries, or, in other words, monopoly.

Which of these systems is likely to be more efficient depends mainly on the question under which of them we can expect that fuller use will be made of the existing knowledge. And this, in turn, depends on whether we are more likely to succeed in putting at the disposal of a single central authority all the knowledge which ought to be used but which is initially dispersed among many different individuals, or in conveying to the individuals such additional knowledge as they need in order to enable them to fit their plans in with those of others.

III

It will at once be evident that on this point the position will be different with respect to different kinds of knowledge; and the answer to our question will therefore largely turn on the relative importance of the different kinds of knowledge; those more likely to be at the disposal of particular individuals and those which we should with greater confidence expect to find in the possession of an authority made up of suitably chosen experts. If it is today so widely assumed that the latter will be in a better position, this is because one kind of knowledge, namely, scientific knowledge, occupies now so prominent a place in public imagination that we tend to forget that it is not the only kind that is relevant. It may be admitted that, so far as scientific knowledge is concerned, a body of suitably chosen experts may be in the best position to command all the best knowledge available—though this is of course merely shifting the difficulty to the problem of selecting the experts. What I wish to point out is that, even assuming that this problem can be readily solved, it is only a small part of the wider problem.

Today it is almost heresy to suggest that scientific knowledge is not the sum of all knowledge. But a little reflection will show that there is beyond question a body of very important but unorganized knowledge which cannot possibly be called scientific in the sense of knowledge of general rules: the knowledge of the particular circumstances of time and place. It is with respect to this that practically every individual has some advantage over all others in that he possess unique information of which beneficial use might be made, but of which use can be made only if the decisions depending on it are left to him or are made with his active coöperation. We need to remember only how much we have to learn in any occupation after we have completed our theoretical training, how big a part of our working life we spend learning particular jobs, and how valuable an asset in all walks of life is knowledge of people, of local conditions, and special circumstances. To know of and put to use a machine not fully employed, or somebody's skill which could be better utilized, or to be aware of a surplus stock which can be drawn upon during an interruption of supplies, is socially quite as useful as the knowledge of better alternative techniques. And the shipper who earns his living from using otherwise empty or half-filled journeys of tramp-steamers, or the estate agent whose whole knowledge is almost exclusively one of temporary opportunities, or the *arbitrageur* who gains from local differences of commodity prices, are all performing eminently useful functions based on special knowledge of circumstances of the fleeting moment not known to others.

It is a curious fact that this sort of knowledge should today be generally regarded with a kind of contempt, and that anyone who by such knowledge gains an advantage over somebody better equipped with theoretical or technical knowledge is thought to have acted almost disreputably. To gain an advantage from better knowledge of facilities of communication or transport is sometimes regarded as almost dishonest, although it is quite as important that society make use of the best opportunities in this respect as in using the latest scientific discoveries. This prejudice has in a considerable measure affected the attitude toward commerce in general compared with that toward production. Even economists who regard themselves as definitely above the crude materialist fallacies of the past constantly commit the same mistake where activities directed toward the acquisition of such practical knowledge are concerned—apparently because in their scheme of things all such knowledge is supposed to be "given." The common idea now seems to be that all such knowledge should as a matter of course be readily at the command of everybody, and the reproach of irrationality leveled against the existing economic order is frequently based on the fact that it is not so available. This view disregards the fact that the method by which such knowledge can be made as widely available as possible is precisely the problem to which we have to find an answer.

IV

If it is fashionable today to minimize the importance of the knowledge of the particular circumstances of time and place, this is closely connected with the smaller importance which is now attached to change as such. Indeed, there are few points on which the assumptions made (usually only implicitly) by the "planners" differ from those of their opponents as much as with regard to the significance and frequency of changes which will make substantial alterations of production plans necessary. Of course, if detailed economic plans could be laid down for fairly long periods in advance and then closely adhered to, so that no further economic decisions of importance would be required, the task of drawing up a comprehensive plan governing all economic activity would appear much less formidable.

It is, perhaps, worth stressing that economic problems arise always and only in consequence of change. So long as things continue as before, or at least as they were expected to, there arise no new problems requiring a decision, no need to form a new plan. The belief that changes, or at least day-to-day adjustments, have become less important in modern times implies the contention that economic problems also have become less important. This belief in the decreasing importance of change is, for that reason, usually held by the same people who argue that the importance of economic considerations has been driven into the background by the growing importance of technological knowledge.

Is it true that, with the elaborate apparatus of modern production, economic decisions are required only at long intervals, as when a new factory is to be erected or a new process to be introduced? Is it true that, once a plant has been built, the rest is all more or less mechanical, determined by the character of the plant, and leaving little to be changed in adapting to the ever-changing circumstances of the moment?

The fairly widespread belief in the affirmative is not, so far as I can ascertain, borne out by the practical experience of the business man. In a competitive industry at any rate—and such an industry alone can serve as a test—the task of keeping cost from rising requires constant struggle, absorbing a great part of the energy of the manager. How easy it is for an inefficient manager to dissipate the differentials on which profitability rests, and that it is possible, with the same technical facilities, to produce with a great variety of costs, are among the commonplaces of business experience which do not seem to be equally familiar in the study of the economist. The very strength of the desire, constantly voiced by producers and engineers, to be able to proceed untrammeled by considerations of money costs, is eloquent testimony to the extent to which these factors enter into their daily work.

One reason why economists are increasingly apt to forget about the constant small changes which make up the whole economic picture is probably their growing preoccupation with statistical aggregates, which show a very much greater stability than the movements of the detail. The comparative stability of the aggregates cannot, however, be accounted for—as the statisticians seem occasionally to be inclined to do—by the "law of large numbers" or the mutual compensation of random changes. The number of elements with which we have to deal is not large enough for such accidental forces to produce stability. The continuous flow of goods and services is maintained by constant deliberate adjustments, by new dispositions made every day in the light of circumstances not known the day before, by B stepping in at once when A fails to deliver. Even the large and highly mechanized plant keeps going largely because of an environment upon which it can draw for all sorts of unexpected needs; tiles for its roof, stationery for its forms, and all the thousand and one kinds of equipment in which it cannot be self-contained and which the plans for the operation of the plant require to be readily available in the market.

This is, perhaps, also the point where I should briefly mention the fact that the sort of knowledge with which I have been concerned is knowledge of the kind which by its nature cannot enter into statistics and therefore cannot be conveyed to any central authority in statistical form. The statistics which such a central authority would have to use would have to be arrived at precisely by abstracting from minor differences between the things, by lumping together, as resources of one kind, items which differ as regards location, quality, and other particulars, in a way which may be very significant for the specific decision. It follows from this that central planning based on statistical information by its nature cannot take direct account of these circumstances of time and place, and that the central planner will have to find some way or other in which the decisions depending on them can be left to the "man on the spot."

V

If we can agree that the economic problem of society is mainly one of rapid adaptation to changes in the particular circumstances of time and place, it would seem to follow that the ultimate decisions must be left to the people who are familiar with these circumstances, who know directly of the relevant changes and of the resources immediately available to meet them. We cannot expect that this problem will be solved by first communicating all this knowledge to a central board which, after integrating *all* knowledge, issues its orders. We must solve it by some form of decentralization. But this answers only part of our problem. We need decentralization because only thus can we ensure that the knowledge of the particular circumstances of time and place will be promptly used. But the "man on the spot" cannot decide solely on the basis of his limited but intimate knowledge of the facts of his immediate surroundings. There still remains the problem of communicating to him such further information as he needs to fit his decisions into the whole pattern of changes of the larger economic system.

How much knowledge does he need to do so successfully? Which of the events which happen beyond the horizon of his immediate knowledge are of relevance to his immediate decision, and how much of them need he know?

There is hardly anything that happens anywhere in the world that *might* not have an effect on the decision he ought to make. But he need not know of these events as such, nor of *all* their effects. It does not matter for him *why* at the particular moment more screws of one size than of another are wanted, *why* paper bags are more readily available than canvas bags, or *why* skilled labor, or particular machine tools, have for the moment become more difficult to acquire. All that is significant for him is *how much more or less* difficult to procure they have become compared with other things with which he is also concerned, or how much more or less urgently wanted are the alternative things he produces or uses. It is always a question of the relative importance of the particular things with which he is concerned, and the causes which alter their relative importance are of no interest to him beyond the effect on those concrete things of his own environment.

It is in this connection that what I have called the economic calculus proper helps us, at least by analogy, to see how this problem can be solved, and in fact is being solved, by the price system. Even the single controlling mind, in possession of all the data for some small, self-contained economic system, would not—every time some small adjustment in the allocation of resources had to be made—go explicitly through all the relations between ends and means which might possibly be affected. It is indeed the great contribution of the pure logic of choice that it has demonstrated conclusively that even such a single mind could solve this kind of problem only by constructing and constantly using rates of equivalence (or "values," or "marginal rates of substitution"), *i.e.,* by attaching to each kind of scarce resource a numerical index which cannot be derived from any property possessed by that particular thing, but which reflects, or in which is condensed, its significance in view of the whole means-end structure. In any small change he will have to consider only these quantitative indices (or "values") in which all the relevant information is concentrated; and by adjusting the quantities one by one, he can appropriately rearrange his dispositions without having to solve the whole puzzle *ab initio,* or without needing at any stage to survey it at once in all its ramifications.

Fundamentally, in a system where the knowledge of the relevant facts is dispersed among many people, prices can act to coördinate the separate actions of different people in the same way as subjective values help the individual to coördinate the parts of his plan. It is worth contemplating for a moment a very simple and commonplace instance of the action of the price system to see what precisely it accomplishes. Assume that somewhere in the world a new opportunity for the use of some raw material, say tin, has arisen, or that one of the sources of supply of tin has been eliminated. It does not matter for our purpose—and it is very significant that it does not matter—which of these two causes has made tin more scarce. All that the users of tin need to know is that some of the tin they used to consume is now more profitably employed elsewhere, and that in consequence they must economize tin. There is no need for the great majority of them even to know where the more urgent need has arisen, or in favor of what other needs they ought to husband the supply. If only some of them know directly of the new demand, and switch resources over to it, and if the people who are aware of the new gap thus created in turn fill it from still other sources, the effect will rapidly spread throughout the whole economic system and influence not only all the uses of tin, but also those of its substitutes and the substitutes of these substitutes, the supply of all the things made of tin, and their substitutes, and so on; and all this without the great majority of those instrumental in bringing about these substitutions knowing anything at all about the original cause of these changes. The whole acts as one market, not because their limited individual fields of vision sufficiently overlap so that through many inter-mediaries the relevant information is communicated to all. The mere fact that there is one price for any commodity—or rather that local prices are connected in a manner determined by the cost of transport, etc.—brings about the solution which (it is just conceptually possible) might have been arrived at by one single mind possessing all the information which is in fact dispersed among all the people involved in the process.

VI

We must look at the price system as such a mechanism for communicating information if we want to understand its real function—a function which, of course, it fulfills less perfectly as prices grow more rigid. (Even when quoted prices have become quite rigid, however, the forces which would operate through changes in price still operate to a considerable extent through changes in the other terms of the contract.) The most significant fact about this system is the economy of knowledge with which it operates, or how little the individual participants need to know in order to be able to take the right action. In abbreviated form, by a kind of symbol, only the most essential information is passed on, and passed on only to those concerned. It is more than a metaphor to describe the price system as a kind of machinery for registering change, or a system of telecommunications which enables individual producers to watch merely the movement of a few pointers, as an engineer might watch the hands of a few dials, in order to adjust their activities to changes of which they may never know more than is reflected in the price movement.

Of course, these adjustments are probably never "perfect" in the sense in which the economist conceives of them in his equilibrium analysis. But I fear that our theoretical habits of approaching the problem with the assumption of more or less perfect knowledge on the part of almost everyone has made us somewhat blind to the true function of the price mechanism and led us to apply rather misleading standards in judging its efficiency. The marvel is that in a case like that of a scarcity of one raw material, without an order being issued, without more than perhaps a handful of people knowing the cause, tens of thousands of people whose identity could not be ascertained by months of investigation, are made to use the material or its products more sparingly; *i.e.,* they move in the right direction. This is enough of a marvel even if, in a constantly changing world, not all will hit it off so perfectly that their profit rates will always be maintained at the same constant or "normal" level.

I have deliberately used the word "marvel" to shock the reader out of the complacency with which we often take the working of this mechanism for granted. I am convinced that if it were the result of deliberate human design, and if the people guided by the price changes understood that their decisions have significance far beyond their immediate aim, this mechanism would have been acclaimed as one of the greatest triumphs of the human mind. Its misfortune is the double one that it is not the product of human design and that the people guided by it usually do not know why they are made to do what they do. But those who clamor for "conscious direction"—and who cannot believe that anything which has evolved without design (and even without our understanding it) should solve problems which we should not be able to solve consciously—should remember this: The problem is precisely how to extend the span of our utilization of resources beyond the span of the control of any one mind; and, therefore, how to dispense with the need of conscious control and how to provide inducements which will make the individuals do the desirable things without anyone having to tell them what to do.

The problem which we meet here is by no means peculiar to economics but arises in connection with nearly all truly social phenomena, with language and most of our cultural inheritance, and constitutes really the central theoretical problem of all social science. As Alfred Whitehead has said in another connection, "It is a profoundly erroneous truism, repeated by all copy-books and by eminent people when they are making speeches, that we should cultivate the habit of thinking what we are doing. The precise opposite is the case. Civilization advances by extending the number of important operations which we can perform without thinking about them." This is of profound significance in the social field. We make constant use of formulas, symbols and rules whose meaning we do not understand and through the use of which we avail ourselves of the assistance of knowledge which individually we do not possess. We have developed these practices and institutions by building upon habits and institutions which have proved successful in their own sphere and which have in turn become the foundation of the civilization we have built up.

The price system is just one of those formations which man has learned to use (though he is still very far from having learned to make the best use of it) after he had stumbled upon it without understanding it. Through it not only a division of labor but also a coördinated utilization of resources based on an equally divided knowledge has become possible. The people who like to deride any suggestion that this may be so usually distort the argument by insinuating that it asserts that by some miracle just that sort of system has spontaneously grown up which is best suited to modern civilization. It is the other way round: man has been able to develop that division of labor on which our civilization is based because he happened to stumble upon a method which made it possible. Had he not done so he might still have developed some other, altogether different, type of civilization, something like the "state" of the terminte ants, or some other altogether unimaginable type. All that we can say is that nobody has yet succeeded in designing an alternative system in which certain features of the existing one can be preserved which are dear even to those who most violently assail it—such as particularly the extent to which the individual can choose his pursuits and consequently freely use his own knowledge and skill.

VII

It is in many ways fortunate that the dispute about the indispensability of the price system for any rational calculation in a complex society is now no longer conducted entirely between camps holding different political views. The thesis that without the price system we could not preserve a society based on such extensive division of labor as ours was greeted with a howl of derision when it was first advanced by von Mises twenty-five years ago. Today the difficulties which some still find in accepting it are no longer mainly political, and this makes for an atmosphere much more conducive to reasonable discussion. When we find Leon Trotsky arguing that "economic accounting is unthinkable without market relations"; when Professor Oscar Lange promises Professor von Mises a statue in the marble halls of the future Central Planning Board; when Professor Abba P. Lerner rediscovers Adam Smith and emphasizes that the essential utility of the price system consists in inducing the individual, while seeking his own interest, to do what is in the general interest, the differences can indeed no longer be ascribed to political prejudice. The remaining dissent seems clearly to be due to purely intellectual, and more particularly methodological, differences.

A recent statement by Professor Joseph Schumpeter in his *Capitalism, Socialism and Democracy* provides a clear illustration of one of the methodological differences which I have in mind. Its author is preeminent among those economists who approach economic phenomena in the light of a certain branch of positivism. To him these phenomena accordingly appear as objectively given quantities of commodities impinging directly upon each other, almost, it would seem, without any intervention of human minds. Only against this background can I account for the following (to me startling) pronouncement. Professor Schumpeter argues that the possibility of a rational calculation in the absence of markets for the factors of production follows for the theorist "from the elementary proposition that consumers in evaluating ('demanding') consumers' goods *ipso facto* also evaluate the means of production which enter into the production of these goods."[1]

---

[1] J. Schumpeter, *Capitalism, Socialism, and Democracy* (New York, Harper, 1942), p. 175. Professor Schumpeter is, I believe, also the original author of the myth that Pareto and Barone have "solved" the problem of socialist calculation. What they, and many others, did was merely to state the conditions which a rational allocation of resources would have to satisfy, and to point out that these were essentially the same as the conditions of equilibrium of a competitive market. This is something altogether different from showing how the allocation of resources satisfying these conditions can be found in practice. Pareto himself (from whom Barone has taken practically everything he has to say), far from claiming to have solved the practical problem, in fact explicitly denies that it can be solved without the help of the market. See his *Manuel d'économie pure* (2nd ed., 1927), pp. 233–34. The relevant passage is quoted in an English translation at the beginning of my article on "Socialist Calculation: The Competitive 'Solution,'" in *Economica*, New Series, Vol. VIII, No. 26 (May, 1940), p. 125.

Taken literally, this statement is simply untrue. The consumers do nothing of the kind. What Professor Schumpeter's *"ipso factor"* presumably means is that the valuation of the factors of production is implied in, or follows necessarily from, the valuation of consumers' goods. But this, too, is not correct. Implication is a logical relationship which can be meaningfully asserted only of propositons simultaneously present to one and the same mind. It is evident, however, that the values of the factors of production do not depend solely on the valuation of the consumers' goods but also on the conditions of supply of the various factors of production. Only to a mind to which all these facts were simultaneously known would the answer necessarily follow from the facts given to it. The practical problem, however, arises precisely because these facts are never so given to a single mind, and because, in consequence, it is necessary that in the solution of the problem knowledge should be used that is dispersed among many people.

The problem is thus in no way solved if we can show that all the facts, *if* they were known to a single mind (as we hypothetically assume them to be given to the observing economist), would uniquely determine the solution; instead we must show how a solution is produced by the interactions of people each of whom possess only partial knowledge. To assume all the knowledge to be given to a single mind in the same manner in which we assume it to be given to us as the explaining economists is to assume the problem away and to disregard everything that is important and significant in the real world.

That an economist of Professor Schumpeter's standing should thus have fallen into a trap which the ambiguity of the term "datum" sets to the unwary can hardly be explained as a simple error. It suggests rather that there is something fundamentally wrong with an approach which habitually disregards an essential part of the phenomena with which we have to deal: the unavoidable imperfection of man's knowledge and the consequent need for a process by which knowledge is constantly communicated and acquired. Any approach, such as that of much of mathematical economics with its simultaneous equations, which in effect starts from the assumption that people's *knowledge* corresponds with the objective *facts* of the situation, systematically leaves out what is our main task to explain. I am far from denying that in our system equilibrium analysis has a useful function to perform. But when it comes to the point where it misleads some of our leading thinkers into believing that the situation which it describes has direct relevance to the solution of practical problems, it is time that we remember that it does not deal with the social process at all and that it is no more than a useful preliminary to the study of the main problem.

MONEY SUPPLY IN THE CONDUCT OF MONETARY POLICY

ARTHUR F. BURNS

*   *   *

Role of Money Supply

For many years economists have debated the role of the money supply in the performance of economic systems. One school of thought, often termed "monetarist," claims that changes in the money supply influence very importantly, perhaps even decisively, the pace of economic activity and the level of prices. Monetarists contend that the monetary authorities should pay principal attention to the money supply, rather than to other financial variables such as interest rates, in the conduct of monetary policy. They also contend that fiscal policy has only a small independent impact on the economy.

Another school of thought places less emphasis on the money supply and assigns more importance to the expenditure and tax policies of the Federal Government as factors influencing real economic activity and the level of prices. This school emphasizes the need for monetary policy to be concerned with interest rates and with conditions in the money and capital markets. Some economic activities, particularly residential building and State and local government construction, depend heavily on borrowed funds, and are therefore influenced greatly by changes in the cost and availability of credit. In other categories of spending—such as business investment in fixed capital and inventories, and consumer purchases of durable goods—credit conditions play a less decisive role, but they are nonetheless important.

Monetarists recognize that monetary policy affects private spending in part through its impact on interest rates and other credit terms. But they believe that primary attention to the growth of the money supply will result in a more appropriate monetary policy than would attention to conditions in the credit markets.

Needless to say, monetary policy is—and has long been—a controversial subject. Even the monetarists do not speak with one voice on monetary policy. Some influential monetarists believe that monetary policy should aim strictly at maintaining a constant rate of growth of the money supply. However, what that constant should be, or how broadly the money supply should be defined, are matters on which monetarists still differ. And there are also monetarists who would allow some—but infrequent—changes in the rate of growth of the money supply, in accordance with changing economic conditions.

A letter sent on November 6, 1973, by Arthur F. Burns, chairman of the board of governors of the Federal Reserve System, to Senator William Proxmire, vice-chairman of the Joint Economic Committee of Congress, and subsequently printed in the *Federal Reserve Bulletin* November 1973. The letter was in response to a request from Senator Proxmire for comment on certain criticisms of monetary policy. It is reprinted here with the permission of Arthur F. Burns.

It seems self-evident that adherence to a rigid growth-rate rule, or even one that is changed infrequently, would practically prevent monetary policy from playing an active role in economic stabilization. Monetarists recognize this. They believe that most economic disturbances tend to be self-correcting, and they therefore argue that a constant or nearly constant rate of growth of the money supply would result in reasonably satisfactory economic performance.

But neither historical evidence nor the thrust of explorations in business-cycle theory over a long century gives support to the notion that our economy is inherently stable. On the contrary, experience has demonstrated repeatedly that blind reliance on the self-correcting properties of our economic system can lead to serious trouble. Discretionary economic policy, while it has at times led to mistakes, has more often proved reasonably successful. The disappearance of business depressions, which in earlier times spelled mass unemployment for workers and mass bankruptcies for businessmen, is largely attributable to the stabilization policies of the last 30 years.

The fact is that the internal workings of a market economy tend of themselves to generate business fluctuations, and most modern economists recognize this. For example, improved prospects for profits often spur unsustainable bursts of investment spending. The flow of personal income in an age of affluence allows ample latitude for changes in discretionary expenditures and in savings rates. During a business-cycle expansion various imbalances tend to develop within the economy—between aggregate inventories and sales, or between aggregate business investment in fixed capital and consumer outlays, or between average unit costs of production and prices. Such imbalances give rise to cyclical movements in the economy. Flexible fiscal and monetary policies, therefore, are often needed to cope with undesirable economic developments, and this need is not diminished by the fact that our available tools of economic stabilization leave something to be desired.

There is general agreement among economists that, as a rule, the effects of stabilization policies occur gradually over time, and that economic forecasts are an essential tool of policy-making. However, no economist—or school of economics—has a monopoly on accurate forecasting. At times, forecasts based largely on the money supply have turned out to be satisfactory. At other times, such forecasts have been quite poor, mainly because of unanticipated changes in the intensity with which the existing money stock is used by business firms and consumers.

Changes in the rate of turnover of money have historically played a large role in economic fluctuations, and they continue to do so. For example, the narrowly defined money stock—that is, demand deposits plus currency in public circulation—grew by 5.7 per cent between the fourth quarter of 1969 and the fourth quarter of 1970. But the turnover of money declined during the year, and the dollar value of gross national product rose only 4.5 per cent. In the following year, the growth rate of the money supply increased to 6.9 per cent, but the turnover of money picked up briskly and the dollar value of GNP accelerated to 9.3 per cent. The movement out of recession in 1970 into recovery in 1971 was thus closely related to the greater intensity in the use of money. Occurrences such as this are very common because the willingness to use the existing stock of money, expressed in its rate of turnover, is a highly dynamic force in economic life.

For this as well as other reasons, the Federal Reserve uses a blend of forecasting techniques. The behavior of the money supply and other financial variables is accorded careful attention. So also are the results of the most recent surveys on plant and equipment spending, consumer attitudes, and inventory plans. Recent trends in key producing and spending sectors are analyzed. The opinions of businessmen and outside economic analysts are canvassed, in part through the nationwide contacts of Federal Reserve Banks. And an assessment is made of the probable course of fiscal policy and also of labor-market and agricultural policies, and their effects on the economy.

Evidence from all these sources is weighed. Efforts are also made to assess economic developments through the use of large-scale econometric models. An eclectic approach is thus taken by the Federal Reserve, in recognition of the fact that the state of economic knowledge does not justify reliance on any single forecasting technique. As economic research has cumulated, it has become increasingly clear that money does indeed matter. But other financial variables also matter.

In recent years, the Federal Reserve has placed somewhat more emphasis on achieving desired growth rates of the monetary aggregates, including the narrowly-defined money supply, in its conduct of monetary policy. But we have continued to give careful attention to other financial indicators, among them the level of interest rates on mortgages and other loans and the liquidity position of financial institutions and the general public. This is necessary because the economic implications of any given monetary growth rate depend on the state of liquidity, the attitudes of businessmen, investors, and consumers toward liquidity, the cost and availability of borrowed funds, and other factors. Also, as the Nation's central bank, the Federal Reserve can never lose sight of its role as a lender of last resort, so that financial crises and panics will be averted.

I recognize that one advantage of maintaining a relatively stable growth rate of the money supply is that a partial offset is thereby provided to unexpected and undesired shifts in the aggregate demand for goods and services. There is always some uncertainty as to the emerging strength of aggregate demand. If money growth is maintained at a rather stable rate, and aggregate demand turns out to be weaker than is consistent with the Nation's economic objectives, interest rates will tend to decline and the easing of credit markets should help to moderate the undesired weakness in demand. Similarly, if the demand for goods and services threatens to outrun productive capacity, a rather stable rate of monetary growth will provide a restraining influence on the supply of credit and thus tend to restrain excessive spending.

However, it would be unwise for monetary policy to aim at all times at a constant or nearly constant rate of growth of money balances. The money growth rate that can contribute most to national objectives will vary with economic conditions. For example, if the aggregate demand for goods and services is unusually weak, or if the demand for liquidity is unusually strong, a rate of increase in the money supply well above the desirable long-term trend may be needed for a time. Again, when the economy is experiencing severe cost-push inflation, a monetary growth rate that is relatively high by a historical yardstick may have to be tolerated for a time. If money growth were severely constrained in order to combat the element of inflation resulting from such a cause, it might well have seriously adverse effects on production and employment. In short, the growth rate of the money supply that is appropriate at any given time cannot be determined simply by extrapolating past trend or by some preconceived arithmetical standard.

Moreover, for purposes of conducting monetary policy, it is never safe to rely on just one concept of money—even if that concept happens to be fashionable. A variety of plausible concepts merit careful attention because a number of financial assets serve as a convenient, safe, and liquid store of purchasing power.

The Federal Reserve publishes data corresponding to three definitions of money and takes all of them into account in determining policy. The three measures are: (a) the narrowly defined money stock (M_1), which encompasses currency and demand deposits held by the nonbank public: (b) a more broadly defined money stock (M_2), which also includes time and savings deposits at commercial banks (other than large negotiable time certificates of deposits); (c) a still broader definition (M_3), which includes savings deposits at mutual savings banks and savings and loan associations. A definition embracing other liquid assets could also be justified—for example, one that would include large-denomination negotiable time CD's, U.S. savings bonds and Treasury bills, commercial paper, and other short-term money market instruments.

There are many assets closely related to cash, and the public can switch readily among these assets. However money may be defined, the task of determining the amount of money needed to maintain high employment and reasonable stability of the general price level is complicated by shifting preferences of the public for cash and other financial assets.

Variability of Money Supply Growth

In the short run, the rate of change in the observed money supply is quite erratic and cannot be trusted as an indicator of the course of monetary policy. This would be so even if there were no errors of measurement.

The record of hearings held by the Joint Economic Committee on June 27, 1973, includes a memorandum that I submitted on problems encountered in controlling the money supply. As indicated there, week-to-week, month-to-month, and even quarter-to-quarter fluctuations in the rate of change of money balances are frequently influenced by international flows of funds, changes in the level of U.S. Government deposits, and sudden changes in the public's attitude toward liquidity. Some of these variations appear to be essentially random—a product of the enormous ebb and flow of funds in our modern economy.

Because the demands of the public for money are subject to rather wide short-term variations, efforts by the Federal Reserve to maintain a constant growth rate of the money supply could lead to sharp short-run swings in interest rates and could risk damage to financial markets and the economy. Uncertainties about financing cost could reduce the fluidity of markets and could increase the costs of financing to borrowers. In addition, wide and erratic movements of interest rates and financial conditions could have undesirable effects on business and consumer spending. These adverse effects may not be of major dimensions, but it is better to avoid them.

In any event, for a variety of reasons explained in the memorandum for the Joint Economic Committee, to which I have previously referred, the Federal Reserve does not have precise control over the money supply. To give one example, a significant part of the money supply consists of deposits lodged in nonmember banks that are not subject to the reserve requirements set by the Federal Reserve. As a result, there is some slippage in monetary control. Furthermore, since deposits at nonmember banks have been reported for only 2 to 4 days in a year, in contrast to daily statistics for member banks, the data on the money supply—which we regularly present on a weekly, monthly, and quarterly basis—are estimates rather than precise measurements. When the infrequent reports from nonmember banks become available, they often necessitate considerable revisions of the money supply figures. In the past 2 years, the revisions were upward, and this may happen again this year.

*   *   *

In our judgment, there is little reason for concern about the short-run variations that occur in the rate of change in the money stock. Such variations have minimal effects on the real economy. For one thing, the outstanding supply of money is very large. It is also quite stable, even when the short-run rate of change is unstable. This October the average outstanding supply of M_1, seasonally adjusted, was about $264 billion. On this base, a monthly rise or fall in the money stock of even $2½ billion would amount to only a 1 per cent change. But when such a temporary change is expressed as an annual rate, as is now commonly done, it comes out as about 12 per cent and attracts attention far beyond its real significance.

The Federal Reserve research staff has investigated carefully the economic implications of variability in the growth of M_1. The experience of the past two decades suggests that even an abnormally large or abnormally small rate of growth of the money stock over a period of up to 6 months or so has a negligible influence on the course of the economy—provided it is subsequently offset. Such short-run variations in the rate of change in the money supply may not at all reflect Federal Reserve policy, and they do not justify the attention they often receive from financial analysts.

The thrust of monetary policy and its probable effects on economic activity can only be determined by observing the course of the money supply and of other monetary aggregates over periods lasting 6 months or so. Even then, care must be taken to measure the growth of money balances in ways that temper the influence of short-term variations. For example, the growth of money balances over a quarter can be measured from the amount outstanding in the last month of the preceding quarter to the last month of the current quarter or from the average amount outstanding during the preceding quarter to the average in the current quarter. The first measure captures the latest tendencies in the money supply, but may be distorted by random changes that have no lasting significance. The second measure tends to average out temporary fluctuations and is comparable to the data provided on a wide range of nonmonetary economic variables, such as GNP and related measures.

*   *   *

Experience of 1972-73

During 1972, it was the responsibility of the Federal Reserve to encourage a rate of economic expansion adequate to reduce unemployment to acceptable levels. At the same time, despite the dampening effects of the wage-price control program, inflationary pressures were gathering. Monetary policy, therefore, had to balance the twin objectives of containing inflationary pressures and encouraging economic growth. These objectives were to some extent conflicting, and monetary policy alone could not be expected to cope with both problems. Continuation of an effective wage-price program and a firmer policy of fiscal restraint were urgently needed.

The narrowly defined money stock increased 7.4 per cent during 1972—measured from the fourth quarter of 1971 to the fourth quarter of 1972. Between the third quarter of 1972 and the third quarter of 1973, the growth rate was 6.1 per cent. By the first half of 1973, the annual growth rate had declined to 5.8 per cent, and a further slowing occurred in the third quarter.

Evaluation of the appropriateness of these growth rates would require full analysis of the economic and financial objectives, conditions, and policies during the past 2 years, if not longer. Such an analysis cannot be undertaken here. Some perspective on monetary developments during 1972–73 may be gained, however, from comparisons with the experience of other industrial countries, and by recalling briefly how domestic economic conditions evolved during this period.

Table 1 compares the growth of M_1 in the United States with that of other industrial countries in 1972 and the first half of 1973. The definitions of M_1 differ somewhat from country to country, but are as nearly comparable as statistical sources permit. It goes without saying that each country faced its own set of economic conditions and problems. Yet it is useful to note that monetary growth in the United States was

Table 1　GROWTH IN MONEY SUPPLY
Percentage change at annual rates

Country	1971 Q4 to 1972 Q4	1972 Q4 to 1973 Q2
Unites States	7.4	5.8
United Kingdom	14.1	10.0
Germany	14.3	4.2
France	15.4	8.7
Japan	23.1	28.2

Table 2 shows, in summary fashion, the rates of change in the money supply of the United States, in its total production, and in the consumer price level during 1972 and 1973. The table is based on the latest data. It may be noted in passing that, according to data available as late as January 1973, the rate of growth of M_1 during 1972 was 7.2 per cent, not 7.4 per cent; and that the rate of increase in real GNP was 7.7 per cent, not 7.0 per cent. In other words, on the basis of the data available during 1972, the rate of growth of M_1 was below the rate of growth of the physical volume of overall production.

Table 2 indicates that growth in M_1 during 1972 and 1973 approximately matched the growth of real output, but was far below the expansion in the dollar value of the Nation's output. Although monetary policy limited the availability of money relative to the growth of transactions demands, it still encouraged a substantial expansion in economic activity; real output rose by about 7 per cent in 1972. Even so, unemployment remained unsatisfactorily high throughout the greater part of the year. It was not until November that the unemployment rate dropped below $5\frac{1}{2}$ per cent. For the year as a whole, the unemployment rate averaged 5.6 per cent. It may be of interest to recall that unemployment averaged 5.5 per cent in 1954 and 1960, which are commonly regarded as recession years.

Table 2　MONEY SUPPLY, GNP, AND PRICES IN THE UNITED STATES
Percentage change at annual rates

Item	1971 Q4 to 1972 Q4	1972 Q4 to—	
		1973 Q2	1973 Q3
Money supply (M_1)	7.4	5.8	5.6
Gross national product			
Current dollars	10.6	12.1	11.7
Constant dollars	7.0	5.4	4.8
Prices			
Consumer price index (CPI)	3.4	7.1	7.8
CPI excluding food	3.0	4.0	4.1

Since the expansion of M_1 in 1972 was low relative to the demands for money and credit, it was accompanied by rising short-term interest rates. Long-term interest rates showed little net change last year, as credit demands were satisfied mainly in the short-term markets.

In 1973, the growth of M_1 moderated while the transactions demands for cash and the turnover of money accelerated. GNP in current dollars rose at a 12 per cent annual rate as prices rose more rapidly. In credit markets, short-term interest rates rose sharply further, while long-term interest rates also moved up, though by substantially less than short-term rates.

The extraordinary upsurge of the price level this year reflects a variety of special influences. First, there has been a worldwide economic boom superimposed on the boom in the United States. Second, we have encountered critical shortages of basic materials. The expansion in industrial capacity needed to produce these materials had not been put in place earlier because of the abnormally low level of profits between 1966 and 1971 and also because of numerous impediments to new investment on ecological grounds. Third, farm product prices escalated sharply as a result of crop failures in many countries last year. Fourth, fuel prices spurted upward, reflecting the developing shortages in the energy field. And fifth, the depreciation of the dollar in foreign exchange markets has served to boost prices of imported goods and to add to the demands pressing on our productive resources.

In view of these powerful special factors and the cyclical expansion of our economy, a sharp advance in our price level would have been practically inevitable in 1973. The upsurge of the price level this year hardly represents either the basic trend of prices or the response of prices to previous monetary or fiscal policies—whatever their shortcomings may have been. In particular, as Table 2 shows, the explosion of food prices that occurred this year is in large part responsible for the accelerated rise in the overall consumer price level.

The severe rate of inflation that we have experienced in 1973 cannot responsibly be attributed to monetary management or to public policies more generally. In retrospect, it may well be that monetary policy should have been a little less expansive in 1972. But a markedly more restrictive policy would have led to a still sharper rise in interest rates and risked a premature ending of the business expansion, without limiting to any significant degree this year's upsurge of the price level.

Concluding Observations

The present inflation is the most serious economic problem facing our country, and it poses great difficulties for economic stabilization policies. We must recognize, I believe, that it will take some time for the forces of inflation, which now engulf our economy and others around the world, to burn themselves out. In today's environment, controls on wages and prices cannot be expected to yield the benefits they did in 1971 and 1972, when economic conditions were much different. Primary reliance in dealing with inflation—both in the near future and over the longer term—will have to be placed on fiscal and monetary policies.

The prospects for regaining price stability would be enhanced by improvements in our monetary and fiscal instruments. The conduct of monetary policy could be improved if steps were taken to increase the precision with which the money supply can be controlled by the Federal Reserve. Part of the present control problem stems from statistical inadequacies—chiefly the paucity of data on deposits at nonmember banks. Also, however, control over the money supply and other monetary aggregates is less precise than it can or should be because nonmember banks are not subject to the same reserve requirements as are member banks.

I hope that the Congress will support efforts to rectify these deficiencies. For its part, the Federal Reserve is even now carrying on discussions with the Federal Deposit Insurance Corporation about the need for better statistics on the Nation's money supply. The Board of Governors also expects shortly to recommend to the Congress legislation that will put demand deposits at commercial banks on a uniform basis from the standpoint of reserve requirements.

Improvements in our fiscal policies are also needed. It is important for the Congress to put an end to fragmented consideration of expenditures, to place a firm ceiling on total Federal expenditures, and to relate these expenditures to prospective revenues and the Nation's economic needs. Fortunately, there is now widespread recognition by Members of the Congress of the need to reform budgetary procedures along these broad lines.

It also is high time for fiscal policy to become a more versatile tool of economic stabilization. Particularly appropriate would be fiscal instruments that could be adapted quickly under special legislative rules, to changing economic conditions—such as a variable tax credit for business investment in fixed capital. Once again I would urge the Congress to give serious consideration to this urgently needed reform.

We must strive also for better understanding of the effects of economic stabilization policies on economic activity and prices. Our knowledge in this area is greater now than it was 5 or 10 years ago, thanks to extensive research undertaken by economists in academic institutions, at the Federal Reserve, and elsewhere. The keen interest of the Joint Economic Committee in improving economic stabilization policies has, I believe, been an influence of great importance in stimulating this widespread research effort.

I look forward to the continued cooperation with the Committee in an effort to achieve the kind of economic performance our citizens expect and deserve.

A STATISTICAL HISTORY OF THE 1974-75 RECESSION-INFLATION

	YEAR	1973		1974				1975		
	QUARTER	3rd	4th	1st	2nd	3rd	4th	1st	2nd	3rd
1 Gross national product		1,308.9	1,344.0	1,358.8	1,383.8	1,416.3	1,430.9	1,416.6	1,440.9	1,497.8
2 Disposable personal income		913.9	939.4	950.6	966.5	993.1	1,008.8	1,015.5	1,078.5	1,079.1
3 Personal consumption expenditures[1]		816.3	823.9	840.6	869.1	901.3	895.8	913.2	938.6	970.0
4 Personal saving		73.2	89.3	84.4	71.5	65.5	86.5	75.9	113.8	82.9
5 Gross private saving[2]		210.3	229.4	224.1	207.3	196.2	227.5	222.6	266.3	
6 Gross private domestic investment		209.0	224.5	210.5	211.8	205.8	209.4	163.1	148.1	174.9
7 Government purchases of goods		276.9	286.4	296.3	304.4	312.3	323.8	331.6	338.1	343.1
8 Federal government expenditures		263.4	270.6	281.0	291.6	304.7	319.3	338.5	355.0	
9 Federal government receipts		261.8	268.3	278.1	288.6	302.8	294.7	284.1	250.5	
10 Federal government deficit		1.7	2.3	2.8	3.0	1.9	24.5	54.4	104.6	
11 Net exports (exports minus imports)		6.7	9.3	11.3	−1.5	−3.1	1.9	8.8	16.2	9.8
12 Gross national product		840.8	845.7	830.5	827.1	823.1	804.0	780.0	783.6	804.6
13 Personal consumption expenditures		555.4	546.3	539.7	542.7	547.2	528.2	531.5	539.7	548.9
14 Personal saving[3]		49.8	59.2	54.2	44.6	39.8	51.0	44.2	65.4	46.9
15 Gross private domestic investment		135.8	145.8	133.3	130.3	122.7	120.5	89.3	80.7	94.9
16 Government purchases of goods		143.7	145.7	146.0	145.8	145.9	146.3	147.7	149.2	149.6
17 Per capita disposable income, 1958 dollars		2,952	2,952	2,887	2,850	2,842	2,798	2,775	2,907	
18 Implicit GNP deflator		155.7	158.9	163.6	167.3	172.1	178.0	181.6	183.9	186.2

Rows 1–11: (in billions of current dollars) (seasonally adjusted annual rates). Rows 12–16: (in billions of 1958 dollars) (seasonally adjusted annual rates).

[1]In the national income and product accounts, disposable personal income is equal to personal *outlays* plus personal saving. Personal consumption expenditures plus interest paid by consumers and personal transfer payments to foreigners comprise personal outlays.

[2]Sum of personal saving, capital consumption allowances, and undistributed corporate profits minus net corporate losses attributable to revaluation of inventory. Personal saving plus gross business saving.

[3]Personal saving in current dollars divided by implicit price deflator for overall personal consumption expenditures.

	YEAR	1973		1974				1975		
	QUARTER	3rd	4th	1st	2nd	3rd	4th	1st	2nd	3rd
	MONTH	Jy Ag Se	Oc No De	Ja Fe Mr	Ap My Je	Jy Ag Se	Oc No De	Ja Fe Mr	Ap My Je	Jy Ag Se
19 Consumer price index		132.7 / 135.1 / 135.5	136.6 / 137.6 / 138.5	139.7 / 141.5 / 143.1	144.0 / 145.5 / 146.9	148.0 / 149.9 / 151.7	153.0 / 154.3 / 155.4	156.1 / 157.2 / 157.8	158.6 / 159.3 / 160.6	162.3 / 162.8 / 163.6
20 Wholesale price index		134.3 / 142.1 / 139.7	138.7 / 139.2 / 141.8	146.6 / 149.5 / 151.4	152.7 / 155.0 / 155.7	161.7 / 167.4 / 167.2	170.2 / 171.9 / 171.5	171.8 / 171.3 / 170.4	172.1 / 173.2 / 173.7·	175.7 / 176.7 / 177.7
21 Money stock: M_1, seasonally adjusted		266.4 / 266.3 / 265.5	266.6 / 269.4 / 271.5	270.9 / 273.1 / 275.2	276.6 / 277.6 / 280.0	280.4 / 280.5 / 280.7	281.6 / 283.6 / 284.4	281.6 / 282.4 / 285.0	285.8 / 288.5 / 293.0	293.5 / 294.2 / 294.6
22 Money stock: M_2, seasonally adjusted		552.1 / 555.1 / 556.8	561.9 / 567.2 / 572.2	575.5 / 580.8 / 585.5	589.4 / 591.5 / 596.7	599.6 / 601.9 / 603.4	607.6 / 611.6 / 613.5	614.8 / 619.1 / 625.1	628.9 / 635.9 / 646.1	650.5 / 653.7 / 656.3
23 Federal funds rate, average of daily rates		10.40 / 10.50 / 10.78	10.01 / 10.03 / 9.95	9.65 / 8.97 / 9.35	10.51 / 11.31 / 11.93	12.92 / 12.01 / 11.34	10.06 / 9.45 / 8.53	7.13 / 6.24 / 5.54	5.49 / 5.22 / 5.55	6.10 / 6.14 / 6.24
24 Prime rate (4–6 months), average of daily rates		9.18 / 10.21 / 10.23	8.92 / 8.94 / 9.08	8.66 / 7.82 / 8.42	9.79 / 10.62 / 10.96	11.72 / 11.65 / 11.23	9.36 / 8.81 / 8.98	7.30 / 6.33 / 6.06	6.15 / 5.82 / 5.79	6.44 / 6.70 / 6.85
25 Noninstitutional population	(in thousands)	148,361 / 148,565 / 148,782	149,001 / 149,208 / 149,436	149,656 / 149,857 / 150,066	150,283 / 150,507 / 150,710	150,922 / 151,135 / 151,367	151,593 / 151,812 / 152,020	152,230 / 152,445 / 152,646	152,840 / 153,051 / 153,278	153,585 / 153,824 / 154,052
26 Civilian labor force, s.a.	(in thousands)	88,902 / 88,816 / 89,223	89,568 / 89,852 / 90,048	90,465 / 90,551 / 90,381	90,324 / 90,753 / 90,857	91,283 / 91,199 / 91,705	91,844 / 91,708 / 91,803	92,091 / 91,511 / 91,829	92,262 / 92,940 / 92,340	92,916 / 93,146 / 93,191
27 Civilian employment, s.a.	(in thousands)	84,679 / 84,582 / 84,983	85,452 / 85,577 / 85,646	85,800 / 85,861 / 85,779	85,787 / 86,062 / 86,088	86,403 / 86,274 / 86,402	86,304 / 85,689 / 85,202	84,562 / 84,027 / 83,849	84,086 / 84,402 / 84,444	85,078 / 85,352 / 85,418
28 Unemployment, s.a.	(in thousands)	4,223 / 4,234 / 4,240	4,116 / 4,275 / 4,402	4,665 / 4,690 / 4,602	4,537 / 4,691 / 4,769	4,880 / 4,925 / 5,303	5,540 / 6,019 / 6,601	7,529 / 7,484 / 7,980	8,176 / 8,538 / 7,896	7,838 / 7,794 / 7,773
29 Employment rate (27 ÷ 25)		57.1 / 56.9 / 57.1	57.3 / 57.4 / 57.3	57.3 / 57.3 / 57.2	57.1 / 57.2 / 57.1	57.3 / 57.1 / 57.1	56.9 / 56.4 / 56.0	55.5 / 55.1 / 54.9	55.0 / 55.1 / 55.1	55.4 / 55.5 / 55.4
30 Unemployment rate (28 ÷ 26)		4.8 / 4.8 / 4.8	4.6 / 4.8 / 4.9	5.2 / 5.2 / 5.1	5.0 / 5.2 / 5.2	5.3 / 5.4 / 5.8	6.0 / 6.6 / 7.2	8.2 / 8.2 / 8.7	8.9 / 9.2 / 8.6	8.4 / 8.4 / 8.3

Sources: Bureau of Economic Analysis; Bureau of Labor Statistics; Board of Governors, Federal Reserve System.

Note: Data for recent quarters and months are subject to minor revisions as more accurate information becomes available. The 1976 benchmark revisions published by the Bureau of Economic Analysis beginning with the January 1976 issues of the *Survey of Current Business* have not been incorporated in the income and product account data of this appendix.

INDEX